Vintage	Red Bordeaux		White Bordeaux		Alsace
	Médoc/Graves	Pom/St-Em	Sauternes & sw	Graves & dry	
2006	6–8	7–9	8–10	8–9	6–8
2005	9–10	9–10	8–10	8–10	8–9
2004	7–8	7–9	5–7	6–7	6–8
2003	5–9	5–8	7–8	6–7	6–7
2002	6–8	5–8	7–8	7–8	7–8
2001	6–8	7–8	8–10	7–9	6–8
2000	8–10	7–9	6–8	6–8	8–10
99	5–7	5–8	6–9	7–10	6–8
98	5–8	6–9	5–8	5–9	7–9
97	5–7	4–7	7–9	4–7	7–9
96	6–8	5–7	7–9	7–10	8–10
95	7–9	6–9	6–8	5–9	7–9
94	5–8	5–8	4–6	5–8	6–9
93	4–6	5–7	2–5	5–7	6–8
92	3–5	3–5	3–5	4–8	5–7
91	3–6	2–4	2–5	6–8	3–5
90	8–10	8–10	8–10	7–8	7–9
89	6–9	7–9	8–10	6–8	7–10
88	6–8	7–9	7–10	7–9	8–10

Vintage	Burgundy			Rhône	
	Côte d'Or red	Côte d'Or white	Chablis	Rhône (N)	Rhône (S)
2006	7–8	8–10	8–9	7–8	7–9
2005	7–9	7–9	7–9	7–8	6–8
2004	6–8	7–8	7–8	6–7	6–7
2003	6–7	6–7	6–7	5–7	6–8
2002	7–8	7–8	7–8	4–6	5–5
2001	6–8	7–9	6–8	7–8	7–9
2000	7–8	6–9	7–9	6–8	7–9
99	7–10	5–7	5–8	7–9	6–9
98	5–8	5–7	7–8	6–8	7–9
97	5–8	5–8	7–9	7–9	5–8
96	6–8	7–9	5–10	5–7	4–6
95	7–9	7–9	6–9	6–8	5–7
94	5–8	5–7	4–7	6–7	5–7
93	6–8				

Beaujolais 06, 05, … now or can wait. … 05, 02, 97, 96, 93, 90 … 6, 05, 04, 02, 00, 99, 97 … , 00, 99 **Muscadet** 06, 05 …

MITCHELL BEAZLEY

Hugh Johnson's
POCKET WINE BOOK
2008

Hugh Johnson's Pocket Wine Book 2008
Edited and designed by Mitchell Beazley, an
imprint of Octopus Publishing Group Limited,
2–4 Heron Quays,
London E14 4JP.

First edition published 1977
Revised editions published 1978, 1979, 1980, 1981,
1982, 1983, 1984, 1985, 1986, 1987, 1988, 1989, 1990,
1991, 1992, 1993, 1994, 1995, 1996,
1997, 1998, 1999, 2000, 2001, 2002(twice), 2003,
2004, 2005, 2006 (twice), 2007

A CIP record for this book is available from the
British Library.

ISBN: 978 184533 320 1

General Editor: Margaret Rand
Editors: Juanne Branquinho, Martyn Page,
Naomi Waters
Proofreader: Jill Cropper
Executive Art Editor: Yasia Williams-Leedham
Editorial Manager: Deirdre Headon
Production Manager: Peter Hunt
Printed and bound in China

Picture credits
Titlte page: Lucy Carolan; 4 Alamy/Bogdan Cioc; 289
Alamy/Cephas Picture Library; 290 Alamy/David Noton
Photography; 291 Claes Lofgren; 294 top Sr Roberto
Conterno, Azienda Vitivinicola Conterno Giacomo;
294 centre Claes Lofgren; 294 bottom Alamy/Cephas
Picture Library; 295 top Marco Felluga SRL; 295
bottom Sr Romano Dal Forno; 296 top Claes Lofgren;
296 centre Attilio Pagli; 296 bottom Falesco Srl Az.
Vin.; 297 top Giampiero Bea; 297 bottom Di
Paolo&C; 298 top Tenuta di Trinoro; 298 centre
Alessandro Saffo; 298 bottom Alessandro Dettori,
Tenute Dettori; 299 left Cephas/Mick Rock; 299 right
Alamy/Cephas Picture Library; 300 left Alamy/Cephas
Picture Library; 300 rightOctopus Publishing Group
Ltd; 301 left VinVino; 301 right Octopus Publishing
Group Ltd

MITCHELL BEAZLEY

Hugh Johnson's

POCKET WINE BOOK

2008

Acknowledgments

This store of detailed recommendations comes partly from my own notes and mainly from those of a great number of kind friends. Without the generous help and cooperation of innumerable winemakers, merchants, and critics, I could not attempt it. I particularly want to thank the following for help with research or in the areas of their special knowledge:

Sarah Ahmed
Geoff Adams
Helena Baker
Phillip Blom
Charles Borden
Gregory Bowden
Stephen Brook
Michael Cooper
Rupert Dean
Michael Edwards
Sarah Jane Evans MW
Jacqueline Friedrich
Rosemary George MW
Robert Gorjak

James Halliday
Annie Kay
Chandra Kurt
Gareth Lawrence
James Lawther MW
Konstantinos Lazarakis
    MW
John Livingstone-
    Learmonth
Nico Manessis
Adam Montefiore
Jasper Morris MW
Shirley Nelson
John and Erica Platter

Jan and Carlos Read
Daniel Rogov
Michele Shah
Stephen Skelton MW
Paul Strang
Gabriella Szlovák
Bostjan Tadel
Marguerite Thomas
Daniel Thomases
Monty Waldin
Larry Walker
Simon Woods

Contents

Front endpaper: Quick reference vintage charts

Hugh Johnson: Point scoring	6
Agenda 2008	9
How to use this book	11
Vintage report 2006	12
A closer look at 2005	13
Hugh Johnson's big brand review	14
France	16
Châteaux of Bordeaux	62
Italy	84
Germany	114
Spain & Portugal	138
Sherry, Port, & Madeira	159
Switzerland	168
Austria	172
Central & Southeast Europe	178
Hungary, Bulgaria, Slovenia, Croatia, Bosnia, Serbia, The Czech Republic, Slovakia, Romania, Greece, Cyprus, Malta	
Other Europe: England & Wales	194
Asia, North Africa, & the Levant	195
North America	198
California	199
The Pacific Northwest	217
East of the Rockies	220
Southwest	223
Canada	225
Central & South America	226
Chile, Argentina, Bolivia, Brazil, Mexico, Peru, Uruguay	
Australia	234
New Zealand	250
South Africa	258
Grape varieties	269
Wine & food	276
Italy today	289

Back endpaper: A little learning/ Temperature

Point Scoring

There can be nobody left who drinks wine regularly who has not encountered the 100-point scoring system invented by Robert Parker, an American lawyer who offered his services, in the 1980s, as America's guide to the world's wines. He scored a bull's eye. He discovered that the imprecision of wine appreciation and the seeming precision of percentage points make perfect partners. He had the confidence to mark the wines he tasted out of 100 and to publish the results. He knew that no-one else would have tasted the same wines in the same way and be in a position to challenge his scores in detail. The magic of the printed word did the rest. I have found the same with this book: when I first wrote it I expected an avalanche of arguments and rebuttals, but the postbag was lean. I expect inertia counts for a lot.

It did not take long for Parker's scores to gain more than local currency. What other guidance was there, after all, in a country with only a handful of wine professionals, as America was at the time? He never intended, he says, his scores to become ready-made marketing tools for a booming industry with few authoritative voices. Others have imitated him, of course, but he remains the gold standard. In the States it seems almost natural, now, that wines should have a percentage number attached to denote their quality.

In my *Pocket Wine Book*, however, I have always taken the diametrically opposite approach to scoring wines. In the minds of most wine drinkers, I argue, it is not the absolute quality of each bottle that determines what we buy – if, indeed, there is such a thing. To investors, yes, who buy wine with a view to selling it, a percentage score is like a share price. But like a share price it has no permanent validity. It is a snapshot of value at one moment: the moment when, in the case of wine, it crossed the critic's gums. The wine from one bottle, that is, out of many thousands of the same wine.

The problems start here. The truest of all wine maxims is "There are no great wines, only great bottles of wine". Variation from bottle to bottle is still an accepted fact in many regions, even if some are trying to eliminate it by means of screwcaps. Bottle variation is an element of risk that many buyers, even of rare and precious bottles, prefer to leave out of account. It is a near certainty that one bottle in a case of twelve will be a dud: not necessarily corked – the random but fatal result of fungus in the cork – but just mysteriously below par. If a critic recognizes a faulty bottle, he or she is duty bound to open another. Ordinary consumers, however, just have to curse their luck.

A critic's opinion of any wine is affected by what comes before. Experience enables you to compensate – but not to taste the tenth wine as you would have done with a fresh mouth. It may be the tenth wine that suffers in the comparison; it may be the first: but it is not the same mouth tasting them both. Nor can you taste two wines for comparative purposes months apart: they develop in their bottles, and you in your skin. Every tasting note should be qualified by the date of tasting. These and other factors (health, mood, atmospheric pressure, the degree of aeration of the wine – the variables are endless) make the perceived precision of a percentage score doubtful, to say the least. Scores expressed on shorter scales are less pretentious. Among British professionals the most commonly used runs to 20 points.

The 20-point scale has been calibrated by a more than respectable magazine, *The World of Fine Wine*, in a way that accurately guides both its users and its interpreters. From 0–7 points means "disagreeable or faulty wine", from 7.5–10, wine which is "sound but dull or boring, of no character or appeal". Wine below the halfway point, in other words, has been rejected. From 10.5–12 points, a wine is "enjoyable, simple and straightforward". From 21.5–14, it is "good, but with no outstanding features". From 14.5–16.5, "very good, with some outstanding features". This is surely as far as most wines, and most of us, need to go. Wines with 17–18.5 points are "outstanding, of great beauty and articulacy". (It was the articulacy of the critic Andrew Jefford that coined these phrases.) At 19–20 points you have met "a great wine, of spellbinding beauty and resonance, leaving the drinker with a sense of wonder". I have not met a clearer statement of what great wine can do, or why it is worth the search.

Twenty points calibrated in this way make seven classes, with ample allowance for nuances within each class. It is an admirable system if scoring is called for, usually in a professional context, and avoids the inbuilt hyperbole as a score gets close to 100.

The consumer magazine *Decanter* pioneered a simple way of scoring out of a mere five possible points. One point designates "poor", two points "fair", three "good", four "very good to excellent" and five "outstanding". The same question, though, has to be asked about all such systems: are they

---

The memory lingers on...

In this edition I have indicated within entries 200 or so of the wines I remember having specially (and in some cases regularly) enjoyed over the past 12 months (that is mid '06–'07). It can be no guide to the future, but with so many alternatives on offer one has to start somewhere, and fragrant memories seem the best place. Lest anyone mistake these for "The World's 200 Best Wines" let me restate my fixed position: taste is personal. I like what I like – and so should you.

The wines are indicated within entries in this way: ***Châteaux Aiguilloux***

applied as absolutes, or in relation to a given group of wines? An outstanding Muscadet, let's say, is a very different proposition from an outstanding First Growth Bordeaux. It is essential, in other words, to know the expectation of the taster giving the points. High expectations lead to low scoring – this is another variable that limits the usefulness of citing scores out of their context.

All these systems are designed to crystallize an opinion of one particular wine at a time. They differ fundamentally, therefore, from the four-point system I devised for this book and which is set out on the front flap. We are not talking here about individual wines but their producers, or in some cases their regions of origin. Any useful judgement of their quality has to be based on an assessment of their whole production in relation to their peers. Hence the bracketing from, for example, two to four stars for a large enterprise whose main production fits the description of "above average" but whose flagship wine is "grand, prestigious, expensive". If the expense is usually justified, the stars are coloured, thereby extending the system to eight possible points. (Or even nine, if you include the inference of no star at all.)

One should always remember that the value of wine is more than a simple (or indeed complex) gustatory pleasure. It is a tapestry of taste and sentiment, expectation and association. Outside the small circle of professional wine judges, who are obliged to strive for objectivity, most of us are readier to enjoy wines with personal links that only we understand. I may have to fight against being subjective in compiling this book. You the reader should embrace it. Love the wines you love, however many points they score.

Agenda 2008

We talk much about vintages in this book. A given year was cool and wet, we say; or was damp in August but cheered up in September; or was successful for those growers who picked before the rain in October. I've always found this last to be of slightly mixed usefulness; how on earth is anybody, myself included most of the time, to know who picked before the rain and who didn't? And when we go into a wine shop, do we take a bottle off the shelf and think: Ah, the year when it cheered up in September? No, on the whole we don't. So what point is there in talking about vintages?

Well, the point is to understand wine, rather than to reduce it to a set of coordinates. I've talked elsewhere in this year's book about my views on points systems, and marking wines out of 20, 100, or whatever amount. If marking a single wine is fraught with difficulties, how much more difficult is it to reduce a whole vintage in a whole region to a number?

We do this, of course, on the front endpapers of this Guide. It's the briefest, most tentative of aides-memoires, and if only it were more exciting. How I long sometimes for decades in which a vintage could be written off with a contemptuous "1", while the next is praised to the skies with "9–10". A mark of 2 or 3 would perhaps damn with faint praise even more conclusively; what gets monotonous is the endless string of 6s and 7s – those perfectly good but not exceptional vintages, where the wines are attractive, even charming, but won't set the world alight. These are the vintages, as often as not, that would have scored 3 or 4 thirty years ago. Modern winemaking and viticulture has made writing a numeric vintage chart a very dull process. And if one compares the scores with the verbal summaries elsewhere in the book, it becomes apparent that whether it rained in August or October makes very little difference to the final score: the wines in the end turn out to be perfectly good, perfectly drinkable. So does any of it matter?

The truth is that vintages matter less than they did. Modern viticulture, providing that a grower knows what he or she is doing, can mitigate the effects of drought or rain. Rot can be controlled; so can most pests and diseases. It's not easy: it means understanding your terroir to the last square metre and knowing which parts dry out and which parts get waterlogged. It means deciding to take off extra leaves to let in more sun, or leave them on to keep it out; or taking them off on one side of the vine, and leaving them on on the other. It means treating each vine as an individual, and watching its progress week by week.

In the winery, it means understanding not just the sugar levels of the grapes as they arrive at the crusher, but also the acidity and tannin levels; it means looking at the thickness of the skins and the darkness of the colour, whether they're shrivelled with overripeness or bloated with water, and adjusting your extraction of colour and tannins accordingly, so that you don't end up with massive tannins in a year of light fruit, or vice versa. It's expertise in these areas that ensures a tedious run of middling-to-rather-good marks in a vintage chart, and ensures that when we take a bottle off the shelf we don't need to worry, most of the time, about the year. There is little chance of the year having been bad enough to worry about.

Yet, in another sense, vintages matter more than ever. Now that good wine is the norm and one has to search hard for bad (British pubs still seem to be especially good at this) we can, if we want, refine our sensitivity to style. The obvious example is the 2003 vintage in most of Europe. If you want big, baked reds with no finish, that's your year. If you don't, avoid it. If you want botrytis-affected sweet wines, then you need to know in which vintages the blessed noble rot filled the vineyards, and in which years it was nowhere to be seen and the grapes were merely shrivelled and overripe. If you're looking for bargains (and aren't we all?) it helps to know which were the uniform vintages, in which you might risk that inexpensive wine from an unknown producer, and which were the uneven ones, in which you should stick to the good names.

But there's another way in which vintages matter more than ever now. In those parts of the world where vintages are closely followed, which means Bordeaux above all, lesser vintages don't sell. And when I say they don't sell, I mean that the négociants still buy them from the châteaux – well, mostly – but that there simply isn't enough demand from consumers to clear them out of the négociants' cellars. The important, hyped-up vintages – 2000, 2005 – move like greased lightning. Everybody wants them. But the 2001s, the 2002s, the 2004s – delicious wines, all of them, but not fashionable vintages – hang fire. The consumers and collectors who are prepared to pay sky-high prices for top years just aren't interested in any vintage that is less than superb. Apart from making one wonder what such people drink with dinner on a wet Monday, it points to a problematic concern with prestige that is driving the market at the top end. Certain vintages, certain properties, are prestigious, and have to be acquired at all costs; others are not, and can be ignored. Those non-prestigious years and wines are better than they have ever been in the whole of their history; at the precise moment when vintages matter less than ever in terms of drinkability, they matter more than ever in terms of saleability. Crazy or what?

And of course it's all tied up with the matter of scores that I talk about elsewhere in this book. If one or two American critics rave about a vintage, it's suddenly fashionable enough to buy. (As Jean-Michel Cazes of Château Lynch-Bages said wickedly after the 2003 vintage, "We didn't think it was very good. But then an American critic said it was fantastic, so then we knew.") The difference in quality of an individual wine between a great vintage and a very good one can be small. All the more reason, then, for explaining in a few well-chosen words the weather that produced the particular style of the year – and for understanding that, in these days where one good year follows another, quality is a matter of incremental steps, not a switch that is either on or off.

How to use this book

The top line of most entries consists of the following information:

①   **③**

Aglianico del Vulture Bas | r dr (s/sw sp) | ★★★ | **96' 97** 98 99' 00 01' 02 (03)

           ②   **④**

① Wine name and the region the wine comes from.

② Whether it is red, rosé or white (or brown/amber), dry, sweet or sparkling, or several of these (and which is most important):

r	red
p	rosé
w	white
br	brown
dr	dry*
sw	sweet
s/sw	semi-sweet
sp	sparkling

( ) brackets here denote a less important wine

*assume wine is dry when **dr** or **sw** are not indicated

③ Its general standing as to quality: a necessarily rough-and-ready guide based on its current reputation as reflected in its prices:

★	plain, everyday quality
★★	above average
★★★	well known, highly reputed
★★★★	grand, prestigious, expensive

So much is more or less objective. Additionally there is a subjective rating:

★ etc   Stars are coloured for any wine which in my experience is usually especially good within its price range. There are good everyday wines as well as good luxury wines. This system helps you find them.

④ Vintage information: which of the recent vintages can be recommended; of these, which are ready to drink this year, and which will probably improve with keeping. Your choice for current drinking should be one of the vintage years printed in **bold** type. Buy light-type years for further maturing.

oo etc   recommended years that may be currently available

96' etc   vintage regarded as particularly successful for the property in question

97 etc   years in **bold** should be ready for drinking (those not in bold will benefit from keeping)

98 etc   vintages in colour are those recommended as first choice for drinking in 2005. (See also Bordeaux introduction, p.80.)

(02) etc   provisional rating

The German vintages work on a different principle again: see p.136.

Other abbreviations

DYA	drink the youngest available
NV	vintage not normally shown on label; in Champagne, means a blend of several vintages for continuity
CHABLIS	properties, areas or terms cross-referred within the section

__Châteaux Aiguilloux__ type so styled within entries indicates wine (mid '06–'07) specially enjoyed by the author.

Vintage report 2006

Is it my imagination, or do vintages come round faster nowadays? We were still swooning over the 2005s when suddenly the 2006 vintage was upon us; and I fear that the fate of the 2006s in many places is to be in the shadow of the earlier, greater year.

Much of that is because Bordeaux is less good than in 2005; and it's still the case that for many people the quality of the vintage in Bordeaux affects their judgement of other regions. A cool summer and a fair amount of rot kept the superlatives away, though the Merlot was healthy enough and alcohol levels don't seem to have fallen appreciably. It's what's often termed a "classic" year in Bordeaux, which means a year of ripe fruit but rather dry tannins. The whites are delicious, and the sweet whites very good indeed. Burgundy, too, was patchy, and again rot was a problem for the reds, although the whites seem to be very good indeed. Champagne was rescued by a good autumn, although the wines may not have enough concentration for the year to be generally declared as a vintage. The Rhône had a healthy year, and rich, balanced wines; the Loire found things more difficult, but mostly survived pretty well.

It was a cool growing season in most places – no bad thing, that, provided the grapes get properly ripe, and on the whole they did. But coolness combined with dampness can bring rot problems, as it did in Germany, requiring growers to be rigorous about selection if they wanted to make good wines. Well, the best German growers were rigorous and made very good wines, even if only in small quantities.

If you want superlatives, try Austria. There they sound very happy indeed: "Wonderful," says Michael Moosbrugger, winemaker at Schloss Gobelsburg in Kamptal. "Unlike most of Europe, we didn't have rain in August. It was cool, so we kept plenty of acidity, and we were able to pick right up until mid-November. I can't say if it was better than 2005, but the general ripeness level was slightly higher in 2006. The wines are outstanding." Over in Rust, Martin Wenzel of Weinbau Wenzel agrees: "We had one rainy day in the whole autumn. In six weeks we got in all the dry wines, all the reds and even the sweet wines."

Italy, too, is talking optimistically. Chianti seems to have made wonderful wines; so does Friuli-Venezia Guilia; so does the Veneto; and so does Piedmont. Spain seems to have made every possible quality from very, very good to pretty dull. Not, perhaps, a year for trying something from that unknown little bodega; stick to the tried and trusted names. And while in Portugal it doesn't seem likely to be a generally declared vintage year for Port, there'll be plenty of soft, ripe, rich table wines for early drinking: the coolness and dampness did not extend this far west, and Portugal had a hot, dry summer.

Across the Atlantic reports from California are cautiously cheerful, while in the southern hemisphere anybody making wine in Eastern Australia (that is, those parts that are not Western Australia) probably had a very good year indeed. Quality in Western Australia is more mixed, with the whites better than the reds. South Africa appears to have had few problems.

A closer look at 2005

In much of Europe, 2005 has already assumed the status of a classic year, even though at the time of writing the wines are only just beginning to hit the shelves. In Burgundy early tastings revealed wines of beautiful balance and length, and reds with the most seductive perfumes for years: if you want to convince anyone of the joys of Pinot Noir, 2005 is the vintage to do it with. The way they combine delicacy and concentration should show any right-thinking person that density, chocolate and prune fruit, and 15 degrees of alcohol are not the only ways for red wine to be. The whites? Almost as good, but not quite. They lack a bit of tension, a bit of nerviness, especially in Chablis. But they're still good.

Naturally, they won't be cheap. In fact the choicest wines will have been snapped up already: interest was keen when merchants held their tastings. Ripeness but not overripeness, structure but not too much muscle: Oh, for more wines like them.

Well, there are more wines like them (except that they're made from Cabernet and Merlot) in Bordeaux this year. Many more. Burgundy is such an elusive creature, with many wines made in tiny quantities, that it's no wonder most of us opt for the simpler option and head to Bordeaux, where we know there'll be enough to go round. Bordeaux shares the characteristics of balance and elegance in 2005: the wines are ripe but not jammy unless the winemaker went out of his way to make them so (some did, inevitably); they're wines that sing. The top wines, the leading classed growths that are in demand internationally, will be expensive – indeed were expensive when the châteaux released them in the spring of 2006. Some of the prices were simply phenomenal. But there'll be plenty of lesser wines that will be affordable and delightful. And it's a great year for Sauternes and other sweet whites.

But is either Burgundy or Bordeaux (excepting Sauternes) enormously better than in 2004? Well, no, actually. They're better, and they're more homogeneous. But they're not streets and streets ahead.

Over in Austria, 2005 seems to have banished the tendency to over-high alcohol that was noticeable for a couple of years: the wines have glorious balance and style. In Germany, too, the vintage seems almost flawless. But over in California early hopes that 2005 would be the best since 2001 seem to have been banished. The wines simply won't be the long-lived classics that had been expected: well, wines do that to you. The first tastings suggest one style; then they do an about-turn and evolve into something else.

In South Africa 2005 showed the continuation of a trend: that if you want wines that combine concentration with elegance and a growing sense of place, the Western Cape is a place to look. There's a brightness to the best wines, red and white, that is not found everywhere in the New World.

Big brand review

What constitutes a wine brand? Discuss. For the purposes of this piece, a brand is taken to be a wine which is widely available in several countries, and generally at the cheaper end of the market. However, as Australia and the USA would tend to dominate under such criteria, some bestselling wines from other countries also appear in the following line-up (all wines were purchased in February 2007).

Whites (plus a lone rosé)

THE BEST

Concha y Toro Casillero del Diablo Sauvignon Blanc 2006, Casablanca, Chile Zesty citrus and herbs, has tang and bite without being an assault on the palate.

Montana Sauvignon Blanc 2006, Marlborough, New Zealand Rich grassy asparagus, with intense herby overtones. Maybe a tad too rich?

Jacob's Creek Semillon/Chardonnay 2005, South Eastern Australia Pithy Semillon and peachy Chardonnay, with a touch of nut, nicely balanced.

Calvet Limited Release Bordeaux Sauvignon Blanc 2005, France Nettle, lemon, lemon-grass, nice texture with length and freshness.

Torres Viña Sol 2006, Penedès, Spain Light, lively citrus notes, simple but tasty, nice crisp finish.

PASSABLE

Robert Mondavi Woodbridge Chardonnay 2005, California Plump and buttery, rather sweet and oily, full of flavour but lacks freshness.

Argento Chardonnay 2006, Mendoza, Argentina Plump peach, nut and cream flavours, slightly lean finish.

Hardy's Stamp Semillon/Sauvignon Blanc 2005, South Eastern Australia Easy-drinking citrus and guava flavours with a slightly nutty edge.

Kumala Colombard/Chardonnay 2006, Western Cape Simple plump pear, melon and peach, hint of ginger but slightly confected.

J P Chenet Chardonnay Vin de Pays d'Oc 2006, France Simple, fresh, lightly fruity, hint of nut.

Lindeman's Bin 65 Chardonnay 2005, South Eastern Australia Rather oily, rich tropical fruit but lacks freshness.

POOR

Blossom Hill Chardonnay 2005, California Very simple, rather thin, vague melon and peach flavours.

Piat d'Or Medium white Vin de Pays du Gers NV, France Tart yet sweet, floral but underripe.

Gallo Sierra Valley Chardonnay 2005, California Thin, dominated by vanilla, little fruit.

Mateus Rosé NV, Portugal Where's the easy berry fruit? This has been better in the past.

Yellow Tail Chardonnay 2005, South Eastern Australia Crude, sweet vanilla, almost like Tia Maria, really not nice.

Blue Nun Tafelwein 2005, Rhein, Germany Stale sweetened grapefruit tinged with ginger, poor.

Reds

THE BEST

Concha y Toro Casillero del Diablo Cabernet Sauvignon 2005, Central Valley, Chile
Classic smoky Chilean blackcurrant, honest, ripe and with potential.
Argento Malbec 2006, Mendoza, Argentina Sweet berry attack, but dry
palate and firm finish with floral notes.
Torres Sangre de Toro 2005, Catalunya, Spain Fresh, herby nose, spicy
berry flavours, slightly jammy, but has bite and structure.
Calvet Limited Release Claret 2005, France Refreshing, tangy black fruit
with an earthy core and ripe tannins.
Jacob's Creek Shiraz/Cabernet 2004, South Eastern Australia Warm pepper
and plum, smoky, almost leathery finish. Again, some potential.
Robert Mondavi Woodbridge Shiraz 2003, California
Maturing, plummy berry and spice, just lacks intensity.

PASSABLE

Lindeman's Bin 50 Shiraz 2006, South Eastern Australia A little sweet and
confected but no shortage of gutsy black fruit.
Kumala Pinotage/Shiraz 2006, Western Cape, South Africa Smoky/rubbery
notes, fleshy ripe fruit, but finish a little clumsy.
Hardy's VR Merlot 2005, South Eastern Australia Simple, stewed fruit,
slightly minty but muddy, vanilla-heavy finish.
J P Chenet Merlot Vin de Pays d'Oc 2005, France Some earthy, plummy grip
here, but overextracted and a sweet finish.

POOR

Montana Merlot/Cabernet Sauvignon 2005, East Coast, New Zealand
Confected jam and oak, sweet, rather crude.
Gallo Sierra Valley Zinfandel 2005, California Vegetal notes dominate
otherwise pleasant fruit, stale finish.
Piat d'Or Vin de Pays d'Oc Red NV, France Artificial fruit flavours, sweet
and insipid.
Blossom Hill Cabernet Sauvignon 2004, California Crude jammy berry and
vanilla, not very pleasant.
Yellow Tail Merlot 2005, South Eastern Australia OK fruit, but dreadful
vanilla dominates – wine for Coke drinkers.

France

More heavily shaded areas
are the wine-growing regions

The following abbreviations
are used in the text:

Al	Alsace
Beauj	Beaujolais
Burg	Burgundy
B'x	Bordeaux
Champ	Champagne
Lo	Loire
Prov	Provence
Pyr	Pyrenees
N/S Rh	North/South Rhône
SW	Southwest
AC	*appellation contrôlée*

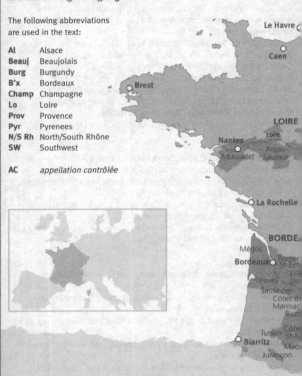

If you were going to invent a wine country from scratch, how closely would it resemble France?

Well, since you're going to be utterly businesslike about it, you'd invent somewhere with low labour costs (you're not a charitable institution) and high volumes, where profits will be healthy and regular. You'd invent somewhere with a safe, regular climate where fashionable, internationally recognizable grape varieties ripen reliably year after year: the last thing you'd want is vintage difference to worry your customers. You'd want nice big vineyards, preferably flat – you don't need to worry too much about mechanization, since labour is so cheap and so readily available, but you like simplicity.

Terroir? Oh, yes, you want to be able to talk about this. But the idea

of making wine in parcels tiny enough actually to reflect the character of the soil and microclimate – well, hmmm.

What you'd have invented, of course, is something like Chile's Central Valley. And it's possible that in time, drinking a succession of low-cost wines with not too much to choose between them, you might hanker after something different. Something more challenging, more complicated: something where wines have evolved without a thought of marketing departments; something eccentric and characterful that makes demands on the drinker; something for grown-ups.

Congratulations. You'd have invented France.

France entries also cross-refer to Châteaux of Bordeaux section.

Recent vintages of the French classics

Red Bordeaux

Médoc/red Graves For some wines bottle age is optional: for these it is indispensable. Minor châteaux from light vintages need only two or three years, but even modest wines of great years can improve for 15 or so, and the great châteaux of these years can profit from double that time.

2006 A cool Aug with rain and rot during harvest meant Cabernet Sauvignon didn't ripen fully. Good colour and alcohol, though. Need to be selective.

2005 Perfect weather conditions throughout the year. Dry season and harvest. Rich, balanced, long-ageing wines from an outstanding vintage.

2004 Dry, sunny Sept and early Oct but rain during the Cabernet harvest. Mixed bag. Abundant vintage, which needed curbing. Good if selective.

2003 Hottest summer on record. Cabernet Sauvignon can be tremendous (St-Estèphe, Pauillac). Atypical but rich, powerful wines at best, unbalanced at worst. Yields right down.

2002 Saved by a dry, sunny Sept. The later-ripening Cabernet Sauvignon benefited most. Yields down. Some good wines if selective. Drink now–2018.

2001 A cool Sept and rain at vintage meant Cabernet Sauvignon had difficulty in ripening fully. Some fine fresh wines to drink now–2012.

2000 Late flowering and a somewhat damp start to the summer looked worrying, but the final product is outstanding – superb wines throughout. Keep.

1999 Vintage rain again diluted ripe juice, so-so wines to drink now–2010.

1998 Rain at vintage *again*. But Aug heat ripened (even roasted) grapes. Good, but the Right Bank is clearly the winner this year. Drink now–2015.

1997 Uneven flowering and summer rain were a double challenge. Top wines still of interest, but the rest have faded.

1996 Cool summer, fine harvest. Good to excellent. Drink now–2020.

1995 Heat-wave and drought; saved by rain. Good to excellent. Now–2015.

1994 Hopes of a supreme year; then heavy vintage rain. The best good, but be careful. Drink now.

1993 Ripe grapes but a wet vintage. Most for drinking up.

1992 Rain at flowering, in Aug, and at vintage. A huge crop; light wines. Avoid.

1991 Frost in April halved crop and rain interrupted vintage. The northern Médoc did best. Drink up.

1990 A paradox: a drought year with a threat of over-production. Self-discipline was essential. Its results are magnificent. To 2015.

1989 Early spring, splendid summer. Top wines classics of the ripe, dark kind: elegance, length. Some better than 1990. Small châteaux uneven. To 2020.

1988 Generally very good; tannic, balanced, drinking well. Keep top wines.

Older fine vintages: 86 85 82 75 70 66 62 61 59 55 53 49 48 47 45 29 28.

St-Emilion/Pomerol

2006 Rain and rot at harvest. Variable. Merlot marginally better than Cabernet Sauvignon this year giving Pomerol the advantage.

2005 Same conditions as the Médoc. An overall success.

2004 Merlot often better than 2003 (Pomerol). Good Cabernet Franc. Variable.

2003 Merlot suffered in the heat, but exceptional Cabernet Franc. Very mixed. Some over-extraction again.

2002 Problems with rot and ripeness; some over-extraction. Modest to good.

2001 Less rain than Médoc during vintage. Some powerful Merlot, but variable.

2000 Similar conditions to Médoc. Less kind to Merlot, but a very good vintage.

1999 Careful, lucky growers made good wines, but rain was again a problem.

1998 Earlier-ripening Merlot largely escaped the rain. Some excellent wines.

1997 Merlot suffered in the rain. Only a handful of wines still of interest.

1996 Cool, fine summer. Vintage rain. Less consistent than Médoc. Now–2015.

1995 Perhaps even better than Médoc/Graves. Now–2015.

1994 Good, especially Pomerol. Drink now.

1993 Pomerol better than Médoc; good despite terrible vintage weather.

1992 Very dilute. Avoid.

1991 A sad story. Many wines not released.

1990 Another chance to make great wine or a lot of wine. Now–2015.

1989 Large, ripe, early harvest; an overall triumph. To 2020.

1988 Generally excellent. But some châteaux over-produced. Drink soon.

Older fine vintages: 85 82 71 70 67 66 64 61 59 53 52 49 47 45.

Red Burgundy

Côte d'Or Côte de Beaune reds generally mature sooner than bigger wines of Côte de Nuits. Earliest drinking dates are for lighter commune wines – *e.g.* Volnay, Beaune; latest for biggest wines of, *e.g.* Chambertin, Romanée. But even the best Burgundies are more attractive young than equivalent red Bordeaux.

2006 Better in Côte de Nuits (less rain); some rot problems in Côte de Beaune.

2005 The best for a generation, potentially outstanding wines everywhere.

2004 Good, except where hail has caused significant damage.

2003 Reds coped with the heat better than the whites. Muscular, rich wines. Best wines outstanding, others short and hot.

2002 Avoided the rains of southern France. A very exciting, stylish vintage to drink and keep.

2001 Just needed a touch more sun for excellence.

2000 Difficult. Much better in Côte de Nuits, delicious to drink now.

1999 Big ripe vintage; good colour, bags of fruit, silky tannins. Wines to keep.

1998 Ripe fruit but dry tannins. Those in balance starting to come round.

1997 Again the gods smiled. Very ripe grapes, with low acidity. Lovely wines mostly ready now.

1996 Fine summer and vintage. Top wines must be kept. 2008–2020.

1995 Small crop, potentially fine but not yet showing its expected class.

1994 Compromised by vintage rain. Generally lean, but exceptions in Côte de Nuits. Drink up.

1993 Impressive fruit to balance the tannins in Côte de Nuits; mostly drying out in Côte de Beaune.

1992 Ripe, plump, pleasing. No great concentration. Drink up.

1991 Very small harvest; some wines very tannic. Côte de Nuits best. Drink soon.

Older fine vintages: 90 88 85 78 71 69 66 64 62 61 59 (all mature).

White Burgundy

Côte de Beaune Well-made wines of good vintages with plenty of acidity as well as fruit. Will improve and gain depth and richness for some years – up to ten. Lesser wines from lighter vintages are ready for drinking after two or three.

2006 Plentiful crop of charming, aromatic wines – 1992-plus.

2005 Small but outstanding crop of dense, concentrated wines.

2004 Really promising for aromatic, balanced wines for medium-term ageing.

2003 Treat with care. Not many keepers from this hot vintage, though best are pleasingly plump.

2002 Ripe healthy grapes; medium-sized crop of great promise. Stylish wines.

2001 Generally good results despite lower sugar levels. Drink soon.

2000 A big crop of ripe, healthy grapes. Exciting wines starting to come round.

1999 Generous vintage of good, well-balanced wines now hitting their stride.

1998 Difficult year for white. Chassagne was successful. Drink up rapidly.

1997 Overall an excellent vintage: forward and charming. Drink soon.

1996 Not developing as well as hoped. Over-acidic.

1995 A potentially great vintage, diluted in places. Now–2010.

The white wines of the Mâconnais (Pouilly-Fuissé, St-Véran, Mâcon-Villages) follow a similar pattern, but do not last as long. They are more appreciated for their freshness than their richness.

Chablis *Grand cru* Chablis of vintages with both strength and acidity can age superbly for up to ten years; *premiers crus* proportionately less.

2006 An early harvest of attractive, aromatically pleasing wines.

2005 Small but outstanding crop of dense, concentrated wines.

2004 Difficult vintage, with mildew a problem, but larger than 2003.

2003 Small crop of ripe wines, but acidity is low and balance in question.

2002 Excellent; may be the equal of 2000.

2001 Too much rain. Relatively weak. Drink up.

2000 Fine weather for harvesting ripe grapes – excellent.

1999 Another ripe vintage, some of it compromised by rain. Drink soon.

1998 Cool weather and some hail. Wines fair to good: not for long keeping.

1997 Another fine vintage; *grands crus* excellent now.

Beaujolais 06: tricky vintage with some rot compromising the fruit. 05: concentrated wines. 04: light, some weak, some pretty. 03: too much heat on the grapes, but some excellent. 02: too much rain for top quality. 01: very good if picked before the rain. 00: excellent. 99: splendid, rich, and deep. 98: very good, if patchy; best *crus* will keep. Older wines should be finished.

Southwest France

2006 A capricious and variable summer. Quality depends on choice of date for picking and selection of grapes at the chais.

2005 Living up to early promise. First class where growers were spared hail.

2004 Spoiled for many by bad Aug. Generally lighter. Excellent in Jurançon.

2003 Fruit often burned by the sun in this heatwave year. Small quantities of unbalanced wines, heavy in fruit, but often with stalky tannins. Drink up.

2002 Light wines, but good Cahors, Madiran, and Jurançon (late pickers).

2001 Big, rich wines in a hot year. Generally very successful. Reds now at their best.

The Midi

2006 Scorching Jun and July, followed by cooler Aug and some rain around harvest, but the best winemakers had fine results.

2005 A beautifully balanced year, with sunshine and rain at the right times throughout the region.

2004 Marked by Aug storms and a fine Sept. Wines are elegantly balanced, with lower alcohol than 03 or 01.

2003 The year of the heat-wave, in sharp contrast to 02, often resulting in a greatly reduced crop, but also many fine wines from skilled winemakers.

2002 Heavy rain in early Sept causing problems. Varies widely from AC to AC, and grower to grower. Good in the Minervois; diluted in Pic St-Loup.

2001 Quantity lower than average. Quality generally very good with a hot summer making for ripe, concentrated wines, drinking well now.

Northern Rhône

2006 Big, healthy crop with wines showing plenty of clear fruit and some sound stuffing. Could be underestimated. Good acidity in the whites.

2005 A great vintage, with wonderful Syrah. Keep the Hermitage, Côte-Rôtie and Cornas for 5+ years, revel now in the St-Joseph and Crozes fruit. Whites are full but can be a little heated – good for mid-term drinking.

2004 Mid-weight, mid-term year, with Côte-Rôtie showing well over time; best reds are from top vineyards. Excellent whites.

2003 A muscled, half-sized crop. Intense sun gave cooked "southern" flavours, high degrees, low acidity. Best reds show genuine richness, are coming together.

2002 Try before you buy. Best growers abandoned half their crop. Decent red St-Josephs, light Hermitage, Côte-Rôtie. Pretty good whites, especially Condrieu.

2001 Very good, lively year if picked before Sept rain. Fresh fruit, good acidity, can age well. Top year at Côte-Rôtie. Often very good whites.

2000 Decent density, quite warm and rich. Some stewed flavours. Hermitage good in parts, Cornas did well, Côte-Rôtie variable. Good Condrieu, sumptuous. Reds simpler than 99/01.

1999 Very successful. Full, ripe fruit. Delicious, likely to live long. More balance than the 98s. Harmony a key word. Ace Côte-Rôties. Sound whites.

1998 Big, robust vintage. More overt tannins than 99, but have fused well, with rich oily textures, now starting a second, gamey phase of life. Good Marsanne-based whites.

Southern Rhône

2006 Rich, ripely fruited wines at Châteauneuf-du-Pape, with summer rainfalls timed to perfection. Fresher style than the 2005s, the roundness of the fruit is present if the grower waited until mid-Sept. Good bistro vintage for the simple wines – Côtes-du-Rhône, Ventoux. Good whites.

2005 Very good, but beware high alcohol levels in prestige wines, with very heady crop, especially Grenache. Punchy wines with greater balance than the 03s. Best sites to the fore again. Whites are big, best drunk young.

2004 Uneven ripening until stable Sept retrieved the situation. Some Côtes du Rhônes have sharp flavours. Good sinew and freshness in the Châteauneufs will suit European palates. Gigondas not always rounded. Be patient; let the wines settle. Good fresh whites.

2003 A classic, chunky, potent, and warm year from the best, e.g. Châteauneuf – better than Gigondas, Vacqueyras. Two-speed ripening, so not all balanced. Go for the best names, best areas.

2002 Nature's payback. Floods around Châteauneuf. Simply-fruited reds (drink early) and acceptable whites. No super-cuvées this year. Gigondas did best.

2001 Excellent classic vintage, where grape, not oak, tannins prevail. Complex reds, lots of life ahead, be patient for top areas. Cracking Châteauneufs.

2000 Tasty wines, led by fruit. Not a long-lived year. Go for leading names. Gigondas may edge Châteauneuf in quality. Best reds are singing now.

1999 Very good overall. Ripe, open fruit with correct structure in the best wines. Châteauneuf reds have moved up a gear with age, very fine fruit on show.

1998 Very good. Big, warm wines, at a funky, cooked-fruit, mineral stage now.

Champagne

2006 Topsy-turvy growing season but fine Sept: sound, ripe base wines but higher permitted yields put question mark over eventual quality.

2005 Almost as big a harvest as 2004 but much less even in quality: some great Chardonnays and selectively good Pinot Noirs – but indifferent Pinot Meuniers.

2004 Exactly what was needed. Record bumper crop giving Champagnes of classic finesse and "tension". Vintage year.

2003 Torrid, difficult year. Tiny harvest, especially from hail-struck Chardonnay. Wines lack acidity – most will be for NV blends.

2002 Ideal harvest yielded rich, complex wines, especially the Pinots. Potentially great.

2000 Fine harvest sun produced decent wines. The best are structured keepers; others can be short on palate. Goodish but not great vintage year.

1999 Warm summer with breaks of refreshing rain. Ripe, expressive wines, ready soon. Exceptional Bollinger Grande Année Rosé.

1998 The vintage to buy now. Really classic wines, some better than 1996; superb Pol Roger Blanc du Chardonnay and Dom Pérignon.

Older fine vintages: 95 90 89 88 85 82

The Loire

2006 A challenging vintage in which only the conscientious succeeded. Dry whites fared well, reds nearly as attractive. Not great for sweet whites.

2005 Excellent across the board. Buy without fear. The sweet wines are more likely to be the product of shrivelled grapes from noble rot.

2004 Huge crop. In general better for reds than whites. Few or no sweet wines in Vouvray/Montlouis. Anjou's whites are fewer and less sweet than usual.

2003 An atypical vintage. Some areas hit by spring frost. Wines are big and supple, though not flaccid. For early drinking. Good year for sweet wines.

2002 Best since 97. Vivid fruit and vibrant acidity in the dry whites. Some fine sweet Chenins. Where yields were kept low, the reds are juicy and deeply coloured. (Beware a whiff of rot in many of the Gamay-based wines.)

2001 Warm, wet winter left soils gorged with water. Best wines are from those who harvested late. But Muscadet perfect. Taste before buying.

Alsace

2006 Hottest recorded July followed by coolest Aug and some rot problems on plains. Skilful growers produced attractive wines.

2005 A large crop of healthy grapes harvested after an Indian summer. Ripe and well-balanced wines. Some good sweet wines, too.

2004 Despite it being a difficult year, growers who picked early and kept yields low produced classic wines.

2003 Earliest harvest since 1893. Small crop of variable wines. Best are ripe, but with low acidity (hence acidification allowed for the first time ever).

2002 Better than most of France. Late-picked wines are good to very good.

2001 Unsettled weather in Sept. Well-balanced wines, good but not great.

2000 Superb – probably best since 90. Very good for Vendanges Tardives and Sélections des Grains Nobles.

Abel-Lepitre Middle-rank CHAMPAGNE house. Very good BRUT Millésimé **96' 98 00** 02.

Abymes Savoie w ★ DYA Hilly area nr Chambéry; light, mild Vin de Savoie AC from Jacquère grape has alpine charm. SAVOIE has many such *crus* for local pleasure.

Agenais SW France r p (w) ★ DYA VIN DE PAYS of Lot-et-Garonne, with good independents (some organic) alongside the co-ops.

Aligoté DYA Second-rank Burgundy white grape and wine. Should be pleasantly tart and fruity with local character when young. BOUZERON has its own appellation – best from de Villaine – but other minerally areas, *e.g.* PERNAND-VERGELESSES also good from top growers.

Alliet, Philippe Lo r w ★★ →★★★ One of best producers of Chinon. Top CUVÉES include barrel-aged Coteau du Noire and a new hill v'yd l'Huissiere. Also a small amount of white.

Aloxe-Corton Burg r w ★★→★★★ 96' 97 98 99' 01 02' 03 05' 06 Village at north end of CÔTE DE BEAUNE famous for two GRANDS CRUS: CORTON (red), CORTON-CHARLEMAGNE (white). Village wines are lighter but to try.

Alsace Al w (r sp sw) ★★→★★★★ Includes eastern foothills of Vosges mountains, especially Strasbourg-Mulhouse. Wines: aromatic, fruity, full-bodied, mostly dry and expressive of variety, but too often sweet. See VENDANGE TARDIVE, SÉLECTION DES GRAINS NOBLES. Much sold by variety (Pinot Bl, Ries, GEWURZ). Matures well (except Pinot Bl, MUSCAT) 5–10 years; GRAND CRU even longer. Good-quality and value CRÉMANT. Pinot N is very good but can be hard to find.

Alsace Grand Cru w ★★★→★★★★ AC restricted to 51 (KAEFFERKOPF added in 2006) of the best-named vineyards (approx 1,600 ha, 800 in production) and four noble grapes (Ries, PINOT GR, GEWURZ, MUSCAT) mainly dry, some sweet. Not without controversy but generally very good, expressive of terroir.

Amirault, Yannick Lo r ★★→★★★ First-rate producer of both Bourgueil and St-Nicholas de Bourgueil. Top CUVÉES include La Petite Cave and Les Quartiers in Bourgueil, and Malagnes and Graviers in St-Nicholas.

Ampeau, Robert Burg ★★★ Exceptional grower and specialist in MEURSAULT and VOLNAY; also POMMARD. Perhaps unique in releasing only long-matured bottles.

André, Pierre Burg ★ NÉGOCIANT at Châteaux Corton-André, ALOXE-CORTON; 38 ha of vineyards in CORTON (good Corton-Charlemagne, Corton Blanc), SAVIGNY, GEVREY-CHAMBERTIN, etc. Definite signs of improvement here. Also owns REINE PEDAUQUE.

d'Angerville, Marquis Burg ★★★★ Top grower with immaculate 14-ha estate all in VOLNAY. Top wines: Champans, and intense, potent Clos des Ducs.

Anjou Lo p r w (sw dr sp) ★→★★★★ Both region and umbrella Loire AC. Many styles: Chenin Bl-based dry whites range from light quaffers to potent agers; juicy reds include surprisingly rich AC Anjou Gamay; juicy Cab Fr-based Anjou rouge; and structured ANJOU-VILLAGES; also strong, usually dry, SAVENNIÈRES; luscious COTEAUX DU LAYON Chenin Bl; dry sweet rosé, and sparkling.

Anjou-Coteaux de la Loire Lo w s/sw sw ★★→★★★ Tiny westernmost Anjou AC for sweet whites made from Chenin Bl that tend to be less rich but nervier than COTEAUX DU LAYON. Especially Musset-Roullier, Château de Putille, Domaines du Fresche, de Putille.

Anjou-Villages Lo r ★→★★★ Superior central ANJOU AC for reds (Cab Fr, some Cab Sauv). Usually ambitious, quality tends to be high and prices reasonable, especially Domaine de Brize, Château de Coulaine, Domaine Philippe Cady, Philippe Delesvaux, Domaine les Grandes Vignes, Ogereau, CHÂTEAU PIERRE-BISE. Sub-AC Anjou-Villages-Brissac covers the same zone as Coteaux de l'Aubance; look for Bablut, Domaine de Haute Perche, Montigilet, RICHOU, Rochelles.

Appellation Contrôlée (AC or AOC) Government control of origin and production (*not* quality) of all the best French wines.

Apremont Savoie w ★★ DYA One of the best villages of SAVOIE for pale, delicate whites, mainly from Jacquère grapes, but recently including CHARD.

Arbin Savoie r ★★ *Deep-coloured lively red from MONDEUSE grapes*, rather like a good Loire Cab Sauv. Ideal après-ski. Drink at 1–2 years.

Arbois Jura r p w (sp) ★★→★★★ Various good and original light but tasty wines; speciality is VIN JAUNE. On the whole, DYA except excellent VIN JAUNE.

l'Ardèche, Coteaux de r p (w) ★→★★ Hilly area west of Rhône, buzzing along well. New DOMAINES; fresh oaked reds; Viognier (*e.g.* Mas de Libian) and Marsanne. Best from pure Syrah, Gamay, Cab Sauv (Serret). Powerful, almost Burgundian CHARD Ardèche by Louis LATOUR; Grand Ardèche is very oaked. Also Domaines du Colombier, Durand, Favette, Flacher, Mazel, Vigier.

Ariège SW r ★ 04 05 (06) Growing VIN DE PAYS from Cab Sauv, Merlot, Côt, and Tannat. Note especially Domaine des Coteaux d'Engravies. Will keep.

l'Arlot, Domaine de ★★★ Leading exponent in CÔTE DE NUITS of whole-bunch fermentation (*i.e.* using stems). Wines pale but aromatically charged and full of fruit. Best vineyards ROMANÉE-ST-VIVANT and NUITS-ST-GEORGES, especially Clos de l'Arlot.

What makes Alsace wine so special?

Alsace is a northerly region that you might expect to be cold and wet, and yet it produces wines of the highest quality. Why? The effect of clouds bumping into the Vosges mountains on their way east makes Colmar the second-driest town in France. Alsace is something of a geologist's paradise and many of the wines (especially Riesling) having an exciting minerality. The chequerboard of varied soil types also means that growers can match each of the eight permitted grape varieties to the ideal soil. Because the ribs of the Vosges run west to east, all the best vineyards have excellent southerly exposure – very important in a northerly region.

Armagnac SW The alternative to COGNAC, and increasingly popular; more tasty, rustic, and peppery. Table wines: CÔTES DE GASCOGNE, GERS, TERROIRS LANDAIS.

Armand, Comte Burg ★★★ Excellent POMMARD wines, especially Clos des Epéneaux. Especially brilliant since 1999.

Aube Southern extension of CHAMPAGNE. Now known as Côte des Bar.

Aujoux, J-M Beauj Substantial grower/merchant of BEAUJOLAIS. Swiss-owned.

Auxey-Duresses Burg r w ★★→★★★ 99' 02' 03 05' 06 Second-rank (but very pretty) CÔTE DE BEAUNE village: affinities with VOLNAY, MEURSAULT. Best examples (red) COMTE ARMAND, HOSPICES DE BEAUNE (Cuvée Boillot), LEROY, Prunier; (white) COMTE ARMAND, Fichet, *LEROY (Les Boutonniers)*.

Avize Champ One of the top Côte des Blancs villages. All CHARD.

Aÿ Champ One of the best Pinot N-growing villages of CHAMPAGNE.

Ayala Once-famous AŸ-based CHAMPAGNE house, now owned by BOLLINGER. Longer ageing on lees and more Pinot in blends are raising quality.

Bandol Prov r p (w) ★★★ Small coastal AC near Toulon; PROVENCE's best. Long-lasting reds mainly from Mourvèdre. Stars include Domaine TEMPIER, Pibarnon, Pradeaux, Mas de la Rouvière, La Suffrène, Lafran Veyrolles. Also rosés from young vines.

Banyuls Pyr br sw ★★→★★★ One of best VINS DOUX NATURELS, mainly Grenache (Banyuls GRAND CRU: over 75% Grenache, aged for 2 years+): a distant relation of port. Best are RANCIOS, with long ageing, from Domaines la Rectorie, du Mas Blanc (★★★), Vial Magnères, at 10–15 years old. Cheap NVs end up in bars.

Barrique The BORDEAUX (and COGNAC) term for an oak barrel holding 225 litres (300 bottles). Barrique-ageing to flavour almost any wine with oak was craze in late 1980s, with some sad results. Current oak prices should urge discretion.

Barsac B'x w sw ★★→★★★★ Neighbour of SAUTERNES with similar superb golden wines from lower-lying limestone soil; generally less powerful with more finesse. Repays long ageing. Top: CLIMENS, COUTET, DOISY-DAËNE, DOISY-VÉDRINES.

Barthod, Ghislaine Burg ★★★→★★★★ Impressive range of archetypal CHAMBOLLE-MUSIGNY. Marvellous poise and delicacy yet with depth and concentration. Les Cras, Fuées, and Beauxbruns best.

Barton & Guestier BORDEAUX shipper since 18th C. Produces a wide range.

Bâtard-Montrachet Burg w ★★★★ 89' 90' 92 93 95 96 97' 99' 00 02' **03** 04' 05' 06' Neighbour of MONTRACHET (22 ha). Should be long-lived: intense flavours, rich texture. Bienvenues-B-M is an adjacent 3.6-ha GRAND CRU; very rare. Criots-Bâtard-Montrachet (1.6 ha) is even rarer. Seek out: BOUCHARD PÈRE & FILS, BOILLOT, CARILLON, DROUHIN, GAGNARD, Louis LATOUR, LEFLAIVE, MOREY, Pernot, RAMONET, SAUZET.

Baudry, Domaine Bernard Lo r p w ★★→★★★ Superb CHINON in every style, from

Chenin Bl-based whites to Cab Fr-based rosés and excellent CHINON CUVÉES of red, from juicy Les Granges to structured Clos Guillot and Croix Boissées.

Baumard, Domaine des Lo ★★→★★★★ Important grower of ANJOU wine, especially Chenin Bl-based whites, including SAVENNIÈRES (Clos St Yves, Clos du Papillon) and QUARTS DE CHAUME. Baumard makes CRÉMANT DE LOIRE and a tangy VIN DE TABLE from VERDELHO.

Béarn SW Fr r p w ★→★★ w p DYA r 04 05 06 Domaine Lapeyre/Guilhémas best in the Pyrenean AC. Also co-op at Bellocq.

Beaujolais r (p w) ★ DYA Simple AC of the very big BEAUJOLAIS region: light short-lived fruity red from Gamay. Beaujolais Supérieur is little different. Best vineyards in the hills around Bois d'Oingt.

Beaujolais Primeur, or Nouveau The Beaujolais of the new vintage, made in a hurry (often only 4–5 days' fermenting) for release at midnight on the third Wednesday in November. Ideally soft, pungent, fruity, and tempting; too often crude, sharp, too alcoholic. More of an event than a drink.

Beaujolais-Villages r ★★ 03 05' 06 Wines from better (northern) half of BEAUJOLAIS; should be much tastier than plain BEAUJOLAIS. The ten (easily) best villages are the *crus*: FLEURIE, ST-AMOUR, JULIÉNAS, CHÉNAS, MOULIN-À-VENT, CHIROUBLES, MORGON, REGNIÉ, CÔTE DE BROUILLY, BROUILLY. Of the 30 others the best lie around Beaujeu. *Crus* cannot be released EN PRIMEUR before 15 December. Best kept until spring (or considerably longer).

Beaumes-de-Venise S Rh br r (p w) ★★→★★★ 01' 03 04 05' 06 for reds. DYA for MUSCAT. Often regarded as France's best dessert MUSCAT, from south CÔTES DU RHÔNE; can be muskily scented, overtly flavoured, subtle, lingering (e.g. Château St Sauveur, Domaines Beaumaric, Bernardins, Durban, JABOULET, Pigeade, VIDAL-FLEURY). Midweight, sometimes austere reds (Château Redortier, Domaine Cassan, du Fenouillet, Durban, Les Goubert, co-op) leave for 3 years. Own since 04 vintage. White and rosé are CÔTES DU RHONE.

Beaumont des Crayères Champ Bijou Côte d'Epernay co-op making excellent Pinot Meunier-based Grande Réserve NV and very fine Fleur de Prestige 98 00 02. Exceptional CHARD-led Cuvée Nostalgie 98 00 02. Fleur de Rosé 02 03.

Beaune Burg r (w) ★★★ Historic wine capital of Burgundy and home to many merchants: BOUCHARD, CHAMPY, DROUHIN, JADOT, LATOUR as well as HOSPICES DE BEAUNE. No GRAND CRU vineyards but sound PREMIER CRUS: e.g. Cras, Grèves, Teurons, Cent Vignes, Clos du Roi, Bressandes for red and an increasing amount of white, of which Drouhin's CLOS DES MOUCHES stands out.

Becker, Caves J ★→★★★ An organic estate. Stylish, well-balanced wines including exceptional MUSCAT GRAND CRU Froehn.

Bellet Prov p r w ★★★ The local wine of Nice; fashionable, expensive, original; especially white from Rolle, with unexpected ageing potential. A few small producers, especially Château de Bellet.

Bellivière, Domaine de Lo r w sw ★→★★★★ Dynamic, eco-friendly grower: riveting Chenin Bl in JASNIERES and COTEAUX DU LOIR and eye-opening PINEAU D'AUNIS.

Bergerac Dordogne r w p dr sw ★→★★★ Good-value Bordeaux annexe making appreciably the same styles. Top properties include ★★★ La Tour des Gendres, Clos de la Colline, Clos des Verdots. Château Masburel. Domaine l'Ancienne Cure, Les Hauts de Caillevel. Otherwise ★★ Les Marnières, Châteaux Belingard-Chayne, Clos de la Colline, Les Fontenelles, Grinou, les Eyssards, Jonc Blanc, de la Mallevieille, Les Miaudoux, le Paradis, Pion, le Raz, Thénac. See also MONBAZILLAC, ROSETTE, SAUSSIGNAC, PECHARMANT, MONTRAVEL.

Besserat de Bellefon CHAMPAGNE house in Epernay, known for lightish wines, not to keep.

Beyer, Léon ★★→★★★★ ALSACE specialist: very fine, intense, dry wines often needing 10 years + bottle age. Superb Ries. Comtes d'Eguisheim, but no mention on label of PFERSIGBERG: Beyer does not recognize GRAND CRU system. Good GEWURZ.

Bichot, Maison Albert Burg One of BEAUNE's largest growers/merchants.

Billecart-Salmon This exemplary family CHAMPAGNE house has hung on to top quality as sales have grown. Exquisite long-lived wines, vintage CUVÉES wholly fermented in wood from 2000. Single-vineyard St-Hilaire BLANC DE NOIRS.

Bize, Simon Burg ★★★ Admirable red burgundy grower; 14 ha at SAVIGNY-LÈS-BEAUNE. Usually model wines in racy, elegant SAVIGNY style; some surprisingly good white.

Blagny Burg r w ★★ →★★★ Austere reds sold as Blagny; fresh, mineral whites, mostly PREMIER CRU, borrow the names of neighbouring MEURSAULT and PULIGNY. AMPEAU, LATOUR, Matrot, and Martelet-Cherisey are good.

Blanc de Blancs Any white wine made from white grapes only, especially CHAMPAGNE. An indication of style, not of quality.

Blanc de Noirs White (or slightly pink or "blush") wine from red grapes.

Blanck, Paul et Fils ★★ →★★★ Grower at Kientzheim, ALSACE, producing huge range of wines. Finest from 6 ha GRAND CRU FURSTENTUM (Ries, GEWURZ, PINOT GR) and GRAND CRU SCHLOSSBERG (Ries). Also good Pinot Bl.

Blanquette de Limoux Midi w sp ★★ Good-value fizz from near Carcassonne; claims older history than CHAMPAGNE. Dry and tasty, with CHARD, Chenin Bl, and improving basic Mauzac, especially in more recent AC CRÉMANT de LIMOUX. Successful co-op, with Sieur d'Arques label.

Blaye B'x r w ★ →★★ **01 03 04** 05' As of 2000, designation for top, concentrated reds (lower yields, longer ageing, etc.) from PREMIÈRES CÔTES DE BLAYE. Also declining AC for simple dry whites.

Boillot Burg Various interconnected Burgundy growers. Look for Jean-Marc (POMMARD) ★★★ for fine oaky reds and whites, Jean (domaine) and Henri (négociant) (VOLNAY) ★★★, Louis (CHAMBOLLE, married to Ghislaine BARTHOD) ★★→★★★, and the late Piere (MEURSAULT) ★★.

Boisset, Jean-Claude Burg Far and away the biggest Burgundy merchant based in NUITS-ST-GEORGES. Owner of Bouchard-Aîné, Lionel Bruck, F Chauvenet, Delaunay, Jaffelin, Morin Père et Fils, de Marcilly, Pierre Ponnelle, Thomas-Bassot, Vienot, CELLIER DES SAMSONS (BEAUJOLAIS), Moreau (CHABLIS), and a share in MOMMESSIN. Now involved in projects in Canada, California, Chile, Uruguay, and the Languedoc. Used to be fairly dire, but Boisset label now resurrected. From 1999 own vineyards separated as Domaine de la VOUGERAIE (★★★). Potentially very good.

Boizel One of CHAMPAGNE's surest values: brilliant, aged BLANC DE BLANCS NV and prestige Joyau de France. Also Grand Vintage Brut and Cuvée Sous Bois.

Bollinger Great individualistic CHAMPAGNE house, especially good in "lesser" vintages (*viz.* 97). Luxury wines: RD, VIEILLES VIGNES Françaises from ungrafted Pinot N vines, La Côte aux Enfants, La Grande Année. See also LANGLOIS-CHÂTEAU.

Bonneau du Martray, Domaine Burg ★★★★ (w) ★★ (r) Two GRAND CRUS made to the highest standard – exemplary, long-lived (10yrs +) CORTON CHARLEMAGNE and significantly improved red CORTON.

Bonnes-Mares Burg r ★★★ →★★★★ 78' 85' 88' 89 90' 91 93 95 96' 97 98 99' 00 01 02' 03 04 05' 06 GRAND CRU (15 ha) between CHAMBOLLE-MUSIGNY and MOREY-ST-DENIS. Sturdy long-lived wines, less fragrant than MUSIGNY; to rival CHAMBERTIN. Best: DUJAC, GROFFIER, JADOT, ROUMIER, Domaine des Varoilles, de VOGÜÉ, VOUGERAIE.

Bonnezeaux Lo w sw ★★★ →★★★★ 88 89 90 95 96 97 02 03 04 05 Profound, sumptuous sweet Chenin Bl, potentially best of COTEAUX DU LAYON. To drink young or age idefinitely. Especially: Ferme de la Sansonnière, CHÂTEAU DE FESLES, Dom les Grandes Vignes, Domaine du Petit Val (Goizil), Château la Fresnaye.

Bordeaux B'x r w (p) ★ →★★ Huge, catch-all AC for generic Bordeaux. Mixed quality, but can be great value when good.

Bordeaux Supérieur B'x r ★→★★ Superior denomination to above. Higher minimum alcohol, lower yield, and longer ageing. 75% of production bottled at the property, the reverse of AC Bordeaux.

Borie-Manoux Admirable BORDEAUX shipper, châteaux-owner. Châteaux include Batailley, BEAU-SITE, Domaine de L'EGLISE, HAUT-BAGES-MONPELOU, TROTTEVIEILLE.

Bouchard Père & Fils Important burgundy shipper (established in 1731) and grower; excellent vineyards (94 ha), mainly CÔTE DE BEAUNE; cellars at Château de Beaune. Revamped since late 1990s; *whites exciting*, reds sound.

Bouches-du-Rhône Prov r p w ★ VINS DE PAYS from Marseille environs. Warming reds from southern varieties, plus Cab Sauv, Syrah, and Merlot.

Bourgeois, Henri Lo ★★→★★★ Key SANCERRE grower/merchant in Chavignol. Also POUILLY-FUMÉ, MENETOU-SALON, QUINCY, COTEAUX GIENNOIS. Top wines include Etienne Clos Henri, MD de Bourgeois, La Bourgeoise (r, w), Jadis, D'Antan Sancerrois, and Le Chêne Etienne (red, white) in New Zealand.

Bourgogne Burg r w (p) ★★ Catch-all AC, with higher standards than basic BORDEAUX. Light, often good flavour, best at 2–4 years. Top growers make bargain beauties from fringes of CÔTE D'OR villages; do not despise. BEAUJOLAIS *crus* (except REGNIÉ) may be labelled Bourgogne, though Gamay.

Bourgogne Grand Ordinaire r (w) ★ DYA Ludicrous name for most basic Burgundy, usually GAMAY for reds and CHARD for white, though may use other grapes.

Bourgogne Passe-Tout-Grains r (p) ★ Age 1–2 years, junior burgundy: min 33% Pinot N, the balance Gamay, mixed in vat. Not as heady as BEAUJOLAIS.

Bourgueil Lo r (p) ★★→★★★(★) **96 02 03** 04 05 06 Burly, full-flavoured TOURAINE reds and big, fragrant rosés based on Cab Fr. The best can age 10 years. Especially YANNICK AMIRAULT, Audebert, Dom de la Butte, Dom de la Chevalerie, Delaunay, Druet, Dom des Ouches. See also ST-NICHOLAS-DE-BOURGUEIL.

Bouvet-Ladubay Lo ★→★★★ Major Important sparkling SAUMUR house purchased by Indian beer company United Breweries in 2006. Best is the barrel-fermented Cuvée Tresor. Also still wines called Les Nonpareils.

Bouzereau Burg ★→★★ Family in MEURSAULT making good whites at attractive prices and ordinary reds. Michel B and Vincent B are the two best domaines.

Bouzeron Burg w ★ CÔTE CHALONNAISE AC specifically for ALIGOTÉ. Age 1–2 years. Top grower: de Villaine.

Bouzy Rouge Champ r ★★★ **90 95 96 97 99** 02 Still red of famous Pinot N village. Like very light Burgundy, but can last well in sunny vintages.

Brocard, J-M Burg ★★→★★★ One of the recent success stories of Chablis with a fine range of wines at all levels. Also on offer: a range of Bourgogne Blancs from different soil types (Kimmeridgian, Jurassic, Portlandian).

Brouilly Beauj r ★★ **03' 05' 06** Biggest of the ten *crus* of BEAUJOLAIS: fruity, round, refreshing wine, can age 3–4 years. CHÂTEAU DE LA CHAIZE is largest estate. Top growers: Michaud, Domaine de Combillaty, Domaine des Grandes Vignes.

Brumont, Alain SW ★★★ Expensive, and once the clear leader in MADIRAN. Specialist in highly extracted and oaked 100% Tannat wines – *e.g.* Le Tyre. Flagship wines: Château Montus, Domaine Bouscassé, and good-value Torus brand.

Brut Term for the dry classic wines of CHAMPAGNE.

Brut Ultra/Zéro Term for bone-dry wines in CHAMPAGNE.

Bugey Savoie r p w sp ★→★★ DYA VDQS for light sparkling, still, or half-sparkling wines from Roussette (or Altesse) and CHARD (good). Best from Montagnieu; also Rosé de Cerdon, mainly Gamay.

Burguet, Alain Burg ★★→★★★ Superb GEVREY-CHAMBERTIN; especially Mes Favorites village wine.

Buxy Burg w Village in AC MONTAGNY with good co-op for CHARD and Pinot N.

Buzet SW France r (w p) ★★ **01' 03 04 05'** One-time Bordeaux satellite, similar wines, sometimes a bit pruney. Co-op changing to more modern styles; single properties (*e.g.* Châteaux de Gueyze, Mazelières). Local character from (independent) ★★★ Domaine de Pech, ★★ Châteaux du Frandat, Tournelles.

Cabardès Midi r (p w) ★ →★★ 00 **01 02 03** 04 05 06 Where Bordeaux and the Midi meet, with blends of Cabernet, Merlot, Syrah, and Grenache. Best is Domaine de Cabrol; also Châteaux Pennautier and Ventenac.

> **Bourgogne** is the generic word for the cheaper end of Burgundy. As well as some indifferent mass-produced wines, it also covers out-lying areas which have their own subdivisions within the AC Bourgogne. **Coulanges-la-Vineuse, Epineuil,** and **Vézélay** (Yonne département), **Chatillonais, Hautes Côtes de Beaune** and **Hautes Côtes de Nuits** (Côte d'Or), **Côte Chalonnaise,** and **Couchois** (Saône et Loire). The best tip is to buy **Bourgogne Rouge,** or **Blanc** from good growers in the famous villages of the Côte d'Or – they will be delicious, simple wines with more style than négociant bottlings.

Cabernet d'Anjou Lo p s/sw ★ DYA Traditionally sweet, often derided, rosé now enjoying a renaissance. Ageworthy. Bablut, Domaine Cady, Domaine Clau de Nell, Domaine les Grandes Vignes, CHÂTEAU PIERRE-BISE.

Cabrières Midi p (r) ★★ DYA COTEAUX DU LANGUEDOC. Tradition for rosé with sound village co-op.

Cady, Domaine Lo r p sw ★★ →★★★★ A reliably excellent ANJOU grower from dry whites to off-dry rosés, to lusciously sweet COTEAUX DE LAYON and CHAUME.

Cahors SW France r ★ →★★★ 89 90' 95 98 00 01' 02 04 (05) All-red AC based on Malbec (at least 70%). Nearly as many styles as growers (200); fruity, easy wines from ★★ Maison Vigoroux "Pigmentum", Château Latuc, Domaine Boliva; more traditional from ★★★ CLOS DE GAMOT (Clos St-Jean), ★★ Coutale, Châteaux du Cayrou, La Coustarelle, La Caminade, Gradou, Les Ifs, Domaines de la Bérengerai, de Cause, Paillas, Pineraie, Les Rigalets, Savarines (organic); more New-World style from Château Lagrézette, ★★★ Châteaux du Cèdre, Lamartine, Clos Triguedina, ★★ Château Eugénie; better control of oak and gentler vinification from cult ★★★ Domaine Cosse-Maisonneuve.

Cairanne S Rh r p w ★★ 98' 00' 01' 03 04' 05' 06 One of two best CÔTES DU RHÔNE-VILLAGES: solid, deep-set, classy fullness, especially Domaines D&D Alary, Ameillaud, Brusset, Castel Mireio, Escaravailles, Hautes Cances, l'Oratoire St-Martin, Rabasse-Charavin, Richaud. Improving, full whites, best with food.

Canard-Duchêne CHAMPAGNE house. Inexpensive, and often tastes it.

Canon-Fronsac B'x r ★★ →★★★ 95 96 98 00' 01 03 05' Full tannic reds of improved quality from west of POMEROL. Try Châteaux Barrabaque, CANON-DE-BREM, Cassagne Haut-Canon, Gaby, Haut-Mazeris, Lamarche Canon Candelaire, Pavillon, La Fleur Caillou, Grand-Renouil, Moulin-Pey-Labrie, Vrai Canon Bouché.

Caramany Pyr r (w) ★ Notionally superior AC for CÔTES DU ROUSSILLON-VILLAGES.

Carillon, Louis Burg ★★★ PULIGNY-MONTRACHET dom consistently in top league.

Cassis Prov w (r p) ★★ DYA Seaside village east of Marseille with reputation for dry whites based on Clairette and Marsanne. Delicious with bouillabaisse (*e.g.* Domaine de la Ferme Blanche, Clos Ste Magdeleine, Clos d'Albizzi). Do not confuse with cassis: blackcurrant liqueur from Dijon.

Cathiard Burg ★★★ Brilliant Vosne-Romanée producer on top form since late 1990s. Perfumed, sensual wines are charming young but will age.

Cave Cellar, or any wine establishment.

Cave coopérative Wine-growers' co-op winery; over half of all French production. Usually well run, well equipped, and wines reasonable value for money.

Cellier des Samsons ★ BEAUJOLAIS/MACONNAIS co-op at Quincié which has 2,000 grower-members. Wines widely distributed; now owned by BOISSET.

Cérons B'x w dr sw ★★ 97' 98 99' **01' 02 03'** 05' Tiny neighbour of SAUTERNES with good sweet, less intense wines, *e.g.* Châteaux de Cérons, Chantegrive, Grand Enclos.

Chablis Burg w ★★ →★★★ Unique, flavoursome, dry, mineral wine of north Burgundy. CHARD. PETIT CHABLIS from a good house can be a good substitute.

Chablis Grand Cru Burg w ★★★ →★★★★ 90' 95' **96'** 97 98 99 00' 02' 03 04 05' 06' In maturity a match for great white burgundy: often dumb in youth, at best with age combines mineral cut with hint of SAUTERNES. Vineyards: Blanchots, Bougros, Clos, Grenouilles, Preuses, Valmur, Vaudésir.

Chablis Premier Cru Burg w ★★★ Technically second-rank but at best excellent; more typical of CHABLIS than its GRANDS CRUS. Can outclass more expensive MEURSAULT and other CÔTE DE BEAUNE. Best vineyards include Côte de Léchet, Fourchaume, Mont de Milieu, Montée de Tonnerre, Montmains, Vaillons.

Chambertin Burg r ★★★★ 78' 85' 88 89 90' 91 93 95 96' **97** 98 99' **00** 01 02' 03 05' 06 A 13-ha GRAND CRU; some of the meatiest, most enduring, best red burgundy. 20 growers including Bertagna, BOUCHARD, CHARLOPIN, Damoy, DROUHIN, LEROY, MORTET, PONSOT, Rossignol-Trapet, ROUSSEAU, Trapet.

Chambertin-Clos de Bèze Burg r ★★★★ 78' 85' 88 89 90' 91 93 95 96' **97** 98 99' **00** 01 02' 03 05' 06 Neighbour of CHAMBERTIN (15 ha). Similarly splendid wines. May legally be sold as CHAMBERTIN. 15 growers, including Bruno CLAIR, Damoy, DROUHIN, Drouhin-Laroze, FAIVELEY, GROFFIER, JADOT, ROUSSEAU.

Chambolle-Musigny Burg r ★★★ →★★★★ 90' 91 93 95' **96'** 97 98 99' **00** 01 02' 03 04 05' 06 CÔTE DE NUITS village (170 ha): fabulously fragrant, complex, but never heavy wine. Best vineyards: Les Amoureuses, part of BONNES-MARES, Les Charmes, MUSIGNY. Growers to note: Amiot-Servelle, BARTHOD, Digoia-Royer, DROUHIN, GROFFIER, HUDELOT-NOËLLAT, JADOT, MUGNIER, RION, ROUMIER, DE VOGÜÉ.

Champagne Sparkling wines of Pinots N and Meunier and/or CHARD, and its region (over 30,000 ha, 145 km/90 miles east of Paris); made by MÉTHODE TRADITIONELLE. Bubbles from elsewhere, however good, cannot be Champagne.

Champs-Fleuris, Domaine des Lo r w p sw ★★ →★★★ Exciting young(ish) domaine Top-notch Saumur Blanc; Saumur-Champigny fine Crémant; pretty rosé; and, when the vintage warrants, a succulent Coteaux du Saumur called Cuvée Sarah.

Champy Père & Cie Burg ★★ →★★★ Oldest négociant, in BEAUNE, rejuvenated by Meurgey family (also brokers DIVA). Range of very well-chosen wines.

Chandon de Briailles, Domaine Burg ★★★ Small estate at SAVIGNY making light, fragrant PERNAND-VERGELESSES, Ile de Vergelesses, and good CORTON red and white.

Chanson Père & Fils Burg ★ →★★★ Old grower-négociant at BEAUNE (45 ha). Especially BEAUNE Clos des Fèves, ***PERNAND-VERGELESSES Les Caradeux***, SAVIGNY, CORTON. Fine quality now.

Chapelle-Chambertin Burg r ★★★ 90' 91 93 95 **96'** 97 98 99' **00** 01 02' 03 04 05' 06 A 5.2-ha neighbour of CHAMBERTIN. Wine more "nervous", not so meaty. Very good in cooler years. Top producers: Damoy, JADOT, Rossignol-Trapet, Trapet.

Chapoutier N Rh ★★ →★★★★ Long-established grower, also trader of full r and w Rhônes; biodynamic. Note special CUVÉES Châteauneuf Barbe Rac, Croix de Bois (r), HERMITAGE: L'Ermite, Le Pavillon (r), L'Ermite, Cuvée d'Orée, Le Méal (w). Also CROZES red Les Varonniers, St-Joseph, white Les Granits. ***Reliable, good-value Meysonniers Crozes***. New holdings in BANYULS, COLLIOURE, COTEAUX DU TRICASTIN, COTEAUX D'AIX-EN-PROVENCE promising. Also Australian joint ventures, especially Jasper Hill.

Chardonnay As well as a white wine grape, also the name of a MÂCON-VILLAGES commune. Hence Mâcon-Chardonnay.

Charlopin, Philippe Burg ★★★ Modern-style GEVREY-CHAMBERTIN estate.

Charmes-Chambertin Burg r ★★★ 90' 91 93 95 **96'** 97 98 99' **00** 01 02' 03 04

05'06 CHAMBERTIN neighbour, including AC MAZOYÈRES-CHAMBERTIN. Supple, rounder wines; especially Bachelet, DROUHIN, DUGAT, DUJAC, LEROY, Perrot-Minot, ROTY, ROUMIER, ROUSSEAU, VOUGERAIE.

Chassagne-Montrachet Burg w r ★★★ →★★★★ CÔTE DE BEAUNE village (304 ha). Sterling, hefty red; excellent rich, dry white rarely with quite the finesse of PULIGNY next door, but often costs less. Best vineyards include part of MONTRACHET, BÂTARD-MONTRACHET, Boudriottes (red, white), Caillerets, CRIOTS-B-M, Morgeot (red, white), Ruchottes, Clos St-Jean (red). Growers include Amiot, Blain-Gagnard, COLIN-DELEGER, DROUHIN, Fontaine-Gagnard, J N GAGNARD, Gagnard-Delagrange, Jouard, Lamy-Pillot, Château de la Maltroye, MOREY, Morey-Coffinet, Niellon, Pillot, RAMONET.

Château d'Arlay ★→★★★ Major JURA estate; 65 ha in skilful hands. Wines include very good VIN JAUNE, VIN DE PAILLE, Pinot N, and MACVIN.

Château de Beaucastel S Rh r w ★★★★ One of biggest, best-run CHÂTEAUNEUF estates. Deep-hued, complex wines, drink first 2 years or from 7–8 years; unusual varietal mix including one-third Mourvèdre. Small amount of wonderful Roussanne: keep 5–14 years. Top-notch CÔTES DU RHÔNE red (lives 8+ years) and white Coudoulet de Beaucastel. Perrin Rasteau, Vinsobres (Les Cornuds, Hauts de Julien) leading quality. Very good organic Perrin Nature CÔTES DU RHÔNE, VACQUEYRAS. (See also Tablas Creek, California.)

Château du Cèdre SW r ★★★ 98 00 01' 02 (04) (05') Leading exponent of modern Cahors. Also delicious white VIN DE PAYS from Viognier.

Château de la Chaize Beauj r ★★★ Best-known BROUILLY estate.

Château Fortia S Rh r w (w) ★★ Traditional 30-ha CHÂTEAUNEUF property. Owner's father, Baron Le Roy, launched AC system in 1920s. Better form, better fruit recently, including special Le Baron and whites.

Château Fuissé Burg w ★★→★★★ Now being challenged as the top estate in POUILLY-FUISSÉ. Numerous CUVÉES, made to mature more rapidly than before.

Château de Meursault Burg r w ★★ 61-ha estate owned by PATRIARCHE; good vineyards and wines in BEAUNE, MEURSAULT, POMMARD, VOLNAY. Cellars open to public.

Château Mont-Redon S Rh r w ★★ Good 100-ha CHÂTEAUNEUF estate. Fine, complex red, always best 6+ years; aromatic, early-drinking white. Also good red (mainly Grenache), white wines from Cantegril vineyard (LIRAC).

Château La Nerthe S Rh r w ★★★ Very high-quality 90-ha CHÂTEAUNEUF estate. Complete, refined modern-style wines, especially special CUVÉES Cadettes (red) and oaked Beauvenir (white). Takes 5 years to show. Also run good Prieuré Montézargues Tavel, Domaine de la Renjarde CÔTES DU RHÔNE, Château Signac Chusclan.

Château Pierre-Bise Lo r w ★★→★★★★ Terroir specialist COTEAUX DU LAYON, including CHAUME, QUARTS DE CHAUME, and SAVENNIERES, particularly Clos de Grand Beaupreau and ROCHE AUX MOINES. Excellent Anjou-Gamay, Anjou Villages.

Château Rayas S Rh r (w) ★★★ Famous, very traditional estate in CHÂTEAUNEUF. Soft, subtle, red fruits. Grenache ages superbly. Traditional-style white Rayas can be very good. Good-value second label: Pignan. Very good Château Fonsalette, CÔTES DU RHÔNE. All benefit from decanting. Also good Château des Tours Vacqueyras.

Château Simone Prov r p w ★★→★★★ Fine old property virtually synonymous with AC PALETTE, outside Aix-en-Provence. Red is warm and spicy; **the white is herbal and rewards bottle-ageing. Delicious rosé.**

Château de Villeneuve Lo r w Leading SAUMUR grower. Masterly Saumur Blanc (especially Les Cormiers) and SAUMUR-CHAMPIGNY (especially VIEILLES VIGNES, Grand Clos).

Château-Chalon Jura w ★★★ Not a château but AC and village. Unique dry, yellow, sherry-like wine (Savagnin grape). Develops *flor* (see Spain) while ageing in barrels for minimum 6 years. Ready to drink when bottled (62-cl clavelin bottle), but ages almost forever. A curiosity.

Château-Grillet N Rh w ★★ 91' 93' 95' 98' 00' 01' 04' 05 06 Single 3.6-ha terraced granite vineyard of Viognier; one of France's smallest ACS. Overpriced, but signs of revival. Mainly cask-reared. Drink 6 years+. Decant first, drink with fish, poultry.

Châteaumeillant Lo r p ★–★★ DYA A minuscule VDQS area south of SANCERRE in Georges Sand country. Gamay and Pinot N for light reds, gris and rosés.

Châteauneuf-du-Pape S Rh r (w) ★★★ 78' 80 81' 83 85 86 88 89' 90' 94 95' 96 98' 99' 00' 01' 03' 04' 05' 06 3,200 ha near Avignon with core of 30 or so domaines for very fine wines (quality variable over remaining 90). Mix of up to 13 red, white varieties led by Grenache, Syrah, Mourvèdre, Clairette. Best are dark, strong, exceptionally long-lived, good value. Increasing number of expensive Prestige wines (old vines, oak). Whites fruity, zesty or rather heavy: many now DYA. Top growers include: CHÂTEAUX DE BEAUCASTEL, FORTIA, Gardine, MONT-REDON, LA NERTHE, RAYAS, Vaudieu; Domaines de Beaurenard, Bosquet des Papes, Les Cailloux, Charvin, Font-de-Michelle, Grand Veneur, Marcoux, Millière, Pegaü, VIEUX TÉLÉGRAPHE, Vieille Julienne, Villeneuve, Henri Bonneau, Clos du Mont-Olivet, CLOS DES PAPES, Clos St-Jean, P Usseglio, Jean Versino, Vieux Donjon.

Champagne growers to watch in 2008

Edmond Barnaut Bouzy. Complex, fine Champagnes mainly from Pinot N culminate in first-rate Sélection Ultra Brut.

Louise Brisson Ace Côtes des Bar (Aube) domaine. Top Cuvée Fût de Chêne (**99 00 02**).

Claude Cazals Cuvée Vive Extra Brut perfect apéritif and lovely single-site Clos Cazals (**96 ★★★★ 98**).

Richard Cheurlin One of best grower/winemakers of the Aube. Rich but balanced Carte d'Or and vintage-dated Cuvée Jeanne (**96 98 00**).

Pierre Cheval-Gatinois Aÿ. Impeccable producer of mono-*cru* Champagnes and excellent still Aÿ Coteaux Champenois (**99 02**).

Michel Genet Fine Chouilly domaine. Fresh yet supple and mature expressions of GRAND CRU CHARD. First-rate Prestige de la Cave (**99 00 02**).

Pierre Gimmonet Leading Côte des Blancs grower at Cuis. ***The complex Le Fleuron (99') is a triumph of elegant complexity.***

Henri Giraud Thoughtful grower/merchant making exceptional Pinot-led Champagne. Excellent Prestige Cuvée (**95 96 98** 99).

Larmandier-Bernier Vertus; top-flight BLANC DE BLANCS grower-maker, especially Terre de Vertus non dosé (**03 04**) and Cramant VIEILLES VIGNES **02 ★★★★**).

Henri Mandois Classy Pinot Meunier/Chard wines from 30-ha estate at Pierry.

Jean Milan Chard Champagnes, very dry – ripeness, minerality, and expression of terroir in perfect balance. Exceptional Symphorine **00 02**.

José Michel Fresh yet mature Carte Blanche NV. Also excellent BLANC DE BLANCS (**98 99**) and vintage (**98 99**).

Châtillon-en-Diois Rh r p w ★ DYA Small, ordinary AC east of Rhône in pre-Alps. Just adequate, largely Gamay reds; white (some ALIGOTÉ) mostly made into sparkling CLAIRETTE DE DIE.

Chave, Gérard and Jean-Louis N Rh r w ★★★★ Wonderful HERMITAGE family domaine. Nine hillside sites. Rich, gourmand, very long-lived wines, especially white, also good occasional VIN DE PAILLE. Fruity new J-L Chave brand ST-JOSEPH Offerus.

FRANCE

Chavignol Picturesque SANCERRE village with famous vineyard, Les Monts Damnés. Chalky soil gives vivid wines that age 4–5 years (or longer); especially from BOURGEOIS, Cotat, and DIDIER DAGENEAU.

Chénas Beauj r ★★★ 03 05' 06 Smallest BEAUJOLAIS *cru* and one of the weightiest; neighbour to MOULIN-À-VENT and JULIÉNAS. Growers include Benon, Champagnon, Charvet, Château Chèvres, DUBOEUF, Lapierre, Robin, Trichard, co-op.

Chevalier-Montrachet Burg w ★★★★ Neighbour of MONTRACHET (6.8 ha) making similarly luxurious wine, perhaps less powerful. Growers include: LATOUR, JADOT, BOUCHARD PÈRE & FILS, COLIN-DELEGER, LEFLAIVE, Niellon, PRIEUR, Château de Puligny.

Cheverny Lo r p w ★ ★★★ 02 04 05 06 Loire AC near Chambord. Pungent dry white from Sauv Bl and CHARD. Also Gamay, Pinot N, or Cab Sauv. Richer, rarer, and

> **Château**
> Means an estate, big or small, good or indifferent, particularly in Bordeaux (see Châteaux of Bordeaux). Elsewhere in France, château tends to mean, literally, castle or great house. In Burgundy, "domaine" is the usual term.

more ageworthy Cour-Cheverny uses local Romorantin grape. Sparkling use CRÉMANT DE LOIRE and TOURAINE ACS. Especially Cazin; Clos Tue-Boeuf; Huards; OISLY & THESÉE; Domaine de la Desoucherie, Domaine du Moulin.

Chevillon, R ★★★ 13-ha estate at NUITS-ST-GEORGES; soft and juicy wines.

Chidaine, Francois Lo dr sw w sp ★★★ Producer of ambitious, very pure, very precise Montlouis. Recently took over Clos Baudoin (formerly Prince Poniatowski), where he makes similarly styled VOUVRAY. Biodynamic principles followed in both DOMAINES.

Chignin Savoie w ★ DYA Light, soft white from Jacquère grapes for alpine summers. Chignin-Bergeron (with Roussanne grapes) is best and liveliest.

Chinon Lo r (p w) ★★–★★★ 89 90 95 96 97 02 03 04 05 06 Juicy, variably rich TOURAINE Cab Fr. Drink cool, young; top vintages from top growers can age 10 years +. An increasing amount of taut dry Chenin Bl. Best include Bernard BAUDRY, ALLIET, Château de Coulaine, Château de la Bonneliere, Domaine du Noire.

Chiroubles Beauj r 03 05' 06 Good but tiny BEAUJOLAIS CRU next to FLEURIE; fresh, fruity, silky wine for early drinking (1–3 years). Growers include: Bouillard, Cheysson, DUBOEUF, Fourneau, Passot, Raousset, co-op.

Chorey-lès-Beaune Burg r (w) ★★99' 01 02' 03 04 05' 06 Minor AC north of BEAUNE. Three fine growers: Arnoux, Germain (Château de Chorey), TOLLOT-BEAUT.

Chusclan S Rh r p w ★ ★★★ 03 04 05' 06 CÔTES DU RHÔNE-VILLAGES with able co-op. Soft textured reds, sound rosés. Labels include CUVÉE de Marcoule, Seigneurie de Gicon. Also good Château Signac (more tannin, can age) and *special cuvées from André Roux*. Drink most young.

Clair, Bruno Burg ★★–★★★★ Leading MARSANNAY estate. Very good wines from there and GEVREY-CHAMBERTIN (especially CLOS DE BÈZE), FIXIN, MOREY-ST-DENIS, SAVIGNY.

Clairet Very light red wine, almost rosé. BORDEAUX Clairet is an AC.

Clairette Traditional white grape of the MIDI. Its low-acid wine was a vermouth base. Revival by Terrasses de Landoc is full and zesty.

Clairette de Bellegarde Midi w ★ DYA Tiny AC near Nîmes: fresh, neutral white.

Clairette de Die Rh w dr s/sw sp ★★ NV Popular dry or (better) semi-sweet good character Tradition MUSCAT-flavoured sparkling wine from pre-Alps in east Rhône; or straight dry CLAIRETTE, can age 3–4 years. Worth trying. Achard-Vincent, A Poulet, J-C Raspail.

Clairette du Languedoc Midi w ★ DYA Near Montpellier. Full-bodied white AC, some barrel-ageing and improving late-harvest wines. Châteaux La

Condamine Bertrand, St-André, and co-ops of Adissan and Cabrières.

Clape, Auguste and Pierre N Rh r (w) ★★★ 97 98' 99' 00 01' **02** 03' 04' 05' 06 _Supreme 5+ ha Syrah vineyard at Cornas, many old vines_. Traditional reds, need 6+ years. Epitome of unspoilt, hands-off winemaking, always good in lesser vintages. Good CÔTES DU RHÔNE, also sound St-Péray.

Clape, La Midi r p w ★★ →★★★ Cru of note in AC COTEAUX DU LANGUEDOC. Warming reds from sun-soaked hills between Narbonne and the Med. Tangy herbal whites age well. Good: Châteaux Rouquette-sur-Mer, Mire l'Etang, Pech-Céléyran, Pech-Redon, _Château de l'Hospitalet_, La Négly, Moyau.

Climat Burgundian word for individually named vineyard, e.g. BEAUNE Grèves.

Clos A term carrying some prestige, reserved for distinct (walled) vineyards, often in one ownership (especially Burgundy and ALSACE).

Clos de Gamot SW France ★★★ 85 89 90' 95 96 98' 00 01' (04) (05') 400-year-old estate. Ultra-traditional, long-lived benchmark wines. Top ★★★★ CUVÉE Clos St Jean is outstanding.

Clos des Lambrays Burg r ★★★ 90' 93 95 99' 00 02 03 04 05' 06 GRAND CRU vineyard (6 ha) at MOREY-ST-DENIS. A virtual monopoly of the Domaine du Clos des Lambrays, in recent years more severe in selecting only the best grapes.

Clos des Mouches Burg r w ★★★ Splendid PREMIER CRU BEAUNE vineyard, largely owned by DROUHIN. _Whites and reds, spicy and memorable – and consistent._ Little-known vineyards of the same name exist in Santenay and Meursault too.

Clos des Papes S Rh r w ★★★ Good 32-ha (18 plots) CHÂTEAUNEUF estate Avril-family-owned for centuries. Long-lived, stylish red (mainly Grenache, Mourvèdre, drink from 6 years) and classy, complex white (5–15 years).

Clos de la Roche Burg r ★★★ 78' 88 90' 91 93' 95 96' 97 98 99' 00 01 02' 03 04 05' 06 MOREY-ST-DENIS GRAND CRU (15 ha). Powerful and complex, like CHAMBERTIN. Amiot, BOUCHARD PÈRE & FILS, DUJAC, LEROY, H Lignier, PONSOT, ROUSSEAU.

Clos du Roi Burg r ★★★ The best vineyard in GRAND CRU CORTON and a PREMIER CRU vineyard in Beaune.

Clos Rougeard Lo r (sw) ★★★ Powerful, unfiltered SAUMUR-CHAMPIGNY dry, quite fine SAUMUR BL, and, vintage permitting, luscious COTEAUX DE SAUMUR.

Clos St-Denis Burg r ★★★ GRAND CRU at MOREY-ST-DENIS (6.4 ha). Splendid sturdy wine growing silky with age. Growers include: Bertagna, DUJAC, and PONSOT.

Clos Ste-Hune Al w ★★★★ Greatest Ries in ALSACE. Very fine, initially austere; needs 5–10+ years ageing. A Trimbach wine from GRAND CRU ROSACKE

Clos St-Jacques Burg r ★★★ 88' 89 90' 91 93 95' 96' 97 98 99' 00 01 02' 03 04 05' 06 6.7-ha hillside PREMIER CRU in GEVREY CHAMBERTIN with perfect southeast exposure. Five excellent producers ESMONIN, JADOT, CLAIR, Fourrier, ROUSSEAU; powerful, velvety red wines often ranked above many GRAND CRUS.

Clos de Tart Burg r ★★★★ 88' 89' 90' 93 95 96' 97 99' 00 02' 03 04 05' 06 GRAND CRU at MOREY-ST-DENIS, owned by MOMMESSIN. Now first-rate but priced accordingly.

Clos de Vougeot Burg r ★★★ 78' 88 89' 90' 91 93' 95 96' 97 98 99' 00 01 02' 03' 04 05' 06 A 50-ha CÔTE DE NUITS GRAND CRU with many owners. Occasionally sublime. Maturity depends on grower's philosophy, technique, and position. Top growers include Château de la Tour, DROUHIN, ENGEL, FAIVELEY, GRIVOT, GROS, HUDELOT-NOËLLAT, JADOT, LEROY, Chantal Lescure, MÉO-CAMUZÉT, MUGNERET, VOUGERAIE.

Coche-Dury Burg ★★★★ 8.4-ha MEURSAULT DOMAINE (plus 0.5 ha of CORTON-CHARLEMAGNE) with the highest reputation for oak-perfumed wines. Even MEURSAULT-Villages is great (with age). Also very good ALIGOTÉ and reds.

Colin-Deléger Burg ★★★ Leading CHASSAGNE-MONTRACHET family, several members of the next generation succeeding either Marc Colin (Pierre-Yves) or Michel Colin-Deleger (Bruno, Philippe).

Collines Rhodaniennes N Rh r w ★ Lively Rhône VIN DE PAYS. Also young vine CÔTE-RÔTIE. Mainly red, mainly Syrah (best), also Merlot, Gamay. Some

Viognier (best), CHARD. Barou (red, white), Bonnefond (red), Chatagnier (red), Cuilleron (white), J-M Gérin (red), Jamet (red), Monier (red), Ogier (red), Perret (white), G Vernay (white).

Collioure Pyr r w ★★ 97 98 99 00 01 02 03 04 05 06 Full-bodied, meaty red from BANYULS area. Tiny production. Top growers include Le Clos des Paulilles Domaines du Mas Blanc, de la Rectorie, La Tour Vieille, Vial-Magnères. Also rosé and new white AC retrospectively from 02 vintage, based on Grenache Bl.

Comté Tolosan SW r p w ★ DYA VIN DE PAYS. Covers multitude of sins and whole of the southwest. ★★ DOMAINE DE RIBONNET (Christian Gerber, south of Toulouse) for experimental use of non-indigenous grape varieties.

Condrieu N Rh w ★★★ 01' 02 03 04' 05 06 Ample, fragrant, floral white of great character (and price) from Viognier. Can be outstanding, but rapid growth of vineyard (now 125 ha; 75 growers) has made quality uneven (except marvellous 04) and increased use of young oak a doubtful move. Best: Y Cuilleron, DELAS, Dumazet, Gangloff, GUIGAL, JABOULET, F Merlin, A Perret, Niéro, C Pichon, G Vernay (especially long-lived Coteau de Vernon), F Villard. Dubious move to VENDANGE TARDIVE style by some growers.

Confuron, J-J Burg r ★★★ Tiny NUITS-ST-GEORGES. Modern-style, full of fruit.

Corbières Midi r (p w) ★★ ↝★★★ Vigorous bargain reds from warm, stony hillsides. AC, with new *cru* Boutenac. Production dominated by co-ops but best estates include ***Châteaux Aiguilloux***, la Baronne, Lastours, ***des Ollieux***, Les Palais, de la Voulte Gasparet, Domaines de Fontsainte, du Vieux Parc, ***de Villemajou***, Villerouge le Château, Cabriac. Co-ops: Embrès-et-Castelmaure, Camplong, Tuchan.

Cornas N Rh r ★★ ↝★★★ Sturdy, mineral-edged very dark Syrah from 105-ha steep granite vineyards south of HERMITAGE. Needs to age 5–15 years but more can be drunk after 4 years now. Top: Allemand, Balthazar (traditional), Colombo (new oak), ***CLAPE (benchmark)***, Courbis (modern), DELAS, Dumien-Serrette (traditional), JABOULET (especially St-Pierre CUVÉE), R Michel (especially Geynale), Tardieu-Laurent (modern, expensive), Voge.

Corsica (Vin de Corse) Characterful wines of all colours. ACS AJACCIO, PATRIMONIO, better *crus* Coteaux du Cap Corse, Sartène, and Calvi. VIN DE PAYS: ILE DE BEAUTÉ. Original Sciacarello reds, good Muscats, brisk rosés, Vermentino whites. Top grower: Peraldi. Also Clos d'Alzeto, Clos Capitoro, Abbatucci, Yves Leccio, Orenga de Gaffory, Montemagni, Vaccelli, Domaine Gentile.

Corton Burg r (w) ★★★ 90' 91 93 95 96' 97 98 99' 00 01 02' 03' 04 05' 06 The only GRAND CRU red of the CÔTE DE BEAUNE. 81 ha in ALOXE-CORTON including CLOS DU ROI, Les Bressandes. Rich and powerful, should age well. Rare white Corton from HOSPICES DE BEAUNE and CHANDON DE BRIAILLES.

Corton-Charlemagne Burg w ★★★★ 89' 90' 92' 95 96 97 98 99' 00' 01 02' 03 04 05' 06 White section (one-third) of CORTON. Rich, spicy, lingering, the GRAND CRU Chablis of the Côte d'Or; ages like a red. Top growers include BONNEAU DU MARTRAY, COCHE-DURY, FAIVELEY, HOSPICES DE BEAUNE, JADOT, Javillier, LATOUR, ROUMIER, VOUGERAIE.

Costières de Nîmes S Rh r p w ★ ↝★★ Mainly warm red with strong fruit and body; best will age. Look for Châteaux de Campuget, Grande Cassagne, Mas Neuf, Mourgues-du-Grès, Nages, d'Or et des Geules, Roubaud, de la Tuilerie, Mas des Bressades, Tardieu-Laurent, Domaine du Vieux Relais. Best reds substantial: 6–8 years. Some stylish whites (including Roussanne) worth a look.

Côte de Beaune Burg r w ★★ ↝★★★★ Used geographically: the south half of the CÔTE D'OR. Applies as an AC only to parts of BEAUNE itself.

Côte de Beaune-Villages Burg r ★★ 99' 02' 03 04 05' 06 Regional APPELLATION for lesser wines of classic area. Cannot be labelled "Côte de Beaune" without either "Villages" or village name added. Red wines only.

> **Champagne – back to grand-père's methods**
> A return to fermenting wines partly or wholly in (old) oak is a
> marked trend among a select band of houses and growers for their
> top cuvées or single-vineyard Champagnes. There should be no
> overt oak flavour, just increased complexity. Try: Billecart-Salmon,
> Jacquesson, Krug, Louis Roederer, Alain Thiénot. The best oak-
> school growers include Clos Cazals (Oger), Henri Giraud (Äy), Alain
> Robert (Le Mesnil), Jacques Selosse (Avize), Tarlant (Oeuilly), Vilmart
> (Rilly la Montagne).

Côte de Brouilly Beauj r ★★ 03' 05' 06 Fruity rich BEAUJOLAIS CRU, one of the best. Try Château Thivin.

Côte Chalonnaise Burg r w sp ★★ Vineyard area between BEAUNE and MÂCON. See also BOUZERON, GIVRY, MERCUREY, MONTAGNY, RULLY. Alias "Région de Mercurey".

Côte de Nuits Burg r (w) ★★→★★★★ north half of CÔTE D'OR. Mostly red wine.

Côte de Nuits-Villages Burg r (w) ★★ 99' 02' 03 04 05' 06 A junior AC for extreme north and south ends of CÔTE DE NUITS; well worth investigating for bargains.

Côte d'Or *Département* name applied to the central and principal Burgundy vineyard slopes: CÔTE DE BEAUNE and CÔTE DE NUITS. Not used on labels.

Côte Roannaise Central France r p ★→★★ 03 04 05 06 Small AC on the high hills outside Roanne, west of Lyon. Silky, focused Gamay. Domaines Lapandéry, du Pavillon, des Millets, Serol.

Côte-Rôtie N Rh r ★★★→★★★★ Finest, most Burgundian Rhône red, from south of Vienne, mainly Syrah, sprinkle of Viognier. Rich, complex softness and finesse with age (especially 5–10+ years). Top growers include: Barge, Bernard, Bonnefond (oak), Burgaud, CHAPOUTIER, Clusel-Roch, DELAS, Gaillard (oak), J-M Gérin (oak), GUIGAL, Jamet, Jasmin, Levet, Ogier (oak), ROSTAING, VIDAL-FLEURY.

Coteaux d'Aix-en-Provence Prov r p w ★→★★★ From hills north of Aix. A mixture of grape varieties. Good properties include: Châteaux Calissanne, Vignelaure, Domaine des Béates (CHAPOUTIER-owned), Domaine du Château Bas. See also COTEAUX DES BAUX-EN-PROVENCE.

Coteaux d'Ancenis Lo r p w (sw) ★ DYA VDQS on the right bank of the Loire, east of Nantes. Chiefly for dry, semi-sec, and sweet Chenin Bl whites made and Malvoisie; also light Gamay reds and rosés . Especially Guindon.

Coteaux de l'Aubance Lo w sw ★★→★★★★ 89 90 **95 96 97 02 03** 04 05 (06) Small AC for sweet whites from Chenin Bl. Nervier and generally less sumptuous than COTEAUX DU LAYON except when SÉLECTIONS DES GRAINS NOBLES. Especially Bablut, Haute-Perche, Montgilet, RICHOU, Rochelles.

Coteaux des Baronnies S Rh r p w ★ DYA Rhône VIN DE PAYS near Nyons. Syrah, Cab Sauv, Merlot, CHARD, plus traditional grapes. Direct wines, from good altitudes. Domaines du Rieu-Frais and Rosière worth a look.

Coteaux des Baux-en-Provence Prov r p ★→★★★ From hills to north and south of Alpilles. Once part of COTEAUX D'AIX, now AC for red and rosé. TRÉVALLON is best of all, but VIN DE PAYS: no Grenache in vineyard so not AC.

Côteaux de Chalosse SW France r p w ★ DYA. VINS DE PAYS from unusual local grapes. Co-op now merged with TURSAN.

Coteaux Champenois Champ r w (p) ★★★ DYA (whites) AC for non-sparkling CHAMPAGNE. Vintages follow those for CHAMPAGNE. Not worth inflated prices.

Coteaux du Giennois Lo r p w ★ DYA Small area north of POUILLY promoted to AC in 1998. Light, potentially powerful red: blend of Gamay and Pinot N; Sauv Bl like a junior SANCERRE. Best: HENRI BOURGEOIS, Cave de Pouilly sur Loire, Paulat.

Coteaux de Glanes SW France r ★★ DYA Lively, good value VIN DE PAYS from upper Dordogne. All from eight grower co-ops. Mostly drunk in local restaurants.

Coteaux du Languedoc Midi r p w ★★→★★★ Large area between Narbonne and

Nimes, numerous sub-divisions, and more recently GRES DE MONTPELLIER and TERRASSES DU LARZAC. PÉZENAS in the pipeline. Numerous fine estates; quality continues to improve apace. AC will disappear, replaced by Languedoc AC.

Coteaux du Layon Lo w s/sw sw ★★–★★★★ Heart of ANJOU: sweet Chenin Bl; lush with admirable acidity, ages almost forever. NEW SÉLECTION DES GRAINS NOBLES; cf ALSACE. Seven villages can add name to AC. Top ACS: BONNEZEAUX, QUARTS DE CHAUME, Coteaux du Layon-Chaume. Growers include Badouin, BAUMARD, Delesvaux, des Forges, DOMAINE LES GRAND VIGNES, Domaine de Juchepie, Ogereau, Papin (CHÂTEAU PIERRE-BISE), Jo Pithon, Guegniard, Château la Fresnaye.

Coteaux du Loir Lo r p w dr sw ★–★★★ 02 03 04 05 The Loir is a northern tributary of the Loire. Small region north of Tours, including JASNIÈRES. Potentially fine, apple-scented Chenin Bl, Gamay, peppery Pineau d'Aunis that marries well with spicy foods and pungent cheeses. Top growers: Chaussard/le Briseau, de Rycke, Fresneau, Gigou, DOMAINE DE BELLIVERE/Nicholas, Robinot.

Coteaux du Lyonnais Beauj r p (w) ★ DYA Junior BEAUJOLAIS. Best EN PRIMEUR.

Coteaux de Pierrevert S Rh r p w ★ Cool area producing easy-drinking co-op red, rosé, fresh white from high vineyards near Manosque. Domaine la Blaque, Château Régusse, Château Rousset. AC since 1998.

Coteaux du Quercy SW France r ★–★★★ 01' 02 03 04 05' (06) South of CAHORS VDQS, queuing for AC. Cab Fr-based wines from ★★ Domaines de Merchien, Lagarde, ★ de la Combarade, d'Aries, de Guyot, de Lafage. Worthy ★ co-op.

Coteaux de Saumur Lo w sw ★★–★★★ Sporadic, potentially fine semi-sweet to fully sweet Chenin Bl. VOUVRAY-like sweet (MOELLEUX) best. Especially CLOS ROUGEARD, Château Tour Grise, DOMAINE DES CHAMPS FLEURIS/Retiveau-Retif, Regis Neau.

Coteaux et Terrasses de Montauban SW France r p ★–★★ DYA Domaine de Montels and ★ Domaine de Biarnès notably better than co-op at LAVILLEDIEU-LE-TEMPLE.

Coteaux du Tricastin S Rh r p w ★★★ 01' 03 04 05' 06 Fringe mid-Rhône AC of some increasing quality. Best include Domaines de Bonetto-Fabrol, Grangeneuve (especially VIEILLES VIGNES), de Montine, St-Luc, and Châteaux La Décelle (including white CÔTES DU RHÔNE).

Coteaux Varois-en-Provence Prov r p w ★–★★ Substantial AC zone, originally Coteaux Varois *tout court*, between COTEAUX D'AIX and CÔTES DE PROVENCE. *Warming red from Routas*, la Calisse, Domaines les Alysses, du Deffends.

Coteaux du Vendômois Lo r p w ★–★★★ DYA Marginal Loire AC west of Vendôme. The most characteristic wines are VINS GRIS from Pinot d'Aunis, which also gives peppery notes to red blends. Whites based on Chenin Bl. Producers include Domaine du Four à Chaux, Cave du Vendôme-Villiers, Patrice Colin, Domaine de Montrieux.

Côtes d'Auvergne Central Fr r r p (w) ★–★★★ DYA Small VDQS. Mainly Gamay, though some Pinot N and CHARD. Best villages: Boudes, Chanturgue, Cateaugay, Corent, and Madargue. Producers: Cave St-Verny and Domaine de Peyra (sells its wines as VIN DE PAYS).

Côtes de Bourg B'x r w ★–★★★ 99 00' 01 02 03 04 05' AC for earthy red and dry white from east of the Gironde. Consistent quality. Top Châteaux Brûlesécaille, Bujan, Falfas, Fougas, Garreau, Guerry, Haut-Guiraud, Haut-Maco, Haut Mondésir, Macay, Mercier, Nodoz, Roc de Cambes, Rousset, Sociondo, Tour de Guiet.

Côtes du Brulhois SW France r p (w) ★–★★★03 04 05' (06) Near Agen. Rapidly improving VDQS centred on Donzac co-op but with promising independents Le Bois de Simon, Château la Bastide, Doms des Thermes and Coujétou-Peyret.

Côtes de Castillon B'x r ★–★★★ 98 99 00' 01 02 03 04 05' Flourishing region east of ST-EMILION; similar wines. Ageing potential. Top châteaux: de l'A, d'Aiguilhe,

Cap de Faugères, La Clarière-Laithwaite, Clos l'Eglise, Clos Les Lunelles, Clos Puy Arnaud, Poupille, Robin, Veyry, Vieux Château Champs de Mars.

Côtes de Duras Dordogne r w p ★→★★★ 02 **04** 05' (06) BORDEAUX satellite. Top include ★★★ Domaines Mouthes-les-Bihan, Petit Malromé, and Châteaux Condom Perceval, ★★ des Allegrets, du Grand Mayne, de Laulan, and Château Lafon. Good co-op (Berticot).

Côtes du Forez lo r p (sp) ★ DYA Uppermost Loire AC near St Etienne for easy-going reds and rosés from Gamay.

Côtes de Francs B'x r w ★★ **98** 00' **01 03 04** 05' Fringe BORDEAUX from east of ST-EMILION. Mainly red but some white: tasty and attractive. Reds can age a little. Top châteaux: Charmes-Godard, Francs, Laclaverie, Marsau, Pelan, PUYGUERAUD, La Prade.

Côtes de Gascogne SW w (r p) ★ DYA VIN DE PAYS. Huge production of very popular wines led by Plaimont co-op and Grassa family (Château de Tariquet). Sancet, de San Guilhem, Château Monluc. Also from MADIRAN growers, notably BRUMONT.

Côtes du Jura r p w (sp) ★ DYA Many light tints/tastes. ARBOIS more substantial.

Côtes du Lubéron S Rh r p w ★→★★ Much improved country wines from south Rhône, often reflect modern techniques. Many new producers including actors and media-magnates. Star is Château de la Canorgue. Others: Domaine de la Citadelle, Château St-Estève de Neri, Val-Joanis, Tardieu Laurent, Cellier de Marrenon.

Côtes de la Malepère Midi r ★ DYA Newly elevated AC on border between Midi and SW, near Limoux, using grape varieties from both. Watch for fresh, eager reds.

Côtes du Marmandais Dordogne r p w ★→★★★ 01 02 **03 04** 05' (06) Rapidly developing AC. ★★★ Cult wines from Elian da Ros (Clos Bacqueys). Very good: ★★ *de Beaulieu* (best are weighty, need ageing). Also ★ Domaine Des Géais.

Côtes de Montravel Dordogne w dr sw ★★ Part of BERGERAC; traditionally med-sweet, now less common. MONTRAVEL SEC is dry, HAUT-MONTRAVEL is sweet.

Côtes de Provence Prov r p w ★→★★★ r 00 01 **02 03** 04 05 06 (p w DYA) Revolutionized by new attitudes and investment. Leaders: Castel Roubine, Commanderie de Peyrassol, Domaines Bernarde, de la Courtade, Domaine Ott with Château de Selle and Clos Mireille, des Planes, Rabiéga, Richeaume, Château Ste-Rosaline. STE VICTOIRE a newly recognized sub-zone. See COTEAUX D'AIX, BANDOL.

Côtes du Rhône S Rh p w ★→★★ Basic Rhône AC mainly Grenache, also Syrah. Best drunk young, even as PRIMEUR. Wide quality variations, Vaucluse area often best: some heavy over-production.

Côtes du Rhône-Villages S Rh r p w ★→★★ Substantial, mainly reliable, sometimes delicious (and very good value). Red base is Grenache, with Syrah, Mourvèdre support. Improving white quality, often with Viognier, Roussanne. See BEAUMES-DE-VENISE, CAIRANNE, CHUSCLAN, LAUDUN, RASTEAU, SABLET, SÉGURET, ST-GERVAIS. New villages from 2005: Massif d'Uchaux, Plan de Dieu, Puyméras, Plateau de Signargues. Good value, *e.g.* Château Fontségune, Signac, Domaines Cabotte, Deforge, Grand Moulas, Grand Veneur, Jérome, Mas Libian, Montbayon, Rabasse-Charavin, Renjarde, Romarins, Ste-Anne, St Siffrein, Saladin, Valériane, Vieux Chêne, Cave Estézargues, Cave Rasteau.

Côtes du Roussillon Pyr r p w ★ →★★ **98 99 00 01 02** 03 04 05 06 East Pyrenees AC. Hefty Carignan red at its best, can pack a punch (*e.g.* Gauby). Some whites.

Côtes du Roussillon-Villages Pyr r ★★ **98 99 00 01 02** 03 04 05 06 Region's best reds, 28 villages. Dominated by Vignerons Catalans. Best labels: Cazes Frères, Domaines des Chênes, la Cazenove, Gauby (also characterful white VIN DE PAYS), Château de Jau, Co-op Lesquerde, Domaine Piquemal, Domaine Seguela.

Côtes du Roussillon des Aspres Newish AC (red only). First wines 03 vintage, based on Grenache Noir, Carignan, Syrah, and Mourvèdre.

Côtes de St-Mont SW France r w p ★★ (r) **04** 05' (06) (w) Gers VDQS seeking AC status. Created by Producteurs Plaimont, the most successful co-op in the southwest. Same grapes as MADIRAN and PACHERENC.

Côtes du Tarn SW France r p w ★ DYA VIN DE PAYS overlaps GAILLAC; same growers but also Dom d'en Segur (not in Gaillac AC).

Côtes de Thongue Midi r w ★ DYA Improving VIN DE PAYS from HERAULT. Dynamic area with reds to age. Domaines Arjolle, les Chemins de Bassac, Coussergues,

> Top Côtes du Rhône producers: Châteaux Courac, La Courançonne, l'Estagnol, Fonsalette, Grand Moulas, Haut-Musiel, Hugues, Montfaucon, St-Estève, Trignon (including Viognier); Co-ops Chantecotes (Ste-Cécile-les-Vignes), Villedieu (especially white); Domaines La Bouvade, Charvin, Combebelle, Coudoulet de Beaucastel (red, white), Cros de la Mûre, Espigouette, Ferrand, Fond-Croze, Gourget, Gramenon, Janasse, Jaume, Perrin, Réméjeanne, St-Siffrein, Soumade, Vieille Julienne, Vieux Chêne; Delas, G Duboeuf, Guigal, Jaboulet.

la Croix Belle, Magellan, Montmarin, Monplézy.

Côtes de Toul E France (Lorraine) p r w ★ DYA Very light wines; mainly VIN GRIS.

Côtes du Ventoux S Rh r p (w) ★★ 01' 03 **04' 05' 06** 6,000+ ha AC between Rhône and PROVENCE for tasty red (café-style to much deeper flavours), rosé, and good white (though oak use growing). Cool flavours from altitude for some. Best: La Vieille Ferme (red) owned by BEAUCASTEL co-op Bédoin, Goult, St-Didier, Domaine Anges, Brusset, Cascavel, Fondrèche, Martinelle, Font-Sane, Murmurium, Verrière, Château La Croix des Pins, Pesquié, Pigeade, Valcombe, JABOULET.

Côtes du Vivarais S Rh r p w ★ **04 05' 06** DYA over 580 ha across several Ardèche villages west of Montélimar; promoted to AC in 1999. Improving simple CUVÉES, strong Syrah fruit impact; substantial oak-aged reds.

Coulée de Serrant Lo w dr sw ★★★★ **95 96 97 98 99** 02 **03** 04 05 A 6.4-ha Chenin Bl vineyard at SAVENNIÈRES. Resolutely biodynamic. Riveting terroir-driven wine even when less than perfect. Decant two hours before drinking – don't chill.

Courcel, Domaine ★★★ Leading POMMARD estate – top PREMIER CRU Rugiens.

Crémant In CHAMPAGNE meant "creaming" (half-sparkling). Since 1975, an AC for quality classic-method sparkling from ALSACE, Loire, BOURGOGNE, and most recently LIMOUX – often a bargain. Term no longer used in CHAMPAGNE.

Crépy Savoie w ★★ DYA Light, soft, Swiss-style white from south shore of Lake Geneva. *Crépitant* has been coined for its faint fizz.

Crozes-Hermitage N Rh r (w) ★★ 95' 98' **99'** 00' 01' **03'** 05 06 Near Hermitage: larger, flatter Syrah vineyards (1,355 ha), mix hill and plain. Most fruity, early-drinking (2–5 years), some cask-aged (4–10 years). Good: Belle, Y Chave, Château Curson, Darnaud, Domaines du Colombier, Combier, des Entrefaux (oak), Hauts-Chassis, Mucyn, Murinais, du Pavillon-Mercurol, de Thalabert of Jaboulet, Chapoutier, Delas. Drink white early (especially good 04).

Cuve close Short-cut method of making sparkling wine in a tank. Sparkle dies away in glass much quicker than with MÉTHODE TRADITIONELLE wine.

Cuvée Wine contained in a *cuve*, or vat. A word of many uses, including synonym for "blend" and first-press wines (as in CHAMPAGNE); in Burgundy interchangeable with *cru*. Often just refers to a "lot" of wine.

Dagueneau, Didier Lo ★★★ →★★★★ Celebrated producer of POUILLY-FUMÉ who has created benchmarks for the AC (especially CUVÉES Silex and Pur Sang) as well as for Sauv Bl – in both Pouilly-Fumé and now SANCERRE with his small vineyard in Chavignol. See also JURANÇON for his Jardins de Babylone.

De Castellane Brut NV; BLANC DE BLANCS; Brut Prestige Florens de Castellane.

Traditional Epernay CHAMPAGNE house. Best for vintage wines; especially CUVÉE Commodore Brut.

Deiss, Domaine Marcel ★★ →★★★ Grower at Bergheim, ALSACE. Favours blends from individual plots but also produces fine varietals from GRANDS CRUS SCHOENENBOURG and Altenberg de Bergheim. Formerly organic, now biodynamic.

Delamotte Fine small CHARD-dominated CHAMPAGNE house at Le Mesnil. Managed with SALON by LAURENT PERRIER.

Delas Frères N Rh ★ →★★★ Old, very reliable Rhône specialists with vineyards at CONDRIEU, CÔTE-RÔTIE, HERMITAGE. Top wines: _CONDRIEU_, CÔTE-RÔTIE Landonne, Hermitage M de Tourette (red, white), Bessards. Owned by ROEDERER. Quality high.

Demi-sec Half-dry: in practice more like half-sweet (_e.g._ of CHAMPAGNE).

Deutz Brut Classic NV; Rosé NV; Brut (**96 98 99** 02); BLANC DE BLANCS (**96 98 99** 02). One of top small CHAMPAGNE houses, ROEDERER-owned. Very dry, classic wines. _Superb CUVÉE William Deutz_ 95 96' 98). See also New Zealand.

Dom Pérignon Cuvée 90' 95 96 98' 99; Rosé 98 99 Luxury CHAMPAGNE of MOËT & CHANDON, named after legendary cellarmaster who first blended CHAMPAGNE. Astonishingly consistent quality and creamy character, especially with 10–15 years bottle-age. Library of late-disgorged oenothèque vintages back to 66.

Domaine Property, particularly in Burgundy and rural France. See under name, _e.g._ TEMPIER, DOMAINE.

Dopff & Irion ★ →★★★ 17th-C ALSACE firm at Riquewihr now part of PFAFFENHEIM. Famed MUSCAT les Amandiers, GEWURZ Les Sorcières. Also good CRÉMANT D'ALSACE.

Dopff au Moulin ★★ Ancient top-class family wine house at Riquewihr, ALSACE. Best: GEWURZ GRANDS CRUS Brand, Sporen; RIES SCHOENENBOURG; Sylvaner de Riquewihr. Pioneers of ALSACE sparkling wine; good CUVÉES: Bartholdi and Julien.

Dourthe, Vins & Vignobles BORDEAUX merchant with wide range and quality emphasis: good notably CHÂTEAUX BELGRAVE, LE BOSCQ, LA GARDE. Beau-Mayne, Pey La Tour, and Dourthe No 1 are well made generic Bordeaux. Essence concentrated, modern.

Doux Sweet.

Drappier, André Outstanding AUBE CHAMPAGNE house. Family-run. Full, Pinot-led NV, BRUT Zéro, Rosé Saignée, Signature BLANC DE BLANCS (**99 00 02**), Millésime d'Exception (**00 02**), superb prestige CUVÉE Grande Sendrée (**98 99 00** 02).

Drouhin, J & Cie Burg ★★★ →★★★★ Deservedly prestigious grower (61 ha). Cellars in BEAUNE; vineyards in Beaune, CHABLIS, CLOS DE VOUGEOT, MUSIGNY, etc., and Oregon, USA. Best include (especially) (white) _BEAUNE-CLOS DES MOUCHES_, CHABLIS LES CLOS, CORTON-CHARLEMAGNE, PULIGNY-MONTRACHET, Les Folatières (red) GRIOTTE-CHAMBERTIN, MUSIGNY, GRANDS-ECHÉZEAUX.

Duboeuf, Georges ★★ →★★★ Top-class merchant at Romanèche-Thorin. Region's leader in every sense; huge range of admirable wines. Also MOULIN-À-VENT atypically aged in new oak, white MÂCONNAIS, etc.

Duclot BORDEAUX négociant; top-growth specialist. Linked with J-P MOUEIX.

Dugat Burg ★★★ Cousins Claude and Bernard (Dugat-Py) both make excellent, deep-coloured wines in GEVREY-CHAMBERTIN under their respective labels.

Dujac, Domaine ★★★ Burgundy grower (Jacques Seysses) at MOREY-ST-DENIS with vineyards in that village and BONNES-MARES, ECHÉZEAUX, GEVREY-CHAMBERTIN, etc. Splendid vivid, long-lived wines. Other top vineyards VOSNE-ROMANÉE, Malconsorts, CHAMBERTIN CLOS DE BEZE purchased in 2005. Also négociant for village wines as Dujac Fils & Père. Also venture in COTEAUX VAROIS.

Dulong BORDEAUX merchant making unorthodox Rebelle blends. Also VINS DE PAYS.

Durup, Jean Burg ★★ →★★★ One of the biggest CHABLIS growers with 152 ha, including Domaine de l'Eglantière and admirable Château de Maligny.

Duval-Leroy Dynamic Côte des Blancs CHAMPAGNE house. 130 ha of good vineyards.

Echézeaux Burg r ★★★ 88' 89' 90' 93 95 96' 97 99' 00 02' 03 04 05' 06 GRAND CRU (30 ha) between VOSNE-ROMANÉE and CLOS DE VOUGEOT. Can be superlative, fragrant. Of middling weight for GRAND CRU.

Ecu, Domaine de l' Lo dr w r ★★★ 89 90 95 96 97 02 03 04 05 06 Superb producer of biodynamic MUSCADET (especially the mineral-rich Cuvée Granite) and Gros Plant. Also small amount of excellent Cab Fr and sparkling.

Edelzwicker ALSACE w ★ DYA Modest blended light white. Popularity has waned.

d'Eguisheim, Cave Vinicole ★★ Very good ALSACE co-op often offering excellent value: fine GRAND CRUS Hatschbourg, HENGST, Ollwiller, Spiegel. Owns Willm. Top label: WOLFBERGER. Best: Grande Réserve, Sigillé, Armorié. Good CRÉMANT and Pinot N.

Engel, R ★★★ Top grower of CLOS DE VOUGEOT, ECHÉZEAUX, GRANDS-ECHÉZEAUX, and VOSNE-ROMANÉE. Bought by François Pinault of CHÂTEAU LATOUR after tragic early death of Philippe Engel in 2005.

Entraygues et Le Fel SW France r p w DYA ★ Fragrant VDQS. Especially white ★★ Domaine Méjannassère and Laurent Mousset's red and rosé.

Entre-Deux-Mers B'x w ★→★★ DYA Improved dry white BORDEAUX from between Rivers Garonne and Dordogne (aka E-2-M). Best Châteaux BONNET, Fontenille, Marjosse, Nardique-la-Gravière, Sainte-Marie, Tour de Mirambeau, Toutigeac.

Esmonin, Sylvie Burg ★★★ Very classy GEVREY-CHAMBERTIN, especially CLOS ST-JACQUES. Now darker and more concentrated.

L'Etoile Jura w dr sp (sw) ★★ Sub-region of the JURA known for stylish whites, including VIN JAUNE, similar to CHÂTEAU-CHALON; good sparkling.

Faiveley, J Burg ★★→★★★★ Family-owned growers and merchants at NUITS-ST-GEORGES. Vineyards (109 ha) in CHAMBERTIN-CLOS DE BEZE, CHAMBOLLE-MUSIGNY, CORTON, MERCUREY, NUITS. Consistent high quality rather than charm.

Faller, Théo/Domaine Weinbach ★★→★★★★ Founded by Capucin monks in 1612, now run by Colette Faller and two daughters. Outstanding concentrated wines now often drier, especially GRANDS CRUS SCHLOSSBERG (Ries), FURSTENTUM (GEWURZ).

Faugères Midi r (p w) ★★ 98 99 00 01 02 03 04 05 06 COTEAUX DU LANGUEDOC village with exceptional terroir based on schist. Reds and pinks gained AC status 1982; white in 2004, from Marsanne, Roussanne, Rolle.

Fessy, Sylvain Beauj ★★ Dynamic BEAUJOLAIS merchant with wide range.

Fèvre, William Burg ★★★ CHABLIS grower with biggest GRAND CRU holding Domaine de la Maladière (18 ha). Outstanding since bought by HENRIOT in 1998.

Fiefs Vendéens Lo r p w ★ DYA VDQS for easy-going, generally unassuming wines from the Vendée, just south of MUSCADET on the Atlantic coast. Wines from CHARD, Chenin Bl, Sauv Bl, Melon (whites), Grolleau (gris), Cab Fr, Cab Sauv, Pinot N, Negrette, and Gamay for reds and rosés. Especially: Coirier, Michon/Domaine St-Nicolas, Château Marie du Fou.

Fitou Midi r ★★ 98 99 00 01 02 03 04 05 06 Powerful red, from hills south of Narbonne as well as coastal vineyards. Ages well. Co-op at Tuchan a pacesetter among co-ops. Experiments with Mourvèdre. Good estates include Château Nouvelles, Domaine Lérys, Rolland.

Fixin Burg r ★★★ 95 96' 97 98 99' 01 02' 03 04 05' 06 Worthy and under-valued northern neighbour of GEVREY-CHAMBERTIN. Often splendid reds. Best vineyards: Clos du Chapitre, Les Hervelets, Clos Napoléon. Growers include CLAIR, FAIVELEY, Gelin, Guyard.

Fleurie Beauj r ★★★ 03 05' 06 The epitome of a BEAUJOLAIS *cru*: should be fruity, scented, silky, racy wines. Especially from Chapelle des Bois, Chignard, Depardon, Després, DUBOEUF, Château de Fleurie, Métras, the co-op.

Floc de Gascogne SW France r w Locally invented Gascon answer to PINEAU DES CHARENTES. Unfermented grape juice blended with ARMAGNAC.

Fronsac B'x r ★→★★★ 95 96 98 00' 01 03 05' Hilly area west of ST-EMILION; one of the best value reds in Bordeaux. Top châteaux: DALEM, LA DAUPHINE, Fontenil, La Grave, Haut-Carles, Mayne-Vieil, Moulin-Haut-Laroque, Richelieu, LA RIVIÈRE, La Rousselle, Tour du Moulin, Les Trois Croix, La Vieille Cure, Villars. See also CANON-FRONSAC.

Frontignan Midi golden sw ★★ NV Small AC for sweet fortified MUSCAT. Experiments with late-harvest unfortified wines. Quality steadily improving.

Fronton SW France r p ★★ **04 05' 06** Red fruits, violets, liquorice earn the nickname "BEAUJOLAIS of Toulouse". Good growers include Doms de Caze, Joliet, du Roc; Châteaux Baudare, *Bellevue-la-Forêt*, Boujac, Cahuzac, Cransac, Plaisance.

Gagnard, Jean-Noel Burg ★★★ At the top of the Gagnard clan. Beautifully expressive GRAND CRU, PREMIER CRU, and village wines in CHASSAGNE-MONTRACHET. Also cousins Blain-Gagnard, Fontaine-Gagnard.

Gaillac SW France r p w dr sw sp ★→★★★ Mostly DYA except oaked reds **03** 04 05' (06) Also sweet whites **01 02 03** 04 05' (06). ★★★ PLAGEOLES, Domaines de Ramaye, Causse-Marines, Rotier, Gineste, ★★ d'Arlus, d'Escausses, La Chanade, Cailloutis, Larroque, Long Pech, Mayragues, Salmes, Sarrabelle. Good all-rounders ★★ Domaines de Labarthe, Mas Pignou, La Vayssette.

Garage *Vins de garage* are (usually) Bordeaux made on such a very small scale. Rigorous winemaking but a bottle costs much the same as a full service.

Gard, Vin de Pays du Languedoc ★ The Gard *département* by mouth of the Rhône is important source of sound VIN DE PAYS production, including Coteaux Flaviens, Coteaux du Pont du Gard, SABLES DU GOLFE DU LION, Duché d'Uzès, Vaunage.

Gers r w p ★ DYA Vin indistinguishable from nearby CÔTES DE GASCOGNE.

Gevrey-Chambertin Burg r ★★★ 90' 93 95 96' 97 98 99' 00 01 02' 03 04 05' 06 Village containing the great CHAMBERTIN, its GRAND CRU cousins and many other noble vineyards (*e.g.* PREMIERS CRUS Cazetiers, Combe aux Moines, Combottes, CLOS ST-JACQUES). Growers include Bachelet, L Boillot, BURGUET, Damoy, DROUHIN, DUGAT, ESMONIN, FAIVELEY, Harmand-Geoffroy, Geantet-Pansiot, JADOT, LEROY, MORTET, Rossignol-Trapet, ROTY, ROUSSEAU, SERAFIN, Trapet, Varoilles.

Gigondas S Rh r p ★★→★★★ 78' 89' 90' 95' 96 97 98' 99' 00' 01' 02 03' 04' 05' 06 Good-quality, robust neighbour to CHÂTEAUNEUF. Full-bodied, chewy, sometimes peppery, largely Grenache. Try: Château de Montmirail, Saint-Cosme, Clos du Joncuas, P Amadieu, Domaine Bouïssière, Cayron, Font-Sane, Goubert, Gour de Chaulé, Grapillon d'Or, les Pallières, Piaugier, Raspail-Ay, Roubine, St-Gayan, Sanat Duc, Tourelles, des Travers. Rosés often too heated.

Ginestet Long-established BORDEAUX négociant now owned by Bernard Taillan.

Girardin, Vincent Burg r w ★★→★★★ Quality grower in SANTENAY, now dynamic merchant, specializing in CÔTE DE BEAUNE ACS. Including Domaine Henri Clerc in PULIGNY. Modern, oak and fruit style.

Givry Burg r w ★★ 02' 03 05' 06 Underrated CÔTE CHALONNAISE village: light, tasty, typical burgundy from, *e.g.* Joblot, L LATOUR, Lumpp, Sarazin, BARON THENARD.

Gorges et Côtes de Millau SW France r p w ★ DYA Improving VDQS country wines: red best. Good co-op at Aguessac. Intrepid private growers include ★★ Domaine Du Vieux Noyer.

Gosset Old small CHAMPAGNE house at AŸ. Traditional full-bodied wine (especially Grand Millésime (**98 99** 00 02). Gosset Celebris (**96' 98 99** 02) is finest CUVÉE.

Gouges, Henri ★★★ Reinvigorated estate for rich, complex NUITS-ST-GEORGES, with great ageing potential.

Grand Cru One of top Burgundy vineyards with its own AC. In ALSACE one of the 51 top vineyards covered by ALSACE GRAND CRU AC, but more vague elsewhere. In ST-EMILION. 60% of the production is covered by the ST-EMILION GRAND CRU AC.

Grande Champagne The AC of the best area of COGNAC. Nothing fizzy about it.

Grande Rue, La Burg r ★★★ 90' 93 95 96' 97 99' 00 02' 03 04 05' 06 VOSNE-ROMANÉE GRAND CRU, neighbour to ROMANÉE-CONTI. Monopoly of Domaine Lamarche.

Grands-Echézeaux Burg r ★★★★ Superlative 8.9-ha GRAND CRU next to CLOS DE

VOUGEOT. Wines not weighty but aromatic. *Viz:* DROUHIN, ENGEL, DRC, GROS.

Gratien, Alfred and **Gratien & Meyer** ★★→★★★ Brut NV; Brut **95 96'** 98; Prestige Cuvée Paradis Brut and Rosé (**98 99** 02). Excellent quirky CHAMPAGNE house, now German owned. ***Fine, very dry, long-lasting wine*** fermented in barrels. Gratien & Meyer is counterpart at SAUMUR. (Good Cuvée Flamme.)

Graves B'x r w ★→★★ **00 01 04** 05' Region south of BORDEAUX city with excellent soft earthy red; dry minerally white. PESSAC-LÉOGNAN is inner zone. Top châteaux: ARCHAMBEAU, CHANTEGRIVE, CLOS FLORIDENE, Vieux-CH Gaubert, Villa Bel Air.

Graves de Vayres B'x r w ★ DYA Small AC within ENTRE-DEUX-MERS zone. No special character.

Grès de Montpellier Midi r p w Recently recognized sub-zone of AC COTEAUX DU LANGUEDOC covering vineyards around Montpellier, including St-Georges d'Orques, la Méjanelle, St-Christol, St-Drézery.

Griotte-Chambertin Burg r ★★★★ 88' 89' 90' 93 95 96' 97 99' 00 02' 03 04 05' 06 A 5.6-ha GRAND CRU adjoining CHAMBERTIN. Similar wine, but less masculine, more "tender". Growers include DUGAT, DROUHIN, PONSOT.

Grivot, Jean Burg ★★★→★★★★ Huge improvements at this VOSNE-ROMANÉE domaine in the past decade. Superb range topped by GRAND CRUS CLOS DE VOUGET, ECHEZEAUX, RICHEBOURG.

Groffier, Robert Burg ★★★ Pure, elegant GEVREY-CHAMBERTIN, CHAMBOLLE-MUSIGNY, especially Les Amoureuses.

Gros, Domaines Burg ★★★→★★★★ Excellent family of *vignerons* in VOSNE-ROMANÉE comprising (at least) Domaines Jean, Michel, Anne, Anne-François Gros, and Gros Frère & Sœur. Wines range from HAUTES CÔTES DE NUITS to RICHEBOURG.

Gros Plant du Pays Nantais Lo w ★ DYA Decidedly junior VDQS cousin of MUSCADET; sharper, lighter; from the COGNAC grape, aka Folle Blanche, Ugni Blanc, etc.

Guffens-Heynen Burg ★★★ Belgian POUILLY-FUISSÉ grower. Tiny quantity, top quality. Heady Glamour. Also CÔTE D'OR wines (bought-in grapes) as VERGET.

Guigal, Ets E N Rh Celebrated grower: 31-ha CÔTE-RÔTIE, also CONDRIEU, HERMITAGE, ST-JOSEPH. Merchant: CONDRIEU, CÔTE-RÔTIE, HERMITAGE, south RHÔNE. Owns Domaine de Bonserine, VIDAL-FLEURY. By ageing single vineyard CÔTE-RÔTIE (La Mouline, La Landonne, La Turque) for 42 months in new oak, Guigal breaks local tradition to please (especially) American palates; all his reds are big-tasting. Standard wines: good value, reliable, especially red, white CÔTES DU RHÔNE. Also full oaky CONDRIEU La Doriane, occasional sweet Luminescence.

Haut-Médoc B'x r ★★→★★★ Big AC Source of good value, minerally, digestible wines. Some variation in soils and wines; sand and gravel in south, so finer; heavier clay and gravel further north, so sturdier. Includes five classed growths (*e.g.* LA LAGUNE).

Haut-Montravel Dordogne w sw ★★ 95' 97' 98' 00 01' 02 03 05' (06) Modestly growing sweet AC, riding crest of foie gras wave. Best are châteaux ★★★ Moulin Caresse, Puy-Servain-Terrement, Roque-Peyre, and Domaine de Libarde.

Haut-Poitou Lo w r ★→★★ DYA VDQS Reds, whites, rosés, and sparkling from numerous grape varieties. Best are Sauv Bl and Gamay, especially from Cave du Haut Poitou (linked with DUBOEUF) and over-achieving wines from Ampelidae.

Hautes-Côtes de Beaune/Nuits r w Burg ★★ red 02' 03' 05' 06 white 02' 03 04 05' 06 ACS for the villages in the hills behind the CÔTE DE BEAUNE. Attractive, lighter reds and whites for early drinking. Best: Cornu, Devevey, Duband, GROS, Jacob, Jayer-Gilles, Mazilly. Also large co-op near BEAUNE.

Heidsieck, Charles Major Reims CHAMPAGNE house. Continuing fine quality, although innovative Mis en Cave range of NV CUVÉES showing year of bottling now (sadly) has lower profile. See also PIPER-HEIDSECK.

Heidsieck, Monopole Once illustrious CHAMPAGNE house. Fair quality.

Hengst Wintzenheim ALSACE GRAND CRU. Excels with top-notch GEWURZ from Albert

MANN; also Pinot-Auxerrois, Chasselas and Pinot N, with no GRAND CRU status.

Henriot Brut Old family CHAMPAGNE house. Very fine, fresh, creamy style. Joseph H also owns BOUCHARD PÈRE & FILS (since 1995) and FÈVRE.

Hérault Midi Biggest vineyard *département*: 96,800 ha and declining. Including Faugères, St-Chinian, Pic St-Loup, and other excellent AC COTEAUX DU LANGUEDOC. Important source of VIN DE PAYS de l'Hérault encompassing full quality spectrum, from pioneering to basic. Also VIN DE TABLE.

Hermitage N Rh r w ★★★ · ★★★★ 61' 66 78' 82 83' 85' 88 89' **90' 91' 94 95' 96 97' 98'** 99' 00 01' 03' 04 05' **06'** Dark, profound. Truest example of Syrah from 131 ha on east bank of Rhône. Thrives on long ageing. Heady, rich white (Marsanne, some Roussanne) best left for 6–7 years; top wines mature for up to 30 years. Best: Belle, CHAPOUTIER, CHAVE, Colombier, DELAS, Desmeure, Faurie, GUIGAL, Habrard (white), JABOULET, Sorrel, Tardieu-Laurent. TAIN co-op good (especially Gambert de Loche).

Hospices de Beaune Burg Auction on third Sunday in November sets the pace for the vintage while raising money for charity. CUVÉES cover the main villages of CÔTE DE BEAUNE plus POUILLY FUISSE, CLOS DE LA ROCHE, MAZIS-CHAMBERTIN. Beware variable standards in recent years, though some very good CUVÉES.

Hudelot-Noëllat, Alain ★★★ Under-appreciated VOUGEOT estate producing some excellent wines, in a light but fine style.

Huet Lo ★★ · ★★★★★ 88 89 90 95 96 97 02 03 04 05 06 Leading estate in VOUVRAY, run on biodynamic principles. Noel Pinguet, Huet's son-in-law continues to tend the vines and make the wines. Single-vineyard wines best: Le Haut Lieu, Le Mont, Clos du Bourg. All great agers: look for ancient vintages like 47 and 59.

Hugel et Fils ★★ · ★★★★ Best-known ALSACE house, making superb late-harvest wines. Three quality levels: Classic, Tradition, Jubilee. Opposed to GRAND CRU system.

Irancy Burg r (p) ★★ 02' 03' **05'** 06 Formerly Bourgogne-Irancy. Light red made near CHABLIS from Pinot N and local César. Best vintages mature well. ***Best: Colinot.***

Irouléguy SW France r p (w) ★★ · ★★★ 01' **02 03 04** (05) Fashionable Basque wines with country accent, less awesome than rival MADIRAN. Dense Tannat-based reds to keep 5 years. Good from Doms Abotia, Ameztia, Arretxea, Brana, Etchegaraya, Ilarria, Mouguy. Excellent co-op, especially white ★★★ Xuri d'Ansa.

Jaboulet Aîné, Paul N Rh Old family firm at TAIN, sold to Swiss investor early 06. Once leading grower of HERMITAGE (especially La Chapelle ★★★), CORNAS St-Pierre, CROZES Thalabert (good value), Roure; merchant of other Rhône wines especially CÔTES DU RHÔNE Parallèle 45, CÔTES DU VENTOUX, VACQUEYRAS. Drink whites young. Quality, prices may now rise, and style more international.

Jacquart Brut NV; Brut Rosé NV (Carte Blanche and Cuvée Spéciale); Brut **96 98 99** Co-op-based CHAMPAGNE marque; in quantity the sixth-largest. Fair quality. Luxury brands: Cuvée Nominée Blanc **98 99 00** 02 and Rosé **99** 02. Fine Mosaïque BLANC DE BLANCS **98** 99 and Rosé **99 00 02.**

Jacquesson Excellent small Dizy CHAMPAGNE house. Superb Avize GRAND CRU 96' **98**; exquisite vintage wines: white (**90** 95 96') and rosé (**96 98**). Corne Bautray, Dizy **00** 02, and ***excellent NV CUVÉES*** 728, 729, 730, and 731.

Jadot, Louis Burg ★★ · ★★★★ Good-quality merchant house with vineyards (63 ha) in BEAUNE, CORTON, Magenta, Château des Jacques (MOULIN À VENT), etc. Sound across the range now.

Jardin de la France Lo w r p DYA One of France's four regional VINS DE PAYS. Covers Loire Valley: mostly single grape (especially CHARD, Gamay, Sauv Bl).

Jasnières Lo w dr (sw)★★ · ★★★ **97 02 03** 04 05 06 Singular, cellar-worthy VOUVRAY-like wine (Chenin Bl), both dry and off-dry from a tiny vineyard north of Tours. Especially Aubert la Chapelle, Chaussard/Le Briseau, Gigou, Nicolas/Domaine de Belliviere, Robinot.

Jobard, François Burg ★★★ Small MEURSAULT DOMAINE; classic, slow-evolving wines. Look out also for nephew Remi Jobard's more modern-style wines.

Joseph Perrier Excellent smaller CHAMPAGNE house at Chalons with good vineyards in Marne Valley. Supple fruity style; top prestige Cuvée Joséphine **95 96' 98**.

Josmeyer ★★→★★★ ALSACE house specializing in fine, elegant, long-lived organic wines in a dry style. Superb Ries GRAND CRU HENGST. Also very good wines from lesser varietals (Chasselas, Auxerrois).

Juliénas Beauj r ★★★ **03' 05' 06** Leading CRU of BEAUJOLAIS: vigorous fruity wine to keep 2–3 years. Growers include Châteaux du Bois de la Salle, des Capitans, de Juliénas, des Vignes; Domaines Bottière, R Monnet, Michel Tête, co-op.

Jurançon N sw dr ★→★★★ SW **95 97 98 00 01 02** 03 **04'** 05' (06) dr **01' 02 03' 04' 05 06** Success story from Pau in Pyrenean foothills. Production of dry and sweet wines increasing every year. Growers: Domaines Bellegarde, Bordenave, Capdevielle, Castéra, de Souch, Cauhapé, Guirouilh, Jolys, Lapeyre, Larredya, Nigri, de Rousse, Uroulat, Bellevue, Cabarrouy, Vignau-la-Juscle. Also ★★★★ Daguenau's Les Jardins de Babylone, co-op especially good for dry white.

Kaefferkopf ALSACE w dr (sw) ★★★ Since 2006 the 51st GRAND CRU of ALSACE at Ammerschwihr. Permitted to make blends as well as varietal wines.

Kientzler, André ★★→★★★ Small, very fine ALSACE grower at Ribeauvillé. Outstanding Ries from GRAND CRUS Osterberg and Geisberg and wonderfully aromatic Gewürz from GRAND CRU Kirchberg. Also very good Auxerrois and sweet wines.

Kreydenweiss Marc ★★→★★★ Fine ALSACE grower: 12 ha at Andlau, especially for PINOT GR (very good GRAND CRU Moenchberg), Pinot Bl, and Ries. Top wine: GRAND CRU Kastelberg (ages 20 years); also fine Auxerrois Kritt Klevner and good VENDANGE TARDIVE. One of first in ALSACE to use new oak. Good Ries/PINOT GR blend Clos du Val d'Eléon. Great believer in terroir and biodynamic viticulture.

Krug Small, supremely prestigious CHAMPAGNE house. Rich, nutty, elegant wines, oak fermented: long ageing, superlative quality. Owned by MOËT-Hennessy.

Kuentz-Bas ★→★★★ ALSACE Famous grower/merchant at Husseren-les Châteaux, especially PINOT GR, GEWURZ. Good VENDANGES TARDIVES. Owned by Caves J-B Adam.

Labouré-Roi Burg ★★→★★★ Reliable, dynamic merchant at NUITS. Mostly white, but now also owns top (mostly red) new-generation merchant Nicolas POTEL.

Ladoix-Serrigny Burg r (w) ★★ Village at north end of COTE DE BEAUNE, including some CORTON and CORTON CHARLEMAGNE. Could deliver more.

Ladoucette, de ★★→★★★ 02 03 04 05 Leading producer of POUILLY-FUMÉ, based at Château de Nozet. Luxury brand Baron de L can be wonderful. Also SANCERRE Comte Lafond, La Poussie, Marc Brédif.

Lafarge, Michel ★★★★ CÔTE DE BEAUNE 10-ha estate with excellent VOLNAYS, in particular Clos des Chênes and now Caillerets. New BEAUNE vineyards (red and white) on stream from 2005.

Lafon, Domaine des Comtes Burg ★★★★ Top estate in MEURSAULT, LE MONTRACHET, VOLNAY. Glorious intense white; extraordinary dark red. Also in the Maconnais.

Laguiche, Marquis de Burg ★★★★ Largest owner of LE MONTRACHET. Superb DROUHIN-made wines.

Lalande de Pomerol B'x r ★★→★★★ Northerly neighbour of POMEROL. Wines similar, but less mellow. New investors and younger generation: improving quality. Top châteaux: des Annereaux, Bertineau-St-Vincent, La Croix-St-André, Les Cruzelles, La Fleur de Boüard, Garraud, Grand Ormeau, Les Hauts Conseillants, Jean de Gué, Perron (La Fleur), La Sergue, TOURNEFEUILLE.

Landron (Domaines) Lo dr w (also Domaine de la Louvetrie) First-rate producer of organic MUSCADET DE SÈVRE ET MAINE with several CUVÉES, bottled by terroir, including ultra-fresh, unfiltered Amphibolite and ageworthy Fief du Breil.

Langlois-Château Lo ★→★★★ A top SAUMUR sparkling houses (especially CREMANT). Also still wines, especially exceptional SAUMUR Bl VIEILLES VIGNES.

Languedoc Midi r p w General term for the Midi and now potential AC to replace COTEAUX DU LANGUEDOC and include Minervois and Corbières.

Lanson Père & Fils Black Label NV; Rosé NV; Brut **96 98 99** 00 02 Important improving CHAMPAGNE house. Long-lived luxury brand: Noble CUVÉE BLANC DE BLANCS (**98 99** 02). Black Label improved by longer ageing.

Laroche ★★→★★★ Important grower and dynamic CHABLIS merchant, including Domaines La Jouchère, Laroche. Top wines: Blanchots (Réserve de l'Obédiencerie ★★★), CLOS VIEILLES VIGNES. Ambitious MIDI range, Domaine La Chevalière.

Latour, Louis Burg ★★→★★★ Famous merchant and grower with vineyards (49 ha) in BEAUNE, CORTON, etc. Very good white: CHEVALIER-MONTRACHET Les Demoiselles, CORTON-CHARLEMAGNE, MONTRACHET, good-value MONTAGNY and ARDECHE CHARD etc. Reds still underperforming. Château de Corton Grancey. Also Pinot N Valmoissine from the Var.

Latour de France r (w) ★→★★ Supposedly superior village in CÔTES DE ROUSSILLON-VILLAGES. Especially Clos de l'Oum, Clos des Fées.

Latricières-Chambertin Burg r ★★★ GRAND CRU neighbour of CHAMBERTIN (6.8 ha). Similar wine but lighter, *e.g.* from FAIVELEY, LEROY, Rossignol-Trapet, Trapet.

Laudun S Rh w r p ★ Village of CÔTES DU RHÔNE-VILLAGES (W bank). Mild reds, pretty rosés. Agreeable wines from Serre de Bernon co-op. Dom Pelaquié best, especially white. Also Château Courac, Domaine Duseigneur, Prieuré St-Pierre.

Laurent-Perrier Dynamic family-owned CHAMPAGNE house at Tours-sur-Marne. Fine minerally NV; excellent luxury brands: Grand Siècle La CUVÉE Lumière du Millésime (**90 96'**), CGS Alexandra Brut Rosé (**96 99** 02). Also Ultra Brut.

Lavilledieu-du-Temple SW France r p w ★ DYA Fruity VDQS mostly from go-ahead co-op near Montauban, reviving old regional varieties. Also independent Domaine de Rouch.

Leflaive, Domaine Burg ★★★★ Among the best white Burgundy growers, at PULIGNY-MONTRACHET. Best vineyards: Bienvenues-, CHEVALIER-MONTRACHET, Folatières, Pucelles, and (since 1991) Le Montrachet. *Also Macon from 2004.* Ever-finer wines on biodynamic principles.

Leflaive, Olivier Burg ★★→★★★ High-quality négociant at PULIGNY-MONTRACHET, cousin of the above. Reliable wines, mostly white, but drink them young.

Leroy, Domaine Burg ★★★★ DOMAINE built around purchase of Noëllat in VOSNE-ROMANÉE in 1988 and Leroy family holdings (known as d'Auvenay). Extraordinary quality (and prices) from tiny biodynamic yields.

Leroy, Maison Burg ★★★★ The ultimate négociant-eleveur at AUXEY-DURESSES with sky-high standards and the finest stocks of expensive old wine in Burgundy.

Liger-Belair Burg ★★★→★★★★ Two recently re-established domaines of high quality. Vicomte Louis-Michel L-B makes brilliantly ethereal wines in VOSNE-ROMANÉE, while cousin Thibault makes plump red wines in NUITS-ST-GEORGES.

Limoux Pyr r w ★★ AC for sparkling BLANQUETTE DE LIMOUX or better CRÉMANT de Limoux, also *méthode ancestrale*. Oak-aged CHARD for white Limoux AC. Red AC since 2003 based on Merlot, plus Syrah, Grenache, Cabernets, Carignan. Pinot N in CRÉMANT and for VIN DE PAYS. Growers: Domaines de Fourn, des Martinolles, Rives Blanques. Good co-op: Sieur d'Arques.

Lirac S Rh r p w ★★ **98' 99' 01' 03 04 05' 06** Next to TAVEL. Approachable, sound-value red (can age 5+ yrs), recently firmer with raised use of Mourvèdre, more CHÂTEAUNEUF-DU-PAPE owners. More focus on red than rosé, especially Domaines Cantegril, Devoy-Martine, Joncier, Lafond Roc-Epine, Maby (Fermade), André Méjan, de la Mordorée, Rocalière, R Sabon, F Zobel, Clos de Sixte, Château d'Aquéria, de Bouchassy, St-Roch, Ségriès. Good whites (5 years).

Listrac-Médoc B'x r ★★→★★★ Neighbour of MOULIS in the southern MÉDOC. Grown-up clarets with tannic grip. Now rounded out with more Merlot. Best châteaux: CLARKE, FONRÉAUD, FOURCAS-DUPRÉ, FOURCAS-HOSTEN, Mayne-Lalande.

Long-Depaquit Burg ★★★ Very good CHABLIS DOMAINE, owned by BICHOT.

Lorentz, Gustave ★★ ALSACE grower and merchant at Bergheim. Especially GEWURZ, Ries from GRAND CRUS Altenberg de Bergheim, Kanzlerberg. Also owns Jerome Lorentz. Equally good for top estate and volume wines.

Loron & Fils ★→★★ Big-scale grower and merchant at Pontanevaux; specialist in BEAUJOLAIS and sound VINS DE TABLE.

Loupiac B'x w sw ★★ Across River Garonne from SAUTERNES. Lighter and fresher in style. Top Clos-Jean, LOUPIAC-GAUDIET, Mémoires, Noble, RICAUD, Les Roques.

Lussac-St-Emilion B'x r ★★ **95 98** 00' 01 03 05' Lighter and more rustic than neighbouring ST-EMILION. Co-op the main producer. Top châteaux: Barbe Blanche, Bel Air, Bellevue, Courlat, la Grenière, Lussac, Mayne-Blanc, LYONNAT.

Macération carbonique Traditional fermentation technique: whole bunches of unbroken grapes in a closed vat. Fermentation induced inside each grape eventually bursts it, giving vivid, fruity, mild wine, not for ageing. Especially in BEAUJOLAIS; now much used in the MIDI and elsewhere, even CHÂTEAUNEUF.

Mâcon Burg r w (p) DYA Sound, usually unremarkable reds (Gamay best), tasty dry (CHARD) whites. Also MÂCON Superieur (similar).

Mâcon-Lugny Burg (r) w sp ★★ **04 05' 06'** Village next to VIRE with huge and very good co-op (4 million bottles). Les Genevrières is sold by LOUIS LATOUR.

Mâcon-Villages Burg w ★★→★★★ **04 05' 06'** Increasingly well-made (when not over-produced). Named after villages, *e.g.* Mâcon-Lugny, -Prissé, -Uchizy. Best co-op: Prissé, Lugny. Best: Vincent (Fuissé), THEVENET, Bonhomme, Guillemot-Michel, Lafon, Merlin (La Roche Vineuse). See VIRÉ-CLESSÉ.

Macvin Jura w sw ★★ AC for "traditional" MARC and grape-juice apéritif.

Madiran SW France r ★★→★★★ 95' 98 00 01' 02 03 04 05' (06) ***Tannat-based hearty red.*** New fruitier style from joint venture between Plaimont and Crouseilles co-ops; but most need ageing. Montus and Bouscassé best known, also Berthoumieu, Chapelle Lenclos, Labranche-Laffont, Laplace, Laffitte-Teston, Capmartin, Barrejat, du Crampilh, Clos Fardet.

Mähler-Besse First-class Dutch négociant in BORDEAUX. Has share in CHÂTEAU PALMER.

Mailly-Champagne Top CHAMPAGNE co-op. Luxury wine: Cuvée des Echansons.

Maire, Henri ★→★★ The biggest grower/merchant of JURA wines, with half of the entire AC. Some top wines, many cheerfully commercial. Fun to visit.

Mann, Albert ★→★★★ Top growers of ALSACE at Wettolsheim: rich, elegant wines. Very good Pinot Bl Auxerrois and Pinot N, and good range of GRANDS CRUS wines from SCHLOSSBERG, HENGST, FURSTENTUM, and Steingrubler.

Maranges Burg r (w) ★★ 99' 02' 03' **04** 05' 06 CÔTE DE BEAUNE AC beyond SANTENAY (243 ha): one-third PREMIER CRU. Best from Contat-Grange, DROUHIN, GIRARDIN.

Marc Grape skins after pressing; also the strong-smelling brandy made from them (the equivalent of Italian grappa; see Italy).

Marcillac SW France r p ★★ DYA Best 3 years or so after vintage. AC from 1990. Violet-hued with grassy red-fruit character. Domaines du Cros, Costes, Mioula Vieux Porche and good co-op.

Margaux B'x r ★★→★★★★ 89 90' 95 96 **98** 99 00' 01 02 03 04 05' Largest communal AC in the southern MÉDOC, grouping vineyards from five villages, including Margaux itself and Cantenac. Known for its elegant, fragrant style. Top châteaux: BRANE-CANTENAC, FERRIERE, MARGAUX, RAUZAN-SÉGLA, PALMER.

Marionnet, Henry Lo ★→★★★ **02 03 04 05** 06 Leading TOURAINE grower with ever-expanding range of wines, including several Sauv Bls (top is Le M de Marionnet) and Gamay, especially the unsulphured Vendange Première. Also ***Provignage, made from ungrafted Romorantin vines***, and juicy Cot.

Marne & Champagne CHAMPAGNE house, and many smaller brands, including BESSERAT DE BELLEFON. Alfred Rothschild brand very good CHARD-based wines.

Marque déposée Trademark.

Marsannay Burg p r (w) ★★ 99' 02' 03 04 05' 06 (rosé DYA) Village with fine, light red and delicate Pinot N rosé. Includes villages of Chenôve, Couchey. Growers: CHARLOPIN, CLAIR, JADOT, MÉO-CAMUZET, ROTY, Trapet.

Mas de Daumas Gassac Midi r w p ★★★ 90 91 92 93 94 95' 96' 97 98' 99 00' 01' 02 03' 04 05 Pioneering estate that set an example of excellence in the Midi, with ___Cabernet-based reds___ produced on apparently unique soil. Quality now rivalled by others. Wines include new super-CUVÉE Emile Peynaud, rosé Frisant, rich, fragrant white blend to drink at 2–3 years. VIN DE PAYS status. Intriguing sweet wine: Vin de Laurence (Sém, MUSCATS, Sercial).

Maury Pyr r sw ★★ NV Red VIN DOUX NATUREL of Grenache from ROUSSILLON. From Grenache grown on an island of schist amid limestone and clay. Much recent improvement, esp from Mas Amiel.

Mazis- (or Mazy) Chambertin Burg r ★★★ 88' 89' 90' 93 95 96' 97 99' 00 02' 03 04 05' 06 GRAND CRU neighbour of CHAMBERTIN (12 ha); can be equally potent. Best from FAIVELEY, HOSPICES DE BEAUNE, LEROY, Maume, ROTY.

Mazoyères-Chambertin See CHARMES-CHAMBERTIN.

Médoc B'x r ★★ 98 00' 02 03 04 05' AC for reds in the flatter, northern part of the MÉDOC peninsula. Good if you're selective. Earthy, with Merlot adding flesh. Top châteaux: GREYSAC, LOUDENNE, LES ORMES-SORBET, POTENSAC, Rollan-de-By (HAUT-CONDISSAS), LA TOUR-DE-BY, TOUR HAUR-CAUSSAN.

Meffre, Gabriel ★★ Biggest south Rhône estate, based at GIGONDAS. Owns mid-range Domaine Longue Toque. Variable quality, recent progress. Also bottles and sells small CHÂTEAUNEUF domaines. Decent north Rhône Laurus (new oak) range, especially CROZES-HERMITAGE.

Mellot, Alphonse Lo ★★→★★★ Nearly impeccable range of SANCERRE (white and red) from leading grower, especially wood-aged CUVÉE Edmond, Génération XIX (red and white), Les Demoiselles and En Grands Champs (red). Also vineyards in Charitois (VdP), both CHARD and Pinot N.

Menetou-Salon Lo r p w ★★ 02 03 04 05 06 Charming, generally reasonably priced wines from a zone west of SANCERRE. Best producers: Clement (Domaine de Chatenoy), Henry Pellé, Jean-Max Roger, BOURGEOIS, Tour St-Martin.

Méo-Camuzet ★★★★ Very fine DOMAINE in CLOS DE VOUGEOT, NUITS-ST-GEORGES, RICHEBOURG, VOSNE-ROMANÉE. JAYER-inspired. Especially VOSNE-ROMANÉE Cros Parantoux. Now also some less expensive négociant CUVÉES.

Mercier & Cie, Champagne Brut NV; Brut Rosé NV; Demi-Sec Brut One of biggest CHAMPAGNE houses at Epernay. Controlled by MOËT & CHANDON. Fair commercial quality, sold mainly in France. Full-bodied Pinot N-led CUVÉE Eugene Mercier.

Mercurey Burg r ★★→★★★ 99' 02' 03' 04 05' 06 Leading red wine village of CÔTE CHALONNAISE. Good middle-rank Burgundy, include improving whites. Try Château de Chamirey, FAIVELEY, M Juillot, Lorenzon, Raquillet, Domaine de Suremain.

Mérode, Domaine Prince de ★★★ Top DOMAINE for CORTON and POMMARD.

Mesnil-sur-Oger, Le Champ ★★★★ One of the top Côte des Blancs villages. Structured CHARD for very long ageing.

Méthode champenoise Traditional laborious method of putting bubbles into CHAMPAGNE by refermenting wine in its bottle. Must use terms "classic method" or "méthode traditionnelle" outside region. Not mentioned on labels.

Méthode traditionnelle See entry above.

Meursault Burg w (r) ★★★ →★★★★ 92 95 97 99' 00' 01 02' 04 05' 06' CÔTE DE BEAUNE village with some of world's greatest whites: savoury, dry, nutty, mellow. Best vineyards: Charmes, Genevrières, Perrières. Also: Goutte d'Or, Meursault-Blagny, Poruzots, Narvaux, Tesson, Tillets. Producers include: AMPEAU, J-M BOILLOT, M BOUZEREAU, V BOUZEREAU, Boyer-Martenot, CHÂTEAU DE MEURSAULT, COCHE-DURY, Ente, Fichet, Grivault, ___P Javillier___, JOBARD, LAFON, LATOUR, O LEFLAIVE, LEROY, Matrot, Mikulski, P MOREY, G ROULOT. See also BLAGNY.

Michel, Louis ★★★ CHABLIS DOMAINE with model unoaked, v. long-lived wines, including **_superb LES CLOS, v. good Montmains, Montée de Tonnerre._**

Microbullage Tiny quantities of oxygen are injected into wine to avoid racking, stimulate aeration, and accelerate maturity.

Midi Broad term covering Languedoc, Roussillon, and even Provence. A melting-pot; quality improves with every vintage. ACS can be intriguing blends; VINS DE PAYS, especially d'OC, are often varietals. Brilliant promise, rewarding drinking.

Minervois Midi r (p w) br sw ★→★★ 98 99 00 01 02 03 04 05 06 Hilly AC region; good, lively wines, especially Château Bonhomme, Coupe-Roses, la Grave, Villerembert-Julien, Oupia, La Tour Boisée, Clos Centeilles Ste Eulalie, Faiteau; co-ops LA LIVINIÈRE, de Peyriac, Pouzols. See ST-JEAN DE MINERVOIS.

Minervois-La Livinière, La Midi r (p w) ★→★★ Quality village (see last entry) only sub-appellation or *cru* in Minervois. Best growers: Abbaye de Tholomies, Borie de Maurel, Combe Blanche, Château de Gourgazaud, Clos Centeilles, Laville-Bertrou, Domaines Maris, Ste-Eulalie, Co-op La Livinière, Vipur.

Mis en bouteille au château/domaine Bottled at the château, property or estate. NB *dans nos caves* (in our cellars) or *dans la région de production* (in the area of production) are often used but mean little.

Moët & Chandon Brut NV; Rosé 99 00 02; Brut Imperial 99 00 02. Largest CHAMPAGNE merchant/grower with cellars in Epernay; branches in Argentina, Australia, Brazil, California, Germany, Spain. Consistent quality, especially vintages. Prestige CUVÉE: DOM PERIGNON. Impressive multi-vintage Esprit du Siècle, GRANDS CRUS Aÿ, Chouilly, Sillery bottlings. Coteaux Champenois Saran: still wine.

Moillard Burg ★★→★★★★ Big family firm in NUITS-ST-GEORGES, making full range, including dark and very tasty wines.

Mommessin, J ★→★★ Major BEAUJOLAIS merchant now owned by BOISSET. Owner of CLOS DE TART. White wines less successful than reds.

Monbazillac Dordogne w sw ★★→★★★★ Golden wine from BERGERAC. Alternative to Sauternes. Top producers: L'Ancienne Cure, Clos des Verdots, Châteaux de Belingard-Chayne, Le Fagé, Les Hauts de Caillavel, Poulvère, Theulet, Tirecul-la-Gravière, and La Grande Maison. Also Château de Monbazillac.

Mondeuse Savoie r ★★ DYA SAVOIE red grape. Potentially good, deep-coloured, wine. Possibly same as Italy's Refosco. Don't miss a chance, *e.g.* G Berlioz.

Monopole A vineyard that is under single ownership.

Montagne-St-Emilion B'x r ★★ 95 98 00' 01 03 05' Largest and possibly best satellite of ST-EMILION. Similar style of wine. Top châteaux: Calon, Faizeau, Maison Blanche, Montaiguillon, Roudier, Teyssier, VIEUX CHÂTEAU-ST-ANDRE.

Montagny Burg w ★★ 04 05' 06' CÔTE CHALONNAISE village. Between MÂCON and MEURSAULT, both geographically and gastronomically. Top producers: Aladame, J-M BOILLOT, Cave de Buxy, Michel, **_Château de la Saule_**.

Monthelie Burg r (w) ★★→★★★★ 99' 02' 03' 04 05' 06 Little-known VOLNAY neighbour, sometimes almost equal. Excellent fragrant red, especially BOUCHARD PÈRE & FILS, COCHE-DURY, LAFON, DROUHIN, Garaudet, Château de Monthelie (Suremain).

de Montille Burg ★★★ Hubert made **_long-lived VOLNAY_**, POMMARD. Son Etienne has expanded domaine with purchases in BEAUNE, NUITS-ST-GEORGES, and potentially outstanding VOSNE-ROMANÉE Malconsorts. Etienne also runs Château de Puligny and is involved with sister Alix in négociant venture Deux Montille (white wines).

Montlouis Lo w dr sw (sp) ★★→★★★ 89 90 95 96 97 02 03 04 05 Directly across the river from VOUVRAY. Makes similar, though leaner, sweet or long-lived dry whites from Chenin Bl, also sparkling. Top growers include Alex-Mathur, Berger, Chidaine, Cossais, Damien Delecheneau/la Grange Tiphaine, Deletang, Moyer, Frantz Saumon, Taille aux Loups.

Montrachet Burg w ★★★★ 1904 35 47 49 59 64 66 71 73 78 79 82 85' 86 88 89' 90 92' 93 95 96' 97 98 99 00' 01 02' 03 04 05' 06 8.01 ha GRAND CRU vineyard in both PULIGNY- and CHASSAGNE-MONTRACHET. Potentially the greatest white burgundy: strong, perfumed, intense, dry yet luscious. Top wines from LAFON, LAGUICHE (DROUHIN), LEFLAIVE, RAMONET, ROMANÉE-CONTI. But THENARD disappointing.

Montravel Dordogne ★★ p dr w DYA r 01 02 03 04 05' (06) Now AC for all colours, adjoins BERGERAC. Similar to BERGERAC. Good examples from Domaines de Krevel, De Bloy, Jonc Blanc, Masmontet, Masburel, Laulerie, Moulin-Caresse. Separate ACs for semi-sweet CÔTES DE MONTRAVEL, sweet HAUT-MONTRAVEL.

Morey, Domaines Burg ★★★ Various family members in CHASSAGNE-MONTRACHET, especially Bernard, including BÂTARD-MONTRACHET. Also Pierre M in MEURSAULT.

Morey-St-Denis Burg r ★★★ Small village with four GRANDS CRUS between GEVREY-CHAMBERTIN and CHAMBOLLE-MUSIGNY. Glorious wine often overlooked. Includes Amiot, DUJAC, H Lignier, Moillard-Grivot, Perrot-Minot, PONSOT, ROUMIER, ROUSSEAU, Serveau.

Morgon Beauj r ★★★ 99' 00 01 03 05' 06 The firmest cru of BEAUJOLAIS, needing time to develop its rich savoury flavour. Try Aucoeur, Château de Bellevue, Desvignes, J Foillard, Lapierre, Château de Pizay. DUBOEUF excellent.

Mortet, Denis ★★★ Dark-coloured and deeply concentrated GEVREY CHAMBERTIN wines until his untimely death in 2006.

Moueix, J-P et Cie B'x Legendary proprietor and merchant of ST-EMILION and POMEROL. Company now run by son Christian. Châteaux include LA FLEUR-PÉTRUS, HOSANNA, MAGDELAINE, PÉTRUS, TROTANOY. Also in California: see Dominus.

Moulin-à-Vent Beauj r ★★★ 95 96' 98 99 00 01 03 05' 06 Biggest and potentially best wine of BEAUJOLAIS. Can be powerful, meaty, long-lived; can even taste like fine Rhône or Burgundy. Many good growers, especially Château du Moulin-à-Vent, Château des Jacques, Domaine des Hospices, Janodet, JADOT, Merlin.

Moulis B'x r ★★→★★★ 95 96 98 00' 01 02 03 04 05' Inland AC in the southern MÉDOC, with several leading CRUS BOURGEOIS: CHASSE-SPLEEN, MAUCAILLOU, POUJEAUX (THEIL). Good hunting ground.

Mouton Cadet Biggest-selling red BORDEAUX brand. Revamped and fruitier since 2004. Also white, rosé, GRAVES AC and MÉDOC AC.

Mugneret/Mugneret-Gibourg Burg ★★★ Superb reds from top CÔTE DE NUITS sites.

Mugnier, J-F Burg ★★★→★★★★ Château de Chambolle estate with first-class delicate CHAMBOLLE-MUSIGNY Les Amoureuses and MUSIGNY. Also BONNES-MARES. From 2004 has reclaimed family's NUITS-ST-GEORGES Clos de la Maréchale.

Mumm, G H & Cie Cordon Rouge NV; Mumm de Cramant NV; Cordon Rouge 96 98 99 00 02; Rosé NV Major CHAMPAGNE grower and merchant. New top GRAND CRU CUVÉE. Also in California, Chile, Argentina, South Africa (Cape Mumm).

Muré, Clos St-Landelin ★★→★★★★ One of ALSACE's great names with 16 ha of GRAND CRU Vorbourg. Unusually ripe Pinot N, full-bodied Ries and GEWURZ, and **fine MUSCAT**. Also very good CRÉMANT.

Muscadet Lo w ★→★★★ DYA (but see below) Popular, good-value, often delicious bone-dry wine from near Nantes. Should never be sharp, but should always be refreshing. Perfect with fish and seafood. Best are from zonal ACs: MUSCADET-COTEAUX DE LA LOIRE, MUSCADET CÔTES DE GRAND LIEU, MUSCADET DE SEVRE-ET-MAINE. Choose a SUR LIE.

Muscadet Côtes de Grand Lieu ★→★★★ Most recent (1995) of MUSCADET's zonal ACs and the closest to the Atlantic coast. Best are SUR LIE from, e.g. Bâtard, Luc Choblet (Domaine des Herbauges), Malidain.

Muscadet-Coteaux de la Loire Lo w ★→★★ Small MUSCADET zone east of Nantes (best SUR LIE). Especially Guindon, Luneau-Papin, Les Vignerons de la Noëlle.

Muscadet de Sèvre-et-Maine ★→★★★★ Largest and best of MUSCADET's delimited zones. Top Guy Bossard (DOMAINE DE L'ECU), Bernard Chereau, Bruno Cormerai, Domaine de la Haute Fevrie, Michel Delhomeau, Douillard, Luneau-Papin. Wines from these properties age beautifully; try 86 or 89.

Muscat Distinctively perfumed and usually sweet wine from the grape of the same name, often fortified as VIN DOUX NATUREL. Dry and not fortified in ALSACE.

Muscat de Lunel Midi golden sw ★★ NV Ditto. Small AC based on MUSCAT, usually fortified, luscious, and sweet. Some experimental late-harvest wines. Look for Domaine Clos Bellevue, Grès St Paul.

Muscat de Mireval Midi sw ★★ NV Tiny Muscat-based AC near Montpellier. Domaine La Capelle.

Muscat de Rivesaltes Midi golden sw ★★ NV Sweet MUSCAT AC wine near Perpignan. Quality variable and popularity waning; best from Cazes Frères, Château de Jau.

Musigny Burg r (w) ★★★★ 85' 88' 89' **90' 91 93 95** 96' 97 98 99' 00 01 02' 03 04 05' 06 GRAND CRU in CHAMBOLLE-MUSIGNY (10 ha). Can be the most beautiful, if not the most powerful, of all red Burgundies. Best growers: DROUHIN, JADOT, LEROY, MUGNIER, PRIEUR, ROUMIER, DE VOGÜÉ, VOUGERAIE.

Négociant-éleveur Merchant who "brings up" (i.e. matures) the wine.

Nuits-St-Georges Burg r ★★ ★★★★ 90' **91 93 95** 96' 97 98 99' 00 01 02' **03** 04 05' 06 Important wine town: wines of all qualities, typically sturdy, tannic, need time. Best vineyards: Les Cailles, Clos de la Maréchale, Clos des Corvées, Les Pruliers, Les St-Georges, Vaucrains. Many merchants and growers: L'ARLOT, Ambroise, J Chauvenet, R CHEVILLON, CONFURON, FAIVELEY, GOUGES, GRIVOT, Lechéneaut, LEROY, Liger-Belair, Machard de Gramont, Michelot, *JF Mugnier* RION.

d'Oc (Vin de Pays d'Oc) Midi r p w ★ ★★★ Regional VIN DE PAYS for LANGUEDOC and ROUSSILLON. Especially single-grape wines and VINS DE PAYS PRIMEURS. Tremendous technical advances recently. Main producers: VAL D'ORBIEU, Jeanjean, Domaines Paul Mas, village co-ops, plus numerous small individual growers.

Orléans Lo r p w ★ DYA Recent (2006) AC for whites (chiefly CHARD), gris, rosé, and reds (Pinot N and particularly Meunier) from small area south of Orléans.

Orléans-Clery Lo r ★ DYA Minuscule recent (2006) AC for lean Cab Fr-based reds.

Pacherenc du Vic-Bilh SW Fr w dr sw ★★ ★★★ The white wine of MADIRAN. Dry (DYA) and (better) sweet (age up to 5 years for oaked versions). For growers see MADIRAN.

Paillard, Bruno Top-flight CHAMPAGNE house. Owns Château de Sarrin in Provence.

Palette Prov r p w ★★ Tiny AC near Aix-en-Provence. Full reds, fragrant rosés, and intriguing whites from CHÂTEAU SIMONE, the only notable producer.

Pasquier-Desvignes ★ ★★★ Very old firm of BEAUJOLAIS merchants near BROUILLY.

Patriarche Burg ★ ★★★ One of the bigger Burgundy merchants. Cellars in BEAUNE; also owns CHÂTEAU DE MEURSAULT (61 ha), sparkling KRITER, etc.

Patrimonio Corsica r w p ★★ ★★★★ Wide range from chalk hills in northern CORSICA. Some of island's best. Characterful reds from Nielluccio, whites from Vermentino. Top growers: Gentile, Yves Leccia, Arena, Pastricciola, Clos de Bernardi.

Pauillac B'x r ★★★ ★★★★ 88' **89'** 90' 93 94 95' **96' 98 99** 00 01 02 03' 04' 05' Communal AC in the MÉDOC with three first-growths (LAFITE, LATOUR, MOUTON). Famous for its powerful, long-lived wines. Other fine châteaux include GRAND-PUY-LACOSTE, LYNCH-BAGES, PICHON-LONGUEVILLE, and PICHON-LALANDE.

Pécharmant Dordogne r ★★ ★★★★ 00' 01 02 04 05' (06) Iron in subsoil differentiates this top area from other BERGERACS. Best: Domaine du Haut-Pécharmant, Les Chemins d'Orient, Clos des Côtes, Châteaux d'Elle, Terre Vieille, de Tilleraie, *de Tiregand*. New-World style from Dom des Costes. Also good Bergerac co-op at Le Fleix.

Pernand-Vergelesses Burg r (w) ★★★ 99' 02' 03' **04** 05' 06 Village next to ALOXE-CORTON containing part of the great CORTON-CHARLEMAGNE and CORTON vineyards. One other top vineyard: Ile des Vergelesses. Growers: CHANDON DE BRIAILLES, CHANSON, Delarche, Dubreuil-Fontaine, JADOT, LATOUR, Rapet, Rollin.

Perrier-Jouët Excellent CHAMPAGNE house at Epernay, the first to make dry

CHAMPAGNE, and once the smartest name of all; now best for vintage wines. Luxury brand: Belle Epoque **96 98** 99 00 (Rosé **99** 02) in a painted bottle.

Pessac-Léognan B'x r w ★★★→★★★★ 90' 95 **96 98** 00' 01 02 04 05' AC for the best part of northern GRAVES, including all the GRANDS CRUS, HAUT-BRION, LA MISSION-HAUT-BRION, PAPE-CLÉMENT, etc. Plump inerally reds and Bordeaux's finest dry whites.

Pézenas Midi r p w COTEAUX DU LANGUEDOC sub-region from vineyards around Molière. Prieuré de St-Jean-de-Bébian, Domaine du Conte des Floris, des Aurelles.

Petit Chablis Burg w ★ DYA Wine from fourth-rank CHABLIS vineyards. Not much character but can be pleasantly fresh. Best: co-op La Chablisienne.

Pfaffenheim ★★ Respectable ALSACE co-op. Strongly individual wines, including good Sylvaner and very good Pinots (N, Gr, Bl).

Pfersigberg Eguisheim ALSACE GRAND CRU with two parcels; very aromatic wines. GEWURZ does very well. Ries, especially Paul Ginglinger, Bruno SORG, and Léon BEYER Comtes d'Eguisheim. Top grower: KUENTZ-BAS.

Philipponnat Small CHAMPAGNE house known for well-structured wines and now owned by BOIZEL Chanoine group. Remarkable single-vineyard Clos des Goisses and charming rosé. Also Le Reflet BRUT NV.

Pic St-Loup Midi ★→★★★ r (p) Notable COTEAUX DU LANGUEDOC *cru*, anticipating own AC. Growers: Châteaux de Cazeneuve, Clos Marie, de Lancyre, Lascaux, Mas Bruguière, Domaine de l'Hortus, Valflaunès.

Picpoul de Pinet Midi w ★→★★ COTEAUX DU LANGUEDOC *cru* expecting own AC, exclusively from the old variety Picpoul. Best growers: AC St Martin de la Garrigue, Félines-Jourdan, Co-ops Pomérols and Pinet.

Pineau des Charentes Strong, sweet apéritif: white grape juice and COGNAC.

Pinon, François Lo w sw sp ★★★ Painstaking, eco-friendly producer of very pure VOUVRAY in all its expressions, including a very good PETILLANT.

Pinot Gris ALSACE grape formerly called Tokay d'Alsace: full-bodied white.

Piper-Heidsieck CHAMPAGNE-makers of old repute at Reims. Much improved Brut NV and fruit-driven Brut Rosé Sauvage; Brut **98 99 00** 02. Excellent CUVÉE Sublime DEMI-SEC, rich yet balanced.

Pithon, Jo (Domaine) Lo w r sw ★★→★★★★ Luscious, concentrated COTEAUX DU LAYON and potent ANJOU BL and SAVENNIERES. Red is a recent addition.

Plageoles, Robert Arch-priest of GAILLAC and defender of the lost grape varieties of the Tarn now having handed over to his son Bernard. Amazingly eccentric wines include a rare big dry white from the Verdanel grape, a sherry-like VIN JAUNE, an ultra-sweet dessert wine (★★★★ Vin d'Autan) from Ondenc. Also a pure Mauzac sparkler called "Mauzac Nature".

Pol Roger Supreme family-owned CHAMPAGNE house at Epernay, now with vines in AVIZE joining 85 ha of family vineyards. Very fine floral NV White Foil, Rosé, and CHARD. Sumptuous CUVÉE: Sir Winston Churchill (**96 98**).

Pomerol B'x r ★★★→★★★★ 88 89' 90' 94 95 **96 98'** 00' 01 04 05' Next village to ST-EMILION but no limestone; only clay, gravel, and sand. Famed for its Merlot-dominated full, rich, unctuous style. Top châteaux: LA CONSEILLANTE, L'EGLISE-CLINET, L'EVANGILE, LAFLEUR, LA FLEUR-PETRUS, PÉTRUS, LE PIN, TROTANOY, VIEUX-CH-CERTAN.

Pommard Burg r ★★★ **88'** 89' 90' 95 96' 97 98 99' 01 02' 03 04 05' 06 The biggest CÔTE D'OR village. Few superlative wines, but many potent, tannic ones to age 10+ years. Best vineyards: Epenots, HOSPICES DE BEAUNE CUVÉES, Rugiens. Growers include COMTE ARMAND, Billard-Gonnet, J-M BOILLOT, DOM DE COURCEL, Gaunoux, LEROY, Machard de Gramont, DE MONTILLE, Château de Pommard, Pothier-Rieusset.

Pommery Brut NV; Rosé NV; Brut **99** 00 02 Historic CHAMPAGNE house; brand now owned by VRANKEN. Outstanding CUVÉE Louise (**96 98**) and Rosé (99 02).

Ponsot ★★★★ Controversial MOREY-ST-DENIS estate. Idiosyncratic high-quality GRANDS CRUS, including CHAMBERTIN, CHAPELLE-CHAMBERTIN, CLOS DE LA ROCHE, CLOS ST-DENIS.

Portes de la Mediterranée New regional VIN DE PAYS from south Rhône/PROVENCE. Facile reds and interesting whites, including Viognier.

Potel, Nicolas Burg ★★·★★★ Delicious, well-priced red wines from BOURGOGNE ROUGE to CHAMBERTIN and now a matching range of classy whites. His own DOMAINE in BEAUNE will come on stream from 2007.

Pouilly-Fuissé Burg w ★★·★★★ **99' 00'** 02' 03 04 05' 06' The best white of the MÂCON region, potent and dense. At its best (*e.g.* Château Fuissé VIEILLES VIGNES) outstanding, but usually over-priced compared with CHABLIS. Top growers: Bret Bros, Ferret, Luquet, Merlin, Château des Rontets, Saumaize, Valette, VERGET, Vincent.

Pouilly-Fumé Lo w ★★·★★★★★ **02 03** 04 05 06 Broad, flavourful white from upper Loire, near SANCERRE. Must be Sauv Bl. Best CUVÉES can improve 5–6 years. Top growers include Cailbourdin, Chatelain, Didier DAGUENEAU, Serge Dagueneau & Filles, Château de Favray, Edmond and André Figeat, Masson-Blondelet, Château de Tracy, CAVE de Pouilly-sur-Loire, Redde.

Pouilly-Loché Burg w ★★ 02' **03 04 05'** 06' POUILLY-FUISSÉ's neighbour. Similar, cheaper; scarce. Can be sold as POUILLY-VINZELLES.

Pouilly-Vinzelles Burg w ★★ 02' **03 04 05'** 06' Superior neighbour to POUILLY-LOCHE, best QUARTS vineyard. Best producers Bret Bros, Valette.

Pouilly-sur-Loire Lo w ★ DYA Neutral wine from the same vineyards as POUILLY-FUMÉ but different grapes (Chasselas). Ever-diminishing though can be delightful. Best from Serge Dagueneau & Filles.

Premier Cru (1er Cru) First-growth in BORDEAUX; second rank of vineyards (after GRAND CRU) in Burgundy.

Premières Côtes de Blaye B'x r w ★·★★ 00' **01** 03 04 05' Mainly red AC east of the Gironde. Varied but improved quality. Top reds labelled BLAYE as of 2000. Best châteaux: Bel Air la Royère, Gigault Cuvée Viva, Haut-Bertinerie, Haut-Colombier, Haut-Grelot, Haut-Sociando, Jonqueyres, Mondésir-Gazin, Montfollet, Roland la Garde, Segonzac, des Tourtes.

Premières Côtes de Bordeaux B'x r w (p) dr sw ★·★★★ **98 00' 01** 03 05' Long, narrow, hilly zone running down the right bank of the River Garonne opposite the GRAVES. Medium-bodied, fresh reds. Quality varied. Best châteaux: Carignan, Carsin, Chelivette, Grand-Mouëys, Lamothe de Haux, Lezongars, Mont-Pérat, Plaisance, Puy Bardens, Reynon, Suau.

Prieur, Domaine Jacques Burg ★★★ 16-ha estate all in top Burgundy sites, including GRAND CRUS from MONTRACHET to CHAMBERTIN. Now 50% owned by ANTONIN RODET. Quality could still improve.

Primeur "Early" wine for refreshment and uplift; especially from BEAUJOLAIS; VINS DE PAYS too. Wine sold *en primeur* is still in barrel for delivery when bottled.

Puisseguin St-Emilion B'x r ★★ **98** 00' 01 03 05' Satellite neighbour of ST-EMILION; Wines firm and solid in style. Top châteaux: Bel Air, Branda, Durand-Laplagne, Fongaban, Laurets, Soleil. Also Roc de Puisseguin from co-op.

Puligny-Montrachet Burg w (r) ★★★·★★★★★ **89' 92' 95** 97 99' 00 01 02' 04 05' Smaller neighbour of CHASSAGNE-MONTRACHET: potentially even finer, more vital and complex wine (apparent finesse can be result of over-production). Vineyards: BÂTARD-MONTRACHET, Bienvenues-BÂTARD-MONTRACHET, Caillerets, CHEVALIER-MONTRACHET, Clavoillon, Les Combettes, MONTRACHET, Pucelles. Producers: AMPEAU, J-M BOILLOT, ***BOUCHARD PÈRE & FILS***, L CARILLON, Chavy, DROUHIN, JADOT, LATOUR, DOMAINE LEFLAIVE, O LEFLAIVE, Pernot, SALIZET.

Pyrénées-Atlantiques SW DYA VIN DE PAYS for wines not qualifying for local ACS MADIRAN, PACHERENC DU VIC BILH, or JURANÇON. ★★ CHARD from Ch Cabidos.

Quarts de Chaume Lo w sw ★★★·★★★★★ **89 90 95 96 97** 02 **03** 04 05 (06) Minuscule, celebrated hillside parcels devoted to Chenin Bl. Immensely long-lived, potent, golden wine with strong mineral undertow. Especially BAUMARD,

Branchereau, Yves Guegniard, Jo PITHON, Claude Papin (CHÂTEAU PIERRE-BISE).

Quatourze Midi r w (p) ★ **98 99 00 01 02** 03 04 05 06 Small *cru* of COTEAUX DE LANGUEDOC on edge of Narbonne. Reputation maintained almost single-handedly by Château Notre Dame du Quatourze as virtually sole producer.

Quincy Lo w ★→★★ DYA Small area: variably dry or tender, depending on the grower, SANCERRE-style Sauv Bl. Worth trying. Growers: Domaine Mardon, Silice de Quincy (whose wines can age), Tatin-Wilk.

Ramonet, Domaine Burg ★★→★★★★ Leading (legendary) estate in CHASSAGNE-MONTRACHET with 17 ha, including some MONTRACHET. Very good Clos St-Jean.

Rancio The most characteristic style of VIN DOUX NATUREL, such as BANYULS, MAURY, RIVERSALTES, wood-aged and exposed to oxygen and heat. The same flavour is a fault in table wine.

Rangen Most southerly GRAND CRU of ALSACE at Thann and Vieux Thann. 18.8 ha, often fantastically steep. Top wines: Ries from ZIND-HUMBRECHT and SCHOFFIT.

Rasteau S Rh r br sw (p w dr) ★★ 98' 01' 03 04' **05' 06** One of the best two COTES DU RHONE villages – robust, quite feisty, especially Beaurenard, CAVE des Vignerons, Château du Trignon, Domaines Didier Charavin, Rabasse-Charavin, Girasols, Gourt de Mautens, Soumade, St-Gayan, Perrin (good white, too). Grenache dessert wine shows signs of revival.

Ratafia de Champagne Sweet apéritif made in CHAMPAGNE of 67% grape juice and 33% brandy. Not unlike PINEAU DES CHARENTES.

Regnié Beauj r ★★ 03 05' 06 *Cru* village between MORGON and BROUILLY. About 730 ha. Try DUBOEUF, Aucoeur, or Rampon.

Reine Pédauque, La Burg ★ Long-established grower-merchant at ALOXE-CORTON. Vineyards in ALOXE-CORTON, SAVIGNY, etc., and CÔTES DU RHÔNE. Owned by Pierre ANDRÉ. Quality not impressive.

Reuilly Lo w (r p) ★→★★ **02 03** 04 05 06 Small AC west of SANCERRE for similar whites and rosés and VIN GRIS made from Pinot N and PINOT GR as well as reds from Pinot N. Best from Claude Lafond, Dom de Reuilly.

Ribonnet, Domaine de SW ★★ Christian Gerber makes pioneering range of VINS DE PAYS (red, rosé, white). The only Marsanne and Roussanne in the SW?

Riceys, Rosé des Champ p ★★★ DYA Minute AC in AUBE for a notable Pinot N rosé. Principal producers: A Bonnet, Jacques Defrance.

Richeaume, Domaine Côte de Prov r ★★ Good Cab Sauv/Syrah. Organic; a model.

Richebourg Burg r ★★★★ 78' 85' 88' 89' 90' 91 93' 95 96' 97 98 99' 00 01 02' 03 05' 06 VOSNE-ROMANÉE GRAND CRU. Powerful, perfumed, expensive wine, among Burgundy's best. Growers: DRC, GRIVOT, J Gros, A Gros, T Liger-Belair, LEROY, MÉO-CAMUZET.

Rion, Domaines Burg ★★★ *Patrice Rion for exceptional CHAMBOLLE-MUSIGNY* Cras and Charmes and NUITS-ST-GEORGES Clos des Argillières. Daniel Rion & Fils for VOSNE-ROMANÉE (Les Chaumes, Les Beaumonts), Nuits PREMIER CRU Les Vignes Rondes and ECHÉZEAUX.

Rivesaltes Midi r w br dr sw ★★ NV Fortified wine made near Perpignan. A tradition very much alive, if struggling these days. Top producers worth seeking out: Domaines Cazes, Sarda-Malet, Vaquer, des Schistes, Château de Jau for delicious old RANCIOS. See MUSCAT DE RIVESALTES.

Roche-aux-Moines, La Lo w sw ★★→★★★ **89 90** 95 96 **97** 99 02 **03** 04 05 06 A 24-ha CRU of SAVENNIÈRES, ANJOU. Potentially powerful, intensely mineral wine; age or drink "on the fruit". Growers include: COULEE DE SERRANT, CH PIERRE-BISE.

Rodet, Antonin Burg ★★→★★★ Quality merchant with 134-ha estate, especially in MERCUREY (Château de Chamirey), Domaine de l'Aigle, near Limoux. See PRIEUR.

Roederer, Louis Brut Premier NV; Rich NV; Brut **95 96 97** 99 02; BLANC DE BLANCS **96** 99 02; Brut Rosé 99 02. Top-drawer family-owned CHAMPAGNE house with enviable 143 ha estate of top vineyards. Magnificent Cristal (can be greatest of all prestige CUVÉES) and Cristal Rosé (90' 95 **96 99**). Also owns DEUTZ, DELAS, CHÂTEAU DE PEZ. See also California.

Rolland, Michel Ubiquitous and fashionable consultant winemaker and Merlot specialist working in Bordeaux and worldwide, favouring super-ripe flavours.

Rolly Gassmann ★★ Distinguished ALSACE grower at Rorschwihr, especially for Auxerrois and MUSCAT from *lieu-dit* Moenchreben. House style is usually off-dry. Made "Eiswein" in 2005.

Romanée, La Burg r ★★★★ 96' 97 98 99' 00 01 02' 03 04 05' 06 GRAND CRU in VOSNE-ROMANÉE (0.8 ha). MONOPOLE of Liger-Belai. Now made with flair by Vicomte Louis-Michel L-B.

Romanée-Conti Burg r ★★★★ 57 59 62 64 66' 71 76 78' 80 85' **88' 89' 90'** 93' 95 96' 97 98 99' 00 01 02' 03 04 05' 06 A 1.7-ha MONOPOLE GRAND CRU in VOSNE-ROMANÉE; 450 cases per annum. The most celebrated and expensive red wine in the world, with reserves of flavour beyond imagination.

Romanée-Conti, Domaine de la (DRC) ★★★★ Grandest estate in Burgundy. Includes the whole of ROMANÉE-CONTI and La TÂCHE, major parts of ECHÉZEAUX, GRANDS ECHÉZEAUX, RICHEBOURG, ROMANÉE-ST-VIVANT, and a tiny part of MONTRACHET. Crown-jewel prices (if you can buy them at all). Keep top vintages for decades.

Romanée-St-Vivant Burg r ★★★★ 78 88' 89' 90' 93 95 96' **97 99'** 00 02' 03 04 05' 06 GRAND CRU in VOSNE-ROMANÉE (9.3 ha). Similar to ROMANÉE-CONTI but lighter and less sumptuous. Cathiard, DRC, DROUHIN, HUDELOT-NOËLLAT, LEROY.

Rosacker ALSACE GRAND CRU of 26 ha at Hunwihr. Produces best Ries in Alsace (see CLOS STE HUNE, SIPP-MACK).

Rosé d'Anjou Lo p ★ DYA Pale, slightly sweet rosé enjoying a comeback in the hands of young vignerons; look for Domaine de la Bergerie, Clau de Nell, Domaine des Sablonnettes, Domaine les Grandes Vignes.

Rosé de Loire Lo p ★→★★ DYA The driest of ANJOU's rosés. Best from same producers as Rosé d'Anjou.

Rosette Dordogne w s/sw ★★ DYA Pocket-sized AC for charming apéritif wines, *e.g.* Clos Romain, Château Puypezat-Rosette, Domaine de la Cardinolle, Coutancie.

Rostaing, René ★★★ N Rh CÔTE-RÔTIE estate with top-grade plots, three wines especially Côte Blonde (elegant, 5% Viognier) and La Landonne (darker fruits, 15–20 years). Accomplished style, turns on finesse; some new oak. Also elegant CONDRIEU and Languedoc.

Roty, Joseph ★★★ Small grower of classic GEVREY-CHAMBERTIN, especially CHARMES-CHAMBERTIN and MAZIS-CHAMBERTIN. Long-lived wines.

Rouget, Emmanuel Burg ★★★★ Inheritor of the legendary estate of HENRI JAYER in ECHÉZEAUX, NUITS-ST-GEORGES, and VOSNE-ROMANÉE. Top wine: VOSNE-ROMANÉE-Cros Parantoux.

Roulot, Domaine G Burg ★★★ Range of seven distinctive MEURSAULTS including Charmes and Perrières. Look out for Tessons Clos de Mon Plaisir.

Roumier, Georges Burg ★★★★ Christophe R makes exceptional long-lived wines in BONNES-MARES, *CHAMBOLLE-MUSIGNY-Amoureuses, MUSIGNY*, etc. High standards.

Rousseau, Domaine A Burg ★★★★ Grower famous for CHAMBERTIN, etc., of highest quality. Wines are intense (not deep-coloured), long-lived, mostly GRAND CRU. Brilliant CLOS ST JACQUES.

Roussette de Savoie w ★★ DYA Tastiest fresh white from south of Lake Geneva.

Roussillon Midi Top region for VINS DOUX NATURELS (*e.g.* MAURY, RIVESALTES, BANYULS). Lighter MUSCATS and younger vintage wines are taking over from darker, heavier wines. See CÔTES DU ROUSSILLON (and Villages), COLLIOURE, for table wines and VIN-DE-PAYS Côtes Catalanes.

Ruchottes-Chambertin Burg r ★★★★ 88' 89' 90' 91 93' 95 96' 97 98 99' **00** 01 02' 03 04 05' 06 GRAND CRU neighbour of CHAMBERTIN. Similar splendid, lasting wine of great finesse. Top growers: LEROY, MUGNERET, ROUMIER, ROUSSEAU.

Ruinart "R" de Ruinart Brut NV; Ruinart Rosé NV; "R" de Ruinart Brut (98 **99**). Oldest CHAMPAGNE house, owned by MOËT-Hennessy. Elegant wines, especially luxury brands: Domaine Ruinart (90' **95** 96' **98** 99), Domaine Ruinart Rosé (90 95 **96** 99). *Minerally BLANC DE BLANCS NV*.

Rully Burg r w (sp) ★★ (r) 02' 03 **05'** 06 (w) **04** 05' 06 CÔTE CHALONNAISE village. Still white and red are light but tasty. Good value, especially white. Growers include *DELORME*, FAIVELEY, Domaine de la Folie, Jacqueson, A RODET.

Sables du Golfe du Lion Midi p r w ★ DYA VIN DE PAYS from Mediterranean sand-dunes: especially Gris de Gris from Carignan, Grenache, Cinsault. Listel almost sole producer.

Sablet S Rh r w (p) ★★ 01 03 **04'** **05'** 06 Attractive, improving CÔTES DU RHÔNE village, often cleanly fruited reds, especially Domaine de Boissan, Cabasse, Espiers, Les Goubert, Piaugier, Domaine de Verquière. Good full whites – aperitif or food.

St-Amour Beauj r ★★ 03 **05'** 06 Northernmost *cru* of BEAUJOLAIS: light, fruity, irresistible (especially on 14 Feb). Growers to try: Janin, Patissier, Revillon.

St-Aubin Burg w r ★★★ (w) 02' 03' 04 05' 06 (r) 99' 02' 03 05' 06 Understated neighbour of CHASSAGNE-MONTRACHET. Several PREMIERS CRUS: light, firm, quite stylish wines; fair prices. Top growers: JADOT, H&O Lamy, Lamy-Pillot, H Prudhon, RAMONET, Thomas.

St-Bris Burg w ★ DYA Recent AC, cousin of SANCERRE, from near CHABLIS. To try. Domaine St-Prix from Domaine Bersan is good. Goisot best.

St-Chinian Midi r ★→★★ 98 99 00 01 02 03 04 05 06 Hilly area of growing reputation in COTEAUX DU LANGUEDOC. AC since 1982 for red, and for white since 2005, plus new *crus* Berlou and Roquebrun. Tasty southern reds, especially co-ops Berlou, Roquebrun; Château de Viranel, Domaine Canet Valette, Madura, Rimbaud, Navarre.

St-Emilion B'x r ★★ →★★★★ 89' 90' **94 95** 96 98' 00' 01 03 04 05' Large, Merlot-dominated district on Bordeaux's Right Bank. ST-EMILION GRAND CRU AC the top designation. Warm, full, rounded style; some long-lived. Top châteaux: ANGELUS, AUSONE, CANON, CHEVAL BLANC, FIGEAC, MAGDELAINE, PAVIE. Also *garagistes* LA MONDOTTE and VALANDRAUD. Good co-op.

St-Estèphe B'x r ★★ →★★★★ 88' **89'** 90' 93 94 95' **96' 98** 99 00' 01 02 **03** 04 05' Most northerly communal AC in the MÉDOC. Solid, structured wines. Top châteaux: COS D'ESTOURNEL, MONTROSE, CALON-SEGUR. A plethora of CRUS BOURGEOIS.

St-Gall Brand name used by Union-Champagne: top CHAMPAGNE growers' co-op at AVIZE. Cuvée Orpale exceptional wine at fair price.

St-Georges-St-Emilion B'x r ★★ **98** 00' 01 03 05' Tiny ST-EMILION satellite. Usually good quality. Best châteaux: Calon, Macquin-St-G, Tour du Pas-St-Georges, Vieux Montaiguillon.

St-Gervais S Rh r (w, p) ★ 03 04 05' 06 West bank Rhône village. Sound co-op, star is excellent, long-lived Domaine Ste-Anne red (marked Mourvèdre flavours); white includes Viognier. Also Domaine Clavel.

St-Jean de Minervois Min w sw ★★ Fine sweet MUSCAT. Much recent progress, especially Domaine de Barroubio, Michel Sigé, village co-op.

St-Joseph N Rh r w ★★ 90' 95 97 98 99' 00' 01' 02 **03' 05'** 06 AC running length of north Rhône (65 km/40 miles). Delicious, fruit-packed wines around Tournon in south; elsewhere quality variable. More structure than CROZES-HERMITAGE, especially from CHAPOUTIER (Les Granits), B Gripa, GUIGAL (Lieu-dit St-Joseph); also CHAVE, Chêne, Chèze, Courbis, Coursodon, Cuilleron, DELAS, B Faurie, P Faury, Gaillard, Gonon, JABOULET, Marsanne, Monier, Paret, A Perret, F Villard. Good aromatic white (mainly Marsanne, drink with food), especially Chapoutier Granits, Cuilleron, Gonon, B Grippa, Faury, A Perret.

St-Julien B'x r ★★★→★★★★ 88' 89' 90' 93 94 95' 96' 98 99 00' 01 02 03 04 05'
Mid-MÉDOC communal AC with 11 classified (1855) estates, including three
LÉOVILLES, BEYCHEVELLE, DUCRU-BEAUCAILLOU, GRUAUD-LAROSE, etc. The epitome of
harmonious, fragrant, and savoury red wine.

St-Nicolas-de-Bourgueil Lo r p ★→★★★ 89 90 95 96 97 02 03 04 05 06 Next to
(and part of) BOURGUEIL: similar range of Cab Fr – from supple and fruity, to
chunky and tannic; the best verge on elegance. Try: Yannick Amirault,
Cognard, *__Mabileau__*, Taluau-Foltzenlogel.

St-Péray N Rh w sp ★★01' 03' 04' 05' 06 White Rhône (mainly Marsanne) from
old granite hills. Some sparkling – *__a curiosity worth trying__*. Still white good
flinty style, can age. Top names: S Chaboud, CHAPOUTIER, CLAPE, Colombo,
B Gripa, J-L Thiers, TAIN co-op, du Tunnel, Voge. JABOULET planting here.

St-Pourçain-sur-Sioule Central Fr r p w ★→★★ DYA Agreeable quaffers from the
Allier. Light red and rosé from Gamay and/or Pinot N, white from Tressalier
and/or CHARD (increasingly popular), or Sauv Bl. Growers include: Ray,
Domaine de Bellevue, Pétillat, Barbara and good co-op with range of styles,
including the drink-me-up CUVÉE Ficelle.

St-Romain Burg w r ★★ (w) 02' 03 04 05' 06 Overlooked village just behind CÔTE
DE BEAUNE. Value, especially for firm fresh whites. Reds have a clean cut. Top
growers: De Chassorney, FÈVRE, Jean Germain, Gras, LEROY.

St-Sardos SW VDQS near Montauban r p w DYA Based on progressive co-op. Also
Domaine de la Tucayne.

St-Véran Burg w ★★ 02' 03 04 05' 06 Next door AC to POUILLY-FUISSÉ. Best nearly
as good; others on unsuitable soil. Try DUBOEUF, Domaines Cordier, Corsin, des
Deux Roches, des Valanges, CHÂTEAU FUISSÉ.

Ste-Croix-du-Mont B'x w sw ★★ 97' 98 99' 01' 02 03' 05' Sweet white AC facing
SAUTERNES across the River Garonne. Well worth trying, especially Châteaux
Crabitan-Bellevue, Loubens, du Mont, Pavillon, la Rame.

Ste-Victoire Prov r p New sub-zone of COTES DE PROVENCE from the southern slopes
of the Montagne Ste-Victoire.

Salon 85 88' 90 95 96 The original BLANC DE BLANCS CHAMPAGNE, from Le Mesnil in
the Côte des Blancs. Awesome reputation for long lived wines – less
consistent recently. Tiny quantities.

Sancerre Lo w (r p) ★→★★★★ The world's benchmark for Sauv Bl, almost
indistinguishable from POUILLY-FUMÉ, its neighbour across the Loire, though often
nervier. Top wines can age 5 years+. Also improving, light Pinot N (best drunk
at 2–5 years) and rosé (do not over-chill). Occasional sweet, curious VENDANGES
TARDIVES. Top growers include: BOURGEOIS, Cotat, Lucien Crochet, André Dezat,
Jolivet, ALPHONSE MELLOT, Vincent Pinard, Roger, Vacheron.

Santenay Burg r (w) ★★★ 99' 02' 03 04 05' 06 Sturdy reds from village south of
CHASSAGNE-MONTRACHET. Best vineyards: La Comme, Les Gravières, Clos de
Tavannes. Top growers: GIRARDIN, Lequin-Roussot, Muzard.

Saumur Lo r w p sp ★→★★★ 02 03 04 05 06 Zone and umbrella AC for mineral
whites plus a few more serious, particularly from SAUMUR-CHAMPIGNY zone; easy-
drinking reds, pleasant rosés, pungent CRÉMANT and Saumur MOUSSEUX.
Producers include: BOUVET-LADUBAY, Cave des Vignerons de Saumur, Domaine St
Just, Château Yvonne, CHÂTEAU DE VILLENEUVE, Château de Targé, DOMAINE DES
CHAMPS FLEURIS/Retiveau-Retif, Château Tour Grise.

Saumur-Champigny Lo r ★★→★★★ 89 95 96 97 02 03 04 05 06 Popular nine-
commune AC for fresh Cab Fr ageing nicely in good vintages. Look for CHÂTEAUX
DE VILLENEUVE, Yvonne; Domaines CHAMPS FLEURIS, Legrand, Nerleux, Roches
Neuves, St Just, Val Brun; CLOS ROUGEARD. *__Château de Targé__*, Cave des Vignerons
de Saumur-St-Cyr-en-Bourg.

Saussignac Dordogne w sw ★★→★★★ 98' 00' 01' 03 04 05' Similar to but with a touch more acidity than MONBAZILLAC. Fully sweet since 2004. No co-op. Best from Domaine de Richard, Châteaux Le Chabrier, Court-les-Muts, La Maurigne, Les Miaudoux, Le Payral, Le Tap, Tourmentine, and Clos d'Yvigne.

Sauternes B'x w sw ★★ →★★★★ 83' 86' 88' 89' 90' 95 96 97' 98 99' 01' 02 03' 05' District of five villages (including BARSAC) that make France's best sweet wine, strong (14%+ alcohol), luscious and golden, demanding to be aged 10 years. Top châteaux are d'YQUEM, GUIRAUD, LAFAURIE-PEYRAGUEY, RIEUSSEC, SUDUIRAUT, LA TOUR BLANCHE, etc. Dry wines cannot be sold as Sauternes.

Sauzet, Etienne Burg ★★★ Top-quality white burgundy estate and merchant at PULIGNY-MONTRACHET. Clearly defined, well-bred wines, better drunk young.

Savennières Lo w dr sw ★★★ →★★★★ 89 90 93 95 96 97 99 02 03 04 05 06 Small ANJOU district for pungent, extremely mineral, long-lived whites. Château de Coulaine (see PIERRE-BISE), Closel, Château d'Epiré, Eric Morgat, Domaine Laureau du Clos Frémur, Tijou, Vincent Ogereau, CHÂTEAU PIERRE-BISE. Top sites: COULÉE DE SERRANT, ROCHE-AUX-MOINES, Clos du Papillon.

Savigny-lès-Beaune Burg r (w) ★★★ 90' 95 96' 98 99' 01 02' 03 04 05' Important village next to BEAUNE; similar mid-weight wines, often deliciously lively, fruity. Top vineyards: Dominode, Guettes, Lavières,

---

Burgundy négociants

The trend towards domaine bottling has caused the old-established merchant houses to raise their game, while those who cannot buy vineyards have to buy in grapes instead. Leading players in various categories include: **Classic Houses:** BOUCHARD PERE, DROUHIN, JADOT, LATOUR. Also CHAMPY, CHANSON. **Commercial success stories:** BICHOT, BOISSET, GIRARDIN, Picard. **White specialists:** Bret Bros, Deux Montille, O LEFLAIVE, Ricjkaert, VERGET. **Outsiders (talent from elsewhere):** Dominique Laurent, Lucien Lemoine, Alex Gambal. **Domaines with négociant activities:** Ambroise, J-M BOILLOT, H BOILLOT, DUJAC, MEO-CAMUZET, Merlin.

Marconnets, Vergelesses; growers: BIZE, Camus, CHANDON DE BRIAILLES, CLAIR, Ecard, Girard, LEROY, Pavelot, TOLLOT-BEAUT.

Savoie E France r w sp ★★ DYA Alpine area with light, dry wines like some Swiss or minor Loires. APREMONT, CRÉPY, and SEYSSEL are best-known whites; ROUSSETTE is more interesting. Also good MONDEUSE red.

Schlossberg ALSACE GRAND CRU of 80 ha at Kientzheim famed since the 15th century. Glorious Ries from FALLER/DOM WEINBACH and Paul BLANCK. Also very good GEWURZ and PINOT GR.

Schlumberger, Domaines ★→★★★ Vast and top-quality ALSACE DOMAINE at Guebwiller owning approx 1% of all ALSACE vineyards. Holdings in GRANDS CRUS Kitterlé, Kessler, Saering, and Spiegel. Range includes rare Ries, signature CUVÉE Ernest, and, latest addition, PINOT GR Grand Cru Kessler.

Schlumberger, Robert de Lo SAUMUR sparkling; by Austrian method. Fruity, delicate.

Schoenenbourg Very rich successful Riquewihr GRAND CRU (ALSACE): PINOT GR, Ries, very fine VENDANGE TARDIVE and SÉLECTION DES GRAINS NOBLES. Especially from MARCEL DEISS and DOPFF AU MOULIN. Also very good MUSCAT.

Schoffit, Domaine ★★→★★★★ Colmar ALSACE house with GRAND CRU RANGEN PINOT GR, GEWURZ of top quality. Chasselas is unusual everyday delight.

Schröder & Schÿler Old BORDEAUX merchant, owner of CHÂTEAU KIRWAN.

Sciacarello Original Corsican grape variety, for red and rosé.

Sec Literally means dry, though CHAMPAGNE so called is medium-sweet (and better at breakfast, teatime, and weddings than BRUT).

Séguret S Rh r w ★★ 01' 03 04 05' 06 Good south Rhône picture-postcard village near GIGONDAS. Peppery, quite full reds; rounded whites. Especially

Château La Courançonne, Domaine de Cabasse, J David, Le Camassot, Garancière, Mourchon, Pourra, Soleil Romain.

Sélection des Grains Nobles Term coined by HUGEL for ALSACE equivalent to German Beerenauslese, and since 1984 subject to very strict regulations (see box, p.124). *Grains nobles* are individual grapes with "noble rot".

Sérafin Burg r ★★★ Christian S has gained a cult following for his intense GEVREY CHAMBERTIN VIEILLES VIGNES and CHARMES-CHAMBERTIN GRAND CRU.

Seyssel Savoie w sp ★★ NV Delicate white, pleasant sparkling. *e.g.* Corbonod.

Sichel & Co One of BORDEAUX's most respected merchant houses, run by five brothers: interests in CHÂTEAUX D'ANGLUDET and PALMER, in CORBIÈRES, and as Bordeaux merchants (Sirius a top brand).

Sipp, Jean & Louis ★★ ALSACE growers in Ribeauvillé (Louis is also a négociant). Both make very good Ries GRAND CRU Kirchberg. Jean's is youthful elegance; Louis's is firmer when mature. Very good GEWURZ from Louis, especially GRAND CRU Osterberg.

Sipp-Mack ★★→★★★ Excellent ALSACE DOMAINE of 20 ha at Hunnawihr (employing integrated pest management in vineyard). Great Ries from GRANDS CRUS ROSACKER and Osterberg; also very good PINOT GR.

Sorg, Bruno ★★→★★★ First-class small ALSACE grower at Eguisheim for GRAND CRUS Florimont (Ries) and PFERSIGBERG (MUSCAT). Also very good Auxerrois.

Sur Lie "On the lees". MUSCADET is often bottled straight from the vat, for maximum zest and character.

Tâche, La Burg r ★★★★ 64 66 71 78' 85' 88' 89' 90' 93' 95 96'97 98 99' 00 01 02' 03 04 05' 06 A 6-ha (1,500-case) GRAND CRU of VOSNE-ROMANÉE and one of best vineyards on earth: big perfumed, luxurious wine. See ROMANÉE-CONTI.

Taille-aux-Loups, Domaine de la Lo w sw sp ★★★ Jacky Blot, formerly a *courtier en vins*, has become a major player in Touraine winemaking – with CUVÉES of barrel-fermented Montlouis and VOUVRAY, from dry to lusciously sweet, Triple Zero Montlouis Petillant and promising reds from Domaine de la Butte in Bourgueil.

Tain, Cave Coopérative de 290 members in north Rhône ACS; owns one-quarter of HERMITAGE. Red Hermitage improved since 91 especially top Gambert de Loche; modern-style CROZES. Sound mainly Marsanne whites. Good value.

Taittinger Brut NV; Rosé NV; Brut **96** 99; Collection Brut **90 95** 96. Once fashionable Reims CHAMPAGNE grower and merchant sold to Crédit Agricole group 06. Distinctive silky, flowery touch, though not always consistent. Excellent luxury brand: Comtes de Champagne BLANC DE BLANCS (**96' 98**), Comtes de Champagne Rosé (**96 99 02**), also good rich Pinot Prestige Rosé NV. New CUVÉES Nocturne and Prélude. (See also California: Domaine Carneros.)

Tavel Rh p ★★ DYA France's most famous, though not best, rosé: strong, very full, and dry – needs food. Best growers: Château d'Aquéria, Domaine Corne-Loup, GUIGAL, Maby, Domaine de la Mordorée, Prieuré de Montézargues, Lafond, Lafond Roc-Epine, Château de Trinquevedel.

Tempier, Domaine r w p ★★★★ The pioneering grower of BANDOL. Quality now challenged by others.

Terrasses du Larzac Midi r w p Part of AC COTEAUX DU LANGUEDOC. Wild, hilly region including Montpeyroux, St Saturnin, and villages near the Lac du Salaou.

Terroirs Landais Gascony r p w ★ VIN DE PAYS, an extension in the *département* of Landes of the CÔTES DE GASCOGNE, a name that many growers prefer to use. Domaine de Laballe is most-seen example.

Thénard, Domaine Burg The major grower of the GIVRY appellation, but best known for his substantial portion (1.6 ha) of LE MONTRACHET. Should be better.

Thevenet, Jean Burg ★★★ Domaine de la Bongran at Clessé stands out for rich, concentrated (even sweet!) white MÂCON. Expensive.

Thézac-Perricard SW Fr r p ★★ 04 05' 06 VIN DE PAYS Extension of but lighter than CAHORS. Independent Domaine de Lancement even better than good co-ops.

Thiénot, Alain Broker-turned-merchant; dynamic force for good in CHAMPAGNE. Ever-improving quality across the range. Impressive, fairly priced Brut NV. Rosé NV Brut 96 99 00 02. Vintage Stanislas BLANC DE BLANCS (99 00 02) and Vigne aux Gamins BLANC DE BLANCS (99 00 02). Top Grande CUVÉE 95 96 98. Also owns Marie Stuart and CANARD-DUCHÊNE in CHAMPAGNE, Château Ricaud in LOUPIAC.

Thorin, J Beauj ★ Grower and major merchant of BEAUJOLAIS.

Thouarsais, Vin de Lo w r p ★ DYA Light Chenin Bl (with 20% CHARD permitted), Gamay, and Cab Sauv from tiny VDQS south of SAUMUR. Especially Gigon.

Tollot-Beaut ★★★ Stylish, consistent Burgundy grower with 20 ha in CÔTE DE BEAUNE, including vineyards at Beaune Grèves, CORTON, SAVIGNY (Les Champs Chevrey), and at its CHOREY-LES-BEAUNE base.

Touraine Lo r p w dr sw sp ★→★★★★ 02 03 04 05 06 Huge region with many ACS (*e.g.* VOUVRAY, CHINON, BOURGUEIL) as well as umbrella AC for zesty reds (Cab Fr, Gamay, Cot), pungent whites (Sauv Bl, Chenin Bl), rosés, and MOUSSEUX. Many good bistro wines, often good value. Producers: Francois Plouzeau/ Domaine de la Garreliere, Clos Roche Blanche; Château de Petit Thouars, MARIONNET, Oisly-Thesée, Jacky Marteau, Puzelat/Clos de Tue-Boeuf, Domaine des Corbillieres, Domaine de la Presle.

Touraine-Amboise Lo r w p ★→★★ Touraine sub-appellation. François Ier is tasty, food-friendly local blend (Gamay/Côt/Cab Fr). Dutertre, Xavier Frissant, Damien Delecheneau/la Grange Tiphaine.

Touraine-Azay-le-Rideau Lo ★→★★ Small Touraine sub-appellation for Chenin Bl-based dry, off-dry white and Grolleau-dominated rosé. Producers: James Paget and Pibaleau Père & Fils.

Touraine-Mesland Lo r w p ★→★★ Touraine sub-appellation best represented by its user-friendly red blends (Gamay/Côt/Cab Fr). Château Gaillard, Clos de la Briderie.

Touraine-Noble Joué Loire p ★→★★ DYA Ancient but recently revived rosé from three Pinots (N, Gr, Meunier) just south of Tours. Especially from ROUSSEAU and Sard. Granted AOC status (Touraine-Noble Joué) in 2000.

Trapet Burg ★★→★★★ A long-established GEVREY CHAMBERTIN domaine now enjoying new life and sensual wines with biodynamic farming. Ditto cousins Rossignol-Trapet – slightly more austere wines.

Trévallon, Domaine de Provence r w ★★★ 88' 89' 90' 91 92 93 94 95' 96 97 98 99 00 01' 03' 04 05 A less-than-humble VIN DE PAYS near Les Baux, fully deserving its huge reputation. Intense Cab Sauv/Syrah to age. Tiny amount of white from Marsanne and Roussanne and a drop of CHARD.

Trimbach, F E ★★★→★★★★ Growers of the greatest Ries in ALSACE (CLOS STE-HUNE) and probably the second-greatest (Cuvée Frédéric-Emile). House style is dry but elegant with great ageing potential. Also very good PINOT GR and GEWURZ. Based in Ribeauvillé; founded 1626.

Turckheim, Cave Vinicole de ★ Important ALSACE co-op with large range of not-always-exciting wines. Vineyard area: 320 ha, including numerous GRANDS CRUS.

Tursan SW France r p w ★★→★★★ (Most DYA) VDQS aspiring to AC. Easy-drinking holiday-style wines. Master-chef Michel Guérard keeps much of his own ★★ wine (now red as well as white) for his famous restaurants at Eugénie-les-Bains, but more traditional ★★ Dom de Perchade is just as good in its own way. Successful co-op the only other producer.

Vacqueyras S Rh r (w, p) ★★ Full, peppery, Grenache-based neighbour to GIGONDAS: finer bodied, should be cheaper. Lives 10+ years. Try JABOULET, Amouriers, Arnoux Vieux Clocher, Châteaux de Montmirail, des Tours; Clos des Cazaux, Domaines Archimbaud-Vache, Charbonnière, Couroulu, Font de

Papier, Fourmone, Garrigue, Grapillon d'Or, Monardière, Montirius, Montvac, Pascal Frères, Perrin, Sang des Cailloux.

Val d'Orbieu, Vignerons du Association of some 200 top growers and co-ops in CORBIÈRES, COTEAUX DU LANGUEDOC, MINERVOIS, ROUSSILLON, etc., marketing a sound range of selected MIDI AC and VIN DE PAYS wines. Cuvée Mythique is flagship.

Valençay Lo r p w ★ Recent AC (VDQS until 2004) in east TOURAINE; light, easy-drinking sometimes sharp wines from similar range of grapes as TOURAINE, especially Sauv Bl. Now AC. Look for the 2005s.

Valréas S Rh r (p w) ★★ 98' 01 03 04 05' 06 CÔTES DU RHÔNE village with big co-op. Good mid-weight red (softer, less body than CAIRANNE, RASTEAU) and improving white. Especially Emmanuel Bouchard, Domaine des Grands Devers, Château la Décelle.

Varichon & Clerc Principal makers and shippers of SAVOIE sparkling wines.

Vaudésir Burg w ★★★★ 90 95' 96' 97 98 99 00' 02' 03 04 05' 06' Arguably the best of seven CHABLIS GRANDS CRUS (but then so are the others).

Vendange Harvest. **Vendange Tardive** Late harvest. ALSACE equivalent to German Auslese (see Quality box, p.124), but usually higher alcohol.

Verget Burg ★★–★★★ The négociant business of J-M GUFFENS-HEYNEN with mixed range from MÂCON to MONTRACHET. Intense wines, often models, bought-in grapes. New Lubéron venture: Verget du Sud. Follow closely.

Veuve Clicquot Historic CHAMPAGNE house of highest standing. Full-bodied, almost rich: one of CHAMPAGNE's surest things. Cellars at Reims. Luxury brands: La Grande Dame (90' 96 98), Rich Réserve (96 99 02), La Grande Dame Rosé (96 98' 99 02).

Veuve Devaux Premium CHAMPAGNE of powerful Union Auboise co-op. Excellent aged Grande Réserve NV, Oeil de Perdrix Rosé, Prestige Cuvée D.

Vidal-Fleury, J N Rh ★–★★★ Long-established GUIGAL-owned shipper of top Rhône wines and grower of CÔTE-RÔTIE, accomplished, elegant La Chatillonne (12% Viognier). Steady quality. Good MUSCAT BEAUMES-DE-VENISE.

Vieille Ferme, La S Rh r w ★★ V. gd brand of CÔTES DU VENTOUX (r) and CÔTES DU LUBERON (w) made by the Perrins, owners of CHÂTEAU DE BEAUCASTEL. Gd value.

Vieux Télégraphe, Domaine du S Rh r w ★★★ 78' 81' 83 85 88 89' 90 94' 95' 96' 97 98' 99' 00 01' 03' 04' 05' 06 A top name, maker of **_vigorous, well-fruited modern red CHÂTEAUNEUF_**, and tasty white (more gourmand since 90s), which age well in lesser years. New good-value second wine: Vieux Mas des Papes. Second DOMAINE: de la Roquète, fruited reds, fresh whites. Owns good GIGONDAS Domaine Les Pallières with US importer Kermit Lynch.

Vin de Paille Wine from grapes dried on straw mats, so very sweet, like Italian _passito_. Esp in the JURA. See also CHAVE and VIN PAILLE DE CORREZE.

Vin de Pays (VDP) Most dynamic category in France (with over 140 regions). The zonal VDPs are best – _e.g._ Côtes de Gascogne, Côtes de Thongue, Haute Vallée de l'Orb, Duché d'Uzès, among others. Enormous variety and sometimes unexpected quality.

Vin de Table Category of standard everyday table wine, not subject to particular regulations about grapes and origin. Can be the source of occasional delights if a talented winemaker uses this category to avoid bureaucratic hassle.

Vin Doux Naturel (VDN) Sweet wine fortified with wine alcohol, so the sweetness is natural, not the strength. The speciality of ROUSSILLON, based on Grenache or MUSCAT. A staple in French bars, but the top wines can be remarkable.

Vin Gris "Grey" wine is very pale pink, made of red grapes pressed before fermentation begins – unlike rosé, which ferments briefly before pressing. Oeil de Perdrix means much the same; so does "blush".

Vin Jaune Jura w ★★★ Speciality of ARBOIS: odd yellow wine like fino sherry.

Normally ready when bottled (after at least 6 years). Best is CHÂTEAU-CHALON. See also PLAGEOLES.

Vin Paillé de Corrèze SW Fr Revival of old-style VIN DE PAILLE near Beaulieur-sur-Dordogne made today from Cab Fr, Cab Sauv, CHARD, Sauv Bl. 25 fanatical growers and small co-op.

Vinsobres S Rh r (p w) ★→★★ Village given full AC status 04 vintage on. Best are openly fruited, quite substantial reds, plenty of Syrah. Look for: Cave La Vinsobraise, Domaines les Aussellons, Bicarelle, Chaume-Arnaud, Coriançon, Deurre, Jaume, Puy de Maupas, Moulin, Peysson, Château Rouanne.

Viré-Clessé Burg w ★★ AC based around two of the best white villages of MÂCON. Extrovert style though residual sugar forbidden. Look for A Bonhomme, Bret Bros, Clos du Chapitre, JADOT, Château de Viré, Merlin, and co-op.

Visan S Rh r p w ★ **03 04 05' 06** Rhône village for fair medium-weight reds, fair whites. Note: Domaine des Grands Devers, Roche-Audran.

Vogüé, Comte Georges de ★★★★ First-class 12-ha BONNES-MARES and MUSIGNY DOMAINE at CHAMBOLLE-MUSIGNY. At best, especially since 90, the ultimate examples. Avoid most of the 80s.

Volnay Burg r ★★★ →★★★★ **88' 89' 90' 91 93 95** 96' **97 98** 99' 02' **03** 04 05' 06 Village between POMMARD and MEURSAULT: often the best reds of the CÔTE DE BEAUNE; structured and silky. Best vineyards: Caillerets, Champans, Clos des Chênes, Santenots, Taillepieds, etc. Best growers: D'ANGERVILLE, J-M BOILLOT, HOSPICES DE BEAUNE, **_LAFARGE_**, LAFON, DE MONTILLE.

Volnay-Santenots Burg r ★★★ Excellent red wine from MEURSAULT is sold under this name. Indistinguishable from other PREMIER CRU VOLNAY. Best growers: AMPEAU, HOSPICES DE BEAUNE, LAFON, LEROY.

Vosne-Romanée Burg r ★★★→★★★★ **88' 89' 90' 91 93 95** 96' **97 98** 99' **00** 01 02' **03** 04 05' 06 Village with Burgundy's grandest *crus* (ROMANÉE-CONTI, LA TÂCHE, etc.). There are (or should be) no common wines in Vosne. Many good growers including: Arnoux, Cathiard , DRC, ENGEL, GRIVOT, GROS, JAYER, LATOUR, LEROY, Liger-Belair, MÉO-CAMUZET, Mongeard-Mugneret, Mugneret, RION.

Vougeot Burg r w ★★★ 90' **91 93 95** 96' **97 98** 99' **00** 01 02' **03** 04 05' 06 Village and PREMIER CRU wines. See CLOS DE VOUGEOT. Exceptional Clos Blanc de Vougeot, white since 12th C. Bertagna and VOUGERAIE best.

Vougeraie, Domaine de la Burg r ★★→★★★ DOMAINE uniting all BOISSET'S vineyard holdings. Good-value BOURGOGNE rouge up to fine MUSIGNY GRAND CRU.

Vouvray Lo w dr sw sp ★★→★★★★ For sweet Vouvray: **89 90 95 96 97 03** 05. For dry Vouvray: **89 90 96 97** 02 **03** 04 05 06. Important AC east of Tours: increasingly good and reliable. DEMI-SEC is classic style, but in good years MOELLEUX can be intensely sweet, almost immortal. Good, dry sparkling: look out for PÉTILLANT. Best producers: Allias, Clos Baudoin, **_Champalou_**, CHIDAINE, (Domaine de la Fontanerie/)Dhoye-Deruet, Foreau, Fouquet (Aubuisière), Château Gaudrelle, Domaine de la Haute Borne, HUET, DOMAINE DE LA TAILLE-AUX-LOUPS, Vigneau-Chevreau, Vincent Careme.

Vranken, Champagne Ever more powerful CHAMPAGNE group created in 1976 by Belgian marketing man. Sound quality. Leading brand: Demoiselle. Owns HEIDSIECK MONOPOLE, POMMERY, and Bricout.

Wolfberger ★★ Principal label of Eguisheim co-op. Exceptional quality for such a large-scale producer. Very important for CRÉMANT.

"Y" (pronounced "ygrec") B'x **79' 80' 85 86 88 94 96** 00 02 04 Intense dry wine produced occasionally at CHÂTEAU D'YQUEM. Most interesting with age. Now changing style and modernizing.

Zind-Humbrecht, Domaine ★★★★ ALSACE DOMAINE founded in 1620. Famed for rich, powerful wines using very low yields. Top wines from single vineyards Clos St. Urbain, Hauserer & Windsbuhl, and GRANDS CRUS RANGEN, HENGST, BRAND & GOLDBERT.

Châteaux of Bordeaux

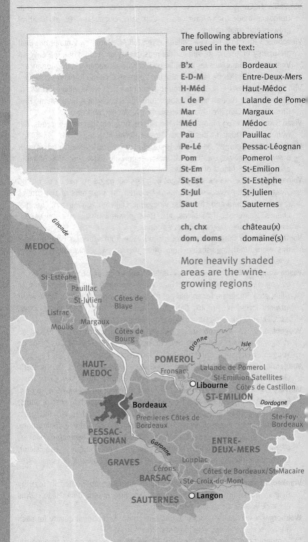

The following abbreviations
are used in the text:

B'x	Bordeaux
E-D-M	Entre-Deux-Mers
H-Méd	Haut-Médoc
L de P	Lalande de Pome
Mar	Margaux
Méd	Médoc
Pau	Pauillac
Pe-Lé	Pessac-Léognan
Pom	Pomerol
St-Em	St-Emilion
St-Est	St-Estèphe
St-Jul	St-Julien
Saut	Sauternes
ch, chx	château(x)
dom, doms	domaine(s)

More heavily shaded
areas are the wine-
growing regions

Hooray! Bordeaux has had a famous and fabulous vintage. I mean the 2005, of course: a vintage hugely in demand across the world, in spite of some spectacular price rises for the top châteaux. It's good news for those who bought it, but it's good news also for the rest of us, because it means that the 2001s and 2004s, the best years between 2005 and the last famous vintage, 2000, now fall into the "overlooked" category. This means that prices might stay reasonable.

Both vintages are highly desirable, if you want wine for drinking rather than investing. And of course there'll be plenty of lesser wines from 2005: not everything from that year will be expensive.

d'Agassac H-Méd r ★★ 98 99 00' 02 03 04 05 "Sleeping Beauty" 14th-C moated fort. 42 ha very near BORDEAUX suburbs. Improved quality since 1997.

Andron-Blanquet St-Est r ★★ 95 96 98 00' 03 04 05' 16-ha CRU BOURGEOIS; sister CHÂTEAU to COS-LABORY. Toughish wines show more charm lately.

Angélus St-Em r ★★★★ 89' 90' 92' 93 94 95 96 97 98' 99 00' 01 02 03' 04 05 Leading PREMIER GRAND CRU CLASSÉ on ST-EMILION CÔTES. Pioneer of the modern style; dark, rich, and sumptuous. Second wine: Le Carillon de L'Angélus.

d'Angludet Cantenac-Mar r ★★★ 90 94 95 96' 98' 00 02 03 04 05 A 32-ha CRU BOURGEOIS SUPÉRIEUR owned and run by négociant Sichel; classed-growth quality. Lively long-living MARGAUX of great style popular in UK. Good value.

Archambeau Graves r w dr (sw) ★★★ (r) 98 00 02 04 05 (w) 00 01 02 04 05 Up-to-date 27-ha property at Illats. Good fruity dry white; fragrant barrel-aged reds (two-thirds of vineyard).

d'Arche Saut w sw ★★ 96 97' 98 99 00 01' 02 03' 05 Much improved 27-ha classed growth. Top vintages are creamy. Château d'Arche-Lafaurie is a richer selection. Also bed-and-breakfast in 17th-C *chartreuse*.

d'Armailhac Pau r ★★★ 88' 89 90' 93 94 95' 96' 98 99 00 01 02 03 04 05' Formerly CHÂTEAU MOUTON BARONNE PHILIPPE. Substantial Fifth Growth under Rothschild ownership. 51 ha: top-quality Pauillac with more finesse than sister CLERC MILON but less power and volume. MOUTON ROTHSCHILD the big brother of both.

L'Arrosée St-Em r ★★★ 95 96 98' 00 01 02 03 04 05' A 9.7-ha CÔTES estate with new owner and investment from 2002. Structured wines with plenty of Cab Fr and Cab Sauv (60%).

Ausone St-Em r ★★★ 85 86' 88 89' 90 93 94 95 96' 97 98' 99 00' 01' 02 03' 04 05' Illustrious First Growth with 6.8 ha (about 2,500 cases); best position on the CÔTES with famous rock-hewn cellars. On superb form since 1996. Long-lived wines with added volume, texture and finesse. Second wine: La Chapelle d'Ausone also excellent.

Bahans-Haut-Brion Pe-Lé r ★★★ 89' 90 93 94 95 96' 98 99 00 01 02 03 04 05' The second wine of CHÂTEAU HAUT-BRION. Serious, Cab Sauv-dominated. Ageing potential of 20 years.

Balestard-la-Tonnelle St-Em r ★★ 95 96 98' 00' 01 03 04 05 Historic 12-ha classed growth on limestone plateau. Fresh, firm, occasionally austere.

Barde-Haut St-Em r ★★ 98 99 00 01 02 03 04 05 'The 17-ha sister property of CLOS L'ÉGLISE and HAUT-BERGEY. Rich, modern and opulent in style.

Bastor-Lamontagne Saut w sw ★★ 95 96' 97' 98 99 01' 02 03' 05 Large (56 ha) Preignac sister to BEAUREGARD. Consistent quality; excellent rich wines. Second

Vintages shown in light type should be opened now only out of curiosity to gauge their future. Vintages in **bold** are deemed (usually by their makers) ready for drinking. Remember, though: the French tend to enjoy the vigour of young wines, and many 88s, 89s, and 90s have at least 10 more years of development in front of them. Vintages marked ' are regarded as particularly successful for the property in question. Vintages in colour are the first choice for 2008.

label: Les Remparts de Bastor. Fruity Caprice (from 2004) for early drinking. Also CHÂTEAU St-Robert at Pujols: red and white GRAVES.

Batailley Pau r ★★★ **94** 95 96 98 00 02 03 04 05' Fifth Growth property (55 ha) bordering PAUILLAC and ST-JULIEN. Fine, firm, strong-flavoured. Good-value PAUILLAC. Even better since 2000. Home of the Castéja family of BORIE-MANOUX.

Beaumont Cussac, H-Méd r ★★ **95** 96 98 00' **02** 04 05' Over 80 ha CRU BOURGEOIS SUPÉRIEUR (see "Médoc" box, p.96); easily enjoyable wines. Second label: Château Moulin d'Arvigny. 40,000 cases. In the same hands as BEYCHEVELLE.

Beauregard Pom r ★★★ 89' 90' 94' 95' 96' 98' 00' 01' **02 03** 04 05' A 17-ha vineyard; fine 17th-C CHÂTEAU near LA CONSEILLANTE. Top-rank rich wines. Advice from consultant Michel ROLLAND. Second label: Benjamin de Beauregard.

Beau-Séjour-Bécot St-Em r ★★★ 89' 90' 94 95' 96 98' 99 00' 01 02 03 04 05' Other half of BEAUSEJOUR-DUFFAU; 18 ha. Controversially demoted in class in 1985 but properly re-promoted to PREMIER GRAND CRU CLASSÉ in 1996. The Bécots also own GRAND-PONTET and LA GOMERIE.

Beauséjour-Duffau St-Em r ★★★ 89' 90' **93'** 94 95 96 **98** 99 00 01 02 **03** 04 05' Part of the old BEAU-SÉJOUR-BÉCOT Premier Grand Cru estate on west slope of the CÔTES. 6.8 ha in old family hands; only 2,000+ cases of firm-structured, concentrated, even hedonistic wine.

Beau-Site St-Est r ★★ 95 96 98 00 03 04 05 CRU BOURGEOIS in same hands as BATAILLEY etc. Usually solid and firm, if unexceptional.

Belair St-Em r ★★★ **88'** 89' 90' 94 95' **96 98** 99 00' 00' 01 02 **03** 04 05' Classed-growth neighbour of AUSONE. Long-time winemaker Pascal Delbeck now the owner. Fine, fragrant, elegant style; deceptively long-lived. Second wine: CHÂTEAU Haut Roc Blanquant.

Bel-Air Marquis d'Aligre Soussans-Mar r ★★ 95' 96' 98' **99** 00' Traditionally run MARGAUX with 13 ha of old vines giving only 3,500 cases. Fine, structured wines that need bottle-age.

Belgrave St-Laurent, H-Méd r ★★ 95 96' 98' 00' 02' 03 04' 05' 60 ha Fifth Growth well managed by CVBG-Dourthe (see LA GARDE, REYSSON). Considerable progress and investment since 1998. Second label: Diane de Belgrave.

Bellefont-Belcier St-Em r ★★ **98** 99 00 01 02 03 04 05' 13.5 ha GRAND CRU CLASSE (2006) on the COTES at St-Laurent-des-Combes. Neighbour of LARCIS-DUCASSE. Taken in hand from 1994. Fine, modern but minerally.

Bel-Orme-Tronquoy-de-Lalande St-Seurin-de-Cadourne, H-Méd r ★★ 95 96 98' 00 **02 03** 04 05 A 24-ha CRU BOURGEOIS north of ST-ESTÈPHE (see "Médoc" box, p.96). Once known for tannic wines; more tempting since 1997.

Berliquet St-Em r ★★ 95 96 97 98' **99** 00' 01 02 03 04 05' A 9.3-ha GRAND CRU CLASSÉ well located on the CÔTES. Moved into top gear from 1997 onwards.

Bernadotte H-Méd-r ★★ 98 99 00' 01 02 **03** 04 05' 30-ha estate managed by PICHON-LALANDE team since 1997. CHAMPAGNE ROEDERER now a major shareholder. Fine, structured wines.

Bertineau St-Vincent L de P r ★★ 98 99 00' **01** 03 04 05 Top oenologist Michel ROLLAND owns this 4-ha estate. Consistent quality. (See also LE BON PASTEUR.)

Beychevelle St-Jul r ★★★ 95 96 **98** 99 00' 01 02 **03** 04 05 Fourth Growth (90 ha) with historic mansion. Greater consistency since 1995. Wines of elegance rather than power. Second wine: Amiral de Beychevelle.

Biston-Brillette Moulis r ★★ 98 00 **01** 02 **03** 04 05' Attractive, fruit-bound, good-value MOULIS. 24 ha in production.

Bonalgue Pom r ★★ 95 96' 98' **99** 00 01 03 04 05 Dark, rich, meaty POMEROL. As good value as it gets. Michel ROLLAND consults.

Bonnet E-D-M r w ★★ (r) 00 01 03 **04 05** (w) DYA Owned by André Lurton. Big producer (270 ha!) of some of the best ENTRE-DEUX-MERS and red BORDEAUX. New CUVÉE Prestige, Divinus from 2000.

Le Bon Pasteur Pom r ★★★ 89' 90' **93**' 94' 95 96' **98**' 99 00 **01** 02 03 04 05' Excellent property on ST-EMILION border, owned by Michel ROLLAND. Concentrated, even creamy wines virtually guaranteed. (See also BERTINEAU ST-VINCENT.)

Le Boscq St-Est r ★★ 95' 96' 98 00 **01** 03 04 05' Leading CRU BOURGEOIS SUPÉRIEUR, owned by CVBG-Dourthe, giving excellent value in tasty ST-ESTÈPHE.

Bourgneuf-Vayron Pom r ★★ 95' 96' 98' 99 00 **01' 03** 04 05' Rich, warm, firm-edged POMEROL from this 9-ha estate on sandy-gravel soils.

Bouscaut Pe-Lé r w ★★ (r) **89 90 94 95** 98 00 **01 02** 04 05' (w) **96 98** 00 **01 02 03 04 05**' Steadily improving classed growth owned by daughter of BRANE-CANTENAC's Lucien Lurton. Hitting its stride since 2000.

Boyd-Cantenac Mar r ★★★ 90 94' 95 96' **98**' 00 02 03 04 05' An 18-ha Third Growth in better form since 2004. Cab Sauv-dominated with a little peppery Petit Verdot. Second wine: Jacques Boyd. See also POUGET.

Branaire-Ducru St-Jul r ★★★ 89' 90' **93**' 94 95 96 **98 99** 00 **01** 02 03 04 05' Fourth Growth ST-JULIEN of 51 ha. Has set the bar of quality and consistency high. Dense, linear, cassis style. Second label: Duluc.

Brane-Cantenac Cantenac-Mar r ★★★ 89' 95 96 **98 99** 00' **01 02 03** 04 05' Big (85-ha) Second Growth. Dense, fragrant MARGAUX. Second label: Baron de Brane.

Brillette Moulis r ★★ 95 96 98 99 00 **02 03** 04 05 A 40-ha CRU BOURGEOIS SUPÉRIEUR. Reliable and attractive. Second label: Berthault Brillette.

Cabanne, La Pom r ★★ 95 96 98' 00 04 05 Well-regarded 10-ha property. More rustic POMEROL in style. Second wine: Domaine de Compostelle.

Cadet-Piola St-Em r ★★ 94' 95 98 00 **01** 03 04 05 Distinguished small property (7 ha) on ST-EMILION's limestone plateau. Fresh, firm, long-lived wines.

Caillou Saut w sw ★★ 88' 89' 90' 95 96 **97 98 99 01'** 02 03' 05 Well-run second-rank 13-ha BARSAC vineyard for firm fruity wine. CUVÉE Reine (**97 99** 01' 03') is a top selection.

Calon-Ségur St-Est r ★★★ 89' 90' 94 95 **96' 98 99** 00' **01** 02 03 04 05' Big (60-ha) Third Growth with great historic reputation. Greater consistency since 1995. Second label: Marquis de Calon.

Cambon La Pelouse H-Méd r ★★ 96' 98' 99 00 **01 02 03** 04 05' Big, accessible CRU BOURGEOIS SUPÉRIEUR. A sure bet for rich typical MÉDOC.

Camensac St-Laurent, H-Méd r ★★ 95 96' 98 00 **01 03** 05 75-ha Fifth Growth. Quite lively if not exactly classic wines. New owner has CHASSE-SPLEEN connection; expect change. Second label: La Closerie de Camensac.

Canon St-Em r ★★★ 96 98' **99** 00 **01** 02 **03** 04 05' Famous first-classed growth with 22 walled-in hectares on plateau west of the town bought in 1996 by (Chanel) owners of RAUZAN-SÉGLA. Investment and restructuring of the vineyard beginning to pay. Elegant, long-lived wines. Second label: Clos Canon.

Canon-de-Brem Canon-Fronsac r ★★ 98 99 00 **01 03** 04 05' Formerly a MOUEIX property but sold to Jean Halley of Carrefour supermarkets in 2000 (DE LA DAUPHINE). Massive recent investment. Firm, pure expression.

Canon La Gaffelière St-Em r ★★★ 89' 90' 94' 95 96 97 **98' 99** 00' **01' 02 03** 04 05' Leading 19-ha GRAND CRU CLASSÉ on the lower slopes of the CÔTES. Same ownership as CLOS DE L'ORATOIRE and LA MONDOTTE. Stéphane Derenoncourt consults. Produces stylish, upfront, impressive wines.

Cantegril Graves r Saut w sw ★★ (r) 00 **02 04** 05 (w) **01 02 03** 04 05' Supple, digestible red and fine, aromatic BARSAC-SAUTERNES from DOISY-DAENE and CLOS FLORIDENE connection.

Cantemerle Macau, H-Méd r ★★★ 89' 90 **95** 96' 98 00 **01** 02 03 04 05' Large 90-ha property in south MÉDOC. Now merits its Fifth Growth status. Sandy-gravel soils so finer style. Second label: Les Allées de Cantemerle.

Cantenac-Brown Cantenac-Mar r ★★ ·★★★ 90' 94 95 96 98 99 00 **01** 02 03 04 05' 42-ha Third Growth sold in 2006 to private investor Simon Halabi; had been owned since late 80s by AXA Millésimes Insurance. Generally powerful, robust but more elegance since 2000. Second label: Brio du Château Cantenac Brown.

Capbern-Gasqueton St-Est r ★★ 95 96 98 00 02 **03** 04 05 Good 34-ha CRU BOURGEOIS (see "Médoc" box, p.96); same owner as CALON-SEGUR.

Cap de Mourlin St-Em r ★★ 95 96 98' 99 00 01 03 05 Well-known 15-ha property of the Capdemourlin family, also owners of CHÂTEAU BALESTARD and CHÂTEAU Roudier, MONTAGNE-ST-EMILION. A vigorous but tasty ST-EMILION.

Carbonnieux Pe-Lé r w ★★★ 90' 95 96 98 99 00 02 04 05' Large (90-ha), historic estate at LÉOGNAN for sterling red and white. The whites, 65% Sauv Bl (e.g. **96 97** 98 99 00 01 02 03 04 05), can age up to 10 years. Châteaux Le Pape and Le Sartre are also in the family. Second label: La Tour-Léognan.

de Carles Fronsac r ★★ 98 99 00 01 02 03 04 05' Haut Carles is the top selection here with its own modern, gravity-fed cellars. Iron fist in a velvet glove. Juicy de Carles now the second wine.

les Carmes-Haut-Brion Pe-Lé r ★★★ 89 90' 94 95 96 98 99 00 01 02 03 04 05' Small (4-ha) neighbour of HAUT-BRION with classed-growth standards. Old vintages show its potential.

Caronne-Ste-Gemme St-Laurent, H-Méd r ★★–★★★★ 95 96' 98 99 00 01 02 03 04 05 CRU BOURGEOIS SUPÉRIEUR (40 ha). Steady, stylish quality repays patience.

Carsin Premières Côtes r w ★★ (r) 00 01 02 03 05 (w) 00 01 02 04 05 Ambitious enterprise: Finnish-owned, Australian-designed winery. Very attractive (especially CUVÉE Prestige and white Etiquette Grise).

Carteau Côtes-Daugay St-Em r ★★ 95 96 98' 99 00 01 02 03 04 05 Consistent, good value, 13-ha GRAND CRU; full-flavoured wines maturing fairly early.

Certan-de-May Pom r ★★★ 90' 94 95 96 98 00' 01' 04 05' Tiny property (1,800 cases) on the POMEROL plateau. Has been inconsistent but 2005 shows the true potential. Opulent with firm, fine tannic frame.

Chambert-Marbuzet St-Est r ★★ –★★★ 95 96 98 99 00 01 02 04 05 HAUT-MARBUZET's tiny (8-ha) sister CHÂTEAU. Mainly Cab Sauv aged in new oak.

Chantegrive Graves r w ★★–★★★★ 98' 99' 00 01 02 03 04 05' With 87 ha, the largest estate in the AC; modern GRAVES of very good quality. CUVÉE Caroline is top white selection (**98'** 99 00 01 02 03 04 05').

Chasse-Spleen Moulis r ★★★ 95 96 98 99 00 01 02 03 04 05' A 80-ha CRU BOURGEOIS EXCEPTIONNEL at classed-growth level (see Médoc box, p.96). Consistently good, often outstanding (e.g. **90' 00'**), long-maturing wine. Second label: Ermitage de Chasse Spleen. One of the surest things in Bordeaux. See also CAMENSAC and GRESSIER-GRAND-POUJEAUX.

Chauvin St-Em r ★★ 95 96 98' 99 00 01 03 04 05 Steady performer; increasingly serious stuff. New vineyards purhased in 1998.

Cheval Blanc St-Em r ★★★★ 85' 86 88 89 90' 93 94 95 96' 97 98' 99 00' 01' 02 **03** 04 05' 40-ha premier GRAND CRU CLASS (A) OF ST-EMILION. High percentage of Cabernet Franc (60%). Rich, fragrant, vigorous wines with some of the voluptuousness of neighbouring POMEROL. Delicious young; lasts a generation. For many, *the* first choice in Bordeaux. Second wine: Le Petit Cheval.

Chevalier, Domaine de Pe-Lé r w ★★★ 89 90' 95 96' 98' 99' 00' 01' 02 03 04' 05' Superb estate of 38 ha at LÉOGNAN. Impressive since 1998, the red has gained in finesse, fruit and texture. Complex white matures slowly and develops rich flavours (89 90' **93** 94 95 96' 97 98' **99** 00 01 02 03 04 05'). Second wine: Esprit de Chevalier. Also look out for Domaine de la Solitude, PESSAC-LÉOGNAN.

Cissac Cissac-Méd r ★★ 90 94' 95 96' **98** 00 02 03 04 05 Pillar of the bourgeoisie. 50-ha CRU BOURGEOIS SUPÉRIEUR (see "Médoc" box, p.96). Steady record for tasty, long-lived wine. Second wine: Les Reflets du Château Cissac.

Citran Avensan, H-Méd r ★★ 90' 94 95 96 98 99 00 02 03 04 05' CRU BOURGEOIS SUPÉRIEUR of 90 ha, back in Villars-Merlaut family since 1996. Now round, ripe, supple; accessible early. Second label: Moulins de Citran. This is one to watch.

Clarke Listrac r (p w) ★★ 89' 90' 95 96' 98' 99 00 01 02 03 04 05' Large (54-ha) CRU BOURGEOIS SUPÉRIEUR. Massive investment. Now very good Merlot-based red. Also a dry white Le Merle Blanc du Château Clarke. CHÂTEAU Malmaison in MOULIS same connection.

Clerc Milon Pau r ★★★ 89' 90' 94 95 96' 98' 99 00 01 02 03 04 05 Once-forgotten Fifth Growth owned by de Rothschilds. Now 30 ha and a top performer; weightier than ARMAILHAC.

Climens Saut w sw ★★★★ 76 78 83' 85' 86' 88' 89 90' 95 96 97' 98 99' 00 01' 02 03' 04 05' A 30-ha BARSAC classed growth making some of the world's most stylish wine (but not the sweetest) for a good 10 years' maturing. (Occasional) second label: Les Cyprès. Owned by Berenice Lurton.

Clinet Pom r ★★★★ 95 96 97' 98' 99 00 01 02 03 04 05' Made a name for intense, sumptuous wines in the 1980s. New owner (1998) continues the style. Michel Rolland consults. New winery 2004. Second label: Fleur de Clinet.

Clos de l'Oratoire St-Em r ★★ 94 95 96 98 99 00' 01' 03 04 05 Serious performer on the northeastern slopes of ST-EMILION. Same stable as CANON-LA-GAFFELIÈRE and LA MONDOTTE, but lighter than both.

Clos des Jacobins St-Em r ★★ 95 96 98 00 01 02 03 04 05' Classed growth with greater stature since 2000. New ownership from 2004; new creamy style. ANGELUS owner consults. Same family owns CHÂTEAU La Commanderie.

Clos du Marquis St-Jul r ★★ ★★★ 90 94 95 96 97 98 99 00 01 02 03 04 05 The second wine of LÉOVILLE-LAS-CASES, cut from the same cloth and regularly a match for many highly classed growths.

Clos Floridène Graves r w ★★ (r) 98' 99 00 01 02 03 04 05 (w) 96' 98 99 00 01' 02 03 04' 05' A sure thing from one of Bordeaux's most famous white-winemakers, Denis Dubourdieu. Oak-fermented Sauv Bl/Sémillon to keep 5+ years; fruity red. See also CHÂTEAUX CANTEGRAIL, DOISY-DAENE and REYNON.

Clos Fourtet St-Em r ★★★ 89 90 94 95 96 97 98 99 00 01 02 03 04 05' Well-placed First Growth on the plateau, cellars almost in town. New owner and investment from 2001. Now on stellar form. Second label: Domaine de Martialis.

Clos Haut-Peyraguey Saut w sw ★★ 86' 88' 89 90' 95' 96 97' 98 99 00 01' 02 03' 04 05' Tiny production (12 ha) of excellent medium-rich wine. Haut-Bommes is the second label.

Clos l'Eglise Pom r ★★ 90' 94 95 96 98 99 00' 01 02 03 04 05' A 6-ha vineyard on one of the best sites in POMEROL. Fine wine with more depth since 1998. Michel ROLLAND consults. Same family owns HAUT-BERGEY.

Clos René Pom r ★★ 94 95 96 98' 00' 01 04 05' Merlot-dominated wine with a little spicy Malbec. Less sensuous than top POMEROL but good value. Alias CHÂTEAU Moulinet-Lasserre.

La Clotte St-Em r ★★ 89 90' 94 95' 96 98' 99 00' 01 02 03 04 05 Tiny CÔTES GRAND CRU CLASSÉ: pungent, supple wine. Drink at owners' ST-EMILION restaurant, Logis de la Cadène. Second label: Clos Bergat Bosson.

Colombier-Monpelou Pau r ★★ 94 95 96 98 99 00' 02 03 04 05 Reliable small CRU BOURGEOIS SUPÉRIEUR; fair standard.

La Conseillante Pom r ★★★★ 85 86 88 89 90' 94 95' 96' 98' 99 00' 01' 02 03 04 05' Historic 12-ha property on plateau between PÉTRUS and CHEVAL BLANC. Some of the noblest and most fragrant POMEROL; drinks well young or old.

Corbin St-Em r ★★ 95 96 98 99 00' 01 02 04 05 Much improved 12-ha GRAND CRU CLASSÉ. New management and investment since 1999. Round and supple with soft, red fruit.

Corbin-Michotte St-Em r ★★ 90 94' 95 96 98' 99 00 01 02 04 05 Well-run, modernized, 7.6-ha classed growth; generous, POMEROL-like wine. In same hands as CHÂTEAUX Calon and Cantelauze.

Cordeillan-Bages Pau r ★★ A mere 1,000 cases of savoury PAUILLAC. Rarely seen outside Bordeaux. Better known for its (Michelin-starred) restaurant and hotel.

Cos d'Estournel St-Est r ★★★★ 88' 89' 90' 94 95 96' 97 98' 00 01 02 03 04 05' A 67-ha Second Growth with eccentric chinoiserie CHAI. Most refined ST-ESTÈPHE and regularly one of the best wines of the MÉDOC. Second label: Les Pagodes de Cos. Same owner as CHÂTEAU MARBUZET and Goulée (Médoc).

Cos-Labory St-Est r ★★ 88 89' 90' 94 95 96' 98' 99 00 02 03 04 05' Little-known Fifth Growth neighbour of COS-D'ESTOURNEL with 15 ha. Recent vintages have more depth and structure. Good value. ANDRON-BLANQUET is sister CHÂTEAU.

Côte(s) In St-Emilion, Côtes distinguishes better valley slopes from plateau.

Coufran St-Seurin-de-Cadourne, H-Méd r ★★ 94 95 96 98 99 00 01 02 03 04 05 CRU BOURGEOIS SUPÉRIEUR Coufran and VERDIGNAN, in the extreme north of the HAUT-MÉDOC, are co-owned. Coufran is mainly Merlot for supple wine. 76 ha. SOUDARS is another, smaller sister.

Couhins-Lurton Pe-Lé w r ★★→★★★ (w) 98' 99 00 01 02 03 04 05 (r) 02 03 04 05 Fine, minerally, long-lived classed-growth white produced from Sauv Bl. Now a little red from 2002. Same family as LA LOUVIÈRE.

La Couspaude St Em r ★★★ 95 96 98 99 00' 01 02 03 04 (05) Classed growth well located on the ST-EMILION plateau. Modern style; rich and creamy with lashings of spicy oak.

Coutet Saut w sw ★★★ 83' 85 86' 88' 89' 90' 95 96 97' 98' 99 01' 02 03' 04 05 Traditional rival to CLIMENS; 37 ha in BARSAC. Usually slightly less rich; at its best equally fine. CUVÉE Madame is a very rich selection in certain years (90 95 01).

Couvent des Jacobins St-Em r ★★ 95 96 98' 99 00' 01 03 04 05 Well-known 10.5-ha vineyard on eastern edge of St-Emilion. Splendid cellars. Lighter, easy style. Second label: Château Beau-Mayne.

Le Crock St-Est r ★★ 89 90' 95 96 98 99 00' 01 02 03 04 05 Outstanding CRU BOURGEOIS SUPÉRIEUR of 30 ha in the same family as LÉOVILLE-POYFERRÉ. Classic, robust ST-ESTEPHE.

La Croix Pom r ★★ 89 90 94 95 96 98 99 00 01 04 05 Well-reputed 10-ha property. Appealing plummy POMEROL. Also La Croix-St-Georges, La Croix-Toulifaut, Castelot, Chambrun, and HAUT-SARPE (ST-EMILION).

La Croix-de-Gay Pom r ★★★ 89 90 94' 95 96 98 99 00' 01' 02 04 05 12 ha in the best part of the commune. Recently on fine form. LA FLEUR-DE-GAY is the best selection. Same family as Quinault L'Enclos and Faizeau.

La Croix du Casse Pom r ★★ 95 96 98 99 00' 01' 04 05 A 9-ha property on sandy-gravel soils in the south of POMEROL. Usually rich and fine in style. Since 2005 owned by BOIRIE-MANOUX.

Croizet-Bages Pau r ★★ 89 90' 95 96' 98 00' 03 04 05 A 26-ha Fifth Growth. Same owners as RAUZAN-GASSIES. A new regime in the cellar is producing richer, more serious wines, but could be better.

Croque-Michotte St-Em r ★★ 95 96 98 00 01 03 04 05 A 14-ha estate on the POMEROL border. Good steady wines but not grand enough to be *classé*.

Cru Bourgeois, Cru Bourgeois Supérieur, Cru Bourgeois Exceptionnel See Médoc classification box, p.96.

de Cruzeau Pe-Lé s r w ★★ (r) 95 96 98 00 01 02 04 05 (w) 00 01 02 03 04 05 Large 97-ha (two-thirds red) PESSAC-LÉOGNAN vineyard developed by André Lurton of LA LOUVIÈRE. Good value wines. Sauv Bl-dominated white.

Dalem Fronsac r ★★ 95 96' 98' 99 00 01 02 03 04 05' Used to be a full-blooded FRONSAC. Now a feminine touch has added more charm. 15 ha: 85% Merlot.

Dassault St-Em r ★★ 95 96 98' 99 00 01 02 03 04 05' Consistent, solid, modern, oak-lined 23-ha GRAND CRU CLASSÉ.

de la Dauphine Fronsac r ★★ 98' 99 00 01 03 04 05 Total makeover since purchased by owner of CANON-DE-BREM in 00. Renovation of château and vineyards plus new, modern winery in 2002. Approachable style.

Dauzac Labarde-Mar r ★★–★★★ 89' 90' **94** 95 96 **98'** 99 00' 01 02 03 04 05 A 49-ha Fifth Growth south of MARGAUX; underachiever for many years but evolution since the 1990s. Owned by an insurance company; managed by André Lurton of LA LOUVIÈRE. Second wine: La Bastide Dauzac.

Desmirail Mar r ★★·★★★ 95 96 98 00' 01 02 03 04 05 Third Growth (30 ha) owned by Denis Lurton, brother of Henri of BRANE CANTENAC. Fine, delicate style.

Destieux St-Em r ★★ 98 99 00' 01 02 03' 04 05' Promoted to GRAND CRU CLASSE in 2006. 8 ha estate to the east of ST-EMILION at St-Hippolyte. New CHAI and investment since 1996. Michel ROLLAND consults. Firm, bold, powerful style.

Doisy-Daëne Barsac w (r) sw dr ★★★ 88' 89' 90' 95 96 **97' 98'** 99 01' 02 03 04 05 Forward-looking 15-ha estate producing a crisp, oaky, dry white and CHÂTEAU CANTEGRIL, but above all renowned for its notably fine (and long-lived) sweet BARSAC. L'Extravagant (90 96 **97** 01 02 03 04 05) is a super-CUVÉE.

Doisy-Dubroca Barsac w sw ★★ 88' 89 90' 95 96 **97'** 99 01 03' 04 05' Tiny (3.4-ha) BARSAC classed growth allied to CHÂTEAU CLIMENS.

Doisy-Védrines Saut w sw ★★★ 88' 89' 90 95 96 **97' 98** 99 01' 03' 04 05 A 20-ha classed growth at BARSAC, near CLIMENS and COUTET. Delicious, sturdy, rich: for keeping. A sure thing for many years.

La Dominique St-Em r ★★★ 89' 90' **94** 95 96 98 99 00' 01 03 04 05' Classed growth with potential for rich, aromatic wines. Owner of VALANDRAUD has consulted since 2006. To watch. Second label: St Paul de Dominique.

Ducluzeau Listrac r ★★ **94** 95 96 00 01 03 04 05 Tiny sister property of DUCRU-BEAUCAILLOU. 4 ha, unusually 90% Merlot.

Ducru-Beaucaillou St-Jul r ★★★★ 82' 83' 85' 94 95' **96'** 98 99 00' 01 02 03 04 05' Outstanding Second Growth, excellent form except for a patch in the late 1980s; 49 ha overlooking the river. Classic cedar-scented claret suited to long ageing. See also LALANDE-BORIE. Second wine: Croix de Beaucaillou.

Duhart-Milon Rothschild Pau r ★★★ 90 **94** 95 96' 98 00' 01 02 03 04' 05' Fourth Growth neighbour of LAFITE, under same management. Greater precision from 2002; increasingly fine quality and reputation. Second label: Moulin de Duhart.

Durfort-Vivens Mar r ★★★ 89' 90 **94** 95 96 98 99 00 01 02 03 04 05' Relatively small (32-ha) Second Growth owned and being improved by Gonzague Lurton, brother of Henri (BRANE CANTENAC) and Denis (DESMIRAIL). Recent wines have structure (lots of Cab Sauv) and finesse.

de l'Eglise, Domaine Pom r ★★ 89 90 95 96 98 99 00 01 02 03 04 05' Small property: stylish, resonant wine distributed by BORIE-MANOUX.

L'Eglise-Clinet Pom r ★★★ 89 90' **93'** **94** 95 96 97 **98'** 99 00' 01' 02 03 04 05' A 6-ha estate. Top-flight POMEROL with great consistency; full, concentrated, fleshy wine. Expensive and limited quantity. Second label: La Petite Eglise.

L'Evangile Pom r ★★★★ 88' 89' 90 95 **96 98'** 99 00' 01 02 03 04' 05' 13 ha between PÉTRUS and CHEVAL BLANC. Deep-veined elegant style in a POMEROL classic. Investment by owners (LAFITE) Rothschild has greatly improved quality. Second wine: Blason de l'Evangile.

de Fargues Saut w sw ★★★ 85' 86 88 89 90 95 96 97 98 99' 01 **02** 03' 04 05' A 15-ha vineyard by ruined castle owned by Lur-Saluces, previous owner of YQUEM. Rich, unctuous wines, but balanced – maturing earlier than YQUEM.

Faurie-de-Souchard St-Em r ★★ 95 96 **98'** 00 01 03 04 05 Underperforming CHÂTEAU on the COTES. Lost classified status in 2006.

de Ferrand St-Em r ★★ 90' 94 95 96 98 00 01 03 04 05 Big (30-ha) plateau estate. Rich oaky wines, with plenty of tannin to age.

Ferrande Graves r (w) ★★ 00 01 02 04 05 Major estate at Castres: over 40 ha. Easy, enjoyable red and good white wine; at their best at 1–4 years.

Ferrière Mar r ★★ →★★★ 89 90 94 95 96 98 99 00 02 03 04 05 In same capable hands as LA GURGUE and HAUT-BAGES-LIBERAL. Dark, firm, perfumed wines.

Feytit-Clinet Pom r ★★ 90' 94 95 96 98 99 00 01 03 04 05' Tiny 6.5-ha property. Once managed by J-P MOUEIX; back with owning Chasseuil family since 2000. Improvements since. Rich, full POMEROL with ageing potential.

Fieuzal Pe-Lé r (w) ★★★ (r) 94 95' 96' 98' 00 01 03 05 (w) 95 96' 97 98' 99 01 02 03 05 Classed-growth at LÉOGNAN. Superb white and red from mid-1980s. Dipped in late 90s. New owner from 2001 with return to winning ways from 05.

Figeac St-Em r ★★★★ 95' 96 98 99 00' 01 02 03 04 05' First growth, 40-ha gravelly vineyard with unusual 70% Cab Fr and Cab Sauv. Rich but elegant wines; deceptively long ageing. Second wine: Grange Neuve de Figeac.

Filhot Saut w sw dr ★★ 90 95 96' 97' 98 99 01' 02 03' 04 05 Second-rank classed growth with splendid CHÂTEAU, 60-ha vineyard. Difficult young, more complex with age. Light and fine in style.

Fleur Cardinale St-Em r ★★ 98 99 00 01 02 03 04 05' 18 ha property east of ST-EMILION. Good from the 1980s but into overdrive since 2001 with new owner and CHAI. GRAND CRU CLASSE in 2006. Ripe, unctuous, modern style.

La Fleur-de-Gay Pom r ★★★ 1000-case super-CUVÉE of CHÂTEAU LA CROIX DE GAY.

La Fleur-Pétrus Pom r ★★★★ 89' 90' 94 95 96 97 98' 99 00' 01 02 03 04 05' A 13-ha vineyard flanking PÉTRUS; same management as J-P MOUEIX. Concentration, richness, finesse. This is POMEROL at its most stylish (and expensive).

Fombrauge St-Em r ★★ →★★★ 89 90 94 95 96 98 99 00' 01' 02 03 04 05 52 ha east of ST-EMILION. Since 1999 rich, dark, chocolatey, full-bodied wines. Second label: Cadran de Fombrauge. Magrez-Fombrauge is its GARAGE wine.

Fonbadet Pau r ★★ 90' 94 95 96' 98' 00' 01 02 03 04 05 CRU BOURGEOIS SUPÉRIEUR of solid reputation. 20 ha. Old vines; sturdy PAUILLAC style. Value.

Fonplégade St-Em r ★★ 95 96 98 00' 01 03 04 05 A 19-ha GRAND CRU CLASSÉ New owner and investment from 2004. Watch for riper, modern, fruit-driven style.

Fonréaud Listrac r ★★ 89 90 94 95 96 98 00' 02 03 04 05 One of the bigger (39 ha) and better CRUS BOURGEOIS of its area. Investment since 1998. 2 ha of white: Le Cygne, barrel-fermented. See LESTAGE.

Fonroque St-Em r ★★ 88 89' 90' 94 95 96 98 01 03 04 05 19 ha on the plateau north of ST-EMILION. Biodynamic culture being introduced. Big, deep, dark wine: drink or (better) keep. Managed by Alain Moueix (see MAZEYRES).

Fontenil Fronsac r ★★ 90 94 95 96 97 98' 99' 00' 01' 02 03 04 05 Leading FRONSAC started by Michel ROLLAND in 1986. Dense, oaky, new-style. Défi de Fontenil is its GARAGE wine.

Les Forts de Latour Pau r ★★★ 85 86 88 89' 90' 93 94 95' 96' 97 98 99 00' 01 02 03 04' 05' The (worthy) second wine of CHÂTEAU LATOUR; the authentic flavour in slightly lighter format. Until 1990 unique in being bottle-aged at least 3 years before release; now offered EN PRIMEUR.

Fourcas-Dupré Listrac r ★★ 89' 90 95 96' 98' 99 00' 01 02 03 04 05 Top-class 46-ha CRU BOURGEOIS SUPÉRIEUR making consistent wine in tight LISTRAC style. Second label: Château Bellevue-Laffont. Complete renovation in 2000.

Fourcas-Hosten Listrac r ★★ →★★★ 89' 90' 95' 96' 98' 00 01 02 03 04 05 A 48-ha CRU BOURGEOIS SUPÉRIEUR. New owners from 2006. Firm wine with a long life.

de France Pe-Lé r w ★★ (r) 90' 95' 96' 98 99 00 02 03 04 05 (w) 96 98 99 00' 01' 02 03 04 05 Well-known GRAVES property (the name helps) making steady progress. Michel ROLLAND consults. Try a top vintage.

Franc-Mayne St-Em r ★★ 89' 90' 94 95 96 98' 99 00' 01 03 04 05 A 7.2-ha GRAND

CRU CLASSÉ. Ambitious new owners in 1996 and again in 2004. Investment and renovation. Round but firmly constituted wines. To watch.

du Gaby Canon-Fronsac r ★★ 00' 01' 03 04 05 Perhaps the finest situation in Bordeaux. Serious wines from dedicated owner.

La Gaffelière St-Em r ★★★ 86' 88' 89' 90' 94 95 96 98' 99 00' 01 03 04 05' A 25-ha First Growth at the foot of the CÔTES. Elegant, not rich wines. Re-equipped and improved since 1998.

Galius St-Em r ★★ 00 01 03 04 05 Oak-aged selection from ST-EMILION CO-op, to a high standard. Formerly Haut Quercus.

La Garde Pe-Lé r w ★★ (r) 96' 98' 99 00 01' 02 03 04 05 (w) 01 02 04 05 Substantial property of 58 ha owned by négociant CVBG-Dourthe; reliable red and improving. More Merlot planted 2000.

Le Gay Pom r ★★★ 89' 90' 95 96 98 99 00 01 03 04 05' Fine 5.6-ha vineyard on northern edge of POMEROL. Major investment, with Michel ROLLAND consulting. Usually impressive tannic wines. Château Montviel same stable and AC.

Gazin Pom r ★★★ 89' 90' 94' 95 96 98' 99 00' 01' 02 03 04 05' Large (for POMEROL): 23 ha, recently shining. Second label: L'Hospitalet de Gazin.

Gilette Saut w sw ★★★ 49 53 55 59 61 67 70 75 76 78 79 81 82 83 85 86 Extraordinary small Preignac CHÂTEAU stores its sumptuous wines in concrete vats to a great age. Only about 5,000 bottles of each. CHÂTEAU Les Justices is its sister (96 97 99 01 02 03' 05).

Giscours Labarde-Mar r ★★★ 85 88 89' 90 94 95 96' 98 99 00' 01 02 03 04 05' Splendid Third Growth south of Cantenac. Excellent vigorous wine in 1970s; 1980s very wobbly; new ownership from 95 and revival since. Second label: La Sirène de Giscours. Château La Houringue is its baby sister in AC HAUT-MÉDOC.

du Glana St-Jul r ★★ 95 96 98 99 00 02 03 04 05 Big CRU BOURGEOIS SUPÉRIEUR. Undemanding; undramatic; value. Second wine: Château Sirène.

Gloria St-Jul r ★★ ·★★★ 89 90 95' 96 98 99 00' 01 02 03 04 05' A 45-ha ST-JULIEN estate that didn't apply for the recent CRU BOURGEOIS classification (see box, p.96). Same ownership as ST-PIERRE. Wines of vigour, with a recent return to long-maturing style. Second label: Peymartin.

La Gomerie St-Em 1,000 cases, 100% Merlot, *garagiste*. See BEAU-SÉJOUR-BÉCOT.

Grand-Corbin-Despagne St-Em r ★★ ·★★★ 89 90' 94 95 96 98 99 00' 01 03 04 05 Demoted from GRAND CRU CLASSÉ in 1996 but reinstated in 2006. In between: investment and hard graft. Aromatic wines now with a riper, fuller edge. Also CHÂTEAU Maison Blanche, MONTAGNE ST-EMILION.

Grand Cru Classé see St-Emilion classification box, p.101.

Grand-Mayne St-Em r ★★★ 88 89' 90' 94 95 96 98 99 00' 01' 02 03 04 05' Leading 16-ha GRAND CRU CLASSÉ on western CÔTES. Noble old CHÂTEAU with wonderfully rich, tasty wines.

Grand-Pontet St-Em r ★★★ 95' 96 98' 99 00' 01 02 03 04 05 A 14-ha estate revitalized since 1985. Quality much improved. See BEAU-SÉJOUR-BÉCOT.

Grand-Puy-Ducasse Pau r ★★★ 89' 90 94 95 96' 98' 99 00 01 02 03 04 05' Fifth Growth enlarged to 40 ha under expert management; improvements in the 1990s, but lacks the vigour of the next entry. Second label: CHÂTEAU Artigues-Arnaud.

Grand-Puy-Lacoste Pau r ★★★ 82' 83 85' 86' 88' 89' 90' 94 95' 96' 97 98 99 00' 01 02 03 04 05' Leading 50-ha Fifth Growth famous for excellent full-bodied, vigorous examples of PAUILLAC. Second label: Lacoste-Borie.

La Grave à Pomerol Pom r ★★★ 88 89' 90 94 95 96 98' 00 01 02 03 04 05 Verdant CHÂTEAU with small but first-class vineyard owned by Christian MOUEIX. Beautifully structured POMEROL of medium richness.

Gressier-Grand-Poujeaux Moulis r ★★ ·★★★ 88 89 90 94 95 96 98 00 01 03 04 05 V. good CRU BOURGEOIS SUPÉRIEUR. Fine firm wine with good track record.

Repays patient cellaring. Since 2003, same owners as CHASSE-SPLEEN.

Greysac Méd r ★★**95 96** 98 00' **02 03 04** 05 Elegant 70-ha CRU BOURGEOIS SUPÉRIEUR. Same management as CANTEMERLE. Fine, consistent style.

Gruaud-Larose St-Jul r ★★★★ 85 86' **88 89' 90' 93 95' 96' 98 99 00' 01** 02 03 04 05' One of the biggest, best-loved Second Growths. 82 ha. Smooth, rich, stylish claret; ages 20+ years. Second wine: Sarget de Gruaud-Larose.

Guadet-St-Julien St-Em ★★ **89 90' 95** 96' **98 00 01** 04 05 Firm, classic style. Poor track record resulted in demotion from GRAND CRU CLASSE in 2006.

Guiraud Saut w (r) sw (dr) ★★★ **86' 88' 89' 90' 95 96' 97' 98 99 01' 02** 03 04 05' Top quality classed growth. Over 100 ha. New owning consortium from 2006 includes existing manager, Xavier Planty, and CANON-LA-GAFFELIERE and DOMAINE DE CHEVALIER connections.

La Gurgue Mar r ★★ **95' 96'** 98 00' **01 02 03** 04 05' Small, well-placed 10-ha property, for MARGAUX of the fruitier sort. Same management as HAUT-BAGES-LIBERAL. Winery renovated in 2000.

Hanteillan Cissac r ★★ **96** 98 00' **02 03** 04 05' Huge 82-ha vineyard: very fair CRU BOURGEOIS SUPÉRIEUR, conscientiously made. Second wine: CHÂTEAU Laborde.

Haut-Bages Averous Pau r ★★ **95 96 98 99 00 02 03** 04 05 The second wine of LYNCH-BAGES. Should be tasty drinking.

Haut-Bages-Libéral Pau r ★★★ 95 **96' 98 99 00 01 02** 03 04 05' Lesser-known Fifth Growth of 28 ha (next to LATOUR) in same stable as LA GURGUE. Results are excellent, full of PAUILLAC vitality.

Haut-Bages-Monpelou Pau r ★★ 95 **96 98 99 00 03** 04 05 A 15-ha CRU BOURGEOIS SUPÉRIEUR stablemate of CHÂTEAU BATAILLEY on former DUHART-MILON land. Good minor PAUILLAC.

Haut-Bailly Graves r ★★★ 88' 89' 90' **94 95 96 98' 99 00' 01** 02 **03** 04 05' Over 28 ha at LÉOGNAN. Since 1979 some of the best savoury, round, intelligently made red GRAVES. New ownership and investment from 1998 has taken it to greater heights. Second label La Parde de Haut-Bailly.

Haut-Batailley Pau r ★★★ **88** 89' 90' 95 96' **98 99 00** 02 **03** 04 05' Smaller part of divided Fifth Growth BATAILLEY: 20 ha. Gentler than sister CHÂTEAU GRAND-PUY-LACOSTE. New cellar in 2005 and more precision. Second wine: La Tour-d'Aspic.

Haut-Beauséjour St-Est r ★★ 95 **98 99 00 01 03** 04 05 Another CRU BOURGEOIS performing well. Owned by CHAMPAGNE house ROEDERER.

Haut-Bergey Pessac-L r (w) ★★ (r) **98 99 00 01** 02 03 04 05 (w) **02 03 04 05** A 26-ha estate now producing a denser, fruit-driven GRAVES with oak overlay. Also a little dry white. Completely renovated in the 1990s. Michel ROLLAND consults. Same ownership as BARDE-HAUT and CLOS L'EGLISE. Sister CHÂTEAU Branon.

Haut Bommes Saut Second label of CLOS HAUT-PEYRAGUEY.

Haut-Brion Pessac, Graves r ★★★★ (r) **75' 76 78' 79' 81 82' 83' 85' 86' 88' 89' 90' 93 94 95' 96' 97 98' 99** 00' 01 02 03 04 05' The oldest great CHÂTEAU of Bordeaux and the only non-MÉDOC First Growth of 1855. 44 ha. Deeply harmonious, never-aggressive wine with endless, honeyed, earthy complexity. Consistently great since 75. A little full dry white: **90 93 94 95 96 97 98 99 00' 01 02 03 04'** 05'. See BAHANS HAUT-BRION, LA MISSION-HAUT-BRION, LAVILLE-HAUT-BRION.

Haut Condissas Méd r ★★ 99 00 01 **02 03** 04 05 Aspiring new *cru* at Bégadan. Old-vine selection from CHÂTEAU Rollan de By. CHX La Clare, La Tour Séran same ownership.

Haut-Marbuzet St-Est r ★★ -★★★ 88 89' 90' **94 95 96' 98 99 00' 01** 02 03 04 05' The best of many good ST-ESTÈPHE CRUS BOURGEOIS. Now CRU BOURGEOIS EXCEPTIONNEL. M Dubosq has reassembled ancient Domaine de Marbuzet, in total 71 ha. Also

OWNS CHAMBERT-MARBUZET, MacCarthy, Tour de Marbuzet. Haut-Marbuzet is 60% Merlot, seductive and remarkably consistent.

Haut-Pontet St-Em r ★★ 98 00 01 03 04 05 Reliable 4.8-ha vineyard of the CÔTES deserving its GRAND CRU status. 2,500 cases.

Haut-Sarpe St-Em r ★★ **88** 89 90' **94** 95 96 **98** 00' **01** 03 04 05 21-ha GRAND CRU CLASSÉ with elegant ch and park, 70% Merlot. Same owner (Janoueix) as CHÂTEAU LA CROIX, POMEROL.

Hortevie St-Jul r ★★ **90** 95 96 98 00 **02** 03 04 05 One of the few non-classified ST-JULIENS. This tiny vineyard and its bigger sister TERREY-GROS-CAILLOU are shining examples. Now hand-harvesting only.

Hosanna Pom r ★★★★ **00** 01 **02** 03 04 05' Formerly Certan-Guiraud until purchased and renamed by J-P MOUEIX. Only best 4.5 ha retained. First vintages confirm its class. Worthy stablemate of PÉTRUS and TROTANOY.

Houissant St-Est r ★★ **90** 95 96 98 00' **02** 03 04 05 Typical robust well-balanced ST-ESTÈPHE CRU BOURGEOIS; well known in Denmark. Same ownership as CRU BOURGEOIS CHÂTEAU Leyssac.

d'Issan Cantenac-Mar r ★★★ 95 96' **98** 99 00' **01** 02 03 04' 05 Beautifully restored moated CHÂTEAU near Gironde with 30-ha Third Growth vineyard. Fragrant wines; more substance since late 90s. Second label: Blason d'Issan.

Kirwan Cantenac-Mar r ★★★**82' 85** 86 **88** 89' **90' 94** 95 96 98 **99 00'** 01 02 03 04 05' A 35-ha Third Growth; from 1997 majority owned by SCHRÖDER & SCHŸLER. Michel ROLLAND advises. Mature vineyards now giving classy wines. Second label: Les Charmes de Kirwan.

Labégorce Mar r ★★ **94** 95 96 **98** 99 00 01 02 03 04 05' Substantial 38-ha CRU BOURGEOIS SUPÉRIEUR north of MARGAUX; long-lived wines of true MARGAUX quality. Significant investment since 1989.

Labégorce-Zédé Mar r ★★ ★★★ **88** 89' **90' 93 94** 95 96' **98 99** 00' **01** 02 03 04 05' CRU BOURGEOIS EXCEPTIONNEL north of MARGAUX (25 ha). Typically delicate, fragrant, classic. Second label: Domaine Zédé. Also 9.3 ha of AC BORDEAUX: "Z".

Lacoste-Borie The second wine of GRAND-PUY-LACOSTE.

Lafaurie-Peyraguey Saut w sw ★★★ 78 82 83' **85** 86' **88' 89'** 90' 95 96' **97** 98 99 **01' 02** 03'04 05' Fine 40-ha classed growth at Bommes; owners Groupe Suez Bank. One of best buys in SAUTERNES. Second wine: La Chapelle de Lafaurie.

Lafite-Rothschild Pau r ★★★★ **82' 83 85 86' 88' 89'** 90' 91 93 94 95 96' **97 98 99** 00' 01' 02 03' 04' 05' First Growth of famous elusive perfume and style, but never huge weight, although more density and sleeker texture from 1996. Great vintages keep for decades. Recent vintages are well up to form. Amazing circular cellars. Joint ventures in Chile (1988), California (1989), Portugal (1992), Argentina (1999), and now the Midi and Italy. Second label: Carruades de Lafite. 91 ha. Also owns CHÂTEAUX DUHART-MILON, l'EVANGILE, RIEUSSEC.

Lafleur Pom r ★★★★ **82' 83 85' 86 88' 89'** 90' 93 94 95 96 **97 98' 99'** 00' 01' 02 03 04' 05' Superb 4.8-ha property. Resounding wine of the elegant, intense, less fleshy kind for long maturing and investment. 50% Cab Fr. Second wine: Pensées de Lafleur.

Lafleur-Gazin Pom r ★★ **89** 90 **94** 95 96 98 00 01 04 05 Distinguished small J-P MOUEIX estate on the NE border of POMEROL.

Lafon-Rochet St-Est r ★★★ 86 **88'** 89' 90' **94** 95 96' **98 99** 00' **01** 02 03' 04 05' Fourth Growth neighbour of COS D'ESTOURNEL, 45 ha. Investment, selection, and a higher percentage of Merlot have made this ST-ESTÈPHE more opulent since 98. Same owner as PONTET-CANET. Second label: Les Pèlerins de Lafon-Rochet.

Lagrange Pom r ★★ **88** 89' 90' **94** 95 96 98 00 01 04 05 An 8-ha vineyard in the centre of POMEROL run by the ubiquitous house of J-P MOUEIX. Good value but not in the same league as HOSANNA, LA FLEUR-PÉTRUS, LATOUR-À-POMEROL, etc..

Lagrange St-Jul r ★★★ **88' 89'** 90' **94** 95 96 **97** 98 99 00' 01 02 03 04 05' Formerly neglected Third Growth inland from ST-JULIEN. 113 ha now in tip-top condition with wines to match. Second wine: Les Fiefs de Lagrange.

La Lagune Ludon, H-Méd r ★★★ 90' 94 95 96' 98 00' 01 02 03 04 05' 80-ha Third Growth in southern MÉDOC with sandy-gravel soils. Dipped in the 1990s but on form from 2000. Fine-edged, now with added structure and depth. New CHAI 2004. Owned by Jean-Jacques Frey, also a shareholder of BILLECART-SALMON.

Lalande-Borie St-Jul r ★★ 96 98 00 01 02 03 04 05 A baby brother of the great DUCRU-BEAUCAILLOU created from part of the former vineyard of CHÂTEAU LAGRANGE. Gracious, easy-drinking wine.

de Lamarque Lamarque, H-Méd r ★★ 89 90' 94 95 96 98 99 00' 02 03 04 05 Splendid medieval fortress in central MÉDOC, 35-ha CRU BOURGEOIS SUPÉRIEUR; competent, mid-term wines. Second wine: Donjon de L.

Lamothe Bergeron H-Méd r ★★ 88 89 90 94 95 96' 98' 00 02 03 04 05 Large 67-ha CRU BOURGEOIS SUPÉRIEUR in Cussac Fort Médoc making reliable claret.

Lanessan Cussac, H-Méd r ★★ 88' 89' 90' 94 95 96' 98 00' 02 03 04 05 Distinguished 44-ha CRU BOURGEOIS SUPÉRIEUR just south of ST-JULIEN. Fine rather than burly, but ages well.

Langoa-Barton St-Jul r ★★★ 90' 94 95' 96' 98 99 00' 01 02 03 04' 05'The 20-ha Third Growth sister CHÂTEAU to LÉOVILLE-BARTON. Very old Barton-family estate; impeccable standards, great value. Second wine: Réserve de Léoville-Barton.

Larcis-Ducasse St-Em r ★★ 85 86 88' 89' 90' 94 95 96 98' 00 02 03 04 05' Top classed-growth property of St-Laurent, eastern neighbour of ST-EMILION, on the CÔTES. 12 ha in a fine situation; wines on an upward swing since management in 2002 (PAVIE-MACQUIN and PUYGUERAUD). To watch.

Larmande St-Em r ★★★ 88' 89' 90' 94 95' 96 98' 00' 01 03 04 05 Substantial 24-ha property. Replanted, re-equipped, and now making rich, strikingly scented wine, silky in time. Second label: CHÂTEAU des Templiers.

Laroque St-Em r ★★ ·★★★ 85 86 88 89 90 94 95 96 98 99 00' 01 02 03 04 05 Important 58-ha vineyard on the ST-EMILION CÔTES in St-Christophe. Promoted to GRAND CRU CLASSÉ in 1996. Well-structured wines for ageing.

Larose-Trintaudon St-Laurent, H-Méd r ★★ 98 00 01 02 03 04 05 The biggest vineyard in the MÉDOC: 172 ha. Modern methods make reliable, fruity and charming CRU BOURGEOIS SUPÉRIEUR wine to drink young. Second label: Larose St-Laurent. Special CUVÉE (from 1996): CRU BOURGEOIS Larose Perganson; from 33-ha parcel.

Laroze St-Em r ★★ 90' 94 95 96' 98' 99 00 01 02 05 Large vineyard (30 ha) on western CÔTES. Fairly light wines from sandy soils, more depth from 1998; approachable when young.

Larrivet-Haut-Brion Pe-Lé r w ★★ (r) 88 89 90 94 95 96' 98' 00 01 02 03 04' 05' LÉOGNAN property with perfectionist standards; Michel ROLLAND consulting. Rich, modern red. Also 4,500 cases of fine, barrel-fermented white (95 96' 98' 99 00 01 02 04' 05). New plantings in 1999.

Lascombes Mar r (p) ★★★ 89' 90' 95 96' 98' 99 00 01 02 03 04 05'A 97-ha Second Growth. Wines have been wobbly, but real improvements from 2001. Michel ROLLAND consults. Second label: Chevalier de Lascombes.

Latour Pau r ★★★★ 70' 75 78' 79 81 82' 83 85 86' 88' 89' 90' 91 92 93 94' 95' 96' 97 98 99 00' 01 02 03' 04' 05' First Growth considered the grandest statement of the MÉDOC. Profound, intense, almost immortal wines in great years; even weaker vintages have the characteristic note of terroir and run for many years. 60 ha sloping to river Gironde. Latour always needs 10 years to show its hand. New state-of-the-art CHAI (2003) allows more precise vinification. Second wine: LES FORTS DE LATOUR; third wine: PAUILLAC.

Latour-à-Pomerol Pom r ★★★ 85' 86 88' 89' 90' 94 95 96 98' 99 00' 01 02 04 05' Top growth of 7.6 ha under MOUEIX management. POMEROL of great power and perfume, yet also ravishing finesse.

Latour-Martillac Pe-Lé r w ★★ (r) 98 00 **01** 02 03 04 05' A 42-ha (three-quarters red) classed-growth property in Martillac. Regular quality (red and white); good value at this level. The white can age admirably (**98'** 99 00 01 02 03 04 05).

des Laurets St-Em r ★★ 98 00 **01** 03 **04** 05 Major property in PUISSEGUIN-ST-EMILION and MONTAGNE-ST-EMILION (to the east), with 72 ha of vineyard evenly split on the CÔTES (40,000 cases).

Laville-Haut-Brion Pe-Lé w ★★★★ 89' 90 92 93' 94 95' 96' 97 98 99 00' 01 02 03 04' 05' Tiny production of very best white GRAVES for long, succulent maturing, made at La Mission-Haut-Brion. Great consistency. Mainly Sémillon.

Léoville-Barton St-Jul r ★★★★ 85' 86' 88' 89' 90' 94' 94 95' 96' 97 98 99 00' 01 02 03' 04 05' A 45-ha portion of the great Second Growth LÉOVILLE vineyard in Anglo-Irish hands of the Barton family for over 150 years. Powerful, classic claret; traditional methods, very fair prices. Major investment raised already high standards to Super Second. See also LANGOA-BARTON.

Léoville-Las-Cases St-Jul r ★★★★ 82' 83' 85' 86' 88 89' 90' 91 93 94 95' 96' 97 98 99 00' 01 02 03' 04' 05' The largest LÉOVILLE; 97 ha with daunting reputation. Elegant, complex, powerful, austere wines, for immortality. Second label CLOS DU MARQUIS is also outstanding.

Léoville-Poyferré St-Jul r ★★★ 86' 88 89' 90' 94 95 96 98 99 00' 01 02 03' 04 05' For years the least outstanding of the Léovilles; high potential rarely realized. Michel ROLLAND consults here; quality now at Second Growth level. 80 ha. Second label: Château Moulin-Riche.

Lestage Listrac r ★★ 89' 90' 95 96 98 00 02 03 04 05 A 42-ha CRU BOURGEOIS SUPÉRIEUR in same hands as CHÂTEAU FONREAUD. Firm, slightly austere claret. Second wine: La Dame du Coeur de Château Lestage.

Lilian Ladouys St-Est r ★★ 95 96 98 00 **01** 02 **03** 04 05 Created in the 1980s: a tiny 9-ha CRU BOURGEOIS SUPÉRIEUR now making consistently good ST-ESTÈPHE.

Liot Barsac w sw ★★ 88 89' 90' 95 96 97' 98 99 01' 02 03 05 Consistent, fairly light, golden wines from 20 ha. Good to drink early, but they last.

Liversan St-Sauveur, H-Méd r ★★ 89' 90' 94 95 96 98 00 02 03 04 05 A 47-ha CRU BOURGEOIS SUPÉRIEUR inland from PAUILLAC. Same owner – Jean-Michel Lapalu – as PATACHE D'AUX. Quality oriented. Second wine: Les Charmes de Liversan.

Loudenne St-Yzans, Méd r ★★ 89' 90 94 95 96' 98 00 00 01 02 03 04 05 Beautiful riverside CHÂTEAU. Michel ROLLAND consults, so wines are getting bigger, denser. Well-made CRU BOURGEOIS SUPÉRIEUR red from 63 ha. Also an oak-scented Sauv Bl white best at 2–4 years (98 99' 00 01 02 04 05).

Loupiac-Gaudiet Loupiac w sw ★★ 96 97 98 99 01 02 03' 05 A reliable source of good-value "almost-SAUTERNES", just across river Garonne.

La Louvière Pe-Lé r w ★★★ (r) 95 96' 98' 99 00' 01 02 03 04 05 (w) 98' 99 00 01 02 03 04' 05' A 55-ha LÉOGNAN estate with classical mansion restored by André Lurton. Excellent white and red of classed-growth standard. See also BONNET, DE CRUZEAU, COUHINS-LURTON, and DE ROCHEMORIN.

de Lussac St-Em r ★★ 99 00 03 04 05 One of the best estates in LUSSAC-ST-EMILION. New owners and technical methods since 2000.

Lynch-Bages Pau r (w) ★★★★ 83' 85' 86' 88' 89' 90' 91 94 95' 96' 98 99 00' 01 02 03 04' 05' Always popular, now a regular star. 90 ha. Rich, robust wine: deliciously dense, brambly; aspiring to greatness. See also HAUT-BAGES-AVEROUS. From 1990, good intense oaky white – Blanc de Lynch-Bages. Same owners (Cazes family) as LES ORMES-DE-PEZ and Villa Bel-Air.

Lynch-Moussas Pau r ★★ 89 90' 94 95' 96' 98 00' 01 02 03 04 05' Fifth Growth restored by the director of Château Batailley. On the up since 2000.

du Lyonnat Lussac-St-Em r ★★ 98 00' 01 03 04 05 A 49-ha estate; well-distributed, reliable wine.

Macquin-St-Georges St-Em r ★★ **95 96 98 99 00 01 03** 04 05 Steady producer of delicious, not weighty, satellite ST-EMILION at ST-GEORGES.

Magdelaine St-Em r ★★★ 85 86 88 89' 90' **94 95 96 98' 99 00 01 02 03** 04 05 Leading CÔTES First Growth: 11 ha owned by J-P MOUEIX. Top-notch, Merlot-led wine; recently powerful and fine.

Malartic-Lagravière Pe-Lé r (w) ★★★ (r) 89 90' **95 96 98 99 00' 01 02** 03 04' 05' (w) **98 99 00 01' 02 03 04' 05'** LÉOGNAN classed growth of 47 ha (majority red). Rich, modern red wine since late 1990s and a little long-ageing Sauv Bl white. Belgian owner (since 96) has revolutionized the property. Michel ROLLAND and Denis Dubourdieu now consulting.

Malescasse Lamarque, H-Méd r ★★ **95' 96 98 00 01 02 03** 04 05 Renovated CRU BOURGEOIS SUPÉRIEUR with 40 well-situated hectares. Second label: La Closerie de Malescasse. Supple wines, accessible early.

Malescot-St-Exupéry Mar r ★★★ 89 90' **94 95 96 98 99 00' 01** 02 03 04 05' Third Growth of 24 ha returned to fine form in the 1990s. Now ripe, fragrant, and finely structured. Michel ROLLAND consults.

de Malle Saut w r sw dr ★★★ (w sw) **88 89'** 90' **94 95 96' 97' 98 99 01' 02** 03' 05 Beautiful Preignac CHÂTEAU of 50 ha. V.fine, medium-bodied SAUTERNES; also M de Malle dry white and GRAVES CHÂTEAU du Cardaillan.

Marbuzet St-Est r ★★ 89 90 94 **95' 96' 98 99** 00' **01 02** 03 04 05' Second label of COS-D'ESTOURNEL until 94. Same owners. Now a separate CRU BOURGEOIS of 7 ha.

Margaux, Château Mar r (w) ★★★★ 82' 83' 85' 86' 88' 89' 90' 91 93 94 **95' 96' 97 98' 99** 00' 01' 02 03' 04' 05' First Growth (85 ha); the most seductive and fabulously perfumed of all in its frequent top vintages. PAVILLON ROUGE (95 96' **98 99 00' 01** 02 03 04' 05') is second wine. Pavillon Blanc is best white (Sauv Bl) of MÉDOC, but expensive (**98 99 00' 01' 02 03 04' 05**).

Marojallia Mar r ★★★ **00' 01 02** 03 04 05' Micro-CHÂTEAU with 2 ha, looking for big prices for big, beefy, un-MARGAUX-like wines. Second wine: Clos Margalaine.

Marquis-d'Alesme-Becker Mar r ★★ **89 90 95 98 00** 01 04 05 17-ha Third Growth. Disappointing in recent years. Purchased by CHÂTEAU LABEGORCE in 2006 so keep an eye out for change.

Marquis-de-Terme Mar r ★★ ·★★★ 89' 90' **95 96 98 99 00' 01 02** 03 04 05' Renovated Fourth Growth of 40 ha. Wobbled in the 1990s but looks better since 2000. Solid rather than elegant MARGAUX.

Martinens Mar r ★★ **96 98 99 00 02 03** 04 05 Worthy 30-ha CRU BOURGEOIS in Cantenac.

Maucaillou Moulis r ★★ **96** 98' 00' **01 02 03** 04 05 An 80-ha CRU BOURGEOIS SUPÉRIEUR with good standards. Cap de Haut-Maucaillou is second wine.

Mazeyres Pom r ★★ **95 96' 98' 99** 00 01 04 05' Consistent, if not exciting lesser POMEROL. 20 ha. Better since 1996. Alain Moueix, cousin of Christian of J-P MOUEIX, manages here. See FONROQUE.

Meyney St-Est r ★★ ·★★★ 89' 90' **94 95 96 98 00 01 02** 03 04 05' Big (50-ha) riverside property in a superb situation. CRU BOURGEOIS SUPÉRIEUR; one of best in ST-ESTÈPHE. Rich, robust, well-structured wines. Second label: Prieur de Meyney.

La Mission-Haut-Brion Pe-Lé r ★★★★ 82' 83 85' 86 88 89' 90' 93 94 95 96' 97 98'

Classification chaos !
The 2003 reclassification of the Crus Bourgeois of the Médoc, having been challenged in court by some 70 châteaux that failed to make the grade (247 got in; 243 were rejected), has now been abandoned. That leaves us with the previous classification, which nobody thought was any good any more. And then the lawyer who had acted for the refusés took on the same cause in St-Emilion.

99 00' **01** 02 03 04' 05' Neighbour and long-time rival to HAUT-BRION; since 1983 in same hands. Consistently grand-scale, full-blooded, long-maturing wine; even bigger than Haut-Brion and sometimes more impressive. 20 ha. Second label: La Chapelle de la Mission. White: LAVILLE-HAUT-BRION.

Monbousquet St-Em r (w) ★★★ **95 96** 97 **98 99 00' 01 02** 03 04 05' Substantial property on gravel revolutionized by new owner. Now super-rich, concentrated, and voluptuous wines. Elevated to GRAND CRU CLASSE in 2006. Rare white (AC BORDEAUX) from 1998. New owners also acquired PAVIE and PAVIE-DECESSE in 1998.

Monbrison Arsac-Mar r ★★→★★★ 86 88' 89' 90 95 96' 98 99 00 01 02 04 05 MARGAUX's most modish CRU BOURGEOIS SUPÉRIEUR. Elegant style. 13 ha.

La Mondotte St-Em r ★★★→★★★★ 96' 97 98' **99 00' 01** 02 03 04' 05' Intense, always fine *garagiste* wines from micro-property owned by Comte Stephen von Neipperg (CANON-LA GAFFELIÈRE, CLOS DE L'ORATOIRE).

Montrose St-Est r ★★★→★★★★ 86' 88 89' 90' 93 94 95 96' 97 **98 99** 00' 01 02 03'04' 05' 64-ha Second Growth famed for deep-coloured, forceful claret. Known as the LATOUR of ST-ESTÈPHE. Vintages 79–85 (except 82) were lighter. After 110 years in same family hands, change of ownership in 2006. Second wine: La Dame de Montrose.

Moulin-à-Vent Moulis r ★★ **95** 96' **98** 00' **02** 03 04 05' A 25-ha CRU BOURGEOIS SUPÉRIEUR; usually regular quality. Lively, forceful wine.

Moulin de la Rose St-Jul r ★★ **95 96** 98 00' **01' 02** 03 04 05 Tiny 4-ha CRU BOURGEOIS SUPÉRIEUR; high standards.

Moulin du Cadet St-Em r p ★★ 95 96 98 **00 01 03** 05 Little 5-ha GRAND CRU CLASSÉ vineyard on the limestone plateau, now managed by Alain Moueix (see also MAZEYRES). Fragrant, medium-bodied wines.

Moulinet Pom r ★★ **95** 96 98 **00** 01 04 05 One of POMEROL's bigger CHÂTEAUX; 18 ha on lightish soil. Denis Durantou of L'ÉGLISE-CLINET consults.

Moulin Pey-Labrie Canon-Fronsac r ★★ 89 90 94 95 96 98' **99** 00' **01 02 03** 04 05' Leading property in FRONSAC. Stylish wines with elegance and structure.

Moulin-St-Georges St-Em r ★★ 95 96 98 99 00' **01 02** 03 04 05 Stylish and rich wine. Classed growth level. Same ownership as AUSONE.

Mouton Baronne Philippe See D'ARMAILHAC. Lightish wines but recent improvements. To watch.

Mouton Rothschild Pau r (w) ★★★★ 75' 76 **78** 82' 83' 85' 86' 88' 89' 90' 93' 94 **95' 96** 97 **98' 99** 00' 01' 02 03 04' 05' Officially a First Growth since 73, though in reality far longer. 71 ha (87% Cab Sauv) can make majestic, rich wine, often MÉDOC's most opulent (also, from 91, white Aile d'Argent). Artists' labels and excellent private museum of art relating to wine. Second wine: Le Petit Mouton from 97. See also Opus One (California) and Almaviva (Chile).

Nairac Saut w sw ★★ 85 86' 88 89 90' 95' 96 97' 98 99 01' 02 03' 04 05' Perfectionist BARSAC classed growth. Rich, intense, botrytized wines from 16-ha. Should age.

Nenin Pom r ★★★ 89 90 94' 95 96 98 **99** 00' 01 02 03 04 05 LÉOVILLE-LAS-CASES ownership since 97. Massive investment. New cellars. 4 ha of former Certan-Giraud acquired in 99. Now a total of 34 ha. On an upward swing. Good-value second wine: Fugue de Nenin.

Olivier Graves r w ★★★ (r) 95 96 98 00 01 02 03 04' 05' (w) 96 97 98' 00 01 02 03 04' 05' A 55-ha classed growth, surrounding a moated castle at LÉOGNAN. A sleeper finally being turned around. Greater purity, expression, and quality from 2002 onwards.

Les Ormes-de-Pez St-Est r ★★ →★★★ 89' 90' 94 95 96 98 99 00' 01 02 03 04 05 Outstanding 29-ha CRU BOURGEOIS EXCEPTIONNEL owned by LYNCH-BAGES. Consistently one of the most delicious ST-ESTÈPHES.

Les Ormes-Sorbet Méd r ★★ **95 96** 98' **99** 00' **01 02** 03' 04 05 Long-time leader in northern MÉDOC. Now 21-ha CRU BOURGEOIS SUPÉRIEUR. Elegant, gently oaked wines that age. Second label: Château de Conques.

Palmer Cantenac-Mar r ★★★★ 75' 76 78' 79' 81 82 83' 85 86' 88' 89 90 93 94 95 96' 98' 99 00 01' 02 03 04' 05' The star of Cantenac: a Third Growth on a par with the Super Seconds. Wine of power, flesh, delicacy, and much Merlot. 52 ha with Dutch, British (the SICHEL family), and French owners. Second wine: **Alter Ego de Palmer (a steal for early drinking)**.

Pape-Clément Pe-Lé r (w) ★★★ ·★★★★ (r) 90' 94 95 96 97 98' 99 00' 01' 02 03 04 05 (w) 01 02 03 04 05' Ancient PESSAC vineyard; record of seductive, scented, not ponderous reds from mid-1890s. 2.5 ha of elegant, barrel-fermented white. Ambitious new-wave direction and more concentration from 2000. Also CHÂTEAU Poumey at Gradignan.

de Parenchère r (w) ★★ 00 01 02 03 04 05 Steady supply of useful AC Ste-Foy BORDEAUX and AC BORDEAUX SUPÉRIEUR from handsome ch with 65 ha. CUVÉE Raphael best.

Patache d'Aux Bégadan, Méd r ★★ 98 99 00 02 03 04 05' A 43-ha CRU BOURGEOIS SUPÉRIEUR of the northern MÉDOC. Fragrant, largely Cab Sauv wine with the earthy quality of its area. See also LIVERSAN.

Pavie St-Em r ★★★ 90' 94 95 96 98' 99 00' 01 02 03' 04 05' Splendidly sited First Growth; 37 ha mid-slope on the CÔTES. Great track record. Bought by owners of MONBOUSQUET, along with adjacent PAVIE-DECESSE. This is new-wave ST-EMILION: thick, intense, sweet, mid-Atlantic, and the subject of heated debate.

Pavie-Decesse St-Em r ★★ 89 90 95 96 98' 99 00' 01' 02 03 04 05' Small 3.6-ha classed growth. Brother to the above and on form since 1998.

Pavie-Macquin St-Em r ★★★ 89' 90' 94 95 96' 98' 99 00' 01 02 03 04 05' Surprise elevation to premier grand cru classe in 2006. 15-ha vineyard on the limestone plateau east of ST-EMILION. Astute management and winemaking by Nicolas Thienpont of PUYGUERAUD and consultant Stéphane Derenoncourt. Powerful, structured wines that need time in bottle.

Pedesclaux Pau r ★★ 95' 96 98' 99 00 02 03 04 05 Fifth Growth on the level of CRU BOURGEOIS. Most goes to Belgium. Second wine: Château Haut-Padarnac.

Petit-Village Pom r ★★★ 90' 94 95 96 98' 99 00' 01 03 04 05 Top property revived. 11 ha; same owner (AXA Insurance) as PICHON-LONGUEVILLE since 1989. Powerful, plummy wine. Second wine: Le Jardin de Petit-Village.

Pétrus Pom r ★★★★ 70' 71' 75' 76 78 79' 81 82' 83 85' 86 88' 89' 90 93' 94 95' 96 97 98' 99 00' 01 02 03 04' 05' The (unofficial) First Growth of POMEROL: Merlot solo in excelsis. 11 ha of gravelly clay giving 5,000 cases of massively rich and concentrated wine, on allocation to the world's millionaires. Each vintage adds lustre.

Peyrabon St-Sauveur, H-Méd r ★★ 98 99 00' 01 02 03 04 05 Serious 53-ha CRU BOURGEOIS owned by Bordeaux négociant. Also La Fleur-Peyrabon in PAUILLAC.

de Pez St-Est r ★★ ·★★★ 89 90' 94 95' 96' 98' 99 00 01 02 03 04 05' Outstanding CRU BOURGEOIS EXCEPTIONNEL of 24 ha. As reliable as any of the village's classed growths, if not quite so fine. Bought in 95 by ROEDERER.

Phélan-Ségur St-Est r ★★ ·★★★ 88' 89' 90' 95 96' 98 99 00' 01 02 03 04 05' Big and important CRU BOURGEOIS EXCEPTIONNEL (89 ha); rivals the last as one of ST-ESTÈPHE's best. From 1986 has built up a strong reputation.

Pibran Pau r ★★ 88 89' 90' 94 95 96 98 99 00' 01 03 04 05' Small CRU BOURGEOIS SUPÉRIEUR allied to PICHON-LONGUEVILLE. Classy wine with PAUILLAC drive.

Pichon-Longueville (formerly Baron de Pichon-Longueville) Pau r ★★★★ 82' 83 85 86' 88' 89' 90' 93 94' 95 96 97 98 99 00' 01 02 03' 04' 05' Second Growth (70 ha) with revitalized powerful PAUILLAC wine on a par with the following entry. Owners AXA Insurance. Second label: Les Tourelles de Longueville.

Pichon-Longueville Comtesse de Lalande (Pichon Lalande) Pau r ★★★★ 75' 76 78'

79' 81 82' 83 85' **86' 88'** 89' 90' 94 95 96 97 98 **99** 00 **01** 02 03' 04 05' Super-second-growth neighbour to LATOUR (75 ha). Always among the very top performers; a long-lived, Merlot-marked wine of fabulous breed, in lesser years. ROEDERER now a partner; same management. Second wine: Réserve de la Comtesse. Other property: CHÂTEAU BERNADOTTE.

Le Pin Pom r ★★★★ 82 83 85 **86** 88 89 90' 94 **95 96** 97 **98' 99** 00 **01** 02 04' 05' The original of the BORDEAUX cult mini-*crus*. A mere 500 cases of Merlot, with same family behind it as VIEUX-CHÂTEAU-CERTAN (a much better buy). Almost as rich as its drinkers, but prices well beyond PÉTRUS are ridiculous.

de Pitray Castillon r ★★ **95 96' 98'** 00' 03 04 05 Large (31-ha) vineyard on CÔTES DE CASTILLON. Flavoursome wines, once the best-known of the AC.

Plince Pom r ★★ **88 89' 90 94** 95 96 **98'** 99 00' 04 05 Reliable 8-ha property near Libourne. Lightish wine from sandy soil.

La Pointe Pom r ★★ →★★★ 89' 90' 95 96 98' 99 00' 01 04 05' Prominent 25-ha estate; wines recently plumper and more pleasing. LA SERRE is in the same hands.

Pontac-Monplaisir Pe-Lé r (w) ★★ 96 98 99 00 02 04 05' 16-ha property nearly lost to Bordeaux urbanization. Useful white and fragrant red of surprising quality.

Pontet-Canet Pau r ★★★ **86' 88 89'** 90' 94' 95 96' 97 **98 99** 00' 01 02' 03 04' 05' An 81-ha neighbour to MOUTON-ROTHSCHILD. Dragged its feet for many years. Old hard tannins were a turn-off. Since mid-90s very fine results. Very PAUILLAC in style. Second wine: Les Hauts de Pontet-Canet.

Potensac Méd r ★★ 89' 90' 94 95 96 **98 99** 00' 01 02 03 04' 05' Well-known CRU BOURGEOIS EXCEPTIONNEL of northern MEDOC. Owned and run by Delon family of LÉOVILLE-LAS-CASES. Class shows, in the form of rich, silky, balanced wines.

Pouget Mar r ★★ 89 90 **94** 95 96 98' 00' 02 03 04 05' An 11-ha Fourth Growth attached to BOYD-CANTENAC. MARGAUX style. New CHAI in 2000.

Poujeaux (Theil) Moulis r ★★ 89' 90' 94' 95' 96' **98 99** 00' 01 02 03 04 05 Family-run CRU BOURGEOIS EXCEPTIONNEL of 52 ha, with CHASSE-SPLEEN and Maucaillou the high-point of Moulis. 20,000-odd cases of characterful tannic and concentrated wine for a long life, year after year. Second label: La Salle de Poujeaux. Also CHÂTEAU Arnauld.

Premier Grand Cru Classé See St-Emilion classification box, p.101.

Prieuré-Lichine Cantenac-Mar r ★★★ 89' 90' 94' 95 **96** 98' **99** 00' 01 02 03 04 05 A 70-ha Fourth Growth brought to the fore by the late Alexis Lichine. New owners 1999; now advised by Stéphane Derenoncourt (see CANON LA GAFFELIÈRE, PAVIE-MACQUIN). Fragrant MARGAUX currently on good form. Second wine: CHÂTEAU de Clairefont. A good white Bordeaux, too.

Puygueraud Côtes de Francs r ★★ **95' 96** 98 99 00' 01' 02 03 04 05' Leading CHÂTEAU of this tiny AC. Wood-aged wines of surprising class. CHÂTEAUX Laclaverie and Les Charmes-Godard follow the same lines. Special CUVÉE George from 2000 with Malbec in blend. Same winemaker as PAVIE-MACQUIN.

Rabaud-Promis Saut w sw ★★→★★★★ **88'** 89' 90 95 **96** 97' **98 99** 01' 02 03' 05' A 30-ha classed growth at Bommes. Near top rank since 86. Rich stuff.

Rahoul Graves r w ★★ (r) 95 96 98' 00' 01 02 04 05 This 30-ha vineyard at Portets is still a sleeper despite long record of good red (60%) and white (96 97 98 99 00 01 02 04' 05).

Ramage-la-Bâtisse H-Méd r ★★ 95 96' 98 99 00' 02 03 04 05' Consistent and widely distributed CRU BOURGEOIS SUPÉRIEUR; 65 ha at St-Sauveur, N of PAUILLAC. CHÂTEAU Tourteran is second wine.

Rauzan-Gassies Mar r ★★ 90' 95 96' **98 99** 00 01' 02 03 04 05' The 30-ha Second Growth neighbour of RAUZAN-SÉGLA that has long lagged behind it. New generation making evident strides since 2000 but still has a long way to go.

Rauzan-Ségla Mar r ★★★★ 85 **86' 88'** 89' 90' 94' 95 96 97 **98 99** 00' 01 02 03 04' 05 A Second Growth (51 ha) famous for its fragrance; owned by owners of

Chanel (see CANON). A great MÉDOC name right at the top, with rebuilt CHÂTEAU and CHAIS. Second wine: Ségla.

Raymond-Lafon Saut w sw ★★★ 83' 85 86' 88 89' 90' 95 96' 97 98 99' 01' 02 03' 04 05 Serious little SAUTERNES estate (18 ha) acquired by YQUEM ex-manager and now run by his children. Rich, complex wines that age. Classed-growth quality.

Rayne Vigneau Saut w sw ★★★ 86' 88' 89 90' 95 96 97 98 99 01' 02 03 05'Large 80-ha classed growth at Bommes. Good but less power and intensity than the top growths. Sweet wine and dry Rayne SEC.

Respide Médeville Graves r w ★★ (r) 99 00' 01 02 03 04 05' (w) 96' 99 00 01 02 04' 05' One of the better unclassified properties for both red and white. Drink the reds at 4–6 years; longer for the better vintages.

Reynon Premières Côtes r w ★★ 40 ha for fragrant white from Sauv Bl 00 01' 02 03 04' 05'; also serious red (98 99 00 01 02 03 04' 05'). Second wine (red): CHÂTEAU Reynon-Peyrat. From 1996 v. good CHÂTEAU Reynon Cadillac liquoreux, too. See also CLOS FLORIDÈNE.

Reysson Vertheuil, H-Méd r ★★ 95 96 00 02 03 04 05 Recently replanted 49-ha CRU BOURGEOIS SUPÉRIEUR; managed by négociant CVBG-Dourthe (see BELGRAVE, LA GARDE). Rich, modern style.

Ricaud Loupiac w sw (r dr) ★★ 95 96 97 99 01' 02 03' 05 Substantial grower of SAUTERNES-like ageworthy wine just across the river.

Rieussec Saut w sw ★★★★ 82 83' 85 86' 88' 89' 90' 95 96' 97' 98 99 01' 02 03' 04 05' Worthy neighbour of YQUEM with 90 ha in Fargues, bought in 1984 by the (LAFITE) Rothschilds. Vinified in oak since 96. Fabulously opulent wine. Also dry "R", now made in new, modern style – with less character? Second wine: Carmes de Rieussec.

Ripeau St-Em r ★★ 95 98 00' 01 04 05' Lesser 16-ha GRAND CRU CLASSÉ on sandy soils near CHEVAL BLANC. Lower yields and some improvement from 2000.

de la Rivière Fronsac r ★★ 89 90 94 95 96' 98' 99 00' 01 02 03 04 05' The biggest and most impressive FRONSAC property, with a Wagnerian castle and cellars. Formerly big, tannic wines have become more refined. New winery in 1999. Michel ROLLAND consults. Special CUVÉE: Aria.

de Rochemorin Pe-Lé r w ★★-★★★ (r) 95 96 98' 99 00' 01 02 03 04 05 (w) 00 01 02 03 04 05 An important restoration at Martillac by the Lurtons of La LOUVIÈRE: 105 ha (three-quarters red) of maturing vines. New state-of-the-art winery in 2004. Fairly consistent quality and widely distributed.

Rol Valentin St-Em r ★★★ 95 96 97 98 99 00' 01 02 03 04 05' New (1994) 7.5-ha estate going for modestly massive style (and price). Owned by former footballer. 1,900 cases. Stéphane Derenoncourt consults (see CANON LA GAFFELIÈRE, PAVE-MACQUIN).

Rouget Pom r ★★ 89' 90 95 96 98' 99 00' 01' 03 04 05' Attractive old estate on the northern edge of POMEROL. 17 ha. New owners in 1992 and plenty of investment since (new cellars). Now excellent; rich, unctuous wines.

Royal St-Emilion Brand name of important, dynamic growers' co-op. See GALIUS.

St-André-Corbin St-Em r ★★ 98' 99 00' 01 03 04 05 A 22-ha estate in MONTAGNE- and

---

Classification chaos II

The latest of the ten-yearly reclassifications here was in 2006. Eleven châteaux were dropped from the previous classification, leaving a total of 61 properties, the smallest number ever. However, legal action has meant that at the time of writing the classification has been suspended for a year: St-Emilion currently has no official classification. Except here, since this book thinks the 06 classification the best guide to performance.

ST-GEORGES-ST-EMILION. Above-average wines.

St-Georges St-Georges-St-Em r ★★ 89' 90' 95' 96 98' 00' 01 03 04 05' Noble 18th-C CHÂTEAU overlooking the ST-EMILION plateau from the hill to the north. 51 ha (25% of St-Georges AC). Good wine sold direct to the public.

St-Pierre St-Jul r ★★★ 82' 85 88 90' 94 95' 96' 98 99 00' 01' 02 03 04 05' Fourth Growth (17 ha). Stylish and consistent classic ST-JULIEN. See GLORIA.

de Sales Pom r ★★ 89' 90' 95 96 98' 00' 01' 04 05 Biggest vineyard of POMEROL (47 ha) on sandy-gravel soils, attached to grandest CHÂTEAU. Never poetry, lighter weight: try top vintages. Second label: CHÂTEAU Chantalouette.

Sansonnet St-Em r ★★ 99 00' 01 02 03 04 05' A small 6.8-ha estate ambitiously run in the new ST-EMILION style (rich, fat) since 1999.

Saransot-Dupré Listrac r (w) ★★ 89 90 95 96 98' 99 00' 01 02 03 04 05 Small 12-ha property with delicious, appetizing wines. Lots of Merlot. Also one of LISTRAC's little band of whites.

Sénéjac H-Méd r (w) ★★ 89' 90' 94 95 96 98 99 00 01 02 03 04 05' A 37-ha CRU BOURGEOIS SUPÉRIEUR in southern MÉDOC recently (1999) bought by the same family as TALBOT. Serious reds to age and unusual all-Sémillon white, also to age Special CUVÉE: Karolus.

La Serre St-Em r ★★ 89 90 94 95 96 98' 99 00' 01 02 03 04 05 Small (6.5-ha) GRAND CRU CLASSÉ, same owner as LA POINTE. Pleasant stylish wines; more flesh and purity of fruit since 2000.

Sigalas-Rabaud Saut w SW ★★★ 83 85 86 88 89' 90' 95' 96' 97' 98 99 01' 02 03' 04 05' The smaller part of the former RABAUD estate: 14 ha in Bommes; same winemaking team as LAFAURIE-PEYRAGUEY. Very fragrant and lovely. Top-ranking now. Second wine: Le Cadet de Sigalas Rabaud.

Siran Labarde-Mar r ★★→★★★ 86 88 89' 90' 95 96 98 99 00' 01 02 03 04 05 A 40-ha property of passionate owner who resents lack of CLASSÉ rank. Given CRU BOURGEOIS EXCEPTIONNEL status in 2003, and deserves it. The wines age well and have masses of flavour: an ambitious property. Michel ROLLAND consults.

Smith-Haut-Lafitte Pe-Lé r (w p) ★★★ (r) 89' 90' 94 95 96 98 99 00 01 02 03 04' 05' (w) 95 96 97 98 99' 00 01 02 03 04 05 Classed growth at Martillac: 56 ha (11 ha make oak-fermented white). Ambitious owners (since 1990) continue to spend hugely to spectacular effect, including a luxurious wine therapy (external!) spa and hotel-restaurant. Second label: Les Hauts de Smith. Also look out for their CHÂTEAU Cantelys, PESSAC-LÉOGNAN.

Sociando-Mallet H-Méd r ★★★ 88' 89' 90' 94 95 96' 97 98' 99 00' 01' 02 03 05' Splendid, widely followed estate at St-Seurin. Classed-growth quality; 75 ha. Conservative big-boned wines to lay down for years. Second wine: Demoiselles de Sociando.

Soudars H-Méd r ★★ 90 94 95 96' 98 99 00' 01 03 04 05 Sister to COUFRAN and VERDIGNAN; recent CRU BOURGEOIS SUPÉRIEUR doing pretty well.

Soutard St-Em r ★★★ 88' 89' 90' 94 95 96 98' 00' 01 02 03 04 05 Potentially excellent 19-ha classed growth on the limestone plateau; 70% Merlot. Potent wines can be long-lived. Now owned by an insurance group (2006). Possible changes. To watch. Second label: CLOS de la Tonnelle.

Suduiraut Saut w SW ★★★★ 79' 81 82' 83 85 86 88' 89' 90' 95 96 97' 98 99' 01' 02 03' 04 05' One of the best classed-growth SAUTERNES: 90 ha with renovated CHÂTEAU and gardens by Le Nôtre. New owner, AXA Insurance, has achieved greater consistency and luscious quality. See PICHON-LONGUEVILLE. Second wine: Castelnau de Suduiraut. New dry wine, S, very promising.

du Tailhas Pom r ★★ 89 90 94 95 96' 98' 99 00 01 04 05 10-ha property, near FIGEAC. POMEROL of the lighter kind.

Taillefer Pom r ★★ 89 90 94 95' 96 98' 00' 01 02 03 04 05' An 11-ha vineyard on the edge of POMEROL. Astutely managed by Catherine Moueix. Less power than top estates but gently harmonious. Good value.

Talbot St-Jul r (w) ✶✶ 86' 88' 89' 90 94 95 96' 98' 99 00' 01 02 03 04 05' Important 102-ha Fourth Growth, for many years younger sister to GRUAUD-LAROSE. Wine similarly attractive: rich, consummately charming, reliable. Second label: Connétable de Talbot. White: Caillou Blanc matures as well as a good GRAVES, but drinks well young. SENEJAC same family ownership. Oenologist also oversees TOUR DE MONS.

Terrey-Gros-Caillou St-Jul r ✶✶ 89 90 94 95 96 98 99 00 02 03 04 05 Sister CHÂTEAU to HORTEVIE; 15 ha; at best, equally noteworthy and stylish.

du Tertre Arsac-Mar r ✶✶✶ 88' 89' 90' 94 95 96' 98' 99 00' 01 02 03 04' 05' Fifth Growth (50 ha) isolated south of MARGAUX. History of undervalued fragrant and fruity wines. Since 97, same owner as CHÂTEAU GISCOURS. New techniques and investment have produced a really concentrated, structured wine.

Tertre Daugay St-Em r ✶✶✶ 88' 89' 90' 94 95 96 98 99 00' 01 03 04 05 Small, spectacularly sited estate. Declassified from GRAND CRU CLASSÉ in 2006. Owner, same as La GAFFELIÈRE, may resort to legal action.

Tertre-Rôteboeuf St-Em r ✶✶✶✶ 85 86 88' 89' 90' 93 94 95 96 97 98' 99 00' 01 02 03' 04 05' A cult star making concentrated, even dramatic, largely Merlot wine since 1983. The prices are frightening. The "roast beef" of the name gives the right idea. Also CÔTES DE BOURG property, Roc de Cambes.

Thieuley E-D-M r p w ✶✶ Supplier of consistent quality red and white AC Bordeaux; fruity CLAIRET; oak-aged red and white CUVÉE Francis Courselle. Also owns CLOS Ste-Anne in PREMIÈRES CÔTES DE BORDEAUX.

La Tour-Blanche Saut w (r) sw ✶✶✶ 83' 85 86 88' 89' 90' 95 96 97' 98 99 01' 02 03 04 05' Historic leader of SAUTERNES, now a government wine college. Coasted in 1970s; since 1988 a top player again.

La Tour-Carnet St-Laurent, H-Méd r ✶✶ 82 85 86 89' 90 94' 95 96 98 99 00' 01 02 03 04' 05' Fourth Growth (65 ha) with medieval moated fortress, long neglected. New ownership (see FOMBRAUGE, PAPE-CLÉMENT) and investment from 2000 have produced richer wines in a more modern style. Second wine: Les Douvres de Château La Tour Carnet.

La Tour-de-By Bégadan, Méd r ✶✶ 89' 90' 94 95 96' 98 00 01 02 03 04 05' Very well-run 74-ha CRU BOURGEOIS SUPÉRIEUR in northern MÉDOC with a name for the most attractive, sturdy wines of the area.

La Tour de Mons Soussans-Mar r ✶✶ 88 89 90' 94 95 96' 98' 99 00 01 02 04 05' Famous CRU BOURGEOIS SUPÉRIEUR of 44 ha, in the same family for three centuries. A long, dull patch but new (1995) TALBOT influence is returning to the old fragrant, vigorous, ageworthy style.

Tour-du-Haut-Moulin Cussac, H-Méd r ✶✶ 86' 88' 89' 90' 94 95 96 98 00' 02 03 04 05' Conservative grower: intense CRU BOURGEOIS SUPÉRIEUR to mature.

Tour-du-Pas-St-Georges St-Em r ✶✶ 95 96 98 99 00' 01 03 04 05 Wine from 16 ha of ST-GEORGES-ST-EMILION made by BELAIR owner.

La Tour du Pin Figeac-Moueix St-Em r ✶✶ 88' 89' 90' 95 96 98 00' 01 04 05 8-ha, formerly part of the FIGEAC estate, now owned by Jean-Michel Moueix. Unimpressive form resulted in demotion from GRAND CRU CLASSÉ in 2006.

La Tour Figeac St-Em r ✶✶ 88 89' 90' 94' 95 96' 98' 99 00' 01' 02 04 05 A 15-ha GRAND CRU CLASSÉ between FIGEAC and POMEROL. California-style ideas since 1994. Biodynamic methods. Keep an eye on this one.

La Tour Haut Brion Graves r ✶✶✶ 89 90 94 95 96' 98' 99 00' 01 02 03 04' 05' Formerly second label of LA MISSION-HAUT-BRION. Up to 1983, a plainer, very tannic wine. Now a separate 4.8-ha vineyard: wines stylish, to keep.

Tour Haut-Caussan Méd r ✶✶ 96 98 00' 01 02 03 04 05' Well-run 16-ha CRU BOURGEOIS SUPÉRIEUR at Blaignan to watch for full, firm wines.

Tournefeuille Lalande de Pom r ✶✶ 95' 98' 99 00' 01' 02 03 04 05 Well-known

Néac CHÂTEAU. 17 ha. On the up-swing since 1998 with new owners.

Tour-St-Bonnet Méd r ★★ 95 96 98 99 00' 02 03 04 (05) Consistently well-made potent northern MÉDOC from St-Christoly. CRU BOURGEOIS; 40 ha.

Tronquoy-Lalande St-Est r ★★ 89 90' 94 95 96 98 99 00' 02 03 04 05 A 16-ha CRU BOURGEOIS SUPÉRIEUR: high-coloured wines to age, but no thrills.

Troplong-Mondot St-Em r ★★★ 88' 89' 90' 94' 95 96' 98' 99 00' 01' 02 03 04 05' Recently promoted PREMIER GRAND CRU CLASSE (2006). Well-sited 30 ha on a high point of the limestone plateau. Wines of power and depth with increasing elegance. Michel ROLLAND consults. Second wine: Mondot.

Trotanoy Pom r ★★★★ 82' 85' 88 89' 90' 93 94 95 96 97 98' 99 00' 01 02 03 04' 05' Potentially the second POMEROL, after PÉTRUS, from the same stable. Only 7 ha: at best (e.g. **98**) a glorious fleshy, structured, perfumed wine. Wobbled a bit in the 1980s, but back on top form since 89.

Trottevieille St-Em r ★★★ 89' 90 94 95 96 98 99 00' 01 02 03' 04 05' First Growth on the limestone plateau. Dragged its feet for years. Same owners as BATAILLEY have raised its game since 2000. Denis Dubourdieu (see REYNON) consults.

Valandraud St-Em r ★★★★ 93 94 95' 96 97 98 99 00' 01' 02 03 04 05' Leader among *garagiste* micro-wines fulfilling aspirations to glory. But silly prices for the sort of thick, vanilla-scented wine California can make. Vineyards now expanded to 20 ha; better terroir and more balance. Second and third wines: Virginie and Axelle.

Valrose St-Est r ★★ 02 03 04 05' A newcomer since 1999, co-owned with CLINET. Special CUVÉE: Aliénor. To watch.

Verdignan Méd r ★★ 95' 96 98 99 00' 01 02 03 04 05 Substantial 60-ha CRU BOURGEOIS SUPÉRIEUR sister to COUFRAN and SOUDARS. More Cab Sauv than Coufran. Good value and ageing potential.

La Vieille Cure Fronsac r ★★ 95 96 98 99 00' 01' 02 03 04 05 A 20-ha property, US-owned, leading the commune. Accessible from 4 years.

Vieux-Château-Certan Pom r ★★★★ 82' 83' 85 86' 88' 89 90' 94 95' 96' 97 98' 99 00' 01 02 04' 05' Traditionally rated close to PÉTRUS in quality, but totally different in style; almost HAUT-BRION build with plenty of finesse. 14 ha. Same (Belgian) family owns tiny LE PIN.

Vieux Château St-André St-Em r ★★ 00' 01 02 03 04 05 Small 6-ha vineyard in MONTAGNE-ST-EMILION owned by winemaker of PÉTRUS. Regular quality.

Villegeorge Avensan, H-Méd r ★★ 89 90 94 95 96' 98' 99 00' 02 03 04 05 A 15-ha CRU BOURGEOIS SUPÉRIEUR north of MARGAUX. Fine, traditional MÉDOC style. Sister CHÂTEAUx Duplessis in MOULIS and La Tour de Bessan in MARGAUX.

Villemaurine St-Em r ★★ 95 96 98 99 00' 03 04 05 Small 8-ha estate with splendid cellars well sited on the limestone plateau by the town. Has not lived up to potential; declassified from GRAND CRU CLASSE in 2006.

Vray Croix de Gay Pom r ★★ 88 89 90 95 96 98' 00' 04 05 Very small (4 ha) but ideally situated vineyard in the best part of POMEROL. Greater efforts from 2004. Sister to Château Siaurac in LALANDE DE POMEROL.

Yon-Figeac St-Em r ★★ 90 95 96 98 99 00' 02 03 04 05 24-ha estate. Vineyard restructured between 1985 and 1995. Improvements from 2000 but too late to prevent declassification from GRAND CRU CLASSE in 2006.

d'Yquem Saut w sw (dr) ★★★★ 75' 76' 79 80' 81' 83' 85 86' 88' 89' 90' 93 94 95' 96 97' 98 99' 00 01' 02 03' 04 05' This is the world's most famous sweet wine estate. 101 ha; only 200 bottles per hectare of very strong, intense, luscious wine, kept 4 years in barrel. Most vintages improve for 15+ years; some live 100+ years in transcendent splendour. After centuries in the Lur-Saluces family, in 1998 control was surrendered to Bernard Arnault of LVMH. The new management is doing well, however, and prices are going sky-high. Also makes dry "Y" (YGREC).

Italy

More heavily shaded areas
are the wine-growing regions

The following abbreviations
are used in the text:

Ab	Abruzzi	Sar	Sardinia
Ap	Apulia	Si	Sicily
Bas	Basilicata	T-AA	Trentino-
Cal	Calabria		Alto Adige
Cam	Campania	Tus	Tuscany
E-R	Emilia-Romagna	Umb	Umbria
F-VG	Friuli-	VdA	Valle d'Aosta
	Venezia Giulia	Ven	Veneto
Lat	Latium		
Lig	Liguria		
Lom	Lombardy	cs	Cantine Sociale
Mar	Marches	fz	frizzante
Pie	Piedmont	pa	passito

VALLE
D'AOSTA

L Com

L Maggiore

Milan

LOMBAR

Turin

PIEDMONT

Genoa

Po

LIGURIA

Ligurian Sea

*C*lassico, or classic, is a term used in many of Italy's major appellations, and it indicates the area of greatest quality. To a certain extent, however, the most recent history of Italy's wines could well be described as a return to a classicism of approach, an attempt to underline the personality that first distinguished the wines, and which only needed a bit of updating.

Classic has been the return to Nebbiolo in Piedmont, the new emphasis on the variety on its own, rather than in blends with Barbera or with international grapes. Classic has been the new interest in Corvina in the Valpolicella and the new emphasis on Sangiovese in the historic areas of Romagna, Tuscany, and Umbria. The re-emergence of Montepulciano has followed the same pattern: once a wine with a certain dignity, then diluted by over-production, it is now showing a new importance in various parts of the Adriatic coast, not only the Abruzzo but also in the Rosso Conero and Rosso Piceno appellations of the Marches and in the north of Apulia as well.

But the most startling developments will soon be coming from even further south. After the quality revolution in Taurasi and the slopes of Mount Vulture, Aglianico is once again providing some of Italy's greatest wines in the centre of Italy's Mezzogiorno, where it is already being called the Nebbiolo of the south. And more is yet to come: extremely impressive wines from the Uva di Troia grapes in various parts of Apulia and equally convincing offerings form the slopes of Mount Etna in Sicily, from ancient bush vines planted on volcanic soil high above the Mediterranean, indicate just what Italy's future will be: in a phrase, its past, the grand tradition which led the ancient world to call the country Enotria, the land of the vine.

Recent Vintages

Tuscany

2006 Generally excellent, though heavy rains in the third week of September may have affected some of the Merlot and some early-ripening Cabernet near the coast.

2005 Much rain and generally irregular results, most successful in the southern part of the coast, less so in Bolgheri. Sangiovese at every quality level imaginable, from first-rate to diluted.

2004 Exceptionally promising along the coast, in Montepulciano, and in Montalcino. Less consistent in cooler parts of the region (Rufina and the higher vineyards of Chianti Classico).

2003 Considerable vine stress from searing heat and three months of drought. Success with late-ripening varieties; less so with Merlot.

2002 Cool Aug, frequent rains in Sept/Oct. Dilution and rot widespread.

2001 A scorching Aug, unusually cool in early Sept, then humid when warm weather returned. Some excellent wines, but much irregularity.

2000 Very hot, dry late summer/early autumn, one of earliest vintages in memory. Full, alcoholic wines, some impressive, some unbalanced.

Older fine vintages: 99 97 95 90

Piedmont

2006 Excellent Dolcetto, very fine Nebbiolo and Barbera; along with 2001 and 2004 the finest vintage of the new millennium.

2005 Pleasurable Dolcetto; spotty for Barbera, with some rot from persistent rains; Nebbiolo rather uneven, though promising wines are not lacking.

2004 Very long growing season, high level of quality for all major red grapes (Dolcetto, Barbera, Nebbiolo), the first since 1999.

2003 Sweltering summer, but nonetheless very positive for Barbera, Dolcetto, and Moscato. Nebbiolo more irregular, with late pickers more successful.

2002 Cool, damp growing season and serious hail damage in Barolo.

2001 Classy and firm Nebbiolo and Barbera, other grapes less successful.

2000 Excellent Barolo, Barbaresco, Barbera. Fifth sound vintage in a row.

Older fine vintages: 97 90 89

Amarone, Veneto

2006 Outstanding, with new record established for the grape tonnage reserved for drying, 30% higher than any previous vintage.

2005 A difficult harvest due to damp weather, but grape-drying technology saved Amarone and Recioto wines. Less successful vintage for Soave and whites.

2004 A damp Nov caused some concern, but a return of drier weather helped avoid rot. Classic, less concentrated and rich than 2003.

2003 The hottest and driest vintage of the post-war period. Very concentrated and sugar-rich grapes; can be outstanding.

2002 Heavy rains throughout the ripening season. A vintage to forget.

2001 Very balanced weather in the growing season. Promising and classic.

2000 Shaping up as a vintage of powerful wines.

Marches & Abruzzo reds

2006 Irregular. Generally positive where hail did not fall; better than 2004 and 2005, but not as good as 2003.

2005 A year of heavy rainfall, saved by a dry second half of October. Wines of good ripeness and structure for those who waited to pick.

2004 Considerable Oct rains; irregular results. Better in Rosso Conero than Rosso Piceno in the Marches; best in Colline Teramane DOCG, Abruzzo.

2003 One of the most successful areas in Italy in 2003, as the Montepulciano grape stood up to the heat and drought, giving first-rate results.

2002 Cool, damp year; only fair results.

2001 Ideal weather, fine balance of power and elegance in the wines, which are fragrant with much complexity and depth.

2000 Properly hot in late Aug and early Sept, a return of the heat after a cooler interval; ripe grapes of good balance; ample and classy wines.

Campania & Basilicata

2006 Rain and problems of rot in lower-lying zones, much sun and a very long growing season in higher vineyards, with predictably superior results.

2005 Traditionally the last grapes to be picked. Aglianico had weight, complexity, and character – perhaps the finest wines of all in 2005.

2004 Slow and uncertain ripening for Aglianico, and only a warm second half of Oct enabled growers to salvage the grapes. Medium-level and spotty.

2003 Scorching and drought-stressed growing conditions, but the altitude of the vineyards worked in Aglianico's favour. Generally a success.

2002 Heavy rains; part of the crop salvaged, but little to crow about.

2001 Hot, dry and very regular from July to the end of Oct; textbook weather. Intense, perfumed, and ageworthy wines.

2000 Hotter than 1999, a powerful impetus to the ripening of the grapes. Potent and alcoholic wines built to last.

Abboccato Semi-sweet.

Aglianico del Vulture Bas DOC r dr (s/sw sp) ★★★97' 98 99' 00' 01' 03' 04' 05' 06 VECCHIO after 3 years, RISERVA after 5 years. Top: Allegretti, Alovini, Basilium, Bisceglia, Francesco Bonifacio, Cantina del Notaio, Cantina di Venosa, Consiglio, Elena Fucci, Lelusi, Lucania, Macarico, Di Palma, PATERNOSTER, Le Querce, Torre degli Svevi, Sasso, and Viticoltori Associati del Vulture.

Alba Major wine city of PIEDMONT, on River Tanaro, southeast of Turin.

Albana di Romagna E-R DOCG w dr s/sw (sp) ★★→★★★ DYA Italy's first white DOCG, a decision that left many incredulous. Albana is the (undistinguished) grape. AMABILE is usually better than dry. ZERBINA and Giovanna Madonia's botrytis-sweet PASSITO outstanding. Tremonti very good.

Alcamo Si DOC w ★ Soft whites and reds. Rapitalà, Ceuso are best brands.

Aleatico Red Muscat-flavoured grape for sweet, aromatic, often fortified wines, chiefly in south Aleatico di Puglia DOC (best: Candido and Santa Lucia) is better and more famous than Aleatico di Gradoli (Latium) DOC, though watch for new effort from Occhipinti. Good Aleatico from Falesco, Massa Vecchia in Monteregio, Cecilia and Le Sughere on ELBA; very good from Jacopo Banti and Brancatelli in VAL DI CORNIA and Sapereta, Acquabona on ELBA.

Alessandria, Gianfranco ★★★ Small producer of high-level ALBA wines at Monteforte d'Alba, esp BAROLO San Giovanni, BARBERA D'ALBA Vittoria, DOLCETTO.

Alezio Ap DOC p (r) ★★ Salento DOC especially for full, flavourful reds and delicate rosés. The top growers are Giuseppe Calò with fine, barrel-aged NEGROAMARO Portulan and Michele Calò with NEGROAMARO IGT Spano.

Allegrini Ven ★★★ Top-quality Veronese producer; outstanding single-vineyard IGT wines (Palazzo della Torre, Grola, and Poja), AMARONE, and RECIOTO.

Altare, Elio Pie ★★★ Pioneering, influential small producer of very good modern BAROLO. Look for BAROLO Arborina, BAROLO Brunate, LANGHE DOC Arborina (Nebbiolo), Larigi (Barbera), La Villa, VDT L'Insieme and DOLCETTO D'ALBA – one of the appellation's best.

Alto Adige T-AA DOC r p w dr sw sp ★→★★★ Alto Adige or SÜDTIROL DOC including almost 50 types of wine: different grapes of different zones (including varietals of VALLE ISARCO/Eisacktal, TERLANO/Terlaner, Val Venosta/Vinschgau, AA STA MADDALENA, AA Bozner Leiten, AA MERANESE DI COLLINA/Meraner).

Ama, Castello di, (Fattoria di Ama) ★★★ One of the best and most consistent modern CHIANTI CLASSICO estates, near Gaiole. La Casuccia and Bellavista are top single-vineyard wines. Good IGTS, Chard, and MERLOT (L'Apparita).

Amabile Means semi-sweet, but usually sweeter than ABBOCCATO.

Amaro Bitter. When prominent on label, contents are not wine but "bitters".

Amarone della Valpolicella (formerly Recioto della Valpolicella Amarone) Ven DOC r ★★★ 88' 90' 93 94 95' 97' 98' 00' 01' 03' 04' 05' 06 Dry version of RECIOTO DELLA VALPOLICELLA: from air-dried VALPOLICELLA grapes; concentrated, long-lived. Best: Stefano Accordini, Aldigheri, Serego Alighieri, ALLEGRINI, Begali, BERTANI, BOLLA, BOSCAINI, BRUNELLI, Buglioni, BUSSOLA, Ca' La Bianca, Campagnola, Castellani, Cesari, Corteforte, Corte Sant Alda, CS Valpantena, CS VALPOLICELLA, DAL FORNO, Farina, Aleardo Ferrari, Guerrieri-Rizzardi, La Costa di Romagnano, LE RAGOSE, LE SALETTE, MASI, Mazzi, Nicolis, Novaia, PASQUA, QUINTARELLI, Roccolo Grassi, Sant'Antonio, Speri, TEDESCHI, Tommasi, Trabucchi, Vaona, Venturini, Villa Monteleone, Viviani, ZENATO, Zeni. Older vintages are still holding, but beginning to show their age.

Anselmi, Roberto ★★★ A leader in SOAVE with his single-vineyard Capitel Foscarino and exceptional sweet dessert RECIOTO i Capitelli, now both IGT.

Antinori, Marchesi L & P ★★→★★★★ Very influential, long-established Florentine house of highest repute (mostly justified), owned by Piero A, sharing management with his three daughters and oenologist Renzo Cotarella. Famous for CHIANTI CLASSICO (Tenute Marchese Antinori and Badia a Passignano), Umbrian (CASTELLO DELLA SALA), and PIEDMONT (PRUNOTTO) wines. Pioneer of new IGT, *e.g.* TIGNANELLO, SOLAIA (TUSCANY), Cervaro della Sala (Umbria). Expanding into south Tuscan MAREMMA, MONTEPULCIANO (La Braccesca), MONTALCINO, in ASTI (for Barbera), in FRANCIACORTA for sparkling (Lombardy), and in APULIA ("Vigneti del Sud"). Very good DOC BOLGHERI Guardo al Tasso.

Apulia Puglia. Italy's heel, producing almost a sixth of Italy's wine, most blended in northern Italy/France. Region to follow in increasing quality/value. Best DOC: CASTEL DEL MONTE, MANDURIA (PRIMITIVO DI), SALICE SALENTO. Producers: ANTINORI, Botromagno, Candido, Cantine Paradiso, Casale Bevagna, Castel di Selva, Giancarlo Ceci, Tenuta Cocevola, Co-op Copertino, Co-op Due Palme, Conti Zecca, Coppadoro, La Corte, Li Veli, D'Alfonso del Sordo, Fatalone, Felline, Gianfranco Fino, Masseria Monaci, Masseria Pepe, Michele Calò, Mille Una, Ognissole, Resta, RIVERA, Rubino, ROSA DEL GOLFO, Santa Lucia, SinfaROSA, TAURINO, Valle dell'Asso, VALLONE.

Aquileia F-VG DOC r w ★→★★ (r) 99' 00 01 03 04 A group of 12 single-varietal wines from around the town of Aquileia. Good REFOSCO, Sauv Bl. Ca' Bolani and Denis Montanar are the ones to watch.

Argiano Top BRUNELLO estate. Castello di Argiano is another.

Argiolas, Antonio ★★→★★★ Important SARDINIAN producer. High-level CANNONAU, NURAGUS, VERMENTINO, Bovale, and red IGTS Turriga (★★★) and Korem.

Arneis Pie DOCG w ★★ DYA Fairly good white from near ALBA: revival of an ancient grape; fragrant, light wine. DOC: ROERO Arneis, northwest of ALBA, normally better than LANGHE Arneis. Try: Almondo, Bric Cencurio, Ca' du Russ, Cascina Chicco, Correggia, Bruno GIACOSA, Malvirà, Monchiero-Carbone, Morra, Angelo Negro, PRUNOTTO.

Assisi Umb r (w) ★→★★ DYA IGT ROSSO and BIANCO di Assisi: very attractive. Sportoletti particularly good.

Asti Spumante Pie DOCG w sw sp ★→★★ NV Charming sweet, white Muscat fizz. Unfortunately, the big Asti houses are not interested in improving production of 80 million bottles. Despite unique potential, Asti is a cheap supermarket product. A few producers care: Walter BERA, CASCINA FONDA, CONTRATTO, Dogliotti-Caudrina, Vignaioli di Santo Stefano (see also MOSCATO D'ASTI).

Avignonesi ★★★ Noble MONTEPULCIANO house; highly ambitious, with a very fine range: VINO NOBILE, Desiderio, 50:50 – a SANGIOVESE/MERLOT joint venture with CAPANNELLE, a white blend, and superlative VIN SANTO (★★★★).

Azienda agricola/agraria Estates (large and small) making wine from own grapes.

Azienda/casa vinicola Négociants making wine from bought-in and own grapes.

Azienda vitivinicola A (specialized) wine estate.

Banfi (Castello or **Villa)** ★★→★★★ Space-age MONTALCINO CANTINA of biggest US importer of Italian wine. Huge plantings at Montalcino, mostly SANGIOVESE; also Syrah, PINOT N, Cab Sauv, Chard, Sauv Bl, etc.: part of a drive for quality plus quantity. Poggio all'Oro and Poggio alle Mura are ★★★ BRUNELLOS. New excellence in Summus and Excelsus in PIEDMONT, also good Banfi Brut, BRACCHETTO D'ACQUI, GAVI, PINOT GR. See also North America.

Barbaresco Pie DOCG r ★★→★★★★ 89' 90' 93 95' 96' 97 98' 99' 00 01' 03 04 05 06 Neighbour of BAROLO; the other great NEBBIOLO wine. Perhaps marginally less sturdy. At best, palate-cleansing, deep, subtle, fine. At 4 years becomes RISERVA. Producers include Marziano Abbona, Antichi PODERI di Gallina, Bera, Piero Busso, Ca' del Baio, Cascina Bruciata, Cascina Luisin, CERETTO, CIGLIUTI, Fontanabianca, FONTANAFREDDA, Fratelli Giacosa, GAJA, Bruno GIACOSA, GRESY, La Ca' Bianca, La Contea, Cortese, Lano, MOCCAGATTA, Montaribaldi, Morassino, Fiorenzo Nada, Paitin, Giorgio Pelissero, PIO CESARE, PRODUTTORI DEL BARBARESCO, PRUNOTTO, Prunset, Ressia, Massimo Rivetti, Roagna, Albino Rocca, Bruno ROCCA, RIVETTI, Ronchi, Serragilli, Sottimano, Vano, Varaldo.

Barbatella, Cascina La ★★★ Top producer of BARBERA D'ASTI: excellent VIGNA dell'Angelo and MONFERRATO Rosso Sonvico (Barbera/Cab Sauv).

Barbera d'Alba Pie DOC r ★★→★★★ 99 00' 01' 03' 04 06 Tasty, fragrant red. Best age up to 7 years. Many excellent wines, often from fine producers of BAROLO and BARBARESCO. Top houses: Marziano Abbona, Gianfranco ALESSANDRIA, Almondo, Baudana, Bric Cencurio, Boglietti, Boroli, Bovio, Bricco Maiolica, I Calici, Cascina Chicco, Cascina Cucco, Cascina Luisin, Caviola, Clerico, Aldo CONTERNO, Giovanni Conterno, Paolo Conterno, Conterno-Fantino, Cordero di Montezemolo, Corino, Damilano, De Stefanis, Gagliaso, Germano, Ghisolfi, Elio GRASSO, Silvio Grasso, Hilberg, MANZONE, Mauro Mascarello, Massolino, Molino, Monchiero-Carbone, Montaribaldi, Paolo Monti, Morra, OBERTO, Paitin, Pelissero, Luigi Pira, Principiano, PRUNOTTO, Revello, Giuseppe Rinaldi, Giorgio Rivetti, Massimo Rivetti, Albino Rocca, Tenuta Rocca, Rocche Costamagna, Ruggieri Corsini, Sandrone, SCAVINO, Seghesio, Edoardo Sobrino, Sottimano, VAJRA, Varaldo, Vietti, Roberto VOERZIO.

Barbera d'Asti Pie DOC r ★★→★★★ 99 00' 01' 03' 04 06 For real Barbera-lovers: Barbera alone, tangy and appetizing, drunk young or aged up to 7–10 years. Top growers: Olim Bauda, BAVA, BERA, Bersano, BERTELLI, Alfiero Boffa, BRAIDA, Brema, Ca' del Fer, Ca' del Prete, Cascina Castlèt, Cascina Ferro, Cascina Garrettina, Cascina Tavijn, Castino, CHIARLO, Contratto, COPPO, CS Nizza, CS Vinchio e Vaglio, Dezzani, Domanda, Il Falchetto, Ferraris, Fidanza, Garetto, La Giribaldina, Mauro Grasso, HASTAE, Hohler, La Barbatella, La Lune del Rospo, La Meridiana, La Morandina, L'Arbiola, L'Armangia, La Tenaglia, Malgrà, Marchesi Alfieri, Marengo, Beppe Marino, Martinetti, Mongetto, Oddero, Agostino Pavia, Pico Maccario, PRUNOTTO, RIVETTI, Bruno Rocca, Scrimaglio, Scagliola, Tenute dei Vallarino, Terre da Vino, VIETTI.

Barbera del Monferrato Pie DOC r ★→★★ DYA Easy-drinking Barbera from Alessandria and ASTI. Pleasant, slightly fizzy, sometimes sweetish. Delimited area is almost identical to BARBERA D'ASTI but style simpler, less ambitious, although serious and more important wines now appearing from Accornero, Bricco Mondlino, Valpane, Vicara.

Barco Reale Tus DOC r ★★ 01 03 04 05 06 DOC for junior wine of CARMIGNANO, using the same grapes.

Bardolino Ven DOC r (p) ★→★★ DYA Pale, summery, slightly bitter red from

Lake Garda. Bardolino CHIARETTO: paler and lighter. Best include Buglioni, Cavalchina, Giovanna Tantini, MONTRESOR, Pantini, ZENATO, Zeni.

Barolo Pie DOCG r ★★★→★★★★ 89' 90' 93' 95 **96' 97'** 98' **99'** 00 01' 03 04 05 06 Small area south of ALBA with one of Italy's supreme reds: rich, tannic, alcoholic (min 13%), dry but dramatically deep and fragrant (also crisp and clean) in the mouth. From NEBBIOLO grapes. Ages for up to 20–25 years (RISERVA after five).

Barolo Chinato A dessert wine made from BAROLO DOCG, alcohol, sugar, herbs, spices, and Peruvian bark. Producers: Cappellano, CERETTO, Giulio Cocchi.

Basciano ★★ Producer of good DOCG CHIANTI RUFINA and IGT wines.

Bava ★★ Producer of BARBERA D'ASTI Piano Alto and Stradivarius, MONFERRATO BIANCO, BAROLO CHINATO; the Bava family controls the old firm Giulio Cocchi in Asti, where it produces good sparkling METODO CLASSICO.

The Barolo role of honour

The classic style: Anselma, Ascheri, Barale, Bergadano, Giacomo Borgogno, Brovia, Cavallotto, Aldo CONTERNO, Giovanni Conterno, Paolo Conterno, Dosio, FONTANAFREDDA, Bruno GIACOSA, Bartolo MASCARELLO, Giuseppe MASCARELLO, Massolino, Monchiero, PRUNOTTO, Renato Ratti, Francesco Rinaldi, Giuseppe Rinaldi, Schiavenza, VIETTI.

A promising new generation: Abbona, Gianfranco ALESSANDRIA, ALTARE, Boglietti, Bongiovanni, Boroli, Brico Cenccurio, Bruna Grimaldi, Cabutto, Camerano, Cascina Ballarin, Cascina Luisin, M CHIARLO, CLERICO, CONTERNO-FANTINO, CORDERO DI MONTEZEMOLO, Corino, Ruggeri Crosini, Damilano, Gagliasso, Ettore Germano, Ghisolfi, Elio GRASSO, Silvio Grasso, Paolo Manzone, Giovanni MANZONE, Giacomo Marengo, MOLINO, OBERTO, PARUSSO, Luigi Pira, Porro, Principiano, Revello, Giorgio Rivetti, Rocche Costamagna, ROCCHE DEI MANZONI, Giovanni Rosso, Sandrone, Saffirio, SCAVINO, Fratelli Seghesio, Tenuta Rocca, VAJRA, Veglio, Gianni Voerzio, Roberto VOERZIO, and many others.

Bellavista ★★★ FRANCIACORTA estate with brisk SPUMANTE (Gran Cuvée Franciacorta is top). Also Satèn (a crémant-style sparkling). TERRE DI FRANCIACORTA DOC and Sebino IGT Solesine (both Cab Sauv/MERLOT blends). Owner Vittorio Moretti also expanding into Tuscan MAREMMA, Val di Cornia, and Monteregio.

Bera, Walter ★★→★★★ Small estate near BARBARESCO. Very good MOSCATO D'ASTI, ASTI, BARBERA D'ASTI, BARBARESCO, and LANGHE NEBBIOLO.

Berlucchi, Guido ★★★ Italy's biggest producer of sparkling METODO CLASSICO.

Bersano Historic wine house in Nizza Monferrato, with BARBERA D'ASTI Generala, and BAROLO Badarina, most PIEDMONT DOC wines including BARBARESCO, MOSCATO D'ASTI, ASTI SPUMANTE.

Bertani ★★→★★★ Well-known, quality wines from VERONA, esp traditional AMARONE.

Bianco White.

Bianco di Custoza Ven DOC w (sp) ★→★★ DYA Twin of SOAVE from VERONA's other side. Good Corte Sant'Arcadio, Le Tende, Le VIGNE di San Pietro, MONTRESOR.

Bibi Graetz Important reds from hills of Fiesole near Florence, *old-vine SANGIOVESE, Canaiolo, and Colorino of character and depth.*

Bisol Top brand of prosecco.

Biondi-Santi ★★★★ Original producer of BRUNELLO DI MONTALCINO, from Il Greppo estate. Absurd prices, but occasional old vintages are very fine.

Boca Pie DOC r ★★ **95 96' 97'** 00 01' 03 04 05 06 Another NEBBIOLO. Look for Le Piane and Poderi ai Valloni (Vigneto Cristiana ★★★).

Boccadigabbia ★★★ Top Marches producer of IGT wines: SANGIOVESE, Cab Sauv, PINOT N, Chard. Proprietor Elvidio Alessandri also owns fine Villamagna estate in ROSSO PICENO DOC.

Bolgheri Tus DOC r p w (sw) ★★→★★★★ Ultra-modish region on the coast south of Livorno. Including seven types of wine: BIANCO, VERMENTINO, Sauv Bl, ROSSO, ROSATO, VIN SANTO, and Occhio di Pernice, plus top IGTS. Newish DOC Bolgheri Rosso: Cab Sauv/MERLOT/SANGIOVESE blend. Top producers: Argentiera, CA' MARCANDA, Caccia al Piano, Giorgio Meletti Cavallari, Campo alla Sughera, Campo al Mare, Casa di Terra, Ceralti, Chiappini, Cipriani, ORNELLAIA, Poggio al Tesoro, San Guido, Enrico Santini, Sapaio, Serni, Terre del Marchesato, Tringali, VIGNA al Cavaliere (SANGIOVESE).

Bolla ★★ Famous VERONA firm for VALPOLICELLA, AMARONE, SOAVE, etc. Also RECIOTO. Top wines: Castellaro, Creso (red and white), Jago. Wines, particularly AMARONE and SOAVE selections, are once again on the upswing.

Bonarda 03 04 06 Minor and confusing red grape or grapes (name often erroneously used for Croatina) widely grown in PIEDMONT, Lombardy, Emilia-Romagna, and blended with Barbera.

Bonarda Lom DOC r ★★ 01 03 04 06 Soft, fresh FRIZZANTE and still wines from OLTREPÒ PAVESE, actually made from Croatina grapes; impressive new wines now appearing from CS Casteggio, Cigognola.

Borgo del Tiglio ★★★→★★★★ FRIULI estate for one of northeast Italy's top MERLOTS, ROSSO della Centa; also superior COLLIO Chard, TOCAI, and BIANCO. Now expanding into Marches with impressive offerings from Sangiovese and Montepulciano.

Boscarelli, Poderi ★★★ Small estate with very good VINO NOBILE DI MONTEPULCIANO and barrel-aged IGT Boscarelli.

Brachetto d'Acqui Pie DOCG r sw (sp) ★★ DYA Sweet, sparkling red with enticing Muscat scent. Can be much better than it sounds. Or dire.

Braida ★★★ The late Giacomo Bologna's estate; for top BARBERA D'ASTI (BRICCO dell'Uccellone, Bricco della Bigotta, Ai Suma).

Bramaterra Pie DOC r ★★ 96 97' 98' 99' 00 01' 03 04 Neighbour to GATTINARA. NEBBIOLO grapes predominate in a blend. Good producer: Sella.

Breganze Ven DOC ★→★★★ (r) 97' 98 99 00 01 Catch-all for many varieties near Vicenza. Best: Cab Sauv, Chard. Top producers: MACULAN, Miotti, Zonta.

Bricco Term for a hilltop (and by implication very good) vineyard in PIEDMONT.

Brindisi Ap DOC r ★★ 97 99 00 01 03 04 Strong NEGROAMARO, especially from Due Palme, Rubino, and forthcoming wines from ZONIN.

Brolio, Castello di ★★→★★★ After a sad period under foreign ownership, the RICASOLI family has taken this legendary 900-year-old estate in hand again. Results are heartening. Very good CHIANTI CLASSICO and IGT Casalferro.

Brunelli ★★→★★★ Very good quality of AMARONE and RECIOTO.

Brunello di Montalcino Tus DOCG r ★★★→★★★★ 93 95' 97' 99 00 01 03 04 With BAROLO, Italy's most celebrated red: strong, full-bodied, high-flavoured, tannic, long-lived. Four years' ageing; after five years becomes RISERVA. Quality is ever improving. MONTALCINO is 25 miles south of Siena. See "Best buys", p.94.

Bussola, Tommaso ★★★ Leading producer of AMARONE and RECIOTO in VALPOLICELLA.

Ca' dei Frati ★★→★★★ The best producer of DOC LUGANA: and very good, dry white blend IGT Pratto, sweet Tre Filer, and red IGT Ronchedone.

Ca' del Bosco ★★★★ FRANCIACORTA estate; *some of Italy's best sparklers* (outstanding DOCG Annamaria Clementi ★★★★), very good Chard, and excellent Cab Sauv blend (MAURIZIO ZANELLA), PINOT N (Pinèro). Intriguing new Carmenère.

Cafaggio, Villa ★★★ Very reliable CHIANTI CLASSICO estate with excellent IGTS San Martino (SANGIOVESE) and Cortaccio (Cab Sauv).

Calatrasi SI ★★→★★★ Good producer of red and white IGT labels, especially D'Istinto range.

Caldaro (Lago di Caldaro) T-AA DOC r ★ DYA Alias Kalterersee. Light, soft, bitter-

> ### Best Brunello di Montalcino to buy
>
> Altesino, ARGIANO, BANFI, Barbi, BIONDI-SANTI, BRUNELLI, La Campana, Campogiovanni, Canalicchio di Sopra, Caparzo, CASANOVA DI NERI, Casanova delle Cerbaie, Casato Prime Donne, CASE BASSE, CASTELGIOCONDO, Castello di Camigliano, Cerbaiona, Cerrino, COL D'ORCIA, Il Colle, Collelceto, Collemattoni, Collosorbo, Corte Pavone, Costanti, EREDI FULIGNI, Fanti-San Filippo, Ferrero, La Fiorita, La Fuga, La Gerla, Gorelli, Lambardi, LISINI, La Magia, La Mannella, Marroneto, Oliveto, Siro PACENTI, Franco Pacenti, Palazzo, Pertimali, Ciacci Piccolomini, PIEVE DI SANTA RESTITUTA, Podere Brizio, La Poderina, POGGIO ANTICO, POGGIONE, La Rasina, Salvioni-Cerbaiola, San Filippo, Scopetone, La Serena, Sesta, Talenti, La Torre, Uccelliera, Valdicava, Vasco Sassetti, Ventolaio, Verbena, Villa Le Prata, Vitanza.

almond SCHIAVA. From a huge area. CLASSICO – smaller area – is better.

Campania Historic centre of Italy's south with capital in Naples. Excellent grape varieties (Aglianico, Falanghina, Fiano, Greco, Piedirosso), volcanic soils, and high, cool vineyards all add up to important potential. Best DOCs are Falerno del Massico, Fiano d'Avellino, Greco di Tufo, Ischia, Taurasi, but many newer areas now coming to the fore. Established producers include Caggiano, Caputo, Colli di Lapio, D' Ambra, De Angelis, Benito Ferrara, Feudi di San Gregorio, Galardi, Mastroberardino, Montevetrano, Mustilli, and Villa Matilde. There are also many new faces are worthy of note: Alois, Cantina del Taburno, Casavecchia, Marisa Cuomo, Felicia, Grotta del Sole, Macchialupa, Molettieri, Amore Perrotta, Poderi Foglia, Quintodecimo, Selvanova, Spada, Torre Gaia, Trabucco, Vesevo, Vestini Campagnano, Villa Raiano, Vinosia, Vuolo.

Ca' Marcanda BOLGHERI estate owned by GAJA since 1996. Focus on international varieties: Cab Sauv, MERLOT, Cab Fr, Syrah.

Cannonau di Sardegna Sar DOC r (p) dr s/sw ★★ 97 98 99 00 01 02 03 04 05 06 Cannonau (Grenache) is the basic red grape of the south. From very potent to fine and mellow. Look for: ARGIOLAS, Contini, Giuseppe Gabbas, Jerzu, Loi, Sedilesu.

Cantalupo, Antichi Vigneti di ★★→★★★ Top GHEMME wines, especially single-vineyard Breclemae and Carellae.

Cantina Cellar or winery. See CS.

Capannelle ★★★ Very good producer of IGT and CHIANTI CLASSICO, plus 50:50 SANGIOVESE/MERLOT joint venture with AVIGNONESI near Gaiole.

Capezzana, Tenuta di (or Villa) ★★★ Tuscan estate of the Contini Bonacossi family. Good CHIANTI Montalbano, **_excellent CARMIGNANO_** (especially Villa Capezzagna, Villa Trefiano). Also very good Bordeaux-style red, Ghiaie Della Furba.

Capichera ★★★ No 1 producer of VERMENTINO DI GALLURA, especially VENDEMMIA Tardiva. Now with excellent red Mantènghja from Carignano grapes.

Caprai ★★★→★★★★ Widely copied, superb DOCG SAGRANTINO, very good DOC ROSSO DI MONTEFALCO. Highly rated.

Capri Cam DOC r p w ★→★★ Legendary island with widely abused name. Only interesting wines are from La Caprense.

Carema Pie DOC r ★★→★★★ 89' 90' 93 95 96' 97' 98 99' 00 01 03 04 05 Old NEBBIOLO speciality from north PIEDMONT. Best: Luigi Ferrando (or CS).

Carignano del Sulcis Sar DOC r p ★★→★★★ Ageworthy red. Best: TERRE BRUNE and Rocca Rubia from CS di SANTADI.

Carmignano Tus DOCG r ★★★ 90' 93 94 95 97' 98 99' 00 01' 03 04 Region west of Florence. CHIANTI grapes plus up to 15% Cab Sauv make distinctive, reliable, excellent red. Best: Ambra, CAPEZZANA, Farnete, PIAGGIA, Le Poggiarelle, Pratesi.

Carpenè-Malvolti Leading producer of classic PROSECCO and other sparkling wines at Conegliano, Veneto. Seen everywhere in Venice.

Carso F-VG DOC r w ★★→★★★ (r) 99' 00 01 02 03 04 DOC near Trieste includes good MALVASIA. Terrano del Carso is a REFOSCO red. Top growers: EDI KANTE, Zidanich.

Cartizze Famous, frequently too expensive, and too sweet DOC PROSECCO of top sub-zone of Valdobbiadene.

Casanova di Neri ★★★ BRUNELLO DI MONTALCINO, Pietradonice (SANGIOVESE/Cab Sauv) and very good ROSSO DI MONTALCINO from Neri family.

Cascina Fonda ★★★ Brothers Marco and Massimo Barbero have risen to the top in MOSCATO D'ASTI DOC. VENDEMMIA Tardiva and METODO CLASSICO ASTI SPUMANTE.

Case Basse ★★★★ Pace-setter at MONTALCINO with sublime BRUNELLO and single-vineyard BRUNELLO Intistieti.

Castel del Monte Ap DOC r p w ★★→★★★ (r) Dry, fresh, well-balanced wines. Rosé best known. Good Pietrabianca and excellent Bocca di Lupo from Vigneti del Sud (ANTINORI). Very good Il Falcone, Puer Apuliae, and Cappellaccio from RIVERA, Le More from Santa Lucia. Interesting new reds from Cocevola, Giancarlo Ceci.

Castelgiocondo ★★★ FRESCOBALDI estate in MONTALCINO: very good BRUNELLO and IGT MERLOT Lamaïone.

Castellare ★★→★★★ Small but admired CHIANTI CLASSICO producer. First-rate SANGIOVESE IGT I Sodi di San Niccoló and sprightly GOVERNO di Castellare: old-style CHIANTI updated. Also Poggio ai Merli (MERLOT) and Coniale (Cab Sauv).

Cataratto Sicilian white grape of high (generally unexplored) promise.

Castell' in Villa ★★★ Very good CHIANTI CLASSICO estate.

Castello Castle. (See under name – e.g. SALA, CASTELLO DELLA.)

Castelluccio ★★→★★★ Pioneering producer of quality SANGIOVESE of Romagna: IGT RONCO dei Ciliegi and RONCO dei Ciliegi. New wine: Massicone.

Caudrina-Dogliotti Romano ★★★ Top MOSCATO D'ASTI: La Galeisa and Caudrina.

Cavalleri ★★→★★★ Very good reliable FRANCIACORTA producer, especially sparkling.

Cavicchioli E-R ★→★★ Large producer of LAMBRUSCO and other sparkling wines: Lambrusco di Sorbara VIGNA del Cristo is best. Also TERRE DI FRANCIACORTA.

Ca' Viola PIEDMONT home base of influential consultant Bepe Caviola. Classy DOLCETTO and Barbera-based wines.

Ca' Vit (Cantina Viticoltori) Group of co-ops near Trento. Top wines: Brune di Monte (red and white) and sparkling Graal.

Cecchi Tus ★→★★ Bottler, producer; La Gavina, Spargolo, CHIANTI CLASSICO RISERVA.

Cerasuolo Ab DOC p ★ The ROSATO version of MONTEPULCIANO D'ABRUZZO.

Cerasuolo di Vittoria Si DOCG p ★★ 01 03 04 05 Garnet, full-bodied, aromatic

---

Who makes really good Chianti Classico?

AMA, Antica Fornace di Ridolfo, ANTINORI, Bibbiano, Bossi, BROLIO, Cacchiano, CAFAGGIO, Candialle, Canonica a Cerreto, Capaccia, CAPANNELLE, Carobbio, Casa Emma, Casafrassi, Casale dello Sparviero, Casaloste, Castello di San Sano, Castel Ruggero, CASTELLARE, Castell'in Villa, Collelungo, Colombaio di Cencio, Coltibuono, Le Corti, Mannucci Droandi, FELSINA-BERARDENGA, Le Filigare, FONTERUTOLI, FONTODI, ISOLE E OLENA, Ispoli, La Cappella, LA MASSA, Lornano, Lucignano, LE CINCIOLE, MONSANTO, NITTARDI, PALAZZINO, PANERETTA, Panzanello, Petroio-Lenzi, Poggerino, Poggiolino, Poggio Amorelli, Poggio al Sole, Poggio Bonelli, Querceto, QUERCIABELLA, RAMPOLLA, RIECINE, Rocca di Montegrossi, Rocca di Castagnoli, RUFFINO, SAN FELICE, SAN GIUSTO A RENTENNANO, Savignola Paolina, Solatione, Selvole, Vecchie Terre di Montefili, VERRAZZANO, Villa Mangiacane, Viticcio, VOLPAIA.

(Frappato and NERO D'AVOLA grapes); try Planeta, Valle dell'Acate, and COS.

Ceretto ★★★ Very good grower of BARBARESCO (BRICCO Asili), BAROLO (BRICCO Rocche, Brunate, Prapò), LANGHE Rosso Monsordo, and ARNEIS. Also very good METODO CLASSICO SPUMANTE La Bernardina.

Chianti Tus DOCG r ★→★★★ Lively local wine of Florence and Siena. At best fresh, fruity, tangy. Of the sub-districts, RUFINA (★★→★★★), COLLI Fiorentini (★→★★★), Chianti Montespertoli can make CLASSICO-style RISERVAS. Montalbano, COLLI Senesi, Aretini, Pisani: lighter wines.

Chianti Classico Tus DOCG r ★★→★★★★ 95 97' 99' 00 01' 03 04' (single-vineyard and RISERVA) 88' 90' 93 95 97' 99 01 03 04 Senior CHIANTI from central area. Old, pale style now rarer; top estates opt for richer, firmer wines. Some are among Italy's best but too much Cab Sauv can spoil style. CONSORZIO members use the badge of a black rooster, but many top firms do not belong.

Chiaretto Rosé (the word means "claret") produced especially around Lake Garda. See BARDOLINO, RIVIERA DEL GARDA BRESCIANO.

Chiarlo, Michele ★★→★★★ Good PIEDMONT producer (BAROLOS Cerequio and Cannubi, BARBERA D'ASTI, LANGHE, and MONFERRATO Rosso). Also BARBARESCO.

Chionetti ★★→★★★ Makes top DOLCETTO di Dogliani (look for Briccolero).

Cigliuti, Renato ★★★ Small, high-quality estate for BARBARESCO and BARBERA D'ALBA.

Cinqueterre Lig DOC w dr sw ★★ Fragrant, fruity white from precipitous coast near La Spezia. PASSITO is known as SCIACCHETRÀ (★★→★★★). Good from Co-op Agricola di Cinqueterre and Forlini Cappellini.

Cirò Cal DOC r (p w) ★→★★★ Strong red from Gaglioppo grapes; light, fruity white (DYA). Best: Caparra, Ippolito, LIBRANDI (Duca San Felice ★★★), San Francesco (Donna Madda, RONCO dei Quattroventi), Santa Venere, Siciliani.

Classico Term for wines from a restricted area within the limits of a DOC. By implication, and often in practice, the best of the district. When applied to sparkling wines, it denotes the classic method (as for Champagne).

Clerico, Domenico ★★★ Constantly evolving PIEDMONT wines; the aim is for international flavour. Especially good for BAROLO.

Col d'Orcia ★★★ Top MONTALCINO estate. Best wine: BRUNELLO.

Colle Santa Mustiola High-level SANGIOVESE from small estate just outside of VINO NOBILE DI MONTEPULCIANO zone.

Colli Hills. Occurs in many wine names.

Colli Berici Ven DOC r p w ★★ 97 99 00 01 03 04 Hills south of Vicenza. Best wine is Cab Sauv. Top producer: Villa Dal Ferro.

Colli Bolognesi E-R DOC r w ★★ Southwest of Bologna, eight wines, five varieties. TERRE ROSSE, the pioneer, now joined by Bonzara (★★→★★★), Santarosa, Vallona.

Colli del Trasimeno Um DOC r w ★→★★★ (r) 97 98 99' 00 01' 03 04 05 Lively white wines from near Perugia, but now more important reds as well. Best: Duca della Corgna, La Fiorita, Pieve del Vescovo, Poggio Bertaio.

Colli Euganei Ven DOC r w dr s/sw (sp) ★→★★★ DYA DOC southwest of Padua for seven wines. Adequate red; white and sparkling are pleasant. Best producers: Ca' Lustra, La Montecchia, Speaia, VIGNALTA.

Colline Novaresi Pie DOC r w ★→★★ DYA New DOC for old region in Novara province. Seven different wines: BIANCO, ROSSO, NEBBIOLO, BONARDA, Vespolina, Croatina, and Barbera. Includes declassified BOCA, FARA, GHEMME, and SIZZANO.

Collio F-VG DOC r w ★★→★★★★ (r) Makes 19 wines, 17 named after their grapes. Very good whites from: Attems, BORGO DEL TIGLIO, Il Carpino, La Castellada, CASTELLO di Spessa, Damijan, Marco FELLUGA, Fiegl, GRAVNER, Renato Keber, LIVON, Aldo Polencic, Primosic, Princic, RONCO dei Tassi, RUSSIZ SUPERIORE, SCHIOPETTO, Tercic, Terpin, Toros, Venica & Venica, VILLA RUSSIZ, Zuani, Casa Zuliani.

Colli Orientali del Friuli F-VG DOC r w dr sw ★★→★★★★ Hills E of Udine.

20 wines (18 named after their grapes). Both white and red can be very good. Best: Angoris, Bastianich, Rosa Bosco, Castello di Buttrio, Centa Sant'Anna, Dorigo, Dri, LE DUE TERRE, Livio FELLUGA, Meroi, Miani, Moschioni, Perusini, Petrussa, Rocca Bernarda, Ronchi di Cialla, Ronchi di Manzano, Ronco delle Betulle, RONCO DEL GNEMIZ, Ronco di Vico, SCHIOPETTO, Scubla, Specogna, Torre di Rosazzo, La Viarte, VIGNA Traverso, LE VIGNE DI ZAMÒ, Vinai dell'Abate, Volpe Pasini.

Colli Piacentini E-R DOC r p w ★→★★ DYA DOC including traditional GUTTURNIO and Monterosso Val d'Arda among 11 types grown south of Piacenza. Good fizzy MALVASIA. Most wines FRIZZANTE. New French and local reds: Montesissa, Mossi, Romagnoli, Solenghi, La Stoppa, Torre Fornello, La Tosa.

Colterenzio CS (or Schreckbichl) T-AA ★★→★★★ Pioneering quality leader among ALTO ADIGE co-ops. Look for: Cornell line of selections; Lafoa Cab Sauv and Sauv Bl; Cornelius red and white blends.

Consorzio In Italy there are two types of association recognized by wine law. One is dedicated to the observance of DOC regulations (*e.g.* Consorzio Tutela del CHIANTI CLASSICO). The second promotes the wines of their members (*e.g.* Consorzio del Marchio Storico of CHIANTI CLASSICO, previously Gallo Nero).

Conterno, Aldo ★★★★ Legendary grower of BAROLO, etc, at Monforte d'Alba. Very good Chard Bussiadoro, BARBERA D'ALBA Conca Tre Pile. Best BAROLOS: Gran Bussia, Cicala, and Colonello. *Langhe Nebbiolo Favot* and Langhe Rosso Quartetto both very good.

Conterno, Giacomo ★★★★ Iconic grower of BAROLO, etc., at Monforte d'Alba. Monfortino BAROLO: long-aged, rare, outstanding. Epitomizes grand tradition.

Conterno-Fantino ★★★ Two families for very good BAROLO etc. at Monforte d'Alba.

Contini, Attilio ★→★★★ Famous SARDINIAN producer of VERNACCIA DI ORISTANO; best is vintage blend Antico Gregori. Also good Cannonau.

Contrada Castelletta Pioneering MONTEPULCIANO/Syrah blend from vineyard of director of Saladini Pilastri in ROSSO PICENO DOC, juicy and rich.

Contratto ★★ At Canelli (owned by GRAPPA-producing family Bocchino); produces very good BARBERA D'ASTI, BAROLO, SPUMANTE, ASTI (De Miranda), MOSCATO D'ASTI.

Copertino Ap DOC r (p) ★★ 99 00 01 04 Savoury, ageworthy, strong red of NEGROAMARO from the heel of Italy. Look for the CS's RISERVA and Masseria Monaci, especially new barrel-aged Le Braci.

Coppo ★★→★★★ Ambitious producers of BARBERA D'ASTI (Pomorosso), Chard.

Cordero di Montezemolo-Monfalletto ★★→★★★ Historic maker of good BAROLO, now with fine BARBERA D'ALBA and Chard.

Corini New house in remote area of Umbria. Produces intriguing, innovative blend of SANGIOVESE/MONTEPULCIANO/MERLOT.

Cortese di Gavi See GAVI. (Cortese is the grape.)

Cortona Tuscan DOC contiguous to Montepulciano's Vino Nobile. Various red and white grapes, best results so far from AVIGNONESI's Desiderio, a Bordeaux blend, and first-rate Syrah from Luigi d'Alessandro, Il Castagno, La Braccesca.

Corzano & Paterno, Fattoria di ★★★ Dynamic CHIANTI COLLI Fiorentini estate. Very good RISERVA, red IGT Corzano, and outstanding VIN SANTO.

CS, Cantina Sociale Cooperative winery.

Dal Forno, Romano ★★★★ Very high-quality VALPOLICELLA, AMARONE, and RECIOTO from perfectionist grower who bottles only the best.

Del Cerro, Fattoria ★★★ Estate with very good DOCG VINO NOBILE DI MONTEPULCIANO (especially RISERVA and Antica Chiusina), red IGTS Manero (SANGIOVESE), and Poggio Golo (MERLOT). Controlled by insurance company SAI. Also owns excellent La Poderina (BRUNELLO DI MONTALCINO) and Colpetrone (MONTEFALCO SAGRANTINO).

Di Majo Norante ★★→★★★ Lone star of Molise, south of Abruzzo, with very good

Biferno ROSSO, Molise MONTEPULCIANO, Ramitello Don Luigi, and AGLIANICO Contado, white blend Falanghina-Greco and Moscato Passito Apianae.

DOC, Denominazione di Origine Controllata Means much the same as *appellation d'origine contrôlée* (see France).

DOCG, Denominazione di Origine Controllata e Garantita Like DOC but with an official "guarantee" of origin.

Dolce Sweet.

Dolcetto ★→★★★ PIEDMONT's earliest-ripening red grape, for very attractive everyday wines: dry, youthful, fruity, fresh, with deep purple colour. Gives its name to several DOCs: d'Acqui; d'Asti; di Diano d'Alba (also Diano DOC), especially Alari, Bricco Maiolica, Cascina Flino, FONTANAFREDDA, and Marco; di Dogliani (especially from M & E Abbona, Francesco Boschis, CHIONETTI, Gillardi, Pecchenino, Poderi Luigi Einaudi, San Fereolo, San Romano); delle Langhe Monregalesi (look for Barone Ricatti); and di Ovada (best from La Gioia, La Guardia, Villa Sparina). Dolcetto d'Alba: ALESSANDRIA, ALTARE, Azelia, Baudana, Boglietti, Brovia, Cabutto, CA' VIOLA, Cavallotto, CLERICO, Aldo CONTERNO, CONTERNO-FANTINO, Corino, De Stefanis, Gagliasso, Gastaldi, Germano, Bruno GIACOSA, GRESY, MANZONE, G. MASCARELLO, Massolino, Mauro Molino, Mossio, Fiorenzo Nada, OBERTO, Pelissero, Luigi Pira, Gianmatteo Pira, PRUNOTTO, Rocche Costamanga, SANDRONE, SCAVINO, Schiavenza, Fratelli Seghesio, Sottimano, VAJRA, Roberto VOERZIO.

Donnafugata Si w r ★★→★★★ Zesty Sicilian whites (best from Chiaranda and VIGNA di Gabri). Solid, improving reds, esp Mille e Una Notte and Tancredi, fine Moscato Passito di Pantellaria Ben Rye. Wines in DOC Contessa Entellina.

Duca di Salaparuta Si ★★ Vini Corvo. Popular SICILIAN wines. Sound, dry reds; pleasant, soft whites. Duca Enrico (★★→★★★) was one of SICILY's pioneeering ambitious reds. Valguarnera is premium oak-aged white.

Elba Tus r w (sp) ★→★★ DYA The island's white is very drinkable with fish. Napoleon in exile here loved the sweet red ALEATICO. Promising new wines from Sapereta, both reds and dessert. Try Acquabona, Acquacalda, Cecilia.

Enoteca Wine library; also wine shop or restaurant with extensive wine list. There are many, the impressive original being the Enoteca Italiana di Siena.

Eredi Fuligni ★★★ Very good producer of BRUNELLO and ROSSO DI MONTALCINO.

Est! Est!! Est!!! Lat DOC w dr s/sw ★ DYA Unextraordinary white from Montefiascone, north of Rome. Trades on its oddball name. See FALESCO.

Etna Si DOC r p w ★★ (r) **95 97** 98 **99** **00** 01 04 Wine from volcanic slopes. New investment in zone from Andrea Franchetti (Trinoro) and broker Marc De Grazia. Good producers: Benanti, Cambria, Bonaccorsi. Newest wines show an important potential for Nerello Mascalese grape.

Falchini ★★★ Producer of good DOCG VERNACCIA DI SAN GIMIGNANO (esp CASTEL Selva and VIGNA a Solatio). Good red IGT Campora (★★★).

Falerno del Massico ★★→★★★ Cam DOC r w ★★ (r) **95 97' 98 99** 00' 01' 03 04 As in Falernum (or Falernian), the best-known wine of ancient times. Times change. Elegant red from AGLIANICO, fruity white from Falanghina. Very good producer: VILLA MATILDE. Other producers: Amore Perrotta, Felicia, Trabucco.

Falesco ★★→★★★ Latium estate, very good MERLOT Montiano and Cab Sauv Marciliano (both ★★★). Good red IGT Vitiano and DOC EST! EST!! EST!!!

Fara Pie DOC r ★★ **90 95' 96'** 97 98 99 00' 01 03 04 Good NEBBIOLO from Novara, north PIEDMONT. Fragrant; worth ageing; especially Dessilani's Caramino and Lochera.

Farnetella, Castello di ★★→★★★ Estate near MONTEPULCIANO where Giuseppe Mazzocolin of FELSINA makes good Sauv Bl and CHIANTI COLLI Senesi. Also very good PINOT N Nero di Nubi and red blend Poggio Granoni.

Faro Si DOC r ★★ **97 98 99** **00** 01 04 05 Interesting full-bodied red from

Messina. Palari wines are exemplary.

Fattoria Central Italian term for an agricultural property, normally wine-producing, of a certain size. (See under name – *e.g.* MONTELLORI, FATTORIA DI.)

Fazi-Battaglia ★★ Well-known producer of VERDICCHIO, best selections: Le Moie, Massaccio, San Sisto. Owns Fassati (producer of VINO NOBILE DI MONTEPULCIANO).

Felluga, Livio ★★★ Substantial estate, consistently fine COLLI ORIENTALI DEL FRIULI wines, especially PINOT GR, Sauv Bl, TOCAI, PICOLIT, and MERLOT/REFOSCO blend.

Felluga, Marco ★★→★★★ The brother of Livio owns a négociant house bearing his name plus RUSSIZ SUPERIORE in COLLIO DOC, Castello di Buttrio in COLLI ORIENTALI DOC. Marco's daughter Patrizia is now owner of Zuani estate in COLLIO.

Felsina-Berardenga ★★★ CHIANTI CLASSICO estate; famous RISERVA VIGNA Rancia, IGT Fontalloro. Regular CHIANTI CLASSICO and RISERVA, less fashionable and less expensive, are more traditional. Also good IGT Chard and Cab Sauv.

Ferrari T-AA ★★→★★★ Cellars making dry sparkling near Trento. Giulio Ferrari RISERVA is best. Improving quality. New reds from TUSCANY and Umbria as well.

Feudi di San Gregorio ★★★→★★★★ Top Campania producer, with DOCG TAURASI, DOC FIANO, Falanghina, *Greco di Tufo*. Red IGT Serpico and Patrimo (MERLOT), white IGT Campanaro. Now active in Basilicata and APULIA as well.

Fiano di Avellino Cam DOCG w ★★→★★★ (DYA) Considered the best white of Campania. Can be intense, slightly honeyed, memorable. Best producers: Caggiano, Caputo, COLLI di Lapio, Benito Ferrara, FEUDI DI SAN GREGORIO, Grotta del Sole, MASTROBERARDINO, Villa Raiano, San Paolo, Vesevo.

Florio The major volume producer of MARSALA, controlled by Illva-Saronno.

Folonari Ambrogio Folonari and son Giovanni have split off from RUFFINO to create their own house. Will continue to make Cabreo (a Chard and a SANGIOVESE/Cab Sauv), wines of NOZZOLE (including Cab Sauv Pareto), BRUNELLO DI MONTALCINO La Fuga, VINO NOBILE DI MONTEPULCIANO Gracciano Svetoni, with new offerings from BOLGHERI, MONTECUCCO, and COLLI ORIENTALI DEL FRIULI.

Fontana Candida ★★ One of the biggest producers of FRASCATI. Single-vineyard Santa Teresa stands out. See also GRUPPO ITALIANO VINI.

Fontanafredda ★★→★★★ Producer of PIEDMONT wines on former royal estates, including single-vineyard BAROLOS and ALBA DOCS. Very good SPUMANTE Brut (especially ★★★ GATTINARA).

Fonterutoli ★★★ Historic CHIANTI CLASSICO estate of the Mazzei family at Castellina. Notable new selection CASTELLO di Fonterutoli (dark, oaky, fashionable CHIANTI), IGT Siepi (SANGIOVESE/MERLOT). Mazzei also own Tenuta di Belguardo in MAREMMA, good MORELLINO DI SCANSANO and IGT wines.

Fontodi ★★★ Top Panzano CHIANTI CLASSICO estate for CHIANTI and RISERVA, especially RISERVA del Sorbo. Very good red IGT Flaccianello, Case Via PINOT N, Case Va Syrah.

Foradori ★★★ Elizabetta F makes best TEROLDEGO. Also oak-aged TEROLDEGO Granato, white IGT Myrto. Wines from new Ampeleia estate in Tuscan MAREMMA already first class.

Forte, Podere Pasquale Forte's Val d'Orcia estate, just south of MONTALCINO, puts cutting-edge technology at the service of ambitious SANGIOVESE and Cab Sauv/MERLOT/Petit Verdot wines.

Forteto della Luja ★★★ Pioneer in LOAZZOLO; very good Barbera/PINOT N Le Grive.

Fossi, Enrico ★★★ High-level small estate in Signa, west of Florence, very fine SANGIOVESE, Cab Sauv, Syrah, Malbec, Gamay, and Chard.

Franciacorta Lom DOCG w (p) sp ★★→★★★★ Small sparkling-wine centre growing in quality and renown. Wines exclusively bottle-fermented. Top producers: Barone Pizzini, BELLAVISTA, CA' DEL BOSCO, Castellino, CAVALLERI, Gatti, UBERTI, VILLA; also very good: Contadi Gastaldi, Cornaleto, Il Mosnel, La Montina, Majolini, Monte Rossa, Monzio Compagnoni, Ricci Curbastri, Ronco Calino, Vezzoli. For white and red, see TERRE DI FRANCIACORTA.

Frascati Lat DOC w dr s/sw sw (sp) ★→★★ DYA Best-known wine of Roman hills: should be soft, limpid, golden, tasting of whole grapes. Most is disappointingly neutral today: look for Conte Zandotti, Villa Simone, or Santa Teresa from FONTANA CANDIDA. Sweet is known as Cannellino.

Freisa Pie r dr s/sw sw (sp) ★★ DYA Usually very dry (except near Turin), often FRIZZANTE red, said to taste of raspberries and roses. With enough acidity it can be highly appetizing, especially with salami. Good wines from Brezza, CIGLIUTI, Clerico, Aldo CONTERNO, COPPO, Franco Martinetti, PARUSSO, Pecchenino, Pelissero, Sebaste, Trinchero, VAJRA, Vigneti Massa, and VOERZIO.

Frescobaldi ★★→★★★★ Ancient noble family, leading CHIANTI RUFINA pioneer at NIPOZZANO, east of Florence. Also POMINO (white) and Mormoreto (red). See MONTESODI. Owner of CASTELGIOCONDO (★★★). Now outright owner of joint venture with Mondavi near MONTALCINO, LUCE, Lucente, and ORNELLAIA. New vineyards in COLLIO DOC and MAREMMA. Important development of vineyards to southeast of Florence near Montespertoli.

Friuli-Venezia Giulia The northeast region on the Slovenian border. Many wines; the DOCS ISONZO, COLLIO, and COLLI ORIENTALI include most of the best.

Frizzante (fz) Semi-sparkling. Used to describe wines such as LAMBRUSCO.

Gaja ★★★★ Old family firm at BARBARESCO under direction of Angelo Gaja. Top-quality – and price – wines, esp BARBARESCO (single-vineyards SORÌ Tildin, Sorì San Lorenzo, Costa Russi), BAROLO Sperss. Chard (Gaia and Rey), Cab Sauv Darmagi. Latest acquisition: Marengo-Marenda estate (BAROLO), commercial Gromis label, PIEVE DI SANTA RESTITUTA (BRUNELLO). Single-vineyard BARBARESCOS and BAROLO now labelled LANGHE DOC. Important new BOLGHERI project: Ca' Marcanda.

Galardi ★★★→★★★★ Producer of Terra di Lavoro, a mind-boggling blend of AGLIANICO and Piedirosso, in north Campania near FALERNO DEL MASSICO DOC.

Gambellara Ven DOC w dr s/sw (sp) ★ DYA Neighbour of SOAVE. Dry wine similar. Sweet (RECIOTO DI GAMBELLARA), nicely fruity. Top producer: La Biancara.

Gancia Famous ASTI house also producing dry sparkling.

Garganega Principal white grape of SOAVE and GAMBELLARA.

Garofoli ★★→★★★ One of quality leaders in the Marches (near Ancona). Notable style in VERDICCHIO Podium, Macrina, and Serra Fiorese. ROSSO CONERO Piancarda and very good Grosso Agontano.

Gattinara Pie DOCG r ★★★ 89' 90' 93 95 96' 97' 98 99' 00 01' 03 04 05 Very tasty NEBBIOLO-based red, historically finest from north PIEDMONT. Best: Travaglini (RISERVA), Antoniolo (single-vineyard wines). Others: Bianchi, Nervi, Torraccia del Piantavigna.

Gavi Pie DOCG w ★→★★★ DYA At (rare) best, subtle dry white of CORTESE grapes. LA SCOLCA is best-known, good from BANFI (especially VIGNA Regale), Castellari Bergaglio, Franco Martinetti, Villa Sparina, Toledana. Broglia, Cascina degli Ulivi, CASTELLO di Tassarolo, CHIARLO, La Giustiniana, PODERE Saulino are also fair.

Geografico ★★ Co-op with *rising-quality CHIANTI CLASSICO*; good RISERVA Montegiachi. IGTS Pulleraia and Ferraiolo.

Ghemme Pie DOCG r ★★ 89 90' 93 95 96 97' 98 99' 00 01 03 04 Neighbour of GATTINARA but not as good. Best: Antichi Vigneti di Cantalupo, Rovellotti, and Torraccia del Piantavigna.

Giacosa, Bruno ★★→★★★★ Inspired loner: outstanding BARBARESCO, BAROLO, and PIEDMONT wines at Neive. Remarkable ARNEIS white and sparkling PINOT N.

Governo Old TUSCAN custom, enjoying mild revival. Dried grapes or must are added to young wine to induce second fermentation and give a slight prickle, sometimes instead of adding must concentrate to increase alcohol.

Gradi Degrees (of alcohol), *i.e.* per cent by volume.

Grappa Pungent and potent spirit made from grape pomace (skins, etc., after pressing), sometimes excellent.

Grasso, Elio ★★★ Very good BAROLO (look for Runcot, Gavarini, Casa Maté), full, barrel-aged BARBERA D'ALBA VIGNA Martina, DOLCETTO D'ALBA, and Chard Educato.

Grave del Friuli F-VG DOC r w ★→★★ (r) 99 00 01 03 DOC covering 15 different wines, 14 named after their grapes, from central part of region. Good REFOSCO, MERLOT, and Cab Sauv. Best producers: Borgo Magredo, Le Fredis, Di Lenardo, Le Monde, Plozner, Vicentini-Orgnani, Villa Chiopris.

Gravner, Josko ★★★ Visionary COLLIO producer, leading drive for low yields, oak ageing, and ageworthy wines. Tirelessly self-critical in his search for new concepts and methods.

Grechetto White grape; more flavour than TREBBIANO, and increasingly seen as its substitute in ORVIETO and in other parts of Umbria. Look for Bigi, Busti, Cardeto, Colli Amerini, FALESCO, Le Poggette, Palazzone, Tudernum.

Greco di Tufo Cam DOCG w (sp) ★★→★★★ (DYA) One of the best whites from the south: fruity, slightly wild in flavour, and ageworthy. Very good examples from Caggiano, Caputo, Benito Ferrara, FEUDI DI SAN GREGORIO, Macchialupa, MASTROBERARDINO (Nuovaserra & Vignadangelo), Vesevo, Villa Raiano.

Gresy, Marchesi di (Cisa Asinari) ★★★ Consistent producer of fine BARBARESCO. Also very good LANGHE Rosso, Sauv Bl, Chard, MOSCATO D'ASTI, BARBERA D'ASTI.

Grevepesa CHIANTI CLASSICO co-op – quality now rising.

Grignolino d'Asti Pie DOC r ★ DYA Lively light red of PIEDMONT. Look for: BRAIDA, Castino, Due Pini, La Luna del Rospo, Marchesi Incisa della Rocchetta.

Grignolino del Monferrato Casalese Much like GRIGNOLINO D'ASTI but firmer. Try: Accornero, BRICCO Mondalino, Colonna, Mongetto, La Scamuzza, La Tenaglia.

Gruppo Italiano Vini (GIV) Complex of co-ops and wineries, including Bigi, Conti Serristori, FOLONARI, FONTANA CANDIDA, LAMBERTI, Macchiavelli, MELINI, Negri, SANTI, and since 1997 controls Ca' Bianca (PIEDMONT) and Vignaioli di San Floriano (FRIULI). Now moving into south with investments in Sicily and Basilicata.

Guerrieri-Gonzaga ★★★ Top TRENTINO estate; especially San Leonardo blend.

Gutturnio dei Colli Piacentini E-R DOC r dr ★→★★ DYA Barbera/BONARDA blend from the hills of Piacenza, often FRIZZANTE. Producers: Cardinali, Castelli del Duca, La Stoppa, La Tosa, Torre Fornello.

Haas, Franz ★★★ ALTO ADIGE producer; very good PINOT N, LAGREIN, and IGT blends.

Hastae ★★★ New super-Barbera from ASTI from group of producers: BRAIDA, CHIARLO, COPPO, PRUNOTTO, VIETTI.

Hofstätter ★★★ ALTO ADIGE producer of top PINOT N. Look for southern Urbano, LAGREIN, Cab Sauv/Petit Verdot, Gewurz.

IGT, Indicazione Geografica Tipica New category for quality wines unable to fit into DOC zones or regulations; replaces the anomaly of glamorous VDTS.

Ischia Cam DOC w (r) ★→★★ DYA Island off Naples. Top producer d'Ambra: DOC red Dedicato a Mario D'Ambra, IGT red Tenuta Montecorvo, IGT white Tenuta Frassitelli, and Piellero. Also good: Il Giardino Mediterraneo, Pietratorcia.

Isole e Olena ★★★→★★★★ Top CHIANTI CLASSICO estate of great beauty with fine red *IGT Cepparello*. Very good VIN SANTO, Cab Sauv, Chard, and L'Eremo Syrah.

Isonzo F-VG DOC r w ★★★ (r) DOC covering 19 wines (17 varietals) in northeast. Best white and MERLOT compare to COLLIO wines. Especially from La Bellanotte, Borgo Conventi, Masut da Rive, LIS NERIS, Pierpaolo Pecorari, RONCO del Gelso, Borgo San Daniele, Sant'Elena, VIE DI ROMANS, Villanova.

Iermann, Silvio ★★→★★★ Family estate with vineyards in COLLIO and ISONZO: top white VDT, including blend Vintage Tunina, oak-aged Capo Martino, and "Were dreams, now is just wine" (yes, really). Now joined by important red Pignacoluse.

Kalterersee German (and local) name for LAGO DI CALDARO.

Kante, Edi ★★→★★★ Leading light of CARSO; fine DOC Chard, Sauv Bl, MALVASIA;

good red Terrano.

Lacryma (or Lacrima) Christi del Vesuvio Cam r p w dr (sw fz) ★→★★ DYA Famous but ordinary wines in great variety from Vesuvius (DOC Vesuvio). MASTROBERARDINO and Caputo wines suggest untapped quality, as do newer offerings from De Angelis and Grotta del Sole.

La Fiorita Lamborghini family property near Lake Trasimeno in Umbria, with touchstone SANGIOVESE/MERLOT blend Campoleone.

Lageder, Alois ★★→★★★ Top ALTO ADIGE producer. Exciting wines include oak-aged Löwengang Chard and Römigberg Cab Sauv. Single-vineyard Lehenhof Sauv Bl, *PINOT GR Benefizium Porer*, PINOT N Krafuss, LAGREIN Lindenberg, TERLANO Tannhammer. Also owns Cason Hirschprunn for very good IGT blends.

Lago di Caldaro See CALDARO.

Lagrein T-AA DOC r p ★★→★★★ 96 97' 98 99 00' 01 02' 03' 04 A grape with a bitter twist. Good, fruity wine – at best, full, minerally, and very appealing. The rosé: Kretzer; the dark: Dunkel. Best from Colterenzio co-op, Gries, Gojer, HAAS, HOFSTÄTTER, LAGEDER, Laimburg, Josephus Mayr, Thomas Mayr, Muri Gries, NIEDERMAYR, Niedrist Estates, St-Magdalena, TERLANO co-op.

La Massa ★★★ Highly rated producer of very good CHIANTI CLASSICO; Giorgio Primo.

Lamberti ★★ Large producer of SOAVE, VALPOLICELLA, BARDOLINO, etc., at Lazise on the eastern shore of Lake Garda.

Lambrusco E-R DOC (or not) r p dr s/sw ★→★★ DYA Popular fizzy red, best known in industrial semi-sweet version. Best is SECCO, traditional with second fermentation in bottle (with sediment). DOCS: L Grasparossa di Castelvetro, L Salamino di Santa Croce, L di Sorbara. Best: Bellei, Caprari, Casali, CAVICCHIOLI, Graziano, Lini Oreste, Medici Ermete (especially Concerto), Rinaldo Rinaldini, Venturini Baldini. Forget your prejudices – try it.

La Morandina ★★★ Small family estate with top MOSCATO and BARBERA D'ASTI.

Langhe The hills of central PIEDMONT, home of BAROLO, BARBARESCO, etc. Has become a name for recent DOC (r w ★★→★★★) for eight different wines: ROSSO, BIANCO, NEBBIOLO, DOLCETTO, FREISA, ARNEIS, Favorita, and Chard. BAROLO and BARBARESCO can now be declassified to DOC Langhe Nebbiolo.

La Scolca ★★ Famous GAVI estate for good GAVI and SPUMANTE.

Latisana F-VG DOC r w ★→★★ (r) DOC for 13 varietal wines from 80 km (50 miles) northeast of Venice. Best wine is TOCAI Friulano. Try wines of Grandi e Gabana.

Le Cinciole ★★★ DOCG CHIANTI CLASSICO, the best is RISERVA Petresco.

Le Due Terre Small producer in COLLI ORIENTALI DEL FRIULI for choice MERLOT, PINOT N Sacrisassi Rosso (Refosco-Schioppettino), and white Sacrisassi Bianco.

Le Fonti ★★★ Very good CHIANTI CLASSICO house in Poggibonsi; look for RISERVA and IGT Vito Arturo (SANGIOVESE).

Le Macchiole ★★★ Outstanding red DOC BOLGHERI Paleo, TOSCANA IGTS Macchiole Rosso (SANGIOVESE/Cab Fr), Messorio (MERLOT), and Scrio (Syrah).

Le Pupille ★★★ Top producer of *MORELLINO DI SCANSANO* (look for Poggio Valente) excellent IGT blend Saffredi (Cab Sauv/MERLOT/ALICANTE).

Le Ragose ★★→★★★ Family estate, one of VALPOLICELLA's best. AMARONE and RECIOTO top quality; Cab Sauv and VALPOLICELLA very good, too.

Le Salette ★★→★★★ Small VALPOLICELLA producer: look for very good AMARONE Pergole Vece and RECIOTO Le Traversagne.

Lessona Pie DOC r ★★ 96' 97' 98 99' 00 01' 03 04 Soft, dry, claret-like wine from Vercelli province. NEBBIOLO, Vespolina, BONARDA grapes. Best producer: Sella plus new estate of Paolo de Marchi of ISOLE E OLENA.

Le Vigne di Zamò ★★★ First-class FRIULI estate for PINOT BIANCO, TOCAI, Pignolo, Cab Sauv, MERLOT, and Picolit from vineyards in three areas of COLLI ORIENTALI DEL FRIULI DOC.

Librandi ★★★ Top Calabria producer. *Very good red CIRÒ* (RISERVA Duca San Felice is ★★★), IGT Gravello (Cab Sauv/Gaglioppo blend), and Magno Megonio from Magliocco grape. New IGT from Efeso from Mantonico grape most impressive.

Liquoroso Means strong; usually sweet and always fortified.

Lisini ★★★→★★★★ Historic small estate for some of the finest BRUNELLO.

Lis Neris ★★★ Top ISONZO estate with bevy of high-quality wines: Chard, PINOT GR, Sauv Bl, a MERLOT-based red, an aromatic Confini white blend, and lovely VDT dessert VERDUZZO.

Livon ★★→★★★ Substantial COLLIO producer, also some COLLI ORIENTALI wines like VERDUZZO. Expanded into the CHIANTI CLASSICO and Montefalco DOCGS.

Loazzolo Pie DOC w sw ★★★ 98' **99'** 00 01' 03 04 05 DOC for MOSCATO dessert wine from botrytized, air-dried grapes: expensive and sweet. Good from Borgo Isolabella, Forteto della Luja, and Pianbello.

Locorotondo Ap DOC w (sp) ★ DYA Pleasantly fresh southern white. ★

Lugana Lom and Ven DOC w (sp) ★→★★ DYA Whites of southern Lake Garda: can be fragrant smooth full of body and flavour. Good from CA' DEI FRATI, ZENATO.

Luce ★★★ Ambitious joint Mondavi/FRESCOBALDI venture launched in 1998, now solely FRESCOBALDI. SANGIOVESE/MERLOT blend. Could become Italy's Opus One.

Lungarotti ★★→★★★ Leading producer of TORGIANO, with cellars, hotel, and museum near Perugia. Good IGT Sangiorgio (SANGIOVESE/Cab Sauv), Aurente (Chard), and Giubilante. Now operating, and very well, in Montefalco as well. See TORGIANO.

Maculan Ven ★★★ Excellent Cab Sauv (Fratta, Ferrata), Chard (Ferrata), MERLOT (Marchesante), and Torcolato (especially RISERVA Acininobili).

Malvasia Widely planted grape; chameleon-like: white or red, sparkling or still, strong or mild, sweet or dry, aromatic or neutral; often IGT, sometimes DOC.

Manduria (Primitivo di) Ap DOC r s/sw ★★→★★★ Dark red, naturally strong, sometimes sweet from near Taranto. Good: Casale Bevagna, Felline, Feudi di San Marzano, Ginafranco Fino, Masseria Pepe, Pervini, Pozzopalo, Sinfarosa.

Manzone, Giovanni ★★★ Very good ALBA wines of personality from Ciabot del Preve estate near Monforte d'Alba. Single-vineyard BAROLO, BARBERA D'ALBA, DOLCETTO.

Marchesi di Barolo ★★ Important ALBA house: BAROLO (especially Cannubi and Sarmassa), BARBARESCO, DOLCETTO D'ALBA, Barbera, FREISA D'ASTI, and GAVI.

Maremma Southern coastal area of TUSCANY in provinces of Livorno and Grosseto. DOCS include BOLGHERI and VAL DI CORNIA (Livorno), MONTECUCCO, MONTEREGIO, MORELLINO DI SCANSANO, PARRINA, SOVANA (Grosseto). Attracting much interest and investment for high-quality potential demonstrated by wines. Maremma IGT, limited to province of Grosseto, now used by many top producers, including new investors, for major wines. Look for: Ampeleia, Belguardo, Casina, Col di Bacche, Fattoria di Magliano, La Carletta, La Parrina, La Selva, Lhosa, Marsiliana, Monteti, MORIS FARMS, Montebelli, Poderi di Ghiaccioforte, Poggio Argentiera, Poggio al Lupo, Poggio Foco, Poggio Paoli, Poggio Verrano, Rascioni e Cecconello, Rocca di Frasinello, San Matteo, Sassotondo, Solomaremma, Suveraia.

Marino Lat DOC w dr s/sw (sp) ★→★★ DYA A neighbour of FRASCATI with similar wine; often a better buy. Look for Di Mauro.

Marsala Sicily's sherry-type wine (★→★★★), invented by Woodhouse Bros from Liverpool in 1773. An excellent apéritif or for dessert, but mostly used in the kitchen for desserts such as *zabaglione*. Dry ("virgin"), sometimes made by the *solera* system, must be 5 years old. Top producers: FLORIO, Pellegrino, Rallo, VECCHIO SAMPERI. Very special old vintages ★★★★.

Martini & Rossi Vermouth and sparkling wine house now controlled by Bacardi group. (Has a fine wine-history museum in Pessione, near Turin.)

Marzemino Trentino, T-AA DOC r ★→★★ **00** 01 03 04 Pleasant local red. Fruity and slightly bitter. Especially from Bossi Fedrigotti, CA' VIT, Gaierhof, Letrari, Longariva, Simoncelli, E Spagnolli, De Tarczal, Vallarom.

Mascarello The name of two top producers of BAROLO, etc.: Bartolo M and Giuseppe M & Figli. Look for the latter's *supreme BAROLO Monprivato*.

Masi ★★→★★★ Fanatical exponent and researcher of VALPOLICELLA, AMARONE, RECIOTO, SOAVE, etc., including fine red Campo Fiorin. Also very good barrel-aged red IGT Toar.

Mastroberardino ★★→★★★ Top Taurasi (look for Historia Naturalis and Radici).

Melini ★★ Long-established producers of CHIANTI CLASSICO at Poggibonsi. Good quality/price; look for single-vineyard CHIANTI CLASSICO Selvanella and RISERVAS La Selvanella and Masovecchio. See GRUPPO ITALIANO VINI.

Meranese di Collina T-AA DOC r ★ DYA Light red of Merano.

Merlot Red grape widely grown in north (especially) and central Italy. Merlot DOCS are abundant. Best producers: BORGO DEL TIGLIO, Livio FELLUGA (Sossò), Renato Keber, LE DUE TERRE, Miani, Radikon, VILLA RUSSIZ (De la Tour) in FRIULI-VENEZIA GIULIA; Bonzara (Rocca di Bonacciara) in E-R; BOCCADIGABBIA in the Marches; FALESCO (Montiano) in Latium; PLANETA in Sicily; FEUDI DI SAN GREGORIO (Patrimo) in Campania; and TUSCAN Super-IGTS AMA (L'Apparita), FRESCOBALDI (Laimaione), La Cappella (Cantico), Cantine Leonardo da Vinci (Artisti), Castello di Bossi (Girolamo), Fattoria del Cerro (Poggio Golo), Macchiole (Messorio), ORNELLAIA (Masseto), Pagani De Marchi (Casa Nocera), Petrolo (Galatrona), San Giusto a Rentennano (La Ricolma), Tua Rita (Redigaffi).

Metodo classico or tradizionale Now mandatory terms to identify classic method sparkling wines. "Metodo Champenois" banned since 1994 and now illegal. (See also CLASSICO.)

Mezzacorona ★★ TRENTINO co-op with good DOC TEROLDEGO, METODO CLASSICO Rotari.

Moccagatta ★★→★★★ Specialist in impressive single-vineyard BARBARESCO: Basarin, Bric Balin (★★★), and VIGNA Cole. Also BARBERA D'ALBA and LANGHE.

Molino ★★★ Talented producer of elegant ALBA wines at La Morra; look for BAROLOS Gancia and Conca, Barbera Gattere, and DOLCETTO.

Monacesca, La ★★→★★★ Fine producer of VERDICCHIO DI MATELICA. Top wine: Mirus.

Monferrato Pie DOC r p w sw ★★ Hills between River Po and Apennines. Name of new DOC; including ROSSO, BIANCO, CHIARETTO, DOLCETTO, Casalese, FREISA, and CORTESE.

Monica di Sardegna Sar DOC r ★→★★ DYA Monica is the grape of light dry red.

Monsanto ★★★ Esteemed CHIANTI CLASSICO estate, especially for Il Poggio vineyard and IGTS Fabrizio Bianchi (SANGIOVESE) and Nemo (Cab Sauv).

Montalcino Small town in province of Siena (TUSCANY), famous for concentrated, expensive BRUNELLO and more approachable, better-value ROSSO DI MONTALCINO.

Montecarlo Tus DOC w r ★★ DYA (w) White, and increasingly red, wine area near Lucca in northern TUSCANY. Whites are smooth, neutral blend of TREBBIANO with range of better grapes; basic reds are CHIANTI-style. Good producers: Buonamico (red IGTS Cercatoja Rosso and Fortino), Carmignani (very good red IGT For Duke), red IGTS of La Torre, Montechiari, Fattoria del Teso.

Montecucco New TUSCAN DOC between MONTALCINO and MORELLINO DI SCANSANO. Try: Basile, Begnardi, Castello di Vicarello, Ciacci Piccolomini, Colli Massari, Fattoria di Montecucco, Montesalario, Poggio Saccone, Poggio Leone, Poggio Mandorlo, Villa Patrizia. Much new investment: FOLONARI, MASI, Pertimali, RIECINE, Talenti.

Montefalco Sagrantino Umb DOCG r dr (sw) ★★★→★★★★ Powerful, long-lasting SECCO wines, plus limited production of sweet PASSITO red from Sagrantino grapes. Good from Alzatura, Antigniano, Antonelli San Marco, Benincasa, CAPRAI, Castelbuono, Colpetrone, Madonna Alta, Martinelli, Le Mura Saracene, Novelli, Pardi, Perticaia, Scacciadiavoli, Spoleto Ducale, Tabarrini,

Terra di Trinci, Terre della Custodia, Tiburzi, Tudernum.

Montellori, Fattoria di ★★→★★★ TUSCAN producer making Chianti, all-SANGIOVESE IGT Dicatum, Cab Sauv/MERLOT blend Salamartano, white IGT Sant'Amato (Sauv Bl), and METODO CLASSICO SPUMANTE.

Montepulciano An important red grape of east central Italy as well as the famous TUSCAN town (see below).

Montepulciano, Vino Nobile di See VINO NOBILE DI MONTEPULCIANO.

Montepulciano d'Abruzzo Ab DOC r p ★→★★★ 95 97' 98' 00' 01' 03' 04 One of Italy's tastiest reds, full of flavour and warmth, from Adriatic coast. Best: Barba, Barone Cornacchia, Nestore Bosco, Caldora, Cataldi-Madonna, Ciccio Zaccagnini, Feuduccio, Filomusi-Guelfi, Illuminati, Marammiero, Masciarelli, Monti, Montori, Nicodemi, Orlandi Contucci Ponno, Terre d'Aligi, Torre dei Beati, La Valentina, VALENTINI, Valle Reale, Valori, Villa Medoro, Ciccio Zaccagnini. *Farnese is the big-value brand*. See also CERASUOLO.

Monteregio Emerging DOC near Massa Marittima in MAREMMA, high-level SANGIOVESE and Cab Sauv wines from Campo Bargello, MORIS FARMS, Massa Vecchia, Montebelli, La Pierotta, Rocca di Frasinello, Suveraia, Tenuta del Fontino. New investors (ANTINORI, BELLAVISTA, Eric de Rothschild, ZONIN) flocking in.

Montescudaio Tus DOC r w ★★ DOC between Pisa and Livorno; best are SANGIOVESE or SANGIOVESE/Cab Sauv blends. Try Aione, Fontemorsi, Marchesi Ginori Lisci, Merlini, Poggio Gagliardo, La Regola, Sorbaiano.

Montevertine Radda estate. IGT Le Pergole Torte a pioneering example of small-barrel-aged SANGIOVESE.

Montevetrano ★★★ Small Campania producer; superb IGT Montevetrano.

Montresor ★★ VERONA wine house: good LUGANA, BIANCO DI CUSTOZA, VALPOLICELLA.

Morellino di Scansano Tus DOC r ★→★★★ 95 97 98 99' 00 01 03 04 05 06 Local SANGIOVESE of the MAREMMA, the south TUSCAN coast. Cherry-red, should be lively and tasty young or matured; many have been over-oaked. Belguardo, Casina, Col di Bacche, Compagnia del Vino, Fattoria di Magliano, Fattorie LE PUPILLE, La Carletta, MORIS FARMS, Mantellasi, Poderi di Ghiaccioforte, Poggio al Lupo, Poggio Argentiera, Poggio Paoli, San Matteo, La Selva, Cantina di Scansano, Terre di Talamo, and Villa Patrizia are producers to try.

Moris Farms ★★★ Very good producer in MONTEREGIO and *MORELLINO DI SCANSANO*, respectively to north and south of Grosseto; look for RISERVA and IGT Avvoltore, a rich SANGIOVESE/Cab Sauv/Syrah blend.

Moscadello di Montalcino Tus DOC w sw (sp) ★★ DYA Revived traditional wine of MONTALCINO, once better known than BRUNELLO. Sweet fizz and sweet to high-octane MOSCATO PASSITO. Best: COL D'ORCIA, La Poderina.

Moscato Fruitily fragrant ubiquitous grape for a diverse range of wines: sparkling or still, light or full-bodied, but always sweet.

Moscato d'Asti Pie DOCG w sp sw ★★→★★★ DYA Similar to DOCG ASTI, but usually better grapes; lower alcohol, sweeter, fruitier, often from small producers. Best DOCG MOSCATO: L Armangia, BERA, BRAIDA, Ca'd'Gal, CASCINA FONDA, Cascina Pian d'Oro, Caudrina, Il Falchetto, FONTANAFREDDA, Forteto della Luja, di GRESY, Icardi, Isolabella, Marino, Marco Negri, La Morandina, Elio Perrone, Rivetti, Saracco, Scagliola, Vajra, Vietti, Vignaioli di Sante Stefano, Viticoltori Acquese.

Moscato Giallo Aromatic ALTO ADIGE grape made into irresistible dry white, especially LAGEDER, CS CALDARO.

Müller-Thurgau Variety of some interest in TRENTINO-ALTO ADIGE and FRIULI. Leading producers: Lavis, LAGEDER, POJER & SANDRI, Zeni.

Murana, Salvatore Si ★★★ Very good MOSCATO and PASSITO di PANTELLERIA.

Muri Gries ★★ Very good producer of DOC ALTO ADIGE, best is DOC LAGREIN.

Nada, Fiorenzo ★★★ Fine producer of smooth, elegant DOCG BARBARESCO.

Nebbiolo The best red grape of PIEDMONT. Also in VALTELLINA (Lombardy).

Nebbiolo d'Alba Pie DOC r dr (s/sw sp) ★★ **96 97 98 99 00 01** 03 04 From ALBA (but not BAROLO, BARBARESCO). Like lighter BAROLO but more approachable. Best from Marziano Abbona, Alario, BRICCO Maiolica, Cascina Chicco, La Contea, Paolo Conterno, Correggia, Damilano, De Marie, FONTANAFREDDA, GIACOSA, Bruna Grimaldi, Hilberg, Mario Marengo, Giuseppe MASCARELLO, Gianmatteo Pira, Paitin, PRUNOTTO, Rizieri, SANDRONE, Tenuta Rocca, VAL DI PRETE. See also ROERO.

Negri See GRUPPO ITALIANO VINI.

Negroamaro Literally "black bitter"; APULIAN red grape with high quality potential. See ALEZIO, BRINDISI, COPERTINO, and SALICE SALENTINO.

Nero d'Avola SICILIAN dark-red grape (Avola is south of Siracusa) with some promise, alone or in blends.

Niedermayr ★★★ Very good DOC ALTO ADIGE, especially LAGREIN, PINOT N, Gewurz, Sauv Bl, and IGT Euforius (LAGREIN/Cab Sauv) and Aureus (sweet white blend).

Niedrist, Ignaz ★★★ Small, gifted producer of white and red ALTO ADIGE wines (especially LAGREIN, PINOT N, PINOT BL, RIES).

Nipozzano, Castello di ★★★ FRESCOBALDI estate in RUFINA east of Florence making _MONTESODI CHIANTI_. The most important outside the CLASSICO zone.

Nittardi ★★→★★★ Reliable source of high-quality CHIANTI CLASSICO.

Nosiola (Trentino) T-AA DOC w dr sw ★ DYA Light, fruity white from Nosiola grapes. Also good VIN SANTO. Best from Castel Noarna, POJER & SANDRI, Giovanni Poli, Pravis, Zeni.

Nozzole ★★→★★★ Famous estate now owned by Ambrogio FOLONARI, in heart of CHIANTI CLASSICO, north of Greve. Also very good Cab Sauv Pareto.

Nuragus di Cagliari Sar DOC w ★★ DYA Lively Sardinian white.

Oasi degli Angeli Benchmark all-MONTEPULCIANO wines from small producer in southern Marches; lush and mouth-filling.

Oberto, Andrea ★★→★★★ Small La Morra producer: top BAROLO, BARBERA D'ALBA.

Oddero ★★→★★★ Well-known La Morra estate for excellent BAROLO (look for Mondocco di Bussia, Rocche di Castiglione, and VIGNA Rionda).

Oltrepò Pavese Lom DOC r w dr sw sp ★→★★★ 14 wines from Pavia province, most named after grapes. Sometimes very good PINOT N and SPUMANTE. Top growers: Anteo, Barbacarlo, Casa Re, Castello di Cigognola, CS Casteggio, Frecciarossa, Le Fracce, La Versa co-op, Monsupello, Mazzolino, Ruiz de Cardenas, Travaglino, Vercesi del Castellazzo.

Ornellaia Tus ★★★★ **90' 93 95' 96** 97' 98 99 01 03 04 Lodovico ANTINORI-founded estate near BOLGHERI on the TUSCAN coast. FRESCOBALDI bought out former joint-venture partner Mondavi. Estate has many prestigious wines: excellent BOLGHERI DOC Ornellaia, superb IGT Masseto (MERLOT), v. good BOLGHERI DOC Le Serre Nuove and IGT Le Volte.

Orvieto Umb DOC w dr s/sw ★→★★ DYA The classic Umbrian golden white, smooth, substantial; once very dull but recently more interesting, especially when sweet. Orvieto CLASSICO is better. Only finest (e.g. Barberani, Co.Vi.O, Decugnano del Barbi, La Carraia, Palazzone, Vi.C.Or) age well. But see Castello della SALA.

Pacenti, Siro ★★★ Very international-style BRUNELLO and ROSSO DI MONTALCINO.

Pagadebit di Romagna E-R DOC w dr s/sw ★ DYA Pleasant traditional "payer of debts" from around Bertinoro.

Pagani De Marchi New face north of BOLGHERI. Impressive IGT varietal wines from Cab Sauv, SANGIOVESE, and in particular, MERLOT.

Palazzino, Podere Il ★★★ Small estate with admirable CHIANTI CLASSICO.

Pancrazi, Marchese ★★→★★★ Estate near Florence: some of Italy's top PINOT N.

Paneretta, Castello della ★★→★★★ To follow for very fine CHIANTI CLASSICO, IGTS Quatrocentenario, Terrine.

Pantelleria Island off the SICILIAN coast noted for MOSCATO, particularly PASSITO.

Watch for Abraxas, Colosi, DONNAFUGATA, Salvatore MURANA, Nuova Agricoltura.

Parrina Tus DOC r w ★★ Grand estate nr classy resorts of Argentario. Good white Ansonica, improving reds (SANGIOVESE/Cab Sauv and MERLOT) from MAREMMA.

Pasqua, Fratelli ★★ Good producer and bottler of VERONA wines: VALPOLICELLA, AMARONE, SOAVE. Also BARDOLINO and RECIOTO.

Passito (pa) Strong, mostly sweet wine from grapes dried on the vine or indoors.

Paternoster ★★★ Top AGLIANICO DEL VULTURE, especially Don Anselmo, Villa Rotondo.

Patriglione ★★★ Dense, strong red IGT (NEGROAMARO/MALVASIA Nera). See TAURINO.

Piaggia Outstanding producer of Carmignano Riserva, IGT Il Sasso and superb new Cabernet Franc Poggio dei Colli.

Piave Ven DOC r w ★→★★ (r) **99'** 00 01' 03 04 (w) DYA Flourishing DOC northwest of Venice for four red and four white wines named after their grapes. Cab Sauv, MERLOT, and RABOSO reds can all age. Good examples from Duca di Castelanza, Molon, Loredan Gasparini, Villa Sandi.

Picolit F-VG DOC w s/sw sw ★★→★★★★ 00 01 03 04 Delicate sweet wine from COLLI ORIENTALI DEL FRIULI, but with an exaggerated reputation. A little like France's Jurançon. Ages up to six years, but very overpriced. Best, and very good, from: Livio FELLUGA, Meroi, Perusini, Specogna, VILLA RUSSIZ, Vinae dell'Abbazia.

Piedmont (Piemonte) With TUSCANY, the most important Italian region for top-quality wine. Turin is the capital, ASTI and ALBA the wine centres. See BARBARESCO, Barbera, BAROLO, DOLCETTO, GRIGNOLINO, MOSCATO, etc.

Piemonte Pie DOC r w p (sp) ★→★★ New all-PIEDMONT blanket-DOC including Barbera, BONARDA, BRACHETTO, CORTESE, GRIGNOLINO, Chard, SPUMANTE, MOSCATO. ★★★

Pieropan ★★★ *Outstanding SOAVE* and RECIOTO: deserving its fame, especially Soave La Rocca and Calvarino, sweet PASSITO della ROCCA.

Pieve di Santa Restituta ★★★ GAJA estate for admirable BRUNELLO DI MONTALCINO.

Pigato Lig DOC w ★★ Often outclasses VERMENTINO as *Liguria's finest white*, with rich texture and structure. Good from Bruna, Colle dei Bardellini, Durin, Feipu, Foresti, Lupi, Poggio die Gorlieri, TERRE ROSSE, Vio.

Pinot Bianco (Pinot Bl) Popular grape in northeast for many DOC wines, generally bland and dry. Best from ALTO ADIGE ★★ (top growers include Colterenzio, HOFSTÄTTER, LAGEDER, NIEDRIST, TERLANO, Termeno), COLLIO ★★→★★★ (very good from Renato Keber, Aldo Polencic, RUSSIZ SUPERIORE, SCHIOPETTO, VILLA RUSSIZ), and COLLI ORIENTALI ★★→★★★ (best from La Viarte, Zamò & Zamò). ISONZO ★★ (from Masut da Rive).

Pinot Grigio Potentially tasty, low-acid white grape popular in northeast. Best from DOCS ALTO ADIGE (SAN MICHELE APPIANO, CALDARO, LAGEDER, Termeno), COLLIO (Renato Keber, LIVON, Aldo Polencic, RUSSIZ SUPERIORE, SCHIOPETTO, Tercic, Terpin, Venica, VILLA RUSSIZ), COLLI ORIENTALI (Livio FELLUGA), and ISONZO (Borgo San Daniele, LIS NERIS, Masut da Rive, Pierpaolo Pecorari, Ronco del Gelso, VIE DI ROMANS).

Pinot Nero (Pinot Noir) Planted in much of northeast Italy. DOC status in ALTO ADIGE (the co-ops of Caldaro, Colterenzio, and Cortaccia, HAAS, Haderburg, HOFSTÄTTER, LAGEDER, Laimburg, NIEDERMAYR, Niedrist, SAN MICHELE APPIANO CO-OP, Termeno co-op) and in OLTREPÒ PAVESE (Frecciarossa, Ruiz de Cardenas). Promising trials elsewhere, *e.g.* FRIULI (LE DUE TERRE, Masut da Riva), TUSCANY (Ama, FARNETELLA, FONTODI, Pancranzi), and on Mount Etna in SICILY. Also fine from several regions: TRENTINO (Lunelli, POJER & SANDRI), Lombardy (CA' DEL BOSCO, Ronco Calino), Umbria (ANTINORI), Marches (BOCCADIGABBIA).

Pio Cesare ★★→★★★ Long-established ALBA producer. Especially BAROLO, BARBARESCO.

Planeta ★★★ Top SICILIAN estate: Segreta Bianco blend, Segreta ROSSO; *outstanding Chard*, Cab Sauv, Fiano, MERLOT, NERO D'AVOLA (Santa Cecilia).

Podere Small TUSCAN farm, once part of a big estate. (See under name – *e.g.* BOSCARELLI, PODERI.)

Poggio Antico ★★★ Admirably consistent, top-level BRUNELLO DI MONTALCINO.

Poggione, Tenuta Il ★★★ Very reliable estate for BRUNELLO, ROSSO DI MONTALCINO.

Pojer & Sandri ★★→★★★ Top TRENTINO producers of both red and white wines, including SPUMANTE.

Poliziano ★★★→★★★★ MONTEPULCIANO estate. Federico Carletti makes superior VINO NOBILE (especially Asinone) and superb IGT Le Stanze (Cab Sauv/MERLOT).

Pomino Tus DOC w r ★★★ r **95 97** 98 99' 01 Fine red and white blends (especially Il Benefizio). Especially from FRESCOBALDI and SELVAPIANA.

Produttori del Barbaresco ★★→★★★ Co-op and one of DOCG's most reliable producers. Often-outstanding single-vineyard wines (Asili, Montefico, Montestefano, Rabajà).

Prosecco di Conegliano-Valdobbiadene Ven DOC w s/sw sp (dr) ★★ DYA Fashionable light sparkling, normally very dry; the dry, faintly bitter; the sweet, fruity. Sweetest are called Superiore di Cartizze. CARPENE-MALVOLTI: best known; also Adami, Bisol, Bortolin, Canevel, Case Bianche, Le Colture, Col Salice, Col Vetoraz, Nino Franco, Gregoletto, Ruggeri, Zardetto.

Prunotto, Alfredo ★★★→★★★★ Very serious ALBA company with top BARBARESCO, BAROLO, NEBBIOLO, BARBERA D'ALBA, DOLCETTO, etc. Since 1999 Prunotto (now controlled by ANTINORI) also produces BARBERA D'ASTI (look for Costamiole) and Monferrato Rosso Mompertone, Barbera-Syrah blend.

Puglia See APULIA.

Querciabella ★★→★★★ Prominent CHIANTI CLASSICO estate with RISERVA, IGT Camartina (SANGIOVESE/Cab Sauv), barrel-fermented white Batàr, new SANGIOVESE/MERLOT.

Quintarelli, Giuseppe ★★★★ True artisan producer of VALPOLICELLA, RECIOTO, and AMARONE. At the top in both quality and price.

Raboso del Piave (now DOC) Ven r ★★ **95 97** 99' 00 01 Powerful, sharp, interesting country red; needs age. Look for Molon.

Rampolla, Castello dei ★★★→★★★★ Fine estate in Panzano in CHIANTI CLASSICO, notable Cab Sauv-based IGT wines Sammarco and Alceo.

Recioto della Valpolicella Ven DOC r s/sw (sp) ★★→★★★★ **95 97** 98 00 01 03 04 Potentially excellent rich and tangy red from half-dried grapes. Very good from Stefano Accordini, Serègo Alighieri, ALLEGRINI, Baltieri, BOLLA, BRUNELLI, BUSSOLA, Campagnola, Ca' Rugate, Castellani, DAL FORNO, Aleardo Ferrari, LE RAGOSE, LE SALETTE, QUINTARELLI, Sant'Alda, Speri, TEDESCHI, Trabucchi, CS VALPOLICELLA, Villa Bellini, Villa Monteleone, Viviani, and Zeldi.

Recioto della Valpolicella Amarone See AMARONE.

Recioto di Gambellara Ven DOC w ssw (sp s/sw DYA) ★ Mostly half-sparkling and industrial. Best is strong and sweet. Look for La Biancara.

Recioto di Soave Ven DOCG w s/sw (sp) ★★★ **93 94 95 97** 98 99 00 01 03 04 SOAVE made from selected half-dried grapes: sweet, fruity, slightly almondy; high alcohol. Outstanding from ANSELMI, Gini, PIEROPAN, Tamellini, and now often very good from Ca' Rugate, Pasqua, Suavia, Trabuchi.

Refosco (dal Peduncolo Rosso) r ★★→★★★ **97'** 99' 00 01 03 04 Interesting, full, dark, tannic red for ageing. Best comes from COLLI ORIENTALI DOC, Moschioni, Le Vigne di Zamo, Volpi Pasini: *very good from Livio FELLUGA* and Miani; good from Dorigo, Ronchi di Manzano, Venica, Ca' Bolani, and Denis Montanara in Aquileia DOC. Often good value.

Regaleali See TASCA D'ALMERITA.

Ribolla Colli Orientali del Friuli and Collio, F-VG DOC w ★→★★ DYA Highly acidic northeastern white. The best comes from COLLIO. Top estates: La Castellada, Damijan, Fliegl, GRAVNER, Il Carpino, Primosic, Radikon, Tercic, Terpin.

Ricasoli Famous TUSCAN family, "inventors" of CHIANTI, whose CHIANTI CLASSICO is named after its BROLIO estate and castle. Other Ricasolis own Castello di Cacchiano and Rocca di Montegrossi.

Riecine Tus r ★★★ First-class CHIANTI CLASSICO estate at Gaiole, created by its late

English owner, John Dunkley. Also fine IGT La Gioia SANGIOVESE.

Riesling Used to mean Riesling Italico or Welschriesling. German (Rhine) Riesling now ascendant. Best: DOC ALTO ADIGE ★★ (especially HOFSTÄTTER, Laimburg, Ignaz NIEDRIST, Kuenhof, La Vis co-op, Unterortl); DOC OLTREPÒ PAVESE (Lom) ★★ (Brega, Frecciarossa, Le Fracce); excellent from RONCO del Gelso and VIE DI ROMANS (DOC ISONZO). Very good from Le Vigne di San Pietro (Ven), JERMANN, VAJRA (Pie).

Ripasso VALPOLICELLA re-fermented on AMARONE grape skins to make a more complex, longer-lived, fuller wine. First-class is MASI's Campo Fiorin.

Riserva Wine aged for a statutory period, usually in casks or barrels.

Riunite One of the world's largest co-op cellars, near Reggio Emilia, producing huge quantities of LAMBRUSCO and other wines.

Rivera ★★→★★★ Reliable winemakers at Andria in APULIA. ★★★ CASTEL DEL MONTE Il Falcone RISERVA; very good Cappellaccio; VIGNA al Monte; Puer Apuliae.

Rivetti, Giorgio (La Spinetta) ★★★ →★★★★ Fine MOSCATO d'Asti, excellent Barbera, interesting IGT Pin, series of top single-vineyard BARBARESCOS. Now owner of vineyards both in the BAROLO and the CHIANTI Colli Pisane DOCGS. First vintages of BAROLO already outstanding.

Riviera del Garda Bresciano Lom DOC w p r (sp) ★→★★ r **97 99** 00 01 Simple, sometimes charming cherry-pink CHIARETTO, neutral white from southwest Garda. Especially from Ca' dei Frati, Comincioli, Costaripa, Monte Cigogna.

Rocca, Bruno ★★★ Young producer with admirable BARBARESCO (Rabajà) and other ALBA wines, now with very fine Barbera d'Asti as well.

Rocche dei Manzoni ★★★ Modernist estate at Monforte d'Alba. Very good oaky BAROLO (especially VIGNA d'la Roul, Cappella di Stefano, Pianpolvere), BRICCO Manzoni (pioneer Barbera/NEBBIOLO blend), Quatr Nas (LANGHE) .

Roero Pie DOCG r ★★ **96 97' 98' 99' 00** 01' 03 04 05 Evolving former "drink-me-quick" NEBBIOLO. Can be firm and delicious. Best: Almondo, Buganza, Ca' Rossa, Cascina Chicco, Correggia, Funtanin, Malvirà, Monchiero-Carbone, Morra, Pace, Pioiero, Taliano, Val di Prete.

Ronco Term for a hillside vineyard in northern Italy, especially FRIULI-VENEZIA GIULIA.

Ronco del Gnemiz ★★★ Small estate, very fine COLLI ORIENTALI DEL FRIULI.

Rosato Rosé; also CHIARETTO, especially around Lake Garda.

Rosato del Salento Ap p ★★ DYA From near BRINDISI; can be strong, but often really juicy and good. See COPERTINO, SALICE SALENTO for producers.

Rossese di Dolceacqua Lig DOC r ★★ DYA Quite rare, fragrant, light red of the Riviera. Good from Foresti, Giuncheo, Guglielmi, Lupi, Terre Bianche.

Rosso Red.

Rosso Conero Mar DOCG r ★★→★★★ 97' **98** 00' 01' 03' 04 *Some of Italy's best MONTEPULCIANO* (the grape, that is): GAROFOLI's Grosso Agontano, Moroder's RC Dorico, TERRE CORTESI MONCARO's Nerone and Vigneti del Parco, Le Terrazze's Sassi Neri and Visions of J. Also good: Casato, FAZI-BATTAGLIA, Lanari, Leopardi Dittajuti, Malacari, Marchetti, Piantate Lunghe, Poggio Morelli, UMANI RONCHI.

Rosso di Montalcino Tus DOC r ★★→★★★ **99' 00 01** 03 04' 05 DOC for younger wines from BRUNELLO grapes. For growers, see BRUNELLO DI MONTALCINO.

Rosso di Montefalco Umb DOC r ★★→★★★ **97' 98 99'** 00' 01' 03 04 05 SANGIOVESE/SAGRANTINO blend. For producers, see MONTEFALCO SAGRANTINO.

Rosso di Montepulciano Tus DOC r ★★ 03 04 05 See previous two entries for VINO NOBILE. For growers see VINO NOBILE DI MONTEPULCIANO. While ROSSO DI MONTALCINO is increasingly expensive, Rosso di Montepulciano offers value.

Rosso Piceno Mar DOC r ★★ **97' 98' 00' 01'** 03' 04 Stylish MONTEPULCIANO/SANGIOVESE, SUPERIORE from classic zone near Ascoli, much improved in recent years. Best include: Aurora, BOCCADIGABBIA, Bucci, Ciù Ciù, COLLI Ripani, Damiani, De Angelis, Fonte della Luna, Forano, Laila, Le Caniette, Laurentina, Montecappone, TERRE CORTESI MONCARO, Saladini Pilastri, San Giovanni, San

Savino, Velenosi Ercole, Villamagna, Villa Ragnola.

Ruchè (also Rouchè/Rouchet) Rare old grape of French origin; fruity, fresh, rich-scented red wine (sweet/semi-sweet). Ruchè di Castagnole MONFERRATO is recent DOC. Look for Biletta, Borgognone, Dezzani, Garetto. SCARPA'S Rouchet Briccorosa: dry (★★★).

Ruffino ★→★★★ Outstanding CHIANTI merchant at Pontassieve, east of Florence. Best are RISERVA Ducale and Santedame. Very good IGT Chard Solatia, SANGIOVESE/Cab Sauv Modus. Owns Lodola Nuova in MONTEPULCIANO for VINO NOBILE DI MONTEPULCIANO, and Greppone Mazzi in MONTALCINO for BRUNELLO DI MONTEPULCIANO. Excellent SANGIOVESE/Colorino blend Romitorio from Santedame estate. Recent purchase: Borgo Conventi estate in FRIULI-VENEZIA GIULIA.

Rufina ★★★ Important sub-region of CHIANTI in the hills east of Florence. Best wines from Basciano, CASTELLO del Trebbio, CASTELLO DI NIPOZZANO (FRESCOBALDI), Colognole, Frascole, SELVAPIANA, Tenuta Bossi, Travignoli.

Sagrantino di Montefalco See MONTEFALCO.

Sala, Castello della ★★→★★★ ANTINORI estate at ORVIETO. Campogrande is the regular white. Top wine is Cervaro della Sala, oak-aged Chard/GRECHETTO. Muffato della Sala was a pioneering example of an Italian botrytis-influenced dessert wine. PINOT N also good.

Salice Salento Ap DOC r ★★→★★★ 95 97' 99' 00 01' 03 04 Resonant but clean and quenching red from NEGROAMARO grapes. RISERVA after 2 years. Top makers: Apollonio, Candido, Castello Monaci, Due Palme, Resya, Tornavento, TAURINO, Valle dell'Asso.

Sandrone, Luciano ★★★ Exponent of new-style BAROLO vogue with very good BAROLO Cannubi Boschi, Le Vigne, DOLCETTO, BARBERA D'ALBA, and NEBBIOLO D'ALBA.

San Felice ★★ Picturesque CHIANTI resort/estate. Fine CLASSICO RISERVA Poggio ROSSO. Also red IGT Vigorello and BRUNELLO DI MONTALCINO Campogiovanni.

San Gimignano Famous TUSCAN city of towers and its dry white VERNACCIA. Also very fine red wines: Cesani, Cusona, FALCHINI, Fontaleoni, La Rampa di Fugnano, Le Calcinaie, Le Tre Stelle, Mormoraia, Palagetto, Palagione, PARADISO.

Sangiovese (Sangioveto) Principal red grape of central Italy. Top performance used to be only in TUSCANY – CHIANTI, VINO NOBILE, BRUNELLO DI MONTALCINO, MORELLINO DI SCANSANO, various fine IGT offerings, etc. – but now competitive bottles are made elsewhere. S di Romagna often well made and very good value from Balia di Zola, Berti, Calonga, Ca' Lunga, Campo del Sole, Tenuta Diavoletto, Drei Donà, La Berta, La Viola, Madonia, Pandolfa, Poderi dal Nespoli, San Patrignano, Santini, San Valentino, Tenuta Valli, Terragens, Tre Monti, Trere (E-R DOC), Uva delle Mura, Zerbina, IGT Ronco del Ginestre, Ronco dei Ciliegi from CASTELLUCCIO. Very good MONTEFALCO ROSSO, TORGIANO (Umbria). Sometimes good from the Marches too: Maria Pia Castelli, BOCCADIGABBIA, Ciù Ciù.

San Giusto a Rentennano ★★★→★★★★ One of the best CHIANTI CLASSICO producers (★★★). Delicious but very rare VIN SANTO. Superb SANGIOVESE IGT Percarlo (★★★★).

San Guido, Tenuta See SASSICAIA.

San Leonardo ★★★ Top estate in TRENTINO, with outstanding San Leonardo (Cab Sauv) and good TRENTINO DOC MERLOT.

San Michele Appiano Top ALTO ADIGE co-op. Look for Sanct Valentin (★★★) selections: Chard, PINOT GR, Sauv Bl, Cab Sauv, PINOT N, Gewurz.

Santadi ★★★ Consistently fine wines from SARDINIAN co-op, especially DOC CARIGNANO DEL SULCIS Grotta Rossa, TERRE BRUNE, Rocca Rubia, and IGT Baie Rosse (Carignano), Vermentino Villa Solais, Villa di Chiesa (VERMENTINO/Chard).

Santa Maddalena (or St-Magdalener) T-AA DOC r ★→★★ DYA Typical SCHIAVA ALTO ADIGE red. Sometimes light with bitter aftertaste; or warm, smooth, and fruity especially: CS St-Magdalena (Huck am Bach), Gojer, Josephus Mayr, Georg Ramoser, Hans Rottensteiner (Premstallerhof), Heinrich Rottensteiner.

Santa Margherita Large Veneto (Portogruaro) merchants: Veneto (Torresella), ALTO ADIGE (Kettmeir), TUSCANY (Lamole di Lamole and Vistarenni), and Lombardy (CA' DEL BOSCO).

Santi See GRUPPO ITALIANO VINI.

Saracco, Paolo ★★★ Small estate with top MOSCATO D'ASTI.

Sardinia (Sardegna) Major potential, at times evidenced in excellent wines, *e.g.* TERRE BRUNE from SANTADI, Turriga from ARGIOLAS, Arbeskia and Dule from Gabbas, VERMENTINO of CAPICHERA, CANNONAU RISERVAS of Jerzu, VERMENTINO and CANNONAU selections from Dettori.

Sartarelli ★★★ One of top VERDICCHIO DEI CASTELLI DI JESI producers (Tralivio); outstanding, rare Verdicchio VENDEMMIA Tardiva (Contrada Balciana).

Sassicaia Tus r ★★★★ **85' 88' 90' 93 95' 96** 97' 98 99 01 03 04 One of the first Cab Sauvs, Italy's best by far in 1970s and 80s. Highly influential, from the Tenuta San Guido at BOLGHERI. Promoted from SUPER TUSCAN VDT to special sub-zone status in BOLGHERI DOC. Conservative style, real finesse.

Satta, Michele ★★★ Very good DOC BOLGHERI, IGT red blend Piastraia and Castagni.

Scarpa ★★→★★★ Old-fashioned house with BARBERA D'ASTI (La Bogliona), rare Rouchet (RUCHÈ), very good DOLCETTO, BAROLO, BARBARESCO.

Scavino, Paolo ★★★ Successful modern-style BAROLO producer. Sought-after single-vineyard wines: Rocche dell'Annunziata, Bric del Fiasc, Cannubi, and Carobric. Also oak-aged Barbera and Langhe Corale.

Schiava High-yielding red grape of TRENTINO and ALTO ADIGE, used for light reds such as LAGO DI CALDARO, SANTA MADDALENA, etc.

Schioppetto, Mario ★★★→★★★★ Legendary late COLLIO pioneer with 25,000-case winery. Very good DOC Sauv Bl, PINOT BL, TOCAI, IGT blend Blanc de Rosis, etc. Rich and elegant new IGT offerings with wine from COLLIO and COLLI ORIENTALI vineyards.

Sciacchetrà See CINQUETERRE.

Secco Dry.

Sella & Mosca ★★ Major SARDINIAN grower and merchant with very pleasant white Torbato and light, fruity VERMENTINO Cala Viola (DYA). Good Alghero DOC Marchese di Villamarina (Cab Sauv), and Tanca Farrà (CANNONAU/Cab Sauv). Also interesting port-like Anghelu Ruju. A safe bet.

Selvapiana ★★★ Top CHIANTI RUFINA estate. Best wines are RISERVA Bucerchiale and IGT Fornace. Also fine red DOC POMINO.

Sforzato See VALTELLINA.

Sicily Island in full creative ferment, both with native grapes (NERO D'AVOLA, Frappato, Inzolia, Grecanico) and international varieties. To watch: Abraxas, Agareno, Benanti, Bonaccorsi, Capocroce, Ceusi, Colosi, COS, Cottanera, CS Corbera, Cusumano, De Bartoli, Di Giovanna, DONNAFUGATA, DUCA DI SALAPARUTA, Fatasci, Fazio, Feudo Maccari, Feudo Montoni, Feudo Santa Teresa, Firriato, Fondo Antico, Fornaci, Grottarossa, Gulfi-Ramada, Miceli, Morgante, MURANA, Passopisciano, Pellegrino, Principe di Butera (ZONIN), PLANETA, Rapitalà, Rudini, Sallier de la Tour, Santa Anastasia, SIV, Spadafora, TASCA D'ALMERITA, Tenuta dell'Abate, Terre Nere, VECCHIO SAMPERI, Zemmer, Zisoli.

Sizzano Pie DOC r ★★ 95 Full-bodied red from Sizzano, (Novara); mostly NEBBIOLO. Ages up to 10 years. Especially: Bianchi, Dessilani.

Soave Ven DOC w ★→★★ DYA Famous white: fresh, smooth, limpid. Standards rising (at last). Soave CLASSICO: intense fruit/minerals. Especially PIEROPAN; also Bolla, Cantina del Castello, La Cappuccina, Cecilia Beretta, Dama del Rovere, Fattori & Graney, Gini, **_Guerrieri-Rizzardi_**, Inama, Montetondo, Portinari, Pra, Ca' Rugate, Sartori, Suavia, Tamellini, TEDESCHI.

Solaia Tus r ★★★★ 85 88 90 **93 94' 95 96** 97' 98 99' 00 01' Very fine Bordeaux-style VDT of Cab Sauv and a little SANGIOVESE from ANTINORI; first made in 1978.

Italy's best Cab Sauv in the 1990s, and a great wine by any standards.

Sorì Term for a high south-, southeast-, or southwest-oriented site in PIEDMONT.

Sovana New MAREMMA DOC; inland near Pitigliano. Look for SANGIOVESE, Ciliegiolo from Tenuta Roccaccia, Pitigliano, Ripa, Sassotondo, Cab Sauv from ANTINORI.

Spanna Local name for NEBBIOLO in a variety of north PIEDMONT zones (BOCA, BRAMATERRA, FARA, GATTINARA, GHEMME, LESSONA, SIZZANO).

Sportoletti ★★★ V. good wines from Spello, near ASSISI, especially Villa Fidelia.

Spumante Sparkling, including both METODO CLASSICO (best from TRENTINO, ALTO ADIGE, FRANCIACORTA, PIEDMONT, OLTREPÒ PAVESE; occasionally good from FRIULI and Veneto) and tank-made cheapos.

Stravecchio Very old.

Südtirol The local name of German-speaking ALTO ADIGE.

Superiore Wine with more ageing than normal DOC and 0.5–1% more alcohol.

Super Tuscan Term coined for innovative wines from TUSCANY, often involving pure SANGIOVESE or international varieties, barriques, and elevated prices.

Tasca d'Almerita ★★★ Historic SICILIAN producer owned by noble family (between Palermo and Caltanissetta to the southeast). Good IGT red, white, and ROSATO Regaleali; very good ROSSO; impressive Chard and Cab Sauv.

Taurasi Cam DOCG r ★★★ 94' 95 97' 98 99 00 01' 03' 04 05 The best Campanian red, and one of Italy's outstanding wines. Tannic when young. RISERVA after 4 years. Very good from Caggiano, Caputo, FEUDI DI SAN GREGORIO, MASTROBERARDINO, Molettieri, Vesevo, and Villa Raiano.

Taurino, Cosimo ★★★ Tip-top producer of Salento-APULIA, very good SALICE SALENTO, VDT Notarpanoro, and IGT PATRIGLIONE ROSSO.

Tedeschi, Fratelli ★★→★★★ Well-known producer of VALPOLICELLA, AMARONE, RECIOTO. Good Capitel San Rocco red IGT.

Tenuta Farm or estate. (See under name – *e.g.* SAN GUIDO, TENUTA.)

Terlano T-AA w ★★→★★★ DYA Terlano DOC incorporated into ALTO ADIGE. AA Terlano DOC is applicable to eight varietal whites, especially Sauv Bl. Terlaner in German. Especially from CS Terlano, LAGEDER, NIEDERMAYR, NIEDRIST.

Teroldego Rotaliano T-AA DOC r p ★★→★★★ Attractive blackberry-scented red; slightly bitter aftertaste; can age very well. ***Especially FORADORI's***. Also good from CA' VIT, Dorigati, Endrizzi, MEZZACORONA'S RISERVA, Zeni.

Terre Brune Sard r ★★★ Splendid earthy Carignano/Boveladda blend from SANTADI, a flag-carrier for SARDINIA.

Terre Cortesi Moncaro Mar ★★★ Marches co-op, now making wines that compete with the best of the region: good VERDICCHIO DEI CASTELLI DI JESI, ROSSO CONERO, and ROSSO PICENO.

Terre da Vino ★→★★★ Association of 27 PIEDMONT co-ops and private estates including most local DOCs. Best: BARBARESCO La Casa in Collina, BAROLO PODERE Parussi, BARBERA D'ASTI La Luna e I Falò.

Terre di Franciacorta Lom DOC r w ★★ 97 99 00 01 Usually pleasant reds (blends of Cab Sauv, Barbera, NEBBIOLO, MERLOT); quite fruity and balanced whites (Chard, PINOT GR). Best producers: see FRANCIACORTA.

Terre Rosse ★★ Pioneering small estate near Bologna. Its Cab Sauv, Chard, PINOT BL, RIES, even Viognier, were trail-blazing wines for the region.

Terriccio, Castello di ★★★ Estate south of Livorno: excellent IGT Lupicaia, very good IGT Tassinaia, both Cab Sauv/MERLOT blends. Impressive new IGT Terriccio, an unusual blend of various French grapes.

Tignanello Tus r ★★★→★★★★ 88 90 93 95 96 97' 98 99' 00 01' 03 Pioneer and leader of international-style TUSCAN reds, made by ANTINORI.

Tocai Mild, smooth white (no relation of Hungarian Tokaji) of northeast. DOC also in Ven and Lom (★→★★), but producers are most proud of it in FRIULI-VENEZIA GIULIA (especially COLLIO and COLLI ORIENTALI) ★★→★★★. Best producers:

Aldo Polencic, BORGO DEL TIGLIO, Borgo San Daniele, LE VIGNE DI ZAMÒ, Livio FELLUGA, Masut da Rive, Meroi, Mirani, Renato Keber, RONCO del Gelso, RONCO DEL GNEMIZ, RUSSIZ SUPERIORE, SCHIOPETTO, Venica & Venica, VILLA RUSSIZ.

Torgiano Umb DOC r w p (sp) ★★ and **Torgiano, Rosso Riserva** Umb DOCG r ★★→★★★ 95 97 99 00' 01' 03 04 Good red from Umbria, resembles CHIANTI CLASSICO in style. RUBESCO: standard. LUNGAROTTI'S RISERVA VIGNA Montecchi was outstanding in vintages such as 75, 79, 85; keeps for many years. Antigniano's Torgiano offers interesting contrast to historic leader LUNGAROTTI.

Traminer Aromatico T-AA DOC w ★★→★★★ DYA (German: Gewürz) Delicate, aromatic, soft. Best from various co-ops (Caldaro, Colterenzio, Prima & Nuova, SAN MICHELE APPIANO, TERLANO, Termeno) plus Abbazia di Novacella, HAAS, HOFSTÄTTER, Kuenhof, LAGEDER, Laimberg, NIEDERMAYR.

Trebbiano Principal white grape of TUSCANY, found all over Italy. Ugni Blanc in French. Sadly, a waste of good vineyard space, with very rare exceptions.

Trebbiano d'Abruzzo Ab DOC w ★→★★ DYA Gentle, neutral, slightly tannic white from Pescara. Best producer: VALENTINI (also MONTEPULCIANO D'ABRUZZO), but challenged by Masciarelli. Nicodemi, La Valentina, and Valori also very good.

Trentino T-AA DOC r w dr sw ★→★★★ DOC for 20 wines, most named after grapes. Best: Chard, PINOT BL, MARZEMINO, TEROLDEGO. Region's capital is Trento.

Triacca ★★→★★★ Very good producer of VALTELLINA; also owns estates in TUSCANY (CHIANTI CLASSICO: La Madonnina; MONTEPULCIANO: Santavenere. All ★★).

Trinoro, Tenuta di ★★★ Isolated and exceptional TUSCAN red wine estate (Bordeaux varieties) in DOC Val d'Orcia between MONTEPULCIANO and MONTALCINO. Early vintages of Cab Sauv/Petit Verdot TRINORO are jaw-dropping. Andrea Franchetti now making wine at Passopisciano estate on Mount Etna.

Tuscany (Toscana) Italy's central wine region, includes DOCS CHIANTI, MONTALCINO, MONTEPULCIANO, etc., regional IGT Toscana, and – of course – SUPER TUSCAN.

Uberti ★★→★★★ Producer of DOCG FRANCIACORTA. Very good TERRE DI FRANCIACORTA (red and white).

Umani Ronchi ★★→★★★ Leading Marches merchant and grower, especially for VERDICCHIO (Casal di Serra, Plenio), ROSSO CONERO Cumaro white IGT Le Busche, red IGT Pelago. Recent wines impressively improved.

Vajra, Giuseppe Domenico ★★★ Very good consistent BAROLO producer, especially for Barbera, BAROLO, DOLCETTO, LANGHE, etc. Also an interesting (not fizzy) FREISA.

Valcalepio Lom DOC r w ★→★★ From near Bergamo. Pleasant red; lightly scented fresh white. Good from Brugherata, CASTELLO di Grumello, Monzio.

Valdadige T-AA DOC r w dr s/sw ★ Name for the simple wines of the valley of the ALTO ADIGE – in German, *Etschtaler*.

Val di Cornia Tus DOC r p w ★★→★★★ 97 98 99' 00 01' 02 03 04 DOC near Livorno, competing in quality with BOLGHERI. SANGIOVESE, Cab Sauv, MERLOT, and MONTEPULCIANO. Look for: Ambrosini, Jacopo Banti, Brancatelli, Bulichella, Tenuta Casadei Casa Dei, Gualdo del Re, Il Bruscello, Incontri, Le Pianacce, Montepeloso (Gabbro, Nardo), Petra, Russo, San Giusto, San Luigi, San Michele, Sant'Agnese, Suveraia, Terricciola, Tua Rita (Redigaffi).

Valentini, Edoardo ★★★ The grand tradition – and, with Gianni Mascerelli, the best maker – of MONTEPULCIANO and TREBBIANO D'ABRUZZO.

Valle d'Aosta (VdA) DOC r w p ★★ Regional DOC for more than 20 Alpine wines, including Premetta, Fumin, Blanc de Morgex et de La Salle, Chambave, Nus Malvoisie, Arnad Montjovet, Torrette, Donnas, and Enfer d'Arvier.

Valle Isarco Eisacktal, T-AA DOC w ★★ DYA AA Valle Isarco DOC is applicable to seven varietal wines made northeast of Bolzano. Good Gewürz, MÜLLER-T, RIES, and Silvaner. Top producers: Abbazia di Novacella, CS Eisacktaler, Kuenhof.

Valpolicella Ven DOC r ★→★★★ (Superiore) 98 00 01 03 04 (Others) DYA

Attractive red from near VERONA. Best are concentrated, complex, and merit higher prices. Delicate nutty scent, slightly bitter taste. Beware big bottles. CLASSICO more restricted; SUPERIORE aged one year. Best (★★★) DAL FORNO, TARELLI. Good: Stefano Accordini, Bertani, BOLLA, BRUNELLI, Buglioni, BUSSOLA, Campagnola, Ca' Rugate, Michele Castellani, Guerrieri-Rizzardi, I Saltari, LE RAGOSE, LE SALETTE, MASI, Mazzi, CS Negrar, PASQUA, Sant'Alda, Sant' Antonio, Sartori, Speri, TEDESCHI, Tommasi, Trabuchi, CS VALPOLICELLA, Vaona, Venturini, Villa Monteleone, Viviani, ZENATO. Interesting IGTS: MASI's Toar and Osar, ALLEGRINI's La Grola, La Poja, Palazzo della Torre (★★★), Zyme's Harlequin, OZ.

Valtellina Lom DOC r ★★→★★★ DOC for tannic wines: mainly from Chiavennasca (NEBBIOLO) in northern Alpine Sondrio province. Very good SUPERIORE DOCG from Grumello, Inferno, Sassella, Valgella vineyards. Best: Caven Camuna, Conti Sertoli-Salis, Fay, Nera, Nino Negri, Plozza, Rainoldi, TRIACCA. Sforzato is the most concentrated type of Valtellina; similar to AMARONE.

VDT, vino da tavola "Table wine": the humblest class of Italian wine. No specific geographical or other claim to fame, but occasionally some excellent wines that do not fit into official categories. See IGT.

Vecchio Old.

Vecchio Samperi Si ★★★ MARSALA-like VDT from outstanding estate. Best is barrel-aged 30 years. Owner Marco De Bartoli also makes top DOC MARSALAS.

Vendemmia Harvest or vintage.

Verdicchio dei Castelli di Jesi Mar DOC w (sp) ★★→★★★ DYA Ancient white from near Ancona, now fruity, well-structured, good value. Also CLASSICO. Best from: Accadia, Bonci-Vallerosa, Brunori, Bucci, Casalfarneto, Cimarelli, Colonnara, Coroncino, FAZI-BATTAGLIA, Fonte della Luna, GAROFOLI, Laila, Lucangeli Aymerich di Laconi, Mancinelli, Montecappone, Monte Shiavo, Santa Barbara, SARTARELLI, TERRE CORTESI MONCARO, UMANI RONCHI.

Verdicchio di Matelica Mar DOC w (sp) ★★→★★★ DYA Similar to above, smaller, less known, longer lasting. Especially Barone Pizzini, Belisario, Bisci, San Biagio, La Monacesca, Pagliano Tre.

Verduno Pie DOC r ★★ (DYA) Pale red with spicy perfume, from Pelavegra grape. Good producers: Alessandria and Castello di Verduno.

Verduzzo Colli Orientali del Friuli, F-VG DOC w dr s/sw sw ★★→★★★ Full-bodied white from native grapes. Ramandolo is highly regarded sub-zone. Top: Dario Coos, Dorigo, Giovanni Dri, Meroi. Superb sweet VDT from LIS NERIS.

Verduzzo del Piave Ven DOC w DYA A dull little white wine.

Vermentino Lig w ★★ DYA Best seafood white of Riviera, especially from Pietra Ligure and San Remo. DOC is Riviera Ligure di Ponente. See PIGATO. Especially good: Colle dei Bardellini, Durin, Lambruschi, La Rocca di San Niccolao, Lunae Bosoni, Lupi, Picedi Benettini, Poggio dei Gorlieri. Also Tuscan coast: ANTINORI, San Giusto, SATTA, Tenuta Vignale, **Terre di Talamo**.

Vermentino di Gallura Sar DOCG w ★★→★★★ DYA Soft, dry, strong white of Sardinia. Especially from CAPICHERA, Depperu, CS di Gallura, CS del Vermentino.

Vernaccia di Oristano Sar DOC w dr (sw fz) ★→★★★ **85' 86' 87 88 90'** 91' 93' 94' 95' 97' 98 99 00 01 Sardinian speciality, like light sherry, a touch bitter, full-bodied. SUPERIORE 15.5% alcohol, 3 years of age. Top: CONTINI.

Vernaccia di San Gimignano Tus DOCG w ★→★★ DYA Formerly ordinary tourist wine; recent renaissance. Newly DOCG with tougher production laws. Best: Cusona, Cesani, FALCHINI, Fontaleoni, Il Paradiso, Le Calcinaie, Le Rote, Mormoraia, Palagetto, Palagione, Rampa di Fugnano, TERUZZI E PUTHOD.

Verrazzano, Castello di ★★ Good CHIANTI CLASSICO estate near Greve.

Vestini Campagnano Small producer north of Naples specializing in forgotten local grapes. Excellent results from Casavecchia, Pallagrello Bianco, and

Pallagrello Nero.

Vicchiomaggio ★★→★★★ CHIANTI CLASSICO estate near Greve.

Vie di Romans ★★★→★★★★ Gifted young producer Gianfranco Gallo has built up his father's ISONZO estate to top FRIULI status. Excellent ISONZO Chard, PINOT GR, Sauv Bl, MALVASIA, RIES, and white blend called Flors di Uis.

Vietti ★★★ Exemplary producer of characterful PIEDMONT wines, including BAROLO, BARBARESCO, BARBERA D'ALBA, and D'ASTI at Castiglione Falletto in BAROLO region.

Vigna or **vigneto** A single vineyard (but, unlike elsewhere in the world, higher quality than that for generic DOC is not required in Italy).

Vignalta ★★ Top producer in COLLI EUGANEI near Padova (Veneto); very good COLLI Euganei Cab Sauv RISERVA and MERLOT/Cab Sauv blend Gemola.

Vignamaggio ★★→★★★ Historic, beautiful, and very good CHIANTI CLASSICO estate near Greve.

Villa ★★→★★★ Worthy producer of DOCG FRANCIACORTA.

Villa Matilde ★★★ Top Campania producer of Falerno ROSSO (Vigna Camararato) and BIANCO (Vigna Caracci), Eleusi PASSITO.

Villa Russiz ★★★ Impressive w DOC COLLIO Goriziano: very good Sauv Bl and MERLOT (especially "de la Tour" selections), PINOT BL, PINOT GR, TOCAI, Chard.

Vino da arrosto "Wine for roast meat" – *i.e.* good, robust, dry red.

Vino Nobile di Montepulciano Tus DOCG r ★★★ **90 93** 95' 97' 98 **99**' 00 01 03 04' Impressive SANGIOVESE with bouquet and style, but often tannic. RISERVA after 3 years. Best estates include AVIGNONESI, Bindella, BOSCARELLI, Canneto, Casanova, Contucci, Dei, I Cipressi, Il Faggeto, Fassati, Fattoria del Cerro, Gavioli, Gracciano della Seta, Gracciano Svetoni, Icario, La Braccesca, La Calonica, La Ciarliana, Le Berne, Le Casalte, Lunadoro, Macchione, Nottola, Palazzo Bandino, Palazzo Vecchio, Paterno, POLIZIANO, Romeo, Salcheto, Tre Berte, Trerose, Valdipiatta, Vecchia Cantina (look for Briareo), Villa Sant'Anna. So far, reasonably priced.

Vino novello Italy's equivalent of France's *primeurs* (as in Beaujolais).

Vin Santo or **Vinsanto**, **Vin(o) Santo** Term for certain strong, sweet wines, especially in TUSCANY: usually PASSITO. Can be very fine both in TUSCANY and TRENTINO.

Vin Santo Toscano Tus w s/sw ★→★★★ Aromatic, rich, and smooth. Aged in very small barrels called *caratelli*. Can be as astonishing as expensive, but a good one is very rare and top producers are always short of it. Best from AVIGNONESI, CAPEZZANA, CORZANO & PATERNO, Fattoria del Cerro, FELSINA, Frascole, ISOLE E OLENA, Rocca di Montegrossi, SAN GIUSTO A RENTENNANO, San Gervasio, SELVAPIANA, Villa Sant'Anna.

Vivaldi-Arunda ★★→★★★ Winemaker Josef Reiterer makes top ALTO ADIGE sparkling wines. Best: Extra Brut RISERVA, Cuvée Marianna.

Voerzio, Roberto ★★★→★★★★ Young BAROLO pace-setter. Top single-vineyard BAROLOS: Brunate, Cerequio, Rocche dell'Annunziata-Torriglione, Sarmassa, Serra; impressive BARBERA D'ALBA.

Volpaia, Castello di ★★→★★★ First-class CHIANTI CLASSICO estate at Radda.

VQPRD Vini di Qualità Prodotti in Regione Delimitata, on DOC labels.

Zenato Ven ★★→★★★ Very reliable estate for VALPOLICELLA, SOAVE, AMARONE.

Zerbina, Fattoria ★★★ New leader in Romagna; best ALBANA DOCG to date (rich PASSITO: Scacco Matto), very good SANGIOVESE; barrique-aged IGT Marzieno.

Zibibbo Si ★★ Local PANTELLERIA name for Muscat of Alexandria. Good: MURANA.

Zonin ★→★★ One of Italy's biggest private estates, based at GAMBELLARA, with DOC and DOCG VALPOLICELLA. Also in ASTI, APULIA, CHIANTI CLASSICO, SAN GIMIGNANO, FRIULI, SICILY, and now Virginia (USA). Quality rising under winemaker Franco Giacosa.

Germany

More heavily shaded areas are the wine-growing regions

The following abbreviations of regional names are used in the text:

Bad	Baden
Frank	Franken
M-M	Mittelmosel
M-S-R	Mosel-Saar-Ruwer
Na	Nahe
Pfz	Pfalz
Rhg	Rheingau
Rhh	Rheinhessen
Würt	Württemberg

I t's not so unusual for the native population of a country to have a different taste in wine from foreigners. But in Germany the difference is so marked as to constitute two different wines – albeit made from the same grape in the same places.

The German taste in Riesling is for ultra purity. Rieslings must be bone dry, fermented in steel and handled reductively so that not a trace of gentle oxidation, the sort that rounds out the wine and adds a bit of flesh and extra complexity, can be detected.

Foreigners, at least English-speaking foreigners, have had difficulty in getting to grips with this style. Outside German-speaking countries the taste tends to be for the style the Germans term "fruity" – that is, with residual sugar. The Germans no doubt think us barbarians for enjoying such old-fashioned flavours; we find them a bit too austere for comfort in their pursuit of steeliness untainted with sugar.

But of course wonderful wines are being made in both styles, and the dry wines have benefited enormously from the warmer summers that Germany has noticed in the past 20 or so years. But what these warmer summers have revealed is that not all German Riesling is suited to extreme dryness. In warmer regions, such as the Pfalz, dry wines can be extremely successful. They are grown on rich soils of marl or loess or volcanic earth, and have high alcohol, and extract to match. They are balanced, big, and punchy. But try and pull the same trick in the Mosel, and you can come unstuck. There the slate soils, the high acidity, and the delicate texture of the wine can mean wines being thrown wildly out of balance if they have the high alcohol that comes with fermenting to dryness.

German wine seems to be on the edge of another evolution of style. Perhaps it will head towards more muscle and power, with the Mosel holding fast to delicacy in the face of fashion. In which case perhaps German Riesling will finally catch the wave of popularity that has carried Austrian and Australian Riesling forward. It would not be before time.

Recent vintages

Mosel-Saar-Ruwer

Mosels (including Saar and Ruwer wines) are so attractive young that their keeping qualities are not often enough explored, and wines older than about eight years are unusual. But well-made Riesling wines of Kabinett class gain from at least five years in bottle and often much more, Spätlese from five to 20, and Auslese and Beerenauslese anything from 10 to 30 years. As a rule, in poor years the Saar and Ruwer make sharp, lean wines, but in the best years, above all with botrytis, they can surpass the whole world for elegance and thrilling, steely "breed".

2006 A cool wet Aug and more poor weather during the autumn dampened expectations; rot was widespread, persuading growers to pick early and fast. There will be some mediocre wines, but the best growers are ecstatic, reporting very high ripeness and vibrant acidity. But ruthless selection means that quantities are very low.

2005 Superb warm autumn weather from late Sep through to Nov brought grapes to very high ripeness levels, but with far better acidity than, say, 2003. An exceptional year, especially in the Saar.

2004 A humid summer led growers to fear the worst, but the vintage was saved by a glorious autumn. At harvest, grapes were healthy and very ripe. A fine year to start drinking.

2003 Hot weather brought high ripeness levels but rather low acidity. Ironically, some great sites suffered from drought, while less-esteemed cooler sites often fared better. So there is considerable variation in quality, with the best, including some powerful dry wines, superb. Some sensational Trockenbeerenauslesen too.

2002 It is a small miracle how the Riesling grapes survived one of the wettest harvests on record to give ripe, succulent, lively wines (mostly Kabinett and Spätlese), attractive drunk young or mature.

2001 Golden Oct resulted in the best Mosel Riesling since 1990. Saar and Ruwer less exciting but still perfect balance. Lots of Spätlesen and Auslesen.

2000 Riesling stood up to harvest rain here better than most other places. Dominated by good QbA and Kabinett. Auslese rarer, but exciting.

1999 Excellent in Saar and Ruwer, lots of Auslesen; generally only good in the Mosel due to high yields. Best drank well young and will age.

1998 Riesling grapes came through a rainy autumn to give astonishingly good results in the Middle Mosel; the Saar and Ruwer were less lucky, with mostly QbA. Plenty of Eiswein.

1997 A generous vintage of consistently fruity, elegant wines from the entire region. Marvellous Auslesen in the Saar and Ruwer.

1996 Variable, with fine Spätlesen and Auslesen, but only from top sites. Many excellent Eisweins.

1995 Excellent vintage, mainly of Spätlesen and Auslesen of firm structure and long ageing potential.

1994 Another good vintage, mostly QmP with unexceptional QbA and Kabinett, but many Auslesen and botrytis wines.

1993 Small, excellent vintage: lots of Auslesen/botrytis; near perfect harmony. Ready to drink except top Auslesen.

1992 A very large crop, with only 30% QmP. To drink soon.

1991 A mixed vintage. Drink up.

1990 Superb vintage, though small.

1989 Often outstanding, with noble rot giving many Auslesen etc. Saar wines best; the Mittelmosel shows some dilution. Except for top Auslesen, ready to drink.

Fine older vintages: 88 76 71 69 64 59 53 49 45 37 34 21.

Rheinhessen, Nahe, Pfalz, Rheingau

Even the best wines can be drunk with pleasure when young, but Kabinett, Spätlese, and Auslese Riesling gain enormously in character by keeping for longer. Rheingau wines tend to be longest-lived, improving for 15 years or more, but best wines from the Nahe and Pfalz can last as long. Rheinhessen wines usually mature sooner, and dry Franken and Baden wines are generally best at three to six years.

2006 Warm, rainy weather in Sept and early Oct forced growers to pick early before rot took too firm a hold. Top estates in the Pfalz and Rheinhessen were obliged to leave rotting fruit unpicked. Grauburgunder (Pinot Gris) worst affected, also Pfalz Riesling. Much of what was picked turned out well, so not a disastrous vintage, though quantities low.

2005 The summer was warm, but rain kept drought at bay. A very fine autumn led to high ripeness levels, accompanied by excellent acidity and extract. A superb year.

2004 After an indifferent summer, a fine autumn delivered ripe healthy grapes throughout the Rhein lands. A larger than average crop, so there could be some dilution, though not at top estates.

2003 Very hot weather led to rich wines in the Rheingau; many lack acidity. The Pfalz produced superb Rieslings. Red wines fared well everywhere.

2002 Few challenge the best from 01, but very good for both classic-style
Kabinett/Spätlese and for dry. Excellent Pinot Noir.

2001 Though more erratic than in the Mosel, here, too, this was often an
exciting vintage for both dry and classic styles; excellent balance.

2000 The further south, the more difficult was the harvest, the Pfalz catching
worst of harvest rain. However, all regions have islands of excellence.

1999 Quality was average where yields were high, but for top growers an
excellent vintage of rich, aromatic wines with lots of charm.

1998 Excellent: rich, balanced wines, many good Spätlesen and Auslesen with
excellent ageing potential. Rain affected much of Baden and Franken.
But a great Eiswein year.

1997 Very clean, ripe grapes gave excellent QbA, Kabinett, Spätlese in dry
and classic styles. Little botrytis, so Auslesen and higher are rare.

1996 An excellent vintage, particularly in the Pfalz and the Rheingau, with
many fine Spätlesen. Great Eiswein.

1995 Rather variable, but some excellent Spätlesen and Auslesen maturing
well – like the 90s. Weak in the Pfalz due to harvest rain.

1994 Good vintage, mostly QmP, with abundant fruit and firm structure.
Some superb sweet wines.

1993 A small vintage of very good to excellent quality. Plenty of rich
Spätlesen and Auslesen, at their peak.

1992 Very large vintage; would have been great but for Oct cold and rain.
A third were QmP of rich, stylish quality. Drink soon.

1991 A middling vintage. Drink soon.

1990 Small and exceptionally fine. Drink now, but will keep for years.

Fine older vintages: 83 76 71 69 64 59 53 49 45 37 34 21.

Achkarren Bad w (r) ★★ Village on the KAISERSTUHL, known especially for
GRAUBURGUNDER. First Class vineyard: Schlossberg. Wines generally best drunk
during first 5 years. Good wines: Dr. HEGER, Michel, and co-op.

Adelmann, Weingut Graf ★★→★★★ Estate based at the idyllic Schaubeck
castle in WÜRTTEMBERG. The specialities are subtle red blends, RIES, and the
rare Muskattrollinger.

Ahr Ahr r ★→★★ **95 97** 98 **99 01 03 04** 05 06 South of Bonn. Light, elegant
SPÄTBURGUNDER, especially from Adeneuer, DEUTZERHOF, Kreuzberg, MEYER-
NÄKEL, Nelles, Stodden.

Aldinger, Weingut Gerhard ★★★ WÜRTTEMBERG's leading red wine estate:

> ### German vintage notation
>
> The vintage notes after entries in the German section are given in
> a different form from those elsewhere in the book. Two styles of
> vintage are indicated:
>
>   **Bold** type (*e.g.* **99**) indicates classic, ripe vintages with a high
> proportion of Spätlesen and Auslesen; or, in the case of red wines,
> good phenolic ripeness and must weights.
>
>   Normal type (*e.g.* 98) indicates a successful but not
> outstanding vintage.
>
> German white wines, especially Riesling, have high acidity and keep
> well, and they display pure fruit qualities because they are
> unoaked. Thus they can be drunk young for their intense fruitiness,
> or kept for a decade or two to develop more aromatic subtlety and
> finesse. This means there is no one ideal moment to drink them,
> so no vintages are specifically recommended for drinking now.

LEMBERGER SPÄTBURGUNDER, and Bordeaux varieties are the specialities Good RIES too.

Amtliche Prüfungsnummer See PRÜFUNGSNUMMER.

APNr Abbreviation of AMTLICHE PRÜFUNGSNUMMER.

Assmannshausen Rhg r ★→★★★ **90 93 95 96** 97 98 **99 01** 02 **03 04 05** 06 Craggy RHEINGAU village known for its usually light SPÄTBURGUNDERS. First Class vineyard: Höllenberg. Growers include KESSELER, Robert König, Hotel KRONE, and the STATE DOMAIN.

Auslese Wines from selective harvest of super-ripe bunches, in many years affected by noble rot (*Edelfäule*) and correspondingly unctuous in flavour. Dry Auslesen are usually too alcoholic and clumsy for me.

Ayl M-S-R (Saar) w ★★★ **89 90 93** 94 **95** 96 **97 99** 00 **01 02 03 04 05** 06 All Ayl vineyards since 71 are known by the name of its historically best site: Kupp. Growers inc BISCHÖFLICHE WEINGUTER, LAUER.

Bacchus Modern, often kitsch grape found mostly in RHEINHESSEN and FRANKEN. Deservedly in decline.

Bacharach w (r) ★→★★★ **90 93 96** 97 98 **01 02** 03 **04 05** 06 Main wine town of MITTELRHEIN. Racy, austere RIES, some very fine. First Class vineyards: Hahn, Posten, Wolfshöhle. Growers include BASTIAN, JOST, Helmut Mades, RATZENBERGER.

Bad Dürkheim Pfz w (r) ★★→★★★ **90 93** 94 95 **96 97 98 99** 01 02 **03 04 05** 06 Main town of MITTELHAARDT, with the world's biggest barrel and an ancient September wine festival. First Class vineyards: Michelsberg, Spielberg. Growers: Darting, Fitz-Ritter, Hensel, Schmitt, Schäfer.

Baden Bad Huge southwest area of scattered vineyards best known for the Pinots, and pockets of RIES, usually dry. Best areas: KAISERSTUHL, ORTENAU.

Badische Bergstrasse/Kraichgau (Bereich) Widespread district of north BADEN. WEISSBURGUNDER and GRAUBURGUNDER make best wines.

Badischer Winzerkeller Germany's (and Europe's) biggest co-op, absorbing the entire crop of 38 other co-ops to produce up to 600 wines each year, accounting for almost half of BADEN's wine: dependably unambitious.

Bad Kreuznach Nahe w ★★ **83 85** 88 **89** 90 92 **93** 94 95 96 97 98 **99** 00 **01 02 03 04 05** Spa town with fine vineyards. First Class: Brückes, Kahlenberg, Krötenpfuhl. Growers inc Anheuser, Carl Finkenauer, von PLETTENBERG.

Bassermann-Jordan ★★★ **89 90 96 97 98 99** 01 02 **03 04 05** 06 MITTELHAARDT estate, under new ownership since 2003, with outstanding vineyards in DEIDESHEIM, FORST, RUPPERTSBERG, etc. Winemaker Ulrich Mell excels at producing *majestic dry RIES* and lavish sweet wines too.

Bastian, Weingut Fritz ★★ 6 ha BACHARACH estate. Racy, austere RIES with MOSEL-like delicacy, especially from the First Class Posten vineyard.

Becker, J B ★★→★★★ The best estate at WALLUF specializing in dry RIES and SPÄTBURGUNDER.

Beerenauslese, BA Luscious sweet wine from exceptionally ripe, individually selected berries, usually concentrated by noble rot. Rare, expensive.

Bercher ★★→★★★ KAISERSTUHL estate; 24 ha of white and red Pinots at Burkheim. Excellent WEISSBURGUNDER, RIES, and SPÄTBURGUNDER.

Bergdolt, Weingut ★★ Just south of NEUSTADT in the PFALZ, Rainer produces outstanding WEISSBURGUNDER (Pinot Bl), as well as good RIES.

Bernkastel M-M w ★→★★★★ **75 83** 88 **89 90 93** 94 95 96 **97** 98 **99** 00 **01 02** 03 **04 05** 06 Top wine town of the MITTELMOSEL; the epitome of RIES. Great First Class (if overpriced) vineyard: Doctor, 3.2 ha; First Class vineyards: Graben, Lay. Top growers include KERPEN, LOOSEN, MOLITOR, PAULY-BERGWEILER, PRÜM, Studert-Prüm, THANISCH, WEGELER.

Bernkastel (Bereich) Inc all the MITTELMOSEL. Wide area of deplorably dim quality and superficial flowery character. Mostly MÜLLER-T. Avoid.

Beulwitz, Weingut von ★★ ··★★★ Reliable 6-ha RUWER estate with wines from Kaseler Nies'chen.

Biffar, Josef ★★··★★★ Important 12-ha estate in DEIDESHEIM and WACHENHEIM. Frequent changes of winemaker have led to some wavering in quality.

Bingen Rhh w ★··★★ 89 90 93 94 **96** 97 **98** 99 01 02 03 **04** 05 06 Rhine/NAHE town. Fine vineyards including First Class Scharlachberg.

Red wines

Perhaps because Germany's trump card has always been white wines, the German population has yearned after reds. Until a dozen years ago, those grown on its own soils, mostly Spätburgunder (Pinot Noir), tended to be weedy, overcropped, and often astringent. Only in the warmest years did the wines taste more red than rosé. Now those warm years make regular appearances, and they certainly add heft to the wines. Pallid Pinot Noir still exists, but so too do ripe, concentrated versions from the Ahr, Pfalz, Franken, and Baden. Thin local specialities such as Württemberg's Trollinger baffle drinkers from outside the region, but other varieties from here, notably Lemberger, can deliver sterling wines. It may continue to be a struggle for Germany to compete internationally with its red wines, but at least these days one can order a Pfalz or Baden red with some confidence and hope of satisfaction.

Bingen (Bereich) District name for northwest RHEINHESSEN.

Bischöfliche Weingüter M-S-R ★★ Famous estate located at TRIER, uniting cathedral's vineyards with those of two other charities, the Bischöfliches Priesterseminar and the Bischöfliches Konvikt. Owns 106 ha of top vineyards, especially in SAAR and RUWER. Routine rather than exciting quality.

Bocksbeutel Squat, inconvenient, flask-shaped bottle used in FRANKEN and north BADEN.

Bodensee (Bereich) Idyllic district of SOUTH BADEN, on Lake Constance. Dry wines are best drunk within 5 years. RIES-like MÜLLER-T a speciality.

Boppard ★··★★★ **90 93** 95 96 97 **98** 01 02 03 **04** 05 06 Important wine town of MITTELRHEIN with best sites all in amphitheatre of vines called Bopparder Hamm. Growers: Toni Lorenz, Matthias Müller, August Perll, WEINGART. Unbeatable value for money.

Brauneberg M-M w ★★★★ 83 88 89 90 93 94 95 96 **97** 98 **99** 00 **01 02** 03 **04 05** 06 Top M-S-R village near BERNKASTEL (304 ha): excellent full-flavoured RIES – grand cru if anything on the Mosel is. Great First Class vineyard: Juffer-SONNENUHR. First Class vineyard: Juffer. Growers: F HAAG, W HAAG, SCHLOSS LIESER, PAULINSHOF, RICHTER, THANISCH.

Breuer, Weingut Georg ★★★··★★★★ Family estate of 24 ha in RUDESHEIM and 7.2 ha in RAUENTHAL, giving superb, full-bodied dry RIES. Superb Sekt too but middling SPÄTBURGUNDER. Pioneering winemaker Bernhard Breuer died

---

Beware of Bereich

District within an *Anbaugebiet* (region). "Bereich" on a label should be treated as a flashing red light. Do not buy. See under Bereich names – *e.g.* BERNKASTEL (BEREICH).

---

suddenly in 04, but the estate stays in his family.

Buhl, Reichsrat von ★★★ Historic PFALZ estate, returning to historic form as of 1994. 55 ha (DEIDESHEIM, FORST, RUPPERTSBERG). Bought in 2005 by businessman Achim Niederberger, who also owns BASSERMANN-JORDAN.

Bundesweinprämierung The German State Wine Award, organized by DLG: gives great (*grosse*), silver, or bronze medallion labels.

Bürgerspital zum Heiligen Geist ★★→★★★ Ancient charitable WÜRZBURG estate. 111 ha. Rich, dry wines, especially SILVANER, RIES, and in some years great TBA.

Bürklin-Wolf, Dr. ★★★→★★★★ Dynamic PFALZ family estate. 85 ha in FORST, DEIDESHEIM, RUPPERTSBERG, and WACHENHEIM, including many First Class sites. The full-bodied dry wines from these are often spectacular. Now biodynamic.

Castell'sches Fürstlich Domänenamt ★→★★★ Historic 58-ha estate in FRANKEN. SILVANER, RIESLANER, dry and sweet, and a growing reputation for red wines.

Chardonnay Now grown throughout Germany; with over 1,020 ha. Quality now more sure-footed. Best: JOHNER, REBHOLZ, DR. WEHRHEIM, WITTMANN.

Christmann ★★★ 15-ha estate in Gimmeldingen (PFALZ) making rich, dry RIES and SPÄTBURGUNDER from First Class vineyards, notably Königsbacher Idig.

Christoffel, J J ★★★ Tiny domain in ERDEN, URZIG. Classic, elegant RIES. Since 2001 leased to Robert Eymael of MÖNCHHOF.

Clüsserath-Weiler, Weingut ★★→★★★ Classic RIES from top TRITTENHEIMER Apotheke and the rare Fährfels vineyard.

Crusius ★★→★★★ 17-ha family estate at TRAISEN, NAHE. Vivid RIES from Bastei and Rotenfels of TRAISEN and SCHLOSSBÖCKELHEIM. Top wines age very well.

Dautel, Weingut Ernst ★★→★★★ Over three decades Dautel has proved himself one of WÜRTTEMBERG'S, and indeed Germany's, few masters of serious red wines, especially SPÄTBURGUNDER and LEMBERGER.

Deidesheim Pfz w (r) ★★→★★★★ 88 89 90 92 94 95 96 97 98 99 01 02 03 04 05 06 Largest top-quality village of the PFALZ (405 ha). Richly flavoured, lively wines. First Class vineyards: Grainhübel, Hohenmorgen, Kalkofen, Kieselberg, Langenmorgen, Leinhöhle. Top growers: BASSERMANN-JORDAN, BIFFAR, BUHL, BÜRKLIN-WOLF, CHRISTMANN, DEINHARD, MOSBACHER, WOLF.

Deinhard In 1997 the WEGELER family sold the 200-year-old merchant house and SEKT producer Deinhard to sparkling wine giant Henkell-Söhnlein. But the splendid Deinhard estates remain in family ownership (see WEGELER).

Deinhard, Dr. ★★★ Fine 35-ha estate: some top sites in DEIDESHEIM and FORST.

Deutscher Tafelwein Officially the term for very humble German wines. Now, confusingly, the flag of convenience for some costly novelties as well, often barrique-aged.

Deutzerhof, Weingut ★★→★★★ AHR estate producing concentrated, BARRIQUE-aged SPÄTBURGUNDER. Fine quality, alarming prices.

Diel, Schlossgut ★★★ Fashionable 17-ha NAHE estate; pioneered ageing GRAUBURGUNDER and WEISSBURGUNDER in BARRIQUES. *Its traditional RIES is often exquisite.* Makes serious SEKT and delectable AUSLESE.

Domäne German for "domain" or "estate". Sometimes used alone to mean the "State Domain" (STAATSWEINGUT, or Staatliche Weinbaudomäne).

Dönnhoff, Weingut Hermann ★★★★ 89 90 94 95 96 97 98 99 00 00 01 02 03 04 05 06 16-ha leading NAHE estate with *magnificent RIES* at all quality levels from NIEDERHAUSEN, Oberhausen, SCHLOSSBÖCKELHEIM. Dazzling EISWEIN.

Dornfelder Red grape making deep-coloured, usually rustic wines. An astonishing 8,250 ha are now planted throughout Germany.

Durbach Baden w (r) ★★→★★★ 94 96 97 98 99 00 01 02 04 05 06 Village with 314 ha of vineyards, of which Plauelrain is First Class. Top growers: LAIBLE, H. Männle, WOLFF METTERNICH. Choose their KLINGELBERGERS (RIES) and Clevners (TRAMINER).

Edel Means "noble". *Edelfäule* means "noble rot".

Egon Müller zu Scharzhof ★★★★ 75 76 79 83 85 88 89 90 92 93 94 95 96 97 98 99 00 01 02 03 04 05 06 Top SAAR estate of 8 ha at WILTINGEN, the vineyards rising steeply behind the Müller's manor house. Its rich and racy

SCHARZHOFBERGER RIES in AUSLESEN vintages is among the world's greatest wines, sublime, honeyed, immortal; best are given gold capsules. Kabinetts are feather-light. Le Gallais is a second 4-ha estate in WILTINGER Braune Kupp; good quality, but the site is less exceptional.

Eiswein Very sweet wine made from frozen grapes with the ice (*i.e.* water content) discarded, producing very concentrated wine in flavour, acidity, and sugar – of BEERENAUSLESE ripeness or more. Alcohol content can be as low as 5.5%. Very expensive. Outstanding Eiswein vintages were 86, 98, and 02.

Eitelsbach M-S-R (Ruwer) w ★★→★★★★ 83 88 89 90 93 94 95 96 **97 98 99** 00 **01 02 03 04 05** 06 RUWER village bordering TRIER, inc superb Great First Class KARTHAUSERHOFBERG vineyard site.

Elbling Grape introduced by the Romans, widely grown on upper MOSEL. Can be sharp and tasteless, but capable of real freshness and vitality in the best conditions (*e.g.* at Nittel or SCHLOSS THORN in the OBERMOSEL).

Eltville Rhg w ★★→★★★ 89 90 93 94 95 96 97 98 99 00 **01 02 03 04 05** 06 Major wine town with cellars of RHEINGAU STAATSWEINGÜTER and LANGWERTH VON SIMMERN estates. First Class vineyard: Sonnenberg.

Emrich-Schönleber ★★★ Located in NAHE village of Monzingen. Since the late 1980s winemaker Werner Schönleber has produced RIES that is now among Germany's finest especially his sumptuous EISWEIN.

Enkirch M-M w ★★ **90 93 94** 96 **97 98 99 01** 02 03 **04 05** 06 Little-known MITTELMOSEL village, often overlooked, but with lovely light, tasty wine. The best grower is IMMICH-BATTERIEBERG.

Erbach Rhg w ★★★ 83 89 90 93 95 96 **98 99** 00 **01 02 03 04 05** 06 RHEINGAU area: big, perfumed, ageworthy wines, including First Class vineyards: Hohenrain, MARCOBRUNN, Siegelsberg, Steinmorgen, Schlossberg. Leading producers: KNYPHAUSEN, LANGWERTH VON SIMMERN, SCHLOSS REINHARTSHAUSEN, SCHLOSS SCHÖNBORN. Also BECKER, Jakob Jung, etc.

Erben Word meaning "heirs", often used on old-established estate labels.

Erden M-M w ★★★ 75 83 88 89 90 93 95 96 **97 98 99** 00 **01** 02 03 **04 05** 06 Village adjoining ÜRZIG: noble, full-flavoured, vigorous wine (more herbal and mineral than the wines of nearby BERNKASTEL and WEHLEN but equally long-living). Great First Class vineyards: Prälat, Treppchen. Growers include BISCHÖFLICHE WEINGÜTER, J J CHRISTOFFEL, Erbes, LOOSEN, Meulenhof, MÖNCHHOF, Peter Nicolay, Weins-Prüm.

Erstes Gewächs Literally translates as "first growth".

Erzeugerabfüllung Bottled by producer. Being replaced by GUTSABFÜLLUNG, but only by estates. Co-ops will continue with *Erzeugerabfüllung*.

Escherndorf Frank w ★★→★★★ **90 93 97** 98 99 **00 01** 02 03 04 **05** 06 Important wine town near WÜRZBURG. Similar tasty, dry wine from RIES and SILVANER. First Class vineyard: Lump. Growers include Michael Fröhlich, JULIUSSPITAL, H SAUER, Rainer Sauer, Egon Schäffer.

Feinherb Imprecisely defined term for wines with around 10–20 g of sugar per litre. Favoured by some as a more flexible alternative to HALBTROCKEN. Used on label by, among others, KERPEN, VON KESSELSTATT, MOLITOR.

Filzen M-S-R (Saar) w ★★ **90 93 94 95 97** 98 **99 01** 02 **03 04 05** 06 Small SAAR village near WILTINGEN. First Class vineyard: Pulchen. Only grower to note: Piedmont.

Forst Pfz w ★★→★★★★ **90 94** 95 96 97 **98 99 01 02 03 04 05** 06 MITTELHAARDT village with over 200 ha of Germany's best vineyards. Ripe, richly fragrant, full-bodied but subtle wines. First Class vineyards: Jesuitengarten,

GERMANY

Kirchenstück, Freundstück, Pechstein, Ungeheuer. Top growers include BASSERMANN-JORDAN, BÜRKLIN-WOLF, DEINHARD, MOSBACHER, Eugen Müller, H Spindler, Werlé, WOLF.

Franken Frank Franconia region of distinctive dry wines, especially SILVANER, always bottled in round-bellied flasks (BOCKSBEUTEL). The centre is WÜRZBURG. Bereich names: MAINDREIECK, STEIGERWALD. Top producers: BÜRGERSPITAL, CASTELL, FÜRST, JULIUSSPITAL, LÖWENSTEIN, RUCK, H SAUER, STAATLICHER HOFKELLER, STÖRRLEIN, WIRSCHING, etc.

Franzen, Weingut Rheinhold ★→★★ From Europe's steepest vineyard, Bremmer Calmont, Franzen makes dependable, sometimes exciting dry RIES and EISWEIN.

Germany's quality levels

The official range of qualities and styles in ascending order are:

1 **Deutscher Tafelwein**: sweetish light wine of no specified character. (From certain producers, can be atypical but excellent.)

2 **Landwein**: dryish Tafelwein with some regional style.

3 **Qualitätswein**: dry or sweetish wine with sugar added before fermentation to increase its strength, but tested for quality and with distinct local and grape character. Don't despair.

4 **Kabinett**: dry or dryish natural (unsugared) wine of distinct personality and distinguishing lightness. Can occasionally be sublime.

5 **Spätlese**: stronger, often sweeter than Kabinett. Full-bodied. Today many top Spätlesen are *trocken* or completely dry.

6 **Auslese**: sweeter, sometimes stronger than Spätlese, often with honey-like flavours, intense and long-lived. Occasionally dry and weighty.

7 **Beerenauslese**: very sweet, sometimes strong, intense. Can be superb.

8 **Eiswein**: from naturally frozen grapes of Beeren- or Trockenbeerenauslese quality: concentrated, sharpish, and very sweet. Some examples are extreme, unharmonious.

9 **Trockenbeerenauslese**: intensely sweet and aromatic; alcohol slight. Extraordinary and everlasting.

Friedrich-Wilhelm Gymnasium ★★ Important charitable estate based in TRIER, with vineyards throughout M-S-R. In 2003 it was leased by the BISCHÖFLICHE WEINGÜTER, but some of its vineyards have been sold off.

Frühburgunder An ancient mutation of Pinot N, found mostly in the Ahr but also in PFALZ and WÜRTTEMBERG, where it is confusingly known as Clevner. Lower acidity and thus more approachable than Pinot N.

Fuhrmann See PFEFFINGEN.

Fürst ★★★ 18-ha estate in Bürgstadt making some of the best wines in FRANKEN, particularly Burgundian SPÄTBURGUNDER (arguably Germany's finest), full flavoured RIES, and oak-aged WEISSBURGUNDER.

Gallais Le See EGON MÜLLER ZU SCHARZHOF.

Geisenheim Rhg w ★★→★★★ 89 90 93 95 96 98 99 00 01 02 03 04 05 06 Home to Germany's best-known wine school and the vineyards produce very good aromatic wines. First Class vineyards: Kläuserweg, Rothenberg. Top growers: JOHANNISHOF, WEGELER. See also HESSISCHE FORSCHUNGSANSTALT.

Gemeinde A commune or parish.

Gewürztraminer (or **Traminer**) Highly aromatic grape, speciality of Alsace, also impressive in Germany, especially in PFALZ, BADEN, SACHSEN, WÜRTTEMBERG.

Gimmeldingen Pfz w ★★ 90 94 96 97 98 99 01 02 03 04 05 06 Village just south of MITTELHAARDT. At best, rich, succulent wines. First-class vineyard: Mandelgarten. Growers include CHRISTMANN, MÜLLER-CATOIR, Weegmüller.

Graach M-M w ★★★ **83 88 89 90 93 94 95** 96 **97** 98 **99 01** 02 **03 04 05** 06 Small village between BERNKASTEL and WEHLEN. First Class vineyards: Domprobst, Himmelreich, Josephshof. Many top growers, including: von KESSELSTATT, Kees-Kieren, LOOSEN, M MOLITOR, J J PRÜM, S A PRÜM, SCHAEFER, SELBACH-OSTER, WEINS-PRÜM.

Grans-Fassian ★★★ Fine MOSEL estate at Leiwen. Vineyards there and in TRITTENHEIM and PIESPORTER. EISWEIN a speciality. Consistently high quality since 1995.

Grauburgunder Or Grauer Burgunder. Both synonyms of RULÄNDER or Pinot Gr: grape giving soft full-bodied wine. Best in BADEN and south PFALZ.

Grosser Ring Group of top (VDP) MOSEL-SAAR-RUWER estates, whose annual September auction often sets world-record prices.

Grosses Gewächs Translates as "great/top growth". This is the top tier in the vineyard classification launched in 2002 by the growers' association VDP, except in the RHEINGAU, which has its own ERSTES GEWÄCHS classification. Wines released as *Grosses Gewächs* must meet strict quality criteria.

Grosslage A collection of individual sites with seemingly similar character.

Gunderloch ★★★·★★★★ **90 93 96 97 98** 99 00 **01** 02 03 **04 05** 06 At this NACKENHEIM estate Fritz Hasselbach makes *some of the finest RIES* on the entire Rhine, especially at AUSLESE level and above. Also owns Balbach estate in NIERSTEIN.

Guntrum, Louis ★★ Large (27-ha) family estate in NIERSTEIN, OPPENHEIM, etc. Good SILVANER and GEWÜRZ as well as RIES. Sound rather than exciting quality.

Gutedel German name for the ancient Chasselas grape, grown in south BADEN. Fresh, but neutral, white wines.

Gutsabfüllung Estate-bottled. Term for genuinely estate-bottled wines.

Haag, Weingut Fritz M-S-R ★★★★ **83 88 89 90 94 95** 96 97 98 **99** 00 **01 02 03 04 05** 06 BRAUNEBERG's top estate, run for decades by MITTELMOSEL veteran Wilhelm Haag. MOSEL *RIES of crystalline purity and racy brilliance* for long ageing. Haag's son runs SCHLOSS LIESER estate.

Haag, Weingut Willi M-S-R ★★ 6-ha BRAUNEBERG estate. Full, old-style RIES. Some fine AUSLESEN.

Haart, Reinhold ★★★★ The best estate in PIESPORT and WINTRICH. Refined, aromatic wines capable of long ageing. Mineral and racy, these are copybook MOSEL RIES.

Hain, Weingut Kurt ★★·★★★ Small but focused PIESPORT estate of steadily increasing quality. See also FEINHERB.

Halbtrocken Medium-dry (literally "semi-dry"), with 9–18 g of unfermented sugar per litre. Popular category, often better balanced than TROCKEN.

Hallgarten Rhg w ★·★★★ **90 93 95** 96 **97** 98 **99** 00 **01** 02 03 **04 05** 06 Village just inland from HATTENHEIM, so vineyards relatively high. Much renowned a century ago, less so today. First class vineyards: Jungfer, Schönhell. Top growers: LÖWENSTEIN, PRINZ.

Hattenheim Rhg w ★★·★★★★ **89 90 93 95** 96 **97** 98 **99** 00 01 02 **03 04 05** 06 Superlative 202-ha wine town, though not all producers achieve full potential. The First Class vineyards are Mannberg, Nussbrunnen, Pfaffenberg, Wisselbrunnen, and, most famously, STEINBERG (ORTSTEIL). Estates include Barth, KNYPHAUSEN, LANG, LANGHERTH VON SIMMERN, RESS, SCHLOSS SCHÖNBORN, STAATSWEINGUT.

Remember that vintage information for German wines is given in a different form from the ready/not ready distinction applying to other countries. See the explanation at the bottom of p.117.

Heger, Dr. ★★★ Leading estate of KAISERSTUHL in BADEN with excellent dry WEISSBURGUNDER, GRAUBURGUNDER, and powerful oak-aged SPÄTBURGUNDER reds. Less emphasis on RIES and Muscat, which can also be very good. Wines from rented vineyards released under Weinhaus Joachim Heger label.

Heilbronn Würt w r ★→★★ 93 96 97 99 01 02 **03 04 05** 06 Wine town with many small growers. Top vineyard: Stiftberg. Best wines are RIES and LEMBERGER. Top growers include Amalienhof, Drautz-Able, Heinrich.

Henkell See DEINHARD.

Hessen, Prinz von ★★→★★★ Famous 42-ha estate in JOHANNISBERG, KIEDRICH, and WINKEL. Improving quality since the late 1990s.

Hessische Bergstrasse w (r) ★★→★★★ **90 93 96** 97 98 **99** 01 02 03 **04 05** 06 Small wine region (436 ha), north of Heidelberg. Pleasant RIES from STAATSWEINGÜTER, Bergsträsser co-op, Simon-Bürkle, and Stadt Bensheim.

Hessische Forschungsanstalt für Wein-Obst & Gartenbau Famous wine school and research establishment at GEISENHEIM, RHEINGAU.

Heyl zu Herrnsheim ★★ Leading NIERSTEIN estate, 80% RIES. Improved under Ahr family ownership in late 90s, but faltered in recent vintages; bought in 2006 by Detlev Meyer. Occasional sweet wines of exceptional quality.

Heymann-Löwenstein ★★★ Estate in Lower Mosel near Koblenz with most consistent dry RIES in MOSEL-SAAR-RUWER and some remarkable AUSLESEN and TROCKENBEERENAUSLESEN. Löwenstein has inspired other WINNINGEN growers to adopt his style. Spectacular wines in 05.

Hochgewächs Supposedly superior level of QBA RIES, especially in MOSEL-SAAR-RUWER. Rarely encountered.

Hochheim Rhg w ★★→★★★★ **89 90 92 93** 94 95 **96 97 98 99** 00 01 02 03 **04 05** 06 242-ha wine town 15 miles east of main RHEINGAU area, once thought of as best on Rhine. Wines with an earthy intensity, body, and fragrance of their own. First Class vineyards: Domdechaney, Hölle, Kirchenstück, Königin Viktoria Berg (5-ha monopoly of Hupfeld family). Growers include Königin-Victoriaberg, KÜNSTLER, W J Schaefer, SCHLOSS SCHÖNBORN, STAATSWEINGUT, WERNER.

Hock Traditional English term for Rhine wine, derived from HOCHHEIM.

Hoensbroech, Weingut Reichsgraf zu ★★ Top KRAICHGAU estate. Dry WEISSBURGUNDER from Michelfelder Himmelberg is the best wine.

Hohenlohe-Oehringen, Weingut Fürst zu ★★ Noble 17-ha estate in Oehringen, WÜRTTEMBERG. Earthy, bone-dry and powerful, structured reds from SPÄTBURGUNDER, LEMBERGER, and other grapes.

Hövel, Weingut von ★★★ Fine SAAR estate at OBEREMMEL (Hütte is 4.8-ha monopoly) and in SCHARZHOFBERG. Erratic quality, but many superb 05s.

Huber, Bernhard ★★★ Leading estate of Breisgau area of BADEN, with powerful long-lived SPÄTBURGUNDER, MUSKATELLER, and Burgundian-style WEISSBURGUNDER, CHARD.

Ihringen Bad r w ★→★★★ **90 93 96** 97 **99** 00 **01 02 03 04 05** 06 Justly celebrated village of the KAISERSTUHL, BADEN. Proud of its SPÄTBURGUNDER red, WEISSHERBST, and GRAUBURGUNDER. Top growers: Dr. HEGER, Konstanzer, Stigler.

Immich-Batterieberg, Weingut ★★ Grown on 7.5 ha of dynamite-blasted slate slopes, this ENKIRCH estate produces good, sometimes excellent, RIES in varying quality.

Ingelheim Rhh r w ★→★★ **90 93 97** 98 **99 01** 02 **03 04 05** 06 Town opposite RHEINGAU historically known for its SPÄTBURGUNDER. Few wines today live up to reputation.

Iphofen Frank w ★★→★★★★ **90 93 97** 98 99 **00 01** 02 03 **04 05** 06 Village near WÜRZBURG renowned for RIES, SILVANER, RIESLANER. First Class vineyards: Julius-Echter-Berg, Kalb. Growers: JULIUSSPITAL, RUCK, WIRSCHING.

Jahrgang Year – as in "vintage".

Johannisberg Rhg w ★★→★★★★ 83 89 90 93 95 96 97 98 99 00 01 02 03 **04** 05 06 A classic RHEINGAU village with superlative long-lived RIES. First Class vineyards: Hölle, Klaus, SCHLOSS JOHANNISBERG. GROSSLAGE: Erntebringer. Top growers: JOHANNISHOF, SCHLOSS JOHANNISBERG, HESSEN.

Johannishof ★★★ JOHANNISBERG family estate RIES that are often the best from the great Johannisberg vineyards. Excellent RÜDESHEIM wines too.

Johner, Karl-Heinz ★★★ 15-ha BADEN estate at Bischoffingen, long specializing in New World-style SPÄTBURGUNDER and oak-aged WEISSBURGUNDER, CHARD, GRAUER BURGUNDER.

Josephshof First Class vineyard at GRAACH, the sole property of von KESSELSTATT.

Jost, Toni ★★★ Leading top estate of the MITTELRHEIN: 9 ha, mainly RIES, in BACHARACH, and also at WALLUF in the RHEINGAU.

Juliusspital ★★★ Ancient WÜRZBURG religious charity with 170 ha of top FRANKEN vineyards. Consistently good quality. Look for its dry SILVANERS and RIES and its top white blend called BT.

Kabinett See "Germany's quality levels" box on p.124.

Kaiserstuhl Outstanding BADEN district, with notably warm climate and volcanic soil. Villages include ACHKARREN, Burkheim, IHRINGEN. Renowned for Pinot varieties, white and red, and some surprising RIES and Muscat.

Kallstadt Pfz w (r) ★★→★★★ 90 93 94 **96 97 98 99** 00 01 02 **03 04** 05 06 Some of the best dry RIES of the north MITTELHAARDT comes from superb Saumagen vineyard. Fine AUSLESE too. Growers include Henninger and KOEHLER-RUPRECHT.

Kanzem M-S-R (Saar) w ★★★ 90 93 94 95 96 **97 99 01** 02 **03 04 05** 06 Small neighbour of WILTINGEN. First Class vineyard: Altenberg. Growers include BISCHÖFLICHE, WEINGÜTER, OTHEGRAVEN, J P Reinert, VEREINIGTE HOSPITIEN.

Karlsmühle ★★★ Small estate with two Lorenzhöfer monopoly sites making classic RUWER RIES; also wines from First Class KASEL vineyards sold under Patheiger label. Consistently excellent quality.

Karthäuserhofberg ★★★★ Outstanding RUWER estate of 19 ha at Eitelsbach. Easily recognized by bottles with only a neck label. Admired if austere TROCKEN wines, but magnificent AUSLESEN and above.

Kasel M-S-R (Ruwer) w ★★★→★★★ 89 90 93 94 95 96 **97** 98 **99** 01 02 **03 04 05** 06 Stunning flowery RIES. First Class vineyards: Kehrnagel, Nies'chen. Top growers: BISCHÖFLICHE, WEINGÜTER, KARLSMÜHLE, von BEULWITZ, von KESSELSTATT.

Keller Wine cellar.

Keller, Weingut ★★★★ Deep in once-derided southern RHEINHESSEN, the Kellers show what can be achieved with scrupulous site selection. Superlative, crystalline GROSSES GEWÄCHS RIES from Dalsheimer Hubacker and two other vineyards. Also astonishing TBA.

Kellerei Winery (*i.e.* a big commercial bottler).

Kerner Modern aromatic grape variety, earlier ripening than RIES. Acceptable wines that lack the inbuilt grace and harmony of RIES. Best in SACHSEN.

Kerpen, Weingut Heribert ★★ Small good estate in BERNKASTEL, GRAACH, WEHLEN, specializing in elegant sweeter styles.

Kesseler, Weingut August Rhg ★★★ 21-ha estate making the best SPÄTBURGUNDER reds in ASSMANNSHAUSEN and RUDESHEIM. Also very good classic-style RIES.

Kesselstatt, von ★★★ The largest private MOSEL estate, 650 years old. Run for two decades by the quality-obsessed Annegret Reh-Gartner. Some 38 ha through MOSEL-SAAR-RUWER producing aromatic, generously fruity MOSELS. Consistently high quality, often magnificent, wines from JOSEPHSHOF monopoly vineyard, PIESPORTER Goldtröpfchen, KASEL, and SCHARZHOFBERG.

Kesten M-M w ★→★★★ **90 93** 94 **95** 96 **97** 98 **99 01** 02 **03 04 05** 06 Neighbour of BRAUNEBERG. Best wines (from Paulinshofberg vineyard) similar. Top growers: Bastgen, Kees-Kieren, PAULINSHOF.

Kiedrich Rhg w ★★→★★★★ **90 93 95** 96 **97** 98 **99** 00 **01** 02 **03 04 05** 06 Neighbour of RAUENTHAL; equally splendid and high-flavoured. First Class vineyards: Gräfenberg, Wasseros. Growers include HESSEN KNYPHAUSEN, Speicher-Schuth. WEIL now top estate.

Klingelberger ORTENAU (BADEN) term for RIES, especially at DURBACH.

Kloster Eberbach Rhg Glorious 12th-C Cistercian abbey in HATTENHEIM forest. Monks planted STEINBERG, Germany's Clos de Vougeot. Now the label of the STAATSWEINGÜTER with a string of great vineyards in ASSMANNHAUSEN, RÜDESHEIM, RAUENTHAL, etc. New director Dieter Greiner has injected new life into a moribund organization. A new winery under construction.

Klüsserath M-M w ★→★★★ **90 93** 95 **97** 98 **99** 00 **01** 02 03 04 **05** 06 Little-known MOSEL village whose wine-growers joined forces to classify its top site, Brüderschaft. Growers: Clüsserath-Eifel, Kirsten, Regnery.

Knebel, Weingut ★★★ WINNINGEN is the top wine village of the Lower MOSEL and Knebel showed how its sites could produce remarkable RIES in all styles. The founder died tragically in 2004; the estate continues.

Knipser, Weingut ★★→★★★ Brothers Werner and Volker specialize in BARRIQUE-aged SPÄTBURGUNDER and other red wines, but dry RIES and some obscure varieties can be worthwhile.

Knyphausen, Weingut Freiherr zu Rhg ★→★★ Noble 22-ha estate on former Cistercian land in ERBACH, HATTENHEIM, and KIEDRICH. Classic RHEINGAU wines yet lacklustre in recent years.

Koehler-Ruprecht ★★★★ **90 93** 94 **96 97** 98 **99** 00 **01** 02 **03 04 05** 06 Outstanding KALLSTADT grower. Bernd Philippi's winemaking is entirely traditional, delivering very long-lived dry RIES from K Saumagen. Outstanding SPÄTBURGUNDER and striking BARRIQUE-aged Pinot varieties under the Philippi label.

Kraichgau Small BADEN region south of Heidelberg. Top growers: Burg Ravensburg, HOENSBROECH.

Krone, Weingut Rhg ★★ The Hotel Krone in ASSMANNHAUSEN has its own 4-ha estate, producing full-bodied SPÄTBURGUNDER in every conceivable style. Best sampled at its own restaurant.

Kröv M-M w ★→★★★ **93 97** 98 **99 01** 02 03 04 **05** 06 Popular tourist resort famous for its GROSSLAGE name: Nacktarsch, or "bare bottom". Be very careful. Best growers: Martin Müllen, Staffelter Hof.

Kruger-Rumpf, Weingut ★★ Most important estate of MÜNSTER, NAHE, with charming RIES and well-crafted SPÄTBURGUNDER. Best enjoyed at the family's inn in MÜNSTER.

Künstler, Franz Rhg ★★★★ 25-ha estate in HOCHHEIM run by the uncompromising Gunter Künstler. Produces superb dry RIES, especially from First Class Domdechaney, Hölle, and Kirchenstück vineyards; also excellent AUSLESE.

Kuntz, Sybille M-S-R ★★ Successful protagonist of untypical dry MOSEL RIES of AUSLESE strength from LIESER.

Laible, Weingut Andreas ★★★ 7-ha DURBACH estate. Limpid, often crystalline dry RIES from Plauelrain vineyard as well as SCHEUREBE and GEWÜRZ. Consistently rewarding quality.

Landwein See "Germany's quality levels" box on p.124.

Lang, Weingut Hans Rhg ★★ Reliable RIES, both dry and sweet, and other varieties from one of HATTENHEIM's most versatile growers.

Langwerth von Simmern, Weingut ★★ Famous ELTVILLE family estate. Top vineyards: Baiken, Mannberg, MARCOBRUNN. After disappointing quality during the 1990s back on form since 01.

.auer, Weingut Peter ★★ The SAAR village of AYL has lacked conscientious growers, until in the early 2000s Florian Lauer began exploring its subtleties with a range of very good parcel selections. NB Lauer's hotel.

.eitz, J ★★★ Fine RÜDESHEIM family estate for rich but _elegant dry and sweet RIES_. Since 1999 Johannes Leitz has won long-overdue recognition.

.eiwen M-M w ★★→★★★ **90 93** 94 95 96 **97** 98 **99** 00 **01 02** 03 **04 05** 06 First Class vineyard: Laurentiuslay. Village between TRITTENHEIM and TRIER. GRANS-FASSIAN, Carl LOEWEN, SANKT URBANS-HOF have put these once overlooked vineyards firmly on the map.

.emberger Red grape variety imported to Germany and Austria in the 18th C, from Hungary, where it is known as Kékfrankos. Blaufränkisch in Austria. Deep-coloured, moderately tannic wines; can be excellent, especially from WÜRTTEMBERG.

.iebfrauenstift A 10.5-ha vineyard in city of Worms; origin of Liebfraumilch.

.ieser M-M w ★★ **90 93 95** 96 **97** 98 **99** 00 **01 02** 03 **04 05** 06 Once-neglected vineyards between BERNKASTEL and BRAUNEBERG. First Class vineyard: Niederberg-Helden. Top grower: SCHLOSS LIESER.

.ingenfelder, Weingut ★→★★ Commercially astute Grosskarlbach (PFALZ) estate: good dry and sweet SCHEUREBE, full-bodied RIES, hit-and-miss SPÄTBURGUNDER.

.oewen, Carl ★★→★★★ Enterprising grower of Leiwen on MOSEL making ravishing AUSLESE from town's First Class Laurentiuslay site, and from Thörnicher Ritsch, a vineyard Loewen rescued from obscurity.

.oosen, Weingut Dr. M-M ★★★★ **90 93 94 95** 96 **97** 98 **99** 00 **01 02 03 04 05** 06 Dynamic 15-ha estate in BERNKASTEL, ERDEN, GRAACH, ÜRZIG, WEHLEN. Deep, _intense classic RIES_ from old vines in some of the MITTELMOSEL's greatest vineyards. Also leases WOLF in the PFALZ since 1996. Joint-venture from 99 Washington State with Ch Ste Michele: TBA-style usually more convincing than Eroica (dry).

.orch Rhg w (r) ★→★★ **89 90** 92 93 **94** 95 96 97 98 99 00 **01 02** 03 **04 05** Extreme west of RHEINGAU. Some fine MITTELRHEIN-like RIES. Best growers: von Kanitz, Kesseler, Ottes.

.öwenstein, Fürst ★★★ Top FRANKEN estate. Tangy savoury SILVANER from historic Homberger Kallmuth, very dramatic slope. Also HALLGARTEN estate rented by SCHLOSS VOLLRADS until 1997.

.ützkendorf, Weingut ★→★★ Leading SAALE-UNSTRUT estate, producing a wide range of varietals.

Maindreieck (Bereich) District name for central FRANKEN, including WÜRZBURG.

Marcobrunn Historic RHEINGAU vineyard; one of Germany's very best. See ERBACH.

Markgräflerland (Bereich) District south of Freiburg, BADEN. Typical GUTEDEL wine can be refreshing when drunk very young, but best wines are the BURGUNDERS: red and white. Also SEKT.

Maximin Grünhaus M-S-R (Ruwer) w ★★★★ **83 88 89 90 93** 94 **95** 96 **97** 98 99 **01** 02 **03 04 05** 06 Supreme RUWER estate of 31 ha at Mertesdorf. Wines, dry and sweet, that are miracles of delicacy, subtlety and longevity. Greatest wines come from Abtsberg vineyard, but Herrenberg can be almost as fine.

Meyer-Näkel, Weingut ★★★★ AHR estate; 15 ha. Fine SPÄTBURGUNDERS in Dernau, Walporzheim, and Bad Neuenahr exemplify modern oak-aged German reds. Expensive.

Mittelhaardt The north central and best part of the PFALZ, inc DEIDESHEIM, FORST, RUPPERTSBERG, WACHENHEIM, largely planted with RIES.

GERMANY

Mittelmosel M-M The central and best part of the MOSEL, including BERNKASTEL PIESPORT, WEHLEN, etc. Its top sites are (or should be) entirely RIES.

Mittelrhein Northern and dramatically scenic Rhine area popular with tourists BACHARACH and BOPPARD are the most important villages of this 465-ha region. Delicate yet steely RIES, often underrated.

Molitor, Markus M-M ★★★ With 38 ha of outstanding vineyards throughou the MOSEL and SAAR, Molitor has since 1995 become a major player in the region. Magisterial sweet RIES, and acclaimed if earthy SPÄTBURGUNDER.

Mönchhof, Weingut M-M ★★ From an exquisite manor house in ÜRZIG, Rober Eymael makes fruity, stylish RIES from ÜRZIG and ERDEN. ERDENER Prälat usually the best wine. Also leases CHRISTOFFEL estate.

Morio-Muskat Stridently aromatic grape variety now on the decline.

Mosbacher, Weingut Pfz ★★★ Fine 15-ha estate for some of best GROSSES GEWÄCHS RIES of FORST. A property going from strength to strength. Decen Sauv Bl.

Moselland, Winzergenossenschaft Huge MOSEL-SAAR-RUWER co-op, at BERNKASTEL including Saar-Winzerverein at WILTINGEN, and, since 2000, a major NAHI co-op too. Its 3,290 members, with a collective 2,400 ha, produce 25% o M-S-R wines (inc classic-method SEKT), but little is above average.

Mosel-Saar-Ruwer M-S-R 9,080-ha region between TRIER and Koblenz includes MITTELMOSEL, RUWER, and SAAR. 58% RIESLING. From 2007 wines from the three regions can only be labelled as Mosel.

Müller-Catoir, Weingut Pfz ★★★→★★★★ 89 90 93 94 96 97 98 99 01 02 03 04 05 06 Since the 70s, this outstanding NEUSTADT estate has bucked conventiona wisdom, focusing on non-interventionist winemaking. Resulting wines are very aromatic and powerful (RIES, SCHEUREBE, GEWÜRZ, RIESLANER, WEISSBURGUNDER GRAUBURGUNDER, MUSKATELLER), with equally impressive dry and sweet.

Müller-Thurgau Fruity, early ripening, usually low-acid grape; most common in PFALZ, RHEINHESSEN, NAHE, BADEN, and FRANKEN; was 21% of German vineyards in 98, but 14% today. Should be banned from all top vineyards.

Münster Nahe w ★→★★★ 90 93 94 96 97 98 99 00 01 02 03 04 05 06 Best north NAHE village; fine, delicate wines. First Class vineyards: Pittersberg Dautenpflänzer, Rheinberg. Top growers: Göttelmann, KRUGER-RUMPF.

Muskateller Ancient aromatic white grape with crisp acidity. A rarity in the PFALZ, BADEN, and WÜRTTEMBERG, where it is mostly made dry.

Nackenheim Rhh w ★→★★★★ 90 93 96 97 98 99 01 02 03 03 04 05 06 NIERSTEIN neighbour also with top Rhine terroir; similar best wines

---

Global warming

Most German growers accept that since 1988 climatic conditions have changed. Grape sugar levels once regarded as exceptional are now considered routine. What are the consequences of these ever-higher ripeness levels? First, wine styles once thought of as marginal in Germany are now feasible: this applies particularly to red wines, which have more body, weight, and extract than in the past. Second, in the more northerly regions, notably the Mosel, "quality" categories such as QbA and Kabinett are becoming parodies of their former selves. In vintages such as 2003 and 2005, all fruit from top growers is being harvested at high Spätlese or Auslese levels. Thus modern Kabinetts are far richer than they would have been 20 years ago, and the ultra-light, ultra-crisp Mosel Kabinetts so much admired and thirstily drunk in the past may soon become extinct. Finally, alcohol levels rise as a consequence of ever-higher ripeness at harvest: dry Rieslings as well as red wines with at least 14% are no longer that rare.

(especially First Class Rothenberg). Top grower: GUNDERLOCH, Kühling-Gillot.

Nahe Na Tributary of the Rhine and a high-quality wine region. Balanced, fresh, clean, but full-bodied, even minerally wines; RIES best. EISWEIN a growing speciality.

Neckar The river with many of WÜRTTEMBERG's finest vineyards, mainly between Stuttgart and HEILBRONN.

Neipperg, Graf von ★★→★★★ Noble estate in Schwaigern, WÜRTTEMBERG: elegant dry RIES and robust LEMBERGER. MUSKATELLER up to BEERENAUSLESE quality a speciality.

Neumagen-Dhron M-M w ★★ Fine neighbour of PIESPORT. Top growers: Eifel, Heinz Schmitt.

Neustadt Central town of PFALZ with a famous wine school. Top growers: MÜLLER-CATOIR, Weegmüller.

Niederhausen Nahe w ★★→★★★★ 90 93 95 96 97 98 99 00 01 02 03 04 05 06 Neighbour of SCHLOSSBÖCKELHEIM. Graceful, powerful RIES. First Class vineyards include Hermannsberg, Hermannshöhle. Growers: especially CRUSIUS, DÖNNHOFF, Gutsverwaltung Niederhausen-Schlossböckelheim, Mathern, J Schneider.

Nierstein Rhh w ★→★★★★ 90 93 96 97 98 99 01 02 03 04 05 06 526 ha. Famous but treacherous village name. Beware GROSSLAGE Gutes Domtal: a supermarket deception now less frequently encountered. Superb First-Class vineyards: Brüdersberg, Glöck, Hipping, Oelberg, Orbel, Pettenthal. Ripe, aromatic, elegant wines, dry and sweet. Try Gehring, GUNTRUM, HEYL ZU HERRNSHEIM, Kühling-Gillot, ST-ANTONY, SCHNEIDER, Strub.

Nobling White crossing created in 39: light fresh wine in BADEN, especially MARKGRÄFLERLAND. In decline.

Norheim Nahe w ★★→★★★ 90 93 95 96 97 98 99 00 01 02 03 04 05 06 Neighbour of NIEDERHAUSEN. Primarily RIES. First Class vineyards: Dellchen, Kafels, Kirschheck. Growers: CRUSIUS, DÖNNHOFF, Mathern.

Oberemmel M-S-R (Saar) w ★★→★★★ 89 90 93 94 95 96 97 98 99 00 01 02 03 04 05 06 Next village to WILTINGEN. Very fine from First Class vineyard Hütte, etc. Growers: von HÖVEL, Willems-Willems.

Obermosel (Bereich) District name for the upper MOSEL above TRIER. Wines from the ELBLING grape, generally uninspiring unless very young.

Ockfen M-S-R (Saar) w ★★→★★★ 89 90 93 94 95 96 97 98 99 00 01 02 03 04 05 06 Superb fragrant, austere wines. First Class vineyard: Bockstein. Growers: Dr. Fischer, Weinhof Herrenberg, SANKT URBANS-HOF, WAGNER, ZILLIKEN.

Oechsle Scale for sugar content of grape juice.

Oestrich Rhg w ★★→★★★ 89 90 93 95 96 97 98 99 00 01 02 03 04 05 06 Big village; variable, but some splendid RIES. First Class vineyards: Doosberg, Lenchen. Top growers: August Eser, Peter Jakob Kühn, Querbach, SPREITZER, WEGELER.

Offene weine "Wines by the glass", the way to order it in wine villages.

Oppenheim Rhh w ★→★★★ 90 93 96 97 98 99 01 02 03 04 05 06 Town south of NIERSTEIN; spectacular 13th-C church. First Class Herrenberg and Sackträger. Growers include: GUNTRUM, Kühling-Gillot. None of these, though, is realizing the full potential of these sites.

Ortenau (Bereich) District just south of Baden-Baden. Good KLINGELBERGER (RIES), SPÄTBURGUNDER, and RULÄNDER. Top village: DURBACH.

Ortsteil Independent part of a community allowed to use its estate vineyard name without the village name – *e.g.* SCHLOSS JOHANNISBERG, STEINBERG.

Othegraven, Weingut von ★★→★★★ Until the late 90s, this KANZEM, SAAR estate was mediocre. In 99 Dr Heidi Kegel inherited the estate, with its superb Altenberg vineyards, and has been restoring its reputation.

Palatinate English for PFALZ.

Paulinshof, Weingut M-M ★★ 8-ha estate, once monastic, in KESTEN and BRAUNEBERG. Unusually for the MITTELMOSEL, the Jüngling family specialize in TROCKEN and HALBTROCKEN wines, as well as fine AUSLESEN.

Pauly-Bergweiler, Dr. ★★★ Fine BERNKASTEL estate. vineyards there and in WEHLEN, etc. Peter Nicolay wines from ÜRZIG and ERDEN are usually best. EISWEIN and TBA can be sensational.

Perlwein Semi-sparkling wine.

Pfalz Pfz 23,400-ha vineyard region south of RHEINHESSEN. Warm climate: grapes ripen fully. The MITTELHAARDT area is the source of full-bodied, often dry RIES. The more southerly SÜDLICHE WEINSTRASSE is better suited to the Pinot varieties, white and red. Biggest RIES area after MOSEL-SAAR-RUWER. Formerly known as the Rheinpfalz.

Pfeffingen, Weingut ★★★ Doris and Jan Eymael make very good RIES and sometimes remarkable SCHEUREBE at UNGSTEIN.

Piesport M-M w ★→★★★★ 89 90 93 94 95 96 **97** 98 **99** 00 **01** 02 03 **04** 05 06 Tiny village with famous vine amphitheatre: at best glorious rich, aromatic RIES. Great First Class vineyards: Goldtröpfchen, Domherr. Treppchen far inferior. GROSSLAGE: Michelsberg (mainly MÜLLER-T; avoid). Especially good as GRANS-FASSIAN, Joh. Haart, R HAART, KURT HAIN, von KESSELSTATT, SANKT URBANS-HOF, Weller-Lehnert.

Portugieser Second-rate red wine grape now often used for WEISSHERBST. Almost 5,000 ha in production.

Prädikat Special attributes or qualities. See QMP.

Prinz, Fred Rhg w ★★ 6 ha of some of the best RIES in village of HALLGARTEN.

Prüfungsnummer Official identifying test-number of a quality wine, the APNR.

Prüm, J J ★★★★ 75 76 79 83 85 **86 88 89** 90 94 **95** 96 **97** 98 **99** 00 **01 02** 03 **04** 05 06 Superlative and legendary 19-ha MOSEL estate in BERNKASTEL, GRAACH, WEHLEN, ZELTINGEN. Delicate but long-lived wines with astonishing finesse, especially in Wehlener SONNENUHR. Long lees-ageing makes the wines hard to taste when young but they reward patience. Good years keep 30 years.

Prüm, S A ★★→★★★ **88 89** 90 94 **95** 96 **97** 98 **99** 00 **01** 02 03 **04** 05 06 If WEHLEN neighbour J J PRÜM is resolutely traditional, Raimond Prüm has dipped his toe into the late 20th C. Sound, if sometimes inconsistent, wines from WEHLEN and GRAACH.

QbA, Qualitätswein bestimmter Anbaugebiete The middle quality of German wine, with sugar added before fermentation (as in French chaptalization), but controlled as to areas, grapes, etc.

QmP, Qualitätswein mit Prädikat Top category, for all wines ripe enough not to need sugaring (KABINETT to TROCKENBEERENAUSLESE).

Randersacker Frank w ★★→★★★ **90 93 94 97** 98 99 **00 01** 02 03 04 **05** 06 Leading village just south of WÜRZBURG known for distinctive dry wine. First Class vineyards include Pfülben, Sonnenstuhl. Top growers include BURGERSPITAL, JULIUSSPITAL, STAATLICHER HOFKELLER, Robert Schmitt, Störrlein, Trockene Schmitts.

Ratzenberger ★★ Estate making racy dry and off-dry RIES in BACHARACH; best from First Class Posten and Steeger St-Jost vineyards. Good SEKT, too.

Rauenthal Rhg w ★★★→★★★★ 90 93 94 95 97 98 99 00 01 02 03 04 05 06 Supreme village on inland slopes: spicy, complex wine. First Class vineyards: Baiken, Gehrn, Nonnenberg, Rothenberg, Wülfen. Top growers: BREUER, KLOSTER EBERBACH, LANGWERTH VON SIMMERN.

Rebholz Pfz ★★★→★★★★ Top SÜDLICHE WEINSTRASSE estate for decades, maintaining extraordinary consistency. Makes some of the best dry MUSKATELLER, GEWÜRZ, CHARD (Burgundian style), and SPÄTBURGUNDER in PFALZ. Outstanding GROSSES GEWÄCHS sites and wines.

Regent New Dark-red grape enjoying considerable success in PFALZ and RHEINHESSEN. 2,160 ha are now planted.

Ress, Balthasar ★★ 35-ha RHEINGAU estate based in HATTENHEIM. Also runs SCHLOSS REICHARTSHAUSEN. Commercially astute, with original artists' labels, but variable-quality wine. Basic "Von Unserm" label, red and white, can offer good value.

Restsüsse Unfermented grape sugar remaining in (or in cheap wines added to) wine to give it sweetness. Can range from 3 grams/litre in a TROCKEN wine to 300 in a TBA.

Rheingau Rhg Best vineyard region of Rhine, west of Wiesbaden. 3,106 ha. Classic, substantial but subtle RIES, yet on the whole recently eclipsed by brilliance elsewhere. Controversially, one-third of the region is classified since 2000 as ERSTES GEWÄCHS (First Growth), subject to some strict regulations. These rules differ from those created by the VDP for GROSSES GEWÄCHS.

Rheinhessen Rhh Vast region (26,230 ha) between Mainz and Worms, bordered by River NAHE to west. Much dross, but includes top RIES from NACKENHEIM, NIERSTEIN, OPPENHEIM, etc. Remarkable spurt in quality in south of region from growers such as KELLER.

Rheinpfalz See PFALZ.

Richter, Weingut Max Ferd ★★→★★★ Top MITTELMOSEL estate, at Mülheim. Fine RIES made from First Class vineyards: BRAUNEBERGER JUFFER-SONNENUHR, GRAACHER Domprobst, Mülheim (Helenenkloster), WEHLENER SONNENUHR. Produces superb EISWEIN from Helenenkloster almost every year. Wines from purchased

> **The Saar**
> With its vineyards located in chilly side valleys, the Saar has always been the source of Germany's leanest, raciest, steeliest Rieslings. And despite the increase in ripeness levels (see Box: Global Warming page 130) throughout Germany, the Saar has retained its typicity more than most regions. The classic Rieslings from producers such as Scharzhof, Zilliken, and Schloss Saarstein have never been more finely honed, and regional quality has been enhanced by the spectacular increase in quality at estates such as Lauer and von Othegraven. A further dimension of excitement is added by growers who aim for a richer, drier style. Arguments will continue to rage over whether such wines are typical or not, but few would deny that the powerful, off-dry Rieslings from producers such as Van Volxem and Herrenberg are exciting wines in their own right.

grapes carry a slightly different label.

Rieslaner Cross between SILVANER and RIES; makes fine AUSLESEN in FRANKEN, where most is grown. Also superb from MÜLLER-CATOIR.

Riesling The best German grape: fragrant, fruity, racy, long-lived. Only CHARD can compete as the world's best white grape.

Ruck, Weingut Johann ★★ Reliable and spicy SILVANER and RIESLANER from

GERMANY

IPHOFEN in FRANKEN.

Rüdesheim Rhg w ★★→★★★★ 83 89 90 92 93 95 **96 97 98 99** 00 01 02 03 04 **05** 06 Rhine resort with First Class vineyards; the three best are called Rüdesheimer Berg. Full-bodied wines, fine-flavoured, often remarkable in off years. Many of the top RHEINGAU estates own some Rüdesheim vineyards. Best growers: BREUER, JOHANNISHOF, KESSELER, LEITZ, RESS, SCHLOSS SCHÖNBORN, STAATSWEINGÜTER.

Ruländer Pinot Gris: now more commonly known as GRAUBURGUNDER.

Ruppertsberg Pfz w ★★→★★★ **90 94 96** 97 **98** 99 01 02 **03 04 05** 06 Southern village of MITTELHAARDT. Patchy quality but First Class vineyards inc Gaisböhl, Linsenbusch, Nussbein, Reiterpfad. Growers include BASSERMANN-JORDAN, BIFFAR, BUHL, BÜRKLIN-WOLF, CHRISTMANN, DR DEINHARD.

Ruwer 76 83 **89** 90 94 95 97 98 **99 01 02 03 04** 05 06 Tributary of MOSEL near TRIER. Very fine, delicate but highly aromatic and well structured wines. RIES both sweet and dry. Villages include EITELSBACH KASEL, Mertesdorf.

Saale-Unstrut 95 97 **00** 01 02 **03** 04 **05** 06 Climatically challenging region of 650 ha around confluence of these two rivers at Naumburg, near Leipzig. The terraced vineyards of WEISSBURGUNDER, SILVANER, GEWÜRZ, RIES, etc., and red SPÄTBURGUNDER have Cistercian origins. Quality leaders: Böhme, Gussek, LÜTZKENDORF, Landesweingut Kloster Pforta, Pawis, Thüringer Weingut.

Saar 76 83 89 90 93 94 95 96 **97** 98 **99** 01 02 **03 04 05** 06 Hill-lined tributary of the MOSEL south of RUWER. Most vineyards located in chilly side valleys. The most brilliant, austere, steely RIES of all. Villages include AYL OCKFEN, Saarburg, SERRIG, WILTINGEN (SCHARZHOFBERG). Many fine estates here.

Sachsen 95 97 **98 99** 00 01 02 **03 04** 05 06 A region of 411 ha in the Elbe Valley around Dresden and Meissen. MÜLLER-T still dominates, but WEISSBURGUNDER, GRAUBURGUNDER, TRAMINER, and RIES give dry wines with real character. Best growers: SCHLOSS PROSCHWITZ, Vincenz Richter, Martin Schwarz, Schloss Wackerbarth, Zimmerling.

St-Antony, Weingut ★★ Once excellent Rheinhessen estate, now faltering. But new owner (same as HEYL ZU HERRNSHEIM) may turn things around. At best rich GROSSES GEWÄCHS RIES from First Class vineyards of NIERSTEIN.

Salm, Prinz zu Owner of SCHLOSS WALLHAUSEN in NAHE and Villa Sachsen in RHEINHESSEN. Until 2006 president of VDP, which implemented the vineyard classification system against some stern opposition.

Salwey, Weingut ★★★ Leading BADEN estate at Oberrotweil, especially for RIES WEISSBURGUNDER, and RULÄNDER. SPÄTBURGUNDER can be very good too, and fruit schnapps are an intriguing sideline.

Samtrot Red WÜRTTEMBERG grape, a mutation of Pinot Meunier. Makes Germany's closest shot at Beaujolais.

Sankt Urbans-Hof ★★★ New star based in LEIWEN, PIESPORT, and OCKFEN. Limpid RIES of impeccable purity and raciness from 38 ha.

Sauer, Horst ★★★ ESCHERNDORFER Lump is one of FRANKEN's top sites, and Sauer is the finest exponent of its *SILVANER* and RIES. Notable dry wines, and sensational TROCKENBEERENAUSLESEN.

Schaefer, Willi ★★★ The finest grower of GRAACH (but only 3 ha). Classic pure MOSEL RIES.

Schäfer-Fröhlich, Weingut ★★★ Increasingly fine RIES, dry and nobly sweet from this 12-ha estate in Nockenau, NAHE.

Scharzhofberg M-S-R (Saar) w ★★★★ 75 76 83 88 89 90 93 94 95 96 97 98 **99** 00 **01 02 03 04 05** 06 Superlative SAAR vineyard: austerely beautiful wines, the perfection of RIES, best in AUSLESEN. Top estates: BISCHÖFLICH WEINGÜTER, EGON MÜLLER, von HÖVEL, von KESSELSTATT, VAN VOLXEM.

Schaumwein Sparkling wine.

Scheurebe Grapefruit-scented grape of high quality (and RIES parentage), especially used in PFALZ. Excellent for botrytis wine (BEERENAUSLESEN, TROCKENBEERENAUSLESEN).

Schillerwein Light red or rosé QBA; speciality of WÜRTTEMBERG (only).

Schlossböckelheim Nahe w ★★→★★★ 83 89 90 93 95 96 97 98 99 00 01 02 03 04 05 06 Village with top NAHE vineyards, including First Class Felsenberg, In den Felsen, Königsfels, Kupfergrube. Firm yet delicate wine that ages well. Top growers: CRUSIUS, DÖNNHOF, Gutsverwaltung NIEDERHAUSEN-SCHLOSSBÖCKELHEIM, SCHÄFER-FRÖHLICH.

Schloss Johannisberg Rhg w ★★→★★★ 89 90 94 95 96 97 98 99 00 01 02 03 04 05 06 Famous RHEINGAU estate of 35 ha, 100% RIES, owned by HENKELL. Deservedly popular tourist destination, but more importantly the original Rhine "first growth". Since 1996 there has been a return to form, though there still seems to be an element of complacency. High prices reflect reputation more than quality.

Schloss Lieser ★★★ 9-ha estate owned by Thomas Haag, from Fritz HAAG estate, making pure racy RIES from underrated vineyards of LIESER.

Schloss Neuweier ★★★ Leading producer of dry RIES in BADEN, from Mauerberg and Schlossberg vineyards near Baden-Baden.

Schloss Proschwitz ★★ A resurrected princely estate at Meissen in SACHSEN, which leads former east Germany in quality, especially with dry *WEISSBURGUNDER* and GRAUBURGUNDER.

Schloss Reichartshausen Rhg 4-ha HATTENHEIM vineyard run by RESS.

Schloss Reinhartshausen Rhg ★★ Fine estate in ERBACH, HATTENHEIM, KIEDRICH, etc. Originally property of Prussian royal family, now in private hands. Model RHEINGAU RIES. The mansion beside the Rhine is now a luxury hotel. Under new management since 2003, the estate is returning to form.

Schloss Saarstein, Weingut ★→★★★ 89 90 93 95 97 99 01 02 03 04 05 06 Steep but chilly vineyards in SERRIG need warm years to succeed but can deliver steely minerally, and long-lived AUSLESE and EISWEIN.

Schloss Schönborn ★★★ Widespread 50-ha RHEINGAU estates, based at HATTENHEIM. Full-flavoured wines, variable, but excellent when at their best. The Schönborn family also own a large wine estate in FRANKEN.

Schloss Sommerhausen, Weingut ★★ Ancient FRANKEN estate producing good dry whites and a dependable range of SEKT.

Schloss Thorn Ancient OBERMOSEL estate; remarkable ELBLING, RIES, and castle.

Schloss Vollrads Rhg w ★★→★★★ 83 89 90 94 98 99 00 01 02 03 04 05 06 One of the greatest historic RHEINGAU estates, owned by a bank since the sudden death of owner Erwein Count Matuschka in 1997. Since 1998, quality, under director Rowald Hepp, is much improved, but the estate's full potential has yet to be defined.

Schloss Wallhausen ★→★★ The 12-ha NAHE estate, among Germany's oldest, of Prince SALM. 60% RIES. The prince's duties as president of the VDP growers' association led to some neglect of quality here, but son Constantin aims to change that.

Schneider, Weingut Georg Albrecht ★★ An impeccably run 14-ha estate. Classic off-dry and sweet RIES in NIERSTEIN, the best from Hipping vineyard.

Schnaitmann, Weingut ★★→★★★ Although this new WÜRTTEMBERG star makes good RIES and SAUV BL, its reputation rests on a broad selection of *full-bodied red wines* from a range of varieties.

Schoppenwein Café (or bar) wine, *i.e.* wine by the glass.

Schwarzer Adler, Weingut ★★→★★★ Fritz Keller makes top BADEN dry GRAU-, WEISS-, and SPÄTBURGUNDER on 51 ha at Oberbergen, KAISERSTUHL.

Schweigen Pfz w r ★★ 96 **97 98 99 01** 02 **03 04 05** 06 Southern PFALZ village. Best growers: Friedrich Becker, especially for SPÄTBURGUNDER, Bernhart, Julg.

Sekt German sparkling wine, best when the label specifies RIES, WEISSBURGUNDER, or SPATBURGUNDER.

Selbach-Oster ★★★ Scrupulous ZELTINGEN estate among MITTELMOSEL leaders. Also makes wine from purchased grapes, but estate bottlings are best.

Serrig M-S-R (Saar) w ★★→★★★ 89 90 93 95 97 99 01 02 03 04 05 06 Village giving steely wines, excellent in sunny years. First Class vineyards: Herrenberg, Schloss Saarstein, Würtzberg. Top growers: SCHLOSS SAARSTEIN, Herrenberg (Siemens).

Silvaner Third-most-planted German white grape variety with 5% of the surface, generally underrated. Best examples in FRANKEN, the closest thing to Chablis in Germany. Worth looking for in RHEINHESSEN and KAISERSTUHL.

Sonnenuhr Sundial. Name of several vineyards, especially First Class sites at WEHLEN and ZELTINGEN.

Spätburgunder Pinot N: the best red wine grape in Germany – especially in BADEN and WÜRTTEMBERG, and increasingly PFALZ – generally improving quality, but most still underflavoured or over-oaked.

Spätlese Late harvest. One better (riper, with more alcohol, more substance and usually more sweetness) than KABINETT. Good examples age at least 7 years, often longer. TROCKEN Spätlesen, often similar in style to GROSSES GEWÄCHS, can be very fine with food.

Spreitzer, Weingut ★★★ Since 1997, brothers Andreas and Bernd Spreitzer in OESTRICH, RHEINGAU, have been making deliciously racy and consistent RIES.

Staatlicher Hofkeller ★★ The Bavarian STATE DOMAIN. 140 ha of the finest FRANKEN vineyards with spectacular cellars under the great baroque Residenz at WÜRZBURG. Quality sound but rarely exciting.

Staatsweingut (or Staatliche Weinbaudomäne) The state wine estates or domains; especially KLOSTER EBERBACH. Some have been privatized in recent years.

State Domain See STAATSWEINGUT.

Stein, Weingut Am ★★ Although this FRANKEN winery is located within the famous WÜRZBURGER STEIN, most of the vines lie to the north, in Stetten. Improving RIES, SILVANER, and REISLANER.

Steinberg Rhg w ★★→★★★ 90 93 95 96 97 99 00 01 02 03 04 05 06 Famous 32-ha HATTENHEIM walled vineyard, planted by Cistercian monks 700 years ago. A monopoly of KLOSTER EBERBACH. Some glorious wines; some in the past were sadly feeble.

Steinwein Wine from WÜRZBURG's best vineyard, Stein.

Südliche Weinstrasse (Bereich) District name for south PFALZ. Quality has improved tremendously in past 25 years. See REBHOLZ, SCHWEIGEN, DR. WEHRHEIM.

Tafelwein See "Germany's quality levels" box on p.124.

Tauberfranken (Bereich) Minor Badisches Frankenland BEREICH of north BADEN: FRANKEN-style wines.

Tesch, Weingut ★★ Once an unremarkable estate in Langenlonsheim, NAHE, this has become a fine source of rich, rounded, dry RIES.

Thanisch, Weingut Dr. H ★★→★★★ BERNKASTEL estate, including part of the Doctor vineyard. Confusingly two estates share the same name: Erben Müller-Burggraef identifies one; Erben Thanisch the other. Little to choose in terms of quality.

Traben-Trarbach M-M w ★★→★★★ 90 93 96 97 98 99 01 02 03 04 05 06 Substantial but underperforming wine town of 324 ha, 87% of it RIES. Top vineyards: Ungsberg, Würzgarten. Top grower: Martin Müllen.

Traisen Nahe w ★★★ 89 90 93 95 96 97 98 99 00 **01 02 03 04 05** 06 Small village including First Class Bastei and Rotenfels vineyards, capable of making RIES of concentration and class. Top grower: CRUSIUS.

Traminer See GEWÜRZTRAMINER.

Trier M-S-R w ★★→★★★ Great wine city of Roman origin, on MOSEL, between RUWER and SAAR. Big Mosel charitable estates have cellars here among imposing Roman ruins. Growers include Deutschherren-Hof.

Trittenheim M-M w ★★★ 89 90 93 95 96 97 98 99 00 01 02 **03 04 05** 06 Attractive south MITTELMOSEL light wines, much improved in quality over past decade. Top vineyards were Altärchen, Apotheke, but now include second-rate flat land; First Class vineyards are Felsenkopf, Leiterchen. Growers include east Clüsserath, Clüsserath-Weiler, GRANS-FASSIAN, Milz.

Trocken Dry. *Trocken* wines have a maximum 9 g of unfermented sugar per litre. Some are austere, others (better) have more body and alcohol. Quality has increased dramatically since the 1980s, when the majority were tart, even sour. Most dependable in PFALZ and points south.

Trockenbeerenauslese (TBA) Sweetest, most expensive category of German wine, extremely rare, with concentrated honey flavour. Made from selected shrivelled grapes affected by noble rot (botrytis). See also EDEL. *Edelbeerenauslese* would be a less confusing name.

Trollinger Pale red grape variety of WÜRTTEMBERG; over-cropped but locally very popular.

Ungstein Pfz w ★★→★★★ 90 93 94 **95 96** 97 **98 99** 00 01 02 03 **04 05** 06 MITTELHAARDT village with fine harmonious wines. First Class vineyards include Herrenberg, Weilberg. Top growers include: Darting, Fitz-Ritter, PFEFFINGEN, Pflüger, Karl Schäfer, Egon Schmitt.

Ürzig M-M w ★★★★ 89 90 92 93 94 **95** 96 **97** 98 **99** 00 01 02 **03 04 05** 06 Village on red sandstone and red slate, famous for firm, full, spicy wine unlike other MOSELS. First Class vineyard: Würzgarten. Growers include CHRISTOFFEL, LOOSEN, MÖNCHHOF, PAULY-BERGWEILER (Peter Nicolay), WEINS-PRÜM.

Van Volxem, Weingut ★★→★★★ Lacklustre SAAR estate revived by brewery heir Roman Niewodniczanski since 1999. Very low yields from top sites result in ultra-ripe dry RIES. Atypical but impressive.

VDP, Verband Deutscher Prädikats und Qualitätsweingüter The pace-making association of premium growers. Look for its eagle insignia on wine labels. President: Steffen CHRISTMANN.

Vereinigte Hospitien ★★ "United Hospices". Ancient charity at TRIER with large holdings in PIESPORT, SERRIG, TRIER, WILTINGEN, etc. Wines recently well below their wonderful potential.

Vollenweider, Weingut ★★★ Newcomer Daniel Vollenweider from Switzerland has since 2000 revived the Wolfer Goldgrube vineyard near TRABEN-TRARBACH. Excellent RIES, but very small quantities.

Wachenheim Pfz w ★★★→★★★★ **94** 95 **96** 97 **98 99** 01 02 03 04 05 06 340 ha, including exceptional RIES. First Class vineyards: Belz, Gerümpel, Goldbächel, Rechbächel, etc. Top growers: BIFFAR, BÜRKLIN-WOLF, and Karl Schäfer, WOLF.

Wagner, Dr. ★★ 9-ha estate with vineyards in Saarburg and OCKFEN. Many fine wines, including TROCKEN.

Wagner-Stempel, Weingut ★★→★★★ 13-ha estate, 50% RIES, near NAHE border in obscure Siefersheim. Recent years have provided excellent wines, great in 2005, both GROSSES GEWÄCHS and nobly sweet.

Walluf Rhg w ★★★ 90 92 94 95 96 **97** 98 **99** 00 **01** 02 03 **04 05** 06 Neighbour of ELTVILLE. Underrated wines. First Class vineyard: Walkenberg. Growers include BECKER, JOST.

Wawern M-S-R (Saar) w ★★→★★★ **90 93 95** 96 **97 99** 01 02 **03 04 05** 06 Small village, fine RIES. First Class vineyard: Herrenberg. Leading grower: Reinert.

Wegeler ★★→★★★ Important family estates in OESTRICH, MITTELHARDT, and BERNKASTEL. The Wegelers owned the merchant house of DEINHARD until 1997. Estate wines remain of high quality.

Wehlen M-M w ★★★→★★★★ **88 89 90 93 94 95** 96 **97** 98 **99** 00 **01 02** 03 **04 05** 06 Neighbour of BERNKASTEL with equally fine, somewhat richer wine. Location of great First Class vineyard: SONNENUHR. The top growers are: KERPEN, LOOSEN, M MOLITOR, J J PRÜM, S A PRÜM, RICHTER, Studert-Prüm, SELBACH-OSTER, WEGELER, WEINS-PRÜM.

Wehrheim, Weingut Dr. ★★★ In the warm SÜDLICHE WEINSTRASSE Pinot varieties and CHAR as well as RIES ripen fully. Both whites and reds are highly successful here.

Weil, Weingut Robert ★★★★ **90 94** 95 **96** 97 **98 99** 00 **01 02** 03 **04 05** 06 Outstanding estate in KIEDRICH; owned since 1988 by Suntory of Japan. Superb EISWEIN, TROCKENBEERENAUSLESEN, BEERENAUSLESEN; ***standard wines also very good*** since 1992. Generally accepted to be RHEINGAU's No 1 in sweet wines, both in quality and price.

Weingart, Weingut ★★→★★★ Outstanding MITTELRHEIN estate, with 11 ha in BOPPARD. Superb value.

Weingut Wine estate.

Weins-Prüm, Dr. ★★→★★★ Classic MITTELMOSEL estate; 4 ha based at WEHLEN. WEHLENER SONNENUHR is usually top wine. Scrupulous winemaking from owner Bert Selbach, who favours a taut, minerally style.

Weinstrasse Wine road: a scenic route through areas of vineyard. Germany has several.

Weissburgunder Pinot Blanc Most reliable grape for TROCKEN wines: low acidity, high extract. Also much used for SEKT.

Weissherbst Usually a pale pink wine, QBA or above and occasionally BEERENAUSLESE, made from a single variety, often SPÄTBURGUNDER. Speciality of BADEN, PFALZ, and WÜRTTEMBERG.

Werner, Domdechant ★★ 12-ha family estate on best HOCHHEIM slopes: top wines excellent; others only fair.

Wiltingen M-S-R (Saar) w ★★→★★★★ **89 90 93 95** 96 **97** 98 **99** 00 **01** 02 **03 04 05** 06 Heartland of the SAAR. 320 ha. Beautifully subtle, austere wine. Great First Class vineyard is SCHARZHOFBERG (ORTSTEIL); and First Class are Braune Kupp, Gottesfuss, Hölle. Top growers: BISCHÖFLICHE WEINGÜTER, EGON MÜLLER, von KESSELSTATT, VAN VOLXEM, etc.

Winkel Rhg w ★★★ **90 93 94 95** 96 97 98 **99** 00 **01** 02 **03 04 05** 06 Village famous for full, fragrant wine. First Class vineyards include Hasensprung, Jesuitengarten, SCHLOSS VOLLRADS, Schlossberg. Growers include Hamm, von HESSEN, SCHLOSS SCHÖNBORN, WEGELER.

Winningen M-S-R w ★★ Lower MOSEL town near Koblenz: excellent dry RIES. First Class vineyards: Röttgen, Uhlen. Top growers: HEYMANN-LÖWENSTEIN, KNEBEL, Richard Richter.

Wintrich M-M w ★★→★★★ **90 92 93 95 97 98 99** 00 **01** 02 03 **04 05** 06 Neighbour of PIESPORT; similar wines. First Class vineyard: Ohligsberg. Top grower: Reinhold HAART.

Winzergenossenschaft (WG) A wine-growers' cooperative, often making sound and reasonably priced wine. Referred to in this text as "co-op". Very important in BADEN and WURTTEMBERG.

Winzerverein The same as above.

Wirsching, Hans ★★→★★★ Estate in IPHOFEN, FRANKEN. Dry RIES and SILVANER can be firm and elegant but quality is variable. 72 ha in First Class vineyards:

Julius-Echter-Berg, Kalb, etc.

Wittmann, Weingut ★★★ Philipp Wittmann since 1999 has propelled this 25-ha organic estate to the top ranks in RHEINHESSEN. Powerful, dry GROSSES GEWÄCHS RIES and magnificent TROCKENBEERENAUSLESEN.

Wöhrwag, Weingut ★★→★★★ Just outside Stuttgart, this 20-ha WÜRTTEMBERG estate produces succulent reds and often brilliant RIES, especially EISWEIN.

Wolf J L ★★★ Estate in WACHENHEIM leased long-term by Ernst LOOSEN of Bernkastel. Firm dry PFALZ RIES with a MOSEL-like finesse. Very consistent.

Wolff Metternich ★★ Noble DURBACH estate: produces some good RIES and SPÄTBURGUNDER.

Wonnegau (Bereich) District name for south RHEINHESSEN.

Württemberg Wurt **90 93 96 97 99** 00 **01** 02 **03** 04 **05** 06 Vast area in the south, little known for wine outside Germany despite some very good RIES (especially NECKAR Valley) and steadily improving reds: LEMBERGER, SAMTROT, TROLLINGER.

Würzburg Frank ★★→★★★★ **90 93 94 97** 98 99 **00 01** 02 03 **04 05** 06 Great baroque city on the Main, centre of FRANKEN wine: fine, full-bodied, dry RIES and SILVANER. First Class vineyards: Abtsleite, Innere Leiste, Stein, Stein-Harfe. See MAINDREIECK. Growers: BÜRGERSPITAL, JULIUSSPITAL, STAATLICHER HOFKELLER, AM STEIN.

Zell M-S-R w ★→★★★ **90 93 95 97** 98 99 **01** 02 **03** 04 05 06 Best-known lower MOSEL village, especially for awful GROSSLAGE: Schwarze Katz (Black Cat). RIES on steep slate gives aromatic wines. Top grower: Kallfelz.

Zeltingen M-M W ★★→★★★★ **89 90 93 95** 96 **97 98 99** 00 **01** 02 **03** 04 05 06 Top but sometimes underrated MOSEL village near WEHLEN. Lively crisp RIES. First Class vineyard: SONNENUHR. Top growers: Markus MOLITOR, J J PRÜM, Schömann, SELBACH-OSTER.

Zilliken, Forstmeister Geltz ★★★ Former estate of Prussian royal forester with 10 ha at Saarburg and OCKFEN, SAAR. Produces intensely minerally RIES from Saarburger Rausch, including superb AUSLESE and EISWEIN with excellent ageing potential.

Luxembourg

Luxembourg has 1,250 hectares of vineyards on limestone soils on the Moselle's left bank. High-yielding Elbling and Rivaner (Müller-Thurgau) have been the dominant varieties, but are in gradual decline; Chardonnay is growing, though primarily for sparkling wine. There are also Riesling, Gewürztraminer, and (usually best) Auxerrois, Pinot Blanc, and Pinot Gris. These give light to medium-bodied (10.5–11.5% alcohol), dry, Alsace-like wines. Perhaps as a result of climatic change, there has been a growth in more full-bodied, richer wines, including some late-harvested Vendanges Tardives and *vins de paille*. Pinot Noir now accounts for 7% of plantings. The most important producer by far is the Vinsmoselle co-op. The Domaine et Tradition association, founded in 88, groups seven estates that impose stricter rules on themselves than the regulations demand. The following vintages were all **good**: 89 90 92 95 97; **outstanding** 97; **average** 98; similar but **softer** 99; **poor** 2000; much **better** 2001 and 2002; **average** 2004; while 2003 and 2005 are good for red as well as white wines. Best from: Bastian, Bentz, Cep d'Or, Abi Duhr, Alice Hartmann, Krier Frères, Krier-WelbesBernard Massard (good classic method sparkling), Schumacher-Knepper, and Sunnen-Hoffmann.

GERMANY

Spain & Portugal

More heavily shaded areas
are the wine-growing regions

The following abbreviations are used in the text:

Alen	Alentejo
Bair	Bairrada
Bul	Bullas
Cos del S	Costers del Segre
El B	El Bierzo
Emp	Empordà-Costa Brava/Ampurdán
Est	Estremadura
La M	La Mancha
Mont-M	Montilla-Moriles
Nav	Navarra
Pen	Penedès
Pri	Priorato/Priorat
Rib del D	Ribera del Duero
Rib del G	Ribera del Guadiana
R Ala	Rioja Alavesa
R Alt	Rioja Alta
RB	Rioja Baja
Set	Setúbal
Som	Somontano
U-R	Utiel-Requena
res	reserva

MADEIRA (off west coast of Africa)

Spain is Europe's slumbering giant. Inward-looking for so long, it is at last adjusting its focus to include international consumers; and is doing so with wines that seek to be universal but maintain their native character.

There are a couple of complications, however. On the one hand there are endless numbers of new Denominations of Origin, often created to encourage – not because they have earned – credibility, and also sometimes created by virtue of the complicated, over-federal nature of a country that was once ruled by dictatorship from the capital. On the other hand, there is an apparently never-ending flow of cash-rich individuals who wish to create wineries for speculative purposes or simply out of vanity.

This latter phenomenon can arise in Portugal, too, although to a lesser degree than in Spain. And Portugal, too, has its complications, but it also has a region clearly ahead of the rest: the Douro's world-class reds. Behind them is a growing band of exciting, modern wines from across Portugal. Alentejo is the leader, with increasingly skilled handling of a diverse portfolio of grape varieties and terroirs. Consistently good everyday wines, especially from Ribatejo, are building a broader fan-base while in the middle ground Estremadura, Dão and Bairrada reinvent themselves.

Navarra
Rioja
Somontano
Ampurdán-Costa Brava
...les
Campo de Borja
Costers del Segre
Conca de Barbera
Ribera del Duero
Calatayud
Carlñena
Alella
Rueda
Montsant
Penedès
Tarragona
Vinos de Madrid
...ntrida
Utiel-Requena
Valencia
Binissalem
La Mancha
Pià i Llevant
Almansa
Valencia
Valdepeñas
Jumilla
Alicante
...lquivir
Bullas
Yecla
...ntilla Moriles
...laga

Sherry, port, and madeira have a separate chapter on p 159.

Spain

Recent vintages of the Spanish classics

Rioja

2006 Biggish harvest with generally favourable weather. Results considered generally positive.

2005 A large, healthy, and plentiful harvest, with exceptionally favourable weather. Quality rated as "exceptional" and "unprecedented".

2004 A large harvest with "magnificent" quality hopes for those who were selective enough given the tricky weather. Most justify initial optimism.

2003 Biggish harvest of fair quality, but it is now obvious that many wines are proving extremely short-lived.

2002 Small harvest of doubtful quality, like a cross between 1999 and 2000 though curiously these are enduring marginally longer than anticipated.

2001 Medium-sized harvest of excellent quality; wines fulfilling their promise, though many are already too austere and drying out.

2000 Huge harvest; wines distinctly bland, with little real flavour or definition.

1999 A difficult harvest, which produced light but very graceful wines that have mainly peaked.

Ribera del Duero

2006 Very complicated indeed: midsummer storms with flash downpours provoking widespread oidium; then intense heat in early September followed by copious rain and the threat of botrytis. Some picked an entire month early, but best picked super-selectively, and finished a month later. Results will be as polarized as 05.

2005 Not only 30% below expectations, with musts of tremendous aromas and extract, but alcohol levels often too high. Those who picked too early have green, unbalanced wines. V. good only for the true professionals.

2004 A better year than in most regions. Despite extremes of temperature in Sept, good quality wines and a plentiful harvest.

2003 A cold winter, mild spring, scorching summer, and Oct rains resulted in a tricky harvest. The best wines are of good colour, glycerine, and alcohol, but low in acidity.

2002 Hot weather followed by heavy rain in late summer led to a large harvest. Quality generally very good.

2001 Medium-sized harvest of excellent quality; wines fulfilling their promise.

2000 Very large harvest but ripening was uneven. Some bodegas made spectacular wines; but in general good.

1999 Almost perfect weather and bumper harvest, but rainfall around harvest time resulted in lack of acidity. Very good, but fading.

Navarra

2006 Complicated, given a wet spring, hot summer and mild and damp autumn. The best have resulting in good fruit, roundness and balance, but moderate alcohol and concentration. Will be good for young wines, but only the most professional will produce wines of any ageing potential.

2005 Possibly the region's best-ever vintage, with perfect climatic conditions and virtually no rain, resulting in optimum ripeness and wines of immense colour, full flavours, and sweet, powerful tannins.

2004 Low spring and summer temperatures with much rain. Good wines for those who picked late and selectively.

2003 The hot, dry summer was followed by extended torrential rain and outbreaks of botrytis and mildew. As in 2002, only the best and most professional producers obtained decent results.

2002 Torrential Aug rains affected the quality of wines from the south of the region; others are excellent.

2001 An excellent year, with big, ripe, well-balanced wines.

2000 Very dry year of prolific yields, calling for rigorous selection. Best wines are big and fleshy, and age well. Very good.

1999 Most frost-afflicted vintage of the decade, with soaring grape prices. Wines are well-structured and long-ageing. Excellent.

Penedès

2006 Healthy and properly developed fruit resulted in v. good acidity and alcohol levels, and the vintage is officially 'excellent' on all levels.

2005 The hardest drought of the last 50 years reduced yields by 30–40%, but thanks to cold summer nights quality was excellent for reds and whites.

2004 A cold spring and late summer rains delayed the harvest, but sunny days and cold nights in autumn resulted in a memorable year for red wines.

2003 A very dry and long summer, refreshed with rains in Aug, then cool nights and sunny days in Sept, resulted in a great vintage.
2002 A splendid Sept gave wines of good quality.
2001 April frosts reduced the yield but warm summer produced very good wines.
2000 Perfect ripening of the grapes gave well-balanced wines. Very good.
1999 Dry summer but abundant harvest. Very good.

Aalto, Bodegas y Viñedos Rib del D r ★★–★★★★ 99 00 01 02 03 Mariano García's newish estate produces two spectacular, lavishly concentrated Tempranillos. Both age well, but top cuvée PS is more than twice the price.

Abadía Retuerta Castilla y León r ★★★ 02 03 04 One of the two most famous non-DO wineries in Spain (the other is Mauro) – and one of the most modern makes an exceptional range of reds from Temp, Cab Sauv, Merlot, Syrah and Petit Verdot. Prices to match. Best wines Rivola (04) and exuberant Negralada (03).

Albariño high-quality, aromatic white grape of GALICIA See GERARDO MÉNDEZ, PALACIO DE FEFIÑANES, PAZO DE BARRANTES, PAZO DE SEÑORANS, RÍAS BAIXAS.

Albet y Noya Pen r w p ★★–★★★★ 98 00 01 05 Spain's most famous organic producer continues to make a wide, old-fashioned selection at big prices.The Col-lecció range is best, in particular the Syrah (still 00) and Cabernet (01).

Alella r w (p) dr sw ★★ DYA Small, demarcated region north of Barcelona best for fresh, lively whites made from Pansa Blanca or Chardonnay. Best producers PARXET, and Alella Vinícola Can Jonc.

Alicante r (w) ★ 02 03 04 DO. Most wines still stringy and over-alcoholic. Best producers: Enrique Mendoza and, for young reds, Bodegas Valle del Carce.

Alión Rib del D r ★★ ·★★★★ 01 03 04. VEGA SICILIA's second BODEGA makes short-lived but wonderfully fragrant 100% Temp aged in French oak.

Allende, Finca R Ala r ★★★ ·★★★★ 00 01 02 03 04 BRIONES-based Miguel Ángel de Gregorio personifies RIOJA's new wave, making since 1995 a series of dark, upfront, broody reds. Best-known Allende is pure Tempranillo; wilder and altogether best Calvario from an old, mixed, single vineyard is his exhilarating, edgy masterpiece; and mega-priced Aurus is showy and Parkeresque. Toasty oak Blanco (04) is good; dya.

Álvaro Palacios Pri r ★★★★ 98 99 00 01 02 03 04 Gifted young emigré from RIOJA, though responsible for the madly overpriced/rated L'Ermita makes the outstanding Finca Dofí which really does age. Also _**Les Terrasses (04)**_ the benchmark 'standard' Priorato.

Artadi Bodegas (Cosecheros Alaveses) R Ala r (w p) ★★★ ·★★★★ 96 98 01 02 03 04 Quality orientated former co-op, especially for good, young, unoaked red Artadi, and serious, pricy, splendid Viñas de Gain, Viña El Pisón, Pagos Viejos and Grandes Añadas.

Astrales, Bodegas Los Rib del D r ★★★ ·★★★★ 01 03 04 New (2000) exciting estate in Anguix making single, pure, vibrant Temp of same name. Formidably intense, fresh and balanced despite lavish new oak ageing and, on limited evidence, develops spectacularly.

Barón de Ley RB r (w) res ★★★ 96 98 01 02 04 Newish (1985) RIOJA BODEGA: agreeably mellow, undemanding single-estate wines. Opt for either Reserva (96 98 or 04) or superior Finca del Monasterio (01 02 04).

Berberana, Bodegas Once a real and great winery with pedigree old vintages. Now just a brand belonging to BODEGAS UNIDAS.

Beronia, Bodegas R Alt r w res ★★ ·★★★ 95 01 03 04 Modern GONZÁLEZ-BYASS-owned BODEGA making reds in traditional, oaky style.

SPAIN

Bierzo 96 98 99 00 01 02 03 04 05 Fashionable DO north of Léon with many new BODEGAS finally popularizing the indigenous black Mencia and sometimes aromatic white Godello too. Top wineries: Luna Beberide, Prada a Tope, Bodegas Pittacum, Bodegas Peique.

Bilbaínas, Bodegas R Alt r w (p) w dr sw sp res ★★→★★★ 99 01 03 04 Historic Haro BODEGA (from 1859), formerly well known for its Viña Pomal and lighter Zaco reds. Newish owner CODORNÍU has taken time to get to grips with its acquisition. Best current offerings La Vicalanda (**99** Gr and **01** Res) and Pomal Reservas **01** and **03**.

Binissalem r w ★★ **01 03 04 05** Best-known MALLORCA DO. Best is Macía Batle.

Blanco White.

Bodega Spanish term for (i) a wineshop; (ii) a concern occupied in the making, blending, and/or shipping of wine; and (iii) a cellar.

Bodegas de Crianza Castilla la Vieja Rueda w dr sp ★★ →★★★ Makes some of RUEDA's liveliest whites from Verdejo, Viura, and Sauv Bl. Main label Palacio de Bornos.

Bodegas Unidas Umbrella organization controlling MARQUÉS DE MONISTROL, and the BERBERANA brand, as well as workmanlike RIOJA Marqués de la Concordia and Durius from RIBERA DEL DUERO. Also controls the MARQUÉS DE GRIGÑON Rioja brand – for some considerable time unrelated to Carlos Falcó.

Bodegas y Viñedos del Jalón Calatayud r (w dr p) ★★ **05 06** Leading brands are very drinkable if muscular Castillo Maluenda and Viña Alarba. Old-vine Garnacha blends, sometimes with Syrah, particularly good.

Briones Small Riojan hill-top town near Haro, peppered with underground cellars. Home to FINCA ALLENDE and one of the most comprehensive wine museums in the world, El Museo de la Cultura de Vino.

Bullas ★→★★ **02 03 04** Small Murcia DO trying hard. Best producer Bodegas Balcona, whose Partal wines are reminiscent of Madiran.

Calatayud ★→★★ **04 05** 06 Aragón DO (one of four): especially Garnacha. Best producers BODEGAS Y VIÑEDOS DEL JALÓN and San Alejandro Coop. The 05 vintage was outstanding.

Campo Viejo See JUAN ALCORTA, and/or PERNOD RICARD.

Canary Islands (Islas Canarias) r w p ★→★★ Best known for occasionally stunning dessert Malvasías (Brumas de Ayosa from the Valle de Güímar) and Moscatels (Bermejo from Lanzarote), despite multiple DOS (6 in Tenerife alone!), modernization and many native varieties – white Listán and Marmajuelo, black Negramoll and Vijariego – given climate and shallow volcanic soils, though worth keeping an eye on, quality still wines still rare.

Can Rafols dels Caus Pen r p w ★★★ **97 98 00 01 02 03** Small, quirky PENEDÈS estate.Three interesting barrel-fermented whites: El Rocallis (01), La Calma (02) and springier Pairal (**04**). Excellent dya Rosado. Two imposing reds: Ad Fines (01) and Can Lubis (98). Wines for those in search of complexity.

Cariñena ★→★★ 01 02 03 04 05 06 Aragón DO with excellent red potential still struggling to make it big-time. Producers to look out for, albeit with mixed offerings: San Valero and Grandes Vinos y Viñedos.

Casa Castillo Jumilla r (w p) ★★→★★★ **02 03 04 05** One of the best wineries in JUMILLA, producing sturdy, brambly, Parkerized styles for semi-immediate drinking: Las Gravas (**02**) and Valtosca Syrah (**05**).

Castaño, Bodegas Yecla r res (w dr) ★★ **02 03 04 05** Still lone quality trailblazer in this remote DO. Sound reliable Monastrell and Cab Sauv /Temp/Merlot/Syrah blends. Best is Pozuelo (**02**) but also v good sweet Monastrell (**04**).

Castell del Remei Cos del S r w p ★★→★★★ 01 02 03 04 Restored historic estate. Best wines: Gotim Bru red blend (**04**), new designer-style Oda Merlot, and top, minerally, long-lasting old-vine cuvée 1780 (**01 03**).

Castilla-la Mancha, Vino de la Tierra In 1999 some 600,000 ha of this vast region were granted VINO DE LA TIERRA status by the EU. Since then dozens of large firms have moved into the area to make wines.

Castillo de Perelada, Caves Emp r w p res sp ★★→★★★ 03 04 05 Large range of still wines and CAVA, including spritzy dya CATALUÑA DO Blanc Pescador and top reds: superb Gran Claustro, Finca Garbet , and Finca Malaveïna.

Castillo de Ygay R Alt r w ★★★★ (r) 54 64 70 89 91 94 97 98 99 01 Legendary top wines from MARQUÉS DE MURRIETA.

Cataluña 00 01 03 04 05 DO covering the whole Catalan area. 193 constituent wineries include such worthies as ALBET I NOYA, MIGUEL TORRES, Bodegas Roqueta, Bodegues Concavins, JEAN LÉON, Mas Gil (with superb Clos d'Agon red), and Mont Marçal.

Cava 'Mobile' DO covering traditional-method fizz up and down Spain; oddly RUEDA and GALICIA are excluded. Most is produced in or around San Sadurní de Noya in PENEDÈS and dominated by FREIXENET and CODORNÍU. Quality is often higher, though with a price tag, from smaller names: Agustí Torelló, CASTILLO DE PERELADA, Covides, Ferret, Giró Ribot, GRAMONA, Llopart, JUVÉ & CAMPS, MARQUES DE MONISTROL, PARXET, RAIMAT, Raventós i Blanc, Rovellats, and Recaredo.

Celler de Cantonella Cos del S r w ★★→★★★ 03 04 05 Small, mountainous estate north of PRIORATO making concentrated, blackcurranty reds and delicious barrel-fermented Macabeo/Chardonnay white Cérvoles.

César Príncipe Cigales r ★★★ 02 03 04 Boutique producer of pricey, dense, sublimely fruity, low-yield, old-vine Tempranillo in a region known for rosé.

Chacolí País Vasco (r) ★★ DYA Now split into 3 separate DOS: Álava, Guetaria (the heartland), and Vizcaya. All produce fragrant but often unduly sharp, pétillant whites. Only one – the historic, Chueca family owned Txomin Etxaniz – truly impresses.

Chivite, Bodegas Julián Nav r w (p) dr sw res ★★★★ 96 01 02 03 04 05 The biggest, most historic and best-known NAVARRA BODEGA. The excellent, popular, benchmark Gran Feudo range is complimented by a pricier *Colección 125* boutique assortment, including an outstanding Tinto Reserva (**02**), barrel-fermented Blanco (04) and *superb Vendimia Tardía Moscatel (04)*.

Clos Mogador Pri r ★★★→★★★★ 99 00 01 02 03 René Barbier (do not confuse with FREIXENET's PENEDÈS table wine) continues to rank as one of PRIORATO's tops. Second wine Manyetes (04) not quite as impressive, but white Clos Nelin (03, 04, 05) is intriguingly savoury.

Codorníu Pen w sp ★★→★★★ One of the two largest CAVA firms owned by the Raventós family. V good Anna de Codorníu and Jaume de Codorníu. Also owns RAÍMAT and BILBAINAS.

Compañía Vinícola del Norte de España (CVNE) R Alt r w (p) ★★→★★ 98 01 02 04 Famous RIOJA BODEGA. Benchmark 20 years ago; quality has declined on all levels: young reds crude and fiery, oaky white Monopole now ordinary. Top cuvée Real de Asúa (02) much heralded in Spain, but best track down pre-1970 light, elegant, high-acid Imperial or fleshier Viña Real. See also CONTINO.

Conca de Barberà w (r p) 01 03 04 05 Small Catalan DO serving as feeder of grapes to large enterprises such as TORRES (superlative Milmanda Chard 04/5 and awesome red Grans Muralles 01/2) yet also home to friendly, modestly priced Concavins wines and the relatively radical output of biodynamic ESCODA-SANAHUJA.

Condado de Haza Rib del D r ★★★ 03 04 Pure, oak-aged Tinto from PESQUERA's Alejandro Fernández but by and large more consistent, richer and better value. Avoid pricy and disappointingly rustic.

Consejo Regulador Organization for the control, promotion, and defence of a DO.

Contino R Ala r res ★★★ 96 99 00 01 02 03 Very fine single-vineyard reds made by a subsidiary of CVNE. Good Graciano and premium Viña del Olivo.

Cosecha Crop or vintage.

Costers del Segre Cos del S r w p sp ★★→★★★ 94 95 96 01 02 03 04 Small demarcated area around city of Lleida (Lérida), famous for vineyards of RAÏMAT CASTELL DEL REMEI, CELLERS DE CANTONELLA, TOMÁS CUSINÉ.

Crianza Literally "nursing"; the ageing of wine. New or unaged wine is *sin crianza* or JOVEN. Reds labelled *crianza* must be at least 2 yrs old (with 1 yr in oak, in some areas 6 months), and must not be released before the third year.

DO, Denominación de Origen Official wine region.

DOCa, Denominación de Origen Calificada Classification for wines of the highest quality; so far only RIOJA (since 1991) and PRIORATO (DOQ – the Catalan equivalent – since 2002) benefit.

Domecq R Ala r (w) res ★★→★★★ 96 00 03 RIOJA outpost of sherry firm, whose adequate but unexciting Marqués de Arienzo is now yet another component of PERNOD RICARD.

Dominio de Tares El B r w ★★★ 04 Up-and-coming producer whose dark, spicy fragrant, purple-scented Bembibre (**04**) and Cepas Viejas (**04**) prove what can be done with Mencía. Sister winery Dominio dos Tares makes the equally impressive Cumal (**04**) – imposing and black.

Dulce Sweet.

Empordà Ampurdán Emp r w p ★→★★ 02 03 04 05 Demarcated region abutting Pyrenees in northeast. Best producers CASTILLO DE PERELADA, Pere Guardiola and the embryonic Espelt.

Escoda-Sanahuja Conca de Barbera r ★★★ Unique, worthwhile and biodynamic. Uncompromising 03s and 04s need decanting; 05s are user friendly. Coll de Sabater (**04**) is Merlot and Cab Franc; La Llopetera (**05**) is Pinot Noir; Les Paradetes (**04/05**) is Sumoll plus Garnacha and Cariñena.

Enate Som DO r w p res ★★★ 01 02 03 04 Best producer in SOMONTANO with excellent DYA Gewurz, *splendid barrel-fermented Chardonnay (03 04)* wonderfully fragrant DYA Rosé, worthwhile Temp/Cabernet/Merlot/Syrah blends and excellent Merlot (03 04).

Espumoso Sparkling (but see CAVA).

Faustino, Bodegas R Ala r w (p) res ★★→★★★ Large, long-established BODEGA, formerly F Martínez, with smooth, reliable reds at all levels: from Faustino V Reserva through to GRAN RES Faustino I and top wine Faustino de Autor.

Finca Farm. (See under name – *e.g.* ALLENDE, FINCA.)

Freixenet, Cavas Pen w sp ★★→★★★ Huge CAVA firm, not only rivalling CODORNÍU in size but also considerably more dynamic. Best-known brands Cordó Negro in black bottles, Brut Barroco, RES Real, and very ordinary Carta Nevada. Also controls Castellblanch, Conde de Caralt, and Segura Viudas.

Galicia Rainy northwest corner of Spain: especially for fresh, aromatic but price w. Reds, made of the Mencia grape, are astringent and best drunk locally and chilled, or avoided. Weirdly, a whole new DO (Ribeira Sacra) is dedicated to this. For excellent w from lesser regional DOS see GUITIÁN and VIÑA MEÍN Otherwise stick to RÍAS BAIXAS or try MONTERREI.

Generoso Apéritif or dessert wine rich in alcohol.

Gerardo Méndez Rías Baixas ★★→★★★ Tiny family estate making modern exuberant new-style ALBARIÑO plus minute production (Cepas Vellas from old vines (200 yrs) with touch of botrytis. Brand name Albariño do Ferreiro.

Gramona Pen r w dr sw res ★★→★★★ Established, sizeable family firm making wide range of varietals. Good Chard and Sauv Bl, but sweet wines are best: Gewurz Riesling (both 04), and Gra a Gra (02). Good.

Gran Reserva See RESERVA.

Guelbenzu, Bodegas r (w) res ★★→★★★ 99 01 02 03 04 05 Non-DO famil enterprise with estates in Navarra (Cascante) and Aragón (Vierlas), specializing in stylish reds: Vierlas, Azul, Evo, La Lombana, and splendid Lautus (**99 01**). Also in Chile.

Guitán Godello Valdeorras w ★★★→★★★★ 04 05 06 Best wines from otherwise sporadic GALICIAN DO (though see also TELMO RODRÍGUEZ), Bodegas La Tapada make three splendidly fragrant and complex Godellos: one in steel, one barrel-fermented, and one lees-aged.

Gutiérrez de la Vega, Bodegas Alicante r (w) res ★★→★★★ 03 04 05 Small estate specializing in excellent sweet whites made from Moscatel. Reds less successful. Brand name Casta Diva.

Haro Spiritual and historic centre of the RIOJA ALTA. Though growing, still infinitely more charming and intimate than commercial capital Logroño.

Inurrieta, Bodega Nav r p w res ★★→★★★ 00 02 03 04 05 Impressive estate near Falces. Good Norte Cabernet-Merlot and Sur Garnacha-Syrah as well as lively Mediodía Rosado. Top wine: Altos de Inurrieta (**03**).

Joven (vino) Young, unoaked wine. Also see CRIANZA.

Juan Alcorta, Bodega R Alt r (w) res ★→★★★ 99 00 01 04 Pernod Ricard concern: all increasingly standardized. Four brands – Campo Viejo, Alcorta, Azpilicueta and Marqués de Villamagna – all perfectly acceptable and correct, deliver reliability while lacking individuality.

Jumilla r (w p) ★→★★★ 02 03 04 05 Arid DO in mountains north of Murcia, best known for dark, fragrant. Monastrell, often blended. Also Tempranillo, Merlot, Cabernet, Syrah and now Petit Verdot. Does not generally age gracefully. Many good producers include Agapito Rico, CASA CASTILLO, Finca Omblancas, Juan Gil, Luzón, and Valle del Carche.

Juvé y Camps Pen w sp ★★★ 01 02 Family firm. Top-quality CAVA from free-run juice only, RES de la Familia and Gran Juvé y Camps are best.

LAN, Bodegas R Alt r (p w) res★→★★★ 99 00 03 04 Large, modern BODEGA. Recently restructured and reorganized, it still fails to convince – its offerings overpriced, over-extracted and over-wooded.

León, Jean Pen r w res ★★★ 97 01 03 04 Now finding its feet having gone from blockbusting intensity into more dilute styles. Best are the intense Petit Chardonnay (**05**) and resonant Zemis (**03**); the wild, rustic Terrasola Syrah/Garnacha (**03**) is also worth a look.

López de Heredia R Alt r w (p) dr sw res ★★ 85 87 88 95 96 01 Picturesque, old-established family BODEGA in HARO that represents the pinnacle of the old style. Long-lasting and traditional wines; best are the really old RES both red and white. Vintage differences notably reduced since c. 1981. *Tondonia* is finer, with more acidity; Bosconia fuller and more imposing.

Luis Cañas, Bodegas R Alav r (w) res ★→★★ 99 03 05 Large, commercial RIOJA concern (founded 1970) producing decent, clean, reliable if unspectacular reds on all levels at fair prices. 1990s peaking.

Málaga Once-famous DO now all but vanished as producers, obliged to bottle within city limits, were forced out by rocketing real-estate values TELMO RODRIGUEZ also has a joint venture here, making clear, subtle, sweet white Molino Real Moscatel, mostly sold in the US.

Mallorca Small, pricey producers. Best are Ánima Negra, tiny Sa Vinya de Can Servera, Hereus de Ribas (outstanding Ribas de Cabrera 2000) and Son Bordils (good Negre 03 and Merlot 04). Stick to reds, usually a blend of traditional varieties (Mantonegro, Callet and Fogoneu) plus Cabernet, Syrah and Merlot. These often have a slightly burnt character. Whites (usually native Prensal plus Chardonnay or Malvasía) less successful. Biggest producer (Franja Roja) seems to have lost the plot.

Mancha, La La M r w ★→★★ 03 04 05 Vast demarcated region north and northeast of VALDEPEÑAS. Its extreme climate results in ordinary, short-lived whites (made mainly from native Airén though efforts are being made to produce Sauvignon); and the area is primarily attempting to concentrate on and improve its reds, which are mainly Cencibel (Tempranillo) based. Best producers are Centro Españolas and Vinícola de Tomelloso, but don't expect too much. See also CASTILLA-LA MANCHA VINO DE LA TIERRA.

Marqués de Cáceres, Bodegas R Alt r p w res ★★★ 94 98 00 03 04 Good, reliable, commercial red RIOJAS made by modern French methods. Top cuvée Gaudium (01) is a keeper so enjoy MC (03 04) in the interim.

Marqués de Griñón Dominio de Valdepusa r w ★★★ 02 03 Enterprising nobleman Carlos Falcó, early graduate of Davis in California, was the first Spaniard to cultivate Cab Sauv, delicious Syrah and Petit Verdot, introduce drip-irrigation and a scientific approach to vineyard management, on his historic estate near Toledo, south of Madrid. Varietals are concentrated – beginners should try the very approachable Summa blend. The Griñón name also appears on a cheap Rioja from Berberana – a leftover from a distribution deal. See BODEGAS UNIDAS.

New money

The cash generated by the Spanish construction boom often gets invested in new wineries. These are sometimes exercises in vanity but more often they are designed to produce expensive, Parkerised, 'boutique' wines for the domestic market.

The interlopers have tended to seize on fashionable or once fashionable regions like Priorato, Rías Baixas, Ribera del Duero, Rueda and Somontano, and have forced prices to unrealistic levels, while often producing quite ordinary wines. It is estimated that within a few years between 30 and 50% of all Spanish wineries may simply disappear. With luck it will be the sound professionals who remain.

Marqués de Monistrol, Bodegas Pen p r sp dr sw res ★★→★★★ 00 01 05 Old BODEGA now owned by BODEGAS UNIDAS. Good, reliable CAVA. Once known for good, young blends of Cab Sauv, Merlot, and Temp; now more emphasis on older, aged styles.

Marqués de Murrieta R Alt r p w res ★★★→★★★★ 98 99 00 01 02 Historic BODEGA at Ygay near Logroño, making intense Reserva reds. Most famous for its magnificent red CASTILLO DE YGAY. Others include odd, wooden white Capellanía Reserva, interesting, savoury Mazuelo (00) and intense, modernist premium red Dalmau (94 98 99 and 00 01 02). See also PAZO DE BARRANTES.

Marqués de Riscal R Ala & Rueda r (p) w dr ★★★→★★★★ 99 00 01 02 03 Best known BODEGA in R Ala, with fantastic new hotel and restaurant designed by Frank Gehry. Good, light but stylish reds and a splendid black Barón de Chirel RES (01 02) made with 50% Cab Sauv. Pioneers in RUEDA with good fragrant Sauvignon Blanc and more savoury barrel-fermented Limousin.

Marqués de Vargas, Bodegas R Ala ★★★ 96 00 01 00 04 Relative newcomer inaccurately heralded as new-style producer, its Reserva Privada and Hacienda Pradolagar (both 01) are outstanding, balanced old-style offerings

Martinez-Bruganda see Valdemar

Mas Martinet Pri r ★★★→★★★★ 00 01 03 04 Maker of Clos Martinet and a pioneer of spectacular boutique PRIORATOS. Daughter Sara continues to maintain excellent standards. Second wine Martinet Bru (04).

Mauro, Bodegas r 00 01 02 04 05 Young BODEGA in Tudela del Duero making good round, fruity TINTO del País (Temp) red (04 05) now with a touch of Syrah; also complex, layered VENDIMIA Seleccionada (00 01 02) and rare awesome, pricy Terreus (01, 03). Not DO, since some of the fruit is from outside RIBERA DEL DUERO. Sister winery Maurodos, in TORO.

Monterrei w ★→★★★ DYA Small but growing DO in O(u)rense, south central GALICIA making interesting, full-flavoured aromatic whites from Treixadura, Godello, and Doña Blanca. Best is Gargalo. Avoid the reds.

Montilla-Moriles w sw ★→★★★ Medium sized DO once best known for unfortified FINO styles but now concentrating on dark, unctuous, often bittersweet dessert wines. Best: Toro Albalá (many old vintages), but Alvear and Pérez Barquero are also in the frame.

Montsant r ★→★★★ 02 03 04 05 Small newish DO (since 2001) in an enclave of PRIORATO. Its best wines share certain similarities but are now as pricey; and its cheaper offerings can be astringent by virtue of different soils. Best: Agrícola Falset-Marçà, Cellers Capafons-Ossó, Celler Laurona; and Celler de Capaçanes, whose approachable styles put the area on the map.

Muga, Bodegas R Alt r (w sp) res ★★★→★★★★ 95 96 98 00 01 02 03 Family firm in HARO, known for **some of RIOJA's most balanced traditional reds**. Good barrel-fermented Viura slightly reminiscent of burgundy; reds light but highly aromatic and – with exception of outstanding GR Prado Enea (95 96 98) which peaks quickly – age well. Top, new-wave cuvées are very fine, delicate Aro (00 01) and concentrated

Navajas, Bodegas R Alt r w res ★★→★★★ 01 02 03 04 Unpretentious family firm making young fruity reds and decently balanced CRIANZAS and RES. Also excellent oak-aged white Viura (04) and Rosado Crianza (03 05).

Navarra Nav r p (w) ★★→★★★ 00 01 02 03 04 05 Extensive DO once known primarily for rosé; many of its 123 BODEGAS now produce reds equal or superior to those of RIOJA – despite often higher yields – partly because of wider spread of varieties including Merlot and Syrah. Also excellent dessert wines. See CHIVITE, INURRIETA, OCHOA, PRÍNCIPE DE VIANA. Also good are Castillo de Monjardín, Otazu, Vinícola Navarra and for dessert wines Camilo Castilla.

Ochoa Nav r p w res ★★→★★★ 98 00 02 04 05 04 Small family BODEGA; Javier Ochoa is ever-reliable and continues to impress, above all with his excellent Moscatel (05), as well as his upmarket Vendimia Seleccionado red (00) and more everyday Garnacha/Graciano (05).

Pago A vineyard or area of limited size giving rise to exceptional wines. The term now has legal status, e.g. DO Dominio de Valdepusa (see MARQUÉS DE GRIÑÓN).

Pago de Carraovejas Rib del D r res ★★★ 99 01 03 04 Large estate. Excellent quality. Enjoy Crianzas (03 04) within three years because of whole-berry fermentation. Reserva (01 03) more intense, imposing and long lived. Top cuvée Cuesta de las Liebres (99 01) is finest and lasts longest. All wines are Tinto Fino/Cabernet blends.

Palacio, Bodegas R Ala r p w res ★★★ 01 02 03 04 05 Good old BODEGA making sound, balanced reds:Gloriosa, Especial, and Cosme Palacio (04).

Palacio de Fefiñanes Rías Baixas w dr ★★★ DYA Oldest BODEGAS of RÍAS BAIXAS, making one of most **delicate excellent ALBARIÑOS**. Two other styles: a creamy barrel-fermented version (1583 – named after the year the winery was founded – 04 05) and a fragrant lees-aged version (III – 03 04).

Parxet Alella w p sp ★★→★★★ DYA Producer of fresh, lively CAVA zesty Cuvée 21, stylish Brut Nature, unusual Titiana Pinot N and expensive dessert version Cuvée Dessert. Best still wine is lively, off-dry MARQUÉS DE ALELLA made from indigenous Pansa Blanca. Also worthy of note is broody, concentrated Tionio (03 04) from outpost in RIBERA DEL DUERO.

Paternina, Bodegas Once great RIOJA BODEGA (from 1896 to early 1970s). The brands, such as Banda Azul, live on, but the quality is ordinary.

Pazo de Barrantes Rías Baixas w ★★★ DYA ALBARIÑO RÍAS BAIXAS; estate owned by MARQUÉS DE MURRIETA. Firm, delicate, exotic, but vintages very variable.

Pazo de Señorans Rías Baixas w dr ★★★ DYA Exceptionally fragrant wines from a BODEGA considered a benchmark of the DO by virtue of its finesse.

Penedès Pen r w sp ★→★★★★ **98 99 00 01 02 03 04 05** Demarcated region best known for CAVA and TORRES. Other good producers are ALBET I NOYA, CAN RÀFOLS DELS CAUS, GRAMONA, Jané Ventura, JEAN LEÓN, MARQUÉS DE MONISTROL and Raventós i Blanc.

Pérez Pascuas Hermanos Rib del D r res ★★★ **94** 01 02 03 04 Immaculate family BODEGA (founded 1980). Its old, slightly 'sheepy' vintages (the result of natural fertilization) triumph in Spain, but younger, more energetic styles (**03** and **04**) are best for a modern audience. Main label Viña Pedrosa and newer Cepa Gavillán.

Pesquera Rib del D r ★★★ **99 02 03 04** Alejandro Fernández was the force that put this region on the map in the late 1980s thanks to the ear of Robert Parker. Good, intense, if somewhat formulaic, upfront, purple styles (see also CONDADO DE HAZA). Also interesting El Vínculo (**02 04**) red from LA MANCHA.

Pingus, Dominio de Rib del D r ★★★ **94 96 98 99** 00 01 02 03 Pingus is available primarily in international auction-rooms, so mere mortals must be content with lesser and often disappointing second label Flor de Pingus (**01 02 03**), which has a much shorter life span.

Piqueras, Bodegas Almansa r (w dr p) ★★→★★★ 00 01 02 03 04 Family BODEGA. Only noteworthy producer here, making chewy but well balanced old-style reds under Castillo de Almansaand Marius labels

Plá i Llevant de Mallorca r w dr ★→★★★ **01 03 04** Just 10 wineries comprise this tiny DO in MALLORCA. Best are Jaime Mesquida, Vins Can Majoral, and Miquel Gelabert.

Príncipe de Viana, Bodegas Nav r w p ★★ Large firm blending and maturing co-op wines as well as using its own 400 ha of Temp. Producers of very sound, basic Pleno range; upmarket Finca d'Albret has yet to find its feet.

Priorato/Priorat Pri br r ★★★ **00 01 03 04** DO enclave of TARRAGONA, once known for Rancio and rustic co-op-produced tarry Garnacha/Cariñena reds. Following initial new wave (including Costers de Siurana – whose sweet Clos L'Obac red is still a must, José Luis Pérez of MAS MARTINET, and CLOS MOGADOR), the area has been invaded by a host of moneyed outsiders. Its best wines are deep and concentrated, but few age beyond two or three years and prices are often unreal. ÁLVARO PALACIOS is great; others include Cims de Porrera, Clos Daphne, Clos Figueras, Grativinum, Mas Doix, Mas Igneus, and Vall-lach. Buil & Giné is fair value, but rustic.

Raïmat Cos del S r w p sp ★★→★★★ **94 95 96 00** 01 02 03 04 05 CODORNÍU-owned estate, one of first in Spain to make varietals in a New World style – using Chard, Tempranillo, Cabernet, Merlot and Syrah. Only to age successfully is Pinot (**00**). Also, good, fresh, appealing CAVA.

Remírez de Ganuza, Bodegas Fernando R Ala w dr r res ★★→★★★ 01 02 03 Agronomist Fernando RdG makes admirable but overpriced wines: DYA Erre Punto, Reserva (**01 02**), Trasnocho (**03**).

Remelluri, La Granja R Ala w dr r res ★★★ **97** 01 02 Small mountainous estate making pedigree RIOJA reds from its own 105 ha. Good RES (**01 02**) and peaking, savoury GR from generally awful year (**97**). Excellent top wine Colección (**02**) and unusual (**04 05**) white made from eight varieties.

Reserva Good-quality wine matured for long periods. Red *reservas* must spend at least 1 yr in cask and 2 in bottle; *gran reservas*, 2 yrs in cask and 3 in bottle. Thereafter, many continue to mature for years.

Rías Baixas w ★★→★★★ DYA Best GALICIAN DO embracing 5 sub-zones – Val do Salnés, O Rosal, and Condado do Tea, Soutomaior and Ribera do Ulla. Best of 183 producers: Condes de Albarei, Adega Maior de Mendoza, Adegas d'Altamira, Adegas Galegas, Agro de Bazán, Bodegas Castro Martín, GERARDO MÉNDEZ, Lusco do Miño, super-commercial Martín Códax, PALACIO DE FEFIÑANES, PAZO DE BARRANTES, PAZO DE SEÑORANS, Santiago Ruiz, Terras Gauda.

Ribera del Duero Rib del D **99 00 01 02 03 04** Fashionable, still-expanding DO (the Duero becomes the Portuguese Douro). Excellent Tinto Fino (Temp) reds, often blended with Cabernet. Many excellent wines, but high prices. See AALTO, ALIÓN, ASTRALES, CONDADO DE HAZA, PAGO DE CARRAOVEJAS, PÉREZ PASCUAS HERMANOS, PESQUERA, PINGUS, VALBUENA, VEGA SICILIA. Also non-DO MAURO. An invasion of new people – there are now 231 BODEGAS – has not necessarily brought exciting new wines. Others: Balbás, Dehesa de los Canónigos, Pago de los Capellanes, and Rodero.

Rioja r p w sp ★★→★★★★ **64 70 75 78 81 82 85 89 91 92 94 95 96 98 99 00 01 02 03 04** North upland region along River Ebro, and Spain's most emblematic wine region due to its comfortingly velvety, oaky offerings. Beware, however, as with now almost 1,200 BODEGAS it pays to be specific. Tempranillo predominates, often with Garnacha, Mazuelo, Graciano and even Cabernet. Best producers: CONTINO, CVNE, FINCA ALLENDE, LÓPEZ DE HEREDIA, LUIS CAÑAS, MARQUÉS DE MURRIETA, MARQUÉS DE CÁCERES, MARQUÉS DE RISCAL, MUGA, NAVAJAS, PALACIO, REMELLURI, RODA, VALDEMAR. Also good: El Coto, Ijalba, Izadi, Montecillo, Palacios Remondo, Pujanza, Sierra Cantabria, Sonsierra, Tobía.

Rioja Alavesa N of the R Ebro, produces fine red wines, mostly light in body

---

Tempranillo and its variants

The queen of Spanish grape varieties is the Tempranillo used in Rioja primarily as a base – plus oxidative Garnacha for colour and power, aromatic plus stringy Graciano for grace, and alcoholic, tannic but rather flavourless Mazuelo/a for structure.

Over the years, however, Tempranillo has found its way to many other regions where it has simply adapted to local conditions to produce quite different wines: Cencibel in Valdepeñas and La Mancha (pale and strawberry-flavoured); Tinto Fino in Ribera del Duero (mainly dark and damson-flavoured though in some sub-zones is more dark strawberry); Tinta de Toro in Toro (robust, black in colour and flavour) and Ull de Llebre (plum coloured, accordingly flavoured though sometimes red-cherry-like in the manner of Rioja).

---

and colour, but particularly aromatic. A political rather than geographical division: some mountain enclaves produce impressively dark wines of substance.

Rioja Alta S of the R Ebro and W of Logroño, grows most of the finest, best-balanced red and white wines; also some rosé.

Rioja Baja Stretching E from Logroño, makes stouter red wines, often from Garnacha and high in alcohol, and often used for blending.

Rioja Alta, Bodegas La R Alt r w (p) dr (sw) res ★★★ **94 95 98 00** Excellent traditional RIOJAS, definitely not moving with the times. All good: light Alberdi Crianza; two RES: lighter Arana and more substantial Ardanza; fine RES 904, and excellent, rarely seen RES 890 (**94**).

Riojanas, Bodegas R Alt r (w p) res ★★→★★★ **98 99 01 02 03 04** Ultra-historic, traditional BODEGA making an extensive range. Its two best known styles are Monte Real and Viña Albina – the former the more robust, the latter very fine

Roda, Bodegas R Alt r ★★★★ **94 98 99 00 01 02 03 04** Newish (1989) BODEGA making sought-after, fine, intense and long-lasting premium RES reds. On an upward scale of intensity and price: Roda (**02**), Roda I(**02**) and Cirsión (**04**).

Rosado Rosé.

Rueda br w ★★⭢★★★★ 96 97 98 99 03 04 DYA Small but growing historic DO producing fresh, crisp styles from Verdejo, Sauvignon Blanc, Viura. Moneyed newcomers now moving in en masse; prices rising. Best producers: BODEGAS DE CRIANZA CASTILLA LA VIEJA, MARQUÉS DE RISCAL, SITIOS DE BODEGA. Look out too for excellent modern styles from Vinos Sanz and quirky, barrel-fermented whites from Belondrade.

Sandoval, Finca Manchuela ★★★ Víctor de la Serna's first and second vintages, (**02 03**), are outstanding: black, wild, minty, chargrilled and rounding out. His 04s (including new second wine Salia) are a touch too powerful.

Seco Dry.

Sitios de Bodega Fifth generation winemaker Ricardo/Richard Sanz and siblings declared independence from BODEGAS DE CRIANZA CASTILLA LA VIEJA in 2006 to launch their own enterprise. Offerings includes modern DYA RUEDA whites (Con Class and Palacio de Menade) as well as Spain's first sweet Tempranillo – la Dolce Tita (**04**) – with much more to come.

Somontano Som ★★⭢★★★★ 01 02 03 04 Fashionable DO in Pyrenean foothills east of Zaragoza that has largely failed to fulfil expectations. Best producers: Bodegas Pirineos, ENATE and VIÑAS DEL VERO.

Telmo Rodríguez, Compañía de Vinos r w ★★⭢★★★★ Gifted oenologist Telmo Rodríguez, formerly of REMELLURI makes and sources a wide range of excellent DO wines from all over Spain inc *MÁLAGA (the outstanding Molina Real Moscatels 03 and 05)*, RIOJA (Lanzaga and Matallana), RUEDA (Basa), TORO (Dehesa Gago, Gago, and Pago la Jara), and Valdeorras (Gaba do Xil).

Tinto Red.

Tomás Cusiné Cos del S r ★★★ 04 05 Former innovating power of CASTELL DEL REMEI and CELLER DE CANTONELLA now on his own making modern, upbeat Vilosell (Temp/Cab/Merlot/Genache/Syrah) and oakier Geol (Temp/Cab/Car).

Toro r ★⭢★★★★ 01 02 03 04 Increasingly fashionable DO west of Valladolid, making tremendously intense reds from Tinta de Toro (acclimatized Temp). Most continue to be clumsy, over-extracted and over-wooded. Two shining exceptions are Maurodos – with Prima (**05**) and San Román (**03 04**) and VEGA SICILIA-owned Pintia (**05**). Also good but not on same level as Sobreño.

Torres, Miguel Pen r w p dr s/sw res ★★⭢★★★★ 01 02 03 04 05 Spain's best-known family firm with historic tentacles in Chile and California too, continues to make a huge range, all good and some outstanding. Best and most consistent PENEDÈS wines are DYA Gran Viña Sol, delightful part barrel-fermented Fransola (**05**); and in reds fragrant Mas Borràs Pinot Noir (**04**), the delicate and stylish Mas la Plana Cab (**02**), and magnificent, massively priced Reserva Real (**01**). Its Mediterranean-style, CATALUÑA Nerola wines are less impressive, but its CONCA DE BARBERÀ duo are quite stunning, and JEAN LEÓN is getting seriously back to form.

Traslanzas Cigales r ★★★ 01 02 Owner oenologist Ana Martín may gunsling for others all over Spain, but it is her own minute production, complex, old-style red that impresses most.

Utiel-Requena U-R r p (w) ★⭢★★★ 96 98 00 01 02 03 04 Satellite region of VALENCIA attempting to forge its own identity by virtue of excellent Bobal variety (also found in LA MANCHA and mistaken for Temp), but hampered by being primarily a feeder for the neighbouring, industrial requirements of nearby VALENCIA. One small producer that tries hard is Casa del Pinar (**03 04**).

Valbuena Rib del D r ★★★★ 90 98 99 00 01 02 Made with the same grapes (Tinto Fino, Cabernet, Merlot, Malbec and a touch of Albillo) as VEGA SICILIA but sold when five years old. ***Best at about 10 yrs; some prefer it to its elder brother.*** For a more modern take see ALIÓN.

Valdemar, Bodegas R Ala r p w res ★★★ 98 00 01 04 05 The Martínez-Bujanda family, from their base in Oyón, have been making wines since 1890 and continue to offer a wide choice of RIOJA styles reliable on all levels.

Valdepeñas La M r (w) ★→★★★ 95 97 98 99 00 01 02 03 04 05 Demarcated region near Andalucían border. Good value, smooth, often oaky lookalike RIOJA reds, high in alcohol but soft in flavour when made from Cencibel grape, the local Temp. Best wines are Viña Albali from Félix Solís and Pata Negra from Los Llanos, who also make a pleasing, simple, fragrant DYA white: Armonioso.

Valencia r w ★ 00 01 03 04 05 Demarcated region exporting vast quantities of clean and drinkable table wine. Also source of budget, orange-marmalade flavoured Moscatel.

Vega Sicilia Rib del D r res ★★★★ 60 62 68 70 81 87 89 90 91 94 95 96 04 Spain's most famous and historic BODEGA, whose costly and sought-after wines are still matured very slowly in oak and best at 12–15 yrs. Wines are deep in colour, with aromatic cedarwood nose, intense and complex in flavour, finishing long. Dense, un-vintaged Reserva Especial can also be spectacular but commands mega prices. See also VALBUENA, ALION, Pintia in TORO, and Oremus Tokaji (Hungary).

Vendimia Vintage.

Viña Literally, a v'yd. But wines such as Tondonia (LÓPEZ DE HEREDIA) are not necessarily made only with grapes from the v'yd named.

Viñas del Vero Som w p r res ★★→★★★ 02 03 04 SOMONTANO estate. Good enjoyable, commercial varietals: esp barrel-fermented Chard and Gewurz. Springy DYA rosé. Best red still the intense and complex Secastilla (**04**).

Viña Meín Ribeiro ★★★ Small estate, in a generally unreliable DO, making two DYA exceptional whites of same name: one in steel and one barrel-fermented; both from some seven local varieties.

Vino común/corriente Ordinary wine.

Vino de la Tierra (VdT) Table wine of superior quality made in a demarcated region without DO.

Vinos de Pago This category, introduced in 2002, awarded DO status to four individualistic estates in the Castilla-La Mancha region: Dehesa del Carrizal, MARQUÉS DE GRIÑÓN, Manuel Manzeneque, and Sánchez Militerno, all of whom can now officially do their own thing.

Portugal

Recent vintages

2006 Another very warm, dry summer. Expect forward reds with soft, ripe fruit and whites with less acidity than usual.

2005 An extraordinarily dry summer, especially in S: unbalanced wines.

2004 A cool, wet summer but a glorious Sept and Oct. Well-balanced reds.

2003 Hot summer produced soft, ripe, early-maturing wines, especially in the South. Best Bairrada for a decade.

2002 Challenging vintage with heavy rain during picking. Better in the South.

2001 Large vintage throughout. Those producers who undertook careful selection made very good wines.

2000 Small harvest in fine weather led to ripe-flavoured wines from all regions.

SPAIN

Adega A cellar or winery.

Alenquer Est r w ★★→★★★ **01 02** 03' 04 05 06 Sheltered DOC making good reds just north of Lisbon. Estate wines from PANCAS and MONTE D'OIRO (Syrah).

Alentejo r (w) 00' 01 02 03 04' 05 06 Vast tract of south Portugal. Most vineyards concentrated around Reguengos, Borba, and Vidigueira. Expansive, southerly DOC divided into sub-regions: Borba, Redondo, Reguengos, Portalegre, Evora, Granja-Amareleja, Vidigueira, and Moura. Dubbed Portugal's "New World", reliably dry climate makes good, ripe-flavoured reds from indigenous and international grape varieties including Syrah and Alicante Bousche. Antão Vaz makes rich flavoursome whites. Estate wines from CARMO (part Rothschild-owned), CARTUXA, CORTES DE CIMA, Herdade de MOUCHÃO, Herdade de MALHADINHA, ZAMBUJEIRO, João RAMOS, José de SOUSA, and ESPORÃO have potency and style. Best co-ops are at BORBA, REDONDO, and REGUENGOS. Now classified as a DOC with BORBA, REDONDO, REGUENGOS, PORTALEGRE, Evora, Granja-Amareleja, Vidigueira, and Moura entitled to their own sub-appellations. Also VINHO REGIONAL Alentejano.

Algarve r w ★→★★ Wines from holiday coast are covered by DOCS Lagos, Tavira, Lagoa, and Portimão. Mostly easy-drinking summer-holiday wines; crooner Cliff Richard has a vineyard near Albufeira.

Aliança, Caves Bair r w sp res ★★→★★★ Large BAIRRADA-based firm making good reds and classic-method sparkling. Also interests in ALENTEJO, DÃO, and the DOURO.

Alorna, Quinta de Ribatejo r w ★→★★ DYA Enterprising estate with a range of good varietals: CASTELÃO, TRINCADEIRA, and Cab Sauv.

Altano Douro DÃO Good new red from Symington family. Look out for RES.

Alvarinho White grape in extreme north of Portugal and increasingly elsewhere making *fragrant, attractive white*. Known as ALBARIÑO in neighbouring Galicia.

Ameal, Quinta do w ★★★ DYA One of best VINHOS VERDES available. 100% LOUREIRO.

Aragonez Successful red grape in ALENTEJO for varietal wines. See TINTA RORIZ.

Arinto White grape. Best from central and south Portugal, where it retains acidity and produces fragrant, crisp, dry white wines.

Arruda r w ★ DOC in ESTREMADURA with large co-op.

Aveleda, Quinta da w ★→★★ DYA Reliable VINHO VERDE made on the Aveleda estate of the Guedes family; also Casal García VINHO VERDE made from bought-in grapes. Also good varietal wines from LOUREIRO, ALVARINHO, and Trajadura. Reds: Charamba (DOURO).

Azevedo, Quinta do w ★★ DYA Superior VINHO VERDE from SOGRAPE. 100% LOUREIRO grapes.

Bacalhoa, Quinta da Set r res ★★★ 00 01 02 03 Estate near SETÚBAL. Its fruity, reliable, mid-weight Cab Sauv/Merlot blend is made by BACALHOA VINHOS. Palaçio de Bacalhoa has more Merlot in the blend.

Bacalhoa Vinhos Set, Est and Alen Formerly JP Vinhos (formerly the producer of João Pires Dry Muscat) has been renamed after its leading estate, Quinta de Bacalhoa. Wide range of well-made reds include BACALHOA, inexpensive JP, Serra de Azeitão, TINTO DA ANFORA from Alentejo, Só (varietal Syrah), JP GARRAFEIRA. Also Cova da Ursa Chard, SETÚBAL dessert wine.

Bairrada Bair r w sp ★→★★★ **90' 94 97' 98 99 00** 01 03' 04 05' 06 DOC in central Portugal. Reputation for solid, unforgiving (astringent) reds from the challenging 100% Baga grape being laid to rest now law permits different grape varieties – see CAMPOLARGO. New DOC Bairrada Classico stipulates minimum 50% Baga. Best Baga wines reward keeping: e.g. CASA DE SAIMA, LUÍS PATO, and Caves SÃO JOÃO will keep for yrs. Most white used by local sparkling-wine industry, but see LUIS PATO.

Barca Velha Douro r res ★★★★ 52 54 58 64 65 66' 78 81 82 85 91' 95' 99 Portugal's most famous red, made in v. limited quantities in the Upper Douro. Intense, complex red with deep bouquet made by FERREIRA which forged the Douro's reputation for stellar wines. Now stiff competition from other modern Douro reds. *Second wine known as Reserva Ferreirinha*.

Beiras ★→★★ VINHO REGIONAL covering DÃO, BAIRRADA, and granite mountain ranges of central Portugal.

Beira Interior ★ Large, isolated DOC near Spain's border. Huge potential from old vineyards.

Boavista, Quinta da Est ★★ DYA Large property near ALENQUER with pioneeringJosé Neiva at helm making good-value range of red and white: Palha Canas, Quinta das Sete Encostas, Espiga, and a Chard, Casa Santos Lima.

Borba Alen r ★→★★ Alentejo sub-region small DOC; also well-managed co-op making fruity reds including varietal range.

Branco White.

Brejoeira, Palácio de w ★★ DYA Best-known ALVARINHO from Portugal; facing increasing competition from VINHO VERDE estates around Monção.

Bright Brothers ★★ DYA Australian flying winemaker based in Portugal: interests as far-flung as Argentina, Sicily, and Spain. Range of well-made wines from DOURO, RIBATEJO, ESTREMADURA, and BEIRAS. See also FIUZA BRIGHT.

Buçaco Beiras r w (p) res ★★★★ (r) 53 59 62 63 70 78 82 85 89 92 Legendary speciality of the Palace Hotel at Buçaco, north of Coimbra, not seen elsewhere. *An experience worth the journey*.

Bucelas Est w ★★ DYA Tiny demarcated region north of Lisbon with three main producers. Quintas da Romeira and da Murta makes racy wines (known as "Lisbon Hock" in 19th-century England) from the ARINTO grape.

Cabriz, Quinta de ★★→★★★ 03 04 Good, well-priced reds. One of five quintas in large, successful venture in south DÃO owned by quality-minded company Dão Sul, which also has wine interests in the Douro, Bairrada, Estremadura, Alentejo and Brazil.

Cadaval, Casa Ribatejo r w ★★ 00 01' 02 03 Good varietal reds especially TRINCADEIRA. Also Pinot N, Cab Sauv, and Merlot. Stunning new red res, Marquês de Cadaval.

Campolargo Bair r w 03 04 Large, quirky estate, until 2004 sold grapes to ALIANÇA, now making exciting reds from local Baga, Cab Sauv, Petit Verdot, and Pinot N.

Carcavelos Est br sw ★★★ NV. Minute DOC west of Lisbon. Rare, sweet apéritif or dessert wines average 19% alcohol and resemble honeyed MADEIRA.

Carmo, Quinta do Alen r w res ★★ 99 00' 01 03 Beautiful, small ALENTEJO ADEGA, partly bought in 1992 by Rothschilds (Lafite). 50 ha, plus cork forests. Fresh white; red better. Second wine: Dom Martinho.

Cartuxa, Herdade da Alen ★★→★★★ r 00 01 03 04 w DYA 200-ha estate near Evora, rather disappointing in recent vintages. Pera Manca (**94 95 97 98**) big but pricey red. Also Foral de Evora, Cerca Nova, EA.

Carvalhais, Quinta dos Dão ★★★ r 99 00 01 03 04 05 w DYA Excellent single-estate SOGRAPE wine. Good red varietals (TOURIGA NACIONAL, Alfrochiero Preto) and white Encruzado.

Casal Branco, Quinta de Ribatejo r w ★★ Large family estate making good reds and whites including entry-level Cork Grove: CASTELÃO with others. Best red: Falcoaria Reserve (00 01 03 04').

Casal García w ★★ DYA Big-selling VINHO VERDE, made at AVELEDA.

Casal Mendes w ★ DYA The VINHO VERDE from Caves ALIANÇA.

Castelão A grape planted throughout south Portugal, particularly in TERRAS DO SADO. Nicknamed PERIQUITA. Makes firm-flavoured, raspberryish reds that take on a tar-like quality with age. Also known as João de Santarem.

Chocapalha Quinta de Est r 03 04 w DYA V. good estate north of Lisbon. Rich-flavoured reds from TOURIGA NACIONAL, TINTA RORIZ, Alicante Bouschet, and Cab Sauv; fine white blend from Chardonnay and Arinto.

Chryseia Douro r ★★★·★★★★ 01' 03' 04 Bruno Prats from Bordeaux has come together with the Symington family to produce a dense yet elegant wine from port grapes now sourced from dedicated vineyard, Quinta de Perdiz. A star in the making. Second wine Post Scriptum (02 04).

Churchill Estates Douro r 02 03 04 Good reds from port shipper Churchill. Single-estate red from Quinta da Gricha.

Colares r ★★ Small DOC on the sandy coast west of Lisbon. Its antique-style, dark-red wines, rigid with tannin, are from ungrafted Ramisco vines. Undergoing a minor revival in fortune. One to watch.

Consumo (vinho) Ordinary (wine).

Cortes de Cima Alen r ★★★ 01 02 03 04 05 Estate near Vidigueira owned by Danish family. Good reds from ARAGONEZ (Temp), TRINCADEIRA, TOURIGA NACIONAL,and PERIQUITA grapes. Chaminé: second label. Also good Syrah bottled under Incognito label.

Côtto, Quinta do Douro r w res ★★·★★★ r 99 00 01 03 w DYA Pioneer of unfortified wines from port country; v. good red Grande Escolha (95 00 01 03)

Crasto, Quinta do Douro r dr sw ★★·★★★★ 99 00 01 02 03' 04 Top estate for excellent oak-aged reds. Excellent, lush, varietal wines (TOURIGA NACIONAL, TINTA RORIZ) and blends; res and two superb single-vineyard wines made only in top vintages from low-yielding old vines: Vinha da Ponte (98 00' 01 03 04) and *María Theresa (98 00' 03')* Also Port.

Dão r w res ★★·★★★★ 00' 01 02 03' 04 05 Established DOC region round town of Viseu in central Portugal. Once dominated by co-ops, investment by quality-focused producers large and small has improved consistency and calibre. Watch out for SOGRAPE'S DUQUE DE VISEU and GRÃO VASCO brands, ALIANÇA Dão Sul and Quintas r ROQUES PELLADA and SAES)Structured, elegant, solid reds of some subtlety and age; substantial, dry whites.

DFJ Vinhos r w ★·★★★ DYA Huge, good-value range. from RIBATEJO and ESTRAMADURA. Premium labels:Grand'Arte-also sourced from the Douro, Dão and Alentejo. Good fruity, entry-level wines Ramada (r w),Segada (r w) Manta Preta (r) and Belafonte labels, and Grand'Arte (r w).

DOC, Denominação de Origem Controlada Demarcated wine region controlled by a Regional Commission. See also IPR, VINHO REGIONAL.

Doce (vinho) Sweet (wine).

Douro r w ★★·★★★★ 95 97 00' 01 02 03' 04' 05' Northern river valley producing port and table wines. BARCA VELHA now eclipsed by a new generation; also a handful of fine whites. New points-based classification for Douro DOC and, is aged at least one year, Douro Reserva or Douro Grandes Reserva. Look for BARCA VELHA, CHRYSEIA, CRASTO, and wines from NIEPOORT (see Port chapter).

Duas Quintas Douro ★★★ r 00 01 02 03' 04 w DYA Good red from port shipper Ramos Pinto. V. good res and outstanding but expensive Reserva Especial

Duque de Viseu Dão ★★ r 02 03 04 w DYA V gd, inexpensive red DÃO from SOGRAPE

Esporão, Herdade do Alen w DYA r ★★·★★★ 00 01 02 03 04 Impressive estate wines made by Aussie David Baverstock. Main brand: Monte Velho (DYA w) Good Verdelho, great-value oaked whites and rich, ripe reds under the Esporão label, especially GARRAFEIRA. Also Vinha da Defesa, Quatro Castas Good varietals: ARAGONEZ, TRINCADEIRA, TOURIGA NACIONAL, Alicante Bouschet, Syrah

Espumante Sparkling.

Esteva Douro r ★ DYA Very drinkable DOURO red from port firm FERREIRA.

Estremadura ★·★★★ VINHO REGIONAL on west coast. Large co-ops. Alta Mesa

Ramada, Portada: good, inexpensive wines from local estates and co-ops; potential for premium wines now being realized by handful of talented, ambitious producers e.g. CHOCAPALHA, MONTE D'OIRO. IPRS: Encostas d'Aire. DOCS: ALENQUER, ARRUDA, Obidos, TORRES VEDRAS.

alua Rib r w p DYA João Portugal RAMOS' state-of-the-art venture. Good entry-level Tagus Creek range of indigenous and international blends, plus more upmarket Tâmara and Conde de Vimioso.

ernão Pires White grape making ripe-flavoured, slightly spicy whites in RIBATEJO. (Known as María Gomes in BAIRRADA.)

erreira Douro r ★→★★★★ SOGRAPE-owned port shipper making a range of good to v. good red DOURO wines: Esteva, Vinha Grande, Callabriga, Quinta de Leda, Reserva Ferreirinha, and BARCA VELHA.

uza & Bright Ribatejo r w ★★ DYA Joint venture between Peter Bright (BRIGHT BROTHERS) and the Fiuza family. Good inexpensive Chard, Merlot, Cab Sauv. And Portuguese varietals.

nseca, José María da Est r w dr sw sp res ★★→★★★ Venerable firm in Azeitão near Lisbon. Huge range of wines including brands LANCERS, Periquita, Pasmados, Quinta de Camerate, Garrafeiras, and the famous dessert SETÚBAL (Alambre). Impressive range of premium reds from new winery opened in 2001: Septimus, Vinya, Primum, and the Domingos Soares Franco Selecção Privado. Top of range: Optimum and Hexagon. Also with interests in DÃO (TERRAS ALTAS), ALENTEJO (José de SOUSA and d'Avillez), DOURO (Domini).

aivosa, Quinta de Douro r ★★★ oo 01 03 04 Leading estate near Régua owned by enterprising Domingos Alves de Sousa. Characterful, concentrated, cask-aged reds from port grapes; Abandonado is v. good, from vines over 80 years old. Other reds include Quinta das Caldas and Vale da Raposa.

arrafeira Label term: merchant's "private reserve", aged for minimum of 2 years in cask and 1 in bottle, often much longer.

atão w ★ DYA Standard Borges & Irmão VINHO VERDE.

azela w ★★ DYA Reliable VINHO VERDE made at Barcelos by SOGRAPE.

neroso Apéritif or dessert wine rich in alcohol.

ão Vasco Dão r w ★★ DYA One of the best and largest brands of DÃO, from SOGRAPE's high-tech ADEGA at Viseu. Fine red GARRAFEIRA; fresh young white.

R Indicação de Proveniência Regulamentada. Portugal's second tier of wine regions: Lafões, Biscoitos, Pico, Graciosa. See also DOC.

goalva, Quinta da r w ★★ 01 02 03 Important RIBATEJO property making good reds from local grapes and Syrah. Second label: Monte da Casta.

ncers p w sp ★ Semi-sweet (semi-sparkling) Rosé, extensively shipped to the USA by José María da FONSECA. Also Lancers ESPUMANTE Brut, a decent sparkler made by a continuous process of Russian invention.

vadores de Feitoria Douro r w Enterprising amalgam of a number of small quality-conscious estates. Principal labels: Meruge, Três Bagos.

ureiro Best VINHO VERDE grape variety after ALVARINHO: crisp, fragrant whites.

adeira br dr sw ★★→★★★★ Portugal's Atlantic island: makes unfortified reds and whites (Terras Madeirenses VINHO REGIONAL and Madeirense DOC), mostly for the local market; whites from Verdelho on the up. See Madeira pages for famous fortified dessert and apéritif wines.

aias, Quinta das Dão ★★ r oo 01 03 w DYA New-wave QUINTA in same ownership as ROQUES: reds to age.

alhadinha Nova, Herdade de Alen r 03' w DYA Newcomer cutting a dash with v. good big reds and rich, oak-aged white in the deep south of the Alentejo.

ateus Rosé Bair p (w) ★ World's best-selling, medium-dry, lightly carbonated rosé, from SOGRAPE. Now made at Anadia in BAIRRADA.

Messias r w ★→★★★ Large BAIRRADA-based firm; interests in DOURO (includir port). Old-school reds best.

Minho River between north Portugal and Spain – lends its name to a VINI REGIONAL.

Monte d'Oiro, Quinta do Est r w ★★★→★★★★ 01 03 Outstanding Rhône-sty reds from Syrah with a touch of Viognier and, since 2004, Madrigal: goc full-bodied Viognier. Good second wine: Vinha da Nora.

Mouchão, Herdade de Alen r res ★★★ 99 00 01 03 The best traditional Alente estate making big, powerful wines dominated by Alicante Bouschet variet **_Outstanding top wine Tonel 3–4._** Second wine Dom Rafael can be goc value but variable.

Mouro, Quinta do Alen r ★★★→★★★★ 98 99 00 04 Fabulous old-style red mostly ALENTEJO grapes. Dry farmed, low yields, concentrated.

Murganheira, Caves ★ Largest producer of ESPUMANTE. Now owns RAPOSEIRA.

Niepoort Douro r w ★★★→★★★★ Family port shipper making exceptiona well-balanced, ageworthy DOURO wines with a mineral core. Vibrant Verten (r), elegant Redoma (r w p) 00 01 03 04 05; Batuta (r) 00 01' 03 04 an sumptuous Charme (r) 00 02. Reds age very well. Also Dado (50% Dãc Quinta da PELLADA (50% Douro) Quinta do Carril.

Palmela Terras do Sado r w ★→★★★ Promising DOC, mostly on sandy soil b incorporating the limestone Serra da Arrabida. Reds from CASTELÃO can I long-lived. Best producers BACALHOA VINHOS and the Cooperativa de Pegõe

Pancas, Quinta das Est r w res ★★→★★★ 00' 01 03 w DYA Go-ahead esta near ALENQUER. Outstanding red Premium (00') and varietals from ARAGONE TOURIGA NACIONAL, Syrah, Cab Sauv, and CASTELÃO.

Passadouro, Quinta do Douro r V. good red joined by layered, concentrate Reserve in 2003 (03, 04') from single parcel of older vines. Also Port.

Pato, Filipa Bair r w sp sw Daughter of LUIS PATO; v. good wines und eponymous label. Ensaios range now joined by innovative "icewine", fi and terroir-driven "Lokal" reds.

Pato, Luís Bair r sp ★★→★★★ 95' 97 99 00 01' 03' 04 Acclaimed Bairra estate though wines now classified as BEIRAS. Skilful exponent of 100 Baga wines that reward ageing: tremendous, **_single vineyard reds Vinh Barrio, Pan and Vinha Barrosa_**, and flagship Quinta do Ribeirinho I Franco (ungrafted vines). Quinta do Ribeirinho 1st Choice is a Baga/TOURI NACIONAL blend: João Pato is 100% TOURIGA NACIONAL.

Pegos Claros r 99 00 01 03 Solid, traditionally made red from PALMELA are Proof at last that PERIQUITA can make substantial wine.

Pellada, Quinta de See SAES.

Periquita The nickname for the CASTELÃO grape. Periquita is also a brand nam for a successful red wine from José María da FONSECA (DYA). Traditional re bottled under Periquita Clássico label (95 01).

Pires, João w DYA Fragrant, off-dry, Muscat-based wine from BACALHOA VINHOS

Planalto Douro w ★★ DYA Good white wine from SOGRAPE.

Poeira Douro r (01 02 03' 04') V. good, structured and elegant red from nor facing slopes of Quinta da Terra Feita de Cima – personal project of Jor Moreira, winemaker at Quinta de la ROSA.

Ponte de Lima, Cooperativa de r w ★ Maker of one of the best bone-dry r VINHOS VERDES, and first-rate dry and fruity white.

Portal, Quinta do Douro r w p ★→★★★ 00 01 03 04 Estate that once belong to Sandeman now making increasingly good red as well as ports.

Portalegre Alen r w ★→★★★ Small DOC with huge potential in the mountains north ALENTEJO. Balanced reds from Monte de Penha and go-ahead local co-o

Quatro Ventos, Quinta dos r Douro 01 02 03 impressive red, especially re from estate belonging to Caves ALIANÇA.

uinta Estate (see under name, *e.g.* PORTAL, QUINTA DO).

amos, João Portugal Alen r w DYA Well-made range from Loios and Vila Santa to premium single varietal range and blends: Quinta da Viçosa and v good Marqués de Borba. Reservas (**01 03**) of the latter fetch a high price.

aposeira Douro w sp ★★ Well-made fizz made by classic method at Lamego.

eal Companhia Velha ★★→★★★ r 00' 01' 02 03 w DYA One-time giant of the port trade; also produces increasingly good range of DOURO wines: Evel (good-value r and w) and more distinguished Evel Grande Escolha, Quinta dos Aciprestes, QUINTA de Cidro. Sweet Granjó from botrytis-affected Sem.

edondo Alen r w ★ DOC in heart of ALENTEJO with well-managed co-op.

eguengos Alen r (w) res ★→★★★ Important DOC near Spanish border. Includes José de SOUSA and ESPORÃO estates, plus large co-op for good reds.

batejo Rib r w The second-largest wine-producing region in Portugal and engine room of good-value wines, now raising its game. Sub-regions: Almeirim, CARTAXO, Coruche, Chamusca, Tomar, Santarem. Mid-weight reds from TOURIGA NACIONAL,TINTA RORIZ, and also a number made from international grapes: Cab Sauv, Syrah, Pinot N, Chard, and Sauv Bl. Rising stars include Pinhal da Torre and FALUA. Also VINHO REGIONAL Ribatejano.

oques, Quinta dos Dão r ★★→★★★ 00 01 03' 04 w DYA V. good estate for big, solid, oaked reds and oaked white Encruzado. Varietal wines from TOURIGA NATIONAL, TINTA RORIZ, Tinta Cão, and Alfrocherio Preto.

oriz, Quinta de Douro r ★★★ 00' 02 03' 04 One of the great QUINTAS of the DOURO, now making fine reds (and vintage port) with the Symingtons. Second wine: Prazo de Roriz.

osa, Quinta de la Douro r w p ★★→★★★ 00 01 02 03' Firm, oak-aged reds from port vineyards. Fine super-concentrated Res; Douro Tinto is v. good value for money. Also red Dourosa. Amarela: lighter second wine.

osado Rosé.

aes, Quinta de Dão r 00' 01 02 03 Small mountain estate belonging to Dão leading light Álvaro Castro. Fine, polished reds Pape and Dado – see NIEPOORT – are among the best DÃO wines around. Quinta de Pellada is under the same ownership and also makes wines to a high standard.

aima, Casa de Bair r (w DYA) sp p ★★★ 99 00 01 02 03' Small, traditional estate; big, long-lasting, tannic reds (especially GARRAFEIRAS 90' 91 95' 97' 01) and *some astounding whites*.

antar, Casa de Dão r ★★★ 00 01 02 03 Well-established estate now making welcome comeback. Reds much better than old-fashioned whites.

io Domingos, Comp dos Vinhos de Est See BOAVISTA.

io João, Caves Bair ★★→★★★ r 95 97 00 01 03 w DYA Small, traditional firm for v. good old-fashioned wines. Reds can age for decades. BAIRRADA: Frei João. DÃO: Porta dos Cavaleiros. Poço do Lobo: well-structured Cab Sauv.

eco Dry.

erradayres ★ DYA Everyday red something of a comeback, having been taken over by Caves Dom TEODÓSIO.

etúbal Set br (r w) sw (dr) ★★★ Tiny demarcated region south of the River Tagus. Dessert wines made predominantly from the Moscatel (Muscat) grape. Two main producers: José Maria da FONSECA and BACALHOA VINHOS also producing v. good reds from CASTELÃO and international varieties.

ezim, Casa de w ★★ DYA Beautiful estate making v. good VINHO VERDE.

ogrape ★→★★★★ Largest wine concern in the country, making VINHO VERDE, DÃO, BAIRRADA, ALENTEJO, MATEUS ROSÉ, and now owners of FERREIRA, Sandeman port, and Offley port in the DOURO. See also BARCA VELHA.

ousa, José de Alen r res ★★→★★★ 00 01 03 Small firm acquired by José María

da FONSECA; wines now slightly lighter in style. Sophisticated, full-bodie
wines from ALENTEJO, especially Mayor, are solid, foot-trodden GARRAFEIRAS ar
fermented in clay amphoras and aged in oak.

Teodósio, Caves Dom r w ★-→★★ Large producer in the RIBATEJO now making
welcome comeback. Everyday wines under the SERRADAYRES label.

Terras Altas Dão r w res ★ DYA Brand of DÃO from José María da FONSECA.

Terras do Sado VINHO REGIONAL covering sandy plains around Sado Estuary.

Tinta Roriz Major port grape (alias Tempranillo) making v. good DOURO wine
Known as ARAGONEZ in ALENTEJO.

Tinto Red.

Tinto da Anfora Alen r ★★-→★★★ 02 03 Reliable red from BACALHOA VINHO
Heavyweight Grande Escolha. Lighter red Monte das Anforas.

Torres Vedras ★ Est r w DOC north of Lisbon, famous for the Duke
Wellington's "lines". Major supplier of bulk wine.

Touriga Nacional Top red grape used for port and DOURO table wines; no
increasingly elsewhere, especially DÃO, ALENTEJO, and ESTREMADURA.

Trás-os-Montes Now DOC with sub-regions Chaves, Valpaços and Planal
Mirandês (was VINHO REGIONAL covering mountains of northeast Portugal
Reds and whites from international grape varieties grown in the DOURO. VINI
REGIONAL re-named Transmontano.

Trincadeira V. good red grape in ALENTEJO for spicy varietal wines.

Tuella r w ★★ DYA Good-value DOURO red from Cockburn (see Port chapter).

Vale Dona Maria, Quinta do ★★★ r 00 01 02 03' 04'. Small, highly regarde
QUINTA run by Cristiano van Zeller. V. good trio of *fruity yet elegant re*
includes CV and Casa Casal de Loivos. Also good port.

Vale Meão, Quinta do Douro r ★★★★ 99 00 01' 03 04 Once the source
legendary BARCA VELHA, now making great wine in its own right. V. goo
second wine: Meandro.

Vallado ★★ r 00' 01 02 03' w DYA Family-owned DOURO estate; v. good-valu
sweet fruited blends, especially Reserve. Also single varietal wines.

Ventozello, Quinta do Douro r 00 01 03 Huge Spanish-owned property in th
heart of the DOURO, making good reds and port.

Verde Green (see VINHO VERDE).

Vidigueira Alen w r ★-→★★★ DOC for traditionally made, unmaturedwhites ar
plummy reds from the hottest part of Portugal. Best producer: CORTES DE CIM

Vinho Regional Larger provincial wine region, with same status as French V
de Pays. They are: ACORES, ALGARVE, ALENTEJANO, BEIRAS, DURIENSE, ESTREMADUR
RIBATEJANO, MINHO, TRÁS-OS-MONTES, TRANSMONTANO, TERRAS MADEIRENSES, TERRAS I
SADO. See also DOC, IPR.

Vinho Verde w ★-→★★★ r ★ DOC between River DOURO and north frontier, f
"green wines" (w or r): made from high-acidity grapes which(originall
underwent secondary fermentation for slight sparkle. Today's large bran
are usually blends with added carbon dioxide. Ready for drinking in sprir
after harvest. Best single QUINTA, single-varietal wines, especially those fro
around Monçâo made from ALVARINHO (e.g. QUINTA Soalheiro) and LOUREII
(e.g. AMEAL).

Wine & Soul Douro r Pintas 01 02 03' 04' w Guru 04 05 Rich, imposing wine
(and single quinta port) from husband and wife team Sandra Tavares ar
Jorge Serôdio Borges, winemakers at Quinta do VALE D. MARIA and Quinta c
PASSADOURO respectively.

Xisto Douro r 03 04 V. good new red from joint venture between Quinta c
CRASTO and Jean-Michel Cazes from Bordeaux.

Sherry, Port, & Madeira

These three constitute the great historic fortified wines of the world. Sherry has experienced a dramatic slide in popularity over the last three decades. Its image has been greatly damaged by the British and Dutch fondness for sweetened or cream sherries. Yet there is a benefit from falling demand. Unsold stocks of Amontillados and Olorosos have been gently developing in the soleras of the Sherry towns. As a result there are exceptional "age-dated" sherries available and at remarkably low prices for their age. There is further reason for optimism in the fact that new bodegas have opened, specializing in top quality aged sherries. Meanwhile Manzanilla, the very driest and lightest of sherries, is enjoying a revival in Spain, and in Japan (as a alternative to Sake), and wherever seafood and shellfish are appreciated.

Madeira swims against the tide of quaffing wines, making sipping wines of singular intensity. Vintage wines and rare solera bottlings represent the pinnacle but the trend for 50cl bottles for premium, canteiro-aged wines, together with the introduction of colheita wines in the mid-nineties, puts fine madeira within everyone's reach.

Better-balanced, more accessible ports reflect hefty investment by major players. As stocks of older wines dry up, classic vintage prices creep up and SQVs from the shippers and a growing number of independent producers offer terrific value for money. These single vintage, single vineyard wines bring the Douro's terroir into sharp focus and, where they form the backbone of leading shippers' classic vintages (e.g. Taylor's Vargellas and Graham's Malvedos), offer an intriguing insight into house style. 2004 is a very good year for them, as in 2005

Recent declared classic port vintages

2003 Hot dry summer. Powerfully ripe, concentrated wines, universally declared. Drink from 2015/2020.

2000 A very fine vintage, universally declared. Rich, well-balanced wines for the long-term. Drink from 2015.

1997 Fine, potentially long-lasting wines with tannic backbone. Most shippers declared. Drink 2012 onwards.

1994 Outstanding vintage with ripe, fleshy fruit disguising underlying structure at the outset. Universal declaration. Drink 2010–2030.

1992 Favoured by a few (especially Taylor and Fonseca) over 91. Richer, more concentrated, a better year than 91. Drink 2008–2025.

1991 Favoured by most shippers (especially Symingtons with Dow, Graham, and Warre) over 92; classic, firm but a little lean in style. Drink now–2020.

1987 Dense wines for drinking over the medium term, but only a handful of shippers declared. Drink now–2015.

1985 Universal declaration which looked good at the outset but has thrown up some disappointments in bottle. Now–2020 for the best wines.

1983 Powerful wines with sinewy tannins. Most shippers declared. Now–2020.

1982 Rather simple, early-maturing wines declared by a few shippers. Drink up.

1980 Lovely fruit-driven wines, perfect to drink now and over the next 15 years. Most shippers declared.

1977 Big, ripe wines declared by all the major shippers except Cockburn, Martinez, and Noval. Lovely now, but don't keep too long.

1975 Soft and early maturing. Drink up.

1970 Classic, tight-knit wines – the best just reaching their peak. Now–2020+.

1966 Wines combine power and elegance. The best rival 1963. Now–2020+.
1963 Classic vintage; some wines past their best, others will go on.

Almacenista Matured, unblended sherry aged by individuals who keep a few barrels and sell them to shippers. Often superb quality and value. See LUSTAU.

Alvaro Domecq ★★·→★★★ Members of five branches of the DOMECQ sherry family purchased the SOLERAS of the Arandas – said to be the oldest bodega in JEREZ – thus re-establishing Domecq as an independent name in sherry. V. good range of 1730 label wines. Best sherry vinegar to be found.

Alvear Largest producer of v. good sherry-like apéritif and sweet wines in MONTILLA.

Andresen Independent, 100% family-owned **_port house making good COLHEITA (68)_**.

Barbadillo, Antonio ★★·→★★★ The largest SANLÚCAR firm with a wide range of MANZANILLAS and sherries, including Muy Fina FINO, Solear MANZANILLA austere Principe AMONTILLADO, Obispo Garcon PALO CORTADO, Cuco dry OLOROSO, Eva Cream, and excellent Reliquia line of AMONTILLADO, PALO CORTADO, OLOROSO seco, and PX. Also the largest producer of table wines with Castillo de San Diego.

Barbeito Managed by Ricardo de Freitas, the founder's dynamic grandson makes intense, finely honed madeiras with no added caramel. Innovative and exciting single-cask COLHEITAS and VERDELHO/BUAL blend ("vb").

Barros Almeida Large port house with several brands (inc Feist, Feuerheerd, KOPKE) owned by Sogevinus: excellent 20-year-old TAWNY and many COLHEITAS.

Barros e Sousa Family-owned madeira producer. Tiny output of extremely fine CANTEIRO-aged rare vintages, and good 10-year-old wines.

Blandy The best-known name of the MADEIRA WINE COMPANY thanks to popular entry-level 3-year-old "Duke" range. Its wines consistently yield fine old vintages (e.g. BUAL 1915, 1964, and 1977). Recent innovations include COLHEITAS (MALMSEY 1999) and Alvada, a moreish blend of BUAL and Malvasia.

Borges, H M Family company; full range. V. good 10-year-olds, COLHEITAS (BUAL & SERCIAL 1995) and vintages, especially SERCIAL.

Bual (or Boal) One of Madeira's traditional grapes, making tangy, smoky, sweet wines; not as rich as MALMSEY.

Burdon English-founded sherry bodega owned by Caballero. Puerto FINO, Don Luis AMONTILLADO, and raisiny Heavenly Cream are top lines.

Burmester Small port house owned by Sogevinus. Fine, soft, sweet 20-year-old TAWNY; also v. good range of COLHEITAS.

Cálem Established port house. Velhotes is the main brand. Fine reputation for COLHEITAS (90) and v. good vintage ports in 66' and 70'; returning to form. Good value single-QUINTA wines from Quinta de Foz.

Canteiro Method of naturally cask-ageing the finest madeira in lodges. Creates subtler, more complex wines than ESTUFAGEM.

Port and madeira: fascinating facts

Port Traditional mixed plantings of up to 30 different grape varieties are giving way to single varietal plantings focused on the Douro's five leading port grape varieties. Tourigas Nacionals, Francesa, Tintas Barocca, Roriz, and Cão. In consequence, today's winemakers can match each variety to soil and climate, harvest at optimum ripeness, and vinify separately.

Madeira Four traditional noble grape varieties define its classic styles (Sercial dry, Verdelho medium dry, Bual medium sweet, and Malvasia sweet) yet represent only 15% of plantings. The balance, which forms the backbone of younger, softer wines, is Tinta Negra Mole, which is now winning greater respect with some fine Colheita wines.

Sherry styles

Fino Along with MANZANILLA the lightest and finest of sherries. Completely dry, pale, delicate, but pungent. Should be drunk cool and fresh. Deteriorates rapidly once opened (always refrigerate and use half bottles if possible). E.g. GONZÁLEZ-BYASS Tío Pepe.

Manzanilla A pale, dry sherry with its own Denomination of Origin; often more delicate than a FINO and matured in the more maritime conditions of SANLÚCAR DE BARRAMEDA (as opposed to the other, more inland sherry towns of El Puerto de Santa Maria or JEREZ). Serving suggestions as with FINO. E.g. HIDALGO'S LA GITANA.

Amontillado A FINO in which the layer of FLOR has died, allowing the wine to oxidize and creating darker, more powerful characteristics. Naturally dry. E.g. VALDESPINO's Tío Diego.

Oloroso Heavier, less brilliant than FINO when young, and not aged under FLOR, but matures to richness and pungency. Naturally dry, often sweetened with PEDRO XIMÉNEZ and sold as an oloroso dulce (sweet oloroso). E.g. DOMECQ Rio Viejo (dry), LUSTAU Old East India (sweet).

Palo Cortado A rare style somewhere between AMONTILLADO and OLOROSO. Dry, rich, complex – worth looking for. E.g. BARBADILLO Obispo Gascon.

Cream Sherry A blended sherry sweetened with grape must, PX, and/or Moscatel for consistent, inexpensive, medium-sweet style. Don't expect much character. E.g. HARVEY'S Bristol Cream.

Pedro Ximénez (or PX) Grapily sweet, dark sherry from partly sun-dried PX grapes. Concentrated, unctuous, decadent, relatively inexpensive. The world's sweetest wine overall. E.g. REY FERNANDO DE CASTILLA's Antique.

Moscatel As with PX above, though it rarely reaches PX's level of concentration or richness. E.g. LUSTAU Centenary Selection Las Cruces.

Other styles Manzanilla Pasada: MANZANILLA aged longer than most, very complex and fascinating. Pale Cream: young, simple FINO sweetened with clarified grape must for dull, commercial appeal; e.g. CROFT.

Age-dated sherries This sub-category applies only to AMONTILLADO, OLOROSO, PALO CORTADO, and PX styles. They are: 12-year-old; 15-year-old; VOS (Very Old Sherry/Vinum Optimum Signatum); VORS (Very Old Rare Sherry/Vinum Optimum Rare Signatum); and Añada (vintage). All the sherry in casks of the second and third categories must be an average of at least 20 and 30 years old, respectively, while sherry in casks of the final category must be of a specific vintage.

Churchill 82 85 **91** 94 97 00 03 Independent, family-owned port shipper founded in 1981. V. good traditional LBV. Quinta da Gricha is the single-QUINTA port (01, 04). Benchmark aged white port.

Cockburn Owned since 2005 by the US Fortune brands, which sold its assets to the Symington family (see DOW) in 2006. Disappointing vintage ports since the early 80s. Vintages: **63** 67 **70 75** 83 **91** 94 97 00 03. Good single-QUINTA wines from Quinta dos Canais (01').

Colheita Vintage-dated port or madeira of a single year, cask-aged at least seven years for port and five years for madeira. Bottling date shown on the label.

Cossart Gordon Top-quality label of the MADEIRA WINE COMPANY; drier style than BLANDY. Best known for the Good Company brand. Also 5-year-old reserves, COLHEITAS (SERCIAL 1988, BUAL 1995, VERDELHO 1995), old vintages (1977 Terrantez, 1908 BUAL).

Crasto, Quinta do Good and improving single port estate, especially LBV; increasingly known for v. good modern table wines; see Portugal.

Croft One of the oldest firms, shipping VINTAGE PORT since 1678. Now part of the

Fladgate Partnership, who reintroduced foot-treading for the much-improved 03 vintage port. Vintages: **63' 66 67** 70 75 77 **82 85** 91 94 00 03'. Lighter QUINTA da Roêda. Triple Crown and Distinction: most popular brands.

Croft Jerez Founded only in 1970 and recently bought by GONZÁLEZ-BYASS. One of the most successful sherry firms. Best known for sweet Original Pale Cream and drier Particular. Also Delicado FINO and first-rate PALO CORTADO.

Crusted Style of port favoured by the British houses, usually blended from several vintages. Bottled young and then aged so it throws a deposit, or "crust", and needs decanting like VINTAGE PORT.

Delaforce Port shipper, part of the Fladgate Partnership. 20-year-old TAWNY: Curious and Ancient and COLHEITAS (64, 79, 88) are jewels in the crown. VINTAGE PORTS are improving: **63 66** 70' 75 77 **82 85** 92' 94 00 03. Single-QUINTA wines from Quinta da Corte.

Delgado, Zuleta ★★→★★★ Old SANLÚCAR firm, best known for marvellous La Goya manzanilla pasada.

Dios Baco ★→★★ New family-owned and run JEREZ bodega with good potential.

Domecq ★★→★★★★ Giant sherry bodega in JEREZ owned by the international conglomerate Beam Brands but still overseen by the supremely knowledgeable Beltran Domecq. La Ina FINO is excellent. Recently: a range of wonderful very old SOLERA sherries. Also in Rioja and Mexico.

Douro Rising in Spain as the Duero, the river Douro flows through port country lending its name to the region, which is divided into the Cima Corgo and Douro Superior, home of the best ports, and the Baixo Corgo.

Dow Brand name of port house Silva & Cosens. Belongs to the Symington family; drier style than other producers in the group (GRAHAM, WARRE, SMITH WOODHOUSE, GOULD CAMPBELL, QUARLES HARRIS, Quinta do VESÚVIO, and Quinta de RORIZ). V. good range, including CRUSTED, 20-year-old TAWNIES, single-QUINTA Bomfim and, since 1998, da Senhora da Ribeira; vintage: **63 66** 70 72 75 77 80 83 85' **91 94** 97 00' 03.

Duff Gordon Sherry shipper best-known for El Cid AMONTILLADO. Good FINO Feria; Niña Medium OLOROSO. OSBORNE-owned; name also second label for Osborne's ports.

Emilio Hildago ★★→★★★★ Small JEREZ bodega making exquisite *Privilegio 1860 PALO CORTADO* and v. good Santa Ana PX. FINO Panesa is good value.

Estufagem Bulk process of slowly heating, then cooling, cheaper madeiras to attain characteristic scorched-earth tang; less subtle than CANTEIRO process.

Ferreira Leading Portuguese-owned shipper belonging to Sogrape. Bestselling brand in Portugal. Fine 10- and 20-year-old TAWNIES, Quinta do Porto and *Duque de Bragança*. Early-maturing vintages : **63 66** 70 75 77 **78 80 82** 83 87 91 94 95 97 00 03.

Flor Spanish word for "flower": refers to the layer of saccharomyces yeast that grows atop FINO/MANZANILLA sherry in barrel, keeping oxidation at bay and changing the wine's flavour, making it aromatic and pungent. When the *flor* dies, the wines are aged further without it, becoming AMONTILLADO.

Fonseca Guimaraens Port shipper; belongs to the Fladgate Partnership. Renowned Bin 27 reserve RUBY joined by organic Terra Prima in 2006. Sumptuous yet structured vintages among best: Fonseca **63'** 66' 70 75 77' **80** 83 85' 92 94 97 00' 03'. Earlier-maturing Fonseca Guimaraens made if no classic declaration. Occasional single-QUINTA do Panascal.

Forrester See OFFLEY.

Frasqueira The official name for "vintage" madeira from a single year. Exceptionally intense wines bottled after at least 20 years in wood. Date of bottling compulsory; the longer in cask, the more concentrated and complex.

Garvey ★→★★★ Famous old sherry shipper in JEREZ Best San Patricio FINO, Tío Guillermo AMONTILLADO, and Ochavico OLOROSO. Also age-dated 1780 line.

SHERRY, PORT, & MADEIRA | Cro–Lea | **163**

González-Byass ★→★★★★ Large family bodega with the most famous and one of the best FINOS: Tío Pepe. Other brands inc La Concha AMONTILLADO, Elegante FINO, El Rocío MANZANILLA, 1847 sweet OLOROSO. Age-dated line inc Del Duque AMONTILLADO, Matúsalem OLOROSO, Apóstoles PALO CORTADO and the ultra-rich Noe PX. Along with WILLIAMS & HUMBERT the only bodega offering old, vintage wines.

Gould Campbell Port shipper belonging to the Symington family. Good-value, full-bodied VINTAGE PORTS **70** 77' 80 83 85' 91 94 97 00 03'.

Gracia Hermanos Mont-M Firm within the same group as PÉREZ BARQUERO and Compañia Vinícola del Sur making good-quality MONTILLAS. Its labels include María del Valle FINO, Montearruit AMONTILLADO, OLOROSO CREAM, and Dulce Viejo PX.

Graham One of port's greatest names, belonging to the Symington family. V. gd range from Six Grapes RESERVE RUBY, LBV and Tawny (reserve) to excellent year-aged TAWNIES from *some of richest, sweetest vintage ports* 63 66 70 75 77 80 83' 85' 91' 94 97 00' 03'. V. gd single-QUINTA vintage: Quinta dos Malvedos.

Gran Cruz The single biggest port brand. Mostly light, inexpensive tawnies.

Guita, La ★→★★★ Especially fine manzanilla pasada made by Pérez Marín in ANLÚCAR with huge presence in Spain. Also owns Gil Luque label for other herries.

Gutiérrez Colosía ★★★ Family-owned and run former ALMACENISTA on the Guadalete river in El Puerto with a very consistent range. Underpriced old PALO CORTADO.

Hartley & Gibson See VALDESPINO.

Harvey's ★→★★★ Important sherry pillar, owned by Beam Brands, along with Domecq and brandy company Terry. World-famous shipper of Bristol Cream (medium-sweet) and Club AMONTILLADO sherries. Also FINO

Henriques, Justino The largest madeira shipper belonging, along with GRAN CRUZ ports, to Martiniquaise. Good 10-year-old and vintage – e.g. 1934 VERDELHO.

Henriques & Henriques Independent madeira shipper. Rich, well-structured wines. Outstanding 15-year-olds; extra-dry apéritif Monte Seco; very fine reserves, vintage and solera wines, inc SERCIAL 1964, Terrantez 1976, *Malvasia 1954, BUAL 1954 & 1957*, Century Malmsey-Solera 1900.

Herederos de Argüeso ★★→★★★ MANZANILLA specialist in SANLÚCAR with v. good San Leon and Las Medallas bottlings; and the desirable VOS AMONTILLADO Viejo.

Hidalgo, La Gitana ★★★→★★★★ Old family sherry firm in SANLÚCAR overseen by the indefatigable Javier Hidalgo. Flagship is the *excellent pale MANZANILLA La Gitana*; also fine OLOROSO, lovely PALO CORTADOS, and mostly organically grown, single vineyard *Pastrana MANZANILLA PASADA* and AMONTILLADO.

Jerez de la Frontera Centre of sherry industry, between Cádiz and Seville. "Sherry" is a corruption of the name, pronounced "hereth". In French, Xérès.

Jordões, Casal dos Certified organic port producers: decent LBV and vintage wines.

Kopke The oldest port house, founded in 1638. Now belongs to BARROS ALMEIDA. Mostly early-maturing, fair-quality vintage wines, but some excellent (**70 74 75 77 78 79 80 82** 83 85 87 89 91 94 97 00 03), and excellent COLHEITAS.

Krohn Port shipper; excellent COLHEITAS (1961 1967), some dating back to 1800s.

Lagare Shallow granite "paddling pool" in which port is trodden by foot – or, these days, increasingly by robot.

LBV (Late Bottled Vintage) Port from a single year kept in wood for twice as long as VINTAGE PORT (about 5 years) so ready to drink on release; much larger volumes, robustly fruity but much less powerful and complex than vintage. No need to decant unless unfiltered wine which can age for 10 years or more (WARRE, SMITH WOODHOUSE, NIEPOORT, CHURCHILL, FERREIRA, NOVAL).

Leacock Volume label of the MADEIRA WINE COMPANY. Main brand is St John, popular in Scandinavia. Older vintages include 1950 SERCIAL, 1934 BUAL, and SOLERA 1860.

Lustau ★★ →★★★★ Sherry house based in jerez and owned by the Caballero group. Wide variety of wines. Best-known as pioneer shipper of excellent *ALMACENISTA* and "landed age" wines; AMONTILLADOS and OLOROSOS aged in elegant bottles before shipping. First to commercialize a vintage sherry with its 1989 sweet OLOROSO.

Madeira Wine Company Formed in 1913 by two firms as the Madeira Wine Association, subsequently to include all 26 British madeira firms; today it produces over 100 different labels. Though cellared together, wines preserve individual house styles; BLANDY and COSSART GORDON lead the pack. Now controlled by the Symington family (see DOW), it has benefitted from improved production facilities following investment. All wines 5-years old plus CANTEIRO-aged traditional grape varieties with exception of Tinta Negra Mole COLHEITA.

Port and madeira selection for 2008

White port CHURCHILL.

Ruby & Reserve Quinta do Passadouro Ruby, FONSECA Bin 27 and Terra Prima, GRAHAM's Six Grapes, DOW's Crusted, WARRE's Warrior.

Late Bottled Vintage FONSECA LBV 2000, WARRE's 1995 LBV, Quinta do Crasto 2000, TAYLOR's LBV 2001.

Tawny & Coleita DELAFORCE, COLHEITA 64, KROHN COLHEITA 67, Quinta do Infantado 10-Year-Old, WARRE's OTIMA 20-Year-Old, GRAHAM's 30-Year-Old, NIEPOORT 20-Year-Old.

Single-quinta ports Quinta do Vale Dona Maria 2000, DOW's Quinta Senhora da Ribeira 01, Quinta do VESÚVIO 96, WARRE's Quinta de Cavadhinha 96, Fonseca Quinta do Panascal 91 and 98, GRAHAM Malvedos 95 and 96, TAYLOR Quinta de Vargellas 95, 96, 98.

Vintage ports FONSECA 63, TAYLOR 63, FONSECA 66, GRAHAM 70, TAYLOR 70, SMITH WOODHOUSE 77, GRAHAM 80, GRAHAM 83, FONSECA 85, GRAHAM 91, TAYLOR 92, NIEPOORT 92, Quinta do NOVAL 94, FONSECA GUIMARAENS 98.

Madeiras BLANDY's BUAL 64, 77, COSSART GORDON SERCIAL COLHEITA 88 Terrantez 1997, BARBEITO's Single Cask COLHEITAS, VB, 81 VERDELHO, HENRIQUES & HENRIQUES 10-yr-old VERDELHO, 15-year-old BUAL and Terrantez 76.

Malmsey or Malvasia The sweetest and richest of traditional madeira grape varieties; dark amber, rich, and honeyed, yet with madeira's unique sharp tang.

Martinez Gassiot Port firm now owned by the Symington family, known especially for excellent rich, and pungent Directors 20-yr-old TAWNY. Good value, ageworthy vintages in drier, traditional style: 63 67 70 75 82 85 87 91 94 97 00 03. V. good single-QUINTA wines from Quinta da Eira Velha.

Medina, José Originally a SANLÚCAR bodega, now a major exporter, especially to the Low Countries. Owns Bodegas Internacionales and WILLIAMS & HUMBERT, also Pérez Megia and Luis Paez: probably the biggest sherry grower and shipper.

Miles Madeira shipper, part of the MADEIRA WINE COMPANY. Basic wines only.

Montecristo Mont-M Brand of big-selling MONTILLAS by Compañía Vinícola del Sur.

Montilla-Moriles Mont-M DO near Córdoba. Not sherry, but close. Its soft FINO and AMONTILLADO, and luscious PX contain 14–17.5% natural alcohol and remain unfortified. At best, singularly toothsome apéritifs. PX sourced from Montilla but aged and bottled in sherry country so it may be called PX sherry.

Niepoort Small family-run port house of Dutch origin; sensational table wines. Consistently fine vintages (63 66 70' 75 77 78 80 82 83 87 91 92 94 97 00 03). Second vintage label: Secundum. Exceptional TAWNIES and COLHEITAS.

Noval, Quinta do Historic port house now French (AXA) owned. Intensely fruity structured, elegant vintage port; around 2.5 ha of ungrafted vines make small quantity of **_Nacional – extraordinarily dark, full, velvety, slow-maturing_**. Also v. good 20-year-old TAWNY and good COLHEITAS. Vintages: **63 66 67 70 75 78 82 85** 87 91 94' 95 97' 00' 03' 04. Second vintage label: Silval. Also v. good LBV.

Offley Brand name belonging to port shipper Forrester. Duke of Oporto is main brand and a big seller in Portugal. Baron de Forrester is good TAWNY. Owns Quinta da Boa Vista. Good early-maturing vintages: **63 66 67 70 72 75 77 80 82 83 85 87 89** 94 95 97 00' 03.

Osborne ★→★★★★ Huge Spanish firm producing sherry, a wide range of Spanish wines, and quality port. Has taken over Bobadilla sherries and brandies. Its instantly recognizable bull logo dots the Spanish countryside. Declared VINTAGE PORTS in95 97 00' 03'.

Paternina, Federico ★★→★★★★ Marcos Eguizabel from Rioja acquired the sherry firm Diez-Merito, retaining three VORS wines for his Paternina label, the excellent and unique FINO Imperial, OLOROSO, Victoria Regina, and PX Vieja SOLERA.

Pedro Romero ★→★★★ Recently expanded SANLÚCAR family operation in a rambling array of bodegas. Very wide range; frustratingly inconsistent.

Pereira d'Oliveira Vinhos Family-owned madeira company since 1850. Good basic range, COLHEITAS and fine old vintages back to 1850 labelled as Reserve.

Pérez Barquero Mont-M Another firm, like GRACIA HERMANOS, once part of Rumasa. Its excellent MONTILLAS include Gran Barquero FINO, AMONTILLADO, and OLOROSO.

Pilar Plá/El Maestro Sierra ★→★★★ Owned by JEREZ's grandest dame Pilar Plá. Wines inconsistent, but some great value at medium ages esp AMONTILLADO.

Poças Portuguese family port firm; v. good TAWNIES and COLHEITAS. good LBV and recent vintages (97 00' 03). Single-QUINTA wines from Quinta Sta Barbera.

Puerto de Santa María The second city and former port of sherry, with important bodegas such as OSBORNE and former ALMACENISTA Gutierrez Colosia.

PX Pedro Ximénez grape, partly sun-dried, either bottled alone as top-class sweet wine, or used for sweetening other sherries.

Quarles Harris One of the oldest port houses, since 1680 , now owned by the Symington family (see DOW). Mellow, well-balanced vintages, often v. good value: **63 66 70 75 77 80 83 85 91** 94 97 00' 03.

Quinta Portuguese for "estate", traditionally denotes VINTAGE PORTS from shipper's single vineyards; declared in good but not exceptional years. An increasing number of independent _quintas_ (growers) make wines from top vintages. Exciting newcomers include Passadouro, Portal, Whytingham's Vale Meão, and Wine & Soul's Pintas.

Ramos Pinto Dynamic port house owned by Champagne house Louis Roederer. Outstanding single-QUINTA de Ervamoira and TAWNIES (de Ervamoira and do Bom Retiro). Rich sweet, generally early maturing vintages.

Reserve/Reserva Premium ports, mostly Reserve RUBY but some Reserve TAWNY, bottled without a vintage date or indication of age but better than the basic style (see boxed selection).

Rey Fernando de Castilla ★★→★★★★ JEREZ veteran Norwegian Jan Pettersen has made a small sherry revolution with his excellent wines, which, although he chooses not to label them Age-Dated, could easily be so. Top Antique line of AMONTILLADO, OLOROSO, and PX; FINOS less so.

Roriz, Quinta de Historic estate now controlled by the Symington family (see DOW).V. good single-QUINTA DOURO wines and ports: 99 00' 01 02 03' 04.

Rosa, Quinta de la V. good single-QUINTA port from the Bergqvist family. Traditional methods and stone LAGARES. Look for **94 95** 00 03' 04 vintages and wines from a small plot of old vines called Vale do Inferno.

Royal Oporto Main port brand within Real Companhia Velha, now focusing on unfortified Douro wines. Some good TAWNIES, COLHEITAS and recent vintages.

Rozès Port shipper owned by Champagne house Vranken alongside São Pedro das Aguias. Very popular in France.

Ruby Youngest and cheapest port style: simple, sweet, red. Best are vigorous, full of flavour; others merely strong, thin, spirity. See also RESERVE.

Sanchez Romate ★★→★★★ Family firm in JEREZ since 1781. Best known in Spanish-speaking world, especially for brandy Cardenal Mendoza. Good sherry: OLOROSO La Sacristía de Romate, PX Duquesa, AMONTILLADO NPU ("Non Plus Ultra").

Sandeman ★→★★★ Large firm, now part of Sogrape group. Founded in 1790 by Scot George Sandeman, who set up twin establishments in Oporto and JEREZ. Scrupulously made sherries include an aged Don FINO, and Armada CREAM. Also dry and sweet Imperial Corregidor and Royal Ambrosante OLOROSOS. Port: good aged TAWNIES, especially 20-year-old. Vintage patchy in recent years (63 66 70 75 77 80 82 85 94 97 00). Second label: Vau Vintage, recommended for drinking young.

Sanlúcar de Barrameda Historic seaside sherry town (see MANZANILLA).

Santa Eufemia, Quinta de Family port estate with v. good old TAWNIES.

Sercial Madeira grape for the driest of the island's wines – supreme apéritif.

Silva, C da Port shipper. Mostly inexpensive RUBIES and TAWNIES, but good aged TAWNIES and COLHEITAS under Dalva label.

Smith Woodhouse Port firm founded in 1784, Mostly a supplier of own-label but v. good unfiltered LBV and some very fine vintages: **63 66 70 75 77' 80 83 85** 91 94 97 00' 03. Occasional single-estate wines from Quinta da Madelena.

Solera System used in ageing sherry. Consists of topping up progressively more mature barrels with slightly younger wine of same sort, the object being continuity in final wine. Most sherries are blends of several soleras. Used to be applied to madeiras; old solera wines in bottle fetch high prices.

Tawny Style of port that implies ageing in wood (hence tawny in colour), though many basic tawnies are little more than attenuated RUBIES. Look for wines with an indication of age: 10-, 20-, 30-, or 40-year-old or RESERVE.

Taylor, Fladgate & Yeatman (Taylor's) One of the best known port shippers, highly rated for its rich, long-lived VINTAGE PORTS. Now a member of the Fladgate Partnership alongside CROFT, DELAFORCE, and FONSECA GUIMARAENS.V. good range including RESERVE (First Estate), LBV and aged TAWNIES. Two prime estates, Vargellas and Terra Feita produce single-QUINTA vintage, and Vargellas "Vinha Velha" (95, 97, 00, 04) from oldest vines (+70 years).

Terry, SA ★→★★ Sherry bodega at PUERTO DE SANTA MARÍA; part of Beam Brands.

Tío Pepe The most famous of FINO sherries (see GONZÁLEZ-BYASS).

Toro Albalá, Bodegas Mont-M Family firm located in a 1920s power station and aptly making Eléctrico FINOS, AMONTILLADOS, and a PX that is among the best in MONTILLA and Spain.

Tradición ★★★→★★★★ Part of the new wave of sherry bodegas focusing exclusively upon small quantities of VOS PX and VORS AMONTILLADO, PALO

CORTADO, and OLOROSO, from a refurbished, art-filled cellar in back streets of JEREZ.

Valdespino ★→★★★★ Famous JEREZ bodega producing Inocente fino from the esteemed Macharnudo v'yd. *Tío Diego is terrific dry AMONTILLADO*; also SOLERA 1842 OLOROSO, Don Tomás AMONTILLADO. Matador is a popular range. In the US its sherries are sold as Hartley & Gibson.

Valdivia ★★ Newest producer of sherry. VOS-and-above levels in stylish bottles.

Vale D Maria, Quinta do Good value, beautifully elegant VINTAGE PORT.

Ventozelo, Quinta de Huge, beautifully situated estate recently acquired and renovated by a Spanish family. Good value single-QUINTA VINTAGE PORTS.

Verdelho Traditional madeira grape for medium-dry wines; pungent but without the searing austerity of SERCIAL. Increasing in popularity for table wines.

Vesúvio, Quinta do Enormous 19th-C estate in the DOURO. Only vintage port: 91 92 94 95' 96' 00' 01 03' 04.

Vila Nova de Gaia City on the S side of the River DOURO from Oporto, where major port shippers traditionally mature their wines in "lodges".

Vintage Port Classic vintages are the best wines declared in exceptional years by shippers between 1 Jan and 30 Sept in the second year after the harvest – e.g. 2003 declared in 2005. Bottled without filtration after 2 years in wood, the wine matures very slowly in bottle throwing a CRUST or deposit so always needs decanting. The best will last over 50 years. Single-QUINTA vintage ports are also drinking earlier.

Warre Oldest of British port shippers (since 1670); owned by the Symington family (see DOW) since 1905. Fine, elegant, long-maturing vintage wines, good RESERVE, vintage character (Warrior), excellent unfiltered, bottle-matured LBV; 10- and 20-year-old Otima TAWNY. Single-QUINTA vintage from Quinta da Cavadinha. Vintages: 63 66 70' 75 77' 80 83 85 91 94 97 00' 03.

White port Port made with white grapes, occasionally sweet (*lagrima*) but mostly off-dry aperitif styles (driest labelled "Dry"). Look for wines with cask age: BARROS, NIEPOORT, CHURCHILL. Since 2006, the designations 10-, 20-, 30-, or 40-year-old can be used. Younger, paler wines can be drunk long with tonic.

Williams & Humbert ★★→★★★★ Famous first-class sherry bodega. Dry Sack (medium AMONTILLADO) is bestseller; Canasta CREAM and Walnut Brown are gd in their class; SOLERA Especial is its famous old PALO CORTADO. Also famous Gran Duque de Alba brandy.

Switzerland

More heavily shaded areas are the wine-growing regions

The big news in Switzerland lately is a deal with the USA, intended to increase trade between the two countries, which will allow the use of oak chips in Swiss wine. This may not seem earth-shattering to the rest of the world but it caused a big rumpus in Switzerland, not least because there is no requirement to say on the label exactly how a wine was produced.

At the moment, very little Swiss wine is exported. The Swiss love their wine, and the average annual consumption is slightly under 40 litres per head. The Swiss are famous for staying within their borders, and they keep their wine with them.

Recent vintages
2006 Very promising and being compared to 2005.
2005 Low in quantity but high in quality.
2004 Less complex than 2003 but very promising.
2003 To drink now. Wines show good maturity.
2002 Not the best year for everybody. Stick to the best producers.

Aargau 04 05 06 Eastern canton for fragrant Müller-THURGAU, rich BLAUBURGUNDER. Best producer: Weingut zum Sternen.

Aigle Vaud r w ★★→★★★ Well known for elegant whites and supple reds.

Amigne Traditional VALAIS white grape, especially of VÉTROZ. Full-bodied, tasty, often sweet. Best producer: André Fontannaz ★★ 04 **05** 06. A new quality rating has been launched, based on residual sugar. One bee – yes, as in the insect – means 0–8 grams per litre RS, two bees mean 9–25g/l RS, three bees mean over 25g/l RS.

Arvine Old VALAIS white grape (also Petite Arvine): *dry and sweet, elegant, long-lasting wines with a salty finish*. Best in SIERRE, SION, Granges, FULLY. Producers: Benoît Dorsaz, Rouvinez, Marie-Thérèse Chappaz, Simon Maye & Fils.

Auvernier Neuchâtel r p w ★★→★★★ Old wine village on Lake NEUCHÂTEL and biggest wine-growing commune of the canton.

Basel Second-largest Swiss town and canton: divided into Basel-Stadt and Basel-Land. Best wines: Müller-THURGAU, PINOT N (104 ha). Look out for wines from the Bacchus grape.

Bern Swiss capital and canton. Vineyards in west (BIELERSEE: CHASSELAS, PINOT N, white SPÉCIALITÉS) and east (Thunersee: BLAUBURGUNDER, Müller-THURGAU); 262 ha.

Bielersee r p w ★→★★ **04 05'** 06 Wine region on northern shore of the Bielersee lake (dry, light CHASSELAS, PINOT N and new specialities such as VIOGNIER and MALBEC). Best producers: Domaine Grillette, Charles Steiner.

Blauburgunder German name for PINOT N; aka Clevner. Wide range of wines, from rosé to heavily oaked reds. Switzerland's main red variety.

Bündner Herrschaft Grisons r p w ★★→★★★ Best German-Swiss region includes top villages: Fläsch, Jenins, Maienfeld, Malans. BLAUBURGUNDER ripens especially well due to warm Föhn wind, cask-aged v. good. Also Chard, Müller-THURGAU, COMPLETER. Best: Gantenbein ★★★, Davaz ★★, Fromm ★★★ **01' 02 03' 04** 05 06. Switzerland's best Blauburgunder is from here.

Chablais Vaud r w ★★→★★★ Sunny wine region on right bank of Rhône and upper end of Lake GENEVA, includes villages AIGLE, Bex, Ollon, VILLENEUVE, YVORNE.

Chasselas (Gutedel in Germany) French cantons, white grape; neutral flavour; takes on local character: elegant (GENEVA); refined, full (VAUD); exotic, racy (VALAIS); pétillant (lakes Bienne, NEUCHÂTEL, Murtensee). Only east of BASEL. Called FENDANT in VALAIS. Accounts for almost a third of Swiss wines but increasingly replaced – a government-financed move. Best: Louis Bovard, Raymont Paccot. The latest fashion is to avoid the malolactic fermentation, thus conserving acidity in the wines.

Completer Native white grape, mostly used in GRISONS, making aromatic wines with high acidity. ("Complet" was a monk's final daily prayer, or "nightcap".) Related to the Valais grape Lafnetscha. Best: Adolf Boner, Malans ★★.

Cornalin ★★→★★★ **03' 04** 05' Local VALAIS speciality that has become more popular since production increased; dark, spicy, very strong red. Best: Denis Mercier, Provins, Jean-René Germanier (★★). Oldest living vine in Switzerland is a Cornalin plant in Leuk, Valais, from 1798 (www.vitisantiqua1798.ch).

Côte, La Vaud r p w ★→★★★ Largest VAUD wine area between LAUSANNE and GENEVA. Traditional whites with elegant finesse; fruity, harmonious reds. Especially from MONT-SUR-ROLLE, Vinzel, Luins, FÉCHY, MORGES, etc.

Côtes de l'Orbe Vaud r p w ★→★★ North VAUD appellation between Lake NEUCHÂTEL and Lake GENEVA especially for light, fruity reds.

Dézaley Vaud w (r) ★★→★★★ Celebrated LAVAUX vineyard on slopes above Lake GENEVA, once tended by Cistercian monks. Unusually potent CHASSELAS, develops especially after ageing. Red Dézaley is a GAMAY/PINOT N/MERLOT/Syrah rarity.

Dôle Valais r ★★→★★★ Appellation for PINOT N, often blended with GAMAY and other reds from the VALAIS: full, supple, often v. good. Lightly pink Dôle Blanche is pressed straight after harvest.

Epesses Vaud w (r) ★→★★★ **05' 06** LAVAUX AC: supple, full-bodied whites.

Ermitage Alias Marsanne; a VALAIS SPÉCIALITÉ. Concentrated, full-bodied dry white, sometimes with residual sugar. Best: Domaine Cornulus, Philippoz Frères.

Féchy Vaud ★→★★ Famous appellation of LA CÔTE, especially elegant whites.

Federweisser German-Swiss name for white wine from BLAUBURGUNDER.

Fendant Valais w ★→★★★ VALAIS appellation for CHASSELAS. The ideal wine for Swiss cheese dishes such as fondue or raclette. All qualities available.

Flétri/Mi-flétri Late-harvested grapes for sweet/slightly sweet wine (respectively).

Fribourg Smallest French-Swiss wine canton (115 ha, near Jura). Especially for PINOT N, CHASSELAS, GAMAY, SPÉCIALITÉS from VULLY, Lake Murten, south Lake NEUCHÂTEL.

Fully Valais r w ★★→★★★ Village near MARTIGNY: excellent ERMITAGE and GAMAY. Best producer: Marie-Thérèse Chappaz sw ★★→★★★ 03' 04 05' 06.

Gamay Beaujolais grape; abounds in French cantons. Mainly thin wine used in blends (SALVAGNIN, DÔLE). Gamay accounts for 14% of grapes in Switzerland.

Geneva Capital, and French-Swiss wine canton; third largest (1,425 ha). Key areas: Mandement, Entre Arve et Rhône, Entre Arve et Lac. Mostly CHASSELAS, GAMAY. Also Gamaret, Chard, PINOT N, Muscat, and good Aligoté. Best: Jean-Michel Novelle ★★★; interesting: Jacques Tatasciere, Domaine de la Rochette ★★.

Germanier, Jean-René VÉTROZ winemaker; Cayas (100% Syrah) ★★★ 01 02 03 04 05'; Mitis (sweet) ★★★ 01' 02 03 04 05'. New release: a pure Cornalin 05'.

Gewurztraminer Grown in Switzerland as a SPÉCIALITÉ variety, especially in VALAIS and the east. Best producer: Jean-Michel Novelle, Satigny 05' 06.

Glacier, Vin du (Gletscherwein) Fabled oxidized, wooded white from rare Rèze grape of Val d'Anniviers. Almost impossible to find on sale.

Grand Cru Quality designation. Implication differs by canton.

Grisons (Graubünden) Mountain canton, mainly in German Switzerland (BÜNDNER HERRSCHAFT, Churer Rheintal; especially BLAUBURGUNDER) and partly south of Alps (Misox, esp MERLOT). 416 ha, primarily PINOT N, also Müller-THURGAU and SPÉCIALITÉS.

Heida (Païen) Old VALAIS white grape (Jura's Savagnin) for country wine of upper Valais (VISPERTERMINEN vineyards at 1,000+ m). Good in lower VALAIS, too. Full-bodied wine with high acidity. Best: Josef-Marie Chanton ★★ 03' 04 05' 06. New release: a Heida from Provins.

Humagne Strong native white grape (VALAIS SPÉCIALITÉ). Humagne Rouge (unrelated, from Aosta Valley) also. Especially from CHAMOSON, LEYTRON, MARTIGNY

Johannisberg Synonym for SYLVANER in the VALAIS.

Landwein (Vin de pays) Traditional light white and red BLAUBURGUNDER from east.

Lausanne Capital of VAUD. No longer with vineyards in town area, but long-time owner of classics: Abbaye de Mont, Château Rochefort (LA CÔTE); Clos des Moines, Clos des Abbayes, Domaine de Burignon (LAVAUX). Pricey.

Lavaux Vaud w (r) ★→★★★ DYA Scenic region on north shore of Lake GENEVA between Montreux and LAUSANNE. Delicate, refined whites, good reds. Best: Calamin, Chardonne, DÉZALEY, EPESSES, Lutry, ST-SAPHORIN, VEVEY-MONTREUX, Villette.

Malvoisie See PINOT GRIS.

Martigny Valais r w ★★ Lower VALAIS commune esp for HUMAGNE ROUGE and Syrah.

MDVS Mémoires des Vins Suisses – a collection of the most important Swiss wines; also older vintages, to protect the country's heritage (www.mdvs.ch)

Merlot Brought to the TICINO in 1907 by the scientist Alderige Fantuzzi (after phylloxera destroyed local varieties): soft to very powerful wines. Also used with Cab Sauv. Best: Castello Luigi, Zanini, Conte di Luna, and Stucky.

Mont d'Or, Domaine du Valais w s/sw sw ★★→★★★ 04 05' 06 Well-sited property near SION: rich, concentrated demi-sec and sweet wines; *notable SYLVANER.*

Mont-sur-Rolle Vaud w (r) ★★ DYA Important appellation within LA CÔTE.

Morges Vaud r p w ★→★★ DYA Largest LA CÔTE/VAUD AOC: CHASSELAS, fruity reds.

Neuchâtel City and canton; 600 ha from Lake Neuchâtel to BIELERSEE. CHASSELAS fragrant, lively (sur lie, sparkling). Good OEIL DE PERDRIX, PINOT NOIR, Chard.

Nostrano Word meaning "ours", applied to red wine of TICINO, made from native and Italian grapes (Bondola, Freisa, Bonarda, etc).

Oeil de Perdrix Pale PINOT N rosé. DYA especially but not only NEUCHÂTEL's; the name can be used anywhere.

Pinot Blanc Weissburgunder Booming variety producing full-bodied, elegant wines.

Pinot Gris Malvoisie Widely planted white grape for dry and residually sweet wines. Makes very fine late-harvest wines in VALAIS (called Malvoisie).

Pinot Noir Blauburgunder Top red grape (33% of vineyards). Especially BÜNDNER HERRSCHAFT, NEUCHÂTEL, THURGAU, VALAIS, ZÜRICH. Try: Gantenbein; Davaz (Fläsch); Kesselring (Ottoberg); Pircher (Eglisau); Baumann (Oberhallau); Meier (Kloster Sion); Fromm (Malans); Christian Obrecht (Jenins) ★★★ 01' 02 03' 04 05' 06.

Rauschling Old white ZÜRICH grape; discreet fruit and elegant acidity.

Riesling Petit Rhin Mainly in the VALAIS. Try Kesseling (Ottoberg) 05' 06.

Riesling-Sylvaner Old name for Müller-THURGAU (top white of the east; a SPÉCIALITÉ in the west). Typically elegant wines with flowery aroma and some acidity. Best producers: Daniel Marugg, Baumann (Oberhallau) ★★ 05 06'.

St-Gallen Eastern wine canton (218 ha). Especially for BLAUBURGUNDER (full-bodied), Müller-THURGAU, SPÉCIALITÉS. Includes Rhine Valley, Oberland, upper Lake ZÜRICH.

St-Saphorin Vaud w (r) ★★→★★★ 05 06' Famous LAVAUX AC for fine, light whites.

Salvagnin Vaud r ★→★★ 03 GAMAY and/or PINOT N appellation. (See also DÔLE.)

Schaffhausen German-Swiss canton and wine town on the Rhine. BLAUBURGUNDER; also Müller-THURGAU and SPÉCIALITÉS. Best: Baumann, Bad Osterfingen ★★. The latest trend is reds and whites with plenty of residual sugar.

Schenk Europe-wide wine giant, founded and based in Rolle (VAUD). Owns firms in France (Burg and Bordeaux), Germany, Italy, and Spain.

Sierre Valais r w ★★→★★★ Sunny resort and famous wine town. Known for FENDANT, PINOT N, ERMITAGE, MALVOISIE. V. good DÔLE.

Sion Valais r w ★★→★★★ Capital/wine centre of VALAIS. Especially FENDANT de Sion.

Spécialités (Spezialitäten) Wines of unusual grapes: vanishing local Gwäss, Himbertscha, Roter Eyholzer, Bondola, etc, ARVINE and AMIGNE, or modish Chenin Bl, Sauv Bl, Cab Sauv, Syrah. Of 47 VALAIS varieties, 43 are spécialités.

Süssdruck Dry rosé/bright-red wine: grapes pressed before fermentation.

Swisswine www.swisswine.ch Wine promotion body, mainly government-financed. Organizes a wine gala competition every two years.

Sylvaner Johannisberg, Gros Rhin White grape especially in warm VALAIS vineyards.

Thurgau German-Swiss canton beside Bodensee Lake (265 ha). Wines from Thur Valley: Weinfelden, Seebach, Nussbaum, and Rhine. South shore of the Untersee. Typical: BLAUBURGUNDER, also good Müller-THURGAU. SPÉCIALITÉS include Kerner, PINOT GRIS, Regent. Best producer: Hans Ulrich Kesselring ★★★ 04 05' 06'.

Ticino Italian-speaking southern Switzerland (with Misox), growing mainly MERLOT (good from mountainous Sopraceneri region) and SPÉCIALITÉS. Trying Cab Sauv (oaked Bordeaux style), Sauv Bl, Semillon, Chard, Merlot white, and rosé (1,020 ha). Best producers: Luigi Zanini, Werner Stucky, Daniel Huber, Adriano Kaufmann, Christian Zündel, Guido Brivio. All ★★★ 02 03' 04 05' 06.

Valais (Wallis) Rhône Valley from German-speaking upper-Valais to French lower-Valais. Largest and most varied wine canton in Switzerland (5,198 ha; source of 30% Swiss wine), now seeing a revival of quality, and ancient grapes. Near-perfect climatic conditions. Wide range: 47 grape varieties, plus many SPÉCIALITÉS. Especially white; FLÉTRI/MI-FLÉTRI wines.

Vaud (Waadt) French Switzerland's second-largest wine canton includes CHABLAIS, LA CÔTE, LAVAUX, BONVILLARS, CÔTES DE L'ORBE, VULLY. CHASSELAS stronghold.

Vétroz Valais w r ★★→★★★ Top village near SION, especially famous for AMIGNE.

Vevey-Montreux Vaud r w ★★ Up-and-coming appellation of LAVAUX. Famous wine festival held about every 30 years.

Villeneuve Vaud w (r) ★★→★★★ Near Lake GENEVA: powerful yet refined whites.

Visperterminen Valais w (r) ★→★★ Upper VALAIS vineyards, especially for SPÉCIALITÉS. The highest vineyards in Europe (at 1,000+ m).

Vully Vaud w (r) ★→★★ Refreshing white from Lake Murten/FRIBOURG area.

Yvorne Vaud w (r) ★★ 04 05 Top CHABLAIS AC for strong, fragrant wines.

Zürich Capital of largest canton. BLAUBURGUNDER mostly; also PINOT GRIS, GEWURZ,

SWITZERLAND

Austria

More heavily shaded areas are the wine-growing regions

If you want to taste Austria's most exciting wines look for those from old, indigenous grape varieties. Recently imported grapes – Cabernet, for example – often produce less unmistakably Austrian styles. Among the reds, Blaufränkisch and Sankt Laurent have the most potential, while Zweigelt will never be more than useful for blending. Pinot Noir is now producing its first excellent results. Most recently the best red producers have moved away from overpowering oak and are exploring individual terroirs. Among the dry whites, Grüner Veltliner, Riesling, Chardonnay and Sauvignon Blanc produce the most prestigious wines, but do not ignore the rose-scented Gelber Muskateller or rarities like Roter Veltliner. Sweet, botrytized wines are made from a variety of obscure grapes, among which Furmint has made a recent comeback.

Recent vintages

2006 An exceptional year. A cold winter was followed by a wet spring and one of the hottest late summers on record. Grape qualities everywhere were very good, but yields were small.

2005 A cool year yielding exceptionally elegant wine, particularly in Lower Austria, but with great discrepancies in quality. Not outstanding for reds, but with wonderful botrytis for dessert wines.

2004 A cooler year. Grüner Veltliner and Riesling fared well, especially in Wachau. Ripe reds in Burgenland.

2003 A hot dry summer, a powerful year for whites and Burgenland reds, especially Blaufränkisch and Zweigelt. Little botrytis for dessert wines.

2002 Though Grüner Veltliner was hit by harvest rains, Riesling and the white Pinots did well. A difficult red-wine vintage, but excellent dessert wines.

2001 Great for dry whites; very good late-harvest wines. Reds more erratic.

2000 Very good vintage in Lower Austria. Mixed in Styria due to harvest rains. In Burgenland, possibly the greatest vintage since 1945.

Achs, Paul r (w) ★★★ Exceptional GOLS estate, especially reds: Pannobile blends, Ungerberg, BLAUFRÄNKISCH and Pinot N.

Alzinger w ★★★★ 93 94 95 97 98 99 00 01 02 03 04 05 Outstanding Wachau estate: deep, mineral Ries and Grüner Veltliner.

Ausbruch PRÄDIKAT wine with sweetness levels between Beerenauslese and Trockenbeerenauslese. Traditionally produced in RUST.

Ausg'steckt ("hung out") HEURIGEN are not open all year; when they are, a green bush is hung above their doors, also to show wine is being served.

Bayer r w ★★★ Cult reds named after star signs: In Signo Leonis, In Signo Sagittarii, In Signo Tauri, plus others. Surprisingly, not just about muscle.

Blauer Burgunder Pinot N. A premium winemaker's favourite, though vintages can vary markedly. Best in BURGENLAND, KAMPTAL, and the THERMENREGION (from growers P ACHS, LOIMER, PITTNAUER, SCHLOSS HALBTURN, PÖCKL, C Preisinger).

Blauer Portugieser Light, fruity wines to drink slightly chilled when young.

Blauer Zweigelt BLAUFRÄNKISCH/ST LAURENT cross High-yielding grape, rich in colour. Lower yields and improved methods can produce appealing, velvety reds. Top HEINRICH, Grassl, Markowitsch, Nittnaus, PITNAUER, PÖCKL, WINKLER-HERMADEN.

Blaufränkisch Lemberger in Germany, Kékfrankos in Hungary. Austria's top-potential red-grape variety, widely planted in MITTELBURGENLAND: good body and structure, peppery acidity, and aromas of eucalyptus and blackberries. Often blended with Cab Sauv. Best from P ACHS, Gesellmann, HEINRICH, Igler, KOLLWENZ, KRUTZLER, Nittnaus, PRIELER SCHIEFER, *TRIEBAUMER*, WENINGER.

Bouvier Indigenous aromatic grape, especially good for Beeren- and Trockenbeerenauslesen.

Bründlmayer, Willi r w sp ★★★★ 99 00 01 02 03 04 05 06 Outstanding Langenlois-KAMPTAL estate. Passionate innovator making excellent RIES, GRÜNER VELTLINER; top international styles, including CHARD. Also Austria's best Sekt.

Burgenland Province and wine region (14,564 ha) in the east bordering Hungary. Warm climate. Ideal conditions for red wines and especially botrytis wines near NEUSIEDLERSEE. Four areas: MITTELBURGENLAND, NEUSIEDLERSEE, NEUSIEDLERSEE-HÜGELLAND, SÜDBURGENLAND.

Buschenschank A wine tavern, often a HEURIGE country cousin.

Carnuntum r w Up-and-coming region southeast of VIENNA now showing good reds. Best: Glatzer, Grassl, G Markowitsch, Pitnauer, Netzl, Weingut Marko.

Chardonnay Both oaked and unoaked, often international in style. Known in STYRIA as MORILLON: strong fruit, lively acidity. Especially BRÜNDLMAYER, GROSS, LOIMER, Malat, KOLLWENTZ, POLZ, SATTLER, STIEGELMAR, TEMENT, VELICH, WIENINGER.

Deutschkreutz r (w) MITTELBURGENLAND red-wine area, especially for BLAUFRÄNKISCH.

Districtus Austriae Controllatus, DAC Austria's first appellation system, introduced in 2003. Similar to France's AC and Italy's DOC. There are currently four DACs: WEINVIERTEL, CARNUNTUM, MITTELBURGENLAND AND TRAISENTHAL.

Donauland (Danube) w (r) Wine region, just west of VIENNA. Includes KLOSTERNEUBURG south of Danube and WAGRAM north of the river. Mainly whites, especially GRÜNER VELTLINER.

Federspiel Medium quality level of the VINEA WACHAU categories, roughly corresponding to Kabinett. Fruity, elegant, dry wines.

Feiler-Artinger Burgenland r w sw ★★★ ·★★★★ 93 94 95 96 97 98 99 00 01 02 03 04 05 06 Outstanding RUST estate with top AUSBRUCH dessert wines. Also good dry whites and exciting red blends. Beautiful baroque house, too.

Freie Weingärtner Wachau w (r) ★★★ 94 95 96 97 98 99 04 05 06 Important growers' co-op in DURNSTEIN. Might now be improving after management problems. V. good GRÜNER VELTLINER and RIES. Domaine Wachau range.

Gemischter Satz A blend of grapes (mostly white) grown, harvested, and vinified together. Traditional wine, still served in HEURIGEN.

Gobelsburg, Schloss ★★★→★★★★ 01 02 03 04 05 06 Renowned KAMPTAL estate revitalized by Michael Moosbrugger. Excellent dry RIES and GRÜNER VELTLINER.

Gols r w dr sw Wine commune on north shore of NEUSIEDLERSEE in BURGENLAND. Top producers: P ACHS, Beck, GSELLMANN & HANS, HEINRICH, A&H Nittnaus, PITTNAUER, Preisinger, Renner, JURIS-STIEGELMAR.

Graf Hardegg r w ★★★ Top WEINVIERTEL estate steered by daring Peter Veyder Malberg, who introduced Austria's first Viognier and port-style Forticus. V. good Syrah, Pinot N and RIES.

Grüner Veltliner Austria's flagship white grape covering 37% of vineyards. Remarkably diverse: from lively spiced fruitiness in youth, to concentrated elegance with age. Best: *BRÜNDLMAYER, HIRTZBERGER,* Högl, KNOLL, LOIMER, MANTLER, NEUMAYER, NIGL, NIKOLAIHOF, OTT, PFAFFL, *FX PICHLER, PRAGER,* Schmelz.

G'spritzer Popular, refreshing summer drink, usually of white wine mixed with soda or mineral water. Especially in HEURIGEN.

Gumpoldskirchen w r dr sw Famous HEURIGE village south of VIENNA, centre of THERMENREGION. Distinctive, tasty, often sweet wines from ZIERFANDLER and ROTGIPFLER grapes. Best producers: Biegler, Spaetrot, Zierer.

Heinrich, Gernot r w dr sw ★★→★★★ 96 97 98 99 00 01 02 03 04 05 06 Top GOLS estate. Especially for Gabarinza and Salzberg labels. Modern winemaking with balance and structure.

Heinrich, Johann r w dr sw ★★★ Leading Mittelburgenland producer. V. good Blaufränkisch Goldberg Reserve.

Heurige Wine of the most recent harvest, called "new wine" for one year. Heurigen are wine taverns in which growers-cum-patrons serve their own wine with simple local food – a Viennese institution.

Hirtzberger, Franz w ★★★★ 95 96 97 98 99 00 01 02 03 04 05 06 Top Wachau producer with 20 ha at SPITZ AN DER DONAU. Fine dry RIES and *GRÜNER VELTLINER.*

Horitschon MITTELBURGENLAND region for reds: Anton Iby, WENINGER.

Illmitz w (r) dr sw SEEWINKEL region famous for Beeren- and Trockenbeeren- auslesen. Best from Angerhof, KRACHER, Martin Haider, Helmut Lang, Opitz.

Jamek, Josef w ★★ Well-known WACHAU estate with restaurant.

Jurtschitsch/Sonnhof w (r) dr (sw) ★★→★★★ 00 01 02 03 04 05 06 KAMPTAL estate run by three brothers: *v. good whites (RIES, GRÜNER VELTLINER, CHARD).*

Kamptal r w Wine region, along River Kamp north of WACHAU. Top vineyards: Langenlois, Strass, Zöbing. Best growers: Angerer, BRÜNDLMAYER, Dolle, Ehn, SCHLOSS GOBELSBURG, Hiedler, Hirsch, JURTSCHITSCH, LOIMER, Sax, Topf.

Kattus ★ Producer of traditional Sekt in VIENNA.

Kerschbaum ★★★ r Mittelburgenland Blaufränkisch specialist, idiosyncratic and often fascinating.

Klosterneuburg r w Main wine town of DONAULAND. Rich in tradition, with a famous Benedictine monastery and a wine college founded in 1860.

KMW Abbreviation for Klosterneuburger Mostwaage ("must level"), the unit used in Austria to measure the sugar content in grape juice.

Knoll, Emmerich w ★★★★ 97 98 99 00 01 02 03 04 05 06 Traditional, highly regarded estate in Loiben, WACHAU. Showpiece GRÜNER VELTLINER and RIES.

Kollwentz-Römerhof w r dr (sw) ★★→★★★ 95 96 97 98 99 00 01 02 03 04 05 06 Innovative producer near EISENSTADT: Sauv Bl, CHARD, Eiswein, v. good reds.

Kracher, Alois w (r) dr (sw) ★★★★ 94 95 96 97 98 99 00 01 02 03 04 05 06 Top-class ILLMITZ producer specializing in botryized PRÄDIKATS (dessert); some barrique-aged (Nouvelle Vague), others in steel (Zwischen den Seen); good reds since 1997. Now right back on top form.

Kremstal w (r) Wine region especially for GRÜNER VELTLINER and RIES. Top growers: Malat, NIGL, SALOMON, S MOSER, WEINGUT STADT KREMS.

Krutzler r ★★★ South Burgenland producer of outstanding Blaufränkisch, especially Perwolff.

Loimer, Fred (r) w ★★★→★★★★ innovative Kamptal producer with biodynamic 31-ha estate, 50% GRÜNER VELTLINER; also RIES, CHARD, Pinot Gr, v. good Pinot N.

Mantlerhof ★★★ Fine Kremstal producer with a well-considered, traditional approach. G Roter Veltliner.

Mittelburgenland r (w) dr (sw) Wine region on Hungarian border protected by three hill ranges. Makes large quantities of red (especially BLAUFRÄNKISCH). Producers: GSELLMANN, J HEINRICH, Iby, Igler, P Kerschbaum, WENINGER.

Morillon Name given in STYRIA to CHARD.

Moser, Lenz ★ Large producer near KREMS. Perfectly all right, but could be better.

Moser, Sepp ★★ Founded with original LENZ MOSER vineyards. RIES, GRÜNER VELTLINER, CHARD, and Sauv Bl are elegant, dry, and highly aromatic.

Muskateller Rare, aromatic grape for dry whites. Best from STYRIA and WACHAU. Top growers: Gross, HIRTZBERGER, Lackner-Tinnacher, FX PICHLER, POLZ, SATTLER.

Muskat-Ottonel Grape for fragrant, often dry whites, interesting PRÄDIKATS.

Neuburger Indigenous white grape with nutty flavour; mainly in the WACHAU (elegant, flowery), THERMENREGION (mellow and ample-bodied), and north BURGENLAND (strong, full). Best from Beck, FREIE WEINGÄRTNER, HIRTZBERGER.

Neumayer w ★★★ Top TRAISENTAL estate making powerful, pithy, dry GRÜNER VELTLINER and RIES.

Neumeister w ★★★ V. good innovative southeast Styrian producer, especially Sauv Bl and Chard.

Neusiedlersee (Lake Neusiedl) Very shallow BURGENLAND lake on Hungarian border. Warm temperatures and autumn mists encourage botrytis. Gives name to wine territories of NEUSIEDLERSEE and NEUSIEDLERSEE-HÜGELLAND.

Neusiedlersee r w dr sw Wine region north and east of Lake Neusiedl. Best growers: ACHS, Beck, HEINRICH, KRACHER, Nittnaus, OPITZ, PÖCKL, UMATHUM, VELICH.

Neusiedlersee-Hügelland r w dr sw Wine region west of NEUSIEDLERSEE based around Oggau, RUST, and Mörbisch on the lake shores, and EISENSTADT in the Leitha Mts foothills. Best producers: FEILER-ARTINGER, KOLLWENTZ, Prieler, Schandl, SCHRÖCK, Sommer, ERNST TRIEBAUMER, WENZEL.

Niederösterreich (Lower Austria) With 58% of Austria's vineyards: CARNUNTUM, DONAULAND, KAMPTAL, KREMSTAL, THERMENREGION, TRAISENTAL, WACHAU, WEINVIERTEL.

Nigl ★★★ w 94 95 96 97 98 99 00 01 02 03 04 05 06 The best in KREMSTAL, making sophisticated dry ageworthy RIES and GRÜNER VELTLINER from Senftenberg vineyard.

Nikolaihof w ★★★ 97 98 99 00 01 02 03 04 05 06 Built on Roman foundations, this biodynamic WACHAU estate produces focused RIES from the Steiner Hund site.

Nittnaus, John r sw ★★★ Searching, organic Neusiedlersee winemaker. Especially elegant and ageworthy reds.

Pfaffl ★★★ 97 98 99 00 01 02 03 04 05 06 WEINVIERTEL estate near VIENNA, in Stetten. Known for wonderful dry GRÜNER VELTLINER (Goldjoch) and RIES (Terrassen Sonnleiten). Also runs nearby Schlossweingut Bockfliess estate.

Pichler, Franz Xavier w ★★★★ 93 94 95 96 97 98 99 00 01 02 03 04 05 06 Top WACHAU producer and one of Austria's best. Very intense, rich RIES and GRÜNER VELTLINER (especially Kellerberg).

Pichler, Rudi ★★★→★★★★ Fine Wachau producer of powerful, expressive RIES and Grüner Veltliner.

Pöckl, Josef & René r (sw) ★★ Father-and-son team in NEUSIEDLERSEE (Mönchhof), each making red gems, especially Admiral, Reve de Jeunesse, and Rosso e Nero. Also good Pinot N and Zweigelt.

Polz, Erich & Walter w ★★★ 93 95 96 97 98 99 00 01 02 03 04 05 06 V. good south STYRIAN (Weinstrasse) growers; especially Hochgrassnitzberg: Sauv Bl, CHARD, Grauburgunder, WEISSBURGUNDER.

Prädikat, Prädikatswein Quality-graded wines from Spätlese upwards (Spätlese, Auslese, Eiswein, Strohwein, Beerenauslese, AUSBRUCH, and Trockenbeerenauslese). See Germany.

Prager, Franz w ★★★★ 99 00 01 02 03 04 05 06 Estate now run by Anton Bodenstein; world-class outstanding RIES and GRÜNER VELTLINER.

Ried Single vineyard.

Riesling On its own, this always means Rhine RIESLING. WELSCHRIESLING is unrelated Top growers: ALZINGER, BRÜNDLMAYER, HIRTZBERGER, Högl, KNOLL, NIGL, NIKOLAIHOF, PFAFFL FX PICHLER, PRAGER, SALOMON.

Rotgipfler *Fragrant, indigenous grape* of *THERMENREGION*. With ZIERFANDLER, makes lively, interesting wine. Especially Biegler, Spaetrot, Stadlmann, Zierer.

Rust w r dr sw BURGENLAND region, famous since 17th C for dessert AUSBRUCH; now also for red and dry white. Especially from FEILER-ARTINGER, Schandl, HEIDI SCHRÖCK, ERNST TRIEBAUMER, Paul Triebaumer, WENZEL.

St Laurent Traditional red grape, v. good potential; possibly related to Pinot N Especially from Fischer, Johanneshof, PITTNAUER, R Schuster, UMATHUM.

Salomon-Undhof w ★★★ V. good KREMS producer: RIES, WEISSBURGUNDER, Traminer

Sattler, Willi w ★★→★★★ 97 98 99 00 01 02 03 04 05 06 Top south STYRIA grower Especially for Sauv Bl, MORILLON with forceful signature.

Schilcher Rosé wine from indigenous Blauer Wildbacher grapes (sharp, dry high acidity). A local taste, or at least an acquired one. Speciality of west STYRIA. Try: Klug, Lukas, Reiterer, Strohmeier.

Schloss Halbturn w r sw ★★→★★★ Recently revitalized estate now creating increasingly beautiful wines with the help of a German and a French winemaker. Especially cuvée Imperial, Pinot N.

Schlumberger Largest sparkling winemaker in Austria (VIENNA); wine is bottle-fermented by unique "Méthode Schlumberger".

Schmelz w ★★→★★★ rising Wachau producer, especially outstanding Riesl Dürnsteiner Freiheit.

Schröck w sw r ★★★→★★★★ Beautiful wines of great purity and focus from an innovative, thoughtful grower. First-class AUSBRUCH.

Seewinkel ("lake corner") Name given to the part of NEUSIEDLERSEE including Apetlon, ILLMITZ, and Podersdorf. Ideal conditions for botrytis.

Smaragd Highest-quality category of VINEA WACHAU, similar to dry Spätlese.

Spätrot-Rotgipfler Typical, two-grape blend of THERMENREGION.

Spitz an der Donau w Cool WACHAU microclimate, especially from Singerriede vineyard. Top growers are: HIRTZBERGER, Högl, Lagler.

Steinfeder VINEA WACHAU quality category for light, fragrant, dry wines.

Styria Steiermark Southernmost wine region of Austria. Some good dry whites, especially Sauv Bl. Including SÜDSTEIERMARK, SÜD-OSTSTEIERMARK, WESTSTEIERMARK (South, Southeast, West Styria).

Südburgenland r w Small south BURGENLAND wine region: good red wines. Best producers: Krutzler, Wachter-Wiesler, Schiefer.

Süd-Oststeiermark SE Styria w (r) STYRIAN region with islands of excellent vineyards. Best producers: Neumeister, Winkler-Hermaden.

Südsteiermark S Styria w Best wine region of STYRIA; makes very popular whites (MORILLON, MUSKATELLER, WELSCHRIESLING, and Sauv Bl). Best: Gross, Jaunegg, Lackner-Tinnacher, POLZ, Potzinger Sabathi, SATTLER, Skoff, TEMENT, Wohlmuth.

Tement, Manfred w ★★★ 97 98 99 00 01 02 03 04 05 06 Renowned south STYRIA estate with beautifully made Steirische Klassik and gently oaked Sauv Bl and MORILLON from Zieregg site. International-style wines, modern reds.

Thermenregion r w d sw Wine/hot-springs region, south of VIENNA. Indigenous grapes (*e.g.* ZIERFANDLER, ROTGIPFLER) and good reds (especially ST LAURENT) from Baden, GUMPOLDSKIRCHEN, Tattendorf, Traiskirchen areas. Producers: Alphart, Biegler, Fischer, Johanneshof, Schafler, Stadelmann, Zierer.

Traisental 700 ha just south of KREMS on Danube. Dry whites can be similar to WACHAU in style, not usually in quality. Top producers: Huber, NEUMAYER.

Triebaumer, Ernst r (w) dr sw ★★★ **97 98 99** 00 **01 02 03** 04 05 06 RUST producer; some of Austria's best reds: BLAUFRÄNKISCH (Mariental), Cab Sauv/Merlot blend. V. good AUSBRUCH. One of several Triebaumers – known as ET.

Umathum, Josef w r dr sw ★★★ V. good and thoughtful NEUSIEDLERSEE producer. V. good reds including Pinot N, ST LAURENT; good whites.

Velich w sw NEUSIEDLERSEE ★★★★ Excellent Burgundian-style Tiglat CHARD (**99** 00 01 02 03) with fine barrel-ageing. Some of top PRÄDIKATS in the SEEWINKEL.

Vienna w (r) ("Wien" in German and on labels) Wine region in suburbs. Generally simple, lively wines, served to busloads of tourists in HEURIGEN, but quality producers on the rise: Christ, WIENINGER, Zahel.

Vinea Wachau WACHAU appellation started by winemakers in 1983 with three categories of dry wine: STEINFEDER, FEDERSPIEL, and the powerful SMARAGD.

Wachau w World-renowned Danube region, home to some of Austria's best wines. Top producers: Alzinger, FREIE WEINGÄRTNER WACHAU, HIRTZBERGER, Högl, JAMEK, KNOLL, Lagler, NIKOLAIHOF, FX PICHLER, R Pichler, PRAGER, Schmelz, Tegernseerhof, Wess.

Weinviertel ("Wine Quarter") w (r) Largest Austrian wine region, between Danube and Czech border. First, and so far only, to adopt DAC appellation status. Mostly refreshing whites, especially from Poysdorf, Retz. Best: Bauer, J Diem, GRAF HARDEGG, Gruber, PFAFFL, Schwarzböck, Weinrieder, Zull.

> ### Going Out
> Austria's very active wine culture ranges from a modest local inn (a "Heurige") to grand gourmet temples. Try the entire range: if you can get a recommendation for a Heurige that is not overrun by busloads of tourists, a late summer's afternoon with a glass of simple Welschriesling and some rustic food can be a great delight.

Weissburgunder Pinot Bl. Ubiquitous: good dry wines and PRÄDIKATS. Especially Beck, Fischer, Gross, HEINRICH, HIRTZBERGER, Lackner-Tinnacher, POLZ, TEMENT.

Welschriesling White grape, not related to RIES, grown in all wine regions: light, fragrant, young-drinking dry wines and good PRÄDIKATS.

Weninger, Franz r (w) ★★★ Top MITTELBURGENLAND (Horitschon) estate, with fine reds, especially BLAUFRÄNKISCH, Merlot.

Wenzel w r sw ★★★ V. good AUSBRUCH and now v. good reds, too. Michael's father Robert pioneered the Furmint revival in RUST.

Weststeiermark W Styria p Small wine region specializing in SCHILCHER. Best from Domaine Müller, Klug, Lukas, Reiterer, Strohmeier.

Wien See VIENNA.

Wieninger, Fritz w r ★★•★★★ 00 03 04 05 06 V. good VIENNA-Stammersdorf grower with HEURIGE: CHARD, BLAUER BURGUNDER, especially good GRÜNER VELTLINER and RIES.

Winkler-Hermaden r w sw ★★★ Outstanding and individual southeast Styrian producer, excellent Traminer and Morillon, also one of the region's few v. good reds, the Zweigelt-based Olivin.

Zierfandler (Spätrot) White variety almost exclusive to THERMENREGION. Often blended with ROTGIPFLER. Best: Biegler, Spaetrot, Stadelmann, Zierer.

Central & Southeast Europe

More heavily shaded areas are the wine-growing regions

Hungary

Hungary is the historic leader of wine culture in Central Europe, with its single great classic region, Tokaji. A new star was needed in all these countries in the 1990s, after the fall of Communism. They are just beginning to emerge into the modern world. Hungary's new system of wine regions is now in place. There are seven of them: Balaton, Duna, Eger, Észak-Dunántúl, Pannon, Sopron, and Tokaj-Hegylja, and they are divided into wine districts. Sopron has no sub-divisions, nor does Tokaji.

Alföld (Duna) Hungary's Great Plain: much everyday wine, some better Incorporates three wine districts: HAJÓS-Baja (Brillant Holding, Koch, Sümegi) Csongrád (Bokrosi, Gulyás, Somodi, Takács), KUNSÁG (Font, Frittmann).

Árvay & Co TOKAJ cellar established in 2000 and headed by former DISZNÓKŐ winemaker János Árvay. ASZÚ (5/6 PUTTONYOS) and *cuvée* Edés Élet, Hétfürtös.

Ászár-Neszmély Wine region in northwest Hungary near the Danube International and native grapes. Hilltop is leading winery (Kamocsay).

Aszú Botrytis-shrivelled grapes and the sweet wine made from them in TOKAJ similar to Sauternes. The wine is graded in sweetness, from 3 PUTTONYOS up.

Aszú Eszencia Tokaj sw ★★★★ 93 96 99 Second TOKAJ quality (see ESZENCIA). 7 PUTTONYOS-plus; should be superb amber elixir, like celestial butterscotch.

Badacsony w dr sw ★★→★★★ Wine district on the north shore of Lake BALATON, home to the native variety KÉKNYELŰ. The basalt soil can give rich, highly flavoured white wines; well-made Ries and SZÜRKEBARÁT have fine mineral flavours. The leader is SZEREMLEY's Szent Orbán winery.

Balaton Hungary's inland sea, Europe's largest freshwater lake. Many good wines take its name. On the northern side are Jásdi Figula, Pántlika, Salánki, and Tamás.

Balatonboglár r w dr sw ★★→★★★ Name of wine district and also a progressive winery owned by Henkell & Söhnlein on south shore of Lake BALATON in Dél-Balaton region. Decent whites (Chard, Sem, Muscat). Also cuve close sparkling. Other producers: Konyári, Katona, Légli, Garamvári, and St Donatus.

Bikavér Eger r ★ "Bull's Blood", historic red wine of EGER: at best full-bodied and well-balanced, but highly variable in export versions today. Now under supervision to protect identity and improve quality (see EGER). Mostly from KÉKFRANKOS, Cab Sauv, Cab Fr, Portugieser, Merlot. Also made in SZEKSZÁRDI BIKAVÉR, where it is based on Kadarka.

Bock, József Family winemaker in VILLÁNY. Hearty reds, both varietal and blends.

Bor "Wine": vörös is red; fehér is white; asztali is table; táj is country, a section of the market that is currently growing.

Dégenfeld, Grof Large TOKAJ estate. Traditional-style wines, plus dry FURMINT.

Disznókő Important first-class TOKAJ estate, owned by French company AXA. The Sauternes-style wines of the early years have given way to a more typically Hungarian note, imparted by a Hungarian, instead of Sauternais, winemaker.

Dobogó Fine small Tokaj estate for ASZÚ

Édes Sweet wine (but not as luscious as ASZÚ).

Eger r w dr sw ★→★★★ Best-known red-wine centre of north Hungary; Baroque city of cellars full of BIKAVÉR. Fresh LEÁNYKA (perhaps its best product), OLASZRIZLING, Chard, Cab Sauv. Top producers: Vilmos Thummerer (consistent BIKAVÉR), Tibor Gál, GIA, Tamás Pók, Ostoros Bor, Béla Vincze, Demeter, Gundel Cellar, and the huge Egervin.

Eszencia ★★★★ The fabulous quintessence of TOKAJ: intensely sweet and aromatic from grapes wizened by botrytis. Properly grape juice of very low, if any, alcoholic strength, reputed to have miraculous properties: raising the dead, and the like. Its sugar content can be over 850 g per litre.

Etyek-Buda (Észak-Dunántúl) Wine region near Budapest. Source of modern-style wines, especially Chard and Sauv Bl. Leading producers: TÖRLEY, Vinarium, Etyeki Kúria, Nyakashegy, György Villa.

Ezerjó Literally "thousand blessings". Widespread traditional grape variety. In MÓR, makes one of the country's top dry whites (especially from István Bozóky), besides Frittman Bro Ezerjó from Soltvadkert. Has great potential: fragrant, with hint of grapefruit.

François President Sparkling-wine brand. Vintage President very drinkable.

Furmint The classic grape of TOKAJ, with great flavour, acidity, and fire, also grown for table wine in Tokaj at Lake BALATON and in SOMLÓ.

Gere, Attila Family winemaker in VILLÁNY with good, forward-looking reds, especially oak-aged Cab Sauv (00) and Cuvée Phoenix (00).

Gundel TOKAJ venture at MÁD, making wines for famous Gundel's restaurant in Budapest. Also vineyards and cellar at EGER.

Hajós Pincék (Duna) Charming village in on River Danube with 1,500 cellars. Mostly traditional, family production. Some quality lighter red wines.

Hárslevelü "Linden-leaved" grape variety used at Debrö and as second grape of TOKAJ. Gentle, mellow wine; peach aroma.

Helvécia (Kecskemét) (Duna) Historic ALFÖLD cellars. Vineyards ungrafted: phylloxera bugs cannot negotiate sandy soil. Whites and rosés modernist; reds traditional.

Hétszőlő Noble first-growth 47-ha TOKAJ estate owned by Grands Millésimes de France and Japanese Suntory. Second label, from purchased grapes: Dessewffy. Fordítás is halfway to ASZÚ in style.

Hilltop Neszmély (Észak-Dunántúl) Winery in ÁSZÁR-NESZMÉLY makes international-style wines, including Review and Woodcutters White from Cserszegi Fuszeres hybrid.

Kadarka Traditional red grape in south, but can produce ample flavour and interesting maturity. Considered by some an essential element of BIKAVÉR.

Kékfrankos Hungarian for Blaufränkisch; reputedly related to Gamay. Most widely planted red variety. Good light or full-bodied reds.

Kéknyelű "Blue stalk". High-flavoured, low-yielding white grape making the best and "stiffest" wine of Mt BADACSONY. Best is flowery and spicy stuff.

Királyudvar Promising TOKAJ winery in old royal cellars at Tarcal. Wines include dry and late-harvest FURMINT, Cuvee Ilona (early-bottled ASZÚ) and Jégbor (Eiswein).

Kunság (Duna) Largest region in ALFÖLD. Good KADARKA especially from Kiskörös. Izsák appellation is special for its Walton-brand sparkling wine. Also Frittmann Bros, Font.

Leányka "Little girl". Native Hungarian white grape. Admirable, aromatic, light, dry wine. Királyleányka ("Royal") is a different variety and supposedly superior.

Mád Old commercial centre of the TOKAJI region. Growers include Vince Gergely, GUNDEL, József Monyok, ROYAL TOKAJI, SZEPSY.

Mátra (Eger) w (r) ★★ District in foothills of Mátra range. Promising, dry SZÜRKEBARÁT (Pinot Gr), Chard, MUSKOTÁLY, Sauv Bl. Foreign investment. Szőke Mátyás and Szőlőskert producers are worth a mention.

Megyer, Château TOKAJ estate bought by Jean-Louis Laborde of Château Clinet in Pomerol. Also owns Château PAJZOS. Megyer is the lighter wine. Quality is fair.

Mézes Mály In TARCAL. This and SZARVAS are historically the best vineyards of TOKAJ.

Minőségi Bor Quality wine. Hungary's *appellation contrôlée* (see France).

Mór (Észak-Dunántúl) N Hungary w ★★→★★★ Region long-famous for fresh, dry EZERJÓ. Now also Ries and Sauv Bl. Wines now mostly exported. István Bozóky is noteworthy.

Muskotály Muscat; usually Ottonel. Muscat Bl à Petits Grains is Muscat Lunel. Makes light, but long-lived wine in TOKAJ and EGER. A little goes into the TOKAJ blend. Very occasionally makes a wonderful ASZÚ wine solo.

Olaszrizling Hungarian name for the Italian Ries or Welschriesling. Better examples can have a burnt-almond aroma.

Oremus Ancient TOKAJ vineyard of founding Rakóczi family, owned by Spain's Vega Sicilia with HQ at Tolcsva. *First-rate ASZÚ*. Also a lesser TOKAJ grape.

Pajzos, Château Bordeaux-owned TOKAJ estate with some fine ASZÚ. See MEGYER

Pécs (Pannon) Mecsek w (r) ★→★★ Newly renamed wine district in southern Hungary, based around the city of Pécs. Known for good whites (sparkling, OLASZRIZLING, Pinot Bl).

Puttonyos Measure of sweetness in TOKAJ ASZÚ. A "puttony" is a 25-kg measure, traditionally a hod of grapes. The number of "putts" per barrel (136 litres) of dry base wine or must determines the final richness of the wine, from 3 putts to 6 (3 putts = 60 g of sugar per litre, 4 = 90 g, 5 = 120 g, 6 = 150 g, 7 = 180 g). See also ASZÚ ESZENCIA and ESZENCIA.

Royal Tokaji Wine Co Pioneer Anglo-Danish-Hungarian venture at MÁD

81 ha, mainly first- or second-growth. First wine (90) a revelation: 91 and (especially) 93 led renaissance of TOKAJ. 99, 00 03 to follow. (I am a co-founder.)

Siklós (Pannon) City in southern Hungary; part of VILLÁNY district. Mainly small producers, known for whites: especially HÁRSLEVELŰ. Ripe, fruity Chard promising; also TRAMINI, OLASZRIZLING.

Somló N Hungary w ★★★ Isolated small district north of BALATON: whites (formerly of high repute) from FURMINT and Juhfark ("sheep's tail") in both traditional barrel-fermented and fresh, fruity styles. Top producers include Fekete, Györgykovács, Inhauser, Tornai.

Sopron W Hungary r ★★→★★★ Historic enclave south of Neusiedlersee (see Austria). Traditionally known for lighter reds like KÉKFRANKOS and sweet wines, but showing promise for whites such as Sauv Bl. Top producer Weininger, promising Ivancsics, Jandl, Lővér, Pfneiszl, Szita, Taschner.

Szamorodni Literally "as it was born"; describes TOKAJ not sorted in the vineyard. Dry or (fairly) sweet, depending on proportion of ASZÚ grapes naturally present. Sold as an apéritif. In vintage TOKAJ ASZÚ years, the sweet style can offer some ASZÚ character at much less cost.

Száraz Dry, especially of TOKAJ SZAMORODNI.

Szarvas TOKAJ vineyard at Tarcal; a top site. Solely owned by TOKAJ TRADING HOUSE and state-run Research Institute for Vine and Wine.

Szekszárd (Pannon) r ★★→★★★ District in south central Hungary; some of country's top reds from KÉKFRANKOS, Cab Sauv, Cab Fr, and Merlot. Also KADARKA which needs age (3–4 years); can also be botrytized ("Nemes Kadar"). Look out for Dúzsi, Fritz, Heiman, Liszt Pincészet, Mészáros, Ribling, Sárosdi, Sebestyén, Szent Gaál Pincészet, Takler, Vesztergombi, and Vida.

Szepsy, István Legendary name and *impeccable small production of long-ageing TOKAJ ASZÚ*. Same family name as the man who created the ASZÚ method in 17th-C, though not related.

Szeremley, Huba *Leader in BADACSONY.* Ries, SZÜRKEBARÁT, KÉKNYELŰ, ZEUSZ are modern models. Fine KÉKFRANKOS. Szent Orbán is another label.

Szürkebarát Literally "Grey Monk": Pinot Gr. Source of sweet tourist wines from BALATON. But this is one of the best: wait for great dry wines.

Tarcal TOKAJ commune with two great first growths and several good producers: Királyudvar, Andrássy Kúria, Gróf Degenfeld.

Tiffán, Ede (Pannon) VILLÁNY grower: full-bodied, oaked reds.

Tokaj w dr sw ★★→★★★★★ Tokaj is the town; Tokay or Tokaji is the wine. Appellation covers 5,967 ha. See ★★, ESZENCIA, FURMINT, PUTTONYOS, SZAMORODNI. Also dry table wine of character.

Tokajbor-Bene New TOKAJ cellar at Bodrogkeresztúr. To watch.

Tokaj Trading House Formerly state-owned TOKAJ company, now reduced to 55 ha inc the magnificent SZARVAS vineyard. Also called Crown Estates. Castle Island is the brand for dry wines. Quality improving; delicious late harvest.

Tolcsva-Bor Kft (Tokaj) Good late harvest wines, and the 5 puttonyos aszú is worth considering.

Törley Large company (previously Hungarovin) international varietals (Chard, Cab Sauv, Merlot), also *cuve close*, transfer, and classic sparkling. Owned by German sekt specialist Henkell.

Tramini Gewürztraminer, especially in SIKLÓS.

Védett eredetű bor Appellation of Origin Controlled wine.

Villány (Pannon) Southern wine region with two main towns. Villány makes mostly red, often good-quality Bordeaux styles. Siklós makes mostly white. High-quality producers: BOCK, Csányi, GERE, Günzer, Jekl, Malatinzky,

Mayer, Polgár, TIFFÁN, Wunderlich, Vylyan.

Zemplén Ridge (TR) Or Zemplén Hegyhát. A less concentrated TOKAJ for younger drinkers. First vintage was 02. Couldn't they just dilute to taste?

Zéta A cross of Bouvier and FURMINT used by some in ASZÚ production.

Bulgaria

Bulgaria's climate and soil are perfect for vines, but until recently neglect and poor management of vineyards hindered quality wine production. Finally the link between well-kept vineyards and good wine has been accepted by new and established winemakers.

Assenovgrad r ★→★★ Cellar near PLOVDIV; ageworthy MAVRUD and RUBIN.

Bessa Valley ★★★ Exciting new winery near Pazardjik. Started by Bordeaux specialist Count Stephan von Neipperg and Karl-Heinz Hauptmann. 135 ha planted with Merlot, Syrah, Petit Verdot, Cab Sauv. Enira label.

Blueridge r w ★→★★ Major Domaine Boyar winery, label.

Burgas w p (r) ★ Easy whites, good young reds, nice rosé (a speciality) from this Black Sea port area.

Controliran Like France's AC. Wine law published in 2000, updated in 2004.

Damianitsa r★★→★★★ Quality-soaring winery specializing in MELNIK grape.

DGO "Quality wines with declared geographical origin".

Dimiat Native white grape. Good examples from BLUERIDGE and POMORIE.

Domaine Boyar Major exporter to UK. Has its own vineyards and wineries in Bulgaria.

Eduardo Miroglio Italian investor with own vineyards.

Gamza Red grape (Kadarka of Hungary) with potential, mainly from Danube region. NOVO SELO, and PLEVEN are specialists.

Haskovo r (w) ★ Thracian Plain winery specializing in Merlot.

Khan Krum Good whites, especially Chard. Now owned by Chateau Rossenovo.

Korten Boutique cellar of DOMAINE BOYAR favouring traditional winemaking styles.

Logodaj New winery at Blagoevgrad. Good Soetto Cab Fr **05**. One to watch.

Mavrud Considered the best indigenous red variety, very popular at home. Can make highly ageworthy, dark, plummy wines, only grown in the south.

Melnik Southwest village and highly prized grape variety grown throughout Struma Valley. Dense reds that can age up to 20 years.

Menada Stara Zagora r Thracian Plain winery, owned by France's Belvedere group. Reserve Cab Sauv and Merlot **03**.

Misket Indigenous grape, mildly aromatic. The basis for most country whites. Sungurlare and Karlovo in the Valley of the Roses are specialists.

Novo Selo Good red GAMZA from the northwest.

Oriachovitza r ★★ Winery owned by Belvedere SA. Also Thracian Plain area for CONTROLIRAN Cab Sauv and Merlot. **_Good Reserve Cab Sauv_**. Richly fruity reds at their best after 4–5 years.

Pamid Light, soft, everyday red in southeast and northwest.

Peruschtitza r Reds-only winery near PLOVDIV. Especially MAVRUD, Cab Sauv, RUBIN.

Pleven Cellar for PAMID, GAMZA, Cab Sauv. Wine research station in Pleven.

Plovdiv City in south; source of good Cab Sauv and MAVRUD. Many Bulgarian oenologists study at the university's Food Technology Dept.

Pomorie w (r) ★Black Sea winery. Especially good Chard and MUSKAT.

Preslav w ★ Large cellar in Black Sea region. Good brandy.

Riesling Rhine Ries is grown, but Italian (Welschriesling; no relation), used for medium and dry whites, dominates.

Rubin Bulgarian cross (Nebbiolo x Syrah); good in blends, but gaining favour in single-varietal niche wines.

Sakar Southeast area with some of Bulgaria's best Merlot.

Santa Sarah ★★ Premium wine brand for fine Cab Sauv, Merlot.

Shumen w r ★ New World-style reds and especially whites from Black Sea-region winery. Good Traminer, popular on home market.

Sliven, Vini r (w) ★★ Thracian Valley winery for Merlot, MISKET, and Chard. Promising barrique-aged Cab Sauv.

Svishtov r (w) ★★ Winery on Danube, renamed Stork's Nest Estates by international owners. Some well-balanced Cab Sauv.

Targovishte w ★ Winery in east. Quality Chard, Sauv Bl, and Traminer.

Telish r Innovative winery in north. Quality Cab Sauv and Merlot.

Terra Tangra r w Newcomer based in the southeast at Harmanli, a good area, and with considerable investment it has produced encouraging first results.

Todoroff Thracian-region high-profile winery (25 ha): Cab Sauv, MAVRUD, Merlot.

Traminer Fine whites with hints of spice. Most popular white in Bulgaria.

Villa Lyubimets New label, vineyard in southeast near Greek-Turkish borders. Mainly reds. Villa Hissar is sister white label.

Vinimpex A major exporter of Bulgarian wines, part of Belvedere group.

Yambol r w ★ Winery in Thracian Plain, specializing in Cab Sauv and Merlot.

Slovenia

Most Slovenian wine is drunk in Slovenia. Goriška Brda, the most forward-thinking district in Slovenia, also has the largest share of internationally established producers. Vintages do not vary greatly, and whites are generally a notch above reds.

Batič ★★ Increasingly organic vineyard in VIPAVA. Top wine: Chard; others also very good.

Bjana ★★ Top GORIŠKA BRDA sparkling producer. Intense, full-bodied wines.

Curin ★★ Legendary pioneer of private wine-growing from early 1970s onwards. Varietal whites and PREDIKATS of very high standards especially top label Pravino ★★★.

Cviček Locally very popular traditional pink blend of POSAVSKI. Low alcohol, high acid. Decent quality from co-op Krško, premium by Frelih (Cviček od fare).

Dveri-Pax ★★★ Excellent, relatively new company based on vineyards that, until Communism, belonged to Benedictine monks. Top wines E (Ries) and Admont (white blend). Recent staff changes may take a toll.

Goriška Brda PRIMORSKI district. Many very good producers, among them BJANA Blažič, Četrtič, Erzetič, JAKONČIČ, Kabaj, Klinec, Klinec, MOVIA, Prinčič, SIMČIČ, Ščurek, Stekar, etc. Slovenia's largest co-op of the same name produces several brands: Bagueri ★★★, Quercus ★★ (REBULA and Cab Sauv). Super-premium red and white blends A+ (★★★).

Istenič ★→★★★ Sparkling wines of all types and prices. NV Barbara and Miha are good value, while Gourmet vintage range is often Slovenia's best.

Izbor Auslese (see PREDIKAT, and box on German quality levels, p.124).

Jagodni izbor Beerenauslese (see PREDIKAT, and box on p.124).

Jakončič ★★★ Improving GORIŠKA BRDA producer. Top wines are red, white, and sparkling Carolina. Varietals lighter, but not to be missed, e.g. MALVAZIJA 05.

Joannes ★★ Fine winery near Maribor. Crisp, well-defined whites, increasingly good MODRI PINOT. Interesting experiments with glass stoppers.

Kogl ★★★ Hilltop winery near Ormož, dating back to 16th C. Replanted 1984. Whites among Slovenia's best, either varietal (since 04 named Mea Culpa) or Duo, Trio, and Quartet blends. Reds since 00. Premium blends (red and white) Magna Domenica. Exceptionally delicate PREDIKATS. Repays ageing.

Koper PRIMORSKI coastal district, known for REFOŠK. SANTOMAS and VINAKOPER excel.

Constantly improving MALAVAZIJA.

Kras PRIMORSKI district. Several TERAN producers. Inc Čotar, Lisjak Boris, RENČEL. Remarkable improvements with whites, especially MALAVAZIJA, also Vitovska.

Kupljen Jože ★★★ Dry wine pioneer near Ormož. Pinot N labelled Modri Burgundec; in better years POZNA TRGATEV. Premium red and white Star of Stiria.

Laški Rizling Welschriesling. Slovenia's most planted variety, but now in decline.

Ledeno vino Icewine. Only in exceptional years and can be sublime.

Ljutomer ★→★★ Traditionally top wine district with neighbouring Ormož. Co-op called Ljutomerčan will see better times: vineyards among Slovenia's best.

Malvazija Slightly bitter yet generous flavour, which goes very well with seafood. *M by VINAKOPER is incredible value*. Also very good from Pucer, Rojac. In recent years successfully grown in GORIŠKA BRDA and KRAS.

Mlečnik ★★★ Disciple of Italy's Joško Gravner from VIPAVA. The closest anyone in Slovenia comes to organics.

Modra Frankinja Austria's Blaufränkisch. Fruity reds mostly in POSAVSKI, best as Metliška črnina by the Metlika co-op in the Bela krajina district.

Movia ★★★★ Best-known Slovenian winery. Releases only mature vintages of its top wines: Veliko Rdeče (red) after 6 years and Belo (white) after 4. Varietals usually very good. New Lunar (REBULA) from 05 and sparkling PURO.

Ormož ★→★★ Top wine district with neighbouring Ljutomer. Co-op named Jeruzalem Ormož. Premium brand Holermuos.

Podravski Traditionally most respected Slovenian region in the northeast. Recent comeback with aromatic whites and increasingly fine reds, mostly Modri Pinot.

Posavski Conservative wine region in the southeast, best known for CVIČEK. Quality producers starting to emerge: look for ISTENIČ, PRUS, Šěkoranja.

Pozna trgatev Late harvest. See PREDIKAT.

Predikat Wines made of botrytis-affected grapes with high sugar content. Term is taken from the German tradition and is used mostly in the PODRAVSKI region as POZNA TRGATEV, IZBOR, JAGODNI IZBOR, SUHI JAGODNI IZBOR, LEDENO VINO.

Primorski Region in the southwest from the Adriatic to GORIŠKA BRDA. The most forward-looking Slovenian wine region for both reds and whites.

Prus Recent star from the Bela Krajina district in POSAVSKI. Best known for PREDIKATS, also very good reds.

Ptujska klet ★→★★ Winery in Ptuj with a collection of vintages from 1917. Recent vintages less notable, but the 80s were fantastic (and still great value).

Radgonske Gorice ★→★★ District near Austrian border, and co-op home to Radgonska Penina, Slovenia's best-known sparkling. Vintage Zlata (golden) is drier and fuller, also ages well; NV Srebrna (silver) often off-dry. Also very popular sweet TRAMINEC and white blend Janževec by Kapela.

Rebula Traditional white variety of GORIŠKA BRDA. Can be exceptional.

Refošk Italy's Refosco. Dark, acidic red; oaked and unoaked. Best: SANTOMAS.

Renčel ★★★★ Outstanding producer of TERAN (tiny quantities); also good whites.

Renski Rizling Ries. PODRAVSKI only. Best: JOANNES, ORMOŽ, KOGL, KUPLEN, Skaza Anton.

Santomas ★★★ KOPER. Good mature REFOŠK and international-style Cab Sauv.

Sauvignonasse White grape in GORIŠKA BRDA until 03 known as TOKAJ. Some believe it may become the most exciting grape in GORIŠKA BRDA.

Ščurek ★★→★★★ Very reliable GORIŠKA BRDA producer (Chard, REBULA, Tokaj, Sauv Bl, Cab Fr). Very particular red (02) and white blends (04) Stara brajda and classy white Dugo. Since 02 excellent premium red blend Up.

Simčič Edi ★★★ Highly reputed GORIŠKA BRDA producer. In particular look for Chard, REBULA, SIVI PINOT. Outstanding red blend Duet Lex 02 (Lex replacing outlawed term "reserva").

Simčič Marjan ★★★★ Excellent GORIŠKA BRDA producer (Chard, SIVI PINOT). REBULAbased blend Teodor is outstanding. A particular gem is Sauv Bl. Exceptional Modri Pinot. In selected years heavenly sweet Leonardo from dried grapes.

Sivi Pinot Italy's Pinot Gr. Increasingly fine, fruity, yet full-bodied wine.

Steyer ★★ Top name from RADGONSKE GORICE. Best known for TRAMINEC, recently also very good Chard, RENSKI RIZLING, SIVI PINOT.

Šturm ★★★★ Long-established, yet lone star of the Bela Krajina district in POSAVSKI. In recent years not as outstanding.

Šuhi jagodni izbor Trockenbeerenauslese (see p.135).

Teran REFOŠK from KRAS. Locally the most popular Slovenian wine after CVIČEK.

Tokaj Italy's Tocai Friulano grape in GORIŠKA BRDA. In 04 and 05 widely rebranded as Tocaj, re-rebranded as SAUVIGNONASSE (aka Chile's Sauvignon Vert) since 06.

Traminec Gewurz, only in PODRAVSKI. Generally sweet – also as PREDIKAT.

Valdhuber ★★★ Dry wine pioneers in PODRAVSKI. Top wine is (dry) TRAMINEC.

Vinag ★→★★ One of largest co-ops in Slovenia, with HQ and immense cellars in Maribor. Many older vintage PREDIKATS. Recently shaky.

Vinakoper ★★★ Large company with own vineyards in KOPER. Many very good varietals: Chard, MALVAZIJA, Muscat (dry and sweet), Cab Sauv, REFOŠK. Premium brands: Capo d'Istria (varietals), Capris (blends).

Vipava ★→★★ PRIMORSKI district. Many fine producers: BATIČ, Lisjak Radivoj, MLEČNIK, Sutor, Tilia. Co-op of same name with premium brand Lanthieri ★★.

Croatia

Few Croatian wines are exported, though the country seems to be doing well with all styles of wine, from dry and sweet whites, to reds and sparkling.

Agrolaguna ★→★★ Co-op at Poreč, ISTRIA. Cab Sauv can be very good.

Babić Dark, long-lived, native red from Primošten (north DALMATIA). Can be of high quality. Best by VINOPLOD. Unique vineyard site.

Badel 1862 ★→★★ Biggest wine producer in the country with wineries from all over. Usually best: IVAN DOLAC, (PZ Svirče), DINGAČ (PZ i Vinarija Dingač).

Coronica, Moreno ★★★ Top MALVAZIJA (DYA) and Gran Malvazija **02 03' 04' 05'** and Gran Teran **03** from ISTRIA. Also Cab Sauv 03 Grabar. Classic.

Dalmacija-vino ★ Giant co-op at Split: very good Faros.

Dalmatia Dalmacija The coast of Croatia is a grower's paradise. Traditionally high in alcohol. Whites struggling, reds improving fast.

Dingač Vineyard designation on PELJEŠAC'S steep southern slopes. "Grand cru" for PLAVAC MALI. Made from partially dried grapes: full-bodied robust, dry red. Look for: Kiridžija, Radovič, and Skaramuča.

Enjingi, Ivan ★★★★ Producer of excellent sweet botrytized and dry whites from Požega. GRAŠEVINA, Sivi Pinot, and superb white blend Venje.

Graševina Welschriesling. Best in SLAVONIA. Look for Adžić, ENJINGI, KRAUTHAKER, Vinarija Daruvar, Djakovačka vina, KUTJEVO.From dry and light to top botrytis wines.

Grgić, Miljenko ★★★ "Paris tasting" winner (see Grgich Hills, California) produces PLAVAC and POŠIP back home at PELJEŠAC peninsula.

Grk Rare white of Korčula. Oldest Croatian native. Try: Cebalo Branimir.

Hvar Beautiful island in mid-Dalmatia. Good reds from PLAVAC MALI from steep southern slopes. Interesting native wines from plateau. Look for: ZLATAN PLAVAC, IVAN DOLAC, Carić Faros, Tomić, PZ Svirče, PLANČIĆ.

Istria North Adriatic peninsula. MALVAZIJA and TERAN reign here. Great for Cab Sauv. Look for CORONICA, Degrassi, Kabola, KOZLOVIČ, MATOŠEVIĆ, Pilato. IQ (Istrian Quality) is a new quality designation.

Ivan Dolac Area on south slopes of HVAR. "Grand cru" for PLAVAC MALI.

Kiridžija, Vedran ★★ Producer of constantly good DINGAČ **03' 04'.**

Korak ★★ Producer of good whites from PLEŠIVICA. Chard 04 and Beli Pinot.

Kozlović ★★★ Good white producer from ISTRIA. Especially MALVAZIJA. Also reds

Krauthaker, Vlado ★★★ Top Croatian producer of dry whites from Kutjevo, esp Chard and GRAŠEVINA. Reds are ★★.

Kutjevo Name shared by a town in SLAVONIJA, centre of GRAŠEVINA. Also the ★★→★★★ co-op. Gewurz, GRAŠEVINA, (De Gotho 04' 05'), and botrytis.

Malvazija Malvasia **04** Planted in ISTRIA. A pleiad of private producers is producing character and style.

Matošević, Ivica ★★→★★★ Pioneer and leader from ISTRIA. MALVAZIJA Alba.

Mendek Selekcija **03' 04'** The most expensive Croatian red. From Pelješac.

Miloš, Frano ★★→★★★ Makes cult brand Stagnum 04' at Pelješac.

Pelješac Beautiful peninsula and region in south DALMATIA. **_Some very good_** _PLAVAC MALI._ Mostly overrated. See GRGIĆ, Mentek, MILOŠ, POSTUP, DINGAČ.

Pjenušac Sparkling. Look for Tomac, Peršurić also Šenpjen.

Plančić ★★ HVAR producer of interesting natives and good Ivan Dolac.

Plavac Mali The best DALMATIAN red grape: wine of body, strength, and ageability. See DINGAČ, GRGIĆ, HVAR, IVAN DOLAC, MENDEK, MILOŠ, PELJEŠAC, POSTUP, ZLATAN OTOK. Promising at island of Brač (Murvica).

Plešivica Quality sub-region near Zagreb, known for whites and sparkling. Look for: KORAK, Režek, Šember Tomac.

Pošip Best DALMATIAN white, mostly on island of Korčula.

Postup Vineyard designation northwest of DINGAČ. Medium- to full-bodied red

Prošek Port-like fortified wine made from dried grapes.

Slavonija Sub-region in north for white. Look out for ENJINGI, Jakobović, KRAUTHAKER, KUTJEVO.

Stolno vino Table wine.

Suho Dry. _Polusuho_ is semi-dry; _poluslatko_ is semi-sweet, sladko is sweet

Teran Stout, dark red pride of ISTRIA, Refosco grape. Try CORONICA.

Vinoplod ★ Co-op from Šibenik in north DALMATIA. BABIĆ ★★★ **03'** 04.

Vrhunsko vino A fairly rigorous designation for premium wines.

Vugava _**Rare white from island of Vis.**_ Linked to Viognier. Try Lipanović.

Zdjelarević ★★ White wine producer from SLAVONIJA, especially Chard.

Zlahtina Native white from island of Krk. Look for Katunar, Toljanić.

Zlatan otok ★★★ HVAR-based winery of Zlatan Plenković, uncrowned king of PLAVAC MALI. His Zlatan Plavac **03'** 04 05 is considered best Croatian red.

Bosnia & Herzegovina

Since the civil war ended in 1995, wine production in Bosnia & Herzegovina has been dominated by small independent family operations.

Blatina Native red grape and wine.

Kameno Vino White of unique, irrigated desert vineyard in Neretva Valley.

Mostar The area around Mostar, the unofficial capital city of Herzegovina, has been the heartland of Herzegovinian wine production since World War II. Cellars such as Ljubuski (the oldest in the country) and Citluk are producing good-quality ZILAVKA white and slightly less impressive BLATINA red.

Samotok Light, red (rosé/_ruzica_) wine from run-off juice (and no pressing).

Zilavka White grape. Potentially dry and pungent. Fruity; faint apricot flavour.

Serbia

Strengths include light, fruity reds made from the Prokupac grape, but international varieties, notably Cabernet Sauvignon and, in the Zapadna Morava region, Sauvignon Blanc, are doing well.

Montenegro

3 July State-run co-op; high-tech Italian kit. VRANAC: high quality.

rmnica Lakeside/coastal vineyards especially for Kadarka grape (see Macedonia).

uklja Late-harvested, semi-sweet version of VRANAC.

rstač Montenegro's top white grape and wine; especially from CRMNICA.

ranac Local vigorous and abundant red grape and wine. Value.

Macedonia

Macedonia comprises three main growing areas: Pcinja-Osogovo, Povardarie Vardar Valley), and Pelagonija-Polog. Wine law, established in 2004, is set to EU standards.

ratosija Red grape also found in Montenegro; sound wines.

lovdina Native grape for mild red, white; especially blended with tastier PROKUPAC.

rokupac Top red grape of Macedonia, Serbia. Makes full reds and dark rosé (*ruzica*) of character. PLOVDINA often added for smoothness.

katsiteli Russian (white) grape often used in blends.

mederevka Widely planted white grape, also found in Serbia and Hungary.

eran Less stylish than the version produced in Istria.

ikveš Macedonia's largest winery in region of same name. Founded in 1946. Strong in exports. Good native SMEDEREVKA and KRATOSIJA grapes.

ranec Local name for Montenegro's red Vranac (qv); quality improving.

rvno Vino Controlled origin designation for quality wines.

The Czech Republic & Slovakia

Amazingly, the wine business in both countries is enjoying a boom, with huge investments in winery equipment, French oak barrels and on-site hospitality facilities to be seen just about everywhere. New wineries are also springing up, seen as a reliable and respectable investment for the newly wealthy. Wines, unknown to the outside world, are improving, though prices commanded by anything with above-average ripeness can reach heights that would embarrass any foreign wine merchant.

Moravia

Vineyards situated in southeast along Austrian and Slovak borders: similar grapes. Look for: Stapleton & Springer (Bořetice), Dobrá Vinice (Nový Šaldorf), Krist (Milotice), all young and now world-standard; **Znovín** Znojmo (modern, internationally recognized; and Vinselekt-Michlovský (Rakvice). Also Baloun (V Pavlovice), Sonberk (Pouzdřany), Spielberg (Archeblov), and Reisten (Pavlov). Moravia also has sparkling: Sekt Domaine Petrák (Kobylí) and Château Bzenec. Icing on the cake is ice and straw wine, but beware highly priced 20-cl bottles.

Bohemia

Same latitude and similar wines to east Germany. Best in the Elbe Valley (north of Prague), notably at Mělník (Ries, Ruländer, Traminer, and Pinot N). Vineyard renewal, especially round Prague, including several small boutique wineries. Producers include: Lobkowicz-Mělník (oak-aged reds, barrel-fermented Chard, *méthode traditionnelle* Château Mělník). Kosher wine production in Chrámce. Sparkling wine is mostly tank-fermented using grapes from Austria. The two biggest players, Bohemia Sekt in Starý Plzenec (Henkell-Söhnlein) and Soare Sekt (Schloss Wachenheim), are still expanding, thanks to foreign investment.

Slovakia

Hungarian and international varieties, with best wines from Malokarpatská region (in foothills of Little Carpathians) and east Slovakia neighbouring Hungary's Tokaj. Leading producers: ***Château Belá*** (Mužla) with Müller-Scharzhof involvement, Masaryk (Skalica), Matyšák (Pezinok), Mrva & Stank (Trnava), J J Ostrožovič (V T ňa, Tokaj), Pavelka – Sobolič (Pezinok), Vinanza (Vráble), Víno Nitra (Nitra), and Karpatská Perla (Šenkvice). For sparkling: J E Hubert and Pálffy Sekt.

Romania

Romania is one of the top 10 viticultural countries of the world. Its long winemaking tradition is being revived after decades of abuse under the old dogmatic mass-production methods and lack of funds and expertise.

Alba Iulia In cool region of TRANSYLVANIA, with aromatic and dry or off-dry whit (RIES ITALIEN, FETEASCĂ, MUSCAT OTTONEL).

Aligoté Pleasantly fresh white especially from Bucium and Sarica-Niculitel.

Băbească Neagră Traditional "black grandmother grape" of the Nicores area; light body and ruby-red colour.

Banat Small wine region on western border, with RIES ITALIEN, SAUV BL, MUSC OTTONEL, local Riesling de Banat; light red Cadarca, Cab Sauv, MERLOT.

Blaj wine region in TÂRNAVE (TRANSYLVANIA), dry or off-dry whites.

Bohotin East Moldavia region famous for local aromatic Busuioacă de Bohotin

Bucium East Moldavia region with dry, off-dry, and sparkling (MUSCAT OTTONEL).

Burgund Mare Varietal name linked to Burgenland (Austria), where grape called Blaufränkisch (Kékfrankos in Hungary).

Buzau Hills Reds (Cab Sauv, FETEASCĂ NEAGRĂ, MERLOT, BURGUND MARE) a northeaster continuation of DEALU MARE.

Carl Reh Innovative German-owned winery with 190-ha vineyard in Oprisc Very good reds, especially La Cetate label.

Cotesti Wine region in Vrancea. Good reds (FETEASCĂ NEAGRĂ, Cab Sauv, MERLO and whites (SAUV BL, FETEASCĂ).

Cotnari Region in northeast with very good botrytis conditions. Famous for mo than 500 years for sweet GRASĂ, FETEASCĂ ALBĂ, TĂMĂIOASĂ, and dry Frâncușă.

Cotnari Winery 1,200 ha in COTNARI region. ***Excellent dessert and modern d whites (Château Cotnari)***.

Cramele Recaș British-Romanian firm with 700 ha vineyards in Banat regio PINOT N with potential. Very good SAUV BL.

Crișana Western region including historical Miniș area (since 15th C): especia red Cadarca; crisp, white Mustoasă. Other areas: Silvania (especia FETEASCĂ), Diosig, Valea lui Mihai.

Da Vino Winery 40 ha in Dealu Mare. Very good labels Domaine Ceptura bla and Domaine Ceptura rouge

Dealu Bujorului Area in middle Moldavia; good reds.

Dealu Mare "The Big Hill". Important well-situated area in southeaste Carpathian foothills. ***Excellent reds, especially FETEASCĂ NEAGRĂ***, Cab Sau MERLOT, PINOT N. Whites from TĂMĂIOASĂ.

Dobrogea Sunny, dry, Black Sea region. Includes MURFATLAR.

DOC Classification for higher-quality wines with denomination of origi DOC-CMD means picked fully ripe; DOC-CT is late harvest; DOC-CÎB noble late harvest, or botrytized.

Domeniile Tohani Winery 800 ha in Dealu Mare. Very good labels Princi (FETEASCĂ NEAGRĂ, Cab Sauv, PINOT N, MERLOT) and sweet Dollete.

Drăgă şani Region on R Olt S of Carpathian. Traditional (Crâmposie Selectionată) and international varieties (esp SAUV BL). Gd MUSCAT OTTONEL.

Fetească White grape with spicy, faintly Muscat aroma. Two types: **F Alba** (same as Hungary's Leányka, ageworthy and with good potential base for sparkling and sweet COTNARI) and **F Regala** (good for sparkling).

Fetească Neagră "Black maiden grape" with potential as showpiece variety. Difficult to handle, but can give deep, full-bodied wines with character.

Grasă Romania's version of Hungarian Furmint grape, featured especially in COTNARI wines. Botrytis-prone. Grasă means "fat".

Halewood Winery British venture producing very good wines, especially reds. Vineyards in Dealu Mare yielding fine FETEASCĂ NEAGRĂ, and PINOT N.

Huşi Wine region in Moldavia, dry and off-dry whites.

Iaşi Region for fresh acidic whites (FETEASCĂ ALBĂ, also RIES ITALIEN, ALIGOTÉ, sparkling MUSCAT OTTONEL): Bucium, Copou. Reds: FETEASCĂ NEAGRĂ, MERLOT, Cab Sauv; in URICANI.

Jidvei Winery in Transylvania (Târnave). Good whites: FETEASCĂ, RIES ITALIEN, SAUV BL, TRAMINER ROZ, and sparkling.

Lacrima lui Ovidiu "Ovidiu's Tear" sweet fortified wine aged for many years in oak barrels until amber coloured, from MURFATLAR.

Lechinta Transylvanian wine area. Good whites FETEASCĂ REGALĂ, Neuburger, MUSCAT OTTONEL noted for bouquet.

Merlot Romania's widely planted, popular red.

Murfatlar Area with vineyards in Drobogea near Black Sea; very good Chard, PINOT GRIS and late-harvest Cab Sauv.

Murfatlar Winery Largest bottled-wine producer. Very good labels Trei Hectare (FETEASCĂ NEAGRĂ, Cab Sauv, Chard) and Ferma Nouă (MERLOT, SAUV BL).

Muscat Ottonel Muscat of eastern Europe; a Romanian speciality, especially in cool Transylvania and in Moldavia dry to sweet wines.

Odobeşti Ancient wine region in Vrancea. Good whites especially from local Galbenă de Odobeşti variety.

Panciu Wine region in Vrancea. Good reds (FETEASCĂ NEAGRĂ, PINOT N), whites, and sparkling (good label Veritas Panciu).

Păuliş Small cellar in town of same name. Fine Cadarca and oak-aged MERLOT.

Pietroasa Area in DEALU MARE known for producing sweet whites, esp TĂMÂIOASĂ ROMÂNEASCĂ.

Pinot Gris Full, slightly aromatic wines, widely grown in Transylvania, MURFATLAR.

Pinot Noir Grown in the south: showing much promise.

Prince Stirbey 20-ha estate in DRĂGĂSANI, returned to Austrian-Romanian noble family (Kripp-Costinescu). V. good dry from local Crâmposie Selectionată, FETEASCĂ REGALĂ, and TĂMÂIOASĂ ROMÂNEASCĂ.

Riesling Italien Widely planted Welschriesling, starting to show potential.

Sauvignon Blanc Very tasty, popular dry and off-dry.

SERVE French-founded DEALU MARE winery and vineyards. Excellent Terra Romana label, especially Cuvée Charlotte (blend of FETEASCĂ NEAGRĂ, Cab Sauv).

Tămâioasă Românească Traditional white "frankincense" grape, with exotic aroma and taste. Often makes fine botrytis wines in COTNARI and PIETROASA.

Târnave (also Tîrnave) Romania's coolest region, in Transylvania, known for SAUV BL and FETEASCĂ REGALĂ. Dry aromatic wines (esp PINOT GR, Gewurz) and sparkling. See JIDVEI, BLAJ.

Uricani Old and famous wine region in eastern Moldavia, near IAŞI. Very good reds (FETEASCĂ NEAGRĂ, Cab Sauv, MERLOT).

Valea Călugărească "Valley of the Monks", part of DEALU MARE. Nice MERLOT, Cab Sauv, PINOT N, RIES ITALIEN, PINOT GR.

Vinarte Winery Comprises three domains: Villa Zorilor in DEALU MARE, Castel

CZECH REPUBLIC/ROMANIA

Bolovanu in DRĂGĂŞANI, Terase Danubiane in MEHEDINTI.

Vin de masă Table wine.

Vincon Vrancea Winery Largest firm in Vrancea region. Very good dry an off-dry label Beciul Domnesc.

Vinterra Dutch/Romanian venture reviving FETEASCĂ NEAGRĂ; also makes goo PINOT N, MERLOT.

Vinuri Dobrogene Winery 700 ha in Sarica-Niculitel (Dobrogea) near Danub delta, fine reds (Cab Sauv, MERLOT, BABEASCĂ NEAGRĂ) and whites (ALIGOTÉ).

Vrancea Important region covering PANCIU, ODOBESTI, and COTESTI.

Greece

There is absolutely no reason why Greece should not be up there in the premier league of wine countries: it has a over 150 indigenous grape varieties, a mild maritime climate (in many cases much cooler than one would imagine), a large number of cutting-edge wineries as well as an army of top-class winemakers.

Aghiorghitiko Quality NEMEA red grape leading Greek wine out of anonymity.

Agioritikos Medium whites and rosés from Agios Oros (Mount Athos Halkidiki's monastic peninsula. Brand name for TSANTALIS.

Aivalis ★★→★★★ Newish boutique NEMEA producer: extracted AGHIORGHITIKO Top (and pricey) wine is "4", from 120-year-old+ vines.

Alpha Estate ★★→★★★ Impressive estate in cooler-climate Amindeo. Ver good barrel-aged Merlot/Syrah/XINOMAVRO blend, pungent Sauv B unfiltered XINOMAVRO from ungrafted vines. Top wine: Alpha 1, astonishin Tannat-Montepulciano 03 that demands ageing.

Antonopoulos ★★→★★★ PATRAS-based winery, with top-class MANTINIA, cris Adoli Ghis, unoaked, nutty Chard, and Cab-based Nea Dris (**97 98 00 01** Top wine: violet-scented Vertzami/Cab Fr. To watch.

Arghyros ★★→★★★ Top SANTORINI producer with exemplary but expensiv Vinsanto aged 20 years in cask. Exciting Ktima white, a popular oak-age Vareli white, and new fragrant (dry) Aidani.

Avantis ★★→★★★ Boutique winery in Evia with (red) vineyards in Boetia. Goo (white) Ktima, dense Syrah. Top wine: elegant single-vineyard Avanti Collection Syrah **02** 03.

Biblia Chora ★★→★★★ Polished New World-style wines. Grapey Sau Bl/Assyrtiko. Floral Syrah Rosé. Oaked Ovilos (white) Sem/Assyrtiko i extremely noteworthy. Tangy red Areti cask-aged AGHIORGHITIKO.

Boutari, J & Son ★→★★ Producers in NAOUSSA. Excellent value wines, popula MOSCHOFILERO. Top oaked Santorini Kalisti, single-vineyard Filiria Goumenissa.

Calliga ★ Good AGHIORGHITIKO sourced for Montenero and Rubis.

Cambas, Andrew ★ Brand owned by BOUTARI. Chard and Cab Sauv.

Carras, Domaine ★ Estate at Sithonia, Halkidiki, with its own OPAP (Côtes d Meliton). Chateau Carras 01. Under new management. Underperforming.

Cava Legal term for cask-aged still white and red table wines – *e.g.* Cav Amethystos Kosta Lazaridi, Cava Hatzimihali.

Cephalonia (Kephalonia) Ionian island: good white Robola, emerging style of sweet Muscat, Mavrodaphne.

Creta-Olympias ★★ Very good Cretan producer. Inexpensive Nea Ghi range very good-value spicy white Xerolithia, red Mirabelo. New Pirorago 0 Syrah/Cab Sauv/Kotsifali blend.

Crete Improving quality. Led by Alexakis, Ekonomou, Lyrarakis, Douloufaki and MANOUSSAKIS.

ougos ★★ From the Olympus area, producing interesting Rhône blends.

riopi ★★★ New venture of TSELEPOS in high NEMEA. Initial vintages are serious (especially single-vineyard Ktima) and of the high-octane style.

mery ★→★★ Historic RHODES producer, specializing in local varieties. Look for brands: Villaré and Grand Rosé. Very good-value Rhodos Athiri. Efreni Muscat.

Gaia ★★★ Top-quality NEMEA-based producer and winery on SANTORINI. Fun Notios label. New World-like AGHIORGHITIKO. Thalassitis SANTORINI. Top wine Gaia Estate (97 98 99 00 01 03 04). New Anatolikos dessert (sun-dried) NEMEA.

Gentilini ★★→★★★ ***Exciting whites including very good Robola***. New Unique Red Blend.

Georgakopoulos ★★ Central Greece, Full-throttle, New World-style reds and rich unoaked Chard.

Gerovassiliou ★★★ Perfectionist miniature estate near Salonika. Look for benchmark Assyrtiko/MALAGOUSIA, smooth Syrah/Merlot blend Herby, red Avaton 03 from rare indigenous varieties. Top wine: Syrah (01 02 03 04).

Goumenissa (OPAP) ★→★★ XINOMAVRO and Negoska oaked red from MACEDONIA. Especially BOUTARI, Tatsis Bros, Aidarinis, and Ligas.

Hatzidakis ★★★ Low-tech but high-class producer. Stunning range across the board. Try the full-throttle Nihteri.

Hatzimichalis, Domaine ★→★★★ Large vineyards and merchant in Atalanti. Huge range. Greek and French varieties. Top red Rahes Galanou Merlot – Cab Fr.

Katoghi-Strofilia ★★ Vineyards and wineries in Attica, Peloponnese, and north Epirus. Mainly Greek varieties, but also Chard, Cab Sauv, and floral Traminer. Top wine: Ktima Averoff.

Katsaros ★★→★★★ Small organic winery of very high standards on Mount Olympus. Ktima red, a Cab Sauv/Merlot has staying power. Supple Chard 05.

Kir-Yanni ★★→★★★ High-quality vineyards in NAOUSSA and at Amindeo. Vibrant white Samaropetra; good Syrah 03; top NAOUSSA Ramnista (98 99 00 01 03).

Kouros ★ Reliable, well-marketed white PATRAS and red NEMEA from KOURTAKIS.

Kourtakis, D ★★ Athenian merchant with *mild RETSINA* and good dark NEMEA.

Ktima Estate, farm. Term not exclusive to wine.

Lazaridis, Domaine Kostas ★★→★★★ Vineyards and wineries in Drama and Kapandriti (near Athens). Quality Amethystos label (white, red rosé). Top wine: unfiltered red CAVA Amethystos (97 98 99 00 01 02). Bordelais Michel Rolland's first Greek consultancy.

Lazaridis, Nico ★★ Spectacular post-modernist winery and vineyards in Drama. Good Trebbiano, even better Late Harvest (dry) Trebbiano. Top wine: Magiko Vouno white, red. New (ultra-premium) range under Perpetuus brand.

Lemnos (OPAP) Aegean island: co-op dessert wines, deliciously fortified, lemony Muscat of Alexandria. New dry Muscats by Kyathos-Honas winery.

Macedonia Quality wine region in the north for XINOMAVRO.

Malagousia Rediscovered perfumed white grape.

Manoussakis ★★→★★★ Impressive newcomer, with Rhône-inspired blends. Impressive range under the Nostos brand, led by Roussanne and Syrah.

Mantinia (OPAP) High central Peloponnese region. Fresh, grapey MOSCHOFILERO.

Matsa, Château ★★→★★★ Historic and prestigious small estate in Attica. Top wine: Ktima Assyrtiko/Sauv Bl. Excellent MALAGOUSIA.

Mavrodaphne (OPE) "Black laurel", and red grape. Cask-aged port/*recioto*-like, concentrated red; fortified. Speciality of PATRAS, north Peloponnese.

Mercouri ★★→★★★ Peloponnese family estate. ***Very fine Refosco***, delicious RODITIS. New CAVA. Classy Refosco dal Penducolo red and fine sweet Belvedere Malvasia.

Mitravelas ★★→★★★ Outstanding new entry in NEMEA, promising great things.

Moraitis ★★ Small quality producer on the island of Paros. Very good smoky (white) Monemvasia, Ktima (white) Monemvasia-Assyrtiko, (red) tanni Moraitis Reserve 01 Monemvasia-Mandelaria blend.

Moschofilero Pink-skinned, rose-scented, high-quality, high-acid grape.

Naoussa (OPAP) r High-quality region for XINOMAVRO. One of two Greek region where a "cru" notion may soon develop.

Nemea (OPAP) r Region in east Peloponnese producing dark, spic AGHIORGHITIKO wines. Recent investment has moved it into higher gear. High Nemea merits its own appellation. Koutsi front-runner for *cru* status.

Oenoforos ★★ Good Peloponnese producer with high vineyards. Leading RODITIS white Asprolithi. Also delicate white Lagorthi, nutty Charc (Burgundian, limited-release, magnum-only), crisp Ries, and stylish Syrah.

OPAP "Appellation of Origin of Higher Quality". In theory equivalent to French VDQS, but in practice where many good appellations and wines belong.

OPE "Appellation of Origin Controlled". In theory equivalent to French AC bu mainly reserved for sweet Muscat and MAVRODAPHNE.

Papaïoannou ★★→★★★ Reliable NEMEA grower. Classy red (including Pinot N) flavourful white. Top wine: Ktima Papaioannou Palea Klimata (old vines) 97 98 00 01 03 and Microklima (a micro-single vineyard) 01.

Patras (OPAP) White wine (based on RODITIS) and wine town facing the Ionian Sea. Home of MAVRODAPHNE. Rio-Patras (OPE) sweet Muscat.

Pavlidis ★★★ Ambitious new vineyards and winery at Kokkinogia near Drama. Good Assyrtiko/ Sauv Bl, very good Assyrtiko. New Syrah and Tempranillo.

Rapsani Interesting oaked red from Mt Olympus. Rasping until rescued by TSANTALIS, but new producers are moving in.

Retsina Attica speciality white with Aleppo pine resin added. Domestic consumption waning.

Rhodes Easternmost island. Home to creamy (dry) Athiri white grape. Top wines inclue Caïr (co-op) Rodos 2400 and Emery's Villare. Also some sparkling.

Roditis White grape grown all over Greece. Good when yields are low.

Samos (OPE) Island near Turkey famed for sweet, golden Muscat. Especially (fortified) Anthemis, (sun-dried) Nectar. Rare old bottlings can be ★★★★.

Santorini Volcanic island north of CRETE: luscious, sweet Vinsanto (sun-dried grapes), mineral-laden, ***bone-dry white from fine Assyrtiko grape***. Oaked examples can be good. Top producers include GAIA, ATZIDAKIS, SIGALAS.

Semeli ★★ Estates near Athens and NEMEA. Value Orinos Helios (w) 05 (r) 04.

Sigalas ★★→★★★ Top SANTORINI estate producing the leading oaked SANTORINI Bareli. Stylish, golden-robed Vinsanto. Also rare red Mavrotragano.

Skouras ★★ Innovative PELOPONNESE wines. Large range. First to introduce screwcaps on Chard Dum Vinum Sperum with most of the white range following suit. Top wine: High Nemea Grande Cuvée 03.

Spiropoulos, Domaine ★★ Organic producer in MANTINIA. Improving oaky, red Porfyros (AGHIORGHITIKO, Cab Sauv, Merlot). Sparkling Odi Panos has potential.

Tetramythos ★★ Exploring the possibilities of cool-climate parts of Peloponnese, a new and promising venture.

TO "Regional Wine", French VdP equivalent. Most exciting Greek wine category .

Tsantalis ★→★★ Merchant and vineyards at Agios Pavlos. AC wines. Good red Metoxi, Rapsani Reserve, and Grande Reserve, and good-value Organic Cab Sauv and top-of-the-range Avaton.

Tselepos ★★→★★★ Top-quality MANTINIA producer and Greece's best Gewurz. Other wines: fresh, oaky Chard, very good Cab Sauv/ Merlot, single-vineyard Avlotopi Cab Sauv. Top wine: single-vineyard Kokinomylos Merlot.

Voyatzi Ktima ★★ Small estate near Kozani. Aromatic white, classy and extremely elegant red.

Xinomavro The tastiest of indigenous red grapes – though name means "acidic-black". Grown in the cooler north, it is the basis for NAOUSSA, GOUMENISSA, and Amindeo. High potential: Greece's answer to Nebbíolo.

Zitsa Mountainous Epirus AC. Delicate Debina white, still or sparkling.

Cyprus

Cyprus has very good natural potential for wine production. The altitude (1,000–1,500 m) of the vineyards located in the Troodos Mountains lessens the Mediterranean heat, and limestone soils have potential for quality. But for much of the 19th and 20th centuries most of the island's production was of basic wine or sherry-style fortified wine from high-yielding local vine varieties. This is now changing to meet the challenges of international competition and EU membership. There is a new emphasis on improving wine quality, with increased use of lower-yielding but better local varieties and more planting of classic, international grapes.

Commandaria Good-quality brown sweet wine traditionally produced in hills north of Limassol. Region limited to 14 villages. Made from sun-dried XYNISTERI and MAVRO grapes. ***Best (as old as 100 years) is superb***.

ETKO One of largest producers: Range includes Salera (red and white) also Shiraz, Merlot, and Chard. Best: Ino Cab Sauv.

KEO Large, go-ahead firm. Range includes single-estate wines Kitma Mallia (red and white), Anerada (white), also Heritage (red), oak-aged MARATHEFTIKO. Production moved from Limassol to regional wineries. COMMANDARIA St John.

Kokkineli Deep-coloured, semi-sweet rosé: the name is related to cochineal.

Loel One of major producers. Reds: Orpho Negro. Mediterranean Cab Sauv and Mediterranean Chard, also COMMANDARIA Alasia and brandies.

Maratheftico Vines of superior quality make concentrated red wine of tannin and colour, close to Cab Sauv; the future grape of Cyprus.

Mavro The black grape of Cyprus. Can produce quality if planted at high altitude; otherwise gives sound, acceptable wines.

Opthalmo Black grape (red/rosé): lighter, sharper than MAVRO.

Palomino Soft, dry white (LOEL, SODAP). Very drinkable ice-cold.

Pitsilia Region south of Mt Olympus. Some of best whites and COMMANDARIA.

SODAP A co-op winery and one of the four largest producers. New ranges made using Australian consultancy: Island Vines (red and white is modern, fresh, and made from native grapes); Mountain Vines (white) is made from "international" varieties. Both are inexpensive. Also regional wines (red and white) from new Kamanterena winery at Paphos.

Xynisteri Native aromatic white grape of Cyprus, making delicate, fruity wines.

Malta

Accession to the EU has seen vineyard, winemaking, and labelling practices slowly improve, though some producers still chaptalize and/or use inferior "eating" or imported grapes. But pioneering estate Meridiana (Antinori-backed) continues, since 1994, to make excellent, quintessentially Maltese Isis and Mistral Chardonnays, Melqart Cabernet Sauvignon/Merlot, Nexus Merlot, ***Bel Syrah***, and premium Celsius Cabernet Sauvignon Reserve from island vines only. Volume producers of note are Delicata, Marsovin, and Camilleri.

To decipher codes, please refer to "Key to symbols" on front flap of jacket, or to "How to use this book" on p.11.

England & Wales

Plantings of the classic Champagne varieties in the past three years
have exceeded all expectations and the rush into fizz seems
unstoppable. Chardonnay and Pinot Noir were, by the end of May 2007,
the two most widely planted UK varieties and will be getting on for 50%
of the vineyard area by 2008–9. Nyetimber, the UK's most prestigious
brand, has quadrupled in size under new ownership and plans are afoot
to build a new winery and launch a non-vintage wine.

Since 1994, the UK has had an official appellation system for still
wines: the best are labelled "Quality Wine" or "Regional Wine". Plain "UK
Table Wine" is best avoided, as is "British Wine" that is made from
imported concentrate.

Astley Stourport-on-Severn, Worcestershire ★★ Wines continue to win awards
and medals. Triassic 05 very good.

Breaky Bottom East Sussex ★★ 99 03 Sparkling wines well worth trying,
especially Cuvée Rémy Alexandre 99 and Cuvée Alex Mercier 03.

Camel Valley Cornwall ★★★ 05 Excellent quality, especially Camel Valley Rosé
05, Bacchus 05 and Pinot Noir Brut sparkling 03. All still wines now in
screwcap. Excellent facilities and very welcoming to visitors.

Denbies Surrey ★★ 04 England's largest vineyard at 106 ha. Impressive winery
worth a visit. Bacchus 04, Redlands 04, and Yew Tree Pinot Noir 03 all good.

English Wines Group Kent ★★★ 04 05 Largest UK producer, including Chapel
Down, Tenterden, and Lamberhurst brands. Wide range of excellent wines.
Bacchus Reserve 04, English Rosé 05, Tenterden Estate Pinot Noir 04 all
gold medal winners. Brut Rosé Sparkling 03 and Bacchus 05 also very
good.

Nyetimber West Sussex ★★★ 98 00 03 Leading UK specialist sparkling-wine
maker; classic Champagne varieties. Most current wines gold medal
winners. Pinot Meunier 03 very good. Much new planting.

RidgeView East Sussex ★★★ 01 03 04 Specialist sparkling-wine producer; classic
Champagne varieties. All wines medal winners. Fitzrovia Rosé 03 very good.

Sharpham Devon ★★★ 04 05, also 01 sparkling Produces consistently very
good wines. Bacchus 05 surprise gold medal winner and excellent.

Stanlake Park Berkshire ★★ Large range of wines of above-average quality but
not such stars as previously.

Three Choirs Gloucestershire ★★ 05 UK's second-largest producer. Wines
sometimes inconsistent, but Noble Rot 03 gold medal winner. Also Stone
Brook 05 and Willow Brook 05 very good.

Other noteworthy producers
Biddenden Kent Long-standing producer. Try Dry Ortega 05.
Brightwell Oxfordshire Up-and-coming producer. Try Bacchus 05.
Davenport Sussex Good organic range, including Limney Dry White 04.
Heart of England Oberon Red worth trying.
Hush Heath Estate Kent Balfour Brut Rosé silver medal winner.
Nutbourne Nutty 04 worth trying.
Throwley Kent Ortega 03 and Brut 01 very good.

Asia, North Africa, & The Levant

Algeria Since independence, the combined effects of Islam and the EU have seen wineries dwindle from more than 3,000 to fewer than 50, and the import of alcohol is banned. Areas and producers of note: Tlemcen (powerful reds, whites, especially rosé – Dom de Sebra), Mascara (Dom El Bordj, Coteaux de Mascara), Dahra (full-bodied reds, rosés – Dom de Khadra), Zaccar (Château Romain), Médéa (Château Tellagh), Tessala, Aïn-Bessem-Bouira.

China With nearly 5% of world production, China is the sixth-largest producer and continues to increase by 15% annually. Twenty-six provinces produce wine from over 400 wineries, especially Shandong, Hebei, Tianjin, Jilin, Xingjiang, Beijing, Henan, Gansu, Ninxia, and Yunan. Four companies dominate – Dynasty, Changyu, Weilong, and Great Wall. Quality producers benefiting from foreign investment such as Huadong (good Chard and Ries) in Shandong and China Grace at Dongjia Village in Shanxi (good Merlot, Cab Sauv, Bordeaux blend, Rosé, Chard) are joined by improving Lou Lan at Turpan (good Chenin Bl and Merlot), Suntime Manas (Xinjiang), Dragon Seal (Cab Sauv and Merlot) and Bodega Langes (Hebei). Others to watch: Tsingtao and Kai Xuan Winery in Shandong, Maotai in Hebei.

India There are 123,000 acres of vines with only a fraction used for wine. Production is centred at Maharashtra, with 30 wineries, including successful Chateau Indage (Omar Khayyam sparkling) and Sula (good Chenin Bl, Sauv Bl, Zin, and Merlot). Grover Vineyards in Bangalore makes good Cab Sauv, Merlot, Shiraz, and Blanc de Blancs Clairette under the guidance of Michel Rolland. Others include ND Wines and Dajeeba Wines in Maharashtra, McDowell, Bangalore, and a new development in Nandi Hills, Karnataka.

Japan Japan has a 135-year history of winemaking and is home to 200 wineries. It has two large wine regions: Yamanashi (near Mount Fuji), the oldest and most important; and Nagano. These are beset with climatic problems (summer rain and high humidity) and excessive soil fertility. Other smaller regions include Yamagata prefectures (north of Tokyo) and Hokkaido, the coldest wine region in the world, which may offer a solution to climatic and fertility issues. Expect better viticulture, and thus better quality, in the future.

Japan is considering an appellation system, as only a fraction of Japanese wines are made locally; the rest are made with imported wine. Production is dominated by Mercian, Suntory, Sapporo (Polaire), Mann, and Kyowa Hakko Kogyo (Ste Neige).

Of the indigenous varieties causing the greatest buzz, Koshu (discovered 1186) is the most prominent, making good crisp, dry whites (good producers: Mercian, Katsunuma, Grace). Others include Shokoshi (Coco Farm, Katsunuma) and the lighter red Yama Sauvignon (Mars).

The most interesting and expensive wines are from international varieties, such as Mann's Chard Solaris Komoro from Nagano, Mercian's Kikyogahara Merlot, Asahi Yoshu's Kainoir, Coco Farm Madiran and Tannat, and Jyonohira Cab Sauv. Smaller wineries to watch include Obuse (Sangiovese/Merlot), Takeda, Alps, Marufuji, and Yamazaki.

Morocco The best vineyards are found on the slopes of the Atlas (Meknes and Fez). Cinsault, Carignan, and Grenache make interesting traditional reds and "Gris", but Syrah, Cab Sauv, Merlot, Sauv Bl, and Chard are now better. Coastal vineyards produce notable light, fruity wines. The area under vine has declined drastically but French investment (especially Castel and William

Pitters) is breathing new life. Best producer Celliers de Meknes makes around 90% of the total; Cépages de Meknes, Cépages de Boulaouane, and Société Thalvin also figure. Best labels include L'Excellence de Bonassia (aged Cab Sauv/Merlot), Les Trois Domaines, El Baraka, Halana, Domaine de Sahari.

Tunisia Substantial foreign investment has prompted a change in style from French to New World. Best producers best include Ceptunes, Reine Elissa, Dom Atlas, Dom Magon, Dom Neferis, Dom Kelibia. Muscat makes the finest traditional whites. The most successful international grapes are Chardonnay, Ugni Blanc, Carignan, Syrah, Merlot, Grenache, Cinsault. The main AC zones lie in Mornag, Kelibia Côteaux d'Utique, Tébourba, Sidi Salem, and Thibar.

Turkey State producer Tekel recently disbanded, leaving Kavaklidere (good Altin Kopuk sparkling, red Yakut) and Doluca (good Kav/V Doluca reds) to dominate. Diren, Melen, Sarafin (very good international varieties), and Kocabag also make good wine. The main area of production is Thrace/Marmara (40%); other districts are central/east/southeast Anatolia and the Black Sea coast. Indigenous Emir and Narince produce good whites; Bogazkere and Oküzgözü make full, powerful reds. International varieties show promise.

The Old Russian Empire

This region's wines are still plagued by their Soviet heritage. Cheap, imported bulk wines sold as local make life difficult for authentic regional wine producers. Large, ex-Soviet wineries dominate. Some good wines are produced by flying winemakers. Known authentic producers are listed below:

Ukraine (including Crimea) Potential for Crimea's dessert and fortified wines was revealed in 1990 by the auction of old wines from the last Tsar's Massandra Collection, near Yalta, where production continues, though now more of a tourist attraction. Classic brut sparkling from Novy Svet (Crimea, served at Tsar's coronation 1896) and Artyomovskoe. Other wineries: Inkermann, Magarach, Sun Valley. Reds: potential (*e.g.* Massandra's Alushta). Whites: Aligoté; Artyomovskoe sparkling.

Georgia Possibly the oldest wine region of all, with a huge number of indigenous grape varieties almost untried. Reluctant to modernize, but newer techniques used for exports (Mukuzani, Tsinandali). Kakheti makes two-thirds of Georgia's wine, especially *__lively, savoury red (the grape is Saperavi)__* and acceptable white (Tibaani, Rkatsiteli, Gurjaani). Foreign investors: Pernod Ricard with GWS brand; US-owned Bagrationi has cheap drinkable sparkling. To watch: Talisman, Suliko, Shumi. As equipment techniques, and attitudes evolve, Georgia could be an export hit, but is currently banned from Russia, its largest market. Definitely to try.

Moldova Most important in size and potential, but poorest, with few signs of recovery. Most wineries are privatized, previously supplied cheap wines to Russia but this is now banned. Wine generates a third of Moldova's income. Regions: Bugeac (most important), Nistrean, Codrean, Northern Grapes include Cab Sauv, Pinot N, Merlot, Saperavi, Ries, Chard, Pinot Gris Aligoté, Rkatsiteli. Top wineries: Purkar, Cahul, Kazayak, Hincesti. Also good: Cricova. New World investment at Hincesti, and by local company Vininvest, has brought modern winemaking. Moldova's most modern Ryman's Hincesti Chard; *__Abastrele__* (white); Legenda (red). Progress has not been smooth but is worth following. Appellations are now in force.

Russia Waking up to wine. But imported cheap bulk wine is bottled as local Krasnodar on Northern Black Sea Coast produces 60% of Russia's authenti wine. Also Château Le Grand Vostock with French winemaker, equipment and French-style blends. Australian winemaker at Myskhako (Novorossiysk making good Aligoté, Chard, Cab Sauv. Largest producer: Fanagoria (Temruk) – Merlot and Cab Sauv. Also sweet Kagor from Vityazevo Winery (Anapa). Abrau Durso Brut (also Prince Golitsyn): classic sparkling since 1896.

The Levant

Israel International expertise, modern technology, and dynamic wineries have ensured continued advances in quality. Best vineyards are in the cooler areas of Upper Galilee, Golan Heights, and Judean Hills.

Amphorae r w ★ Seeking return to early promise. Viognier of interest.

Barkan r w ★→★★ Barkan and Segal reds good value at every price point.

Bazelet ha Golan Golan r ★ Excellent Cab Sauv – ripe, rounded, approachable.

Binyamina r w ★ Traditional winery placing new emphasis on quality.

Carmel r w sp ★→★★★ Founded in 1882 by a Rothschild. New winery and vineyards in Upper Galilee. Elegant Limited Edition (**02** 03' 04). Smoky, tarry Cab Sauv from Kayoumi vineyard. Luscious sweet Gewurz.

Castel Judean Hills r w ★★★★ Small family estate in Jerusalem mountains. _**Characterful complex Grand Vin**_ (**00' 02** 03' 04). Second label, Petit Castel. Outstanding, well-balanced Chard – "C" Blanc du Castel.

Chateau Golan Golan r (w) ★ Extravagant, showy winery with innovative wines.

Clos de Gat ★★ Judean Hills r w Estate winery: buttery Chard and spicy Shiraz.

Dalton Upper Galilee r w ★→★★ Consistent wines. Reserve Cab Sauv best.

Ella Valley Judean Hills r w ★★ Well-made wines. Cab Fr showing finesse.

Flam r (w) ★★→★★★★ Intense Cab Sauv, tight Merlot, earthy, herbal Syrah Cab.

Galil Mountain Upper Galilee r w ★★→★★★ Concentrated Yiron Bordeaux blend; successful Pinot N. Unoaked Cab Sauv and Merlot very good value.

Margalit r ★★→★★★ Rich, ripe, Bordeaux blend, Enigma. Excellent Merlot.

Recanati r w ★ Good competition wines, very New World in style.

Saslove r (w) ★★ Aviv reds are flavourful; reserve red more sophisticated.

Tabor Galilee r w ★ Crisp, aromatic Sauv Bl. All wines very good value.

Teperberg r w ★ Efrat reborn – new winery, new name, and better wines.

Tishbi r w sp ★ Grower turned winemaker. Still a family operation.

Yarden Golan Heights r w sp ★★→★★★★ Pioneering winery. Cab Sauv always good; rare Bordeaux blend red Katzrin (**93 96** 00' 03'); oaky Chard. Sweet wines and sparkling wines high quality. Gamla fruit-forward second label.

Yatir Judean Hills r (w) ★★★ Rich, velvety, concentrated red (**01'** 02 03') from 900 m Yatir Forest vineyards, made by Australian-trained winemaker.

Lebanon New, quality wineries are challenging the old order. Most vineyards lie in the Bekaa Valley. Wines are mainly made from Bordeaux and Mediterranean varieties.

Chateau Musar r (w) ★★★★ Unique, raisiny, long-lasting Cab Sauv/Cinsault/Carigan red (94 95 98). Legendary to some; past its best to others. Hochar red is fruitier. Also oaky white from indigenous Obaideh Merwah.

Clos St Thomas r (w) ★ Deep but silky red wines. Les Emirs good quality.

Kefraya r w ★★★ Spicy, minerally Comte de M (**99** 00' 01) from Cab, Syrah, and Mourvèdre. Delicious sweet Lacrima d'Oro. Also fragrant rosé.

Ksara r w ★★ 150 years old but still progressive with excellent-value wines.

Massaya r w ★→★★ Young, forward-looking winery. New Lebanon.

Wardy r w ★ Les Cèdres oaky red. Crisp, fresh Chard and Sauv Bl.

North America

California

More heavily shaded areas are the wine-growing regions

California is now the fourth-largest wine producer in the world, after France, Italy and Spain. Although Napa, where Cabernet Sauvignon is king, remains the best-known growing area, savvy wine consumers are finding excellent quality and value in wines from other regions. The fascination with Rhône varieties is paying off for growers, with very good bottlings from the Central Coast and from the Lodi American Viticultural Area (AVA) in northern Joaquin Valley, east of San Francisco. Zinfandel remains a strong suit all over California, with distinctive styles coming from areas as diverse as the Sierra Foothills and the North Coast. The trend toward Pinot Noir is still strong, with successful wines coming from ever-cooler parts of Sonoma and other coastal regions. Chardonnay remains the top-selling varietal, with very good examples from Sonoma, Carneros, and the Central Coast. Another major story currently unfolding is the move toward organically grown grapes and biodynamic farming of vineyards. Organic and/or biodynamic wines have consistently outperformed traditional wines in several US tastings. The downside is price. Good Californian wines, even with a cheap dollar, are rarely competitive with, for example, French.

The principal Californian vineyard areas

Central Coast
An umbrella region stretching from San Francisco Bay south almost to Los Angeles. Important sub-AVAs include:

Arroyo Grande San Luis Obispo County. A coolish growing region with Pacific influence. Good Pinot N, Viognier. Zin at higher and warmer elevations away from the coast.

Arroyo Seco Monterey County. Excellent Ries both dry and late harvest, citrus Chard and Cab Sauv from warmer canyons in the Santa Lucia mountains.

Edna Valley San Luis Obispo County. Cool winds whip through a gap in the coastal range off Morro Bay. Excellent minerally Chard.

Paso Robles San Luis Obispo County. Large, productive area east of coastal range. Known for Zin. Promising plantings of Syrah and Rhône varieties.

Santa Lucia Highands Monterey County. AVA above the Salinas Valley, east of the Santa Lucia mountains. Excellent Syrah and Ries; outstanding Pinot N.

Santa Maria Valley Santa Barbara County. Outstanding Pinot N, good Chard, Viognier, and Syrah.

Santa Rita Hills New AVA in Santa Barbara County offering very good Pinot N.

Santa Ynez Valley Santa Barbara County. Like Santa Maria but warmer inland regions. Rhône grapes, Pinot N, Chard in cool areas. Sauv Bl a good bet.

North Coast
Lake, Mendocino, Napa, Sonoma counties, all north of San Francisco. Ranges from very cool climate near San Francisco Bay and the coast to very warm interior regions. Soils vary from volcanic to sandy loam. Includes the following key regions:

Alexander Valley Sonoma County. Fairly warm AVA bordering Russian River. Excellent Cab Sauv in a ripe, juicy style. Good Sauv Bl near the river.

Anderson Valley Mendocino County. Cool valley opening to the Pacific along the Navarro River. Outstanding sparkling wine, very good Gewurz and Pinot N. Hillside vineyards above the fog produce terrific old-vine Zin.

Carneros Napa and Sonoma Counties. Cool and foggy region bordering San Francisco Bay. Top site for Pinot N and Chard. Very good sparkling wine.

Dry Creek Valley Sonoma County. Relatively warm region offering distinctive Zin and Sauv Bl, with Cab Sauv a winner on rocky hillsides.

Lake County Warm to hot mountainous region centred around Clear Lake. Good

Zin, Sauv Bl near the lake, and lush, fruity Cab Sauv on cooler hillsides.

Mendocino County Large region north of Sonoma County with a wide range of growing regions from hot interior valleys to cooler regions near the coast.

Mount Veeder Napa County. High-altitude AVA (vineyards planted up to 730 m) best known for concentrated Cab Sauv and rich Chard.

Napa Valley Napa's vineyard land has become the most expensive outside of Europe. Great diversity of soil, climate, and topography in such a small area can produce a wide range of wines, especially the red Bordeaux varieties. Wines have achieved international acclaim, and are priced to match.

Oakville Napa County. Located in mid-Valley, the heart of Cab Sauv County.

Redwood Valley Mendocino County. Warm interior region. Good basic Cab Sauv, excellent Zin, everyday Chard, and Sauv Bl. Also good plantings of Syrah.

Russian River Valley Sonoma County. Very cool, often fog-bound until noon. Maybe best Pinot N in California; Zin and Cab Sauv on hillside vineyards. Green Valley is a small super-cool AVA located within the Russian River AVA.

Rutherford Napa County. Rivals Oakville as Cab Sauv heartland. Long-lived reds from hillside vineyards; lush, dazzling Merlots and other near Napa River.

St Helena Very good Cab Sauv with bright, elegant fruit and a silky mouthfeel from the north of Napa Valley.

Sonoma Coast Sonoma County. Trendy new region borders the Pacific. Very cool climate, very poor soils. New plantings of Pinot N show great promise.

Sonoma Valley This is Jack London's Valley of the Moon. Varied growing regions produce everything from Chard to Zin. Sub-AVA Sonoma Mountain good for powerful Cab Sauv.

Spring Mountain Napa County. Very good Cab Sauv with pockets of delicious Sauv Bl at lower elevations, plus good Ries.

Stags Leap Napa County. East of Napa River, distinctive Cab Sauv and Merlot.

Bay Area

Urban sprawl has wiped out most of the vineyards that once surrounded San Francisco Bay.

Contra Costa County Historic growing district east of the Bay now succumbing to homes and shopping malls. Fine Zins, red Rhônes.

Livermore East and south of San Francisco Bay, valley soils are gravel and stone. Surprisingly good Cab Sauv; outstanding Sauv Bl and Sem.

Marin County Old (1820s) growing region being revived with new plantings of Pinot N and Chard near the coast.

Santa Cruz County Pierce's Disease has wiped out many vineyards, but a few remain, yielding good Cab Sauv and some Pinot N from Santa Cruz Mountains.

Central Valley

About 60% of California's vineyards are in this huge region that runs north to south for several hundred miles. Now shedding its image as a low-quality producer, as Valley growers realize they must go for quality to keep up.

Clarksburg Sacramento, Solano, and Yolo counties. Just outside the state capital Sacramento, running along the Sacramento River. Viognier, Syrah, and Sauv Bl are strong.

Lodi San Joaquin and Sacramento counties. More than a decade ago this AVA began a push for quality. It has paid off in a major way. Strengths are Zin, Sauv Bl, Muscat (sweet), and fruit-forward Chard grown near Sacramento River. New plantings of Rhônes and Spanish varietals show promise.

San Joaquin Valley Hot heart of the Central Valley. Source of most jug, bag-in-a-box, and fortified dessert wine from the state. Many growers now process their own grapes, making fruity, easy-drinking varietals at a bargain price.

Sierra Foothills

Grapes were first planted here during Gold Rush days in the 1850s. Best regions include:

Amador County Warm region famous for old Zin vineyards producing jammy, intense wines, as well as crisp Sauv Bl. Top Rhône reds and Italian varietals as well.

Fiddletown Amador County. High-elevation vineyards produce a more understated, elegant Zin than much of Amador.

Shenandoah Valley Amador County. Source of powerful Zins and increasingly well-regarded Syrah.

Recent vintages

Because of its size and wide range of microclimates, it is impossible to produce a one-size-fits-all vintage report for California. California's climate is not as consistent as its "land of sunshine" reputation suggests, and although grapes ripen regularly, they are often subject to spring frosts, sometimes a wet harvest time, and (too often) drought. Wines from the Central Valley tend to be most consistent. The Central Coast region, with its much cooler maritime mesoclimate has a different pattern of vintage quality from the North Coast or Sierra Foothills. That said, the following vintage assessment relies most heavily on evaluation of Cab Sauv from North Coast regions. For Chard, the best vintages are: 01 03 04.

2006 Early results mixed; summer heat cut crop size. Long harvest ripening could result in balanced wines. Needs some time to come around.

2005 After sorting out this vintage some of the early promise has faded. Wines likely to be for short-term consumption.

2004 Scant winter rains and a warm spring led to bud-break and bloom at least 3 weeks early. Grapes developed evenly through the summer and it was looking good until a prolonged heat-wave hit the North Coast in late Aug. Grapes ripened quickly with uneven quality. At best it looks average.

2003 A difficult year all around. Spring was wet and cool, with a series of heat spikes during the summer and some harvest rains. The size of the crop is down and quality is spotty on the North Coast, although Napa Cab Sauv looking better than expected.

2002 Average winter rainfall and slightly delayed bud-break with some frost damage. Heavy rain in May, cool growing season but no rain until Nov. Average-sized crop with superior quality and showing well with age.

2001 Little winter rain, sporadic heat in March, severe April frost, hottest May on record, and no rain until Oct. Excellent quality with Cab Sauv showing potential for ageing up to a decade.

2000 Scares included a threatened storm from the south in early Sept, but damage was minimal. Biggest harvest on record. OK quality.

1999 Very cold spring and summer created late harvest, but absence of autumn rain left crop unscathed. Intensely flavoured and coloured wines. Outstanding quality, which is looking even better with a little age.

1998 Erratic harvest stumbled into Nov. Wines are adequate to dismal.

1997 Huge crop that looked good early. May be peaking now.

1996 Tiny crop, lots of structure, lacks aromatic charm. Vintage is fading fast.

1995 Tiny crop, great vitality but slow to unfold. Good Zins, great Cabs. Best vintage for cellaring since 90.

1994 Mild growing season; dry, late harvest. Superb Zins, but a bit long in the tooth now; drink Cab Sauv now.

1993 Modest, plain-faced, serviceable year in the North Coast, but spectacular in Sierra Foothills with concentrated Zins, refreshing acidity. Drink up.

1991 Supple, balanced wines, best still drinking nicely.

1990 Cab Sauv at its peak; drink now.

Abreu Vineyards Napa ★★★ Cultish producer of huge, concentrated Cab Sauv that does come round after a decade.

Acacia Carneros ★★★ (Chard) 03 (Pinot N) 01 02 CARNEROS pioneer in Chard and Pinot N, moving towards darker Pinot N fruit with emphasis on single-vineyard wines. New bottling of Viognier very good.

Acorn Russian River Valley ★★→★★★ Outstanding Zin from Heritage vines. Also very good Sangiovese and Syrah.

Alban Edna Valley ★★→★★★ Pioneer Rhône-variety planter, and (with CALERA) California benchmark for Viognier. Excellent Grenache, Roussanne, Marsanne.

Alexander Valley Vineyards Sonoma ★★ Juicy approachable Cab Sauv and Zin. Chard much improved.

Altamura Vineyards Napa ★★★ 99 00 Elegant and luscious Cab Sauv. Sangiovese is one of the state's best.

Amador Foothills Winery Amador ★★ Ripe and delicious Zin and bright Sauv Bl, often blended with Sem.

Andrew Murray Sta Barbara ★★★ Small winery with a goal of producing only Rhône varietals. Good Syrah, Roussanne, and Viognier.

Araujo Napa ★★★ 96 97 Powerful, sleek, cultish Cab Sauv made from Eisele vineyard, bottled for years by Joseph PHELPS as a single-vineyard wine.

Armida Sonoma ★★→★★★ RUSSIAN RIVER VALLEY winery with solid Merlot, good Pinot N, and a zippy Zin made from DRY CREEK VALLEY grapes.

Arthur Earl Sta Barbara ★★→★★★ Small producer of Rhône and southern French varietals. Very good Mourvèdre, Grenache.

Atlas Peak Napa ★ Former Sangiovese specialist under Antinori influence, now putting emphasis on Cab Sauv, with mixed results.

Au Bon Climat Sta Barbara ★★★ Owner Jim Clendenen listens to his private drummer: ultra-toasty Chard, flavourful Pinot N, light-hearted Pinot Bl. Vita Nova label for Bordeaux varieties, Podere dellos Olivos for Italianates. See also QUPÉ.

Babcock Vineyards Sta Barbara ★★★ Very cool location in west SANTA YNEZ VALLEY. Good for Pinot N and Chard; Eleven Oaks Sauv Bl is one of California's best.

Baxter Napa ★★★ Veteran Napa winemaker Phil Baxter is making single-vineyard beauties. His Napa Valley Merlot is very good.

Beaulieu Vineyard Napa ★★★ 97 99 00 Under André Tchelistcheff in the 1940s and 1950s, Beaulieu set the style for NAPA Cab Sauv. Not the jewel it was, but still quite good, especially the Georges de Latour Private Reserve Cab Sauv.

Benessere Napa ★★★ Sangiovese and Syrah worth a try. New Super Tuscan-style blend called Phenomenon is outstanding.

Benziger Family Winery Sonoma ★★★ Family began converting vines to biodynamism in the mid-1990s. Steady improvement in wines, especially Chard and a soft, delicious Merlot.

Beringer Blass (Foster's Wine Estates) Napa ★→★★★★ (CAB) 97 98 A NAPA classic. Single-vineyard Cab Sauv Reserves can be over-the-top, but marvellous. Velvety but powerful Howell Mountain Merlot one of the best. Look for Founder's Estate bargain line from North Coast and Central Coast grapes. Also owns CHATEAU ST JEAN, ETUDE, MERIDIAN, ST CLEMENT, STAGS' LEAP WINERY, and Taz, a ★★→★★★ Pinot from Santa Barbara.

Bernardus Carmel Valley ★★★ Strong Meritage wines from densely planted, high-altitude vineyard above the valley floor. Brilliant Sauv Bl.

Biale Napa ★★→★★★ Small Zin specialist using mostly NAPA fruit.

Boeger El Dorado ★★ First El Dorado winery after Prohibition. Mostly estate wines. Attractive Merlot, Barbera, Zin, and Meritage. More understated than many in SIERRA FOOTHILLS.

Bogle Vineyards Yolo ★→★★★ Major growers in the SACRAMENTO Delta, Bogle family makes an attractive line of budget varietals and an excellent old-vine Zin.

Bokisch Lodi ★★→★★★ Makes wine only from Spanish varieties. Very good Garnacha, brilliant Albariño and one of the state's best Tempranillos.

Bonny Doon Sta Cruz Mtns ★★★ Original Rhône Ranger Randall Grahm sold his budget Big House Red and Big House White brand to concentrate on biodynamic production. Tops is Cigare Volant, his homage to Châteauneuf-du-Pape. Pacific Rim Ries is brilliant.

Bouchaine Vineyards Napa Carneros ★★→★★★ Winery has had some ups and downs since its founding in 1980. Now on an up-swing with classic, sleek Chard and juicy but serious single-vineyard Pinot N.

Bridlewood Santa Barbara ★★→★★★ A Rhône specialist, serious about Syrah – no Shiraz, please – and one of the state's best Viogniers for a bonus.

> **New AVAs springing up**
>
> As California wine-growers fine-tune the art of putting the right vine in the right place, a rash of new American Viticultural Areas (AVAs) have appeared. Seven new AVAs have been added in the Lodi area alone. Paso Robles is now debating how to split up that basic AVA into two or three parts. There is talk in Napa of an AVA for Calistoga and at least two in Pope Valley, to the east of Napa proper. The idea is not only to distinguish terroir but to appeal to increasingly well-informed wine consumers.

Bruce, David Sta Cruz Mtns ★★★ Powerful Chard keeps getting better; Pinot N always near the top.

Buena Vista Napa, Carneros ★★→★★★ After stumbling for a few years, Buena Vista is back on track with very good Estate Cab Sauv and good Sauv Bl from Lake County. Chard also worth a look.

Burgess Cellars Napa ★★★ (CAB) 95 97 99 Emphasis on dark, weighty Cab Sauv made from hillside vines on Howell Mountain. Powerful Zin.

Bynum, Davis Sonoma ★★★ Marvellous single-vineyard Pinot N from RUSSIAN RIVER VALLEY. Lean, minerally Chard is a treat.

Cain Cellars Napa ★★★ 95 97 99 Stylish, supple Cain Five anchored in estate plantings of Cab Sauv and four Bordeaux cousins on SPRING MOUNTAIN; Cain Cuvée (declassified Cain Five) can rival the big brother.

Cafaro Napa ★★★ Winemaker label for sturdy-to-solid Cab and Merlot.

Cakebread Napa ★★★ (Chard) 02 03 (Cab) 91 97 Powerful Cab Sauv with well-integrated if sometimes obvious oak. One of the best Sauv Bls in the state. Chard sometimes too oaky.

Calera San Benito ★★★★ Yale and Oxford graduate Josh Jensen went in search of the holy grail of Pinot N and found it in the dry, hot hills of San Benito. Three Pinot Ns named after vineyard blocks: Reed, Seleck, and Jensen; also, intense, flowery Viognier.

Campion Winery Napa ★★→★★★ Pinot N guru Larry Brooks is making only Pinot N and only single-vineyard Pinot N. Very promising beginning.

Caymus Napa ★★★→★★★★ 90 91 97 99 The Special Selection Cab Sauv is consistently one of California's best: rich, intense, slow to mature. Also a quite good regular bottling, balanced and a little lighter. Good Chard from Mer Soleil winery in Monterey, owned by Caymus.

Ceago Vinegarden Lake ★★→★★★ Jim Fetzer's new winery on the north shore of Clear Lake in Lake County. Very good. Sauv Bl and Cab Sauv made from biodynamic and organic vineyards on the estate and from Mendocino County. Keep an eye on this one.

Ceja Vineyards Napa ★★→★★★ Established in 1999 and already making a mark with balanced, focused Cab Sauv and delicious Chard from vineyards in Napa and Sonoma.

Chalk Hill Sonoma ★★→★★★ Large estate that has been up and down over the years. Usually reliable Cab Sauv made for ageing and a pleasing Chard.

Chalone Monterey ★★★→★★★★ (Pinot) **00 01 02** Mountain estate on east edge of MONTEREY. Marvellous flinty Chard and rich, intense Pinot N. Also makes a good Chenin Bl (unusual in California) and a tasty Pinot Bl.

Chappellet Napa ★★★ Ageworthy Cab Sauv has new grace-notes, especially Signature label. ***Chenin Bl: a NAPA classic, dry and succulent***. Pleasing, understated Chard; good Cab Fr, Merlot.

Château Montelena Napa ★★★→★★★★ (Chard) **97 99** (Cab) **99** Understated ageworthy Chard, and Calistoga Estate Cab Sauv built for long-term ageing.

Château Potelle Napa ★★★ Ex-pat French couple produce quietly impressive Chard (Reserve edition toastier) and vigorous Cab Sauv from MOUNT VEEDER estate. Outrageously good Zin from estate-owned vineyards in PASO ROBLES.

Château St Jean Sonoma ★★→★★★ Pioneered single-vineyard Chard in California under Richard Arrowood in the 1970s, still outstanding; good Sauv Bl. Red wine now a priority. Cinq Cepage, made from the five Bordeaux varieties is good. Reliable bottlings of Sonoma County Cab Sauv and Chard.

Chimney Rock Napa ★★★→★★★★ (Cab) **97 99** STAGS LEAP AVA producer of elegant, sometimes understated Cab Sauv capable of long ageing.

Clark-Claudon Napa ★★★ Newish producer of hillside Cab Sauv from estate vineyard on the eastern slope of Howell Mountain. Balanced and complex with layers of flavour. Very good unoaked Sauv Bl from Pope Valley.

Cline Cellars Carneros ★→★★ Originally Contra Costa (important vineyards still there), now in SONOMA/CARNEROS and still dedicated mostly to rustic-style Rhône blends and sturdy Zin.

Clos du Bois Sonoma ★★→★★★ Large-scale Sonoma producer of quaffable everyday wines, with the exception of a single-vineyard Cab Sauv (Briarcrest) and Calcaire Chard, which can be very good.

Clos du Val Napa ★★★★ (Cab) **95 97** Consistently elegant Cab Sauvs that are among the best ageing candidates in the state. Chard is a delight and a Sem/Sauv Bl blend called Ariadne is a charmer.

Clos LaChance Santa Cruz ★★ Relative newcomers showing good Zin and bright Chard from sourced fruit and own vineyards.

Clos Pegase Napa ★★→★★★ Post-modernist winery/museum makes a spare, wiry NAPA CARNEROS Chard and a sleek Cab Sauv from north NAPA grapes.

Cohn, B R Sonoma ★★→★★★ Mostly estate Cab Sauvs; hard-edged and awkward in the 1990s, now showing good juicy base and ageing potential.

Conn Creek Napa ★★★ Very good Cab Sauv sourced from several different vineyards; elegant wines with good structure and long ageing potential.

Constellation ★→★★★★ Owns wineries in California, NY, Washington State, Canada, Chile, Australia, and New Zealand. Produces 90 million cases of wine annually, selling more wine than any other winery in the world. Once a bottom feeder, now going for the top. Bought MONDAVI at the end of 2004 and also owns FRANCISCAN, ESTANCIA, Mount Veeder, SIMI, and RAVENSWOOD among others.

Corison Napa ★★★★ (Cab) **97** Long-time winemaker at CHAPPELLET makes supple, flavoursome Cab Sauv promising to age well.

Cosentino Napa ★★→★★★ Irrepressible winemaker-owner Mitch Cosentino always full tilt. Results sometimes odd, sometimes brilliant, never dull. Cab

Sauv always worth a look; Chard can be very good.

Coturri & Sons, H Sonoma ★ Organic, no-sulphite but unreliable wines. Sometimes good Zin with an attitude. Has a cult following.

Cuvaison Napa ★★★ (Chard) **02** (Merlot) **99 00 01** Good to very good Chard, Merlot, Syrah from Carneros. Impressive new Cab Sauv called Brandlin (after the vineyard) from Mt Veeder.

David Noyes Wines ★★★ Sonoma Former Ridge and Kunde Estate winemaker out on his own with elegant Pinot N and a delicious Tocai Friulano.

Dalla Valle Napa ★★★★ **97 99** Hillside estate is that rare thing: a cult classic with a track record. Maya is a Cab Sauv-based brawny, and Pietre Rosso, from Sangiovese, is a brilliant showcase for that variety.

Dehlinger Sonoma ★★★★ (Pinot) **00 01** Outstanding Pinot N from estate Russian Valley vineyard. Also good Chard, Syrah.

Delicato Vineyards San Joaquin ★→★★ One-time CENTRAL VALLEY jug producer has moved up-scale with purchase of MONTEREY vineyards and several new bottlings from LODI. Watch this brand for good quality at everyday price.

Diamond Creek Napa ★★★★ **94 95** Austere, stunning cult Cabs from hilly vineyard near Calistoga go by names of vineyard blocks: Gravelly Meadow, Volcanic Hill, Red Block Terrace. Wines age beautifully.

Domaine Carneros Carneros ★★★ Showy US outpost of Taittinger in CARNEROS echoes austere style of its parent in Champagne (see France) but with a delicious dollop of California fruit. Vintage Blanc de Blancs very good. La Rêve the luxury *cuvée*. Still Pinot N and Chard also impressive.

Domaine Chandon Napa ★★→★★★ Maturing vineyards, maturing style, broadening range taking Moët & Chandon's California arm to new heights. Look for NV Reserve, étoile rosé. Still wines a recent and welcome addition.

Dominus Napa ★★★★ 95 97 **98 99** 00 01 02 03' Christian Moueix of Pomerol produces red Bordeaux blend that is slow to open but ages beautifully; packed with power inside a silk glove. Big jump in quality in the mid-1990s. Second wine is Napanook.

Dry Creek Vineyard Sonoma ★★ Sauv (Fumé) Bl set standard for California for decades. Still impressive. Pleasing Chenin Bl; good Zin.

Duckhorn Vineyards Napa ★★★ ·★★★★ (Merlot) **97 00** Known for dark, tannic, almost plummy-ripe, single-vineyard Merlots (especially Three Palms) and Cab Sauv-based blend Howell Mountain. New winery in ANDERSON VALLEY for Golden Eye Pinot N in a robust style that would raise eyebrows in Burgundy. New Paraduxx Winery in Napa produces bold Zin-Cab Sauv blend.

Dunn Vineyards Napa ★★★★ 85 87 89 Owner-winemaker Randy Dunn makes dark, iconic Cab Sauv from Howell Mountain, which ages magnificently, slightly milder bottling from valley floor.

Dutton-Goldfield Western Sonoma Co ★★★ Adroitly crafted Burgundian varieties from several top sites. Likely to reach four stars soon.

Duxoup Sonoma ★★★ Quirky producer of excellent Rhône-style Syrah (don't look for Shiraz here) and inky, old-vine Charbono. A promising Sangiovese under the Gennaio label. Limited production but worth seeking out.

Eberle Winery San Luis Obispo ★★→★★★ Burly ex-footballer makes Cab Sauv and Zin in his own image: plenty of knock-your-socks-off power but, behind that, good balance and a supple concentration.

Echelon Napa Good-value label featuring good CENTRAL COAST Chard.

Edna Valley Vineyard San Luis Obispo ★★★ Much improved in past few vintages; very good Chard, crisp and fruity, lovely Sauv Bl. Recent Syrah impressive.

Estancia FRANCISCAN label: good value MONTEREY Chard, Sauv, Pinot N, Cab Sauv.

Etude Napa ★★★ ·★★★★ Rich Pinot N made from Carneros fruit.

CALIFORNIA

Failla Vineyards Napa ★★⭢★★★ The winery is on the Silverado trail in NAPA, but Failla is scoring big with SONOMA COAST and RUSSIAN RIVER VALLEY Pinot N and Chard. The Keefer Ranch Pinot N is especially impressive.

Far Niente Napa ★★★ (Chard) **00 01 02** 03 04 (Cab) **95 97** Opulence is the goal in both Cab Sauv and Chard from luxury NAPA estate. Can go over the top Nickel & Nickel, owned by Far Niente owners, makes several good-to-very-good single-vineyard Cab Sauvs.

Farrell, Gary Sonoma ★★★⭢★★★★ After years of sharing working space at David BYNUM winery while making legendary RUSSIAN RIVER Pinot N, Farrell now has his own winery. Also look for Zin and Chard.

Ferrari-Carano Sonoma ★★★ Dry Creek producer draws on estate vineyards in NAPA and SONOMA to make range of above-average wines, Merlot being the best, but don't overlook Sauv Bl and toasty Chard.

Fess Parker Sta Barbara ★★★ Owned by actor who played title role in TV's *Daniel Boone*; son Eli is winemaker. Good Chard in tropical-fruit style, impressive Pinot N and Syrah, surprisingly good Ries. Parker Station Pinot N is a luscious little wine made from young vines.

Fetzer Mendocino ★★⭢★★★ A leader in the organic/sustainable viticulture movement, Fetzer has produced consistently good-value wines from least expensive range (Sundial, Valley Oaks) to brilliant Reserve wines. Fetzer also owns Bonterra Vineyards (all organic grapes) where Roussanne and Marsanne are stars. Wines from McNabb Ranch line now farmed biodynamically.

Pinot Noir with a Californian accent

In the past decade, Pinot Noir has become very popular in California – that is no secret. But an odd thing has happened to the wine recently: a new wave of huge, fruit-forward and high-alcohol Pinot Noir has pushed its way to the front of the line. These wines – some call them "populist Pinots" – are a big hit with younger drinkers who also favour super-concentrated Cabernets. Examples include Duckhorn's Goldeneye from Anderson Valley and Kosta Browne Russian River Valley.

Ficklin Vineyards Madera, Central Valley Lush and delicious port-style dessert wines made from the classic Portuguese varieties.

Fiddlehead San Luis Obispo ★★★ Winemaker Kathy Joseph makes Pinot N that is always near the top; also very good Sauv Bl in a minerally Bordeaux style.

Firestone Sta Barbara ★★ Fine Chard overshadows but does not outshine *delicious Ries*. Good Merlot as well.

Fisher Sonoma ★★⭢★★★ Hill-top SONOMA grapes for often-fine Chard; NAPA grapes dominate steady Cab Sauv.

Flora Springs Wine Co Napa ★★★ Best here are the two Meritage wines, a red blend called Trilogy and a white called Soliloquy. Juicy Merlot also worth a look. Chard can be too oaky.

Flowers Vineyard & Winery Sonoma ★★★ Intense, terroir-driven Pinot N and Chard from very cool-climate vines only a few miles from the Pacific. Flowers has won early critical acclaim and is clearly a winery to watch.

Foley Estates Vineyard Santa Barbara ★★⭢★★★ Established in 1997; making a name for itself with balanced and delicious Chard and Pinot N.

Foppiano Sonoma ★★ Long-established wine family turns out fine reds (especially Petite Sirah, Zin) under family name. Responsible for leading the mini-renaissance in Petite Sirah, "petty sir".

Forman Napa ★★★★ (Cab) **97 99** Winemaker who found fame for STERLING in the 1970s now makes his own excellent Cab Sauv and Chard.

Foxen Sta Barbara ★★★ Tiny winery nestled between SANTA YNEZ and SANTA MARIA

VALLEYS. Always bold, frequently brilliant Pinot N overshadows stylish Chard.

Franciscan Vineyard Napa ★★★ Solid producer of reliable Cab Sauv and Merlot, complex yet supple Chard. Austere Cab Sauv and red Meritage from MOUNT VEEDER label. Now owned by CONSTELLATION.

Franzia San Joaquin Penny-saver wines under Franzia, Corbett Canyon, NAPA Ridge, Charles Shaw ("Two-Buck Chuck"), and other labels. Largest bag-in-box producer.

Freeman Russian River Valley ★★ New producer showing great promise with cool-climate Pinot N (Akiko's Cuvée from SONOMA COAST AVA) and RUSSIAN RIVER Pinot N. Keep an eye on this exciting new estate.

Freemark Abbey Napa ★★★ (Cab) 97 00 Underrated but consistent producer of *stylish Cab Sauv* (especially single-vineyard Sycamore and Bosché). Very good, deliciously true-to-variety Chard.

Fritz Dry Creek Valley ★★ Consistently good Zin from DRY CREEK and RUSSIAN RIVER AVAs, sometimes rising to ★★★. Good Pinot N and a reliable Cab Sauv.

Frog's Leap Napa ★★★ →★★★★ 97 99 Small winery, as charming as its name (and T-shirts) suggest. Lean, minerally Sauv Bl, toasty Chard, spicy Zin. Supple and delicious Merlot, Cab Sauv. Converting to organic and biodynamic.

Gallo, E & J San Joaquin ★ Having mastered the world of commodity wines, this huge family firm is now unleashing a blizzard of regional varietals under such names as Anapauma, Marcellina, Turning Leaf, Zabaco, and more; some from Modesto, some via GALLO SONOMA, all mostly forgettable.

Gallo Sonoma Sonoma ★★→★★★ (Cab) 99 00 DRY CREEK VALLEY winery bottles several wines from SONOMA, NORTH COAST. Cab Sauv can be very good, especially the single-vineyard ones. SONOMA line impressive for value.

Geyser Peak Sonoma ★★→★★★ Reliable producer of toasty Chard, powerful, sleek Cab Sauv, juicy Shiraz. A blend of Bordeaux reds can be very good. Interesting new bottlings of single-vineyard wines worth looking out for.

Gloria Ferrer Sonoma, Carneros ★★★ Built by Spain's Freixenet for sparkling wine, now producing spicy Chard and bright, silky Pinot N, all from CARNEROS fruit. Bubbly quality remains high, especially the Royal Cuvée, inspired by a visit from King Juan Carlos of Spain.

Grace Family Vineyard Napa ★★★★ 97 Stunning Cab Sauv. Shaped for long ageing. One of the few cult wines actually worth the price.

Greenwood Ridge Mendocino ★★→★★★ Winery well above the floor of ANDERSON VALLEY made its name as producer of off-dry, perfumy Ries. Reds, especially Cab Sauv and Pinot N, also very good.

Girgich Hills Cellars Napa ★★★→★★★★ (Chard) 99 Vastly underrated NAPA producer of supple Chard (which can age); balanced, elegant Cab Sauv; jammy, ripe Zin from SONOMA grapes. Good Sauv Bl in minerally style.

Groth Vineyards Napa ★★★★ (Cab) 95 97 99 OAKVILLE estate Cab Sauv has been consistently four-star quality for a decade, with big, wrap-around flavours made for ageing. Chard also excellent.

Gundlach-Bundschu Sonoma ★★→★★★ Versatile Rhinefarm estate vineyard signals memorably individual Gewurz, Merlot, Zin. Much-improved Cab Sauv recently from hillside vines.

Hagafen Napa ★★ One of the first serious California kosher producers. Especially Chard and crisp Sauv Bl.

Handley Cellars Mendocino ★★★ Winemaker Mila Handley makes excellent ANDERSON VALLEY Chard, Gewurz, Pinot N. Also very good DRY CREEK VALLEY Sauv Bl and Chard from her family's vines. She produces a small amount of intense sparkling wine, which is well worth a look.

Hanna Winery Sonoma ★★★ Has been flirting with four-star status for yrs. Recent vintages of Cab Sauv and well-made Sauv Bl are excellent.

Hanzell Sonoma ★★★★ (Chard) **oo** (Pinot N) **oo** Small producer of outstanding terroir-driven Chard and Pinot N from estate vines. Always good; quality level has risen sharply in the past few years. Deserves to be ranked with the best of California.

Harlan Estate Napa ★★★★ **97 99** Concentrated, sleek, cult Cab Sauv from small estate commanding luxury prices.

Harrison Napa ★★→★★★ Located near LONG VINEYARDS and the cult Cab Sauv of Bryant family. Predictably specializing in Cab Sauv.

Hartford Court Sonoma ★★★ Part of KENDALL JACKSON's Artisans & Estates group showing very good single-vineyard Pinot Ns, tight coastal-grown Chard, and wonderful old-vine RUSSIAN RIVER Zins.

HDV Carneros Chard from grower Larry Hyde's vineyard in conjunction with Aubert de Villaine of Domaine Romanée-Conti (see France).

Heitz Napa ★★★→★★★★ **95 97** Rich, supple, deeply flavoured, minty Cab Sauv from Martha's Vineyard. Bella Oaks and newer Trailside Vineyard rival but can't match Martha. Some feel quality has slipped in recent vintages.

Heller Estate Carmel Valley, Monterey ★★★ **97 99** Dark and powerful wines (especially the past few years as vines mature) are acquiring something of a cult status. Chenin Bl is charming.

Hess Collection, The Napa ★★★→★★★★ (Cab) **97** Owned by Swiss art collector Donald Hess, who has installed a very good museum. New Cab Sauv from vineyards in Mt Veeder AVA step up to new quality level. Chard crisp and bright. Budget Hess Select label is very good value.

Honig Napa ★★★ Big jump in quality after switching to organic farming. Very good Cab Sauv in classic NAPA style and seriously delicious Sauv Bl.

Hop Kiln Sonoma ★★★ A new direction for this well-regarded winery with a brand called HK Generations. Chard is superb, Pinot N excellent, both made from RUSSIAN RIVER VALLEY grapes. Also good Zin.

Iron Horse Vineyards Sonoma ★★★→★★★★★ RUSSIAN RIVER family estate producing *some of California's best bubbly*, especially a series of late-disgorged beauties. Chard from cool RUSSIAN RIVER VALLEY is outstanding, and an above-average Cab Sauv from ALEXANDER VALLEY vineyards.

Jade Mountain Napa ★★→★★★ Outstanding producer of Rhône-style wines, especially Syrah, Mourvèdre.

Jessie's Grove Lodi ★★ Old Zin vines work well for farming family's venture.

Jordan Sonoma ★★★★ (Cab) **94 95 97** Extravagant ALEXANDER VALLEY estate models its Cab Sauv on supplest Bordeaux. And it lasts. Minerally Chard is made in a Burgundian style.

J Sonoma ★★★ Born part of JORDAN, now on its own in RUSSIAN RIVER VALLEY. Creamy, classic-method Brut the foundation. Still, Pinot N and Pinot Gr worth a look.

Judd's Hill Napa Valley ★★★ Founders of Whitehall Lane now have their own winery, making elegant Cab Sauv that should age very well.

Kautz-Ironstone Lodi and Calaveras County ★ Showplace destination in SIERRA FOOTHILLS attracts visitors from all over the state. Honestly priced broad range led by fine Cab Fr.

Keenan Winery, Robert Napa ★★★ Winery on SPRING MOUNTAIN: supple, restrained Cab Sauv, Merlot; also Chard.

Kendall-Jackson Sonoma ★★→★★★ Staggeringly successful style aimed at widest market, especially broadly sourced off-dry toasty Chard. Even more noteworthy for the development of a diversity of wineries under the umbrella of Kendall-Jackson's Artisans & Estates (see HARTFORD COURT).

Kenwood Vineyards Sonoma ★★→★★★ (Jack London Cab) **97 99** Single-vineyard

Jack London Cab Sauv, Zin (several) the high points. Sauv Bl is reliable value.

Kistler Vineyards Sonoma ★★★ (Chard) Still chasing the Burgundian model of single-vineyard Pinot N, most from RUSSIAN RIVER, with mixed success. Chards can be very toasty, buttery, and over-the-top, though they have a loyal following.

Konigsgaard Napa ★★★ Small production of Chard, Syrah, and Roussanne from former NEWTON winemaker.

Korbel Sonoma ★★★ Long-established sparkling specialist emphasizes bold fruit flavours, intense fizz; Natural tops the line.

Krug, Charles Napa ★★ Historically important winery with sound wines. Cabs at head of list, although Sauv Bl has stepped forward in past few vintages.

Kunde Estate Sonoma ★★★ Solid producer with an elegant, understated Chard, flavourful Sauv Bl, peachy Viognier, and silky Merlot. All estate-bottled.

La Jota Napa ★★→★★★ Huge, long-lived Cab Sauv from Howell Mountain. Owned by MARKHAM vineyards.

Lambert Bridge Dry Creek, Sonoma ★★★ Seductive Merlot, zesty Zin, and brilliant Sauv Bl in a "Bordeaux meets New Zealand" style.

Lamborn Howell Mountain, Napa ★★★ Vineyard planted on historic 19th-C site. Big juicy Zin, Cab Sauv coming along for this cult winery.

Landmark Sonoma ★★→★★★ Early promise of elegant Burgundian-style Chard blunted by oaky-toasty flavours for a time in the late 1990s. Recent bottlings seem to be back on track.

Lang & Reed Napa ★★★ Specialist focusing on delicious Loire-style Cab Fr.

Laurel Glen Sonoma ★★★★ (Cab) **91 94 95** Floral, well-etched Cab Sauv with a sense of place from steep vineyard on SONOMA MOUNTAIN.

Lava Cap El Dorado ★★ Sierra producer making a wide range of mostly estate wines. Cab Sauv is good, but Zin is outstanding.

Livingston Moffett St Helena, Napa ★★★ Noteworthy Cab Sauv from Rutherford Ranch vineyards. Syrah also very good.

Lockwood Monterey ★ S Salinas Valley vineyard. Good value in Chard, Sauv Bl.

Lohr, J Central Coast ★★→★★★ Large winery with extensive vineyards; very good PASO ROBLES Cab Sauv Seven Oaks. Recent series of Meritage-style reds best yet. Commodity line is Cypress.

Lolonis Mendocino ★★ Pre-Prohibition MENDOCINO growers, founded winery in 1982. Good, solid Zin, Merlot, spicy Chard.

Long Meadow Napa ★★★ Elegant, silky Cab Sauv better with each vintage. Vineyard is organically farmed. Potential cult status.

Longoria Winery Sta Barbara (★★→★★★) Rick Longoria makes brilliant Pinot N from top vineyards in the area.

Long Vineyards Napa ★★★ (Chard) **oo o1** Small estate owned by legendary winemakers Robert and Zelma Long. Luscious Chard, silky Cab Sauv, and velvety Ries at top prices.

MacRostie Sonoma, Carneros ★★★ Toasty, ripe Chard with some complexity is flagship. Also Merlot, Pinot N from single-vineyards. New Syrah is very good.

Madonna Estate Napa Carneros ★★→★★★ Outstanding single-vineyard Pinot N; Cab Sauv, Chard seldom rise above two stars. Formerly Mont St John Cellars.

Mahoney Vineyards Napa, Carneros ★★→★★★ Founder of CARNEROS CREEK, one of the Carneros pioneers and an early Pinot N enthusiast, now producing under own label. Very good Vermentino, excellent single-vineyard Pinot N.

Marcassin Sonoma Coast Cult consultant Helen Turley's own tiny label. Worth so much at auction that few ever drink it. Concentrated Chard and dense Pinot N. Chard so densely concentrated, those who do taste it never forget.

Markham Napa ★★★ (Merlot) **98 01** Greatly underrated producer of balanced, elegant Merlot and solid Cab Sauv.

Martinelli Russian River ★★★ Family growers from fog-shrouded western hills of

Sonoma, famous for old-vine Jackass Hill Vineyard Zin. Sought-after Pinot N and Chard made under Helen Turley's consulting eye.

Martini, Louis M Napa ★★→★★★ Long history-making, ageworthy Cab Sauv, Zin, Barbera from fine vineyards (Monte Rosso, Los Vinedos, Glen Oaks, etc.) in NAPA and SONOMA. On downslide for several years. Now on the way back after purchase by GALLO in 2002 with recent bottlings of Cab Sauv showing very well.

Matanzas Creek Sonoma ★★ Excellent Sauv Bl has slipped of late. Merlot outstanding; Chard good. Owned by KENDALL-JACKSON.

Mayacamas Napa ★★★ Pioneer boutique vineyard with rich Chard and firm (but no longer steel-hard) Cab Sauv, capable of long ageing.

Merry Edwards Russian River ★★★★ Superstar consultant has planted her own Pinot N vineyard in RUSSIAN RIVER district and buys in grapes. Already one of the top Pinot N producers in California. Also lovely, true-to-varietal Sauv Bl.

Merryvale Napa ★★★ Best at Cab Sauv and Merlot, which have elegant balance and supple finish. Chard being revitalized, moving away from oaky-toast to a more complex Burgundian model. Sauv Bl can be very good.

Mettler Family Vineyards Lodi ★★ Long-time growers now producing a sleek and tangy Cab Sauv and a powerful Petite Sirah. On the way up.

Michael, Peter Sonoma ★★★→★★★★ Stunning, complex Chard from Howell Mountain in a powerful style, and a more supple ALEXANDER VALLEY bottling. Cab Sauv on the tight side.

Michel-Schlumberger Sonoma ★★→★★★ Excellent ageing potential in supple Cab Sauv usually blended with Merlot from hillside vines.

Milano Mendocino ★★ Small producer of Zin, Cab Sauv, worth seeking out.

Mitchell Katz Livermore Valley ★★→★★★ An upcoming winery on the site of Ruby Hill, an historic Livermore winery. Makes very good Cab Sauv and blockbuster Petite Sirah. Watch for more.

Mondavi, Robert Napa ★★→★★★★ Brilliant innovator bought in 2004 by CONSTELLATION, has wine at all price/quality ranges. At the top are the NAPA VALLEY Reserves (bold, prices to match), NAPA VALLEY appellation series (e.g. CARNEROS Chard, OAKVILLE Cab Sauv, etc.), NAPA VALLEY (basic production). At the low end are various Central Coast wines and Robert Mondavi-Woodbridge from Lodi. Mondavi insiders say quality is on the way up of late.

Monteviña Amador ★★ Ripe and fruit-forward SIERRA Zin and a very good Barbera. Owned by SUTTER HOME. Top of line called Terra d'Oro.

Monticello Cellars Napa ★★★ (Cab) **95 97** Consistently worth seeking out. Basic line under Monticello label, reserves under Corley. Both include Chard and Cab Sauv.

Morgan Monterey ★★★★ Top-end, single-vineyard Pinot Ns and Chards from very good SANTA LUCIA HIGHLANDS vineyards. Especially fine unoaked Chard called Metallico. Estate Double L vineyard is now farmed organically.

Mount Eden Santa Cruz Mountains ★★★ Founded by California wine guru Martin Ray in the 1940s, Mount Eden produces ageworthy Chard – rare in California – and intense Pinot N.

Mumm Napa Valley Napa ★★★ Stylish bubbly, especially delicious Blanc de Noirs and a rich, complex DVX single-vineyard fizz, which does improve with a few years in the bottle.

Murphy-Goode Sonoma ★★ Large ALEXANDER VALLEY estate. Sauv Bl, Zin are tops; Merlot better than average. Tin Roof (screwcap) line offers refreshing Sauv Bl and Chard *sans* oak, in contrast to lavishly oaked Reserve line.

Nalle Sonoma ★★★ Doug Nalle makes lovely Zins from Dry Creek fruit, that are juicy and delicious when young and will also mature gracefully for years.

Napa Wine Company Napa ★★★ Largest organic grape grower in Napa sells most of the fruit and operates a custom crush facility for several small premium producers. Offers three-star Cab Sauv under own label.

Navarro Vineyards Mendocino ★★★→★★★★ From ANDERSON VALLEY, splendidly ageworthy Chard, perhaps the grandest Gewurz in state. Even more special: late-harvest Ries, Gewurz. Pinot N in two styles, homage to Burgundy from ANDERSON VALLEY grapes, plus a brisk and juicy bottling from bought-in grapes.

Newton Vineyards Napa ★★★→★★★★ (Cab) 95 **97** (Merlot) **97 99** Mountain estate makes some of California's best Merlot. Lush Chard and a supple Cab Sauv.

Meyers Napa ★★→★★★ Good quality overall; great Syrah and a lovely Chard.

Niebaum-Coppola Estate Napa ★★★ (Rubicon) **97 98 99** "Godfather" Coppola has proven he is as serious about making wine as making movies. Now owns the historic Inglenook Estate vineyard and winery (but not the brand). Flagship Rubicon ranks with the state's best Bordeaux red blends. Edizone Pennino concentrates on delightfully old-fashioned Zin; good-value Diamond series always worth a look.

Ojai Ventura ★★★ Former AU BON CLIMAT partner Adam Tolmach on his own since early 1990s makes wide range of excellent wines, especially Syrah.

Opus One Napa ★★★ **95 97 99** There have been a lot of in-and-out years at Opus, but the trend has been up for the last few vintages. In some ways the winery seems to be marking time, awaiting a firm hand to put it right.

Pahlmeyer Napa ★★★ Cultish producer of dense, tannic Cab Sauv and more supple, fruity Merlot.

Paradigm Napa ★★★ Westside OAKVILLE vineyard with an impressive Merlot and a bright, supple Cab Sauv.

Paraiso Monterey ★★→★★★ Up-and-comer owned by large grower in Salinas, making luscious Ries and Pinot Bl. More recently bright and balanced Pinot N from SANTA LUCIA HIGHLANDS fruit and a supple Syrah.

Patianna Vineyards Russian River ★★★ Biodynamic vineyards farmed by Patty Fetzer. Also sources grapes from organic vineyards in MENDOCINO. Lovely Sauv Bl and very good Syrah are main strengths.

Peachy Canyon Paso Robles ★★→★★★ Big bold Zin is a story worth telling.

Pedroncelli Sonoma ★★ Old-hand in DRY CREEK producing agreeable Zin, Cab Sauv, and a solid Chard.

Periano Lodi ★★ Good example of the new look of Lodi wines. Outstanding Barbera, brilliant Viognier, and very good Chard.

Perry Creek Eldorado ★★→★★★ An extraordinary Syrah from high-elevation vines and above-average Cab Sauv.

Phelps, Joseph Napa ★★★★ (Insignia) **95 97** Phelps has emerged as one of the top six Cab Sauv houses in California. Very good Chard, Cab Sauv (especially Backus), and Cab Sauv-based Insignia. Also look for fine Rhône series under Vin du Mistral label. Expect great things from a Pinot N-only winery Phelps has built in coastal SONOMA. Beginning to farm biodynamically.

Philips, R H Yolo, Dunnigan Hills ★→★★★ The only winery in the Dunnigan Hills AVA makes a wide range of wines. Excellent job with Rhône varieties under the EXP label and good-value Toasted Head Chard.

Philip Togni Vineyards Napa ★★★→★★★★★ **97 99** Veteran Napa winemaker makes outstanding Cab Sauv from small estate vineyard on Spring Mountain.

Pine Ridge Napa ★★★ Tannic and concentrated Cab Sauvs from several NAPA AVAs which may be worthy of ageing. The just off-dry Chenin Bl is a treat.

Preston Dry Creek Valley, Sonoma ★★★ Lou Preston is a demanding terroirist, making outstanding DRY CREEK VALLEY icons like Zin and fruity, marvellous Barbera. His Sauv Bl is delicious. New line of Rhône varietals show promise.

Pride Mountain Napa ★★★ Top hillside location on Spring Mountain contributes bright fruit characters to fine Bordeaux-variety offerings; ageing potential.

Provenance Napa ★★★ Lovely, elegant, and supple Cab Sauv from heart of NAPA estate. Winemaker Tom Rinaldi also makes a superb Hewitt Vineyard Cab Sauv. A winery on the way up.

Quady Winery San Joaquin. Imaginative Madera Muscat dessert wines include celebrated orangey Essencia, rose-petal-flavoured Elysium, and Moscato d'Asti-like Electra.

Quintessa Napa ★★★ Splendid new estate on Silverado Trail, developed by the Huneeus wine family of Chile and linked to FRANCISCAN and CONSTELLATION. Early releases of red Meritage-style show tremendous promise. Converting to biodynamic farming.

Quivira Sonoma ★★★ Sauv Bl, Zin, and others, from DRY CREEK VALLEY estate Vineyards farmed biodynamically.

Qupé Sta Barbara ★★★ Never-a-dull-moment cellar-mate of AU BON CLIMAT. *Marsanne, Pinot Bl, Syrah are all well worth trying*.

Rafanelli, A Sonoma ★★★→★★★★ Extraordinary Dry Creek Zin is strong suit. It will age, but it's so delightful when young, why bother?

Ramey Wine Cellars Russian River ★★★→★★★★ Veteran winemaker is making outstanding single-vineyard Cab Sauv, sourced mostly from NAPA, and incredibly rich and complex Chard from cooler vineyards.

Rasmussen, Kent Carneros ★★★ Crisp, lingering Chard and delicious Pinot N. Ramsay is an alternative label for small production lots.

Ravenswood Sonoma ★★★→★★★★ Zin Master Joel Peterson pioneered single-vineyard Zin. Affordable line of SONOMA and Vintners Reserve Zin and Merlot. Now owned by CONSTELLATION, but quality appears to be holding firm.

Raymond Vineyards and Cellar Napa ★★★ (Cab) **97 99** Underrated Cab Sauv from family vineyards. Potential for long-term ageing.

Ridge Sta Cruz Mtns ★★★★ (Cab) **87 91 94** Winery of highest repute among connoisseurs. Drawing from NAPA (York Creek) and its own mountain vineyard (*Montebello) for lithe, harmonious Cab Sauvs* worthy of long maturing, and from SONOMA, NAPA, Sierra Foothills, and PASO ROBLES for amazing single-vineyard Zin. Most Zin has good ageing potential, but why bother? Outstanding Chard from wild-yeast fermentation is often overlooked.

Rochioli, J Sonoma ★★★→★★★★ Long-time RUSSIAN RIVER grower sells most of his fruit to GARY FARRELL and other top Pinot N producers, but makes several own-label Pinot Ns every year that are simply super. Also very good Zin.

Roederer Estate Mendocino ★★★★ ANDERSON VALLEY branch of Champagne house (established 1988). Supple, elegant house style. Easily one of the top three sparklers in California and hands-down the best rosé. Top-of-the-line luxury *cuvée* l'Ermitage superb.

Rosenblum Cellars San Francisco Bay ★★→★★★★ Makes 7–8 single-vineyard Zin in any given year sourced from all over the state, many from old vines. Quality varies, but always well above average.

Rutz Cellars Sonoma ★★→★★★★ Early Chard outstanding but has strayed into over-the-top bottlings of late. Very good Pinot N with more guts than most from RUSSIAN RIVER vineyards.

Saddleback Cellars Napa ★★★→★★★★ (Cab) **95 97 99** Owner-winemaker Nils Venge is a legend in NAPA. Lush Zin and long-lived Cab Sauv.

St Clement Napa ★★★→★★★★ (Cab) **95 97** Supple, long-lived Oroppas, a Cab Sauv-based blend, is the go-to wine here. Merlot and Chard also outstanding. New winemaker Danielle Cyrot has a terroir-driven approach that speaks well for the future.

St Francis Sonoma ★★★ (Merlot) **99 00** Deep and concentrated Cab Sauv; fruity and lively Merlot. The old-vine Zin is super.

St-Supéry Napa ★★→★★★★ Sleek and graceful Merlot; Cab Sauv can be outstanding, as is red Meritage. Sauv Bl one of best in state. Sources some grapes from warmer Pope Valley east of NAPA VALLEY. French-owned (Skalli).

aintsbury Carneros ★★★ →★★★★ (Chard) **00 01** (Pinot N) **99 00 01** Outstanding Pinot N, denser than most from CARNEROS. Chard full-flavoured and oak-shy. *Garnet Pinot N, made from younger vines, is a light-hearted treat*.

Sanford Sta Barbara ★★→★★★ Founder Richard Sanford was one of the first to plant Pinot N in Santa Barbara, but wines have hit a rough patch under new owners. However, the Pinot N and Sauv Bl are still worth a look.

Santa Cruz Mountain Vineyard Santa Cruz ★★→★★★ (Cab) **95** Produces wines of strong varietal character from estate grapes, including single very good Pinot N and an exceptional Cab Sauv – big and concentrated, and capable of extended ageing.

Sattui, V Napa ★★ King of direct-only sales (*i.e.* winery door or mail order). Wines made in a rustic, drink-now style. Reds are best, especially Cab Sauv, Zin.

Sausal Sonoma ★★→★★★ ALEXANDER VALLEY estate noted for its Zin and Cab Sauv. Century Vine Zin is a stunning example of old-vine Zin.

Scherrer Sonoma ★★→★★★ Ripe, California-style Pinot N and Chard from RUSSIAN RIVER, as well as mouth-filling, old-vine Zin from ALEXANDER VALLEY.

Schramsberg Napa ★★★★ Sparkling wine that stands the test of time. The first to make a true *methode champenoise* in the state in commercial quantity. Historic caves. Reserve is splendid; *Blanc de Noirs outstanding* (2–10 years). Luxury *cuvée* J Schram is America's Krug. Now making a very good Cab Sauv from mountain estate vines.

Schug Cellars Carneros ★★★ German-born and trained owner-winemaker dabbles in other types, but CARNEROS Chard and Pinot N are his main interests and wines. Pinot N is always near the top.

Screaming Eagle Napa Small lots of cult Cab Sauv at luxury prices for those who like that kind of thing.

Sebastiani Sonoma ★ Former jug-wine king has tried to go upscale with vineyard wines with limited success. Don Sebastiani with his sons also producing crowd-pleasing everyday wines, such as Screw Kappa Napa.

Seghesio Sonoma ★★★ Concentrating now on superb, ageworthy Zins from own old vineyards in ALEXANDER and DRY CREEK VALLEYS, but don't overlook smaller lots of Sangiovese.

Selene Napa ★★★→★★★★★ Ace winemaker Mia Klein makes rich and concentrated Merlot and brilliant Sauv Bl.

Sequoia Grove Napa ★★★ Estate Cab Sauvs are intense and long-lived, and the trend in the past few years is clearly towards a fourth star. Chard is a cut above and can age.

Shafer Vineyards Napa ★★★★ (Cab) **87 90 91** (Merlot) **97 99** Always in the top range for Merlot and Cab Sauv, especially the Hillside Select from STAGS LEAP. CARNEROS Chard (Red Shoulder Ranch) breaking out of oak shackles. A solid California "first growth".

Sierra Vista El Dorado ★★→★★★ Dedicated Rhôneist in SIERRA FOOTHILLS. Style is elegant, mid-weight, and fruit driven, with emphasis on varietal typicity.

Signorello Napa ★★★ Fairly high-end Cab Sauvs and Chards, noteworthy Pinot N from RUSSIAN RIVER, very good Sem/Sauv Bl blend is best value. All could do with a bit less oak.

Silverado Vineyards Napa ★★★→★★★★ (Cab) **95 97** Showy hilltop STAGS LEAP district winery offering supple Cab Sauv, lean and minerally Chard, and distinctive Sangiovese.

Silver Oak Napa/Sonoma ★★★→★★★★ (Cab Napa) **97** Separate wineries in NAPA and ALEXANDER VALLEYS make Cab Sauv only. Owners have ridden extreme American-oaked style to pinnacle of critical acclaim among those who admire such wines. Alexander Valley a bit more supple than Napa.

Simi Sonoma ★★-★★★★ Up-and-down historic winery makes a wide range of varietals. Long-lived Cab Sauv and very good Chard still the heart of the matter. White Meritage Sendal is super.

Sinskey Vineyards Napa ★★★ Ex-ACACIA partner started winery. Chard with a good acidic bite and luscious Pinot N are the highlights.

Smith & Hook Monterey ★★-★★★★ Rich, fruity Pinot N from Santa Lucia Highlands vineyard leads the way followed by a good Chard. Budget line is Hahn Estate.

Smith-Madrone Napa ★★ High up on SPRING MOUNTAIN, the Smith brothers craft a *superb off-dry Ries* and a lean Chard.

Sonoma-Cutrer Vineyards Sonoma ★★ Chard specialist is back on track after a few down years. New Pinot N release is very good.

Spencer Roloson ★★ Négociant producer of stylish Zin and Tempranillo from single vineyards. To watch.

Spottswoode Napa ★★★ (Cab) **94 95** *Outstanding Cab Sauv* from estate vineyard is long-lasting, balanced, and harmonious. Another California "first growth". Brilliant Sauv Bl is a bonus.

Spring Mountain Napa ★★★-★★★★ Famed on TV as "Falcon Crest", this historic mountain estate is on a winning path. Excellent Cab Sauv and outstanding Sauv Bl from estate vines.

Stag's Leap Wine Cellars Napa ★★★★ (Cab) **91 94 95** Celebrated for silky, seductive Cab Sauvs (SLV, Fay, top-of-line Cask 23) and Merlots. Good Chard is often overlooked. Holding the line for balance and harmony against the onslaught of over-the-top, super-concentrated Napa Cab.

Stags' Leap Winery Napa ★★ Historic estate being revived by BERINGER BLASS. Important for Petite Sirah.

Staglin Napa ★★★ (Cab) **97 99** Silky, elegant Cab Sauv from Rutherford Bench.

Steele Wines Lake ★★-★★★★ Jed Steele is a genius at sourcing vineyards for a series of single-vineyard wines under main label and a second label called Shooting Star. Chard can get a little oaky, but Pinot N and some speciality wines, such as Washington State Lemberger, are outstanding.

Sterling Napa ★★-★★★★ Scenic NAPA estate now owned by Diageo Chateau & Estate Wines. Good basic Chard and understated single-vineyard Cab Sauv. Sterling has never seemed to fulfil potential, despite good vineyard sources.

Stony Hill Napa ★★★★ (Chard) **90 91 95 97** Amazing hillside Chard for past 50 years, made in an elegant "homage to Chablis" style. Most wine sold from mailing list. Stony Hill was Napa's first cult winery. Wines are very long-lived.

Storybook Mountain Napa ★★ Dedicated Zin specialist makes taut and tannic Estate and Reserve wines from Calistoga vineyard.

Strong Vineyard Sonoma ★-★★ Cab Sauv from single-vineyard bottlings good to very good; good RUSSIAN RIVER Pinot N and a pleasing heritage-vine Zin.

Sutter Home Napa ★-★★★ Famous for white Zin and rustic Amador red Zin. New upscale Signature Series and M Trinchero a solid step up, especially Cab Sauv.

Swan, Joseph Sonoma ★★★ Long-time RUSSIAN RIVER producer of intense Zin and classy Pinot N capable of ageing in the 10-year range.

Tablas Creek Paso Robles ★★★ Joint venture between owners of Château Beaucastel and importer Robert Hass. Vineyard based on cuttings from Châteauneuf vineyards. Early results promising.

Talbott, R Monterey ★★★ Chard from single vineyards in MONTEREY is the name of the game, with the famed Sleepy Hollow vineyard in the Santa Lucia Highlands AVA at the heart. Approach is Burgundian.

Tanner, Lane Santa Barbara ★★★-★★★★ (Pinot N) **00 01** Owner-winemaker makes hands-on and often-superb single-vineyard Pinot N (Bien Nacido, Sierra Madre Plateau) reflecting terroir with a quiet, understated elegance.

The Terraces Napa ★★★ High above the Silverado trail, this is the home of outstanding Zin and Cab Sauv with supple style.

Thomas Fogarty Santa Cruz Mountains ★★→★★★ Go here for a rich, complex Chardonnay that ages fairly well. Also good Pinot N from estate vineyards and a delightful Gewurz from Monterey grapes.

Torres Estate, Marimar Sonoma ★★★★ (Chard) 00 01 (Pinot N) 99 00 Edgy Chard (ages magnificently), lovely Pinot N from RUSSIAN RIVER VALLEY. Wines from new Pinot N plantings on coast are superb. Vineyards now farmed organically and moving toward biodynamics.

Trefethen Napa ★★★ Respected family winery. Good off-dry Ries, balanced Chard for ageing, although recent releases have not shown as well. ***Cab Sauv shows increasing depths and complexity with a few years in bottle***.

Tres Sabores Rutherford, ★★★ Newcomer making Zin and Cab Sauv from organically grown estate grapes. Wines are consistently balanced and elegant. Should age vry well.

Truchard Carneros ★★★→★★★★ From the warmer north end of CARNEROS comes one of the flavoury, firmly built Merlots that give the AVA identity. Cab Sauv and Syrah even better, and the tangy lemony Chard is a must-drink. New bottlings of Tempranillo outstanding and a very good Roussanne.

Turley Alexander Valley ★★★ Former partner in FROG'S LEAP, now specializing in hefty, heady, single-vineyard Zin and Petite Sirah from old vines.

Viader Estate Napa ★★★★ (Cab Sauv) 95 97 A blend of Cab Sauv and Cab Fr from Howell Mountain hillside estate. Powerful wines, yet balanced and elegant in best years. Ages well. Also look for new series of small-lot bottlings, including Syrah, Tempranillo.

Volker Eisele Family Estate Napa ★★★→★★★★ 95 99 Sleek luscious blend of Cab Sauv and Cab Fr is highlight. Also look for a spicy Sauv Bl.

Wellington Sonoma ★★→★★★★ Vivid old-vine Zin and sleek, powerful Cab Sauv from selected vineyards.

Wente Vineyards Livermore and Monterey ★★→★★★★ Historic specialist in whites, ***especially LIVERMORE Sauv Bl*** and Sem. But LIVERMORE estate Cab Sauv is also very good. Monterey sweet Ries can be exceptional. A little classic sparkling.

Williams Selyem Sonoma Intense smoky RUSSIAN RIVER Pinot N, especially Rochioli and Allen vineyards. Now reaching to SONOMA COAST, MENDOCINO for grapes. Cultish favourite.

Young, Robert Sonoma ★★★ Outstanding Chard, Cab Sauv from famed vineyard, source of CHATEAU ST JEAN Chard for many years.

York Creek Spring Mtn, Napa ★★★ Exceptional vineyard owned by Fritz Maytag, father of microbrew revolution in US with his Anchor Steam beer. Sells to RIDGE and now has own label. Mostly good, always interesting.

Zaca Mesa Sta Barbara ★★→★★★★ Now turning away from Chard and Pinot N to concentrate on Rhône grapes (especially Marsanne and Syrah) and blends (Cuvée Z) grown on estate.

Zahtila Vineyards Napa ★★★ Newcomer in north NAPA specializes in elegant and inviting Cab Sauv and intense Zin (one from estate vineyard near Calistoga). Also makes DRY CREEK and RUSSIAN RIVER Zins from SONOMA COUNTY. To watch.

ZD Napa ★★ Lusty Chard tattooed by American oak is ZD signature wine.

The Pacific Northwest

Some of the most exciting wines in North America are coming out of the Pacific Northwest. In Washington, Oregon, and to some degree in Idaho, winemakers are matching grapes to vineyard site and producing wines of elegance and complexity. There was no wine to speak of in the region 40 years ago, which makes the new wines even more remarkable. Today's winemakers have built on pioneering efforts of the 1970s and 1980s, bringing new technical skills and knowledge of what is possible.

Oregon is, of course, well known for its Pinot Noir but that is only part of the story. Newer plantings of Pinot Gris look very promising and Oregon Chardonnay, made in an almost austere Chablis style, has many fans. And don't overlook very good Oregon Riesling.

Washington continues to define its growing areas and varieties, turning out an astonishing range of wines, including Sauv Blanc, Semillon, and Chardonnay, as well as classic Riesling. In reds, the Bordeaux varieties are still tops – Cabernet Sauvignon, Merlot, and more and more excellent Cabernet Franc. Syrah is also a winner, especially in warmer areas. It is still early days in Idaho, but Cabernet Sauvignon seems to be a good bet. Some very good Icewine is being made in Washington and in Idaho.

Recent vintages

It is impossible to patch together a vintage chart that covers the Pacific Northwest because of the great variations in climate and soils. The Rogue River Valley of southern Oregon, for example, has more in common with Napa and Sonoma in California than it has with the Willamette Valley only a few hundred miles north. There are great variations between the Columbia Valley and the Yakima Valley in Washington. Idaho is another story entirely. In general, Oregon Pinot Noir has been on the plus side since 1999.

2006 The century is young, but when talk turns to vintage of the century, this is it so far for Oregon. Incredible quality across the board. Washington and Idaho reporting similar quality.

2005 This is turning out to be a rather amazing vintage, if the winery paid attention. It was a cool harvest with some rain, but if the grapes were picked at the right time, the wines are looking very good. Oregon Pinot N, Washington Cab Sauv, Merlot, could be exceptional.

2004 Rain during flowering led to a small crop in some cases, but in general grape quality was high. Wines range from below average to well above average, depending on the site.

2003 A potentially mixed vintage after a season of heat and water stress.

2002 Wines with full expression and elegance.

2001 Lower acidity and less concentration than previous three years.

Oregon

Abacela Vineyards Umpqua Valley ★★★ New producer is performing well in unfashionable area of Oregon. Tempranillo Dolcetto, Cab Fr, Syrah stand out.

Adelsheim Vineyard Yamhill County ★★★ ·★★★★★ Smoothly balanced Pinot N. New Dijon clone Chard, Ries, top Pinots Gr and Bl: clean, bracing.

Amity Willamette ★★ ·★★★ Pioneer in Oregon with exceptional Ries and Pinot Bl. The Pinot often rises to ★★★.

Andrew Rich (Tabula Rasa) Willamette ★★ Ex-California winemaker. Small lots of artisan wines, including Pinot N and exceptional Syrah, solid rosé.

Argyle Yamhill County ★★ ·★★★ An **_outstanding sparkling wine_** (especially the vintage brut) and ★★★ Pinot N form a solid base for this winery, founded by Aussie superstar winemaker Brian Croser.

Beaux Frères Yamhill County ★★ Pinot N has more power than most Oregon offerings, if that's what you are looking for. Part-owned by Robert Parker.

Bethel Heights Willamette ★★ ·★★★ 00 01 Deftly made estate Pinot N. Also notable Chard, Pinot Bl, Pinot Gr.

Brick House Yamhill County ★★★ 01 02 Huge estate Pinot N. Dark and brooding when young with older vintages more balanced.

Cameron Yamhill County ★★ (Pinot N) Eclectic producer of powerful, unfiltered Pinot N, Chard: some great. Also very good Pinot Bl.

Chehalem Yamhill County ★★→★★ Outstanding Chard with ageing potential sometimes rising to ★★★. Very good Ries, Pinot Gr.

Cooper Mountain Willamette ★★→★★★ Outstanding Pinot Gr and Pinot N on a steady upward curve. Certified biodynamic vineyards.

Cuneo Oregon ★★ Sources grapes from Columbia Valley, Washington, and Rouge River Valley, Oregon. Emphasis is on Italian and Bordeaux varietals. One of best is Cana's Feast, a Bordeaux blend from Red Mountain AVA in Washington.

Domaine Drouhin Willamette ★★★→★★★★ 00 01 *Outstanding Pinot N*, silky and elegant, improving with each vintage. Chard also a winner.

Domaine Serene Willamette ★★★★ 00 01 Traditional Pinot N in a rich echo of Burgundy. Bottled unfiltered. Well worth seeking out.

Elk Cove Vineyards Willamette ★★→★★★ Outstanding Ries including a late harvest. Pinot N often near the top; some recent improvements in Chard.

Erath Vineyards Yamhill County ★★→★★★ 01 02 Oregon pioneer, established 1968. Very good Chard, Pinot Gr, Gewurz, Pinot Bl. Pinots and Ries age well.

Evesham Wood Willamette ★★★ Small family winery with fine Pinot N, Pinot Gr, and dry Gewurz. Pinot N leaping ahead in recent vintages. Organic.

Eyrie Vineyards Willamette ★★★ 98 01 Pioneer (1965) winery. Chards and Pinot Gr: rich yet crisp. All wines age beautifully.

Foris Rouge Valley ★→★★ A lovely Pinot Bl and a classic red-cherry Pinot N top the list.

Freja Willamette Valley ★★★ Only estate-grown Pinot N, the best flirting with four stars. Wines are silky on the palate but with an underlying power.

Henry Estate Rouge Valley ★→★★ Big but never clumsy Cab Sauv and a light, crisp Müller-T.

Ken Wright Cellars Yamhill County ★★ Floral Pinot N and a very good Chard from single vineyards.

King Estate S Willamette ★★★→★★★★ 01 02 One of Oregon's largest wineries, now converting to biodynamic viticulture. Lovely and constantly improving Pinot N, outstanding Chard, better-than-average Zin.

Lachini Vineyards ★★★ New producer of outstanding Pinot N and Pinot Gr. Vineyards farmed biodynamically. A coming star. Outstanding Pinot Gr and very good Pinot N.

Lange Winery Yamhill County ★★ Pinot N has become richer, more intense as vineyards mature. Very good Pinot Gr.

Panther Creek Willamette ★→★★ 97 Concentrated, meaty, vineyard Pinot N and pleasant Melon de Bourgogne.

Oak Knoll Willamette ★★ Pinot is the big story here, with intense but balanced bottlings. Also a very good off-dry Ries.

Patricia Green Cellars Yamhill County ★★→★★★ Exciting, intense Pinot N from a newish winery. Small production, but worth seeking out.

Penner-Ash Yamhill County ★★★ REX HILL winemaker Lynn Penner-Ash and her husband are making great Pinot N in a bolder style than many in Oregon.

Ponzi Vineyards Willamette Valley ★★★ 99 00 01 Small pioneering winery well known for Pinot Gr, Chard, Pinot N.

Rex Hill Willamette ★★→★★★ Excellent Pinot N, Pinot Gr, and Chard from several N Willamette vineyards. Reserves rank high.

Sokol Blosser Willamette ★★→★★★ Outstanding Pinot N, Chard, and Gewurz, usually balanced and harmonious. Intriguing Müller-T.

Stoller Estate Dundee Hills ★★★ Long regarded as an outstanding source of grapes, Stoller began producing its own wine in 2002. Pinot N. is very good with fruit matched with a spicy earthiness. A winery to watch.

Torii Mor Yamhill County ★★★ Several very good single-vineyard Pinot N bottlings and a superior Pinot Gr.

Tyee S Willamette ★★ Small producer; very good Pinot N, Pinot Gr, tasty Gewurz.

Van Duzer Winery Willamette Valley ★→★★ Bright, fruity Pinot N, delicious Pinot Gr, from one of the cooler parts of the Willamette Valley. Steadily improving.

Willakenzie Estate Yamhill County ★★ Outstanding, sometimes ★★★ Pinot N. Very good Pinot Bl.

Willamette Farms Vercingetorix Willamette ★★→★★★ Star turn here is the _complex Pinot Gr, easily_ ★★★ Pinot N has ups and downs but worth trying.

Willamette Valley Vineyards Willamette ★→★★ Large (for Oregon) winery near Salem. Moderate- to very high-quality Chard, Ries, Pinot N. Also owns and produces very good Griffin Creek and Tualatin brands.

Washington & Idaho

Alexandria Nicole Cellars Columbia ★★→★★★ Founded in 1998 with a double focus on Syrah and a Bordeaux blend. A very good beginning.

Andrew Will Puget Sound, Washington ★★★★ **96 97 00** Owner Chris Camarda sources Bordeaux varietals from Red Mountain, making outstanding single-vineyard reds: balanced, elegant, tremendous ageing potential.

Arbor Crest Spokane, Washington ★★ The top draw here is the Chard, followed closely by a floral Sauv Bl. Cab Sauv is steadily improving.

Badger Mountain Columbia Valley, Washington ★★ Washington's first organic vineyard, producing impressive Cab Sauv and good Chard.

Barnard Griffin Columbia Valley, Washington ★★→★★★ Small producer: well-made Merlot, Chard (especially barrel-fermented), Sem, Sauv Bl. Top Syrah.

Basel Cellars Columbia Valley ★★★→★★★★ Newcomer sweeping the board with exciting Bordeaux varieties and a four-star Syrah. A tremendous beginning.

Baer Woodinville ★★→★★★★ Artisan producer of Bordeaux varietal wines. Top marks to Ursa, an elegant wine with good ageing potential.

Bergevin Lane Columbia Valley ★★★ Another newcomer off to a fast start. Viognier is good, Syrah very good. Best to come.

Brian Carter Cellars Woodinville ★★ Wines include a "Super Tuscan", two Bordeaux blends and a Rhône blend. All good; Byzance Rhône blend is a real treat.

Bunnell Cellars Yakima Valley ★★★ A series of single-vineyard Syrahs are best-foot-forward here, plus a very good Viognier.

Buty Walla Walla Valley Focus is on Bordeaux blends, sometimes with Syrah. California wine ace Zelma Long consults. Cab Sauv/Syrah blend from Columbia Valley called Rediviva is very good.

Cayuse Walla Walla ★★→★★★★ Striking Syrah and Viognier with loyal following.

Cedergreen Cellars Kirkland ★★→★★★ A striking Sauv Bl and a richly complex blend of Merlot and Cab Sauv called Thuja are both very good.

Château Ste-Michelle Woodinville, Washington ★★→★★★★★ Washington's largest winery; also owns COLUMBIA CREST, Northstar (top Merlot), Domaine Ste-Michelle, and Snoqualmie, among others. Major vineyard holdings, first-rate equipment, and skilled winemakers keep wide range of varieties in front ranks. Very good vineyard-designated Cab Sauv, Merlot, and Chard.

Chinook Wines Yakima Valley, Washington ★★★ (Merlot) **99 00 01** Lovely, elegant Merlot and Cab Sauv; outstanding Cab Fr.

Columbia Crest Columbia Valley, Washington ★★→★★★ Separately run CHÂTEAU STE-MICHELLE label for delicious, well-made, top-value wines. Cab Sauv, Merlot,

Syrah, and Sauv Bl best. Also very good reserve wines.

Columbia Winery Woodinville, Washington ★★★ (Cab) **99 00** Pioneer (1962, as Associated Vintners) and still a leader. MW David Lake makes balanced, stylish, understated single-vineyard wines. Marvellous Syrah.

DeLille Cellars Woodinville ★★★→★★★★ 98 99 00 Exciting winery for very good red Bordeaux blends: ageworthy Chaleur Estate, D2 (more forward, affordable). Excellent barrel-fermented white. Look for new Syrah, Doyenne.

Di Stefano Woodinville ★★→★★★ Best here are the Bordeaux varieties, including a very good, elegant Cab Sauv; also a bright and juicy Syrah.

Dunham Cellars Walla Walla, Washington ★★→★★★ A silky Syrah tops the list.

> ### Oregon's alternative Pinot
>
> Oregon has a reputation for Pinot Noir, and Pinot Gris is becoming known as the "other" Oregon wine. The grapes are close cousins, and both thrive in the cool climate of Oregon. Pinot Gris seems to achieve complexity and depth of flavour. Many have compared Oregon's version with Alsace Pinot Gris.

Extracted Cab Sauv has a strong following.

Glen Fiona Walla Walla, Washington ★★→★★★ Rhône specialist with good Syrahs and Syrah blends, especially the Syrah/Cinsault/Counoise *cuvée*.

Hedges Cellars Yakima Valley, Washington ★★★→★★★★ Outstanding Bordeaux reds from Red Mountain AVA. Also very good second label CMS Cellars.

Hogue Cellars, The Yakima Valley, Washington ★→★★ Large reliable producer known for excellent, good-value wines, especially Ries, Chard, Merlot, Cab Sauv. Produces quintessential Washington Sauv Bl.

Hyatt Vineyards Yakima Valley, Washington ★★→★★★ Stylish Merlot is among the state's best. Seek Black Muscat Icewine when conditions are right.

Indian Creek Idaho ★→★★ Top wine here is Pinot N backed by a very good Ries and successful Cab Sauv.

Kiona Vineyards Yakima Valley ★→★★ Solid Red Mountain producer. Easy-drinking wines; good value and quality. Juicy Lemberger and reliable Cab Sauv.

Lake Chelan Winery Columbia Valley ★★ A promising new winery producing good to very good Cabernet Sauv and an attractive Syrah.

L'Ecole No 41 Walla Walla ★★★→★★★★ (Merlot) **99 00** Blockbuster but balanced reds (Merlot, Cab Sauv, and super Meritage blend) with forward, ageworthy fruit. Good barrel-fermented Sem.

Leonetti Walla Walla ★★★→★★★★ *Harmonious Cab Sauv: fine and big-boned*. Bold and ageworthy Merlot. Wines are in great demand.

Long Shadows Columbia Valley ★★→★★★ Former Château Ste-Michelle CEO Allen Shoup led leading international winemakers producing Washington wine under a separate label. Very good early releases including Poet's Leap Ries; Pirouette, an amazing red; Chester-Kidder, a more concentrated, New Worldish red; and a bold Australian-style Syrah. Expect great things here.

McCrea Puget Sound ★★★ Look for good Viognier, Syrah, and Grenache sourced from top Washington vineyards from this Rhône specialist.

Nicolas Cole Cellars Columbia Valley ★★→★★★ A rising star winery with very good, balanced, and elegant Bordeaux-style reds that show promise of ageing.

Nota Bene Cellars Puget Sound ★★→★★★ Amazing wines from Bordeaux varietals sourced in Red Mountain AVA and other top Washington vineyards. Hard to find now, but well worth looking for.

Owen Roe Washington ★★→★★★ Look for the Yakima Valley Chard and Ries, and reds, especially Bordeaux varieties, from Columbia Valley.

Pepper Bridge Walla Walla Valley ★★→★★★ Bordeaux-style Cab Sauv and Merlot.

Quilceda Creek Vintners Puget Sound ★★★→★★★★ (Cab) **97 98** Expertly crafted, ripe, well-oaked Cab Sauv from Columbia Valley grapes is the speciality. Exceptional finesse and ageability.

Reininger Walla Walla, Washington ★★→★★★ Small, focused producer of outstanding Merlot and exceptional Syrah. Helix Columbia Valley Merlot is firting with ★★★★.

Ste Chapelle Caldwell, Idaho ★★ Pleasant, forward Chard, Ries, Cab Sauv, Merlot, and Syrah from local and east Washington vineyards. Attractive sparkling wine: good value and improving quality.

Sandhill Winery Columbia Valley ★★★ Estate-only wines from the Red Mountain AVA. Outstanding Cab Sauv and Merlot and a very good Pinot Gr.

Saviah Cellars Walla Walla ★★ Very good Bordeaux blends, especially Big Sky Cuvée and outstanding Syrah.

Sawtooth Cellars Idaho ★★ Good Cab Sauv with new plantings of Syrah and Viognier showing promise.

Seven Hills Walla Walla ★★ Ciel du Cheval Bordeaux blend very good, also Pentad (Bordeaux varietals with a splash of Carmenère.

Woodward Canyon Walla Walla, Washington ★★★→★★★★ (Cab) **97 98** Ripe, intense, but elegant Cab, Chard, and blends. Merlot coming on strong.

East of the Rockies

The eastern United States had a relatively thriving wine culture until it was decimated by Prohibition in the 1930s. Not until the 1970s did it begin to reinvent itself. Because of disease and a challenging climate, hardy native grapes and French-American hybrids dominated the scene for years, but today vinifera is being raised successfully in every Eastern state. Viticulturists are still discovering which grapes are best suited to the Eastern terroirs. So far, Chardonnay and the Bordeaux grapes have been successful almost everywhere.

Recent vintages

1998 and 1999 were generally outstanding years in the Eastern US, but few of those wines are still around. 2001 and 2002 were excellent years, but 2000 and 2003 were disappointing. 2004 and 2005 were good, but meagre due to winter damage and hurricanes. 2006 was bountiful, with good-to-great quality.

Allegro Pennsylvania ★★ 04 05 06 Worthy Chard, Cab Sauv, and Merlot.

Anthony Road Finger Lakes, NY ★★★ Fine Ries; Pinot Gr, late-harvest Vignoles.

Barboursville Virginia ★★★★ Oldest of the state's modern-era wineries. Excellent Chard, Cab Fr, Barbera, Nebbiolo, Pinot Gr. Elegant inn and restaurant.

Bedell Long Island, NY ★★★ **02** 03 04 05 06 Excellent Merlot and Cab Sauv.

Blenheim Young Virginia estate. Very good Chard, Petit Verdot, Bordeaux blend.

Breaux Virginia ★★★ 02 04 05 06 Beautiful 35 ha vineyard 1 hr from Washington, DC. Good Chard, Sauv Bl.

Chaddsford Pennsylvania ★★★ 02 04 05 06 Solid producer since 1982, especially Barbera and Rubino, a Cab/Sangiovese blend.

Chamard ★★ 03 04 05 06 Connecticut's best winery, founded by Tiffany chairman. Top Chard. AVA is Southeastern New England.

Chateau LaFayette Reneau Finger Lakes, NY ★★★ 04' 05' 06 Stylish Chard, Ries, and Cab Sauv from established producer. Stunning lakeside setting.

Chrysalis Virginia ★★★ Top Viognier, v. good Petit Manseng, and native Norton.

Clinton Vineyards Hudson River, NY ★★ 05 06 Clean, good dry Seyval (still and sparkling). Exceptional cassis, sparkling, and peach wine.

Debonné Vineyards Lake Erie, Ohio ★★ 04 05 06 Largest OHIO estate winery. Chard, Ries, Pinot Gr, and some hybrids: Chambourcin and Vidal.

Ferrantes Winery & Ristorante Venerable estate (since 1937) has emerged as quality leader with fine Chard, Cab Sauv, Ries, and Merlot.

Finger Lakes Beautiful, cool, upstate NY region, source of most of state's wines. Top wineries: ANTHONY ROAD, CHATEAU LAFAYETTE RENEAU, DR. FRANK, FOX RUN, Heron Hill, King Ferry, Lakewood, RED NEWT, Shalestone, STANDING STONE, Swedish Hill, and WIEMER.

Firelands Lake Erie, Ohio ★★ OHIO estate making Cab Sauv, Gewurz, Pinot Gr.

Fox Run Finger Lakes, NY ★★★ 04 05 06 Some of region's best Chard, Gewurz, Ries, and Pinot N.

Frank, Dr. Konstantin (Vinifera Wine Cellars) Finger Lakes, NY ★★★★ 01 02 04 05 06 Continues to set the pace for serious winemaking. The late Dr. F was a pioneer in growing European vines in the FINGER LAKES. Excellent Ries, Gewurz; good Chard, Cab Sauv, and Pinot N. Also very good Chateau Frank sparkling.

Glenora Wine Cellars Finger Lakes ★ 04 05 Good sparkling , Chard, and Ries.

Hamptons, The (aka South Fork) LONG ISLAND AVA. The top winery is moneyed WÖLFFER ESTATE. Showcase Duck Walk owns 130 acres of vines, Channing Daughters fast improving.

Heron Hill Finger Lakes ★★ Great Ries and dessert wines by Thomas Laszlo.

Horton Virginia ★★★ 04 05 06 Established early 90s. Good Viognier, Mourvèdre, Cab Fr, Norton.

Hudson River Region America's oldest wine-growing district (37 producers) and NY's first AVA. Straddles the river, 2 hours' drive north of Manhattan.

Jefferson Virginia ★★★ 01' 02' 04 05 06 Near Thomas Jefferson's landmark estate Monticello, fine Pinot Gr, Viognier, Petit Verdot, Bordeaux blend.

Keswick Virginia ★★★ 04 05 06 Young winery already establishing reputation for elegant Chard, very good Viognier, Touriga, and Cab-based blend.

King Family Estate/Michael Shaps Wines Virginia ★★★★ Excellent Chard, Viognier, Merlot, Cab Fr, Bordeaux blend by Burgundy-trained oenologist.

King Ferry Finger Lakes, NY ★★★ 05 06 Great Ries, stylish Chards.

Kluge Virginia ★★ 04 05 06 Showplace estate, ambitious wines include Viognier and Bordeaux blend.

Lake Erie Largest grape-growing district in the eastern US; 10,117 ha along shore of Lake Erie, includes portions of New York, Pennsylvania, and OHIO. Also name of a tri-state AVA: NY's sector has 12 wineries, Pennsylvania's seven and OHIO's 32. OHIO's Harpersfield sets standards for quality.

Lamoreaux Landing Finger Lakes, NY ★★★ 03 04 05 06 Promising Chard, Ries, and Cab Fr from striking Greek-revival winery.

Lenz ★★★ 02' 04 05 06 Classy winery of NORTH FORK AVA. ***Fine austere Chard in the Chablis mode***, also Gewurz, Merlot, and sparkling wine.

Linden Virginia ★★★★ 99' 00 01 02 04 05 06 Small (5,000 cases) Virginia producer in mountains 100 km (65 miles) west of Washington, DC. Impressive Sauv Bl, Cab Fr, Petit Verdot, and Bordeaux-style "claret".

Long Island, New York Exciting wine region east of the Rockies and a hothouse of experimentation. Currently 1,200 ha, all vinifera (35% Merlot) and three AVAs (LONG ISLAND, NORTH FORK, THE HAMPTONS). Most of its 43 wineries are on the North Fork. Best varieties: Chard, Cab Sauv, Merlot. A long growing season; almost frost-free but hurricane-prone. The youngest generation of wineries include Ackerly Pond, Comtesse Thérèse, Diliberto (good reds), Martha Clara, Old Fields Shinn (owned by proprietors of acclaimed Manhattan restaurant Home), Sherwood House (Chard and Merlot), Raphael.

Maryland Has more than 25 wineries in four distinct growing regions. Best-known producer and oldest family-run winery is Boordy Vineyards, making very good Vidal Blanc, Chard, and Cab Sauv. Basignani for good Cab Sauv, Ries, and Seyval. Fiore: good Chambourcin, Merlot, Cab Sauv, and Vidal Blanc. Woodhall has good Chard and Barbera.

Michigan In addition to fine cool-climate Ries, impressive Gewurz, Pinot N, and Cab Fr are emerging; 49 commercial wineries using Michigan grapes and four AVAs. Best include Brys, Black Star, Château Grand Traverse, Peninsula Cellars (especially dry Gewurz), Château Chantal, Willow, and Tabor Hill. Mawby Vineyards known for outstanding sparkling Fenn Valley, St. Julian and Lemon Creek have large following. Up-and-coming: Round Barn, Longview, Dom Berrien, and Cherry Creek.

Millbrook Hudson River, NY ★★ 04 05 06 Chards modelled on Burgundy; Cab Fr can be delicious.

Naked Mountain Virginia 05 06 Established 1981; known for big, buttery Chard.

Niagara Escarpment New York's newest AVA (Sept 05); currently 12 wineries.

North Carolina Look for Chard, Viognier, Cab Fr. 61 wineries. Leaders include Biltmore Estate, Childress, Duplin (for Muscadine), Hanover Park, Iron Gate, Laurel Gray, Old North State, RagApple, Lassie, RayLen, Shelton.

North Fork LONG ISLAND AVA (of three). Top wineries: Bedell, Macari, Lieb, LENZ, PALMER, PAUMANOK, PELLEGRINI, PINDAR. 2.5 hours' drive from Manhattan.

Ohio 96 wineries, five AVAs, notably LAKE ERIE and Ohio Valley. Notable progress with Pinot Gr, Ries, Pinot N, Cab Fr, Icewine.

Palmer Long Island, NY ★★★ 04 05 06 Superior NORTH FORK producer and byword in Darwinian metropolitan market. Tasty Chard, Sauv Bl, Chinon-like Cab Fr.

Paumanok Long Island, NY ★★★★ 98' 99' 00 01 04 05 06 NORTH FORK winery; impressive Ries, Chard, Merlot, Cab Sauv; outstanding Chenin Bl; savoury late-harvest Sauv Bl.

Pellegrini Long Island, NY ★★★★ 99' 00 02 04 05 06 An enchantingly designed winery on NORTH FORK. Opulent Merlot, stylish Chard, Bordeaux-like Cab Sauv.

Pindar Vineyards Long Island, NY ★★★ 01 02 04 05 06 A 116-ha operation at NORTH FORK (Island's largest). Wide range of blends and popular varietals, including Chard, Merlot, sparkling, very good Bordeaux-style red blend, Mythology. Popular with tourists.

Red Newt Finger Lakes, NY ★★★ 04 05 06 Turns out top Chard, Ries, Cab Fr, Merlot, and Bordeaux-inspired red blend. Popular bistro.

Sakonnet Little Compton, Rhode Island ★★ 04 05 06 Largest New England winery. Very drinkable wines; delicious sparkling brut *cuvée*.

Standing Stone Finger Lakes, NY ★★ 04 05 06 One of the region's finest wineries with very good Ries, Gewurz, and Bordeaux-type blend.

Tomasello New Jersey ★★ Good Chambourcin, Pinot N, Cab Sauv, and Merlot.

Unionville Vineyards New Jersey ★★ Nice Chard and good Bordeaux-style red.

Valhalla Virginia ★★★ 01 02 04 05 06 Vineyard at 600 m (2,000 ft) atop a granite mountain yields fine Alicante Bouschet, spicy Sangiovese, and good red blend of all five Bordeaux grapes.

Veritas Virginia ★★★ 04 05 06 Good Chard, Cab Fr, Viognier, *gutsy Petit Verdot*.

Villa Appalaccia Virginia ★★★ 04 05 06 Italian-inspired winery in the Blue Ridge Mountains making limited amounts (3,000 cases total) of Primitivo, Sangiovese, Malvasia, Pinot Gr.

Virginia With 109 bonded wineries and six AVAs, Virginia is turning out some of the best wines in the east. The modern winemaking era now encompasses virtually every part of the state, with emphasis on vinifera.

Wagner Vineyards Finger Lakes, NY ★★ 04 05 06 Chard, dry and sweet Ries, Bordeaux blend, and Icewine. Also has micro-brewery and restaurant.

Westport Rivers SE New England ★★ 00 02 05 06 Massachusetts house established in 1989. Good Chard and elegant sparkling.

Whitehall Virginia ★★★★ 03 04 05 A handsome estate near Charlottesville. Impeccable Gewurz, lush Petit Manseng, top Chard, Cab Fr, and Cab blend.

Wiemer, Hermann J Finger Lakes, NY ★★ →★★★ 05 06 Creative, German-born owner/winemaker. Outstanding Ries; very good Chard.

Wölffer Estate Long Island ★★★ 02 03 04 05 06 Modish Chard and Merlot from German-born winemaker. Good wine *can* be made on the South Fork.

Wollersheim Wisconsin ★★ 05 06 Winery specializing in variations of Maréchal Foch. Prairie Fumé (Seyval Bl) is a commercial success.

Southeast & central states

Missouri Continues to expand, with over 50 producers in three AVAs: **Augusta, Hermann**, and **Ozark Highlands**. Best wines are Seyval Blanc Vidal, Vignoles (sweet and dry versions), and Chambourcin. **Stone Hill** in Hermann produces very good Chardonel (a frost-hardy hybrid of Seyval Blanc and Chardonnay), Norton, and good Seyval Blanc and Vidal Blanc. **Hermannhof** is also drawing notice for Vignoles, Chardonel, and Norton. Also notable: **St James** for Vignoles, Seyval, Norton; **Mount Pleasant** in Augusta for rich "port" and Norton; **Adam Puchta** for good port-style wines and Norton, Vignoles, Vidal Blanc; **Augusta Winery** for Chambourcin, Chardonel, Icewine; **Les Bourgeois**, good Syrah, Norton, Chardonel, Montelle, very good Cynthiana and Chambourcin.

Georgia There are now over a dozen wineries here. Look for: **Three Sisters** (Dahlonega), **Habersham Vineyards**, and **Chateau Elan** (Braselton), which features southern splendour with vineyards, wine, and a resort.

Southwest

Texas

Texas continues to grow in wine quality and in the number of wineries; it now has over 100. New Mexico is up to 30 wineries; Colorado has over 65. Arizona now has 20 wineries and vineyards, and Oklahoma has 30.

Becker Vineyards Stonewall ★★★ Very good Cab Sauv, Ries, Sauv Bl, Prairie Roti (red blend), Viognier.

Delaney Vineyards Near Dallas ★ Good Cynthiana and Sauv Bl.

Driftwood Vineyards Texas Hill Country ★★ Very good Muscat Canelli, Viognier, and red blends.

Fall Creek Texas Hill Country ★★ Very good Chenin Bl, Sauv Bl, Viognier, Cab Sauv.

Flat Creek Estate Texas Hill Country ★★ Very good Sangiovese, Moscato Bianco, and "Port" style.

Fredericksburg Winery Offers dry to dessert wines; very good Orange Muscat, good "port" and "sherry" styles.

Haak Vineyard & Winery Galveston County ★ Very good Blanc du Bois and Cab Sauv.

Llano Estacado Near Lubbock ★★★ The pioneer continues on award-winning track with Chard, Merlot, and Signature Series (red and white blends).

Lost Creek Vineyard Texas Hill Country Very good Chard; good Merlot and blends.

McPherson Cellars Lubbock New and promising; very good Sangiovese, Viognier and red blends.

Messina Hof Wine Cellars Bryan ★★★ Most award-winning wines in the state. Excellent Ries, Cab Sauv, and Muscat Canelli. Very good port-style wines.

Pheasant Ridge Near Lubbock Very good Chard and Cab Sauv.

Pleasant Hill Brenham Good Cab Sauv, Blanc du Bois, blends.
Sister Creek Boerne Boutique winery with good Pinot N, Chard, Muscat Canelli.
Stone House Spicewood Good blends and port-style wines.

New Mexico, etc.

New Mexico Continues with emphasis on vinifera grapes, though some French
hybrids still used, primarily in northern areas. More than 30 wineries. **Black
Mesa:** ★★ Very good Cab Sauv, Seyval Bl, Merlot; good blends, especially
Coyote (red). **Casa Rondeña:** ★★ Very good Cab Fr, Cab Sauv, Meritage (red).
Corrales: ★★ Very good Cab Sauv, Ries. Gruet: ★★★ Excellent sparkling; very
good Chard, Pinot N. **La Chiripada:** ★★ Very good Ries and blends; good
port-style wine. **Milagro Vineyards:** very good Chard, Cab Sauv. **Ponderosa
Valley:** ★★ Very good Ries, Merlot, and blends, especially Summer Sage
(white) and Jemez Red. **La Viña:** ★★ Very good Chard, Zin; good blends. St
Clair, Blue Teal Vineyards, Mademoiselle Vineyards, D H Lescombes, and
Santa Rita Cellars all under winemaker **Florent Lescombes** have a good
variety of wines. **Luna Rosa** very good Zin, Symphony, Merlot, Nini (red
blend). Jacona Valley Winery: new, specializing in Pinot N.

Colorado Focus is on vinifera grapes, with over 250 ha planted, ranging from
the Grand Valley on the Western Slope, over the Rocky Mountains to the
Front Range. Has over 65 wineries **Carlson Cellars:** ★★★ Very good Gewurz,
Ries, fruit wines. **Canyon Wind:** Good Chard, Cab Sauv, Merlot. **Garfield
Estates:** Very good Sauv Bl and Cab Fr. **Plum Creek:** ★★★ Very good Ries and
Sauv Bl; Chard, Merlot. **Terror Creek:** ★★ Small with very good Ries, Gewurz.
Trail Ridge: Gewurz, Ries. **Two Rivers:** Very good Cab Sauv, Chard, Merlot.
Verso Cellars: Very good Cab Sauv. **Balistreri:** Good Cab Sauv, Syrah,
Sangiovese. **Stoney Mesa** Good Cab Sauv, Riesling. **Debeque Canyon** Very
good Malbec.

Arizona Continues to grow with over 20 vineyards and wineries. **Callaghan
Vineyards:** ★★ Very good Syrah, Cab Sauv, blends. **Dos Cabezas:** ★ Very good
Cab Sauv, Petite Sirah, Sangiovese. **Colibri:** new, promising boutique winery,
good Viognier, Roussanne, Syrah. **Kokopelli:** sound, reasonably priced.

Oklahoma Expanded to over 30 wineries, emphasizing vinifera, although some
wineries include native American grapes. **Greenfield Vineyard** Chandler:
Good Merlot, Sauv Bl. **Stone Bluff Cellars** Haskell: Good Vignoles, Cynthiana,
blends. **Panther Hills** Bessie: ★★ Boutique very good Cab Sauv, good
Pinot N. **Tidal School Vineyards** Drumright: The largest; good blends. **Oak
Hills Winery** Chelsea: Very good Catawba; **Nuyaka Creek** Bristow good
grape, fruit, berry wines and pleasing cordial-style selections, especially
Petite Pecan.

Utah **Spanish Valley** (Moab) Very good Ries and Cab Sauv.

Nevada **Pahrump Valley** Near Las Vegas Good Symphony, red blends. **Tahoe
Ridge** (N Nevada) continues with experimental plans; good Sem.

Canada

Recent vintages

With a few exceptions, pre-1998 is essentially obsolete, 1998 still showing
well for top reds. 2002 excellent all around with reserve reds drinking well
now. 2003–2005 were challenging vintages with mostly good whites and
some reds for early drinking. 2006 variable vintage with good early ripening
whites, Riesling and some late reds.

British Columbia

The biggest concentration of wineries is in the warm, dry Okanagan Valley around a vast lake, 400 km (245 miles) east of Vancouver, especially in the desert-like southernmost part of the region. There are over 130 wineries in four appellations: Okanagan Valley, Fraser Valley, Similkameen Valley, Vancouver Island. Up-and-coming: Thornhaven (Sauv Bl), Golden Mile (Pinot N, Chard), Nk'Mip Cellars (Merlot, Ries, Icewine), Lake Breeze, Blasted Church (Chard), Tantalus (Ries).

Blue Mountain Excellent Pinot N and sparkling.

Burrowing Owl Excellent Cab Fr and Syrah.

Calona-Sandhill Vineyards ★★★ Good Pinot Gr, Cab Fr, Syrah, Merlot.

Cedar Creek ★★★ Outstanding Chard, Pinot N, Meritage, and Merlot.

Inniskillin Okanagan ★★★ Excellent Chard, Viognier, Pinot Bl.

Jackson-Triggs Okanagan ★★★ Very good Cab Sauv, Meritage, Shiraz, Ries, Icewine.

Mission Hill ★ → ★★★ Acclaimed Chard, Sauv Bl/Sem, Syrah, Merlot, and flagship Oculus. High culinary standards on dining terrace.

Osoyoos Larose Remarkably fine Bordeaux blend red.

Quails' Gate ★★ Ries, Late Harvest Optima, and Old Vines Foch.

Sumac Ridge ★★ Gewurz, Sauv Bl, sparkling "Stellar's Jay" among region's best. Notable Meritage. (Owned by CONSTELLATION.)

Ontario

Includes Canada's largest viticultural area Niagara Peninsula. Around 100 wineries. Proximity of the lake and diverse soils create distinctive growing conditions. Emerging quality-driven wineries include: Le Clos Jordanne, Hidden Bench, Norman Hardie, Clossen Chase, and Tawse. Icewine is the region's international flagship. In 2005, 12 new sub-appellations were approved within the larger Niagara Peninsula appellation.

Andres Largest Canadian-owned winery. Includes HILLEBRAND ESTATES and Peller Estates.

Cave Spring Cellars ★★★ Benchmark Ries, sophisticated Chard from old vines, exceptional Late Harvest and Icewines.

Château des Charmes ★★★ Showplace château-style winery. Fine Chard, Bordeaux-style blend, Icewines, sparkling.

Creekside Consistently top producer of fine Pinot N, Sauv Bl, Bordeaux-blend.

Henry of Pelham ★★★ Respected family-owned winery with elegant Chard and Ries; Bordeaux-style reds, distinctive Baco Noir, Icewine.

Hillebrand Estates ★ → ★★★ Large producer of good sparkling and Bordeaux-style red blend.

Inniskillin ★★★★ Important producer that spearheaded birth of modern Ontario wine industry. Skilful Burgundy-style Chard, Pinot N; also Bordeaux-style red and Ries, Icewine specialists, some of them truly bizarre.

Jackson Triggs ★★★ State-of--art winery, fine Ries, Chard, and Bordeaux-style reds.

Malivoire Small, innovative gravity-flow winery with very good Pinot N, Chard, and Gamay. Some organic.

Peninsula Ridge ★★★ Est 2000. Good Chard, Sauv Bl, and Merlot.

Pillitteri Large family-owned winery with very good Cab Fr and Merlot. Prolific Icewine producer.

Vincor International ★ → ★★ Recently purchased by Constellation. Wineries include JACKSON-TRIGGS, INNISKILLIN, Nk'Mip, Le Clos Jordanne, Osooyos Larose.

Vineland Estates ★★★ Dry and semi-dry Ries; Gewurz much admired. Vidal Icewine good. Chard, Cab Sauv, Sauv Bl, and Bordeaux-style red.

Vintners Quality Alliance (VQA) Canada's appellation body. Its rigid standards rapidly raised respect and awareness of Canadian wines.

Central & South America

More heavily shaded areas
are the wine-growing regions

Chile

Which country claims to be home to both the world's largest biodynamic vineyard and the world's biggest producer of Pinot Noir? Yes, it's Chile (with Emiliana Organicos and Cono Sur respectively). Once a source of correct but soulless wines, Chile now has more Latin passion.

Given the arid conditions – all but a handful of the vineyards survive only thanks to irrigation – the move towards organic and biodynamic viticulture is understandable. But it's the surge in appreciation of viticulture that is notable. Hand in hand with this are developments in regions where vines have never been cultivated. Indeed, it's a struggle to keep up. San Antonio and Elqui are now last year's news as producers expand their horizons.

Together with this has come a realization that what Chile needs isn't an influx of different grape varieties but a better understanding of those it already has. Cabernet Sauvignon remains the trump card – which other country offers more consistency at the entry level? – while Pinot Noir and Syrah are enjoying a rise in fortunes. At the same time, enthusiasm for Carmenère has tempered. On the white front, Sauvignon Blanc, usually from Casablanca, leads the pack but, thanks to some excellent examples from Casablanca, San Antonio and Limari, Chardonnay is finally finding its feet, while the number of fine Rieslings and Viogniers is increasing. As Chile pursues complexity rather than loudness in its wine, expect further improvements in the years to come.

South American vintages

Vintages do differ but not to the same extent as in Europe. Whites are almost without exception at their best within two years of vintage, reds within three years. The most ambitious reds (Chilean Cabernet-based wines, Argentine Cabernets and Malbecs) can confidently be kept for a decade or more but it is debatable whether they improve rather than get older beyond their fifth year. Curiously, odd years have been the best for Chilean reds in recent years, although currently the producer is of far greater importance than the vintage.

Aconcagua Northernmost quality region. Inc CASABLANCA, Panquehue, SAN ANTONIO.

Almaviva ★★★ Expensive but classy, claret-style MAIPO red – a joint venture between CONCHA Y TORO and BARON PHILIPPE DE ROTHSCHILD.

Altaïr ★★→★★★ Ambitious joint venture between Ch Dassault (St-Emilion) and SAN PEDRO. Pascal Chatonnet of Bordeaux is consultant; *grand vin* (mostly Cab Sauv, Carmenère) complex and earthy, 2nd wine Sideral for earlier drinking.

Anakena Cachapoal ★→★★ Solid range. Flagship wines under Ona label include punchy Syrah; Single Vineyard bottlings and Reserve Chard also good.

Antiyal ★★→★★★ Alvaro Espinoza's own estate, making fine, complex red from biodynamically grown Cab Sauv, Syrah, Carmenère. Second wine Kuyen.

Apaltagua ★★→★★★ Carmenère specialist drawing on old-vine fruit from Apalta (Colchagua). Grial is rich, herbal flagship wine.

Aquitania, Viña ★★→★★★ Chilean/French joint venture making v. good Lazuli Cab Sauv (MAIPO) and Sol de Sol Chard from Malleco. Also Paul Bruno MAIPO Cab Sauv (Paul Pontallier and Bruno Prats from Bordeaux are partners).

Arboleda, Viña ★★ Part of the ERRÁZURIZ/CALITERRA stable, sourcing fruit from several regions, and impressing with Cab Sauv, Syrah, Carmenère, Sauv Bl, Chard.

Baron Philippe de Rothschild ★→★★ Bordeaux company making simple varietal range, better Escudo Rojo red blend. Also see ALMAVIVA.

Bío-Bío Promising southern region. Potential for good whites and Pinot N.

Botalcura ★★→★★★ Curicó venture involving French winemaker Philippe Debrus, formerly of VALDIVIESO. Grand Reserve Cab Fr is the star.

Calina, Viña ★→★★ Kendall-Jackson (California) venture. Better reds especially Selección de Las Lomas Cab Sauv) than whites; Elite Cab Sauv the pick.

Caliterra ★→★★ Sister winery of ERRÁZURIZ. Chard and Sauv Bl improving (more CASABLANCA grapes), reds becoming less one-dimensional, especially Res.

Cánepa, José Colchagua ★★ Solid range. Lemony Semillon, spicy Zin among the more unusual wines. Best include juicy Malbec and fragrant Syrah Res.

Carmen, Viña ★★→★★★ MAIPO winery; same ownership as SANTA RITA. Ripe, fresh Special Res CASABLANCA Chard and late-harvest MAIPO Semillon top whites. Reds even better; esp RAPEL Merlot, MAIPO Petite Sirah, Gold Res Cab Sauv.

Carta Vieja ★→★★ MAULE winery owned by one family for six generations. Reds better than whites; but Antigua Selección Chard is good.

Casablanca Cool-climate region between Santiago and coast. Little water: drip irrigation essential. Top-class Chard, Sauv Bl; promising Merlot, Pinot N.

Casablanca, Viña ★→★★ RAPEL and MAIPO fruit used for some reds; but better wines – Merlot, Sauv Bl, Chard, Gewurz – from CASABLANCA. Look for super-*cuvée* Neblus and new Nimbus Estate varietals.

Casa Lapostolle ★★→★★★★ Money from the family of Grand Marnier and advice from Michel Rolland (see France) result in fine range. Bordeaux-style Sauv Bl good, Cuvée Alexandre reds and Carmenère-based Clos Apalta even better.

Casa Marín ★★★ Dynamic San Antonio white specialist, v. good Gewurz and superb Sauv Bl. First Syrah and Pinot N promising.

Casa Rivas Maipo ★★ Part of group that includes TARAPACA, VIÑA MAR, Missiones de Rengo. Best: Sappy Sauv Bl; gentle, citrus Chard Res; blackcurrantpastille-y Cab Sauv; generously fruity Maria Pinto Syrah/Cab Sauv Res.

Casas del Bosque ★→★★ CASABLANCA winery, also using Cab Sauv from Cachapoal for elegant range including juicy underated Sauv Bl, svelte Pinot N and peppery *Syrah Res*.

Casa Silva ★★ Colchagua estate with solid range topped by silky, complex Altura red and Quinta Generación Red and White. Also commendable Doña Dominga range; Carmenère is v. good.

Casas del Toqui ★→★★ RAPEL venture by Médoc Château Larose-Trintaudon under the Las Casas del Toqui and Viña Alamosa labels. Silky top-end Leyenda red blend and Prestige Cab Sauv.

Concha y Toro ★→★★★ Mammoth, quality-minded operation. Best: subtle Amelia Chard (CASABLANCA); inky *Don Melchor Cab Sauv*; Terrunyo; Winemaker Lot single-vineyard range; and new, complex Carmin de Peumo (Carmenère). Marqués de Casa Concha, Trio, Explorer, Casillero del Diablo offer v. good value. See also BARON PHILIPPE DE ROTHSCHILD, CONO SUR, TRIVENTO (Argentina).

Cono Sur Chimbarongo, Colchagua ★★→★★★ V. good Pinot N, headed by Ocio. Other top releases appear as 20 Barrels selection; new innovations under Visión label (BÍO-BÍO Ries is superb). Also dense, fruity Cab Sauv, delicious Viognier, rose-petal Gewurz, impressive new Syrah. Second label Isla Negra.

Córpora Dynamic organization that owns GRACIA DE CHILE, Augustinos (peppery Grand Reserve Malbec), Veranda (joint venture with Boisset of Burgundy), PORTA and now Cantata in Bío-Bío. See also GRAZIA DE CHILE.

Cousiño Macul ★★→★★★ MAIPO producer now relocated to Buin. Now more modern in style, but better? Reliable Antiguas Res Cab Sauv; zesty Sauv Gris; new top-of-the-range blend Lota. Cab Sauv rosé v. refreshing.

de Martino Maipo ★★→★★★ Ambitious Carmenère pioneer; one of west MAIPO's best wineries, esp for v. good premium *cuvée*, Gran Familia Cab Sauv.

Domus Maipo ★★→★★★ Ambitious winery making good Chard and v. good Domus Aurea Cab Sauv; sister Cabs Stella Aurea and Peñalolen also tasty.

Echeverría ★★ Boutique Curicó (MAULE) winery. Reliable Res Cab Sauv; good oaked and unoaked Chard; improving Sauv Bl; elegant, fragrant Carmenère.

Edwards, Luís Felipé ★★ Colchagua winery. Citrus Chard, silky Res Cab Sauv. Shiraz a speciality.

El Principal, Viña ★★★ Pirque (MAIPO) estate that has gone rather quiet under new ownership. Earlier vintages of Bordeaux-blend El Principal and second wine Memorias are excellent.

Emiliana Orgánicos ★→★★★ Organic/biodynamic specialist involving Alvaro Espinoza (see ANTIYAL). Complex, Syrah-heavy "G" and Coyam show almost Mediterranean-style wildness; cheaper Novas range v. good for affordable complexity. See also GEO WINES.

Errázuriz ★→★★★ Main winery in ACONCAGUA's Panquehue district. Complex Wild Ferment Chard; brooding La Cumbre Syrah; best Sangiovese in Chile. Award-winning VIÑEDO CHADWICK (00), Seña (00 01). See also ARBOLEDA, CALITERRA, SEÑA.

Falernia, Viña ★★ Winery in far N Elquí Valley, v'yds lie at around 2,000 m. Alta Tierra Syrah and Chard show potential; good Sauv Bl, Carmenère, Merlot.

Fortuna, Viña La Lontué Valley ★★ Established winery with attractive range.

Garcés Silva Leyda ★★→★★★ Exciting newcomer with Amayna range; SAN ANTONIO Sauv Bl is among Chile's finest; Pinot N and Chard also commendable.

Geo Wines Umbrella under which Alvaro Espinoza makes wines for several new wineries. Look for earthy Chono San Lorenzo MAIPO red blend and tangy Quintay BÍO-BÍO Ries.

Gracia de Chile ★→★★ Winery with v'yds from ACONCAGUA down to BÍO-BÍO. Reserva Lo Mejor Cab Sauv and Syrah (both ACONCAGUA), BÍO-BÍO Sauv Bl are best.

Hacienda Araucano ★★→★★★ The Lurton brothers' Chilean enterprise. Complex

Gran Araucano Sauv Bl (CASABLANCA), refined Carmenère/Cab Sauv blend Clos de Lolol, and heady Alka Carmenère. Look out for new Humo Blanc Pinot N.

Haras de Pirque ★★→★★★ Pirque (MAIPO) estate. Smoky Sauv Bl, stylish Chard, dense Cab Sauv/Merlot. Top wine Albis (Cab Sauv/Carmenère) is solid, smoky red made in joint venture with Antinori (see Italy).

Leyda, Viña ★★→★★★ San Antonio pioneers producing elegant Chard (Lot 5 Wild Yeasts is the pick), lush Pinot N (especially Lot 21 cuvée and lively rosé), tangy Garuma Sauv Bl. Decent MAIPO Cab Sauv and RAPEL Merlot.

Limarí Northerly, high-altitude region, so quite chilly (for Chile); already impressing with Syrah and Chard. TABALÍ and Tamaya are best wineries.

Maipo Famous wine region close to Santiago. Chile's best Cab Sauvs often come from higher, eastern sub-regions such as Pirque and Puente Alto.

Matetic San Antonio ★★★ Decent Pinot N and Chard from exciting winery. Stars are fragrant, zesty Sauv Bl and spicy, berry EQ Syrah. Second label Corralillo.

Maule Southernmost region in Central Valley. Claro, Loncomilla, Tutuven Valleys.

Montes ★★→★★★★ Alpha Cab Sauv can be brilliant; Merlot, Syrah, Malbec fine; Chard v. good. Bordeaux blend Montes Alpha M improves each year; _**Folly Syrah**_ one of the best in Chile; Purple Angel is Carmenère at its most intense.

MontGras ★★→★★★ State-of-the-art Colchagua winery with fine limited-edition wines, incl Syrah and Zin. High-class flagships Ninquén Cab Sauv and Altu Ninquén Syrah. Good value organic Soleus and excellent Amaral whites.

Morande ★★ Vast range including César, Cinsault, Bouschet, Carignan. Limited Edition are top wines, inc a spicy Syrah/Cab Sauv, inky Malbec. Good value.

Neyen New project in Alpata for Patrick Valette, making intense old-vine Carmenère/Cab Sauv blend.

Odfjell ★→★★★ MAIPO-based, Norwegian-owned red specialist. Top wine: Aliara Cab Sauv. Orzada range, including entry-level Armador, also v. good.

Pérez Cruz ★★★ MAIPO winery with Alvaro Espinoza (see ANTIYAL) in charge of winemaking. Fresh spicy Syrah, aromatic Cot, and stylish Liguai red blend.

Porta, Viña ★→★★★ MAIPO winery. Range inc supple, spicy Cab Sauv. See CÓRPORA.

Rapel Central quality region divided into Colchagua and Cachapoal valleys. Great "Merlot" (much is actually Carmenère). Watch for sub-region Marchihue.

La Rosa, Viña ★★ Reliable RAPEL Chard, Merlot, and Cab Sauv under La Palmeria and Cornellana labels. Don Reca reds are the stars.

San Antonio Coastal region west of Santiago benefiting from sea breezes; very promising for whites, Syrah, and Pinot N. Leyda is a sub-zone.

San Pedro ★→★★★ Massive Curicó-based producer. 35 South (35 Sur) for affordable varietals; Castello di Molina a step up. Best are 1865 reds and elegant Cabo de Hornos. See also ALTAÏR, TABALÍ, VIÑA LEYDA.

Santa Carolina, Viña ★★→★★★ Historic bodega. Quality ladder goes Varietal, Reserva, Barrica Selection, Reserva de las Familia, and new VSC Cab Sauv/Syrah/Petit Verdot blends. Syrah and Carmenère good at all levels.

Santa Inés ★★ Successful small family winery in Isla de MAIPO making ripe, blackcurranty Legado de Armida Cab Sauv. Part of DE MARTINO stable.

Santa Mónica ★→★★ Rancagua (RAPEL) winery; the best label is Tierra del Sol. Ries, Semillon, and Merlot under Santa Mónica label also good.

Santa Rita ★★→★★★★ Quality-conscious MAIPO bodega. Best: Casa Real MAIPO Cab Sauv; but Triple C (Cab Sauv/Cab Fr/Carmenère) nearly as good.

Selentia ★★ New Chilean/Spanish venture. Res Special Cab Sauv is fine.

Seña Polished Cab Sauv/Merlot/Carmenère blend from the ERRÁZURIZ stable; vineyards in the process of biodynamic conversion.

Tabalí Limarí ★★ Winery partly owned by SAN PEDRO, making refined Chard and earthy, peppery Syrah. Look out for fine newcomers Viognier and Pinot N.

Tarapacá, Viña ★★ MAIPO winery improved after investment, but inconsistent.

Terramater ★→★★ Wines from all over Central Valley, inc v. gd Altum range. Patrick Valette now consults here.

Terranoble ★→★★ Talca winery specializing in grassy Sauv Bl and light, peppery Merlot. Range now includes v. good spicy Carmenère Gran Res.

Torreón de Paredes ★→★★ Attractive, crisp Chard, ageworthy Res Cab Sauv from this RAPEL bodega. Flagship Don Amedo Cab Sauv could be better.

Torres, Miguel ★★→★★★ Fresh whites and good reds, especially sturdy Manso del Velasco single-vineyard Cab Sauv and Cariñena-based Cordillera. Conde de Superunda is rare top cuvée. See also Spain.

Undurraga ★→★★ Traditional MAIPO estate known for its Pinot N. Top wines: Res Chard, refreshing, limey Gewurz, peachy Late Harvest Semillon.

Valdivieso ★→★★★ Major producer with new Lontué winery. Single-vineyard bottlings include fine new Chard and NV blend Caballo Loco. Res bottlings also good; basic range much improved in recent vintages.

Vascos, Los ★→★★ Lafite-Rothschild venture making Cab Sauv in Bordeaux mould. Recent vintages show more fruit. Top Le Dix and Grande Réserve.

Veramonte ★★ Whites from CASABLANCA fruit, red from Central Valley grapes – all good. Top wine: *Primus red blend*.

Villard ★★ Sophisticated wines made by French-born Thierry Villard. Good MAIPO reds, esp heady Merlot, Equis Cab Sauv, and CASABLANCA whites.

Viña Mar Casablanca ★→★★ Bordeaux-style reds are a little scrawny, but Pinot N, Sauv Bl, and Chard all show Casablanca at its best. See CASA RIVAS.

Viñedo Chadwick Maipo ★★★ Stylish Cab Sauv improving with each vintage from vineyard owned by Eduardo Chadwick, chairman of ERRÁZURIZ.

Viu Manent ★→★★ Emerging Colchagua winery. Dense, fragrant Viu 1 tops range; Secreto Malbec and Viognier also v. good. Late Harvest Semillon top notch.

Von Siebenthal ★★★ Small (in Chilean terms) Swiss-owned ACONCAGUA winery. V. Good Carabantes Syrah and Bordeaux-inspired reds, the best of which is elegant Cab Sauv/Petit Verdot/Carmenère blend Montelig.

Argentina

A decade ago, many predicted that Argentina would soon ease ahead of Chile on the world wine stage. Yet despite the generations of winemaking experience, an enticingly eclectic portfolio of grape varieties and a genuinely world-class wine style in the form of old-vine Malbec, this hasn't happened. True, there are still some producers who aim to impress with excess ripeness and oak, but in general, the cheaper wines combine authentic varietal flavours with a European freshness, while more ambitious cuvées offer combination of alluring fruit and terroir character. Malbec is still tops, but after years of underperforming, Cab-Sauv is now capable of turning heads.

Achaval Ferrer ★★★→★★★★ MENDOZA. Super-concentrated Altamira, Bella Vista, and Mirador single-vineyard Malbecs and Quimera Malbec/Cab/Merlot blends.

Alta Vista ★→★★★ French-owned MENDOZA venture specializing in Malbec. Dense, spicy *Alto* among best wines in the country. Also fresh, zesty Torrontés. Sister winery Navarrita makes fine Winemakers Selection Malbec.

Altos las Hormigas ★★★ Italian-owned Malbec specialist, wines made by consultant Alberto Antonini (ex-Italy's Antinori). Best: Viña las Hormigas Res.

Antucura ★★★ Valle de Uco bodega with beautifully balanced, spicy Cab Sauv/Merlot blend. Antucura is second label.

Argento ★→★★ CATENA offshoot making good commercial wine under the Libertad, Malambo and Argento labels.

Balbi, Bodegas ★★ Pernod-Ricard-owned San Rafael producer. Juicy Malbec, Chard, and delicious Syrah (red and rosé). Red blend Barbaro also v. good.

Bianchi, Valentin ★ San Rafael red specialist. Enzo Bianchi (Cab Sauv/Merlot/Malbec) is excellent flagship. Good-value Elsa's Vineyard including meaty Barbera. Pithy Sauv Bl; also decent sparkling.

Bodega del Fin del Mundo ★★ First winery in the province of Neuquén; Malbec a speciality, top wine Special Blend is Merlot/Malbec/Cab Sauv.

Bressia ★★→★★★ Tiny new winery already on form with classy Malbec-dominated Profundo from Agrelo and Conjuro Malbec from Tupungato.

Cabernet de los Andes ★★ Promising organic (and partly biodynamic) Catamarca estate with big, fragrant, balanced reds under Vicien and Tizac labels.

Canale, Bodegas Humberto ★★ Premier Río Negro winery known for its Sauv Bl and Pinot N, but Merlot and Malbec (esp Black River label) are the stars.

Cassone, Bodega ★★ Mendoza enterprise now benefiting from Alberto Antonini's winemaking expertise (ALTOS LAS HORMIGAS, Renacer, Melipal). Watch out for Obra Prima Malbec.

Catena ★★→★★★★ Style can be a little international, but quality is always good. Range rises from Alamos through Catena, Catena Alta, to flagship Nicolas Catena Zapata and 5 fine single-vineyard Malbecs (see ARGENTINO). Also joint venture with the Rothschilds of Lafite: classy *Caro* and younger Amancaya.

Clos de los Siete ★★ Seven parcels of French-owned vines in MENDOZA, run by Michel Rolland (see France). A juicy Malbec already exists, but each site will produce its own wine (see MONTEVIEJO).

Chakana ★★ Agrelo winery to watch for joyful Malbec, Cab Sauv, Syrah.

Chandon, Bodegas ★→★★ Makers of Baron B and M Chandon sparkling under Moët & Chandon supervision; promising Pinot N/Chard blend. See TERRAZAS.

Cobos, Viña ★★★ Stunning Marchiori Vineyard old-vine Malbec.

Colomé, Bodega ★★→★★★ SALTA bodega owned by California's Hess Collection. Pure, intense, biodynamic Malbec-based reds, lively Torrontés.

Dominio del Plata ★→★★★★ EX-CATENA husband-and-wife pair Susana Balbo and Pedro Marchevsky produce superior wines under the Crios, Susana Balbo, BenMarco, Anubis and Budini labels.

Doña Paula ★ Luján de Cuyo estate owned by Santa Rita (see Chile). Elegant, structured Malbec; modern fleshy Cab Sauv; tangy Los Cardos Sauv Bl.

Etchart ★★→★★★★ Reds good, topped by plummy Cafayate Cab Sauv. Torrontés also one of the best, with intriguing late-harvest Tardío.

Fabre Montmayou ★★ French-owned Luján de Cuyo (MENDOZA) bodega; fine reds and advice from Michel Rolland (see France). Also decent Chard. Infinitus is sister bodega in Rio Negro making supple Gran Res Merlot.

Familia Schroeder ★★ Confident Neuquén estate impressing with reds and whites. V. Good Saurus Select range includes sappy Sauv Bl, earthy Merlot and fragrant Malbec.

Familia Zuccardi ★→★★★ Dynamic MENDOZA estate producing gd-value Santa Julia range, led by new blend Magna, better Q label (impressive Malbec, Merlot, Tempranillo), and deep yet elegant Zeta (Malbec/Tempranillo).

Finca La Anita ★★→★★★★ MENDOZA estate making high-class reds, esp Syrah and Malbec, and intriguing whites, including Semillon and Tocai Friulano.

Finca El Retiro ★→★★★ MENDOZA bodega for good Malbec, Bonarda, Tempranillo.

Finca Flichman ★★ Long-established company. Good-value Syrah. Best: Dedicado blend (mostly Cab Sauv/Syrah). Paisaje de Tupungato (Bordeaux blend), Paisaje de Barrancas (Syrah-based) v. good.

Finca Las Moras ★★ San Juan bodega with chunky Tannat, chewy Malbec Res, and plump, fragrant Malbec/Bonarda blend Mora Negra.

Finca Sophenia Tupungato bodega. Advice from Michel Rolland (see France).

Malbec and Cab Sauv shine; good Altosur entry-level range; top Synthesis.

Kaikén ★★→★★★ Mendoza venture for Aurelio Montes (see Chile) making user-friendly range topped by Ultra Cab Sauv and Malbec.

Luigi Bosca ★★→★★★ Small MENDOZA bodega with three tiers of quality – Finca La Linda, Luigi Bosca Res, and High Range. Esp good Finca Los Nobles Malbec/Verdot and Cab Sauv/Bouchet, plus impressive new Gala blends.

Lurton, Bodegas J & F ★→★★★ MENDOZA venture of Lurton brothers. Juicy, concentrated Piedra Negra Malbec and complex, earthy Chacayes (Malbec) head range; new Flor de Torrontés more serious than most.

Marguery, Familia Top-class Malbec from old vines in the Tupungato district.

Masi Tupungato ★★→★★★ MENDOZA enterprise for the well-known Valpolicella producer (see Italy). Passo Doble is fine *ripasso*-style Malbec/Corvina/Merlot blend; Corbec is even better Amarone lookalike (Corvina/Malbec).

Mendel ★★★ Former Terrazas winemaker Roberta de la Mota makes plummy Malbec and graceful Unus blend from old Luján de Cuyo vines.

Mendoza Most important province for wine (over 70% of plantings). Best sub-regions: Agrelo, Valle de Uco (includes Tupungato), Luján de Cuyo, Maipú.

Monteviejo ★★→★★★ One of the vineyards of CLOS DE LOS SIETE, now with top-class range of reds headed by wonderfully textured Monteviejo blend (Malbec/Merlot/Cab Sauv/Syrah); Lindaflor Malbec also v. good.

Navarro Correas ★★ Good if sometimes over-oaked reds, esp Col Privada Cab Sauv. Also reasonable whites, inc very oaky Chard and Deutz-inspired fizz.

Neuquén Patagonian region to watch: huge developments since 2000.

Nieto Senetiner, Bodegas ★★ Luján de Cuyo-based bodega. Quality rises from tasty entry-level Santa Isabel through Reserva to top-of-range Cadus reds.

Noemia Old-vine RÍO NEGRO Malbec from Hans Vinding-Diers and Noemi Cinzano. J Alberto and A Lisa new second labels. (Chacra Pinot N from nearby is another promising Vinding-Diers project.)

Norton, Bodegas ★★★ Old bodega, now Austrian-owned. Good whites; v. good reds, esp Malbec and **excellent value Privada** (Merlot/Cab Sauv/Malbec).

O Fournier ★→★★★ Spanish-owned Valle de Uco bodega. Urban Uco v. good entry-level range; then come B Crux and Alfa Crux, both fine Tempranillo/Merlot/Malbec blends. Also fragrant but rare Syrah.

Peñaflor ★→★★★ Argentina's biggest wine company. Labels include Andean Vineyards and, finer, TRAPICHE, FINCA LAS MORAS, SANTA ANA and MICHEL TORINO.

Poesia ★★→★★★ Exciting Luján de Cuyo producer under same ownership as Clos l'Eglise of Bordeaux; stylish Poesia (Cab Sauv/Malbec), chunkier but fine Clos des Andes (Malbec), and juicy Pasodoble Malbec/Syrah/Cab Sauv blend.

Pulenta Estate ★★→★★★ Luján de Cuyo winery. Good Sauv Bl and v. good reds. Best: Gran Corte (Cab Sauv/Malbec/Merlot/Petit Verdot) and Malbec.

Río Negro Patagonia's oldest wine region, good for Pinot N and Malbec.

Salentein, Bodegas ★★ MENDOZA bodega, impressing with Cab Sauv, Malbec, Merlot, Primus Pinot N. Finca El Portillo (a separate estate) good for cheaper wines; also Bodegas Callia in San Juan, where Shiraz is the focus.

Salta Northerly province with some of the world's highest vineyards. Sub-region Cafayate renowned for Torrontés.

San Juan Second largest wine region, home to promising Shiraz and Tannat.

San Pedro de Yacochuya ★★★ SALTA collaboration between Michel Rolland (see France) and the ETCHART family. Ripe but fragrant Torrontés; dense, earthy Malbec; and powerful, stunning Yacochuya Malbec from oldest vines.

Santa Ana, Bodegas ★→★★ Old-established firm at Guaymallen, MENDOZA. New La Mascota range a distinct improvement, with weighty Cab Sauv being the pick; also bright, friendly Cepas Privadas Viognier.

San Telmo ★★ Modern winery making fresh, full-flavoured Chard, Chenin Bl,

Merlot. Best: Malbec and Cab Sauv Cruz de Piedra-Maipú.

Tacuil, Bodegas ★★→★★★ 33 de Davalos is spicy Cab Sauv/Malbec blend.

Terrazas de los Andes ★★→★★★ CHANDON enterprise for still wines made from Malbec, Cab Sauv, Chard, Syrah. Three ranges: entry-level Terrazas (juicy Cab Sauv is the star), mid-price Res, and top-of-the-tree Afincado. Joint venture with Ch Cheval Blanc of Bordeaux making superb _Cheval des Andes_ blend.

Torino, Michel ★★ Rapidly improving organic Cafayate enterprise; Don David Malbec and Cab Sauv v. good. Altimus is rather oaky flagship.

Toso, Pascual ★★→★★★ Californian Paul Hobbs heads a team making g. value, tasty range inc ripe but finely structured Magdalena Toso (mostly Malbec).

Trapiche ★★→★★★ PEÑAFLOR premium label in ascending order of quality: Astica, Trapiche (Oak Cask Syrah), Fond de Cave (gd Malbec Reserva), Medalla (Cab Sauv), pricy red blend Iscay, and new trio of single-v'yd Malbecs.

Trivento ★→★★ Owned by CONCHA Y TORO of Chile, making good-value range, with Viognier standing out; also under Otra Vida label.

Val de Flores ★★★★ Another Michel Rolland-driven enterprise close to CLOS DE LOS SIETE for compelling yet elegant (and biodynamic) old-vine Malbec.

Viniterra ★→★★ Clean, modern wines under Omnium, Bykos, Viniterra labels.

Weinert, Bodegas ★→★★ Potentially fine reds, esp Cavas de Weinert blend (Cab Sauv/Merlot/Malbec), are often spoiled by extended ageing in old oak.

Other Central & South American wines

Bolivia With just a handful of wineries, this hot, humid country is not a major wine producer. Even so, wines such as Cepas de Altura Cab Sauv from **Vinos y Viñedos La Concepción** show what is possible. The vineyards, 1,000 km south of La Paz, are the highest in the world.

Brazil New plantings of better grapes are transforming a big, booming industry. International investment, especially in Rio Grande do Sul and Santana do Liuramento, notably from France and Italy, are significant. The sandy Frontera region and Sierra Gaucha hills (Italian-style sparkling) to watch. Continuous harvesting is possible in some equatorial vineyards. Of the wines that do leave Brazil, 95% are made by **Vinicola Aurora** (**Bento Gonçalves**), sometimes under the **Amazon** label. Look out for **Rio Sol, Miolo**.

Mexico Oldest Latin American wine industry is reviving, with investment from abroad (e.g. Freixenet, Martell, Domecq) and California influence via UC Davis. Best in Baja California (with Valle de Guadeloupe among the best sub-zones), Querétaro, and on the Aguascalientes and Zacatecas plateaux. Lack of water is a problem countrywide. Top Baja C producers are **Casa de Piedra** (impressive Tempranillo/Cab Sauv), **L A Cetto** (Valle de Guadeloupe, the largest, esp for Cab Sauv, Nebbiolo, Petite Sirah), **Doña Lupe** (organic specialist), **Bodegas Santo Tomás** (working with California's Wente Brothers to make Duetto, grapes from both sides of the border), **Monte Xanic** (with Napa award-winning Cab Sauv), **Bodegas San Antonio, Cavas de Valmar**.

Peru Viña Tacama exports some pleasant wines, esp the Gran Vino Blanco white; also Cab Sauv and classic-method sparkling. Chincha, Moquegua, and Tacha regions are making progress, but phylloxera is a serious problem.

Uruguay Point of difference here is the rugged, tannic grape Tannat, producing a sturdy, plummy red, best blended with Merlot and Ca **Carrau/ Castel Pujol** is among the most impressive wineries: Amat Gran Tradición 1752 and Las Violetas Reserva show Tannat at its most fragrant. Juanicó is equally impressive, with flagship red blend Preludio and joint venture with Bernard Magrez of Château Pape Clement to produce Gran Casa Magrez de Uruguay. Others: Bruzzone & Sciutto, Casa Filguera, Castillo Viejo, De Lucca,

Australia

More heavily shaded areas
are the wine-growing regions

The gods, it seems, are angry. Two munificent vintages (04 and 05) were followed by a third (06), exacerbating the surplus of grapes and wine. The outcome was up to 100,000 tonnes of grapes left unpicked, and an even greater amount sold at or below the cost of production. Tens of millions of dollars were offered by the largest wineries to growers as compensation for the termination of long-term grape supply contracts. Growers either removed lesser-quality vineyards or mothballed their vines.

Even as this was happening, the drought variously described as the worst in 100 or even 1,000 years tightened its grip, with the worst frosts ever experienced in the eastern states.

These frosts – which struck Australia's premium regions all the way from Tasmania to Canberra, but left the engine rooms of the Murray and Riverina largely untouched – have not only destroyed the 2007 crop, but will likely reduce the 2008 harvest. In the latter two regions cold weather and ever-decreasing irrigation-water allocations have cut yields. It may sound like bad news all round, but the very good 2005 vintage and even better 2006 vintage wines will help bridge the gap. Producers from other New World countries are currently rubbing their hands with glee, hoping to fill any shortfall; well, we shall see.

Recent vintages

New South Wales (NSW)

2006 A burst of extreme heat around Christmas in some regions did not leave a lasting mark on a vintage of overall high quality.

2005 A very good to exceptional year across almost all districts, especially the Hunter, Mudgee, and Orange.

2004 Hunter Valley suffered; other regions good to very good outcomes.

2003 Continued drought broken by heavy rain in Jan/Feb; variable outcomes.

2002 Heavy Feb rain caused problems in all but two areas. Riverina outstanding.

2001 Extreme summer heat and ill-timed rain set the tone; remarkably, Hunter Valley Semillon shone.

2000 A perfect growing season for the Hunter Valley, but dire for the rest of the state; extreme heat followed by rain during the harvest.

1999 Another Hunter success; rain when needed. Other regions variable.

Victoria (Vic)

2006 One of the earliest and most compressed vintages on record; paradoxically fruit flavour came even earlier. A charmed year.

2005 Rain up to end of Feb was followed by a freakish three-month Indian summer giving superb fruit.

2004 Near perfect weather throughout ripened generous yields.

2003 Overall, fared better than other states, except for bushfire-ravaged Alpine Valleys.

2002 Extremely cool weather led to tiny yields, but wines of high quality.

2001 Did not escape the heat; a fair to good red vintage, whites more variable.

2000 Southern and central regions flourished in warm and dry conditions; terrific reds. Northeast poor; vintage rain.

1999 Utterly schizophrenic; Yarra disastrous (vintage rain); some other southern and central regions superb; northeast up and down.

South Australia (SA)

2006 A great Cabernet year; for other reds those picked before Easter rains did best. Here, too, flavour ripeness came early.

2005 Clare Valley, Coonawarra, Wrattonbully, and Langhorne Creek did best in what was a large but high-quality vintage with reds to the fore.

2004 Excellent summer and autumn weather helped offset large crops (big bunches/berries); heavy crop-thinning needed.

2003 A curate's egg. The good: Limestone Coast and Clare Riesling (yet again); the bad: rain-split Shiraz.

2002 Very cool weather led to much-reduced yields in the south and to a great Riverland vintage in both yield and quality. Fine Riesling again.

2001 Far better than 2000; Clare Valley Riesling an improbable success.

2000 The culmination of a four-year drought impacted on both yield and quality, the Limestone Coast Zone faring the best.

1999 Continuing drought was perversely spoiled by ill-timed March rainfall; Limestone Coast and Clare reds the few bright spots.

Western Australia (WA)

2006 Complete opposite to Eastern Australia; a cool, wet and late vintage – gave good whites, dubious reds.

2005 Heavy rain in late March and April spoiled what would have been the vintage of a generation for Cabernet and Shiraz in the south; whites uniformly excellent.

2004 More of the same; mild weather, long autumn. Good flavours, some lacking intensity.

2003 An in-between year, with ill-timed rainfall nipping greatness in the bud.

2002 Best since 84 in Swan District. In the south, quality is variable.

2001 Great Southern, the best vintage since 95; good elsewhere.

2000 Margaret River excellent, variation elsewhere; the Swan Valley ordinary.

1999 An outstanding vintage for Margaret River and Swan reds (best in more than a decade) and pretty handy elsewhere, other than the Great Southern.

Abercorn Mudgee, NSW r ★★ Dedicated, self-taught winemaker acquired neighbouring HUNTINGTON ESTATE late 2005. Identities to be kept separate.

Adelaide Hills SA Spearheaded by PETALUMA: cool, 450 m sites in Mt Lofty ranges.

Alkoomi Mount Barker, WA r w ★★★ (RIES) **01' 02 03** 04 05' 06 (CAB SAUV) 97 99 01 02' 04 A veteran of 35 years making fine RIES and long-lived reds.

All Saints Rutherglen, Vic r w b ★★ Historic producer making creditable table wines; great fortifieds.

Alpine Valleys Vic Geographically similar to KING VALLEY and similar use of grapes.

Amberley Estate Margaret R r w ★★ Successful maker of a full range of regional styles now improving. Now a tiny part of Constellation.

Andrew Pirie N Tas r w sp ★★→★★★ A phoenix arisen, with own brand and responsibility for TAMAR RIDGE and Rosevears Estate.

Angove's SA r w (br) ★→★★ Large, long-established MURRAY VALLEY family business. Good-value range white and red varietals.

> ### Dealing with drought
> The rapidly escalating water shortages in Australia are of alarming proportions, and demand immediate responses. Fortunately, viticulture provides a high economic return per megalitre of water, and there are numerous ways that current technology can significantly increase that return. The same cannot be said for crops such as rice and cotton, which make major impacts on eastern Australia's crumbling, increasingly saline, but still major, water source, the Murray Darling basin.

Annie's Lane Clare V, SA r w ★★→★★★ Part of FWE. Consistently good, boldly flavoured wines; flagship Copper Trail excellent, especially RIES.

Arrowfield Hunter V, NSW r w ★→★★ Has sold Upper Hunter winery and vineyards to coalminer and relocated. Eviscerated Rothbury brand retained by FWE.

Ashbrook Estate Margaret R, WA r w ★★★ Minimum of fuss; consistently makes 8,000 cases of exemplary SEM, CHARD, SAUV BL, VERDELHO, and CAB SAUV.

Ashton Hills Adelaide Hills, SA r w (sp) ★★★ Fine, racy, long-lived RIES and compelling PINOT N crafted by Stephen George from 25-year-old vineyards.

Bailey's NE Vic r w b ★★ Rich SHIRAZ, and magnificent dessert Muscat (★★★★) and "Tokay". Part of FWE.

Balgownie Estate Bendigo and Yarra V, Vic r w ★★→★★★ Rejuvenated producer of very well-balanced wines now with separate YARRA VALLEY arm.

Balnaves of Coonawarra SA r w ★★★ Grape-grower since 1975; winery since 1996. Very good CHARD; excellent supple, medium-bodied SHIRAZ, MERLOT, CAB SAUV.

Bannockburn Geelong r w ★★★ (CHARD) **97' 99** 98' 00 02' 03' 04 (PINOT N) **97' 99** 02' 03' 04' (05') Intense, complex CHARD and PINOT N produced using Burgundian techniques. New winemaker Michael Glover is a whizz.

Banrock Station Riverland, SA r w ★→★★ Almost 1,600-ha property on MURRAY RIVER, 243-ha vineyard, owned by HARDYS. Impressive budget wines.

Barossa Valley SA Australia's most important winery (but not vineyard) area; grapes from diverse sources make diverse wines. Local specialities: very old-vine SHIRAZ, Mourvèdre, and GRENACHE.

Bass Phillip Gippsland, Vic r ★★★→★★★★ (PINOT N) 91' 94' 96 97' 99' 02' 03 04 (05') Tiny amounts of stylish, eagerly sought-after PINOT N in three quality grades; very Burgundian in style, though quality can be erratic.

Bay of Fires N Tas r w sp ★★★ Pipers River outpost of HARDYS empire. Produces stylish table wines and Arras super-*cuvée* sparkler.

Beechworth Vic Trendy region; Castagna and GIACONDA are best-known wineries.

Bellarmine Wines Pemberton WA w (r) ★★★ German Schumacher family is long-distance owner of this 20-ha, seven-variety vineyard: (*inter alia*) startling Mosel-like RIES at various sweetness/alcohol levels, at ridiculously low prices.

Bendigo Vic Widespread 34 small vineyards, some very good quality. Notable: BALGOWNIE, PONDALOWIE, Passing Clouds, Turner's Crossing, and Water Wheel.

Beringer Blass Barossa, SA r w (sp, sw, br) ★★★ (CAB SAUV blend) 90' 91' 94 96' 98' 00 02' 04 (05) Founded by the ebullient Wolf Blass, now swallowed up by FWE (see also Beringer Blass, California). It is well served by winemakers Chris Hatcher (chief) and Caroline Dunn (reds).

Best's Grampians, Vic r w ★★→★★★ (SHIRAZ) 92' 94' 97' 98 01' 02' 03' 04' (05') Conservative old family winery; very good mid-weight reds. Thomson Family SHIRAZ from 120-year-old vines is super.

Big Rivers Zone NSW and Vic The continuation of South Australia's Riverland, including the MURRAY DARLING, Perricoota, and Swan Hill regions.

Bindi Macedon, Vic r w ★★★→★★★★ Ultra-fastidious, *terroir*-driven maker of outstanding, long-lived PINOT N and CHARD.

Bloodwood, Orange, NSW ★★★ r w Old dog (1983) in up-and-coming cool, high-altitude, and picturesque region. CHARD, RIES, and Big Men in Tights Rosé always good.

Blue Pyrenees Pyrenees, Vic r w sp ★★ 180 ha of mature vineyards are being better utilized across a broad range of wines.

Botobolar Mudgee, NSW r w ★★ Marvellously eccentric little organic winery.

Brand's of Coonawarra Coonawarra, SA r w ★★★ 90' 91' 94 96' 98' 02 03 04 (05) Owned by McWILLIAM's. Super-premium Stentiford's SHIRAZ (100-year-old vines) and Patron's CAB SAUV are tops.

Bremerton Langhorne Creek, SA r w ★★ Regularly produces attractively priced red wines with silky, soft mouthfeel and stacks of flavour.

Brini Estate McLaren Vale, SA r ★★→★★★ Family grape-growers for 50 years now have pick of the crop contract-made into velvety SHIRAZ and GRENACHE.

Brokenwood Hunter V, NSW r w ★★★ (ILR Res SEM) 97' 99' 03' 04 (05') (06') (Graveyard SHIRAZ) 83' 85' 86' 87' 93' 97' 98' 00' (02') (03') Exciting CAB SAUV; SHIRAZ since 1973 – _**Graveyard SHIRAZ outstanding**_. SEM and Cricket Pitch SEM/SAUV BL fuel sales.

Brookland Valley Margaret R, WA r w ★★→★★★ Superbly sited winery (with a restaurant) doing great things, especially with SAUV BL. Owned by HARDYS.

Brown Brothers King V, Vic r w dr br sp sw ★→★★★ (Noble RIES) 98 99' 02' Old family firm, with new ideas. Wide range of delicate, varietal wines, many from cool mountain districts, including CHARD and RIES. Dry white Muscat is outstanding. CAB SAUV blend is best red.

Bullers Calliope Rutherglen, Vic br ★★★★ Rated for superb Rare Liqueur Muscat and "Tokay" (Muscadelle).

Buring, Leo Barossa, SA w ★★★ 73' 79' 84' 91' 94' 95 98 02' 04' 05' Part of

> **Brettanomyces**
>
> Brett (for short, but also sometimes called dekkera) can variously be described as giving wet-sticking-plaster or meaty aromas and a metallic finish to the palate. It used to be regarded as a foreign (Old World or Californian) disease, but lower sulphur levels allowed it to populate Australian wines. Brett police, armed with brettometers, are now vigilantes, savaging any wine with the presumption of guilt, not innocence. The police, coupled with higher sulphur additions, have led to a marked reduction in its occurrence.

FWE. Happily, now exclusive RIES producer; Leonay to label, ages superbly. Has moved to screwcap.

By Farr/Farr Rising Geelong, Vic r w ★★★ Father Gary and son Nick's own, after departure from Bannockburn. CHARD and PINOT N are minor masterpieces.

Cabernet Sauvignon 28,621 ha; 284,062 tonnes. Grown in all wine regions, best in COONAWARRA. From herbaceous green pepper in coolest regions, through blackcurrant and mulberry, to dark chocolate and redcurrant in warmer areas.

Campbells of Rutherglen NE Vic r br (w) ★★ Smooth, ripe reds and good fortified wines; Merchant Prince Rare Muscat and Isabella Rare Tokay very good.

Canberra District NSW Both quality and quantity on the increase; altitude-dependent, site selection important.

Capel Vale Geographe, WA r w ★★★ Very successful with good whites, including RIES. Also top-end SHIRAZ and CAB SAUV.

Cape Mentelle Margaret R, WA r w ★★★ Robust CAB SAUV good, CHARD even better; also ZIN and very popular SAUV BL/SEM. LVMH Veuve Clicquot owner; also Cloudy Bay (see New Zealand).

Capercaillie Hunter V, NSW r w ★★→★★★ Veteran Alasdair Sutherland goes from strength to strength, supplementing local grapes with purchases from elsewhere, including ORANGE, MCLAREN VALE, etc.

Carlei Estate Yarra V, Vic r w ★★ Mercurial winemaker Sergio Carlei sources PINOT N and CHARD from various vineyards and cool regions to make wines with abundant character.

Casella Riverina, NSW r w ★ The (yellow tail) phenomenon has swept all before it with multimillion-case sales in US. Like Fanta: soft and sweet.

Centennial Vineyards Southern Highlands, NSW r w ★★ So far, sources much of its best grapes from ORANGE, but the winemaking skills and a large investment chequebook are there.

Central Ranges Zone NSW Encompasses MUDGEE, ORANGE, and Cowra regions, expanding in high-altitude, moderately cool to warm climates.

Chain of Ponds Adelaide Hills, SA r w ★★ Impeccably made, full, flavoursome wines. SEM, SAUV BL, and CHARD to the fore.

Chalkers Crossing Hilltops, NSW r w ★★→★★★ Beautifully balanced cool-climate wines made by French-trained Celine Rousseau.

Chambers' Rosewood NE Vic br (r w) ★★→★★★ Viewed with MORRIS as the greatest maker of "Tokay" and Muscat.

Chapel Hill McLaren Vale, SA r w ★★ (r) Now owned by Swiss Schmidheiny group with multinational interests including Napa's Cuvaison in California.

Chardonnay 30,507 ha; 378,287 tonnes. Best known for fast-developing, buttery, peachy, sometimes syrupy wines, but cooler regions produce more elegant, tightly structured, ageworthy examples. Oak is less heavy-handed.

Charles Melton Barossa, SA r w (sp) ★★★ Tiny winery with bold, luscious reds, especially Nine Popes, an old-vine GRENACHE/SHIRAZ blend.

Cheviot Bridge Long Flat, SE Aus r w ★★ Fast-moving part of new corporate empire that bought the Long Flat brand from TYRRELL'S.

Clare Valley (Clare V), SA Small high-quality area 90 miles north of Adelaide. Best for RIES; also SHIRAZ and CAB SAUV.

Clarendon Hills McLaren Vale, SA r (w) ★★★ Monumental (and expensive) reds from small parcels of contract grapes around Adelaide.

Clonakilla Canberra District, NSW r w ★★★ Deserved leader of the SHIRAZ/Viognier brigade. RIES and other wines also very good.

Coldstream Hills Yarra V, Vic r w (sp) ★★★ (CHARD) 88' **92 96'** 02' 03 04' 05' (06') (PINOT N Reserve) **91'** 92' 96' **97** 02' 04' 05' (06') (CAB SAUV) **91'** 92' 98' 00' 02 04 (05') Established in 1985 by wine critic James Halliday. Delicious PINOT N to drink young, and Reserve to age leads Australia. Very good CHARD (especially Reserve wines), fruity CAB SAUV, and (from 97) MERLOT. Part of FWE.

Coonawarra SA Southernmost and perhaps finest vineyards of state: home to most of Australia's best CAB SAUV; successful CHARD, RIES, and SHIRAZ. Newer arrivals including Murdock and Reschke.

Coriole McLaren Vale r w ★★→★★★ (Lloyd Reserve SHIRAZ) **90' 91' 96'** 97 98' 02' 04 (05') To watch, especially for old-vine SHIRAZ Lloyd Reserve.

Craiglee Macedon Vic r w ★★★ (SHIRAZ) 90' 91' **93' 96'** 97 00' 02' 04' 05' Re-creation of famous 19th-C estate. Fragrant, peppery SHIRAZ, CHARD.

Cullen Wines Margaret R, WA r w ★★★★ (CHARD) 99' **00'** 02' 03 04' 05' (CAB SAUV/MERLOT) **86' 87' 90' 91' 94'** 95' 96' 97' 98' 99' 01' 02 04' (05') Vanya Cullen makes strongly structured *CAB SAUV/MERLOT (Australia's best)*, substantial but subtle SEM/SAUV BL, and bold CHARD: all real characters.

> **New varieties and varietal choice**
> In the past 20 years or so the number of varieties in commercial production has quadrupled. Vines from Russia to Portugal – and every country in between – have sprung up everywhere; the varietal count is now in excess of 115. There is Italian Fiano, and French Aucerot and Petit Meslier among the whites, and Russian Saperavi and Italian Marzemino among the reds. So far choice seems to have been somewhat haphazard, but the need for varieties that perform well in warm-to-hot climates, will clarify people's ideas.

Cumulus Orange, NSW r w ★★ The reborn Reynolds Wines, with much venture capital, the production skills of Philip Shaw (ex ROSEMOUNT), and slick marketing to push its 550,000-case production.

Cuttaway Hill Southern Highlands, NSW r w Leads the region in the production of estate-grown wines, especially CHARD, SAUV BL, Pinot Gr.

Dalwhinnie Pyrenees, Vic r w ★★★ (CHARD) **96' 98'** 00' 03' 04' 05 (SHIRAZ) 97' **98'** 99' 00' 02 03 04' Rich CHARD and SHIRAZ. CAB SAUV best in PYRENEES.

d'Arenberg McLaren Vale, SA r w (sw br sp) ★★→★★★ Old firm with new lease of life; sumptuous SHIRAZ and GRENACHE, lots of varieties and wacky labels.

Deakin Estate Murray Darling r w ★ Part of KATNOOK group, producing 500,000 cases of very decent varietal table wines.

De Bortoli Griffith, NSW r w dr sw (br) ★→★★★★ (Noble SEM) Irrigation-area winery. Standard red and white but splendid sweet botrytized Sauternes-style Noble SEM. See also next entry.

De Bortoli Yarra V, Vic r w ★★→★★★★ (CHARD) **01' 02'** 04 05' (06') (CAB SAUV) **92' 94' 98'** 02' 03 04 YARRA VALLEY's largest producer. Main label is quite good; second label Gulf Station and third label Windy Peak very good value.

Delatite Upper Goldburn (r) w (sp) ★★ (RIES) 00 01 **02'** 04 05 06' RIES, Gewurz, CAB SAUV, and SAUV BL are specialities of this cool mountainside vineyard.

Devil's Lair Margaret R, WA r w ★★★ Opulently concentrated CHARD and CAB SAUV/MERLOT. Fifth Leg is trendy second label. Part of FWE.

Diamond Valley Yarra V, Vic r w ★★→★★★ (PINOT N) 96' 98' 01' 02' 04' 05 Outstanding PINOT N in significant quantities; others good, especially CHARD.

Domaine A S Tas r w ★★★ Swiss owners/winemakers Peter and Ruth Althaus are ultimate perfectionists; SAUV BL (Fume Blanc) and CAB SAUV are picks.

Domaine Chandon Yarra V, Vic sp (r w) ★★★ Classic sparkling wine from grapes grown in cooler wine regions, supported by owner Moët & Chandon. Well known in UK as Green Point (label also used for table wine)

Dominique Portet Yarra V, Vic r w ★★→★★ After 25-year career at TALTARNI, now in his own winery for the first time, going from strength to strength.

Dromana Estate Mornington Pen, Vic r w ★★→★★★ (CHARD) 00' 01 02' 03 04 (05') Light, fragrant CAB SAUV, PINOT N, and CHARD. Now taking Italian varieties (grown elsewhere) very seriously.

Eden Valley (Eden V), SA Hilly region home to HENSCHKE and PEWSEY VALE; RIES and SHIRAZ of very high quality.

Elderton Barossa r w (sp br) ★★ Old vines; flashy, rich, oaked CAB SAUV and SHIRAZ.

Evans & Tate Margaret R, WA r w ★★→★★★ (CAB) 95' 96' 99' 00 01' 02 04' Fine elegant SEM, CHARD, CAB SAUV, MERLOT from MARGARET RIVER, Redbrook. Has suffered financial blues and stock write-downs.

Evans Family Hunter V, NSW r w ★★★ (CHARD) 00' 01' 02 03' 05' Excellent CHARD from small vineyard owned by family of Len Evans. Fermented in new oak. Repays cellaring. See also TOWER ESTATE.

Ferngrove Vineyards Great Southern, WA r w ★★★ Cattle farmer Murray Burton's syndicate has established more than 400 ha of vines since 1997; great RIES.

Fox Creek McLaren Vale, SA r (w) ★★★ Produces 36,000 cases of flashy, full-flavoured wines, which are inveterate wine-show winners.

Freycinet Tas r w (sp) ★★★ (PINOT N) 97' 98' 99 00' 01' 02' 03 04 05' (06') East coast winery producing voluptuous, rich PINOT N and good CHARD.

FWE (Fosters Wine Estates) Official name of the merged Beringer Blass and Southcorp wine groups. Has 41 brands in Australia, more than any other, excluding the virtual brands (which use contract grapes, contract wineries, contract staff) that come and go like mushrooms after spring rain.

Gapsted Wines Alpine V, Vic r w ★★ Brand of large winery that crushes grapes for 50 growers.

Geelong Vic Once-famous area destroyed by phylloxera, re-established in the mid-1960s. Very cool, dry climate: firm table wines from good-quality grapes. Names including BANNOCKBURN, SCOTCHMANS HILL, BY FARR, Curlewis.

Gemtree Vineyards McLaren Vale, SA r (w) ★★ Top-class SHIRAZ alongside Tempranillo, Bordeaux blends and other exotica, linked by quality.

Geoff Merrill McLaren Vale, SA r w ★★ Ebullient maker of Geoff Merrill and Mt Hurtle. A questing enthusiast; his best are excellent, others unashamedly mass-market oriented. TAHBILK owns 50%.

Geoff Weaver Adelaide Hills, SA r w ★★★ An 8-ha estate at Lenswood. Very fine SAUV BL, CHARD, RIES, and CAB SAUV/MERLOT blend. Marvellous label design.

Giaconda Beechworth, Vic r w ★★★ (CHARD) Australia's answer to Kistler (see California). CHARD is considered by many to be the best in Australia – certainly the 96 is one of the all-time greats. PINOT N is very variable; newly introduced SHIRAZ better.

Glaetzer Wines Barossa r ★★★ Hyper-rich, unfiltered, very ripe old-vine SHIRAZ headed by iconic Amon-Ra. Very good examples of high-octane style much admired by US critics.

Goulburn Valley (Goulburn V), Vic Very old (TAHBILK) and relatively new (MITCHELTON) wineries in temperate mid-Victoria region. Full-bodied table wines.

Goundrey Wines Great Southern WA r w ★★ Recent expansion has caused quality to be variable. Bought by Canada's Vincor International in 2003.

Grampians Vic Region previously known as Great Western. Temperate region in central west of state. High quality, especially SHIRAZ.

Granite Belt Qld High-altitude, (relatively) cool region just north of Qld/NSW border. Especially spicy SHIRAZ and rich SEM.

Granite Hills Macedon, Vic r w ★★→★★★ 30-year-old family vineyard and winery has regained original class with fine elegant RIES and spicy SHIRAZ.

Grant Burge Barossa, SA r w (sp sw br) ★★→★★★ 200,000 cases of silky-smooth reds and whites from the best grapes of Burge's large vineyard holdings.

Great Southern WA Remote, cool area; FERNGROVE and GOUNDREY are the largest wineries. Albany, Denmark, Frankland River, Mount Barker, and Porongurup are official sub-regions.

Regions: Geographical Indications

The process of formally defining the boundaries of the zones, regions, and sub-regions, known compendiously as Geographic Indications (GIs), continues. These correspond to the French ACs, and AVAs in the United States. It means every aspect of the labelling of Australian wines has a legal framework that, in all respects, complies with EC laws and requirements. The guarantee of quality comes through the mandatory analysis certificate for, and the tasting (by expert panels) of, each and every wine exported from Australia.

Grenache 2,097 ha; 25,418 tonnes. Produces thin wine if overcropped, but can do much better. Growing interest in old BAROSSA and MCLAREN VALE plantings.

Grosset Clare, SA r w ★★★→★★★★ (RIES) 97' 99' 00' 01 02' 03' 04' 05 06' (Gaia) 90' 91' 92 **94'** 96' 98' 99 01' 02' 03' 04' (05) Fastidious winemaker. _Foremost Australian RIES, lovely CHARD, PINOT N, and exceptional Gaia CAB SAUV/MERLOT_ from dry vineyard high on MOUNT HORROCKS.

Haan Wines Barossa, SA r w ★★★ Low yields and meticulous winemaking ensure top results for Viognier, MERLOT, SHIRAZ, and Bordeaux blend (Wilhelmus).

Hamelin Bay Margaret R, WA ★★ 15-year-old estate plantings (25 ha) are paying dividends, with top-flight CHARD leading the way.

Hanging Rock Macedon, Vic r w sp ★→★★★ (Heathcote SHIRAZ) 91' 97' 98' 99 00' 01' 02' 03 has successfully moved upmarket with sparkling Macedon and HEATHCOTE SHIRAZ; bread and butter comes from contract winemaking.

Hardys r w sp (sw) ★★→★★★★★ (Eileen CHARD) 99' 00 00' 01' 02' 03 04' 05' (Eileen Shiraz) 70' **95'** 96' 98' 99' 00 01' 02' 04 Historic company blending wines from several areas. Best are Eileen Hardy and Thomas Hardy series and (Australia's best) "Vintage Ports". Part of Constellation, world's largest wine group.

Heathcote Vic The 500-million-year-old, blood-red Cambrian soil has seemingly unlimited potential to produce reds, especially SHIRAZ, of the highest quality.

Heathcote Estate Heathcote, Vic r ★★★ SHIRAZ specialist brimming with potential for small group of owners/executive winemakers; overlaps with YABBY LAKE.

Heggies Eden V, SA r w dr (sw w) ★★ (RIES) 98 99 00 02' 04 **05** vineyard at 500 m owned by S SMITH & SONS, like PEWSEY VALE with superb ageworthy RIES, but adds Viognier and CHARD to its portfolio.

Henschke Eden Valley, SA r w ★★★★ (SHIRAZ) 58' 61' 84' 86' 88 90' 91' 93' 96' 98' 99' 01' 02' (04') (CAB SAUV) 80' **85** 86' **88** 90' **91' 93** 94 96' 98 99' 01' 02' (04') A 139-year-old family business, perhaps Australia's best, known for delectable Hill of Grace (SHIRAZ), very good CAB SAUV and red blends, and value whites, including RIES. Lenswood vineyards in ADELAIDE HILLS add excitement. Fervent opponent of corks for reds, too.

Hewitson SE Aus r (w) ★★★ The virtual winery of ex-PETALUMA/ex-flying winemaker Dean Hewitson, sourcing parcels of 60–100-year-old vines and making wines (with great skill) in rented space.

Hollick Coonawarra, SA r w (sp) ★★→★★★★ (CAB SAUV/MERLOT) **91' 93 96' 98'** 99 01 02' 03 Has expanded estate vineyards, two in COONAWARRA, most recently in WRATTON BULLY. Main focus on CAB, SAUV, SHIRAZ, and MERLOT. Top-class winery restaurant too.

Hope Estate Lower Hunter V ★★ Snapped up Rothbury Estate Winery from FWE; also owns Virgin Hills and WA vineyards.

Houghton Swan V, WA r w ★→★★★ The most famous old winery of WA. Soft, ripe Supreme is top-selling, ageworthy white; a national classic. Also excellent CAB SAUV, VERDELHO, SHIRAZ, etc., sourced from MARGARET RIVER and GREAT SOUTHERN. See HARDYS.

Howard Park Mount Barker and Margaret R, WA r w ★★★ (RIES) **86' 91' 95' 97' 99' 02'** 03' 05' (06) (CAB SAUV) **88' 90 94' 96' 98'** 99' 01' 02' 03' 04 (05') (CHARD) **97' 98' 02' 03** 04' 05 (06') Scented RIES, CHARD; spicy CAB SAUV. Second label: MadFish Bay is excellent value.

Hunter Valley NSW Great name in NSW. Broad, soft, earthy SHIRAZ and gentle SEM that live for 30 years. CAB SAUV not important; CHARD is.

Huntington Estate Mudgee NSW r w ★★→★★★★ (CAB SAUV) **93 94' 95' 96' 97' 99'** 01' 02' 35-year-old vineyards (mainly SHIRAZ and CAB SAUV) on some of the best soil in the region, recently acquired by quality-conscious neighbour ABERCORN. Separate identity will be retained.

Jasper Hill Heathcote, Vic r w ★★★→★★★★ (SHIRAZ) **83' 85' 90' 91'** 92' 93 96' 97' 99' 00' 03 04' (05') Emily's Paddock SHIRAZ/Cab Fr blend and Georgia's Paddock SHIRAZ from dry-land estate are intense, long-lived, and much admired.

Jim Barry Clare V, SA r w ★★→★★★★ Some great vineyards provide good RIES, McCrae Wood SHIRAZ, and richly robed and oaked The Armagh.

John Duval Wines Barossa V r ★★★ The eponymous business of former chief red-wine maker for Penfolds (and Grange), making delicious reds that are supple and smooth, yet amply structured.

Kaesler Barossa, NSW r (w) ★★→★★★★ Old Bastard SHIRAZ (A$180) outranks Old Vine SHIRAZ (a mere A$60). Wine in the glass good, too (in heroic style).

Katnook Estate Coonawarra, SA r w (sp sw w) ★★★ (CAB SAUV) **91' 92' 94 96'** 97' 98' 00' 02' Excellent, pricey CAB SAUV, SHIRAZ, and CHARD. Also RIES and SAUV BL.

Keith Tulloch Hunter, NSW r w ★★★ Ex-Rothbury winemaker fastidiously crafting elegant yet complex SEM, SHIRAZ, etc.

Killikanoon Clare V, SA ★★→★★★★ r w RIES and SHIRAZ have been awesome performers in shows over past years. Portfolio now extends to Barossa V.

Kingston Estate SE Aus ★→★★★ Kalaedoscopic array of varietal wines from all over the place, consistency and value providing the glue.

King Valley Vic Altitude between 155 m and 860 m has massive impact on varieties and styles, and prolonged legal wrangling over GI boundaries. 21 wineries headed by Brown Bros, and important supplier to many others.

Knappstein Wines Clare V, SA r w ★★→★★★★ Reliable RIES, CAB SAUV/MERLOT SHIRAZ, and CAB SAUV. Owned by LION NATHAN.

Lake Breeze Langhorne Ck, SA r (w) ★★ Long-term grape-growers turned winemakers, producing succulently smooth SHIRAZ and CAB SAUV.

Lake's Folly Hunter V, NSW r w ★★★★ (CHARD) **89' 97' 99' 00' 02'** 03' 04' 05 (CAB SAUV) **69 81 89' 91 93 97'** 98' 00 02 03' (05') Founded by Max Lake the pioneer of HUNTER CAB SAUV. New owners since 2000. CHARD usually better than CAB SAUV these days.

Lamont's Swan V, WA r w ★★ Winery and superb restaurant owned by Corin Lamont (daughter of legendary Jack Mann) and husband. Delicious wines

Leasingham Clare V, SA r w ★★→★★★ Important mid-sized quality winery bought by HARDYS in 1987. Good RIES, SHIRAZ, and CAB SAUV/Malbec blend. Various labels.

Leeuwin Estate Margaret R, WA r w ★★★★ (CHARD) 82' 85' 87' 89 92' 95' 97' 98 99' 01' 02' 03 04' Leading W Australia estate, lavishly equipped. Superb, ageworthy (and expensive) Art Series CHARD, SAUV BL, RIES, and CAB SAUV also good.

Limestone Coast Zone SA Important zone including Bordertown, COONAWARRA, Mount Benson, Mount Gambier, PADTHAWAY, Robe, and WRATTONBULLY. All regions suffered significant frost damage in 2006.

Lindemans r w ★→★★ One of the oldest firms, now owned by FWE. Low-price Bin range (especially Bin 65 CHARD) now its main focus, a far cry from former glory.

Lion Nathan New Zealand brewery; owns PETALUMA, STONIER, TATACHILLA, MITCHELTON, Smithbrook, ST HALLET, and KNAPPSTEIN.

Macedon and **Sunbury** Vic Adjacent regions, Macedon at higher elevation, Sunbury near Melbourne airport. CRAIGLEE, HANGING ROCK, VIRGIN HILLS, GRANITE HILLS.

Majella Coonawarra, SA r (w) ★★★→★★★★ Rising to the top of COONAWARRA cream. The Malleea is outstanding CAB SAUV/SHIRAZ super-premium red. SHIRAZ and CAB SAUV also very good.

Margaret River, WA Temperate coastal area south of Perth, with superbly elegant wines. Australia's most vibrant tourist wine (and surfing) region.

Len Evans

The sudden death of Len Evans, AO, OBE, a few days before his 75th birthday in August 2006, robbed Australia, his family, and his many hundreds of friends of a man of unique talents and unlimited vision. To the last, he continued to urge Australian winemakers to make ever-better wines, and to learn from the greatest of France and elsewhere. One legacy of which he was particularly proud was the annual Len Evans Tutorial, an intensive five-day, 12-hours-a-day series of master-classes and blind tastings for 12 of the best young palates chosen from Australian winemakers, sommeliers, retailers, journalists/educators, and importers/distributors. His fellow teachers and trustees of the Tutorial are determined to make it a perpetual memorial to this great man.

McGuigan Simeon Hunter V, NSW ★→★★★ Nominal Hunter base of Australia's fifth-largest wine group, recently adding Miranda scalp to its collection. Has been buffeted by stormy financial climate, abrogating innumerable grape-purchase contracts.

McLaren Vale SA Historic region on the southern outskirts of Adelaide. Big, alcoholic, flavoursome reds have great appeal to US, but Coriole, WIRRA WIRRA, and others show flavour can be gained without sacrificing elegance.

McWilliam's Riverina, Hunter V, COONAWARRA, HILLTOPS NSW r w (sw br) ★★→★★★★ (Elizabeth SEM) 84' 86' 87' 93 94' 95 96 98 99' 00' 01' 02 03' 04 Still family-owned (Gallo lurking with 10% of shares) but has reinvented itself with great flair, always over-delivering. Elizabeth SEM the darling of Sydney, cheaper HANWOOD blends in many parts of the world. *Elizabeth and Lovedale SEMS* so consistent that vintages irrelevant.

Merlot The star of the new millennium; from 9,000 tonnes in 1996, to 132,586 tonnes in 2005. Grown everywhere, but shouldn't be, and beginning to show signs of fading.

Mitchell Clare V, SA r w ★★→★★★ (RIES) 00' 01' 03 04 05' Small family winery for excellent CAB SAUV and firmly structured dry RIES, under screwcap since 00.

Mitchelton Goulburn V, Vic r w (sw w) ★★ Reliable producer of RIES, SHIRAZ,

CAB at several price points, plus specialty of MARSANNE and ROUSSANNE.

Mitolo McLaren Vale/Barossa, SA r ★★★ One of the best "virtual wineries" (*i.e.* contract vineyards, contract wineries, contract winemaker), paying top dollar for top-quality SHIRAZ and CAB; quality oak and winemaking by Ben Glaetzer. Heroic but (virtually) irresistible wines.

Moorilla Estate Tas r w (sp) ★★★ Senior winery on outskirts of Hobart on Derwent River: very good RIES, Gewurz, and CHARD; PINOT N now in the ascendant. Superb restaurant.

Moorooduc Estate Mornington Pen, Vic r w ★★★ Stylish and sophisticated (wild yeast, etc.) producer of top-flight CHARD and PINOT N.

Mornington Peninsula Vic Exciting wines in new cool coastal area 25 miles south of Melbourne; 1,000 ha. Many high-quality, boutique wineries.

Morris NE Vic br (r w) ★★→★★★★ Old winery at RUTHERGLEN for some of Australia's greatest dessert Muscats and "Tokays".

Moss Wood Margaret R, WA r w ★★★★ (CAB SAUV) 75' 77' 80' 85' 88 90' 91' 94 95' 96' 99' 01' 02 03 04' To many, the best MARGARET RIVER winery (11.7 ha) SEM, CAB SAUV, CHARD, all with rich fruit flavours.

Mount Horrocks Clare V, SA w r ★★★→★★★★ *Finest dry RIES* and sweet Cordon Cut RIES; CHARD best in region.

Mount Langi Ghiran Grampians, Vic r w ★★★ (SHIRAZ) 81 84 88 89' 93' 95 96' 98 03' 04' 05' Especially for superb, rich, peppery, Rhône-like SHIRAZ, one of Australia's best cool-climate versions. Now owned by YERING STATION.

Mount Mary Yarra V, Vic r w ★★★★ (PINOT N) 97' 99 00' 02' 05' (06') (Quintet 88' 90' 92' 94 95' 96' 97' 98' 99 00' 02 03 04 The late Dr. John Middleton made tiny amounts of suave CHARD, vivid PINOT N, and (best of all) CAB SAUV blend: Australia's most Bordeaux-like "claret". All will age impeccably.

Mudgee NSW Long-established region northwest of Sydney. Big reds, surprisingly fine SEM, and full CHARD.

Murdock Coonawarra, SA r ★★★ Long-term grower now making classic CAB SAUV.

Murray Valley SA, Vic and NSW Vast irrigated vineyards. Principally making "cask" table wines. 40% of total Australian wine production.

Nepenthe Adelaide Hills, SA r w ★★→★★★ State-of-the-art kit, excellent vineyards, skilled winemaking, and sophisticated wines (especially SAUV BI CHARD, and SEM).

Ninth Island See PIPERS BROOK.

O'Leary Walker Wines Clare V, SA r w ★★★ Two whizz-kids have mid-life crisis and leave BERINGER BLASS to do their own thing – very well.

Orange NSW Cool-climate, high-elevation region giving lively CHARD, CAB SAUV MERLOT, SHIRAZ.

Orlando (Jacob's Creek), Barossa, SA r w sp (br sw) ★★→★★★ (St Hugo Cab 90' 91 96' 98' 99 01 02 03' (05') Great pioneering company, now owned by Pernod Ricard. Almost totally focused on three tiers of Jacob's Creek wines covering all varieties and prices, all tied historically to Jacob Gramp and his eponymous creek.

Padthaway SA Large area developed as overspill of COONAWARRA. Cool climate, good CHARD and excellent SHIRAZ (Orlando). Severe frost damage in 2006.

Paringa Estate Mornington Pen, Vic r w ★★★★ Maker of quite spectacular CHARD, PINOT N, and (late-picked) SHIRAZ, winning innumerable trophies.

Parker Estate Coonawarra, SA r ★★★ Small estate making very good CAB SAUV, especially Terra Rossa First Growth. Acquired by YERING STATION mid-2004.

Pemberton WA Region between MARGARET RIVER and GREAT SOUTHERN; initi enthusiasm for PINOT N replaced by MERLOT and SHIRAZ.

Penfolds Originally Adelaide, now everywhere r w (sp br) ★★→★★★★ (Grange (Bin 707) (Grange) 52' 53' 55' 62' 63' 66' 71' 76' 78' 80' 83' 86' 90' 91' 9

96' 98' 99' 01' (02') (Cab S Bin 707) **64' 76' 86' 90' 91' 96' 02' (04')** Consistently Australia's best red wine company, if you can decode its labels. Its Grange (was called Hermitage) is deservedly ★★★★. Yattarna CHARD was released in 98. Bin 707 CAB SAUV not far behind. Other bin-numbered wines (*e.g.* Kalimna Bin 28 SHIRAZ) can be very good. Rawson's Retreat brings up the rear.

Penley Estate Coonawarra, SA r w ★★★ High-profile, no-expense-spared winery. Rich, textured, fruit-and-oak CAB SAUV; SHIRAZ/CAB SAUV blend; CHARD.

Perth Hills WA Fledgling area 19 miles east of Perth with a larger number of growers on mild hillside sites. Millbrook and Western Range best.

Petaluma Adelaide Hills, SA r w sp ★★★★ (RIES) 80' **87' 94' 02'** 03 **04' 05'** (CHARD) **92'** 01 02 03' 04' (05') (CAB SAUV COONAWARRA) 79' 90' **91' 95' 98'** 99 00' 03' A rocket-like 1980s' success with COONAWARRA CAB SAUV, ADELAIDE HILLS CHARD, Croser CLARE VALLEY RIES, all processed at winery in ADELAIDE HILLS. Created by the fearsome intellect and energy of (now-retired) Brian Croser. Red wines richer from 1988 on. Fell prey to LION NATHAN 2002.

Peter Lehmann Wines Barossa, SA r w (sp br sw w) ★★–★★★★ Defender of BAROSSA faith; fought off Allied-Domecq by marriage with Swiss Hess group. Consistently well-priced wines in substantial quantities. Try Stonewell SHIRAZ and dry RIES, especially with age.

Pewsey Vale Adelaide Hills, SA w ★★★→★★★★ Glorious RIES, especially The Contours, released with screwcap, 5 years bottle-age and multiple trophies.

Pierro Margaret R, WA r w ★★★ (CHARD) **95' 96' 99'** 00' 01' 02' 03 Highly rated producer of expensive, tangy SEM/SAUV BL and very good barrel-fermented CHARD.

Pinot Noir 4,231 ha; 36,887 tonnes. Mostly used in sparkling. Exciting wines from south Victoria, TASMANIA, and ADELAIDE HILLS; plantings are increasing.

Pipers Brook Tas r w sp ★★★ (RIES) **98' 99' 00' 01' 02'** 04' 06 (CHARD) **97 99' 00'** 02' Cool-area pioneer; very good RIES, PINOT N, restrained CHARD, and sparkling from Tamar Valley. Second label: Ninth Island. Owned by Belgian Kreglinger family, owners of Vieux-Château-Certan (see Bordeaux).

Pirramimma McLaren Vale, SA r w ★★ Century-old family business with large vineyards is now moving with the times; snappy new labels and packaging, the wines not forgotten.

Plantagenet Mount Barker, WA r w (sp) ★★★ (Reds) 95 98' 01' 03 (05') The region's elder statesman: wide range of varieties, especially rich CHARD, SHIRAZ, and vibrant, potent CAB SAUV.

Pondalowie Bendigo, Vic r ★★★ Flying winemakers with exciting SHIRAZ/Viognier/Tempranillo in various combinations.

Primo Estate Adelaide Plains, SA r w dr (w sw) ★★★ Joe Grilli is a miracle-worker given the climate; successes including very good botrytized RIES, tangy Colombard, and potent Joseph CAB SAUV/MERLOT.

Pyrenees Vic Central Vic region producing rich, often slightly minty reds.

Red Hill Estate Mornington Pen, Vic r w sp ★★→★★★★ One of the larger and more important wineries; notably elegant wines.

Redman Coonawarra, SA r ★ Famous old name in COONAWARRA; red specialist: SHIRAZ, CAB SAUV, CAB SAUV/MERLOT. Wine fails to do justice to vineyard quality.

Richmond Grove Barossa r w ★→★★★★ Master winemaker John Vickery produces great RIES at bargain prices; other wines are OK. Owned by ORLANDO WYNDHAM.

Riesling 4,326 ha; 41,237 tonnes. Has a special place in the BAROSSA, EDEN, and CLARE valleys. Usually made bone-dry; can be glorious with up to 20 years bottle-age. Screwcaps now the only accepted closure.

Riverina NSW Large-volume irrigated zone centred around Griffith. Good-quality "cask" wines (especially white) and great sweet, botrytized SEM. Watch for reduced yields and better quality, *e.g.* the marvellous 02 wines.

Robert Channon Wines Granite Belt, Qld r w ★→★★ Lawyer turned *vigneron* has 6.8 ha of permanently netted, immaculately trained vineyard producing very good VERDELHO (plus usual others).

Rockford Barossa r w sp ★★→★★★★ Small producer from old, low-yielding vineyards; reds best, also iconic sparkling Black SHIRAZ.

Rosemount Estate Upper Hunter, McLaren Vale, Coonwarra, SA r w (sp) ★★ Rich, Roxburgh CHARD, McLAREN VALE Balmoral Syrah, MUDGEE Mountain Blue CAB SAUV/SHIRAZ, and COONAWARRA CAB SAUV lead the wide range. Part of FWE.

Rutherglen and **Glenrowan** Vic Two of four regions in the NE Vic Zone, justly famous for weighty reds and magnificent, fortified dessert wines.

St Hallett Barossa, SA r w ★★★ (Old Block) 86' 90' 91' 96 98' 99 01 02' 04' (05') Old Block SHIRAZ the star; rest of range is smooth, stylish. LION NATHAN-owned.

St Sheila's SA p sw sp **36 22 38** Full-bodied fizzer. Ripper grog, too.

Saltram Barossa, SA r w ★★→★★★ Mamre Brook (SHIRAZ, CAB SAUV, CHARD) and No 1 SHIRAZ are leaders. Metala is associated Stonyfell label for Langhorne Creek CAB SAUV/SHIRAZ. An FWE brand.

Sandalford Swan V, WA r w (br) ★→★★★ Fine old winery with contrasting styles of red and white single-grape wines from SWAN and MARGARET RIVER areas.

Sauvignon Blanc 4,152 ha; 38,355 tonnes. Usually not as distinctive as in New Zealand, but amazingly popular. Many styles, from bland to pungent.

Scotchmans Hill Geelong, Vic r w ★★ Makes significant quantities of stylish PINOT N, good CHARD, and spicy SHIRAZ.

Appellation Contrôlée and Global Warming

There seems to be broad agreement that the effect of global warming will be greater in the northern hemisphere than the southern. The ratio of water to land mass is greater in the southern hemisphere, and water is a temperature (and carbon) sink. Paradoxically, Australia, New Zealand, and South Africa cannot move vineyards much further south (if at all), although Chile and Argentina can. Australia shares with those two the opportunity of planting at higher altitudes, and its island state of Tasmania (like New Zealand) has less to fear. But, in a sense, this all misses the point: Australia can and will change varietal plantings at will, and adopt techniques such as water mist sprays to drop canopy temperatures. By contrast, even at the most basic level, tradition and appellation contrôlée law may delay changes in France.

Semillon 6,282 ha; 96,727 tonnes. Before the arrival of CHARD, Sem was the HUNTER VALLEY's answer to South Australia's RIES. Traditionally made without oak and extremely long-lived. Brief affair with oak terminated.

Seppelt Bendigo, Grampians, Henty r w sp br (sw w) ★★★ (St Peter's SHIRAZ) 71' 85' 86' 91' 96' 97' 99' 02' 03' 04' (05) Being broken up and sold by FWE, notably Seppeltsfield and amazing range of 100-year-old-plus fortifieds. GRAMPIANS winery and table wines retained, notably SHIRAZ, all sourced from premium Vic regions.

Sevenhill Clare V, SA r w (br) ★★ Owned by the Jesuitical Manresa Society since 1851. Consistently good wine; SHIRAZ and RIES can be outstanding.

Seville Estate Yarra V, Vic r w ★★★ (SHIRAZ) 90 91' 94 97' 00' 02' 03' 04' (05') Multiple ownership changes have not affected quality of CHARD, SHIRAZ, PINOT N.

Shadowfax Geelong, Vic r w ★★→★★★ Stylish new winery, part of Werribee Park; also hotel based on 1880s' mansion. Very good CHARD, PINOT N, SHIRAZ.

Shantell Yarra V, Vic r w ★★→★★★ Underrated producer with 30-year-old vineyard. SEM, CHARD, PINOT N, CAB SAUV.

Shaw & Smith McLaren Vale, SA w (r) ★★★ Founded by Martin Shaw and

Australia's first MW, Michael Hill Smith. Crisp SAUV BL, complex, barrel-fermented Reserve CHARD, MERLOT and, of course, SHIRAZ.

Shelmerdine Vineyards Heathcote/Yarra V, Vic r w ★★→★★★ Well-known family with high-quality wines from estate in the YARRA VALLEY and HEATHCOTE, the latter with unusual elegance and relatively low alcohol levels.

Shiraz 48,508 ha; 415,421 tonnes. Hugely flexible: velvety/earthy in the HUNTER; spicy, peppery, and Rhône-like in central and south Vic; or brambly, rum-sweet, and luscious in BAROSSA and environs (e.g. PENFOLDS' Grange).

Sirromet Queensland Coast r w ★★ A striking (100-ha) 75,000-case winery, with a 200-seat restaurant; biggest of many such new ventures. Wines from 100-plus ha of estate vineyards in GRANITE BELT consistently good.

South Burnett Now Queensland's second region with 14 wineries and more births (and some deaths) imminent, symptomatic of southeast corner of the state.

South Coast NSW Zone including Shoalhaven Coast and Southern Highlands.

Southcorp The former giant of the industry; now part of FWE. Owns PENFOLDS, LINDEMANS, SEPPELT, Seaview, WYNNS, ROSEMOUNT.

Southern NSW Zone including CANBERRA, Gundagai, Hilltops, Tumbarumba.

S Smith & Sons (alias Yalumba) Barossa, SA r w sp br (sw w) ★★→★★★ Big old family firm with considerable verve. Full spectrum of high-quality wines, including PEWSEY VALE, HEGGIES, and YALUMBA. Angas Brut, a good-value sparkling wine, and Oxford Landing varietals are now world brands.

Stanton & Killeen Rutherglen, Vic br r ★★★ Grandson Chris Killeen has a modernist palate, makes a great dry red, outstanding "Vintage Port", and Muscat.

Stefano Lubiana S Tas r w sp ★★→★★★ Beautiful vineyards on the banks of the Derwent River 20 mins from Hobart. Sparkling wine specialist, but also very good table wines including PINOT N.

Stonehaven Padthaway, SA r w ★★ First large (A$20m) winery in PADTHAWAY region, built by HARDYS, servicing whole LIMESTONE COAST ZONE production.

Stonier Wines Mornington Pen, Vic r w ★★★ (CHARD) 00' 01 02 03' 04 04' (05') (PINOT N) 00' 02' 03 04' 05 Consistently very good; Reserves outstanding. Owned by LION NATHAN.

Suckfizzle/Stella Bella/Skuttlebutt Margaret R, WA r w ★★★ Avant-garde label designs and names shouldn't obscure deadly serious commitment to quality. CAB SAUV, SEM/SAUV BL, CHARD, SHIRAZ, SANGIOVESE/CAB all shine.

Summerfield Pyrenees, Vic r (w) ★★ Consistent producer of estate-grown, blockbuster SHIRAZ and CAB SAUV, especially in reserve appellation.

Swan Valley (Swan V), WA Located 20 minutes north of Perth. Birthplace of wine in the west. Hot climate makes strong, low-acid table wines; being rejuvenated for wine tourism.

Tahbilk Goulburn V, Vic r w ★★→★★★ (Marsanne) 74' 75' 82' 92' 97' 98' 99' 01' 03' 05' (SHIRAZ) 68' 71' 76' 86 98' 00 02' 03 04' Beautiful historic family estate: long-ageing reds, also RIES and *Marsanne*. Reserve CAB SAUV outstanding; value for money ditto. Rare 1860 Vines SHIRAZ, too.

Taltarni Pyrenees, Vic r w (sp) ★★ New management and winemaking team producing more sophisticated reds, especially Cephas.

Tamar Ridge N Tas r w (sp) ★★→★★★ Public-company ownership, Dr. Richard Smart as viticulturist, Dr. Andrew Pirie as CEO/chief winemaker, and 230-plus ha of vines make this a major player – if not the major player – in TASMANIA.

Tapanappa SA r ★★ New WRATTONBULLY collaboration between Brian Croser, Bollinger, and J-M Cazes of Pauillac (see France). To watch.

Tarrawarra Yarra V, Vic r w ★★★ (CHARD) 00 01' 02' 03' 04' (05') (PINOT N) 00 01'

02' 03 04 (05) Has moved from idiosyncratic to elegant, mainstream CHARD and PINOT N. Tin Cows is the second label.

Tarrington Henty, Vic r w ★★★ Cameo winery producing jewel-like CHARD (intense, no oak) and PINOT N in miniscule quantities.

Tasmania Production continues to surge, but still tiny. Great potential for sparkling, CHARD, PINOT N, and RIES in cool climate. Only region to report excess demand for grapes in 06; frost will exacerbate imbalance in 07.

Tatachilla McLaren Vale, SA r w ★★→★★★ Significant (250,000 cases) production of nice whites and very good reds. Acquired by LION NATHAN in 2002.

Taylors Wines Clare V, SA r w ★★→★★★ 400,000 case production of much-improved RIES, SHIRAZ, CAB SAUV. Exports under Wakefield Wines brand (trademark issues with Taylors of Oporto).

Ten Minutes by Tractor Mornington Pen, Vic r w ★★ Amusing name and sophisticated packaging links three family vineyards that are – yes, you've guessed. SAUV BL, CHARD, PINOT N are all good.

T'Gallant Mornington Pen, Vic w (r) ★★ Improbable name and avant-garde labels for Australia's top Pinot Gris/Grigio producer. Also makes a fragrant unwooded CHARD. Quixotic acquisition by FWE.

The Islander Estate Kangaroo Island, SA r w ★★ New, full-scale development by Jacques Lurton, planned as likely retirement venture. Flagship estate wine an esoteric blend of Sangiovese, Cabernet Fr, and Malbec. Watch this space.

Torbreck Barossa, SA ★★★ r (w) The most stylish of the cult wineries beloved of the US; focus on old-vine Rhône varieties.

Tower Estate Hunter V, NSW r w ★★★→★★★★ Offers luxury convention facilities and portfolio of 10 wines made from grapes grown in the best parts of Australia. Impressive stuff.

Trentham Estate Murray Darling (r) w ★→★★★ 65,000 cases of family-grown and made, sensibly priced wines from "boutique" winery on R Murray; good restaurant, too.

Turkey Flat Barossa, SA r p ★★★ Icon producer of rosé, GRENACHE, and SHIRAZ from core of 150-year-old vineyard. Top stuff; controlled alcohol and oak.

Two Hands Barossa, SA r ★★→★★★ Savvy wine execs have created very successful virtual winery with top SHIRAZ from PADTHAWAY, MCLAREN VALE, LANGHORNE CREEK, BAROSSA, and HEATHCOTE stuffed full of alcohol, rich fruit, oak, and the kitchen sink.

Tyrrell's Hunter V, NSW r w ★★★ (SEM) **94' 95' 96' 97' 98' 99'** 00' 01' 03' 05' (*CHARD Vat 47*) 79' **96' 97' 98 99' 00'** 02' 04' 05' Australia's greatest maker of SEM, Vat 1 now joined with a series of individual vineyard or sub-regional wines, one or more of which will stand out in any given vintage, hence the unusual vintage ratings for the SEMS. Vat 47, too, continues to defy the climactic odds, albeit in a different style to LAKES POLLY.

Upper Hunter NSW Established in early 1960s; irrigated vines (mainly whites), lighter and quicker developing than Lower Hunter's.

Vasse Felix Margaret R, WA r w ★★★ (CAB SAUV) **96 97 98'** 99' 01 02 03' 04' 05' With CULLEN, pioneer of MARGARET RIVER. Elegant CAB SAUV, notable for mid-weight balance.

Verdelho 1,603 ha, 18,627 tonnes. Old white grape used in large volumes, unoaked and slightly sweet; cash cow.

Voyager Estate Margaret R, WA r w ★★★ 30,000 cases of estate-grown, rich, powerful SEM, SAUV BL, CHARD, CAB SAUV/MERLOT.

Wendouree Clare V, SA r ★★★★ Treasured maker (tiny quantities) of Australia's most powerful and concentrated reds, based on SHIRAZ, CAB SAUV,

Mourvèdre, and Malbec. Immensely long-lived, so much so that any wine less than 20 years old will not have reached maturity, and all of the six different wines would justify slightly different ratings.

Willow Creek Mornington Peninsula Vic r w ★★★ Impressive producer of CHARD and PINOT N in particular, with echoes of Burgundy. Perhaps it's the wine list at the excellent Salix restaurant with all 31 grand cru vineyards on offer.

Wirra Wirra McLaren Vale, SA r w (sp sw w) ★★★ (RSW SHIRAZ) 98' 99' 00' 01' 02' 03' 04' (05') (Angelus CAB SAUV) 97' 98' **99** 00 01' 02' 04' (05') High-quality wines making a big impact. RSW SHIRAZ has edged in front of Angelus CAB SAUV; both superb.

Woodlands Margaret R, WA r (w) ★★★→★★★★ 7 ha of 30-plus-year-old CAB SAUV among top vineyards in region, joined by younger but still very good plantings of other Bordeaux reds. Still family-owned and run, but consultancy advice has lifted quality to sensational levels, especially single-barrel Réserve du Cave releases.

Wrattonbully SA Important grape-growing region in LIMESTONE COAST ZONE for 30 years; profile lifted by recent arrival of TAPANAPPA.

Wyndham Estate Hunter V, NSW r w (sp) ★→★★ Originally HUNTER/MUDGEE, but now no wineries there, just brands: Poet's Corner, Montrose, and RICHMOND GROVE. Part of Orlando Wyndham, owned by Pernod Ricard.

Wynns Coonawarra, SA r w ★★★ (SHIRAZ) 55' 63 86' 90' 91' 94' 96' 97 98' 99' 00 02 04 (05') (CAB SAUV) 57' 60' 82' 85' 86' 90' 91' 94' 96' 98' 99' 00 02 04 (05') SOUTHCORP-owned COONAWARRA classic. RIES, CHARD, SHIRAZ, and CAB SAUV are all very good, especially *John Riddoch CAB SAUV* and Michael SHIRAZ.

Yabby Lake Mornington Pen, Vic r w ★★★ Joint venture between movie-distribution magnate Robert Kirby, Larry McKenna (ex-Martinborough), and Tod Dexter (ex STONIER WINES) (affiliated to HEATHCOTE estate), utterly driven by the goal of quality.

Yalumba See S SMITH & SONS.

Yarra Burn Yarra V, Vic r w sp ★★→★★★ Estate making SEM, SAUV BL, CHARD, sparkling PINOT N/CHARD/Pinot Meunier, and CAB SAUV. Acquired by HARDYS in 1995. Bastard Hill CHARD and PINOT N legitimate flag-bearers.

Yarra Valley Superb historic area near Melbourne. Growing emphasis on very successful PINOT N, CHARD, SHIRAZ, MERLOT, and sparkling. Lower-altitude vineyards, unprecedented frost damage in November 2006, followed by the discovery of phylloxera.

Yarra Yarra Yarra V, Vic r w ★★★ Recently increased to 7 ha, giving greater access to fine SEM/SAUV BL and CAB SAUV, each in classic Bordeaux style.

Yarra Yering Yarra V, Vic r w ★★★→★★★★ (Dry Reds) 80' 81' 82' 83 84 85 90' 91' 93' 94' 95 96 97' 99' 00' 01 02' 03 04' 05' (06') Best-known Lilydale boutique winery. Especially racy, powerful PINOT N; deep, herby CAB SAUV (Dry Red No 1); SHIRAZ (Dry Red No 2). Luscious, daring flavours in red and white. Also fortified "Port-Sorts" from the correct grapes.

Yeringberg Yarra V, Vic r w ★★★ (*Marsanne*) 91' 92 94' 95 97 98 00 02' 04 05' (CAB SAUV) 77' 80 81' 84' 88' 90 97' 98 00' 02' 04 (05') Dreamlike, historic estate still in the hands of founding family. Makes small quantities of very high-quality Marsanne, Roussanne, CHARD, CAB SAUV, and PINOT N.

Yering Station/Yarrabank Yarra V, Vic r w sp ★★★ On site of Vic's first vineyard; replanted after 80-year gap. Extraordinary joint venture: Yering Station table wines (Reserve CHARD, PINOT N, SHIRAZ, VIOGNIER); Yarrabank (especially fine sparkling wines for Champagne Devaux). Decimated by frost, but has enough stock to weather the storm.

Zema Estate Coonawarra, SA r ★★→★★★ One of the last bastions of hand-pruning in COONAWARRA; silkily powerful, disarmingly straightforward reds.

AUSTRALIA

New Zealand

More heavily shaded areas
are the wine-growing regions

Awash with garden-fresh, pungently herbaceous aromas and flavours,
Sauvignon Blanc from New Zealand has exploded onto the world stage
since the 1980s. The sunny but nocturnally cool Marlborough region, where
over half the country's vines are grown, now promotes itself as "the
Sauvignon Blanc capital of the world" – with few voices dissenting. High
hopes are also held for Pinot Noir, which yields deliciously perfumed, rich and
supple wines in Martinborough and throughout the South Island. The top
Merlot and Cabernet Sauvignon-based reds from the relatively warm Hawke's
Bay region show a Bordeaux-like fragrance and finesse, and its notably
aromatic, spicy Syrahs are also generating excitement. Pinot Gris is fast-
expanding and fashionable.

Recent vintages

2006 Record crop. In the North Island some reds were caught by autumn rains.
Average to good Marlborough Sauvignon; some lack pungency.

2005 Much lower-yielding than 2004, due to exceptionally cold, wet, early
summer. Late summer and autumn variable but often good. Excellent
Marlborough Sauvignon Blanc and Pinot Noir.

2004 Record crop, reflecting fast-expanding vineyard area and heavy yields.
Exceptionally wet Feb, but cool, dry autumn. Variable quality, with some
Sauvignon Blanc lacking depth.

2003 Frost-affected season, yielding the lightest crop yet. Unripe flavours in
some wines; excellent intensity in others.

2002 Bumper crop (50% heavier than previous record). Outstanding
Chardonnay and variable reds in Hawke's Bay.

Akarua Central Otago ★★ Large vineyard at Bannockburn, producing classy,
exuberantly fruity Pinot N, buttery Chard, and crisp appley Pinot Gr.
Supple, charming, second-tier Pinot N, labelled The Gullies.

Allan Scott Marlborough ★★ Excellent Ries (from vines more than 20 years old), good Chard, Sauv Bl; sturdy spicy Pinot N.

Alpha Domus Hawke's Bay ★★ Good Chard and concentrated reds, especially savoury Merlot-based The Navigator, and notably dark rich Cab Sauv-based The Aviator. Top wines labelled AD.

Amisfield Central Otago ★★ Impressive fleshy, smooth Pinot Gr and powerful, complex Pinot N. Lake Hayes is lower-tier label.

Astrolabe Marlborough ★★ Label owned by WHITEHAVEN winemaker Simon Waghorn. Strikingly intense harmonious Sauv Bl.

Ata Rangi Martinborough ★★★ Small but highly respected winery. Outstanding Pinot N (00 03' 05) and very good young-vine Crimson Pinot N. Rich, concentrated Craighall Chard and Lismore Pinot Gr.

Auckland Largest city in NZ. Henderson, Huapai, Kumeu, Matakana, Clevedon, Waiheke Island districts – pricey, variable Bordeaux-style reds – nearby.

Awatere Valley Marlborough Important sub-region, slightly cooler than the larger WAIRAU VALLEY, with racy herbaceous, minerally Sauv Bl.

Babich Henderson (Auckland) ★★ ·★★★ Mid-size family firm, established 1916; quality, value. AUCKLAND, HAWKE'S BAY, and MARLBOROUGH vineyards. Refined, slow-maturing Irongate Chard (02') and tight elegant Irongate Cab Sauv/Merlot (single vineyard). Ripe, dry MARLBOROUGH Sauv Bl.

Bilancia Hawke's Bay ★★ Small producer of classy Syrah (including brilliant, hill-grown La Collina) and rich Viognier, Pinot Gr.

Brancott Vineyards ★·★★★ Brand used by PERNOD RICARD NEW ZEALAND in US.

Brookfield Hawke's Bay ★★ Outstanding "gold label" Cab Sauv/Merlot; good Chard, Pinot Gr, and Gewurz. "Hillside" Syrah is a winner.

Cable Bay Waiheke Island ★★ Sizeable newcomer, first vintage 2002. Tight, refined Waiheke Chard and spicy, savoury, Five Hills red; subtle, finely textured MARLBOROUGH Sauv Bl. Second label is Culley.

Canterbury NZ's fifth-largest wine region; most top vineyards in warm, sheltered Waipara district. Long, dry summers favour Pinot N, Ries.

Carrick Central Otago ★★ Bannockburn winery with flinty, flavourful whites (Pinot Gr, Sauv Bl, Chard, Ries) and classy, densely packed Pinot N.

Central Otago (r) 03' 06 (w) 06 Fast-expanding, cool, mountainous region in southern South Island. Scented, crisp Ries and Pinot Gr; Pinot N perfumed and silky, with notably intense character, but best drunk young.

Chard Farm Central Otago ★★ Fresh, vibrant Ries, Pinot Gr, and good Pinot N.

Church Road Hawke's Bay ★★ ·★★★ PERNOD RICARD NEW ZEALAND winery. Rich Chard and elegant Merlot/Cab Sauv. Top Reserve wines; prestige, claret-style red, Tom.

Churton Marlborough ★★ Owned by English wine merchant turned winemaker Sam Weaver. Subtle, complex, finely textured Sauv Bl; fragrant, spicy, very harmonious Pinot N.

Clearview Hawke's Bay ★★ ·★★★ Burly, flavour-packed Reserve Chard; dark, rich Reserve Cab Fr, Enigma (Merlot-based), Old Olive Block (Cab Sauv blend).

Clifford Bay Marlborough ★★ Single-vineyard, Awatere Valley producer of fresh, lively Chard, Ries, Pinot N. Scented, intense Sauv Bl is best.

Clos Henri Marlborough ★★ ·★★★ Established by Henri Bourgeois (see France). First vintage 2003. Deliciously weighty, rich, rounded Sauv Bl and vibrant, supple Pinot N.

Cloudy Bay Marlborough ★★★ Large-volume Sauv Bl, Chard, and Pinot N are very good. Pelorus sparkling impressive. Rarer Gewurz, Late-Harvest Ries, and Te Koko (oak-aged Sauv Bl) now the finest wines. Pinot Gr is in the wings.

Collard Brothers Auckland ★★ Long-established small family winery. Whites, especially Rothesay Vineyard Chard.

Cooper's Creek Auckland ★★ Excellent Swamp Reserve Chard; very good MARLBOROUGH Sauv Bl, Ries; top-value Viognier; floral slightly spicy 06 Arneis (NZ's first).

Corbans Auckland ★→★★★ Established 1902, now PERNOD RICARD NEW ZEALAND BRAND. Best wines: Cottage Block; Private Bin. Quality from basic to outstanding.

Craggy Range Hawke's Bay ★★→★★★ Mid-sized winery with vineyards in MARTINBOROUGH and HAWKE'S BAY. Restrained Sauv Bl, stylish Chard, Pinot N; notably dense, ripe firm Merlot and Syrah.

Daniel Le Brun Marlborough ★★ Small winery: best known for citrus, yeasty Brut NV. New owner (Mahi Wines) in 2006.

Delegat's Auckland ★★ Large, fast-expanding family winery. Vineyards at MARLBOROUGH. Reserve Chard, Merlot, and Cab Sauv/Merlot offer v gd quality and value. OYSTER BAY brand: fresh fruit-driven Chard and Sauv Bl, elegant Pinot N.

Delta Marlborough ★★ Promising new producer with substantial, graceful Pinot N. Top label: Hatter's Hill.

Deutz Auckland ★★★ Champagne company gives name to fine sparkling from MARLBOROUGH by PERNOD RICARD NEW ZEALAND. NV: lively, yeasty, flinty. Vintage Blanc de Blancs: finely focused, citrus, piercing.

Dog Point Marlborough ★★ Grape-grower Ivan Sutherland and winemaker James Healy (both ex-CLOUDY BAY) produce unusually complex, finely textured, oak-aged Sauv Bl (Section 94), Chard, and Pinot N.

Dry River Martinborough ★★★ Tiny winery. Penetrating, long-lived Chard, Ries, Pinot Gr (NZ's finest), Gewurz, and ripe, powerful Pinot N (00 01 **03' 04**).

Escarpment Martinborough ★★ Sturdy, rich, Alsace-like Pinot Gr and muscular, dense Pinot N from Larry McKenna, ex-MARTINBOROUGH VINEYARD. Top label: Kupe.

Esk Valley Hawke's Bay ★★→★★★ Owned by VILLA MARIA. Some of NZ's most voluptuous Merlot-based reds (especially Reserve label 00' 02', 04) very good Merlot rosé, Chenin Bl, satisfying Chards, and Sauv Bl.

**Felton Road** Central Otago ★★★ Star winery in warm Bannockburn area. Bold, supple Pinot N Block 3 and 5 and light, intense Ries outstanding; excellent Chard and regular Pinot N.

Firstland Waikato ★→★★ Previously De Redcliffe; now owned by expatriate American. Hotel du Vin attached. Good MARLBOROUGH whites. Improving HAWKE'S BAY reds.

Forrest Marlborough ★★ Mid-size winery; easy-drinking Chard, Sauv Bl, Ries; gorgeous botrytised Ries; flavour-crammed HAWKE'S BAY Cornerstone Vineyard Cab Sauv/Merlot/Malbec.

Foxes Island Marlborough ★★ Small producer of rich, smooth Chard, finely textured Sauv Bl, and elegant, supple Pinot N.

Framingham Marlborough ★★ Owned by PERNOD RICARD NEW ZEALAND. Superb aromatic whites, _**notably intense zesty Ries**_, and lush slightly sweet Pinot Gr, Gewurz. Rich, dry Sauv Bl. Scented, silky Pinot N.

Fromm Marlborough ★★★ Swiss-founded, focusing on very powerful red wines. Sturdy, firm, long-lived Pinot N, especially under Fromm Vineyard and Clayvin Vineyard labels.

Gibbston Valley Central Otago ★★ Pioneer winery with popular restaurant. Greatest strength is Pinot N, especially robust, exuberantly fruity Reserve (**01 02'**). Racy local whites (Chard, Ries, Pinot Gr).

Giesen Estate Canterbury ★ German family winery. Good, slightly honeyed Ries, but bulk of production is now average-quality MARLBOROUGH Sauv Bl.

Gimblett Gravels Hawke's Bay Defined area with very free-draining soils, noted for rich, ripe, Bordeaux-style reds and Syrah.

Gisborne (r) 04' 05 (w) 05 NZ's third-largest region. Abundant sunshine and rain, with fertile soils. Key strength is Chard (typically deliciously fragrant, ripe, and soft in its youth). Good Gewurz and Viognier; Merlot more variable.

Goldwater Waiheke Island ★★→★★★ Region's pioneer Cab Sauv/Merlot Goldie (oo' o2) is still one of NZ's finest: Médoc-like finesse. Also crisp, citrus Chard and solid Sauv Bl, both grown in MARLBOROUGH. Sold in 2006 to NZ Wine Fund (also owns Vavasour).

Gravitas Marlborough ★★ First o2 vintage yielded exceptionally rich Sauv and Chard. Subsequent wines less memorable.

Greenhough Nelson ★★→★★★ One of region's top producers, with immaculate and deep-flavoured Ries, Sauv, Chard, Pinot N. Top label: Hope Vineyard.

Grove Mill Marlborough ★★→★★★ Attractive whites, including vibrant Chard; excellent Ries, Sauv, and slightly sweet Pinot Gr. Good, lower-tier Sanctuary brand.

Hawke's Bay (r) oo' o2' o4 (w) o4' o6 NZ's second-largest region. Long history of winemaking in sunny climate; shingly and heavier soils. Full, rich Merlot and Cab Sauv-based reds in good vintages; Syrah a fast-rising star; powerful Chard; rounded Sauv Bl.

Herzog Marlborough ★★★ Established by Swiss immigrants. Power-packed, pricey, but classy Merlot/Cab Sauv, Montepulciano, Pinot N, Chard, Viognier, and Pinot Gr. Now sold under Hans brand in Europe and US.

Highfield Marlborough ★★ Japanese owned with quality Ries, Chard, Sauv Bl, and Pinot N. Also piercing, flinty, yeasty Elstree sparkling.

Huia Marlborough ★★ Mouth-filling, subtle wines that age well, including savoury, rounded Chard and perfumed, well-spiced Gewurz.

Hunter's Marlborough ★★→★★★ Top name in intense, immaculate Sauv Bl. Fine, delicate Chard. Excellent sparkling, Ries, Gewurz; light, elegant Pinot N.

Isabel Estate Marlborough ★★★ Family estate with limey clay soil. Formerly outstanding Pinot N, Sauv Bl, and Chard, but lately very disappointing.

Jackson Estate Marlborough ★★ Rich Sauv Bl, good Chard, and attractive Dry Ries. Lightish Pinot N.

Johanneshof Marlborough ★★ Small, low-profile winery with outstandingly perfumed, lush Gewurz.

Kaituna Valley Canterbury ★★→★★★ Small producer with vineyards near Christchurch and in MARLBOROUGH. Consistently very powerful, multi-award-winning Pinot N.

Karikari Northland ★★ NZ's northernmost vineyard and winery, American owned, with rich, ripe Bordeaux-style reds, Pinotage, and Syrah.

Kemblefield Hawke's Bay ★→★★ US-owned winery. Solid reds; ripely herbal, oak-aged Sauv Bl; soft, peppery Gewurz; and fleshy, lush Chard.

Kim Crawford Hawke's Bay ★★ Now part of US-based Constellation empire. Numerous labels, including rich, oaky GISBORNE Chard and scented, strong-flavoured MARLBOROUGH Sauv Bl. Top range labelled SP (Small Parcel).

Kumeu River Auckland ★★→★★★ Rich, refined Kumeu Chard (o5' o6); single-vineyard Mate's Vineyard Chard even more opulent. Fresh, immaculate Pinot Gr. Distinctive, minerally MARLBOROUGH Sauv Bl since o4. Second label: Kumeu River Village.

Lake Chalice Marlborough ★★ Small producer with bold, creamy-rich, softly textured Chard and incisive, slightly sweet Ries; Sauv Bl of excellent quality. Platinum premium label.

Lawson's Dry Hills Marlborough ★★→★★★ Weighty wines with rich, intense flavours. Distinguished Sauv Bl and Gewurz; good Pinot Gr and Ries.

Lincoln Auckland ★ Long-established family winery. Good-value varietals of improving quality: buttery GISBORNE Chard (top label Reserve).

Lindauer See PERNOD RICARD NEW ZEALAND.

Longridge ★ Former CORBANS brand, now owned by PERNOD RICARD NEW ZEALAND. Reliable, moderately priced wines (including citrus, lightly oaked Chard) typically from HAWKE'S BAY.

Margrain Martinborough ★★ Small winery with firm, concentrated Chard, Ries, Pinot Gr, Merlot, and Pinot N, all of which reward bottle-age.

Marlborough (r) 03 04 05' (w) 04 05 NZ's largest region (more than half of all plantings). Warm days and cool nights give intense, crisp whites. Intense Sauv Bl, from sharp, green capsicum to ripe tropical fruit. Fresh, limey Ries; very promising Pinot Gr and Gewurz; Chard leaner, more appley than HAWKE'S BAY. High-quality sparkling and botrytised Ries. Pinot N best are among NZ's finest.

Martinborough (r) 01 03' (w) 03' Small, high-quality area in south WAIRARAPA (foot of North Island). Warm summers, dry autumns, gravelly soils. Success with white grapes, but most renowned for sturdy, rich, long-lived Pinot N.

Martinborough Vineyard Martinborough ★★★ Distinguished small winery; one of NZ's top Pinot Noirs (03' 05). Rich, biscuity Chard and intense Ries.

Matakana Estate Auckland ★→★★ Largest producer in Matakana district. Average to good Chard, Pinot Gr, Sem, Syrah, and Merlot/Cab Sauv blend. Volume label: Goldridge.

Matariki Hawke's Bay ★★ Stylish white and red, extensive vineyards in stony Gimblett Road. Rich, ripe Sauv Bl; robust, spicy Quintology red blend.

Matua Valley Auckland ★★→★★★ Highly rated, large winery, owned by Beringer Blass (see California), with vineyards in four regions. Top range Ararimu includes fat, savoury Chard and dark, rich Merlot/Cab Sauv. Numerous attractive GISBORNE (especially Judd Chard), HAWKE'S BAY, and MARLBOROUGH wines (Shingle Peak). Shingle Peak Sauv Bl top value.

Mills Reef Bay of Plenty ★★→★★★ The Preston family produces impressive wines from HAWKE'S BAY grapes. Top Elspeth range includes dense, rich Bordeaux-style reds and Syrah. Reserve range also impressive.

Millton Gisborne ★★→★★★ Region's top small winery: mostly organic. Soft, savoury Chard (single-vineyard Clos de Ste Anne is superb). Rich, long-lived Chenin Bl is NZ's finest.

The Wither Hills Scandal

In late 2006, the prestigious Wither Hills winery sent to competitions and magazine tastings a batch of its hugely popular 2006 Marlborough Sauvignon Blanc that was different to the wine widely available in retail stores. Yet the two wines had identical labels.

Only 2,228 cases of the now-famous batch BR315, sent to show organizers, were made, out of the total output of Wither Hills Marlborough Sauvignon Blanc 2006 of 130,000 cases. At best, consumers had a one in 50 chance of buying the wine entered in shows, which won two silver and three gold medals in New Zealand competitions.

The public defence of Wither Hills – owned by Lion Nathan – was left to the company's founder and chief winemaker, Brent Marris. He argued that the samples sent to the shows were from an early batch produced to keep the market supplied, prior to the release of the main blend. Marris claimed samples of the relatively small-volume batch had been sent by mistake.

Stoking the fire was Marris's role as chairman of judges at the industry's own competition, the Air New Zealand Wine Awards. After a media furore, during which the wine was stripped of another top award, Marris resigned his judging post and Wither Hills surrendered its remaining silver and gold medals.

Mission Hawke's Bay ★→★★★ NZ's oldest wine producer, established 1851, still run by Catholic Society of Mary. Solid varietals: sweetish, perfumed Ries is especially good value. Reserve range includes good Bordeaux-style reds and Chard. Top label: Jewelstone.

Montana Auckland ★→★★★ Formerly name of NZ wine giant, now a key brand of PERNOD RICARD NEW ZEALAND. Top wines labelled Estate; Reserve is second tier. Big-selling varietals include smooth, peachy, lightly oaked GISBORNE Chard and crisp, grassy MARLBOROUGH Sauv Bl.

Morton Estate Bay of Plenty ★★ Respected mid-size producer with vineyards in HAWKE'S BAY and MARLBOROUGH. Refined Black Label Chard is one of NZ's best (**02'**). White Label Chard also very good and top value.

Mount Riley Marlborough ★→★★ Fast-growing company. Easy-drinking Chard; punchy Sauv Bl; dark, flavoursome Merlot/Malbec. Top wines labelled Seventeen Valley. All good value.

Mt Difficulty Central Otago ★★ Quality producer in relatively hot Bannockburn area. Best known for vibrant, flinty Ries and very refined, intense Pinot N.

Mud House Marlborough ★→★★ Punchy, vibrant Sauv Bl and solid Pinot Gr, Ries, Merlot, and Pinot N. Purchased in 2006 by WAIPARA HILLS.

Muddy Water Waipara ★★ Small, high-quality producer with beautifully intense Ries, minerally Chard, and savoury, subtle Pinot N.

Nautilus Marlborough ★★ Small range of distributors Négociants (NZ), owned by S SMITH & SON of Australia. Top wines include stylish, finely balanced Sauv Bl, savoury Pinot N, and fragrant sparkler. Lower-tier: Twin Islands.

Nelson (r) **03** 06 (w) **06** Small, fast-growing region west of MARLBOROUGH; climate wetter. Clay soils of Upper Moutere hills and silty Waimea Plains. Strengths in whites, especially Ries, Sauv Bl, Chard. Pinot N is best red.

Neudorf Nelson ★★★ A top, smallish winery. Strapping, creamy-rich Chard (**03 04** 05), superb Pinot N, Sauv Bl, Ries.

Nga Waka Martinborough ★★ Dry, steely whites of high quality. Outstanding Sauv Bl; piercingly flavoured Ries; robust, savoury Chard. Pinot N scented and supple.

Ngatarawa Hawke's Bay ★★→★★★ Mid-sized. Top Alwyn Reserve range, including powerful Chard, Cab Sauv, Merlot. Mid-range Glazebrook also excellent.

Nobilo Auckland ★→★★★ NZ's second-largest wine company, now owned by Hardy's (see Australia). MARLBOROUGH Sauv Bl is good but sharply priced. Superior varietals labelled Icon. Very good Drylands Sauv Bl. Cheaper wines labelled Fernleaf and Fall Harvest. See also SELAKS.

Okahu Estate Northland ★→★★ One of NZ's northernmost wineries, at Kaitaia. Hot, humid climate. Warm, ripe reds; complex, creamy Chard.

Omaka Springs Marlborough ★→★★ Punchy, herbaceous Sauv Bl, solid Ries, Chard, and leafy reds.

Oyster Bay See DELEGAT'S.

Palliser Estate Martinborough ★★→★★★ One of the area's largest and best wineries. Superb tropical-fruit-flavoured Sauv Bl, excellent Chard, Ries, Pinot N. Top wines: Palliser Estate. Lower tier: Pencarrow.

Pask, C J Hawke's Bay ★★→★★★ Mid-size winery, extensive vineyards. Good to excellent Chard. Cab Sauv and Merlot-based reds fast improving. Top wines labelled Declaration.

Pegasus Bay Waipara ★★→★★★ Small but distinguished range: notably taut, cool-climate Chard; lush, complex, oaked Sauv Bl/Sem; very rich, zingy Ries. Merlot-based reds are region's finest. Pinot N lush and silky (especially Prima Donna).

Peregrine Central Otago ★★ Crisp, cool-climate Ries, Pinot Gr, Gewurz of variable quality, and beautifully rich, silky, good-value Pinot N.

Pernod Ricard New Zealand Auckland ★→★★★ NZ wine giant, formerly called Allied Domecq Wines (NZ) and, before that, MONTANA. Wineries in AUCKLAND, GISBORNE, HAWKE'S BAY, and MARLBOROUGH. Extensive co-owned vineyards for

MARLBOROUGH whites, including top-value MONTANA Sauv Bl, Ries, and Chard (Reserve range especially good). Strength in sparkling, including DEUTZ, and stylish, fine-value Lindauer. Elegant CHURCH ROAD reds and quality Chard. Other key brands: CORBANS, LONGRIDGE, STONELEIGH, Saints. New brand Triplebank offers intense, racy AWATERE VALLEY wines.

Providence Auckland ★★★ Rare, Merlot-based red from Matakana district. Perfumed, lush, and silky; very high-priced.

Quartz Reef Central Otago ★★ Quality producer with weighty, flinty Pinot Gr; substantial rich Pinot N; *yeasty, lingering, Champagne-like sparkler, Chauvet.*

Rimu Grove Nelson ★★ Small, American-owned, coastal vineyard. Concentrated, minerally Chard and Pinot Gr; rich, spicy Pinot N.

Rippon Vineyard Central Otago ★★→★★★ Stunning vineyard. Fine-scented, very fruity Pinot N and slowly evolving whites, including steely, appley Ries.

Rockburn Central Otago ★→★★ Crisp, racy Chard, Pinot Gr, Gewurz, Ries, Sauv Bl. Fragrant, supple, rich Pinot N is best.

Sacred Hill Hawke's Bay ★★→★★★ Sound Whitecliff varietals; good, oaked Sauv Bl (Sauvage). Good Basket Press Merlot and barrel-fermented Chard. Highly distinguished Riflemans Chard and Brokenstone Merlot. Punchy, off-dry MARLBOROUGH Sauv Bl.

Saint Clair Marlborough ★★→★★★ Fast-growing, export-led producer with substantial vineyards. Prolific award winner. Punchy Sauv Bl, fragrant Ries, easy Chard, and plummy, early-drinking Merlot. Rich Reserve, Chard, Merlot, Pinot N. Exceptional Wairau Reserve Sauv Blanc.

St Helena Canterbury ★ The region's oldest winery, founded near Christchurch in 1978. Light, supple Pinot N (Reserve is bolder). Chard variable but good in better vintages. MARLBOROUGH Sauv Bl solid.

Seifried Estate Nelson ★★ Region's biggest winery, founded by an Austrian. Known initially for well-priced Ries and Gewurz; now also producing good-value, often excellent Sauv Bl and Chard. Best wines: Winemakers Collection.

Selaks ★→★★ Mid-size family firm bought by NOBILO in 1998. Sauv Bl, Ries, and Chard are its strengths; reds are mostly plain but improving.

Seresin Marlborough ★★→★★★ Established by NZ film producer Michael Seresin. Stylish, immaculate Sauv, Chard, Pinots N and Gr, Ries, Noble Ries.

Sileni Hawke's Bay ★★ Major winery with extensive vineyards and classy Chard and Merlot. Top wines: EV (Exceptional Vintage), then Estate Selection, and Cellar Selection.

Southbank Hawke's Bay ★→★★ Fast-growing new producer. Creamy, rich HAWKE'S BAY Chard and penetrating MARLBOROUGH Sauv Bl are best.

Spy Valley Marlborough ★★ Fast-growing company with extensive vineyards. Sauv Bl, Chard, Ries, Gewurz, Pinot Gr, and Pinot N are all very good and priced right.

Staete Landt Marlborough ★★ Dutch immigrants, producing refined Chard, Sauv Bl, and Pinot Gr; and graceful, supple Pinot N.

Stonecroft Hawke's Bay ★★→★★★ Small winery. Dark, concentrated Syrah, more Rhône than Australia. Very good red blend Ruhanui, Chard, very rich Gewurz.

Stoneleigh Former CORBANS brand, now owned by PERNOD RICARD NEW ZEALAND. Impressive MARLBOROUGH whites and Pinot N, especially Rapaura Reserve.

Stonyridge Waiheke Island ★★★★ Boutique winery. Famous for exceptional Bordeaux-style red, Larose (99 00' 04' 05'). Also Rhône-style blend, Pilgrim, and super-charged Luna Negra Malbec. 2nd label: Fallen Angel.

Tasman Bay Nelson ★→★★★ Best known for rich, creamy-smooth Chard. Top, single-vineyard wines sold as Spencer Hill.

Te Awa Hawke's Bay ★★ US-owned large estate vineyard. Classy Chard and Boundary (Merlot-based blend); good larger-volume Longlands labels.

Te Kairanga Martinborough ★→★★ One of district's larger wineries. Big, flinty Chard (richer Reserve); perfumed, supple Pinot N (complex, powerful Reserve).

Te Mata Hawke's Bay ★★★→★★★★★ Prestigious winery. Fine, powerful Elston Chard; stylish very Bordeaux-like Coleraine Cab/Merlot (95' **98'** oo' o2). Syrah and Viognier among NZ's finest. Woodthorpe range for early drinking; Rymer's Change is third tier.

Te Motu Waiheke Island ★★ Top wine of Waiheke Vineyards, owned by Dunleavy and Buffalora families. Concentrated, brambly red. Dunleavy second label.

Te Whau Tiny Waiheke Island winery/restaurant. Fine Chard and The Point Bordeaux blend.

Terra Vin Marlborough ★★ Weighty, dry, tropical-fruit-flavoured Sauv Bl and rich, firmly structured, complex Pinot N, especially Hillside Sel.

Tohu ★→★★ Maori-owned venture with extensive vineyards. Punchy, racy Sauv Bl and moderately complex Pinot N, both from MARLBOROUGH; full-flavoured GISBORNE Chard.

Torlesse Waipara ★→★★ Small, good-value CANTERBURY producer of fresh, flinty Ries and firm, toasty, citrus Chard. Mid-weight Pinot N.

Trinity Hill Hawke's Bay ★★→★★★ Firm, concentrated reds since 96, and top-flight Chard. New Homage range since o2: very stylish and expensive (Chard, Syrah, Merlot-based). Very promising Tempranillo. NZ's best Viognier.

Unison Hawke's Bay ★★→★★★ Red specialist with dark, spicy, flavour-crammed blends of Merlot, Cab Sauv, Syrah. Selection label is oak-aged the longest.

Vavasour Marlborough ★★ Based in AWATERE VALLEY. Immaculate, intense Chard and Sauv Bl; promising Pinot N and Pinot Gr. Dashwood is the second label.

Vidal Hawke's Bay ★★→★★★ Part of VILLA MARIA. Reserves (Chard, Cab Sauv/Merlot, Syrah) uniformly high standard.

Villa Maria Auckland ★★→★★★ One of NZ's three largest wine companies, includes VIDAL and ESK VALLEY. Top ranges: Reserve (Pinot N is powerful, lush) and Single Vineyard; Cellar Selection: middle-tier (less oak) is often excellent; third-tier Private Bin wines can be very good and top value (especially Ries, Sauv Bl, Gewurz). Brilliant track record in competitions.

Waimea Nelson ★→★★ Fresh, grassy Sauv Bl; rich, gently sweet Classic Ries; and bold, lush Bolitho Reserve Chard. Reds variable; Pinot N best.

Waipara Hills Canterbury ★★ Publicly owned, sizeable producer of MARLBOROUGH and CANTERBURY wines, especially nettly, zingy MARLBOROUGH Sauv Bl. Top-flight Waipara Ries and Pinot Gr in 2006.

Waipara Springs Canterbury ★★ Small producer with lively, cool-climate Ries, Sauv Bl, and Chard; concentrated Reserve Pinot N.

Waipara West Canterbury ★★ Finely scented, lively Ries; freshly acidic, herbaceous Sauv Bl; firm, citrus Chard; increasingly ripe, substantial Pinot N.

Wairarapa NZ's sixth-largest wine region. Includes East Taratahi and Gladstone. See also MARTINBOROUGH.

Wairau River Marlborough ★★ Intense Sauv Bl. Home Block is top label.

Wairau Valley MARLBOROUGH's largest district, with most of the region's vineyards and the vast majority of its wineries.

Wellington Capital city and name of region; includes WAIRARAPA, Te Horo, MARTINBOROUGH.

West Brook Auckland ★★ Underrated, richly flavoured Chard, Sauv Bl, Ries.

Whitehaven Marlborough ★★ Excellent wines: racy Ries; scented, very pure and harmonious Sauv Bl; flavourful, easy Chard. Gallo is part-owner.

Wither Hills Marlborough ★★→★★★ Rich, toasty Chard; big-selling fragrant, fleshy Sauv Bl; serious, concentrated, spicy Pinot N. See box, p.254.

South Africa

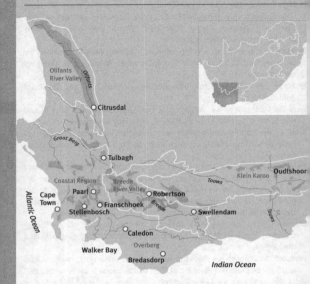

Like much of the wine-producing world, South Africa is overflowing with wine. Good wine it cannot sell profitably. Yet each vintage seems to get bigger and better and investment continues to pour in. Winery startups run at more than 50 a year and there's now a choice of more than 6,000 labels. Competition, quality, and choice at the top end have improved dramatically as a consequence – although alcohol levels have shot up too (it seems de rigueur for competition winners to be heady 15-degree, knock-me-over wines).

But for the first time in 13 years, exports have dipped ominously, by double digits in key markets, after soaring from 22 to 282 million litres a year in that time. That's a reflection of global oversupply. But domestic per capita consumption (at only about seven litres a year) is also in decline, in a hot, largely beer-drinking country.

Present surpluses and vanishing margins notwithstanding, the government is injecting more than a frisson of excitement – perhaps opportunity – into what has been a virtually all-white business: affirmative action legislation, with a barrage of carrot-and-stick prodding, is demanding that growers begin sharing equity with black partners. The new wine-drinking classes to revive Cape wine?

Recent vintages

2007 An almost perfect run-up to harvest: cool, wet winter; dry, largely disease-free summer. A general heatwave – soaring above 40ºC – just before picking rushed the ripening and pushed up alcohol.

2006 Dry, warm winter but a trouble-free, hot, longer summer than 2005 – by about two weeks – with average yields, slightly lower alcohols; the fourth sound vintage in a row.

2005 Early, short harvest after an exceptionally dry, hot season. Small, thick-skinned berries, concentrated reds for keeping.

2004 Drawn-out, hot year, above-average quality across most varieties. Intense reds, especially Shiraz, Pinotage.

2003 Excellent: hot, dry, generally disease-free. Concentrated, rich reds, for longer keeping.

Vineyard practices and cellar techniques are improving each vintage: a producer's reputation is usually a better guide to wine quality than the vintage. The Cape generally experiences warm to hot summers. Most Cape dry whites are best drunk within 2-3 years.

Adoro Wines St'bosch r w ★★ →★★★ Acclaimed debut for new labels from seasoned winemaker Ian Naudé (ex-Dornier) buying in selected parcels; Chenin Bl/Semillon dry white **06**', and finely scented red 04 (Merlot blended with Mourvèdre/Grenache).

Alto Estate St'bosch r ★★ Old estate (exporting since 1920s) Cab Sauv reputation for long life, slow maturation. Luscious and smoky Shiraz. Also popular Alto Rouge (blend Cab Sauv/Cab Fr/Shiraz).

Anthony de Jager Wines r ★★★ PAARL-based FAIRVIEW Estate winemaker's own label; supple, complex Shiraz/Viognier blend called Homtini Shiraz.

Anwilka St'bosch r ★★★ Joint venture: Bruno Prats and Hubert de Bouard (Château Angelus) with South Africa's Lowell Jooste (KLEIN CONSTANTIA). 40 ha. Cab Sauv/Shiraz. Launched with understated, pricy 05.

Asara St'bosch r w sw ★★ Good, improving quality across wide range, including Chard Reserve, botrytis dessert; Cape Fusion Blend including Pinotage/Merlot/Cab Sauv and rated Shiraz.

Ataraxia Mountain Vineyards Walker Bay r w ★★ →★★★ Fresh, austere style Chard and red blend Ataraxia – by Kevin Grant, ex-Hamilton Russell Vineyards.

Axe Hill r sw ★★★ Outstanding tiny specialist producer of vintage port-style at Calitzdorp. Touriga Nacional, Tinta Barocca **99 00 01 02 03** 04.

Backsberg r w sw ★★ PAARL estate. Among Cape's oldest, largest, crushing 1,000 tons of grapes a year; well-priced spread of 20+ labels in 4 ranges, including Kosher wine. Top remains Babylonstoren Cab/Merlot, Chard and Viognier.

Beaumont r w sw ★★★ Walker Bay. Traditional-looking winery now blazing a trail with finer version of old-vine Pinotage **01 02** 03 04'. Also dense, Mourvèdre **02 03** 04' and Shiraz **02 03** 04. Among Cape's best Chenin Bls, dry and dessert.

Bellingham r w ★ →★★★ Long-established, popular brand, many ranges/labels – including Maverick range (Syrah, Viognier). Popular whites (all DYA).

Beyerskloof St'bosch r ★★ →★★★ A top specialist PINOTAGE grower – Reserve **02 03** 04; deep-flavoured Cab Sauv/Merlot blend **01 03** 04. Firm, bold Cape blend (PINOTAGE/Cab Sauv/Merlot) Synergy Reserve **02 03** 04.

Bilton St'bosch r w ★★ Improving selection reds: Shiraz/Merlot/Petit Verdot blend Matt Black 04; fruit-rich Shiraz 04 and complex Merlot 04. Gaining reputation for Pinotage. Also Sauv Bl.

Boekenhoutskloof Franschhoek r w ★★★ Highly rated grower/producer, consistently ranked among top five Cape labels by local critics, specializing in unfiltered, native-yeast ferments. Three rich, ripe reds: spicy Syrah **00 01' 02' 03** 04'; intense, minerally Cab Sauv **00 01' 02 03** 04'; supple Chocolate Box belnd Syrah-Grenache-Cinsault-Viognier **02 03** 04 05. Also fine Semillon and good value second label Porcupine Ridge.

Bon Courage Robertson r w sw sp ★★ Lively array of Chard-driven sparkling wines and two outstanding desserts: botrytis Riesling and white Muscadel.

Boplaas Family Vineyards r w sw ★★ Estate in dry, hot Karoo. Earthy, deep Cape Vintage Res port-style **91 94 96 97 99 01** 03' 04, fortified Muscadels, and Cape Vintner's Reserve Tawny Port.

Boschendal r w sp ★★ Cape's biggest single estate (250,000 cases p.a.) near Franschhoek, specializing in Shiraz **02** 03; and Sauv Bl (DYA) in recently revamped labels, under Cecil John range and Reserve Collection.

Bouchard-Finlayson Walker Bay r w ★★★ Among South Africa's few good Pinot N growers with solid reputation for two top labels: Galpin Peak and Tête de Cuvée. Impressive Chard sparkling Missionvale label, also Kaaimansgat.

Buitenverwachting r w sp ★★→★★★ Historic estate in Constantia suburbs. ***Standout Sauv Bl,*** generally DYA, Chard (Hussey's Vlei 05), Bordeaux blend Christine, Cab Sauv.

Cabrière Estate Franschhoek ★★ Good NV sparkling under Pierre Jourdan label (Brut Sauvage; Belle Rosé). Fine Pinot N in some years **00 02 04**.

Camberley Wines St'bosch r w ★★→★★★ Family-run red specialist: striking Shiraz **03** 04; impressive, full Cab Sauv/Merlot blend (Philosopher's Stone) **02 03** 04; massive, dark, plummy PINOTAGE 04'.

Capaia Wines Philadelphia r w ★★→★★★ Recent French-German collaboration: supple, rich-berry Capaia Bordeaux blend **03** 04 05 winning local plaudits.

Cape Bay ★★ Among most successful, easy-priced export ranges, ready-drinking Cab Sauv and PINOTAGE-based blends, quaffable Chard, Chenin Bl, Sauv Bl. Driven by NEWTON-JOHNSON family.

Cape Chamonix Franschhoek r w sp ★★ Recently improved reds: Pinot N 04; Cab Sauv, Cab Fr, Merlot "Troika" **03** 04. Consistently good Chard Res 04 and two Méthode Cap Classique Chard-based sparkling.

Cape Point Vineyards w ★★★ Premium white wine label, from Atlantic-cooled vineyards on the slim tip of Cape Town's Peninsula. Elegant, complex flagship Sauv Bl/Semillon blend Isliedh; and outstanding, minerally Semillon **05' 06**; crisp Sauv Bl (DYA).

Cape Winemaker's Guild (CWG) Stages a benchmarking annual auction of limited, premium bottlings by 38 of the Cape's leading growers, each producing usually no more than a barrel or two under the CWG label. Portion of proceeds goes to disadvantaged winelands' communities.

Cederberg Wines Cederberg r w ★★→★★★ High altitude vineyards. Fruity, crisp whites: Sauv Bl, Reserve V Generations Chenin Bl. Cab Sauv-based blend V Generations **01 03 04'**. Exceptional Shiraz **02 03** 04.

Château Libertas Blend of mainly Cab Sauv made by STELLENBOSCH FARMERS' WINERY.

Cloof Darling r w ★★ Rising new label; best is concentrated Crucible Shiraz **03'** 04, also good PINOTAGE and Cab Sauv-based blends.

Clos Malverne St'bosch ★★→★★★ Small estate, with reputation for PINOTAGE Res **00** **02** 03, Cab Sauv/Merlot/PINOTAGE blend Auret **01** 03.

Coleraine Wines Paarl r ★★ Opulent, inky reds, winning plaudits, local medals: Culraithin Syrah **02** 04; Culraithin Merlot **03** 04.

Constantia Once the world's most famous sweet, Muscat-based wines (both red and white). See KLEIN CONSTANTIA.

Constantia Uitsig r w ★★→★★★ White specialist; picks are Semillon Reserve, Chard Res and "Constantia White" Semillon/Sauv Bl from premium CONSTANTIA v'yds.

Cordoba St'bosch r w ★★→★★★ Highly regarded winery/v'yds on Helderberg mountains. Usually late-developing, Cab Fr-based claret blend labelled Crescendo **00 01 02** 03; plus Merlot **01'** 02.

Dalla Cia Wine & Spirit Company St'bosch r w ★★→★★★ New, striking, fine Bordeaux blend Giorgio **02 03'**; also Chard and Sauv Bl. Producers of intense grappa-style digestifs.

David Frost Paarl r ★★ South African golfing legend's increasingly respected small range reds led by Res Cab Sauv and ***Bordeaux blend Par Excellence***.

De Krans Estate ★★→★★★ Old family-run Karoo semi-desert vineyards make rich, full, impressive Vintage Reserve port-style **97 99 02** 03' 04. Also Cape Tawny

"Port" and traditional fortified sweet red and Muscadels.

De Toren St'bosch r ★★→★★★ Elegant Bordeaux blend (Cab Sauv, Sauv Bl, Merlot, Petit Verdot, Malbec) Fusion V **01 02** 03' 04 and Merlot-based blend "Z" 04

De Trafford Wines St'bosch r w sw ★★★ Exceptional boutique grower. David Trafford's international reputation, and knack, for bold but elegant wines (unfiltered, wild-yeast fermented) makes them scarce. Bordeaux blend Elevation "393", Cab Sauv; Shiraz. Also tiny quantities Pinot N, Merlot and dry CHENIN BL in oak and dessert Vin de Paille (also Chenin) worth cellaring.

De Waal Wines r w ★★→★★★ From Uiterwyk, old estate southwest of STELLENBOSCH. single-vineyard PINOTAGE Top of the Hill **01 02** 04 among Cape's best, from 50-year-old vines. V. good "Cape blend" Merlot/Shiraz/PINOTAGE.

De Wetshof Robertson w sw ★★ Large-scale producer, including Chards – flagships are barrel-selected Bateleur and Finesse. Sauv Bl, Gewurz, Rhine Ries, Edeloes botrytis dessert. Dependable, unoaked Limestone Hill Chard mainly for export.

Delaire Winery St'bosch r w ★★ Mountain v'yds at Helshoogte Pass. Spectacular hilltop winery. Delaire flagship Bordeaux blend – rich, intense 03 04. Cab Sauv Botmaskop **00 02** 04. Also barrel-fermented Chard and fresh Sauv Bl DYA.

Delheim St'bosch r w dr sw ★★ Family winery. Acclaimed Vera Cruz Shiraz **01 02** 04; plummy Grand Res Bordeaux blend **99 00 01** 03 04. Also Chard and Sauv Bl. Following for botrytis Edelspatz; since 06 from single vineyard Ries.

Diemersfontein Wines Wellington r w ★★ Growing reputation for power-packed PINOTAGE **03** 04 in Carpe Diem range.

Distell STELLENBOSCH-based conglomerate, merging Distillers and STELLENBOSCH FARMERS' WINERY, dwarfing other wholesalers. Many brands, spanning quality scales: Capenheimer, Cellar Cask, CHÂTEAU LIBERTAS, FLEUR DU CAP, Kellerprinz, MONIS, NEDERBURG, Overmeer, Tassenberg, Two Oceans, ZONNEBLOEM, etc.

Dornier Wines St'bosch r w ★★→★★★ Imposing Bordeaux blend, Cab Fr/Merlot Donatus **02** 03, 04, worth cellaring. Slightly oaked, fruity/flinty white blend – CHENIN BL. Sauv Bl, Semillon **03**. Since 04, Chenin/Semillon only.

Durbanville Hills r w ★★ Fashionably maritime-cooled vineyards owned by giant DISTELL. Best is Single-vineyard Range Caapman Cab Sauv/Merlot **99 01**. Also Rhinofields Range with good Chard and Sauv Bl DYA.

Du Toitskloof Winery r w sw Rawsonville ★→★★ Specialist in various well-priced dessert Muscats. Regular winner of local good-value awards.

Edelkeur ★★★ Intensely sweet noble-rot white from CHENIN BL by NEDERBURG. Like all full-blown Cape botrytis desserts, officially designated Noble Late Harvest.

Ernie Els Wines r ★★★ South African golfing great's rich aromatic Bordeaux blend with fruit from Helderberg/STELLENBOSCH vineyards. Cape's priciest wine. Also "Engelbrecht-Els Proprietor's Blend". Partnership between Ernie Els and Jean Engelbrecht (ex-Rust-en-Vrede) sourcing widely, selectively for Cab Sauv/Shiraz blend. Good Guardian Peak range: Syrah/Mourvèdre/Grenache.

Estate Wine Official term for wines grown and made (not necessarily bottled) exclusively on registered estates. Not a quality designation.

Fairview r w dr sw ★★→★★★★ Dynamic, export-savvy proprietor Charles Back, produces never-ending innovations, but with emphasis on Rhône varieties, and open, generous, ready-to-drink wines. Top Range Red Seal, with Caldera, Solitude, Beacon Block, Jakkalsfontein, featuring Shiraz; PINOTAGE Primo. Pegleg Carignan; Oom Pagel Semillon. Regular labels include Cape's first and still v. good Viognier. Recently also Italian varieties – Barbera, Sangiovese, Primitivo – in Agostinello range. Successful with Rhône-style and Bordeaux blends (white, red, rosé) Goats do Roam, Goat-Roti, Bored Doe, The Goatfather etc – taunting, gimmicky labels that usually overdeliver. (Protests from French authorities gratefully received.)

First Cape Vineyards Worcester/Walker Bay r w ★★ Fastest-growing Cape export

> **Chenin Blanc**
> Chenin Blanc has earned a new role. Long considered a white *vin ordinaire* staple – it is South Africa's most planted variety – Chenin Blanc is now being vinified more carefully and is being used to produce wines of restrained quality and greater longevity. On wine lists, Chenin Blanc often represents better value than Chards and Sauvignon Blancs.
>
> A selection of producers: Rudera, Ken Forrester, Cederberg, Jean Daneel, Villiera, Mulderbosch, De Trafford, Beaumont

brand to UK in past two years, at one million (12-bottle) cases a year. Excellent price/quality in three, tiered ranges: First Selection (Shiraz; Shiraz/Cab Sauv; Shiraz Rosé; Chard; and Chard/Viognier). Limited Release and First Cape range features Cab Sauv, PINOTAGE, Shiraz, Merlot Chenin Bl, Semillon and Sauv Bl as varietals and blends. Joint venture of NEWTON-JOHNSON WINES, Brand Phoenix in Surrey, UK, and De Wet, Goudini, Badsberg, Stettyn and Aan de Doorns wineries based in Worcester, Cape.

Flagstone r w ★★→★★★ Expanding, modern Cape star, with 30-plus labels in six ranges: most named with cheerful idiosyncrasy by proprietor/winemaker Bruce Jack (e.g. Cellar Hand Backchat Blend, good quaffing red, melange of seven grape varieties). Grapes sourced from many individual, often far-flung vineyards. Best: Bowwood Cab/Merlot. Mary Le Bow, Cab/Shiraz/Merlot. Regular youthful standout: The Berrio Sauv Bl. Also: The Berrio Cab Sauv; Dark Horse Shiraz; Longitude Shiraz/Merlot/PINOTAGE; Writer's Block PINOTAGE; Fiona Sauv Bl Reserve.

Fleur du Cap St'bosch r w sw ★★ Giant producer DISTELL's flagship label, includes good Unfiltered Collection. Cab Sauv, Merlot; Sauv Bl Limited Release; also Chard, Semillon and Viognier Limited Release.

Gilga Wines St'bosch r ★★→★★★ Boutique label, intense, spicy Syrah. Shiraz/CabSauv blend Amurabi.

Glen Carlou r w ★★★ 1st-rate Cape winery, vineyards at PAARL, owned by Donald Hess (see California), with fine-art gallery. Standout, spicy Syrah; Gravel Quarry Cab Sauv; also fine Bordeaux blend Grand Classique and full Pinot N. Three excellent Chards, led by Quartz Stone label.

Graham Beck Wines Robertson/Franschhoek r w sp ★★→★★★ Avant-garde properties of mining, horse-racing, art-collecting tycoon Graham Beck, making classy sparkling including vintage Blanc de Blancs Chard. Also outstanding single-vineyard bottlings of The Ridge Syrah; Coffeestone Cab Sauv; "Peasants Run" Sauv Bl; and sumptuous dessert Rhona Muscadel. Good new Viognier.

Grangehurst St'bosch r ★★→★★★ Small, top red specialist, buying in grapes. Cape blend Cab Sauv/PINOTAGE/Merlot Nikela. Good PINOTAGE, and concentrated Cab Sauv/Merlot; Shiraz/Cab Sauv.

Groot Constantia r w ★→★★★ Historic government-owned estate near Cape Town. Legendary red and white Muscat desserts in early 19th C. Grand Constance revives tradition, with same red/white Muscat grape. Also good Bordeaux blend Gouverneur's Reserve; Shiraz, Chard Res, sweet Weisser (Rhine) Ries.

Groote Post Vineyards Darling r w ★★ Coastal, cool-climate benefits for Chard (oaked and unwooded) and intense Shiraz; also Sauv Bl Reserve.

Hamilton Russell Vineyards Walker Bay r w ★★★ Cape's Burgundian-style specialist estate at Hermanus. *Fine Pinot N 99 00 01' 03' 04. Classy Chard 01 02 03 04 05'*. Small yields, French-inspired vinification, careful barrelling. Also v.gd Sauv Bls and Pinotages under HRV-owned Southern Right and Ashbourne labels.

Hartenberg St'bosch r w ★★★ Cape front-ranker. The McKenzie Bordeaux blend 03'. Always serious Shiraz **01 02 03** 04, also flagship single-v'yd The Stork Shiraz **03** 04'. Fine Merlot **02 03 04'** 05. Award-winning Chards, top is The Eleanor.

Havana Hills Durbanville r w ★★→★★★ Well-structured, fruity, intense reds in the

Du Plessis Reserve range: Du Plessis Bordeaux blend and Shiraz.

Ingwe Stellenbosch r w ★★→★★★ Alain Moueix (of the Pomerol dynasty) among early 1990s French investors; elegant, minerally Merlot-based Bordeaux blend Ingwe – **02 03**; Sauv Bl/Semillon Amehlo white. For export.

Jack & Knox Winecraft Somerset West r w ★★→★★★ Excellent dry Frostline Ries and subtle Green on Green Semillon.

J C le Roux St'bosch sp ★★ South Africa's largest sparkling-wine house. All METHODE CAP CLASSIQUE. Top is "Desiderius" in Pongràcz range: and Scintilla (both Chard/Pinot N); also Pinot N; Blanc de Blancs Chard, long (5–9 years) maturation in bottle. Well-priced NV Pongràcz.

Jean Daneel Wines Napier r w ★★★ *Outstanding Signature Series CHENIN BL 03' 04 05'*. Chard Brut METHODE CAP CLASSIQUE sparkling.

Joostenberg Wines Paarl r w ★★ Botrytis dessert from CHENIN BL **03 04 05**; also good Cab Sauv/Merlot/Shiraz blend **01 03** 04, particularly good Shiraz/Viognier **04** 05.

Jordan Vineyards St'bosch r w ★★★ A bright star. Flagship Chard Nine Yards Res **03' 04** 05. Cab Sauv blend Cobbler's Hill **00 01** 03'; Cab Sauv **00 01 03** 04; Merlot **99 00 01 02** 03; v. good Sauv Bl (DYA) and botrytis dessert Mellifera.

J P Bredell St'bosch ★★→★★★ Rich Cape Vintage Res port-style (Tinta Barocca, Touriga Nacional and Souzão). A Cape benchmark. Also Late Bottled Vintage.

Kaapzicht Estate St'bosch r w ★★★ Acclaimed family-run red wine specialist. Signature is ripe, concentrated Steytler Vision (blend PINOTAGE/Cab Sauv/Merlot); Steytler PINOTAGE. Well-crafted Kaapzicht Cab Sauv.

Kanonkop St'bosch r ★★★ Grand local status past three decades, mainly with two labels: oak-finished PINOTAGE and, with a fanatic following, Bordeaux-style blend Paul Sauer plus Cab Sauv.

Kanu Wines St'bosch r w sw ★★→★★★ Best known for barrel-aged CHENIN BL; also v. good Chard and Sauv Bl (DYA); botrytis dessert wine Kia Ora.

Ken Forrester Vineyards St'bosch r w sw ★★→★★★ Helderberg producer. Benchmark Cape CHENIN BL in "Ken Forrester" proprietorial range; also oustanding, luscious off-dry Forrester-Meinert CHENIN BL, labelled FMC, from 30-year-old+ bush vines in Icon Range, a punter's favourite. Hearty but fine Grenache/Shiraz/PINOTAGE, called 'Gypsy'. Botrytis CHENIN BL named T.

Klein Constantia Estate r w sw ★★→★★★ Led resurgence of historic Constantia area, now also in joint venture with Bordeaux's Bruno Prats (ANWILKA). From 1886, with Vin de Constance, recreated legendary 18th-C Cape icon dessert from Muscat de Frontignan. Only about 500 cases p.a. Dependably luscious, rich, penetrating (non-botrytis). Bold Sauv Bl, DYA but can hang in for years; solid Chard. Ageworthy, just-off-dry Ries.

Kleine Zalze Wines St'bosch r w ★★ Family Reserve Shiraz tops good reds including Cab Sauv and Merlot. Also barrel-fermented CHENIN BL and Chard.

Kloovenburg Wines Swartland r w ★★ Peppery Shiraz, forward Chard.

Krone Brut ★★ Two fine. light bubblies: Borealis (Chard/Pinot N) and Rosé (Pinot N, from one of Cape's oldest farms, Twee Jonegzellen at Tulbagh).

Kumala r w sp Underperforming range now under the giant Constellation umbrella. Quality has plummeted.

KWV International Paarl r w sw ★→★★★ Kooperatieve Wijnbouwers Vereniging, formerly South Africa's national wine co-op and controlling body: now partly (25.1%) black-owned. Top ranges are Laborie Estate and Cathedral Cellar: Cab Sauv. Bordeaux blend Triptych, Shiraz, and Chard. Regular KWV labels include traditional blend Roodeberg and a vast range of dry whites. Sherry and port-styles, fortified, mainly Muscat-based desserts. MÉTHODE CAP CLASSIQUE sparkling.

La Motte Franschhoel r w ★★→★★★ Multifaceted estate (art collections, music concerts, fragrant oils) run by the Ruperts, a leading Cape wine (and international business) family. Fine, distinctive "Pierneef Collection"

Shiraz/Viognier and assertively fruity Sauv Bl. Also fine La Motte range Bordeaux-style blend Millennium; consistently friendly Shiraz.

L'Avenir St'bosch r w ★★→★★★ Acquired by Michel Laroche of Chablis in 2005 – adding to properties in Chile. His passion for Cape Pinotage showing now in specially matured 04 named Gran Vin Pinotage, firm and built to last. Also among Cape's consistently top dry Chenin Bls. Solid, dependable range of other labels – a red named Cabernet-dominated "Stellenbosch Classic" 04 and full Chard botrytis dessert Vin de Meurveur, Cape Vintage port-style.

Lanzerac St'bosch r w ★★ Old vineyards (and grand hotel) expensively refurbished, replanted by banking/retailing magnate Christo Wiese. Early-drinking Merlot, forward, oaky Chard.

Le Riche Wines St'bosch r ★★★ Fine Cab Sauv-based boutique wines, hand-crafted by respected Etienne le Riche. Cab Sauv Res. From 06 also Chard.

Long Mountain Wine ★→★★ Pernod Ricard label, buying grapes from Breede River co-ops, exporting to 35 countries. Well-priced Cab Sauv, Ruby Cab, Cab Sauv/Merlot Res, Chard, CHENIN BL. Chard/Pinot N MCC sparkling recently added.

Lourensford St'bosch r w Vast vineyards/winery/tourism project – 285 ha – owned by banking tycoon Christo Wiese (LANZERAC). Best bottlings: delicately peachy Viognier 04 05, dessert from Semillon, promising Cab Sauv and Sauv Bl.

L'Ormarins Private Cellar r w sw ★★ Revamp, replantings underway at this high-profile Rupert family property near Franschhoek (see LA MOTTE). Best red is Bordeaux blend Optima. Good Cab Sauv, Merlot, Chard, Sauv Bl. Quaffers from Sangiovese and Pinot Grigio in Terra del Capo range.

Lynx Wines Franschhoek r ★★ Rich Shiraz. Also Cab Sauv and Bordeaux blend Xanache.

Meerlust Estate St'bosch r w ★★→★★★ Prestigious old estate, probably South Africa's best-known quality red label, still in the control of the Myburgh family after 250 years. New winemaker Chris Williams is stressing elegance over impact. Flagship Rubicon Bordeaux blend with Cab Sauv about 75% plus Merlot, Cab Fr; Merlot; Pinot N. Also good limey-minerally Chard. Good-value 2nd label Meerlust Red, for years when Rubicon "declassified".

Meinert Wines St'bosch r ★★→★★★ Small-scale producer/consultant Martin Meinert does two fine blends, Devon Crest (Bordeaux) and Synchronicity (Cab Sauv/Cab Fr/Merlot/PINOTAGE) 01 03. Merlot 01 03 from Devon Valley vineyards.

Méthode Cap Classique (MCC) S African term for classic-method sparkling wine.

Monis Paarl DISTELL-owned: enduring quality from oldest (1906) fortified wine producer of tawny-port-styles and Muscadels.

Moreson Franschhoek r w ★★ Powerful, prize-winning Pinotage 03 04 05; elegant Bordeaux blend Magia, and reliable, elegant Premium Chard.

Morgenhof Estate St'bosch r w sw sp ★★★ Anne Cointreau (of the French Cointreau dynasty) pioneered modern French investment in Cape wine and turned this 75-ha property into a top Cape estate. Big reputation for three reds: Merlot Res, Bordeaux blend Première Sélection and Cab Sauv Res. V.gd whites and ageworthy CHENIN BL, dry and botrytis; port-style LBV and Vintage; Brut Res MCC from Chard/Pinot N. Gd value Fantail range.

Morgenster Estate St'bosch r ★★★ Pierre Lurton of Bordeaux (Cheval Blanc) consulting. Bordeaux blend is fine; supple proprietary label. Lourens River Valley blend is similarly restrained 2nd label.

Mulderbosch Vineyards St'bosch r w ★★★ Penetrating – usually scintillating too – Sauv Bl. Two Chards: oak-fermented and fresh, less oaky. V. good barrel-fermented CHENIN BL Steen op Hout. Easy, Bordeaux-style blend, Faithful Hound.

Mvemve Raats St'bosch r ★★ New partnership between Mzokhana Mvemve, South Africa's first university-qualified black winemaker, and Bruwer Raats (Raats Family Wines). Maiden release Bordeaux blend De Compostella 04. Also promising Sagila, dry Chenin Bl by Mvemve going solo. Both boutique-scale labels to watch.

Nederburg Paarl r w p dr sw s/sw sp ★→★★★ Large winery est 1937. Headed by Romanian Razvan Macici. Sound Classic Range reds include Edelrood blend **01** 04 and Cab Sauv **01 03**. Also Chard, Sauv Bl, Ries, and sparkling. Also excellent botrytis dessert Noble Late Harvest, mostly Chenin Bl spiced with Muscat (see also EDELKEUR). Small quantities of Limited Vintage, Private Bins for auction, some outstanding. Stages Cape's annual wine event, the Nederburg Auction.

Neethlingshof St'bosch r w sw ★★ Large estate, many labels. Best in flagship Lord Neethling range Laurentius (Cab Sauv/Cab Fr, Shiraz); also gd PINOTAGE; Shiraz; Chard, and Gewurz, blush Blanc de Noirs, botrytis Weisser Riesling.

Neil Ellis Wines St'bosch r w ★★★ Sourcing single-vineyard grapes for site expression. Forthright wines. Top-flight Res Vineyard Selection Cab Sauv, Syrah,

---

WineBiodiversity Initiative (WBI)

Scores of producers are signing up to conserve threatened natural vegetation in and around wine farms through scientific biodiversity guidelines – reinforcing the government's encouragement to adopt Integrated Wine Production (IWP) techniques to grow wine in environmentally sustainable ways. There is also a small but growing list of recognized biodynamic producers.

---

oak-fermented Sauv Bl. Premium STELLENBOSCH range. Always excellent Cab Sauv, PINOTAGE, Shiraz and (unoaked) Sauv Bl, including Groenkloof and Elgin, and full, bold Chards from STELLENBOSCH and Elgin.

Newton-Johnson Wines r w ★★→★★★ Family winery, with vineyards at Walker Bay, sourcing grapes widely. Among few v. good Cape Pinot N growers. Lemony Chard, intense Sauv Bl. Delicious peppery Shiraz/Mourvèdre blend. See also FIRST CAPE VINEYARDS, CAPE BAY.

Nitida Cellars Durbanville r w ★★ Small v. good range, sea-cooled vyds; fresh, vital Sauv Bl (DYA) and Semillon. Also good Cab Sauv, Bordeaux blend Calligraphy.

Overgaauw Estate St'bosch r w ★★→★★★ Old (1783) family estate. Dependable Merlot and Bordeaux blend Tria Corda; v. good Cab Sauv. Two excellent port-styles: outstanding Cape Vintage and Reserve.

Paarl Town 30 miles northeast of Cape Town and the wine district around it.

Paul Cluver Estate r w ★★ Good Pinot N **03 04** from these cooler upland vineyards east of Cape Town. Also elegant Chard; intense botrytis dessert from Weisser (Rhine) Riesling **03 04' 05**; also off-dry Ries. Aromatic off-dry Gewurz.

Plaisir de Merle r w ★★ Grand, DISTELL-owned cellar, vineyards near PAARL. Approachable Merlot, weightier Grand Plaisir Bordeaux blend. Recently single-vineyard Cab Fr.

Raats Family St'bosch r w ★★→★★★ Deep-scented, minerally Cab Franc **01 02 03** 04 and two oaked and unoaked, CHENIN BL, both worth keeping a few years.

Raka Walker Bay r w ★★→★★★ Award-winning, powerful Shiraz **02 03 04' 05**, plus hearty, opulent, full, five-varieties Bordeaux blend with touch Pinotage named Figurehead 04, deep-flavoured, long-lasting Merlot 05 and racy Sauv Bl.

Remhoogte Estate Stellenbosch r ★★→★★★ Classically styled Bonne Nouvelle (Cab Sauv/Merlot/PINOTAGE) joint-venture between proprietor Murray Boustred and Michel Rolland; also Bordeaux blend Estate Wine and Cab Sauv.

Ridgeback Wines Paarl r w ★★→★★★ Standout Shiraz **02 03** 04, Cab Fr/Merlot **03** 04, and Viognier.

Rijk's Private Cellar Tulbagh r w ★★★ Small-scale, big-impact winery. Depth, intensity in Cab Sauv and Shiraz matched by emphatic Semillon and CHENIN BL.

Robertson District Inland from Cape. Mainly dessert (notably Muscat) and white wines. Determined effort now to increase red vineyards.

Robertson Winery Robertson r w sw ★→★★ Good value from warm-climate, co-op-scale (29,000 tons p.a.) winery. Vineyard Selection range: two good Shiraz labels, Constitution Rd and Wolfkloof; Phanto Ridge PINOTAGE; King's River Chard. Ries Wide River Noble Late Harvest can be superb.

Rudera Wines St'bosch r w ★★★ Local stardom based on owner/winemaker Teddy Hall's passion for Chenin Bl. Various labels, styles, all outstanding: fresh, dry, oak-fermented, native-yeast fermented, and dessert botrytis Noble Late Harvest. Also excellent Cab Sauv, Syrah.

Rupert & Rothschild Vignerons r w ★★★ Top vineyards, cellar at Simondium, Paarl. Joint venture between Baron Benjamin Rothschild and the Ruperts, two old French and South African wine families. Roving French guru Michel Rolland is consultant. Mellow, impressive Bordeaux blend **01** 03 named Baron Edmond since 1998. Chard Baroness Nadine is a deep-flavoured classic.

Rustenberg Wines r w ★★★ Prestigious STELLENBOSCH estate, founded 300 years ago, making wine continuously for more than 100 years. Flagship is single-vineyard unfiltered _**Peter Barlow Cab Sauv 99' 01' 03 04**_: Rustenberg Bordeaux blend John X Merriman **01** 03 04. Outstanding Chard Five Soldiers (single vineyard). Also top 2nd label Brampton.

Rust en Vrede Estate r ★★★ Estate east of STELLENBOSCH: known for strong, individual red Cab Sauv-led blend Rust en Vrede Estate Wine **00 01 03**. Solid Cab Sauv and Shiraz.

Sadie Family Wines Swartland r ★★★ Biodynamically grown, trendily/traditionally-made (wild-yeast fermented, unfined, unfiltered) Columella (Shiraz/Mourvèdre) **01 02 03** 04 now spoken of as Cape benchmark. Complex, intriguing (citrus/apricots) white blend Palladius **04'** (Viognier, CHENIN BL, Chard, Grenache Blanc). Star winemaker Eben Sadie.

Saronsberg Tulbagh r w ★★ Growing reputation for Rhône-style blend, led by Shiraz; also unblended Shiraz and Sauv Bl.

Saxenberg Wines St'bosch w dr sw sp ★★→★★★ Swiss-owned vineyards and winery jointly run with French Château Capion. Powerful reds: sparkling flagship Shiraz Select and Private Collection Shiraz. Robust Pinotage, Cab Sauv. Also Merlot, Chard, Sauv Bl, and sweet Gewurz.

Seidelberg Estate Paarl r w ★★ "Roland's" Reserve Merlot **01** 03, Syrah 04, Bordeaux blend Un Deux Trois 00 03, Chard, promising Viognier, and CHENIN BL.

Ses'Fikile St'bosch r w ★★★ Front-ranker among first of Cape's new black-controlled wine ventures; all-woman business in partnership with Flagstone. Good Sauv Bl, Chard, and Shiraz Res.

Signal Hill Cape Town r w sw ★★ French flair in lively range, widely sourced grapes, for new city-centre Cape Town winery, Jean-Vincent Ridon assisted by winemaker Khulekani Buthelezi. Malbec, Petit Verdot, Furmint (Tokaji lookalike Mathilde Aszu), Muscat and PINOTAGE all feature; several ageworthy desserts, including botrytis.

Simonsig Estate St'bosch r w sp sw ★★→★★★ Malan family winery run by three brothers. Extensive but serious top-end range including red Bordeaux blend Tiara, much-decorated Merindol Syrah, Frans Malan Reserve Pinotage-dominated blend, Red Hill Pinotage, v. good Chard, and dessert-style Gewurz. First (30 years ago); new Auction Reserve Viognier from 04. Also Cape MÉTHODE CAP CLASSIQUE, Kaapse Vonkel brut from Pinot N/Chard.

Simonsvlei International r w p sw sp ★ Leading co-op cellar, just outside PAARL. Many tiers of quality, from Hercules Paragon (Merlot) to Mount Marble.

Solms-Delta Franschhoek r w ★★→★★★ Rising reputation for spicy, Rhône-style red Shiraz/Mourvèdre/Grenache etc, named Hiervandaan; intrguing rosé and Viognier/Grenache Blanc dry white.

Spice Route Wine Company Malmesbury r w ★★★ Front-running Cape specialist in Rhône style; top label is Malabar (Syrah/PINOTAGE/Mourvèdre/Grenache/Viognier). Also rich "Flagship Syrah", Merlot, PINOTAGE; full, barrel-fermented CHENIN BL and Viognier.

Spier Cellars St'bosch r w ★★ Well-made ranges, best in Private Collection Cab Sauv, Merlot, plus PINOTAGE/Shiraz, CHENIN BL/Viognier and dessert botrytis Ries/CHENIN BL. Recently award-winning CHENIN BL. Pan-African restaurant Moyo, golf course, wildlife and conference centre, hotel.

Springfield Estate Robertson ★★→★★★ Individual wines from whole-berry and native yeast fermentation. Three v. good, softer-style Cab Sauvs, unfiltered, unfined: "Whole Berry", "Méthode Ancienne" (native yeast) and "The Work of Time" (Bordeaux blend). Also two crisp, minerally Sauv Bls – best is "Special Cuvée" **06**, and rich, wild yeast Chard "Méthode Ancienne".

Stark-Condé St'bosch r ★★→★★★ Ripe, full, single-v'yd Cab Sauv and serious, peppery Syrah.

Steenberg Vineyards Constantia r w ★★★ Showcase Cape winery/vineyards under winemaker John Loubser. Serious, elegant Merlot and savoury, leanish red flagship blend (Merlot, Cab Sauv, Cab Fr, Shiraz; even Nebbiolo in latest) Catharina. Best-known for its superb arresting Sauv Bls: flinty single-v'yd Res and fruitier Regular. Two single-v'yd Semillons, oaked and unoaked. Gd sparkling Steenberg Brut 1682 NV. One of Cape's few Nebbiolos (minerally, taut).

Stellenbosch St'bosch. Oak-shaded university town, second oldest in South Africa, and demarcated wine district 30 miles east of Cape Town. Heart of the wine industry – the Napa of the Cape. Many top estates, especially for reds, tucked into mountain valleys and foothills; extensive wine routes, many restaurants.

Stellenbosch Farmers' Winery (SFW) Part of South Africa's biggest wine conglomerate Distell: equivalent of 14 million cases per year. Ranges include NEDERBURG; ZONNEBLOEM. Wide selection of mid- and low-price wines.

Stellenzicht St'bosch ★★ Modern winery, mountainside vineyards. V. good Syrah, consistent Bordeaux blend Stellenzicht, Semillon Res.

Thandi r w →★★ Among early black wine joint ventures: good Cab/Merlot, improving Pinot N, Chard, and Sauv Bl/Semillon blends. Currently under aegis of The Company of Wine People.

The Company of Wine People (formerly Omnia Wines) ★→★★★ A 2.5-million-case-a-year STELLENBOSCH operation with more than 40 labels in eight brands/ranges. Best is Kumkani range, with good Shiraz and Shiraz/Cab Sauv, good-value Pinotage, Sauv Bl Lanner Hill and dry white blend VVS (Viognier/Verdelho/Sauv Bl); Credo range; Arniston Bay range (mainly entry-level export); Inglewood range; etc.

The Foundry St'bosch r ★★★ Meerlust winemaker Chris Williams' small-scale production, buying in site-specific parcels for outstanding Syrah and Viognier.

The Observatory Paarl r ★★→★★★ Expanding Rhône-style specialist with organic/biodynamic methods. Perfumed Syrah; juicy, Carignan/Syrah, and elegant PINOTAGE/Syrah. Chenin Bl-Chard from 05.

The Winery of Good Hope (formerly Radford-Dale, The Winery) r w ★★→★★★ Australian-French winemaking team for this premium export label. Unfiltered Shiraz, Merlot-and Gravity (Merlot/Cab/Shiraz) and Shiraz-Viognier, Viognier. Also Chard. Very promising Pinot N and first-rate Chenin Bl in other ranges: Vinum, Black Rock, New World.

Thelema Mountain Vineyards St'bosch r w ★★★→★★★★ After three decades, winemaker Gyles Webb and Thelema's star is undimmed; one of v. few iconic Cape names. *Cab Sauv* **99 00 01 03 04**, "The Mint" Cab Sauv from 04 showing off Thelema's trademark ripe-sweet minty intensity; rich Merlot Res, two elegant Shiraz (Thelema V'yd), and Arumdale (Elgin v'yd); excellent Chard, and Sauv Bl and Sutherland Sauv Bl from Elgin V'yd. Individual, spicy, rich Ed's Reserve Chard.

Tokara St'bosch r w ★★★ Showcase winery, v'yds under direction of Gyles Webb (THELEMA). Outstanding, lightly oaked Tokara White (Sauv Bl) and fresh unoaked Sauv Bl; elegant Cab Sauv/Merlot/Petit Verdot/Cab Fr blend, and Chard. Second label Zondernaam Sauv Bl (DYA). Also gd Cab Sauv, Shiraz and PINOTAGE.

Uva Mira St'bosch r w ★★ Recently outstanding – limey/peachy – Chard from high Helderber vineyards; and Cab Sauv and Cab fr/Merlot/Shiraz.

Veenwouden r ★★ •★★★ PAARL property. Reputation for Merlot and Bordeaux blend Veenwouden Classic.

Vergelegen St'bosch r w ★★★ •★★★★ Heads Cape wine's leader board. Inspired, irreverent, unconventional winemaker André van Rensburg given his head by owners, mining giant Anglo-American Corp. Luxury-priced flagship is Vergelegen V (Cab Sauv/Merlot) – forsakes restraint for power and impact; but stablemate Bordeaux blend Vergelegen offers sumptuous, lower-key alternative. Ditto Cab Sauv, Merlot, exceptional Shiraz. Estate White is taut but ample, minerally barrel-fermented Semillon-led blend. Superb, lemony Chard, and standout, racy Schaapenberg Sauv Bl and Sauv Bl; botrytis Ries dessert.

Vilafonté Paarl r ★★★ First US-South African joint venture. California's Zelma Long (ex-Simi) and Phil Freese (ex-Mondavi viticulturalist) teaming up with WARWICK ESTATE's Mike Ratcliffe. Two very focused Bordeaux blends: mainly Cab Sauv C Series and mainly Merlot M Series, both fine, supple – C more firmly structured for longer keeping. Top international notices for maiden 03 04 releases.

Villiera Wines St'bosch r w sp ★★ •★★★ Big family-run v'yds and winery with excellent quality/value range. Five MÉTHODE CAP CLASSIQUE bubblies include: Brut Natural, virtually organic Blanc de Blancs and Monro Brut Première Cuvée Sound red Bordeaux blend Monro. Consistently good single-v'yd Bush Vine Sauv Bl (DYA); and Merlot, Chenin Bl in serious "Cellar Door" range; also two excellent dessert botrytis from Ries and CHENIN BL port-style Fired Earth.

Vins D'Orrance Constantia r w ★★ •★★★ Excellent small-scale producer of Syrah Cuvée Ameena 03 04 05, and complex Chard Cuvée Anais.

Vredendal Cooperative r w dr sw ★ South Africa's largest co-op winery in warm Olifants River region. Improving reds, including Shiraz Mt Maskam. Huge range mostly white. Big exporter of various supermarket labels.

Vriesenhof Vineyards St'bosch r w ★★★ Run by Cape wine (and rugby) legend, Jan Boland Coetzee. Highly rated, includes Talana Hill (Bordeaux blend Royale and Chard) and Paradyskloof labels. Bordeaux blend Kallista is flagship. Pinot N o1 04' 05; PINOTAGE-based blend Enthopio 01 02' 03 04.

Warwick Estate St'bosch r w ★★ •★★★ *Consistently good Bordeaux blend Trilogy* Estate Reserve and Cape blend Three Ladies Cab Sauv/Merlot/PINOTAGE. Fine Cab Fr. Old Bush Vines PINOTAGE has following. V. good Chard, Sauv Bl Prof Black.

Waterford St'bosch r w ★★★ Outstanding v'yds, with top rank status under veteran Kevin Arnold. Eponymous Shiraz is Cape classic, partnered with Mourvedre minerally Cab Sauv. Lately among finest Cape Chards. V. good Sauv Bl (DYA) and dessert Chard, Semillon, Muscat.

Welgemeend Estate Paarl r ★★ •★★★ Boutique estate: Bordeaux-style blend (the Cape's first) Estate Reserve. Malbec-based blend Douelle.

Weltevrede Robertson r w sw ★★ Old estate, reviving reputation with three well crafted, individual Chards, emphasizing single-vineyard limestone terroirs and native-yeast fermentation.

Wine of Origin The Cape's "AC", but without French crop-yield etc. restrictions. Certifies vintage, variety, region of origin.

Zonnebloem r w sw ★★ STELLENBOSCH FARMERS' WINERY's top range, widely sourced Generally good value: Bordeaux blend Laureat plus dependable if unremarkable PINOTAGE, Shiraz, Cab Sauv. Easy drinking, well-priced Chard, Sauv Bl and Blanc de Blanc (CHENIN BL/Sauv Bl).

Grape varieties

In the past two decades a radical change has come about in all except the most long-established wine countries: the names of a handful of grape varieties have become the ready reference to wine. In senior wine countries, above all France and Italy (between them producing nearly half the world's wine), more complex traditions prevail. All wine of old prestige is known by its origin, more or less narrowly defined, not just the particular fruit-juice that fermented.

For the present the two notions are in rivalry. Eventually the primacy of place over fruit will become obvious, at least for wines of quality. But for now, for most people, grape tastes are the easy reference-point – despite the fact that they are often confused by the added taste of oak. If grape flavours were really all that mattered this would be a very short book.

But of course they do matter, and a knowledge of them both guides you to flavours you enjoy and helps comparisons between regions. Hence the originally Californian term "varietal wine" – meaning, in principle, from one grape variety.

At least seven varieties – Cabernet Sauvignon, Pinot Noir, Riesling, Sauvignon Blanc, Chardonnay, Gewurztraminer, and Muscat – have tastes and smells distinct and memorable enough to form international categories of wine. To these you can add Merlot, Malbec, Syrah, Sémillon, Chenin Blanc, Pinots Blanc and Gris, Sylvaner, Viognier, Nebbiolo, Sangiovese, Tempranillo... The following are the best and/or most popular wine grapes.

Grapes for red wine

Agiorgitiko (St George) Versatile Greek (Nemea) variety with juicy damson fruit and velvety tannins. Sufficient structure for serious ageing.

Baga Bairrada (Portugal) grape. Dark and tannic. Has great potential, but hard to grow.

Barbera Widely grown in Italy, at its best in Piedmont, giving dark, fruity, often sharp wine. Fashionable in California and Australia; promising in Argentina.

Blaufränkisch Mostly Austrian; can be light and juicy but at best (in Burgenland) a considerable red. LEMBERGER in Germany, KEKFRANKOS in Hungary.

Brunello Alias for SANGIOVESE, splendid at Montalcino.

Cabernet Franc, alias Bouchet (Cab Fr) The lesser of two sorts of Cabernet grown in Bordeaux but dominant (as "Bouchet") in St-Emilion. The Cabernet of the Loire, making Chinon, Saumur, Champigny, and rosé. Used for blending with CABERNET SAUVIGNON, etc., or increasingly, alone, in California, Australia.

Cabernet Sauvignon (Cab Sauv) Grape of great character: spicy, herby, tannic, with characteristic blackcurrant aroma. The first grape of the Médoc; also makes most of the best California, South American, East European reds. Vies with Shiraz in Australia. Its wine almost always needs ageing; usually benefits from blending with e.g. MERLOT, CABERNET FRANC, SYRAH, TEMPRANILLO, SANGIOVESE etc.. Makes aromatic rosé.

Cannonau GRENACHE in its Sardinian manifestation: can be very fine, potent.

Carignan In decline in France. Needs low yields, old vines; best in Corbières. Otherwise dull but harmless. Common in North Africa, Spain, and California.

Carmènere An old Bordeaux variety now extremely rare in France. Widely used in Chile where until recently it was often mistaken for MERLOT.

Cinsault/Cinsaut Usually bulk-producing grape of Southern France; in South Africa crossed with PINOT NOIR to make PINOTAGE. Pale wine, but quality potential.

Dolcetto Source of soft seductive dry red in Piedmont. Now high fashion.

Gamay The Beaujolais grape: light, very fragrant wines, at their best young. Makes even lighter wine in the Loire Valley, in central France, and in Switzerland and Savoie. Known as "Napa Gamay" in California.

Grenache, alias Garnacha, Cannonau Useful grape for strong and fruity but pale wine: good rosé and *vin doux naturel* – especially in the South of France, Spain, and California – but also the mainstay of beefy Priorato. Old-vine versions are prized in South Australia. Usually blended with other varieties (*e.g.* in Châteauneuf-du-Pape).

Grignolino Makes one of the good everyday table wines of Piedmont.

Kadarka, alias Gamza Makes healthy, sound, agreeable reds in East Europe.

Kékfrankos Hungarian BLAUFRÄNKISCH; similar lightish reds.

Lambrusco Productive grape of the lower Po Valley, giving quintessentially Italian, cheerful, sweet, and fizzy red.

Lemberger See BLAUFRÄNKISCH. Württemberg's red.

Malbec, alias Côt Minor in Bordeaux, major in Cahors (alias Auxerrois) and especially in Argentina. Dark, dense, tannic wine capable of real quality.

Merlot Adaptable grape making the great fragrant and plummy wines of Pomerol and (with CABERNET FRANC) St-Emilion, an important element in Médoc reds, soft and strong (and à la mode) in California, Washington, Chile, Australia. Lighter but often good in North Italy, Italian Switzerland, Slovenia, Argentina, South Africa, New Zealand etc.. Grassy when not fully ripe.

Montepulciano A good central-eastern Italian grape, and a Tuscan town.

Morellino Alias for SANGIOVESE in Scansano, southern Tuscany.

Mourvèdre, alias Mataro Excellent dark aromatic tannic grape used mainly for blending in Provence (but solo in Bandol) and the Midi. Enjoying new interest in, for example, South Australia and California.

Nebbiolo, alias Spanna and Chiavennasca One of Italy's best red grapes; makes Barolo, Barbaresco, Gattinara, and Valtellina. Intense, nobly fruity, perfumed wine but very tannic: improves for years.

Periquita Ubiquitous in Portugal for firm-flavoured reds. Often blended with CABERNET SAUVIGNON and also known as Castelão.

Petit Verdot Excellent but awkward Médoc grape, now increasingly planted in Cabernet areas worldwide for extra fragrance.

Pinot Noir (Pinot N) The glory of Burgundy's Côte d'Or, with scent, flavour, and texture that are unmatched anywhere. Makes light wines rarely of much distinction in Switzerland and Hungary. Improving in Germany and Austria. But now also splendid results in California's Sonoma, Carneros, and Central Coast, as well as Oregon, Ontario, Yarra Valley, Adelaide Hills, Tasmania, and New Zealand's South Island.

Pinotage Singular South African grape (PINOT NOIR X CINSAUT). Can be very fruity and can age interestingly, but often jammy. Good rosé.

Primitivo Southern Italian grape making big, rustic wines, now fashionable because genetically identical to ZINFANDEL.

Refosco In northeast Italy possibly a synonym for Mondeuse of Savoie. Deep, flavoursome and age-worthy wines, especially in warmer climates.

Sagrantino Italian grape found in Umbria for powerful cherry-flavoured wines.

Sangiovese (or Sangioveto) Main red grape of Chianti and much of central Italy. Aliases include BRUNELLO and MORELLINO. Interesting in Australia.

Saperavi Makes good, sharp, very long-lived wine in Georgia, Ukraine etc. Blends very well with CAB SAUV (*e.g.* in Moldova).

Spätburgunder German for PINOT N. Quality is variable, seldom wildly exciting.

St-Laurent Dark, smooth and full-flavoured Austrian speciality. Also in the Pfalz.

Syrah, alias Shiraz The great Rhône red grape: tannic, purple, peppery wine which matures superbly. Very important as Shiraz in Australia, and under either name in California, Washington State, South Africa, Chile, and elsewhere.

Tannat Raspberry-perfumed, highly tannic force behind Madiran, Tursan, and other firm reds from Southwest France. Also rosé. Now the star of Uruguay.

Tempranillo Aromatic fine Rioja grape, called Ull de Llebre in Catalonia, Cencibel in La Mancha, Tinto Fino in Ribera del Duero, Tinta Roriz in Douro, Aragonez in southern Portugal. Now Australia, too. Very fashionable; elegant in cool climates, beefy in warm. Early ripening.

Touriga Nacional Top port grape grown in the Douro Valley. Also makes full-bodied reds in south Portugal.

Zinfandel (Zin) Fruity adaptable grape of California (though identical to PRIMITIVO) with blackberry-like, and sometimes metallic, flavour. Can be structured and gloriously lush, but also makes "blush" white wine.

Grapes for white wine

Albariño The Spanish name for North Portugal's Alvarinho, making excellent fresh and fragrant wine in Galicia. Both fashionable and expensive in Spain.

Aligoté Burgundy's second-rank white grape. Crisp (often sharp) wine, needs drinking in 1–3 years. Perfect for mixing with cassis (blackcurrant liqueur) to make "Kir". Widely planted in East Europe, especially Russia.

Arinto White central Portuguese grape for crisp, fragrant dry whites.

Arneis Aromatic, high-priced grape, DOC in Roero, Piedmont.

Blanc Fumé Occasional (New World) alias of SAUVIGNON BLANC, referring to its smoky smell, particularly from the Loire (Sancerre and Pouilly). In California used for oak-aged Sauvignon and reversed to "Fumé Blanc". (The smoke is oak.)

Bourboulenc This and the rare Rolle make some of the Midi's best wines.

Bual Makes top-quality sweet madeira wines, not quite so rich as malmsey.

Chardonnay (Chard) The white grape of Burgundy, Champagne, and the New World, partly because it is one of the easiest to grow and vinify. All regions are trying it, mostly aged (or, better, fermented) in oak to reproduce the flavours of burgundy. Australia and California make classics (but also much dross). Italy, Spain, New Zealand, South Africa, New York State, Argentina, Chile, Hungary and the Midi are all coming on strong. Called Morillon in Austria.

Chasselas Prolific early-ripening grape with little aroma, mainly grown for eating. AKA Fendant in Switzerland (where it is supreme), Gutedel in Germany.

Chenin Blanc (Chenin Bl) Great white grape of the middle Loire (Vouvray, Layon, etc). Wine can be dry or sweet (or very sweet), but with plenty of acidity. Bulk wine in California, but increasingly serious in South Africa. See also STEEN.

Clairette A low-acid grape, part of many southern French blends.

Colombard Slightly fruity, nicely sharp grape, makes everyday wine in South Africa, California, and Southwest France.

Fendant See CHASSELAS.

Fiano High quality grape giving peachy, spicy wine in Campania.

Folle Blanche High acid/little flavour make this ideal for brandy. Called Gros Plant in Brittany, Picpoul in Armagnac. Also respectable in California.

Friulano See Tocai Friulano.

Furmint A grape of great character: the trademark of Hungary both as the principal grape in Tokáj and as vivid, vigorous table wine with an appley flavour. Called Sipon in Slovenia. Some grown in Austria.

Garganega The best grape in the Soave blend. Top wines, especially sweet ones, age well.

Gewürztraminer, alias Traminer (Gewurz) One of the most pungent grapes, distinctively spicy with aromas like rose petals and grapefruit. Wines are often rich and soft, even when fully dry. Best in Alsace; but also good in Germany (Gewürztraminer), East Europe, Australia, California, Pacific Northwest, and New Zealand.

Grauburgunder See PINOT GRIS.

Grechetto or Greco Ancient grape of central and south Italy noted for the vitality and stylishness of its wine.

Grüner Veltliner Austria's favourite. Around Vienna and in the Wachau and Weinviertel (also in Moravia) it can be delicious: light but structured, dry, peppery and lively. Excellent young, but the best age five years or so.

Hárslevelü Other main grape of Tokáj (with FURMINT). Adds softness and body.

Kéknyelü Low-yielding, flavourful grape giving one of Hungary's best whites. Has the potential for fieriness and spice. To be watched.

Kerner The most successful of recent German varieties, mostly RIESLING X SILVANER, but in this case Riesling x (red) Trollinger. Early-ripening, flowery (but often too blatant) wine with good acidity. Popular in Pfalz, Rheinhessen, etc.

Laski Rizling Grown in northern Italy and Eastern Europe. Much inferior to Rhine RIESLING, with lower acidity, best in sweet wines. Alias Welschriesling, Riesling Italico, Olaszrizling (no longer legally labelled simply "Riesling").

Loureiro The best and most fragrant Vinho Verde variety in Portugal.

Macabeo The workhorse white grape of north Spain, widespread in Rioja (alias Viura) and in Catalan cava country. Good quality potential.

Malvasia A family of grapes rather than a single variety, found all over Italy and Iberia. May be red, white, or pink. Usually plump, soft wine. Malvoisie in France is unrelated.

Marsanne Principal white grape (with ROUSSANNE) of the northern Rhône (*e.g.* in Hermitage, St-Joseph, St-Péray). Also good in Australia, California, and (as Ermitage Blanc) the Valais. Soft full wines that age very well.

Moschofilero Good, aromatic pink Greek grape. Makes white or rosé wine.

Müller-Thurgau (Müller-T) Dominant in Germany's Rheinhessen and Pfalz and too common on the Mosel. It was thought to be a cross between RIESLING and Chasselas de Courtellier, but recent studies suggests otherwise. Soft aromatic wines for drinking young. Makes good sweet wines but usually dull, often coarse, dry ones. Should have no place in top vineyards.

Muscadelle Adds aroma to white Bordeaux, especially Sauternes. In Victoria as Tokay it is used (with MUSCAT, to which it is unrelated) for Rutherglen Muscat.

Muscadet, alias Melon de Bourgogne Makes light, refreshing, very dry wines with a seaside tang round Nantes in Brittany.

Muscat (Many varieties; the best is Muscat Blanc à Petits Grains.) Widely grown, easily recognized, pungent grapes, mostly made into perfumed sweet wines, often fortified (as in France's *vins doux naturels*). Superb in Australia. The third element in Tokáj Aszú. Rarely (*e.g.* Alsace) made dry.

Palomino, alias Listán Makes all the best sherry but poor table wine.

Pedro Ximénez, alias PX Makes very strong wine in Montilla and Málaga. Used in blending sweet sherries. Also grown in Argentina, the Canaries, Australia, California, and South Africa.

Petit (and Gros) Manseng The secret weapon of the French Basque country: vital for Jurançon; increasingly blended elsewhere in the Southwest.

Pinot Blanc (Pinot Bl) A cousin of PINOT NOIR, similar to but milder than CHARDONNAY: light, fresh, fruity, not aromatic, to drink young. Good for Italian spumante. Grown in Alsace, northern Italy, south Germany, and East Europe. Weissburgunder in Germany. See also MUSCADET.

Pinot Gris (Pinot Gr) Best in Alsace for full-bodied whites with a certain spicy style. In Germany can be alias Ruländer (sweet) or GRAUBURGUNDER (dry); Pinot Grigio in Italy, where it is newly popular for rosé. Also found in Hungary, Slovenia, Canada, Oregon, New Zealand...

> ### Riesling (Ries)
>
> Riesling is making its re-entrance on the world-stage through, as it were, the back door. Riesling stands level with Chardonnay as the world's best white wine grape, though in diametrically opposite style. Chardonnay gives full-bodied but aromatically discreet wines, while Riesling offers a range from steely to voluptuous, always positively perfumed, and with more ageing potential than Chardonnay. Germany makes the greatest Riesling in all styles. Yet its popularity is being revived in, of all places, South Australia, where this cool-climate grape does its best to ape Chardonnay. Holding the middle ground, with forceful but still steely wines, is Austria. While lovers of light and fragrant, often piercingly refreshing Rieslings have the Mosel as their exclusive playground. Also grown in Alsace (but nowhere else in France), Pacific Northwest, Ontario, California, New Zealand, and South Africa.

Pinot Noir (Pinot N) Superlative black grape used in Champagne and else where (*e.g.* California, Australia) for making white, sparkling, or very pale pink "vin gris".

Roussanne Rhône grape of great finesse, now popping up in California and Australia. Can age well.

Sauvignon Blanc (Sauv Bl) Makes very distinctive aromatic grassy wines, pungent in New Zealand, often mineral in Sancerre, riper in Australia; good in Rueda, Austria, north Italy, Chile's Casablanca Valley, and South Africa. Blended with SEMILLON in Bordeaux. Can be austere or buxom. May be called BLANC FUMÉ.

Savagnin The grape of *vin jaune* of Savoie: related to TRAMINER?

Scheurebe Spicy-flavoured German RIES X SILVANER (possibly), very successful in Pfalz, especially for Auslese. Can be weedy: must be very ripe to be good.

Semillon (Sem) Contributes the lusciousness to Sauternes and increasingly important for Graves and other dry white Bordeaux. Grassy if not fully ripe, but can make soft dry wine of great ageing potential. Superb in Australia: old Hunter Valley Sem, though light, can be great wine. Promising in New Zealand.

Sercial Makes the driest madeira (where myth used to identify it with RIESLING).

Seyval Blanc (Seyval Bl) French-made hybrid of French and American vines. Very hardy and attractively fruity. Popular and reasonably successful in eastern States and England but dogmatically banned by EU from "quality" wines.

Steen South African alias for CHENIN BLANC, not used for better examples.

Silvaner, alias Sylvaner Germany's former workhorse grape. Rarely fine except in Franken – where it is savoury and ages admirably – and in Rheinhessen and Pfalz, where it is enjoying a renaissance. Good in the Italian Tyrol; now declining in popularity in Alsace. Very good (and powerful) as Johannisberg in the Valais, Switzerland.

Tocai Friulano North Italian grape with a flavour best described as "subtle". Now to be called plain Friulano.

Tokay Supposedly Hungarian grape in Australia and a table grape in California. The wine Tokay (Tokáj) is FURMINT, HARSLEVELU and MUSCAT.

Torrontes Strongly aromatic, MUSCAT-like Argentine speciality, usually dry.

Trebbiano Important but mediocre grape of central Italy (Orvieto, Soave etc.). Also grown in southern France as Ugni Blanc, and Cognac as St-Emilion. Mostly thin, bland wine; needs blending (and more careful growing).

Ugni Blanc (Ugni Bl) See TREBBIANO.

Verdejo The grape of Rueda in Castile, potentially fine and long-lived.

Verdelho Madeira grape making excellent medium-sweet wine; in Australia, fresh soft dry wine of great character.

Verdicchio Potentially good dry wine in central-eastern Italy.

Vermentino Italian, sprightly with satisfying texture and ageing capacity.

Vernaccia Name given to many unrelated grapes in Italy. Vernaccia di San Gimignano is crisp, lively; Vernaccia di Oristano is sherry-like.

Viognier Ultra-fashionable Rhône grape, finest in Condrieu, less fine but still aromatic in the Midi. Good examples from California and Australia.

Viura See MACABEO.

Welschriesling See LASKI RIZLING.

Wine & food

The dilemma is most acute in restaurants. Four people have chosen different dishes. The host calculates. A bottle of white and then one of red is conventional, regardless of the food. The formula works up to a point. But it can be refined – or replaced with something more original, something to really bring out the flavours of both food and wine.

Remarkably little ink has been spilt on this byway of knowledge, but thirty years of experimentation and the ideas of many friends have gone into making this list. It is perhaps most useful for menu-planning at home. But used with the rest of the book, it may ease menu-stress in restaurants, too. At the very least, it will broaden your mind.

Before the meal – apéritifs

The conventional apéritif wines are either sparkling (epitomized by Champagne) or fortified (epitomized by sherry in Britain, port in France, vermouth in Italy, etc.). A glass of white or rosé (or in France red) table wine before eating is presently in vogue. It calls for something light and stimulating, fairly dry but not acidic, with a degree of character; Chenin Blanc or Riesling rather than Chardonnay.

Warning: Avoid peanuts; they destroy wine flavours. Olives are also too piquant for many wines; they need sherry or a Martini. Eat almonds, pistachios or walnuts, plain crisps or cheese straws instead.

Food A–Z

Abalone Dry or medium white: Sauv Bl, Côte de Beaune Blanc, Pinot Gr, or Grüner Veltliner. Chinese style: try vintage Champagne.

Aïoli A thirst-quencher is needed for its garlic heat. Rhône, sparkling dry white; Provence rosé, Verdicchio.

Anchovies A robust white – or fino sherry.

Antipasti Dry white: Italian (Arneis, Soave, Pinot Grigio, prosecco, Vermentino); light red (Dolcetto, Franciacorta, young Chianti); fino sherry.

Apples, Cox's Orange Pippins Vintage port (55 60 63 66 70 75 82).

Artichoke vinaigrette An incisive dry white: New Zealand Sauv Bl; Côtes de Gascogne or a modern Greek; young red: Bordeaux, Côtes du Rhône. **With hollandaise** Full-bodied slightly crisp dry white: Pouilly-Fuissé, Pfalz Spätlese, or a Carneros or Yarra Valley Chard.

Asparagus A difficult flavour for wine, being slightly bitter. Sauv Bl echoes the flavour, but needs to be ripe, as in Chile. Sem beats Chard, esp Australian, but Chard works well with melted butter or hollandaise. Alsace Pinot Gr, even dry Muscat is gd, or Jurançon Sec.

Aubergine purée (Melitzanosalata) Crisp New World Sauv Bl e.g. from South Africa or New Zealand; or modern Greek or Sicilian dry white. Or try Bardolino red or Chiaretto. Baked aubergine dishes can need sturdier reds: Shiraz, Zin.

Avocado with seafood Dry or slightly sharp white: Rheingau or Pfalz Kabinett, Grüner Veltliner, Wachau Ries, Sancerre, Pinot Gr; Sonoma or Australian Chard or Sauv Bl, or a dry rosé. Or Chablis Premier Cru.

Avocado with vinaigrette Manzanilla sherry.

Barbecues The local wine would be Australian. Or south Italian, Tempranillo, Zin or Argentine Malbec. Bandol for a real treat.

Beef, boiled Red: Bordeaux (Bourg or Fronsac), Roussillon, Gevrey-Chambertin, or Côte-Rôtie. Medium-ranking white burgundy is gd, *e.g.*. Auxey-Duresses. Or top-notch beer. Mustard softens tannic reds, and horseradish kills everything – but can be worth the sacrifice.
roast Ideal partner for fine red wine of any kind, esp Cab Sauv.

Beef stew Sturdy red: Pomerol or St-Emilion, Hermitage, Cornas, Barbera, Shiraz, Napa Cab Sauv, Ribera del Duero or Douro red.

Beef Stroganoff Dramatic red: Barolo, Valpolicella Amarone, Cahors, Hermitage, late-harvest Zin – even Moldovan Negru de Purkar.

Beurre blanc, fish with A top-notch Muscadet-sur-lie, a Sauv Bl/Sem blend, Chablis Premier Cru, Vouvray or a Rheingau Riesling.

Bisques Dry white with plenty of body: Pinot Gr, Chard, Gruner Veltliner. Fino or dry amontillado sherry, or montilla. West Australian Sem.

Boudin noir (blood sausage) Local Sauv Bl or Chenin Bl – esp in the Loire. Or Beaujolais Cru, esp Morgon.
blanc Loire Chenin Bl, esp when served with apples: dry Vouvray, Saumur or Savennières. Mature red Côtes de Beaune, if without apple.

Bouillabaisse Savoury dry white, Marsanne from the Midi or Rhône, Corsican or Spanish rosé, or Cassis, Verdicchio, South African Sauv Bl.

Brandade Chablis, Sancerre Rouge or New Zealand Pinot Noir.

Bread-and-butter pudding Fine 10-yr-old Barsac, Tokáj Azsú or Australian botrytized Sem.

Brill Very delicate: hence a top fish for fine old Puligny and the like.

Cajun food Works well with Fleurie, Brouilly or Sauv Bl. With gumbo: amontillado or Mexican beer.

Carpaccio, beef Seems to work well with the flavour of most wines. Top Tuscan is appropriate, but fine Chards are gd. So are vintage and pink Champagnes.

Cassoulet Red from southwest France (Gaillac, Minervois, Corbières, St-Chinian or Fitou) or Shiraz. But best of all is Beaujolais Cru or young Tempranillo.

Cauliflower cheese Crisp aromatic white: Sancerre, Ries Spätlese, Muscat, English Seyval Bl, or Schönburger.

Caviar Iced vodka. If you prefer Champagne, it should be full-bodied (*e.g.* Bollinger, Krug).

Ceviche Try Australian Ries or Verdelho; South African or New Zealand Sauv Bl.

Charcuterie Young Beaujolais-Villages, Loire reds such as Saumur, Swiss or Oregon Pinot N. Young Argentine or Italian reds. Sauv Bl can work well too.

Chicken/turkey/guinea fowl, roast Virtually any wine, including very best bottles of dry to medium white and finest old reds (esp burgundy). The meat of fowl can be adapted with sauces to match almost any fine wine (*e.g. coq au vin* with red or white burgundy). Try sparkling Shiraz with strong, sweet, or spicy stuffings and trimmings.

Chicken Kiev Alsace or Pfalz Ries, Hungarian Furmint, young Pinot N.

Cheesecake Sweet white: Vouvray or Anjou or fizz, refreshing but nothing special.

Cheese fondue Dry white: Valais Fendant or any other Swiss Chasselas, Roussette de Savoie, Grüner Veltliner, Alsace Ries, or Pinot Gr. Or a Beaujolais Cru. For Wine & cheese, see p.27.

Chilli con carne Young red: Beaujolais, Zin, or Argentine Malbec.

Chinese Food
Canton or Peking style Dry to medium-dry white – Mosel Ries Kabinett or Spätlese trocken – can be gd throughout a Chinese banquet. Light Monbazillac, too. Gewurz is often suggested but rarely works (but brilliant with ginger), yet Chasselas and Pinot Gr are attractive alternatives. Dry or off-dry sparkling cuts the oil and matches sweetness. Eschew sweet-and-sour dishes but try St-Emilion ★★, New World Pinot N, or Châteauneuf-du-Pape with duck. I often serve both white and red wines concurrently during Chinese meals. **Szechuan style** Verdicchio, Alsace Pinot Blanc or very cold beer.

Chocolate Generally only powerful flavours can compete. California Orange Muscat, Bual, Tokáj Aszú, Australian Liqueur Muscat, 10-yr-old tawny port; Asti for light, fluffy mousses. Experiment with rich, ripe reds: Syrah, Zin, even sparkling Shiraz. Médoc can match bitter black chocolate. Banyuls for a weightier partnership. Or a tot of good rum.

Chowders Big-scale white, not necessarily bone dry: Pinot Gr, Rhine Spätlese, Albariño, Australian Sem, buttery Chard. Or fino sherry.

Choucroute garni Alsace Pinot Blanc, Pinot Gris, Ries. Or beer.

Christmas pudding, mince pies Tawny port, cream sherry, or liquid Christmas pudding itself, Pedro Ximénez sherry. Asti or Banyuls.

Cold meats Generally better with full-flavoured white than red. Mosel Spätlese or Hochheimer and Côte Chalonnaise are v.gd, as is Beaujolais. Leftover cold beef with leftover Champagne is bliss.

Cod If roast, a good neutral background for fine dry whites: Chablis, Meursault, Corton-Charlemagne, cru classé Graves, Grüner Veltliner, German (medium) Kabinett or dry Spätlesen or a gd light red, *e.g.* Beaune.

Coffee desserts Sweet Muscat inc Australia liqueur or Tokáj Aszú.

Confit d'oie/de canard Young tannic red Bordeaux Cru Bourgeois, California Cab Sauv and Merlot, and Priorato all cut the richness. Choose Alsace Pinot Gr or Gewurz to match it.

Consommé Medium-dry amontillado sherry or sercial madeira.

Coq au vin Red burgundy. In an ideal world, one bottle of Chambertin in the dish, two on the table.

Crab Crab and Ries are part of the Creator's plan.
cioppino Sauv Bl; but West Coast friends insist on Zin. Also California

sparkling wine – or any other full-bodied sparkler.
cold, with salad Alsace, Austrian or Rhine Ries; dry Australian Ries or
Condrieu. Show off your favourite white.
softshell Top Chard or top-quality German Ries Spätlese.
with black bean sauce A big Barossa Shiraz/Syrah.

Creams, custards, fools, syllabubs See also Chocolate, Coffee, Ginger,
and Rum. Sauternes, Loupiac, Ste-Croix-du-Mont, or Monbazillac.

Crème brûlée Sauternes or Rhine Beerenauslese, best Madeira or Tokáj.
(With concealed fruit, a more modest sweet wine.)

Crêpes Suzette Sweet Champagne, Orange Muscat or Asti.

Crostini Morellino di Scansano, Montepulciano d'Abruzzo, Valpolicella,
or a dry Italian white such as Verdicchio or Orvieto.

Crudités Light red or rosé: Côtes du Rhône, Minervois, Chianti, Pinot N;
or fino sherry. For whites: Alsace Sylvaner or Pinot Blanc.

Dim-Sum Classically, China tea. For fun: Pinot Grigio or Ries; light red
(Bardolino or Loire). NV Champagne or gd New World fizz.

Duck or goose Rather rich white: Pfalz Spätlese or off-dry Alsace Grand
Cru. Or mature gamey red: Morey-St-Denis, Côte-Rôtie, Bordeaux, or
burgundy. With oranges or peaches, the Sauternais propose drinking
Sauternes, others Monbazillac or Ries Auslese.
Peking See Chinese food.
wild duck Big-scale red such as Hermitage, Bandol, California or
South African Cab Sauv, or Barossa Shiraz – Grange if you can find it.
with olives Top-notch Chianti or other Tuscans.

Eel, jellied NV Champagne or a nice cup of (Ceylon) tea.
smoked Strong/sharp wine: fino sherry or Bourgogne Aligoté. Schnapps.

Eggs See also Soufflés. Difficult: eggs clash with most wines and
can actually spoil gd ones. But local wine with local egg dishes is
a safe bet. So ★→★★ of whatever is going. Try Pinot Bl or not too
oaky Chard. As a last resort I can bring myself to drink Champagne
with scrambled eggs.
Quail's eggs Blanc de Blancs Champagne.
Seagull's (or gull's) eggs Mature white burgundy or vintage Champagne.
Oeufs en meurette Burgundian genius: eggs in red wine calls for wine
of the same.

Escargots Rhône reds (Gigondas, Vacqueyras), St-Véran or Aligoté. In
the Midi, v.gd Petits-Gris go with local white, rosé or red. In Alsace, Pinot
Bl or Muscat.

Fennel-based dishes Sauv Bl, or young, fresh red like Beaujolais.

Fish and chips, fritto misto (or tempura) Chablis, white Bordeaux, Sauv
Bl, Pinot Bl, Gavi, fino, montilla, Koshu, tea; or NV Champagne and Cava.

Fish baked in a salt crust Full-bodied white or rosé; Meursault, Rioja,
Albariño, Sicily, Côtes de Lubéron or Minervois.

Fish pie (with creamy sauce) Albariño, Soave Classico, Pinot Gr d'Alsace.

Fish terrine Pfalz Ries Spätlese Trocken, Grüner Veltliner, Chablis
Premier Cru, Clare Valley Ries, Sonoma Chard; or manzanilla.

Foie gras White. In Bordeaux they drink Sauternes. Others prefer a late-harvest Pinot Gr or Ries (inc New World), Vouvray, Montlouis, Jurançon Moelleux or Gewurz. Tokáj Aszú 5 puttonyos is a Lucullan choice. Old dry amontillado can be sublime. If the foie gras is served hot, mature vintage Champagne. But never Chard or Sauv Bl.

Frankfurters German Ries, Beaujolais or light Pinot N. Or Budweiser (Budvar) beer.

Fruit
fresh Sweet Coteaux du Layon or light sweet Muscat.
poached Sweet Muscatel: try Muscat de Beaumes- de-Venise, Moscato di Pantelleria or Spanish dessert Tarragona.
dried fruit (and compotes) Banyuls, Rivesaltes or Maury.
flans and tarts Sauternes, Monbazillac; sweet Vouvray or Anjou.
salads A fine sweet sherry or any Muscat-based wine.

Game birds, young, plain-roasted The best red you can afford.
older birds in casseroles Red (Gevrey-Chambertin, Pommard, Santenay or Grand Cru St-Emilion, Napa Valley Cab Sauv or Rhône).
well-hung game Vega Sicilia, great red Rhône, Lebanon's Chateau Musar.
cold game Mature vintage Champagne.

Game pie, hot Red: Oregon Pinot N.
cold Gd quality white burgundy, cru Beaujolais or Champagne.

Gazpacho A glass of fino before and after. Or Sauv Bl.

Ginger desserts Sweet Muscats, New World botrytized Ries and Sem.

Goat's cheese (warm) Sancerre, Pouilly-Fumé or New World Sauv Bl. Chilled Chinon, Saumur-Champigny or Provence rosé. Australian sparkling Shiraz or strong east Mediterranean reds: *e.g.* Greek or Turkish.

Goulash Flavoursome young red such as Hungarian Zin, Uruguayan Tannat, Morellino di Scansano or a young Australian Shiraz.

Gravadlax Akvavit or iced sake. Grand Cru Chablis; California, Washington or Margaret River Chard; Mosel Spätlese (not Trocken).

Guacamole California Chard, Sauv Blanc, dry Muscat or NV Champagne. Or Mexican beer.

Haddock Rich dry whites: Meursault, California or New Zealand Chard, Marsanne or Albariño.
smoked, mousse or brandade A wonderful dish for showing off any stylish full-bodied white, inc Grand Cru Chablis or Chard from Sonoma or New Zealand.

Haggis Fruity red, eg young claret, Châteauneuf-du-Pape or New World Cab Sauv. Or of course malt whisky.

Hake Sauv Bl or any fresh fruity white: Pacherenc, Tursan, white Navarra.

Halibut As for turbot.

Ham, raw or cured Alsace Grand Cru Pinot Gr, crisp Italian white or sweetish German white (Rhine Spätlese). Soft Pinot Noir or lightish Cab Sauv. With Spanish *pata negra* or *jamon*, try fino sherry or tawny port.

Hamburger Young red: Beaujolais or Australian Cab Sauv, Chianti or Zin.

Hare Calls for flavourful red: not-too-old burgundy or Bordeaux, Rhône (*e.g.* Gigondas), Bandol, Barbaresco, Ribero del Duero or Rioja Reserva. Australia's Grange would be an experience.

Herrings, raw or pickled Dutch gin (young, not aged) or Scandinavian akvavit, and cold beer. If wine is essential, try Muscadet 2003.
fried/grilled Need a white with some acidity to cut their richness. Rully, Chablis, Bourgogne Aligoté, Greek white or dry Sauv Bl. Or try cider.

Houmous Pungent, spicy dry white, *e.g.* Furmint or modern Greek white.

Ice-creams and sorbets Fortified wine (Australian liqueur Muscat, Banyuls, PX sherry); sweet Asti or sparkling Moscato. Amaretto liqueur with vanilla; rum with chocolate.

Indian food Medium-sweet white, very cold: Orvieto Abboccato, South African Chenin Bl, Alsace Pinot Bl, Indian sparkling, Mateus Rosé, cava and NV Champagne. Or emphasize the heat with a tannic Barolo or Barbaresco, or deep-flavoured reds such as Châteauneuf-du-Pape, Cornas, Australian Grenache or Mourvèdre, or Valpolicella Amarone.

Kedgeree Full white, still or sparkling: Mâcon-Villages, South African Chard. At breakfast: Champagne.

Kidneys Red: St-Emilion or Fronsac: Nuits-St-Georges, Cornas, Barbaresco, Rioja, Spanish or Australian Cab Sauv or top Alentejo.

Kippers A good cup of tea, preferably Ceylon (milk, no sugar). Scotch? Dry oloroso sherry is surprisingly good.

Lamb, roast One of the traditional and best partners for v.gd red Bordeaux – or its Cab Sauv equivalents from the New World, esp Napa and Coonawarra. In Spain, the partner of the finest old Rioja and Ribera del Duero Reservas. New Zealand Pinot N for spicy lamb dishes.
cutlets or chops As for roast lamb, but a little less grand.

Lamproie à la Bordelaise 5-yr-old St-Emilion or Fronsac. Or Douro reds with Portuguese lampreys.

Lemon desserts For dishes like Tarte au Citron, sweet Ries from Germany or Austria, or Tokáj Aszú; the sharper the lemon, the sweeter the wine.

Lentil dishes Sturdy reds such as southern French, or Zin or Shiraz.

Liver Choose a young red: Beaujolais-Villages, St-Joseph, Cab Sauv, Merlot, Zin or Portuguese.
Calf's Red Rioja crianza, Salice Salentino Riserva or Fleurie.

Lobster, richly sauced Vintage Champagne, fine white burgundy, cru classé Graves, California Chard or Australian Ries, Pfalz Spätlese.
salad NV Champagne, Alsace Ries, Chablis Premier Cru, Condrieu, Mosel Spätlese, Penedès Chard or Cava.

Mackerel Hard or sharp white: Sauv Bl from Touraine, Gaillac, Vinho Verde, white Rioja or English white. Guinness is gd.
smoked An oily wine-destroyer. Manzanilla sherry, proper dry Vinho Verde or Schnapps, peppered or bison-grass vodka. Or lager.

Mediterranean vegetable dishes Vigorous young red: Chianti, New Zealand Cab Sauv or Merlot; young red Bordeaux, Gigondas or Coteaux du Languedoc. Or characterful white.

Meringues Recioto di Soave, Asti or Champagne doux.

Mezze A selection of hot and cold vegetable dishes. Sparkling is a gd all-purpose choice, as is rosé from the Languedoc or Provence. Fino sherry is in its element.

Mille-feuille desserts Delicate sweet sparkling white such as Moscato d'Asti or demi-sec Champagne.

Monkfish Often roasted, which needs fuller rather than leaner wines. Try Australian/New Zealand Chard, Oregon Pinot N or Chilean Merlot.

Moussaka Red or rosé: Naoussa from Greece, Sangiovese, Corbières, Côtes de Provence, Ajaccio or New Zealand Pinot N.

Mullet, red A chameleon, adaptable to gd white or red, esp Pinot N.

Mullet, grey Verdicchio, Rully or unoaked Chard.

Mussels Muscadet-sur-lie, Chablis Premier Cru or a lightly oaked Chard.

Nuts Finest oloroso sherry, madeira, vintage or tawny port (nature's match for walnuts), Vin Santo or Setúbal Moscatel.

Orange desserts Experiment with old Sauternes, Tokáj Aszú, or California Orange Muscat.

Osso buco Low tannin, supple red, such as Dolcetto d'Alba or Pinot N. Or dry Italian whites such as Soave and Lugana.

Oxtail Match with a rather rich French red such as St-Emilion, Pomerol, Pommard, Nuits-St-Georges, Barolo, Châteauneuf-du-Pape. Or Rioja Reserva or Ribera del Duero. Or California or Coonawarra Cab Sauv.

Oysters, raw NV Champagne, Chablis Premier Cru, Muscadet, white Graves, Sauv Bl or Guinness.
cooked Puligny-Montrachet or gd New World Chard. Champagne is gd with either.

Paella Young Spanish wines: red, dry white or rosé from Penedès, Somontano, Navarra or Rioja.

Panettone Jurançon moelleux, late-harvest Ries, Barsac, Vin Santo or Tokáj Aszú.

Pasta Red or white according to the sauce or trimmings:
cream sauce Orvieto, Frascati or Alto Adige Chard.
meat sauce Montepulciano d'Abruzzo, Salice Salentino or Merlot.
pesto (basil) sauce Barbera, Ligurian Vermentino, New Zealand Sauv Bl, Hungarian Hárslevelü or Furmint.
seafood sauce (*e.g.* vongole) Verdicchio, Soave, top white Rioja, Cirò, or Sauv Bl.
tomato sauce Barbera, south Italian red, Zin, or South Australian Grenache.

Pastrami Alsace Ries, young Sangiovese, or Cab Fr.

Pâté
chicken liver Calls for pungent white (Alsace Pinot Gr or Marsanne), a smooth red like a light Pomerol or Volnay, or even amontillado sherry.
duck pâté Châteauneuf-du-Pape, Cornas, Chianti Classico, or Pomerol.
fish pâté Muscadet, Mâcon-Villages, or Australian Chard (unoaked).
Pâté de campagne A dry white ★★: Gd vin de pays, Graves, Pfalz Ries.

Pears in red wine A pause before the port. Or try Rivesaltes, Banyuls or Ries Beerenauslese.

Pecan pie Orange Muscat or Australian liqueur Muscat.

Peperonata Dry Australian Ries, Western Australia Sem or New Zealand Sauv Bl. Red drinkers can try Tempranillo or Grenache.

Perch, sandre Exquisite freshwater fish for finest wines: top white burgundy, Alsace Ries Grand Cru or noble Mosels. Or try top Swiss Fendant or Johannisberg.

Pigeon Lively reds: Savigny, Chambolle-Musigny; Crozes-Hermitage, Chianti Classico, or California Pinot N. Or try Franken Silvaner Spätlese.
squab Fine white or red burgundy, Alsace Ries Grand Cru or mature claret.

Pipérade Rosé, or dry South Australian Ries.

Pimentos, roasted Sauv Bl, or light reds.

Pizza Any ★★ dry Italian red. Or Rioja, Australian Shiraz, southern French red or Douro red.

Pork, roast A gd rich neutral background to a fairly light red or rich white. It deserves ★★ treatment – Médoc is fine. Portugal's suckling pig is eaten with Bairrada Garrafeira. Chinese is gd with Pinot N.

Pot au feu, bollito misto, cocido Rustic red wines from the region of origin; Sangiovese di Romagna, Chusclan, Lirac, Rasteau, Portuguese Alentejo or Yecla and Jumilla from Spain.

Pumpkin/Squash dishes Full-bodied fruity dry or off-dry white: Viognier or Marsanne, demi-sec Vouvray, Gavi or South African Chenin Bl.

Prawns, shrimps or langoustines Fine dry white: burgundy, Graves, New Zealand Chard, Pfalz Ries – even fine mature Champagne. ("Cocktail sauce" kills wine, and in time, people.)

Quail Alsace Ries Grand Cru, Rioja Reserva, mature claret or Pinot N.

Quiches Dry full-bodied white: Alsace, Graves, Sauv Bl, dry Rheingau; or young red (Tempranillo, Periquita), according to ingredients.

Rabbit Lively medium-bodied young Italian red or Aglianico del Vulture; Chiroubles, Chinon, Saumur-Champigny, or New Zealand Pinot Noir.

Raspberries (no cream, little sugar) Excellent with fine reds which themselves taste of raspberries: young Juliénas, Regnié, even Pomerol.

Risotto, with seafood Pinot Gr from Friuli, Gavi, youngish Sem, Dolcetto or Barbera d'Alba.
with fungi porcini Finest mature Barolo or Barbaresco.

Rum desserts (baba, mousses, ice-cream) Muscat – from Asti to Australian liqueur, according to weight of dish.

Salads As a first course, esp with blue cheese dressing, any dry and appetizing white wine.
salade niçoise Very dry, ★★, not too light or flowery white or rosé: Provençal, Rhône, or Corsican; Fernão Pires, Sauv Bl.
NB Vinegar in salad dressings destroys the flavour of wine. If you want salad at a meal with fine wine, dress the salad with wine or a little lemon juice instead of vinegar.

Salmon, seared or grilled Fine white burgundy: Puligny- or Chassagne-Montrachet, Meursault, Corton-Charlemagne, Chablis Grand Cru; Grüner Veltliner, Condrieu, California, Idaho or New Zealand Chard, Rheingau Kabinett/Spätlese, Australian Ries. Young Pinot N can be gd. Salmon fishcakes call for similar, but less grand, wines.
smoked A dry but pungent white: fino sherry, Alsace Pinot Gr, Chablis Grand Cru, Pouilly-Fumé, Pfalz Ries Spätlese or vintage Champagne. Also vodka, schnapps or akvavit.
carpaccio Puligny-Montrachet, Condrieu, California Chard or New Zealand Sauv Bl.

Sand-dabs This sublime fish can handle your fullest Chard (not oaky).

Sardines, fresh grilled Very dry white: Vinho Verde, Soave, Muscadet, or modern Greek.

Sashimi If you are prepared to forego the wasabi, sparkling wines will match. Or Washington or Tasmanian Chard, Chablis Grand Cru, Rheingau Ries and English Seyval Bl. Otherwise, iced sake, fino sherry or beer. Trials have matched 5-putt Tokáj with fat tuna, sea urchin and anago (eel).

Satay Australia's McLaren Vale Shiraz. Gewurz from Alsace or New Zealand.

Sauerkraut (German) Lager or Pils. But a Ries Auslese can be amazing.

Scallops An inherently slightly sweet dish, best with finest whites.
in cream sauces German Spätlese, Montrachet, top Australian Chard, or dry Vouvray.
grilled or seared Hermitage Blanc, Grüner Veltliner, Entre-Deux-Mers, vintage Champagne, or Pinot N.
with Asian seasoning New Zealand, South African Sauv Bl, Verdelho, Australian Ries, or Gewurz.

Sea bass Weissburgunder from Baden or Pfalz. V.gd for any fine or delicate white: Clare Valley dry Ries, Chablis or Châteauneuf-du-Pape.

Shark's fin soup Add a teaspoon of Cognac. Sip amontillado.

Shellfish Dry white with plain boiled shellfish, richer wines with richer sauces. With *plateaux de fruits de mer*: Muscadet, Chablis, unoaked Chard or dry Ries.

Skate with brown butter White with some pungency (*e.g.* Pinot Gr d'Alsace), or a clean straightforward wine like Muscadet or Verdicchio.

Snapper Sauv Bl if cooked with Oriental flavours; white Rhône with Mediterranean flavours.

Sole, plaice, etc.: plain, grilled or fried Perfect with fine wines: white burgundy, or its equivalent.
with sauce Depending on the ingredients: sharp dry wine for tomato sauce, fairly rich for sole *véronique* with its sweet grapes, etc.

Soufflés As show dishes these deserve ★★★ wines.
fish Dry white: ★★★ Burgundy, Bordeaux, Alsace, Chard, etc.
cheese Red burgundy or mature Cab Sauv.
spinach (tougher on wine) Light Chard (Mâcon-Villages, St-Véran), or Valpolicella. Champagne can also be gd with many kinds of soufflé.
sweet soufflés Sauternes or Vouvray moelleux. Or a sweet (or rich) Champagne.

Steak au poivre A fairly young Rhône red or Cab Sauv.

Steak tartare Vodka or light young red: Beaujolais, Bergerac or Valpolicella.

Korean Yuk Whe (The world's best steak tartare.) Sake.

filet, tournedos, T-bone, fiorentina (bistecca) Any top red (but not old wines with Béarnaise sauce: top Californian Chard is better). My choice: Château Haut-Brion.

Steak and kidney pie or pudding Red Rioja Reserva, Douro red, or mature Cabernet.

Stews and casseroles Red burgundy comes into its own; otherwise lusty full-flavoured red, such as Toro, Corbières, Barbera, Shiraz, or Zin.

Strawberries and cream Sauternes or similar sweet Bordeaux, Vouvray Moelleux or Jurançon Vendange Tardive.

Strawberries, wild (no cream) Serve with red Bordeaux (most exquisitely Margaux) poured over.

Summer pudding Fairly young Sauternes of a gd vintage (95 96 97 98).

Sushi Hot wasabi is usually hidden in every piece. German QbA trocken wines, simple Chablis, or NV brut Champ. Or, of course, sake or beer.

Sweetbreads A grand dish, so grand wine, but not too dry: Rhine Ries or Franken Silvaner Spätlese, top Alsace Pinot Gr or Condrieu, depending on the sauce.

Swordfish Full-bodied dry white of the country. Nothing grand.

Tagines These vary enormously, but fruity young reds are a gd bet: Beaujolais, Tempranillo, Sangiovese, Merlot and Shiraz.

Tapas Perfect with fino sherry, which can cope with the wide range of flavours in both hot and cold dishes.

Tapenade Manzanilla or fino sherry, or any sharpish dry white or rosé.

Taramasalata A rustic southern white with personality. Fino sherry works well. Try white Rioja or a Marsanne. The bland supermarket version goes well with any delicate white or Champagne.

Thai food Ginger and lemongrass call for pungent Sauv Bl (Loire, South Africa, Australia, New Zealand) or Ries (German Spätlese or Australian). **coconut milk** Hunter Valley or other ripe, oaked Chards; Alsace Pinot Bl for refreshment; Gewurz or Verdelho. And of course sparkling.

Tiramisú This Italian dessert works best with Vin Santo, but also with young tawny port, Muscat de Beaumes-de-Venise or Sauternes and Australian Liqueur Muscats.

Tongue Gd for any red or white of abundant character, esp Italian. Also Beaujolais, Loire reds, New Zealand reds and full dry rosés.

Trifle Should be sufficiently vibrant with its internal sherry.

Tripe Red (e.g. Corbières, Roussillon) or rather sweet white (e.g. German Spätlese). Better: Western Australian Sem/Chard, or cut with pungent dry white such as Pouilly-Fumé or fresh red such as Saumur-Champigny.

Trout Delicate white wine, e.g. Mosel (Saar or Ruwer), Alsace Pinot Bl.

smoked Sancerre, California or South African Sauv Bl. Rully or Bourgogne Aligoté, Chablis or Champagne. But Mosel Spätlese is best.

Tuna, grilled or seared White, red, or rosé of fairly fruity character; a top St-Véran, white Hermitage, or Côtes du Rhône would be fine. Pinot N or a light Merlot are the best reds to try.
carpaccio Viognier, California Chard or New Zealand Sauv Bl.

Turbot Serve with your best rich dry white: Meursault or Chassagne-Montrachet, mature Chablis or its California, Australian or New Zealand equivalent. Condrieu. Mature Rheingau, Mosel or Nahe Spätlese or Auslese (not trocken).

Veal, roast A good neutral background dish for any fine old red which may have faded with age (e.g. a Rioja Reserva), a German or Austrian Ries, or Vouvray, or Alsace Pinot Gr.

Venison Big-scale reds inc Mourvèdre – solo as in Bandol, or in blends – Rhône, Bordeaux or California Cab of a mature vintage; or rather rich whites (Pfalz Spätlese or Hunter Semillon).

Vitello tonnato Full-bodied whites esp Chard; or light reds (e.g. young Cabernet or Valpolicella) served cool.

Whitebait Crisp dry whites: Chablis, Verdicchio, Greek, Touraine Sauv Bl, or fino sherry.

Zabaglione Light-gold marsala, Australian botrytized Sem or Asti.

Wine & cheese

The notion that wine and cheese were married in heaven is not born out by experience. Fine red wines are slaughtered by strong cheeses: only sharp or sweet white wines survive. Principles to remember, despite exceptions, are first: the harder the cheese the more tannin the wine can have. And second: the creamier the cheese is the more acidity is needed in the wine. The main exception constitutes a third principle: wines and cheeses of a region usually sympathise. Cheese is classified by its texture and the nature of its rind, so its appearance is a guide to the type of wine to match it. Individual cheeses mentioned below are only examples taken from the hundreds sold in good cheese shops.

Fresh, no rind – cream cheese, crème fraîche, Mozzarella
Light crisp white – Simple Bordeaux Blanc, Bergerac, English unoaked whites; or rosé – Anjou, Rhône; or very light, very young, very fresh red such as Bordeaux, Bardolino or Beaujolais.

Hard cheeses, waxed or oiled, often showing marks from cheesecloth – Gruyère family, Manchego and other Spanish cheeses, Parmesan, Cantal, Comté, old Gouda, Cheddar and most "traditional" English cheeses
Particularly hard to generalize here; Gouda, Gruyère, some Spanish, and a few English cheeses complement fine claret or Cab Sauv and great Shiraz/Syrah wines. But strong cheeses need less refined wines, and preferably local ones. Sugary, granular old Dutch red Mimolette or Beaufort are gd for finest mature Bordeaux. Also for Tokáj Aszú.

Blue cheeses Roquefort can be wonderful with Sauternes, but don't extend the idea to other blues. It is the sweetness of Sauternes, esp aged, which complements the saltiness. Stilton and port, preferably tawny, is a classic. Intensely flavoured old oloroso, amontillado, madeira, marsala, and other fortified wines go with most blues. The acidity of Tokáj Aszú also works well.

Natural rind (goat's or sheep's cheese) with bluish-grey mould (the rind is wrinkled when mature), sometimes dusted with ash – St-Marcellin
Sancerre, Valençay, light fresh Sauv Bl, Jurançon, Savoie, Soave, Italian Chard or English whites.

Bloomy rind soft cheeses, pure white rind if pasteurized, or dotted with red: Brie, Camembert, Chaource, Bougon (goat's milk 'Camembert')
Full dry white burgundy or Rhône if the cheese is white and immature; powerful, fruity St-Emilion, young Australian (or Rhône) Shiraz/ Syrah or Grenache if it's mature.

Washed-rind pungent soft cheeses, with rather sticky orange-red rind – Langres, mature Epoisses, Maroilles, Carré de l'Est, Milleens, Munster
Local reds, esp for Burgundy cheeses; vigorous Languedoc, Cahors, Côtes du Frontonnais, Corsican, southern Italian, Sicilian or Bairrada. Also powerful whites, esp Alsace Gewurz and Muscat.

Semi-soft cheeses, grey-pink thickish rind – Livarot, Pont l'Evêque, Reblochon, Tomme de Savoie, St-Nectaire
Powerful white Bordeaux, Chard, Alsace Pinot Gr, dryish Ries, southern Italian and Sicilian whites, aged white Rioja or dry oloroso sherry. But the strongest of these cheeses kill most wines.

Food & finest wine

With very special bottles, the wine sometimes guides the choice of food rather than the usual way around. The following suggestions are based largely on the gastronomic conventions of the wine regions producing these treasures, plus much diligent research. They should help bring out the best in your best wines.

Red wines

Red Bordeaux and other Cabernet Sauvignon-based wines (very old, light and delicate: e.g. pre-60)
Leg or rack of young lamb, roast with a hint of herbs (but not garlic); entrecôte; roast partridge or grouse, sweetbreads; or cheese soufflé after the meat has been served.

Fully mature great vintages (e.g. Bordeaux 61 66 75) Shoulder or saddle of lamb, roast with a touch of garlic, roast ribs, or grilled rump of beef.

Mature but still vigorous (e.g. 85 86 89) Shoulder or saddle of lamb (inc kidneys) with rich sauce. Fillet of beef *marchand de vin* (with wine and bone-marrow). Avoid Beef Wellington: pastry dulls the palate.

Merlot-based Bordeaux (Pomerol, St-Emilion) Beef as above (fillet is richest) or venison.

Côte d'Or red burgundy (Consider the weight and texture, which grow lighter/more velvety with age. Also the character of the wine: Nuits is earthy, Musigny flowery, great Romanées can be exotic, Pommard renowned for its four-squareness, etc.). Roast chicken, or better, capon, is a safe standard with red burgundy; guinea-fowl for slightly stronger wines, then partridge, grouse, or woodcock for those progressively more rich and pungent. Hare and venison (*chevreuil*) are alternatives.
great old burgundy The classic Burgundian formula is cheese: Epoisses (unfermented). A fabulous cheese but a terrible waste of fine old wines.
vigorous younger burgundy Duck or goose roasted to minimize fat.

Great Syrahs: Hermitage, Côte-Rôtie, Grange; or Vega Sicilia
Beef, venison, well-hung game; bone-marrow on toast; English cheese (esp best farm Cheddar) but also hard goat's milk and ewe's milk cheeses such as Berkswell and Ticklemore.

Rioja Gran Reserva, Pesquera... Richly flavoured roasts: wild boar, mutton, saddle of hare, or whole suckling pig.

Barolo, Barbaresco Risotto with white truffles; pasta with game sauce (*e.g. pappardelle alla lepre*); porcini mushrooms; Parmesan.

White wines

Top Chablis, white burgundy, other top Chards
White fish simply grilled or *meunière*. Dover sole, turbot, halibut are best; brill, drenched in butter, can be excellent.

Supreme white burgundy (Le Montrachet, Corton-Charlemagne) or equivalent Graves Roast veal, organic chicken stuffed with truffles or herbs under the skin, or sweetbreads; richly sauced white fish or scallops as above. Or lobster or wild salmon.

Condrieu, Château-Grillet or Hermitage Blanc Very light pasta scented with herbs and tiny peas or broad beans.

Grand Cru Alsace
Ries Truite au bleu, smoked salmon or choucroute garni.
Pinot Gris Roast or grilled veal.
Gewurztraminer Cheese soufflé (Münster cheese).
Vendange Tardive Foie gras or Tarte Tatin.

Sauternes Simple crisp buttery biscuits (*e.g.* Langue-de-Chat), white peaches, nectarines, strawberries (without cream). Not tropical fruit. Pan-seared foie-gras. Experiment with blue cheeses.

Supreme Vouvray moelleux, etc. Buttery biscuits, apples, or apple tart.

Beerenauslese/Trockenbeerenauslese Biscuits, peaches, greengages. Desserts made from rhubarb, gooseberries, quince, or apples.

Tokáj Aszú (4–6 putts) Foie gras is thoroughly recommended. Fruit desserts, cream desserts, even chocolate can be wonderful.

Great vintage port or madeira Walnuts or pecans. A Cox's Orange Pippin and a digestive biscuit is a classic English accompaniment.

Old vintage Champagne (not Blanc de Blancs) As an apéritif, or with cold partridge, grouse or woodcock.

Italy today

Italy and its regions

Is it possible to stand on a hilltop anywhere in Italy and not see vines? Well, probably it is: there are places in the industrialized north where all vegetation has been squeezed out by concrete; and the centre of Naples doesn't boast many vineyards. But in most places vines are commonplace. They march alongside motorways and advance up hills to the medieval fortifications of old city-states. You have to had vines, for most of Italian history. Otherwise what else would you have drunk?

Italian wine is regional, always was regional, and, in spite of the pressures of globalization of wine flavours, stands a pretty good chance of staying regional. Yes, wine was exported in previous centuries, but there was no equivalent of Bordeaux, for example, to become known worldwide and bring foreigners and their new ideas flooding into a region. Italian wines were mostly drunk locally, and evolved to suit local tastes.

For most people today, Chianti is still the archetypal Italian red – and it's come a long way since we first got to know it. Well, we aim to show how tradition and modernity, regionality and internationalism, are interacting in Italian wine today. We want to show you the people behind contemporary Italian wine, and the local dishes with which it's drunk. We want to point you towards a few bottles you might not have thought of, and towards a few must-haves (or at least must-tastes). And if this sends you off on your own voyage of exploration, be it along the back roads of Tuscany or the back shelves of your local wine merchant, well, that's the idea.

2006: a great vintage

Over the past five years Italy has seen a mixed bag of vintages from very good to rather weak; but most regions agree that 2006 is a five-star year. Dino Illuminati in Abruzzo went as far as to describe it as "the best vintage I have seen in the past 50 years", and Gianni Masciarelli, who hates making predictions about the quality of a vintage, is calling 2006 a "stunner".

It was a cool summer in most places. Umbria and Tuscany had their share of snow, and spring was late to arrive in the hills of Piedmont – and here, as elsewhere, the traditional Italian heat never quite materialized. But then warm sunny days and cool nights lasted throughout September and October, giving even, gentle ripening that produced well-extracted, full-bodied, round, juicy reds and wonderful zesty, crisp, aromatic whites.

All across northern Italy, from the high-altitude vineyards of Alto Adige and Trentino, northeast to cool Friuli, producers welcomed healthy, aromatic Pinot Grigio, Traminer, Ribolla Gialla, Tocai, and others. The Veneto likewise, apart from a moment of panic at the end of July because of a drought followed by thunderstorms, is boasting of perfect balance in Amarone di Valpolicella and in Soave.

Tuscan Sangiovese, like many other of Italy's indigenous grape varieties – Sagrantino in Umbria, Nebbiolo in Piedmont, and Aglianico and Greco in Campania – can be rather temperamental in reaching full ripeness. The long ripening season of 2006 was just what these grapes needed to show their full potential as structured, ageworthy wines. Marco Pallanti of Castello di Ama reckons that "2006 is the best vintage in the past 20 years for Chianti Classico".

Down in the south, Alessio Planeta of Sicily was moved to poetry: it's a "luminous and solar vintage", he says, "with beautifully extracted reds, especially Nero d'Avola and Syrah".

Italians to try in 2008

PIEDMONT
Riserva Rabajà 2001, Produttori del Barbaresco, Barbaresco,
Vigna Elena 2001, Cogno, Barolo
Granbussia Riserva 2000, Poderi Aldo Conterno, Barolo
Le Rocche del Falletto di Serralunga d'Alba Riserva 2000,
  Bruno Giacosa, Barolo
Bricco Boschis Vignolo Riserva 2000, F.lli Cavalotto, Barolo
Monprivato Cà d'Morissio Riserva 1996, Giuseppe Mascarello, Barolo
Riserva Monfortino 1999, Giacomo Conterno, Barolo
Bricco della Bigotta 2004, Giacomo Bologna, Barbera d'Asti

LOMBARDY
Cuvée Anna Maria Clementi 1999, Cà del Bosco, Franciacorta

TRENTINO
Brut Riserva del Fondatore 1997, Giulio Ferrari, Trentino
Villa Gresti 2003, Tenuta San Leonardo
Bianco Faye 2003, Pojer & Sandri

ALTO ADIGE
Valle Isarco Kerner Praepositus 2005, Abbazia di Novacella, Alto Adige
Gewürztraminer Nussbaumer 2005, Produttori Termeno, Alto Adige
Barthenau Vigna S. Urbano Pinot Nero 2003, Hofstätter, Alto Adige
Abtei Muri Riserva 2003, Lagrein, Muri-Gries, Alto Adige,

VENETO
Vigneto di Monte Lodoletta 2001, Romano dal Forno, Amarone della
  Valpolicella,
Classico Mazzano 2001, Masi, Amarone della Valpolicella
Villa Rizzardi 2001, Classico, Guerrieri Rizzardi, Amarone della
  Valpolicella
Monte Fiorentine 2005, Ca' Rugate, Soave Classico
La Rocca 2004, Leonildo Pieropan, Soave Classico

FRIULI VENEZIA GIULIA
Pinot Bianco 2005, Picéch, Collio
Carso Malvasia 2004, Zidarich
Bianco Terre Alte 2004, Livio Felluga, Colli Orientali del Friuli
Berg Anfora 2002, Josko Gravner
Gräfin de la Tour 2004, Villa Russiz, Collio Chardonnay

TUSCANY
Ugolaia 2000, Lisini, Brunello di Montalcino
Brunello di Montalcino 2001, Fuligni
Tenuta Nuova 2001, Casanova di Neri, Brunello di Montalcino
Riserva 1999, Poggio di Sotto, Brunello di Montalcino

Vigneto Bellavista 2001, Castello di Ama, Chianti Classico
Riserva Rancia 2003, Felsina, Chianti Classico
Cepparello 2003, Isole e Olena
Tenuta di Valgiano 2003, Tenuta di Valgiano, Colline Lucchesi,
Flaccianello della Pieve 2003, Fontodi
Le Pergole Torte 2003, Montevertine
Paleo Rosso 2003, Le Macchiole
Ornellaia 2003, Tenuta dell'Ornellaia, Bolgheri Superiore
Sassicaia 2003, Tenuta San Guido, Bolgheri
Solaia 2003, Antinori
Nocio dei Boscarelli 2003, Boscarelli, Vino Nobile di Montepulciano
Avvoltore 2004, Morris Farms
Galatrona 2004, Petrolo
Vin Santo Occhio di Pernice 1995, Avignonesi

MARCHE
Mirum Riserva 2004, Fattoria La Monacesca, Verdicchio di Matelica
Verdicchio dei Castelli di Jesi Classico Riserva 2004, Villa Bucci

UMBRIA
Montefalco Sagrantino 1999, Paolo Bea
Montefalco Sagrantino 2003, Antonelli

ABRUZZO
Montepulciano d'Abruzzo 2001, Emidio Pepe
Trebbiano d'Abruzzo 2002, Valentini

CAMPANIA
Montevetrano 2004, Montevetrano
Fatica Contadina 2001, Terredora, Taurasi
Vigna Cinque Querce Riserva 2001, Salvatore Molettieri, Taurasi
Nova Serra 2004, Mastroberardino, Greco di Tufo
Pietraincatenata 2004, Maffini

BASILICATA
Vigna Caselle Riserva 2001, d'Angelo, Aglianico del Vulture
Il Repertorio 2004, Cantine del Notaio, Aglianico del Vulture

SICILY
Feudo di Mezzo 2004, Terre Nere, Etna Rosso
Pietramarina 2002, Benanti, Etna Bianco
Nerobufaleffj 2003, Gulfi
Passopisciaro 2004, Passopisciaro

SARDINIA
Vernaccia di Oristano Antico, Gregori Attilio Contini
Turriga 2002, Argiolas
Vendemmia Tardiva 2004, Capichera, Vermentino di Gallur

Dramatis personae

Piedmont

Some years ago Barolo's winemakers divided into two camps, modernist and traditionalist. The boundaries between the two have since blurred, but there is still a difference between modernist interpretations of Barolo, which show deeper colour and bolder fruit and are generally more approachable younger, and the most traditional Barolo, which takes a good decade or more to lose its initial tannic hardness. How to tell the difference in the winery? Look for barriques – they're the key sign.

Giacomo Conterno in Monforte d'Alba is one of Barolo's leading traditionalists, and ages his wine in large, old Slovenian oak barrels. "It is important to avoid any additional tannins coming from the barrels," says Roberto Conterno (left), winemaker and nephew to Giacomo. The process is as natural as can be. "The result is a complex layer of subtle flavours which evolve and with time show great class," he says. WINES & VINTAGES: Monfortino Riserva 1999, Conterno, Barolo; Cascina Francia 2004, Conterno, Barbera d'Alba

Enrico Scavino (bottom left) from the Paolo Scavino estate in Castiglione Falletto was a pioneer of modernism – one of the first, in fact, to break ranks and experiment with barriques. "Initial trials were a disaster," says Scavino. "I was about to give up, but then I moved to French oak. Barriques give colour." Scavino has seen 55 harvests in Langhe, and each year he experiments with at least ten different coopers. "French oak suits Nebbiolo best, giving it sweeter, finer tannins. It integrates perfectly, and allows the tipicity of the wine and its terroir to surface." WINES & VINTAGES: Rocche dell'Annunziata Riserva 2000, Scavino, Barolo; Dolcetto d'Alba 2005, Scavino

Friuli

Josko Gravner (left) looks to the past. He's an iconoclast and a relentless experimenter, uncompromising to the point of gruffness. Today's white wines lack flavour and depth of character, he says; and his dissatisfaction with technology has led him to embrace biodynamics. But he goes further still in his pursuit of authenticity: he abjures temperature control during fermentation, he won't filter his wines, and he leaves them on their skins to macerate in, of all things, large clay amphorae for up to seven months. In lesser hands the results could be disastrous; his wines, though, are compelling, if controversial: rich, evolved, and weighty with quite a bite. WINES & VINTAGES: Bianco Breg Anfora 2002, Gravner; Ribolla Anfora 2002, Gravner

Eighty-year-old **Marco Felluga** (left) of the Russiz Superiore estate, one of the most respected producers in Friuli, sees the way forward as being within modernity. "I believe in the richness of our territory. Our wines have great minerality and aromatic allure," he says. He used his presidency of the local vinous ruling body, the Consorzio, to carry out a detailed soil study of the area, and broadened the terms of the Collio DOC to include all the white varieties grown in the region; until then they had been limited to Tocai, Ribolla, and Malvasia. "We need to embrace innovation without losing track of tradition." WINES & VINTAGES: Col Dosre 2004, Russiz Superiore, Collio Bianco; Collio Rosso degli Orzoni Riserva 2002, Russiz Superiore

Veneto

Leonildo Pieropan, Nino to his friends, is the third generation of a family that pioneered the idea of single-estate wines in Soave; when they started, the idea of serious Soave seemed ludicrous to many. Nino, in turn, explored single-vineyard wines and the use of small French barriques for fermentation and maturation, and his wines have a depth of fruit and structure that few can match. His Soaves are based on Garganega, the best grape of the region, and display seductive – floral aromas, followed by great length on the palate. WINES & VINTAGES: La Rocca 2004, Pieropan, Soave Classico; Passito della Rocca 2001, Pieropan

Over in Valpolicella, on the other side of the Veneto hills, is **Romano Dal Forno** (left). He has attracted attention for his extremism: for example, he plants his vines more densely than anyone else in the region – 13,000 vines per hectare – and takes tiny yields of just 500 grams per vine. He seeks, he says, "emotion" from his Amarone. "This concentration alone is an extreme feat of nature," says Dal Forno. "There must be nothing heavy about such a wine. I look for the perfect balance between concentration, fine tannins, and freshness." He ages the wine in barriques made from American oak and the results are dense, immensely rich, immensely powerful, and utterly unlike most people's idea of Amarone della Valpolicella. Is he leading the way or going off at a tangent? WINES & VINTAGES: Vigneto di Monte Lodoletta 2001, Dal Forno; Valpolicella Superiore di Vigneto di Monte Lodoletta 2002, Dal Forno

Tuscany

Tuscan born and bred, **Carlo Ferrini** (overleaf top) is one of that most modern breed, the consultant winemaker. His philosophy is one of "weight, structure, balance, and elegance". Tuscan Sangiovese is his passion: "It's as temperamental as a pure-bred horse, but when you get it right there are few wines that can match its class," he says. But if he can't have pure Sangiovese, he'd prefer to have a blend than any other

grape on its own. "It's like a painting, the more colours you have, the better the complexity of the final blend." He also loves simply to walk in the vineyards. "This is where life starts: fine wine originates from well-tended vineyards." WINES & VINTAGES: Siepi 1997, Fonterutoli; Tenuta Nova 2001, Casanova dei Neri, Brunello di Montalcino; Asinone 1997, Poliziano, Vino Nobile di Montepulciano

Attilio Pagli (left), a fellow consultant winemaker, shares Ferrini's love of Sangiovese. "Sangiovese is among Italy's top varieties and one of its best," he says. "It is a difficult variety that needs perfect ripening. It takes time to get to know it and cultivate it, but when you get it right there is no other variety like it. It is really extraordinary." Pagli's philosophy is one of respect for the individual terroir and its indigenous grape varieties, whether in Tuscany or anywhere else in Italy. "Today Tuscany is reversing the trend of concentrated wines to that of elegance and balance. It is producing wines that are recognizably, uniquely Tuscan." WINES & VINTAGES: Vigneto San Marcellino 2003, Rocca di Montegrossi, Chianti Classico; Avvoltore 2004, Moris Farms; Giovin Re 2005, Michele Satta

Umbria/Lazio

Umbrian through and through, consultant winemaker **Riccardo Cotarella** (left) is a fan of international varieties like Merlot. "Neither Lazio nor Umbria boast a great viticultural patrimony with the exception of the Sagrantino and Grechetto vines," he comments. "Merlot does particularly well in Lazio and Umbria; I believe in making wines that will sell, wines that give pleasure, and to me this means a wine that is not aggressive, herbaceous, or bitter, but a wine that is fruity, soft, round, and supple – which explains why I am a Merlot enthusiast." WINES & VINTAGES: Montevetrano, 2004; Falesco Ferentano, 2004; Feudi di San Gregorio, Serpico, 2004

Where Cotarella looks to the future with Merlot, the reclusive **Paolo Bea** prefers tradition, and the traditional Sagrantino grape. He is the quintessential artisanal producer, whose tiny estate is a labour of love, his wines still hand-crafted. The 73-year-old Bea is still the guiding force behind the estate, assisted by his son Giampiero (left). They are essentially biodynamic in the vineyard and completely non-interventionist in the cellar. Giampiero shuns barriques, temperature control, fining, and filtration. His aim is to produce a "tamed Sagrantino with a soul, which expresses authenticity". **WINES & VINTAGES:** Sagrantino Montefalco 2003, Bea; Passico 2001, Bea, Sagrantino Montefalco

Abruzzi

It would be difficult to talk about the Abruzzi without mentioning two of the region's benchmark producers: Valentini, a die-hard traditionalist, praised for his ageworthy Trebbiano; and Masciarelli, a dynamic, passionate innovator with a Montepulciano that is a statement of power and finesse.

The legendary **Valentini** estate is the grandaddy of Abruzzi DOC wines. It boasts a unique clone of Trebbiano d'Abruzzo, which is vastly better than any other Trebbiano – normally rather a neutral grape. "These 40-year-old Trebbiano vines represent the true, indigenous Trebbiano, which, over centuries, has acclimatized to our region," explains Francesco Paolo Valentini. Valentini's wines display a profound individual personality, often taking years to develop their full profile. This is all perfectly in keeping with one of Valentini's favourite lines: "*Natura non facit saltus*", or "Nature doesn't leap". **WINES & VINTAGES:** Montepulciano d'Abruzzo 2001, Valentini; Trebbiano d'Abruzzo 2002, Valentini

Gianni Masciarelli (left) is the first producer to embrace modern viticulture by replacing his high-trained pergola vines with vines trained lower, on wires, as is the norm in most of the world. Yields are lower this way, and quality higher. He produces eight separate *crus* of Montepulciano d'Abruzzo, all aged in new barriques, all with an unparalleled richness. According to Masciarelli, the key is empirical knowledge; and he maintains that "Abruzzi's great potential is still to be seen". **WINES & VINTAGES:** Villa Gemma 2001, Masciarelli, Montepulciano d'Abruzzo; Marina Cvetic 2004, Masciarelli, Trebbiano d'Abruzzo

Campania/Basilicata/Puglia

Ask **Luigi Moio** how he got into wine, and he'll tell you that he was born in a vat. He comes from five generations of winemakers in Campania. But unlike his father Michele, Luigi got a degree in agriculture – followed by a PhD in biochemistry. He taught oenology at the University of Foggia in Puglia for five years and is also professor of oenology at Naples University. He did a stint in Burgundy researching wine aromas, and this is his passion: wines can and should have distinct aromas, he says. It's a matter of researching different grape varieties and a matter, too, of planting them in specific terroirs.

Sicily

Andrea Franchetti (left), best known for his isolated southern Tuscan property, Tenuta di Trinoro, also believes resolutely in Sicilian wines. Like the Sicilians themselves, his Sicilian wines have soul. When Andrea restored the abandoned Pisciopassaro vineyard most people thought him crazy. Not only is it just under an old spill of black lava on the north side of Etna, but it's 1,000 metres up. His terraced plots, planted on thin layers of dusty lava, are a real triumph over nature. "The wines are harsh and need endless handling," says Franchetti, "but the upsides are the starry nights, and incredible ripeness." WINES & VINTAGES: Tenuta di Trinoro 2004; Passopisciaro 2005, Tenuta di Trinoro

Etna-born **Salvo Foti** (left) is among Sicily's finest winemakers, especially when it comes to the indigenous Nero d'Avola grape. His philosophy is to follow the viticultural traditions taught by his forefathers, expressed through vines planted on dry-stone terraces and sometimes still worked by mule. "I believe in continuation and improving what was already achieved generations ago," says Foti. "With the exception of Etna, the Sicilian climate is too warm to produce wines of complexity, and not all wines need to be complex. Nero d'Avola grown in its native terroir is an authentic example of Sicilian wine, driven by pure fruit." WINES & VINTAGES: Nerobufaleffj 2003, Gulfi

Sardinia

Alessandro Dettori (left), young and uncompromising, is inspired by the red Cannonau grape. "I like to sail against the wind," he says. "I am not interested in following market trends, I want to produce a wine with a soul, though it may be old style and imperfect; this is the expression of Cannonau that reflects our terroir." The vines are 80 years old, yields are low, and alcohol high in the finished wines – up to 17.5 degrees. Their appeal is much like that of port. WINES & VINTAGES: Chimbanta 2004, Dettori; Tuderi 2003, Dettori

The Italian Feast

Italy's cuisine, like its wines, is based on territorial diversity and seasonal produce. Local ingredients go into traditional recipes, "*cucina tipica*", handed down from generation to generation. And just as Italian food is expected to be washed down with wine, so Italian wine is made to go with food: Italians will happily serve you wine without food if you want, but it's not what wine is for here.

The North

Northern Italy boasts the nation's richest diet, both in abundance and variety; and hilly, foggy Piedmont has some of Italy's finest cuisine. The ultimate luxury is the white truffle, sniffed out by dogs in the Langhe and shaved raw over pastas, risottos, meats, and fondues. Either Dolcetto or a sturdier Barbera or Barolo is the usual accompaniment: richness upon richness.

Meat takes pride of place throughout the north, and in most places butter and lard are the traditional fats. Aostans, like the people of Trentino, thrive on hearty meat dishes, the richest of which is the local venison stew accompanied by polenta. These dishes require robust, generous reds – and plenty of uphill walking. The local Teroldego and Marzemino reds have the structure to cope and the brightness of fruit to be refreshing. (Don Giovanni partnered Marzemino with cold pheasant, and very good it must have been, too.) Near Verona you might be offered horse, perhaps in the form of dark, silky, and delicious Pastissada a caval. Valpolicella is naturally a light red, so what have the locals done since time immemorial to satisfy their need for a serious red wine? Dried their grapes to produce Amarone, with its baked-cherry flavours and endless depth.

But if you regard eating horse as akin to cannibalism, you can stick to the Veneto's risottos and the fresh fish from the Venetian lagoon, or from Lake Garda, depending on where you are. Soave is the obvious partner for the likes of fritto misto, or perhaps pasta with crustaceans from lake or lagoon: a simple Classico for the lighter dishes, and single-vineyard versions, perhaps with some bottle age, for special occasions.

PIEDMONT

Agnolotti Piemontesi Pasta filled with lean white meat and herbs, served with sage leaves sautéed in butter and Parmigiano. Pair with Dolcetto di Dogliani or, if you want white, Arneis.

Brasato al Barolo Beef stewed very slowly in Barolo. Pair with Barolo (obviously) or Gattinara.

Crudo di Vitella delle Langhe battuta col coltello Finely chopped lean, raw veal, seasoned with salt, pepper, lemon juice, and olive oil, and perhaps garlic. Pair with young Barbera or Grignolino.

Fonduta di Toma con uovo e tartufo Fondue of cheese with a poached egg and plenty of white truffle shavings. Pair with Nebbiolo or Barbaresco, and take the rest of the day off.

LIGURIA

Pansùuti con la salsa di noci Pasta filled with ricotta and preboggion, a type of wild spinach, topped with a creamy walnut sauce with Parmigiano Reggiano. This needs white to balance its richness of texture and delicacy of flavour: pair with Vermentino or Pigato.

Cima alla genovese Veal breast stuffed with vegetables, nuts, eggs, and cheese. Served in thin slices, preferably with a glass of Cinqueterre.

Stoccafisso Dried cod simmered in white wine and tomato sauce with pine nuts, olives, potatoes, herbs, and anchovies. This needs something refreshing, with some bite, like Rossese di Dolceacqua.

VENETO

Risotto al nero di seppia Rice cooked with squid ink. The flavour is subtle, and doesn't want to be dominated by the wine: go for Soave Classico Superiore or Bianco di Custoza.

Fegato alla veneziana Calves' liver cooked in wine with onions. Bright fruit and lightness of weight is the key here, and Valpolicella Classico or Bardolino are perfect.

Pastissada a caval Horsemeat cooked slowly with wine, and served with gnocchi or polenta. This needs the deep, dark flavours of Amarone or Valpolicella Ripasso.

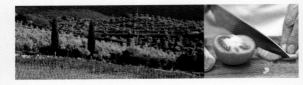

The Centre

The food of Tuscany, Umbria, and Lazio is rooted in hunting, with plenty of wild boar, perhaps turned into a stew; hare, often with pasta; and game birds; but also the tamer roast pork – as in porchetta – and the Chianina beefsteaks, which provide the legendary bistecca alla fiorentina. Bread plays a key role in the simpler peasant foods like ribollita – country soup with beans, black cabbage, and other vegetables, often thickened with stale bread; and panzanella – stale bread soaked with water and crumbled with chopped tomatoes, onions, basil, oil, and vinegar in a sort of salad. It's inland food, sturdy and often simple; like living off the land, only better.

As one descends further south to Rome, spaghetti, bucatini, and rigatoni play a vital role in the staple diet, and the central Apennines are a major source for truffles, both the prized white varieties found in the Marches and parts of Tuscany, and the black varieties that thrive in Umbria. On either side of the peninsula there is local fish, like cacciucco alla livornese, fish soup from the Tuscan coast. And of course the wines come in all shades of richness, from the lightness of young Chianti to the weight of Vino Nobile de Montepulciano. Most are made from Sangiovese: it's inescapable in central Italy, though in Umbria there is the option of cherry-fruited Morellino. All have good acidity and generally some tannin: it's what you need for this sort of food.

TUSCANY

Trippa alla Fiorentina Tripe stewed in tomato sauce with beans or potatoes, and served ideally with Chianti or Chianti Classico, combining freshness and some earthy weight.

Cinghiale in agrodolce Wild boar in sweet and sour sauce. This is a treat, and deserves something special; something as stylish as Carmignano Riserva or Brunello di Montalcino.

Pappardelle alla lepre Flat, wide tagliatelle with rich hare sauce. This needs a red with some real flavour to cope with its smoky richness. Try it with Rosso di Montalcino or Nobile di Montepulciano Riserva.

UMBRIA

Palombacci alla ghiotta Spit-roasted pigeons with an elaborate sauce of wine, lemon, vinegar, sage, garlic, rosemary, juniper berries, and chicken livers. Drink Sagrantino di Montefalco or Torgiano Rosso Riserva.

Spaghetti alla Norcina Sausages and onion in a creamy sauce, which may be topped with grated cheese or white truffles. This needs either a gentle white like Orvieto to complement it, or a young red like Rosso di Montefalco to balance its richness.

LAZIO

Coda alla vaccinara Oxtail braised with onion, tomatoes, lots of celery, and wine. A pretty straightforward dish to match, this: try Merlot or Cabernet Sauvignon.

Pasta e ceci Chickpea soup with garlic, rosemary, and pasta. Frascati will wash it down with elegance.

Saltimbocca alla romana Veal fillets rolled together with prosciutto and sage, sautéed in butter. Pair with light, bright, fruity red from the local Cesanese grape.

The South

The southern regions of Abruzzi, Puglia, Campania, Basilicata, Sicily, and Sardinia are celebrated for their sun-drenched, fertile plains and Mediterranean shores. Olive oil is the essence of all dishes, but the real symbol of southern cooking is the tomato, along with peppers, zucchini, beans, and aubergine, or egg-plant. The irresistible piquancy of southern food comes from herbs, spices, garlic, and above all from the piquant pimento known as peperoncino or diavolicchio.

The Arabs in Sicily established a pasta industry in the Middle Ages, using durum wheat for lasagne, macheroni, and orecchiette, often baked in the oven with fresh buffalo mozzarella. The Tyrrhenian and Ionian seas provide tuna, swordfish, anchovies, and sardines, along with shellfish served as fresh antipasti di mare. Meat was scarce in the south, with the exception of lamb from the hills – grilled, roasted, braised, or stewed in ragouts, and often served with pasta.

The soft, even luscious reds of the region will marry with the lamb and even cope with the pungent flavours of tuna and sardines, and if you want aged red – for, perhaps, some roasted spring lamb – Aglianico can fit the bill. But there are startlingly aromatic whites here, too, like Fiano di Avellino or Falanghina, or the elegant, mineral, nutty Greco di Tufo. You wouldn't expect such elegance from such a relentlessly hot landscape, but cool nights up in the hills are the key. Hills and coast come together to provide perfect balance.

CAMPANIA/BASILICATA

Coniglio all'ischitana Rabbit braised with tomatoes, rosemary, and basil in Ischian white wine. Greco di Tufo has the weight and freshness.

Empepata di cozze Mussels cooked in their juice with lemon, parsley, and black pepper. Fiano di Avellino is a great match: perfumed but not overwhelming.

Strangulapreuti (priest stranglers) Little dumplings similar to gnocchi and often kneaded with vegetables. Drink Falerno del Massico.

ABRUZZI/PUGLIA

Polpi in purgatorio Octopus cooked with tomato, garlic, parsley, and diavolicchio. A gutsy, flavoursome dish that needs gutsy, no-nonsense red: Salice Salentino or Locorotondo.

Indocca Pungent stew of pork ribs, feet, and ears simmered with rosemary, bay leaf, peppers, and vinegar. Try with Montepulciano d'Abruzzo.

Orecchiette con cime di rapa Ear-shaped pasta shells with turnip greens, garlic, and chilli peppers. Pink wine is the answer to this; for example Castel del Monte Rosato.

SICILY

Agghiotta di pesce spada Swordfish simmered with tomatoes, pine nuts, raisins, olives, and herbs. This can take a flavoursome red, so try Etna Rosso or Nero d'Avola.

Gnocculli Semolina gnocchi with ricotta and meat sauce. Cerasuolo di Vittoria is a good match.

Peperonata Bell peppers stewed with onion, tomato, and olives. This needs wine with bags of flavour and some assertiveness, so try Syrah.

SARDINIA

Agnello con finocchietti Baby lamb stewed with onion, tomato, and wild fennel. Red is the answer, but one with some perfume and weight, like Cannonau or Carignano.

Cassùla Up to a dozen types of fish, shellfish, and shrimps cooked with tomato and spices and served as a piquant soup. It needs a white with some weight: try Vernaccia di Oristano or Vermentino di Gallura.

Twenty Italian bottles to drink before you die

GRANBUSSIA RISERVA 1999, PODERI ALDO CONTERNO, BAROLO

There are many excellent Barolos, but this is in a class of its own. Ripe berries, roses, spice, and tobacco on the nose, and a balanced palate, richly layered with depth, harmony, and length. Drink this red by 2016.

MONFORTINO RISERVA 1995, GIACOMO CONTERNO, BAROLO

A monument to Barolo's traditional style. Robust and structured. A floral bouquet and ripe berries mingle with hints of tobacco. Ample tannins give depth, complexity, and length. A red to drink by 2020.

SORÌ SAN LORENZO 1998, ANGELO GAJA, LANGHE NEBBIOLO

Undoubtedly the best Nebbiolo in Piedmont, with an intense bouquet of vanilla, ripe cherries, and violets. Round, structured, and elegant on the palate. Drink this red by 2015.

MONPRIVATO 1990, GIUSEPPE MASCARELLO, BAROLO

Barolo from one of Langhe's prime single vineyards. Complexity and elegance mingle with berries, liquorice, and tobacco, warm and round with fine tannins and length. Drink by 2015.

BRIC DÈL FIASC 1999, PAOLO SCAVINO, BAROLO

When Barolo is as good as this it is unbeatable. Vibrant, floral, berry and spice complexity. Fine, rich, warm, and full on the palate. Drink by 2015.

ANTICO GREGORI, VERNACCIA DI ORISTANO RISERVA

Solera-style Vernaccia; a white wine with huge complexity and a toasted-almond finish. Drink by 2020.

CUVÉE ANNAMARIA CLEMENTI 1999, CÀ DEL BOSCO, FRANCIACORTA

Rich, complex and elegant sparkling wine of an unsurpassed and unique style. Drink by 2012.

VIN SANTO OCCHIO DI PERNICE 1994, AVIGNONESI

If I were confined to a desert island I would insist on having this with me: it's a wine for contemplation. Sensuous and sumptuous white dessert wine with intense bouquet and full palate. Drink by 2020.

PIETRAMARINA 1997, BENANTI, ETNA BIANCO SUPERIORE

There's something wildly romantic about a white wine grown on the slopes of Mount Etna. But it's also a wine of great vitality, mineral notes, and layers of complexity, with ripe fruit and persistence. Drink by 2010.

BARTHENAU PINOT NERO 2001, VIGNA SANT'URBANO, HOFSTATTER, ALTO ADIGE

When Pinot Noir is this good it takes you into a world of nuances and subtleties. Light berry fruit mingles with tobacco and spice. Subtle, layered depth with firm, silky tannins, very persistent. Drink by 2020.

VALPOLICELLA CLASSICO SUPERIORE 2000, QUINTARELLI

No other Valpolicella producer makes wines with as much character as Quintarelli. Rich, opulent crushed berries with hints of dark chocolate. Drink by 2012.

KASTELAZ GEWÜRZTRAMINER 2005, ALTO ADIGE BIANCO, ELENA WALCH

One of Elena Walch's signature wines. Soaring aromas and opulent fruit. This is an all-time classic, a perfectly crafted wine.

GIULIO FERRARI RISERVA DEL FONDATORE TALENTO 1995, TRENTINO, FERRARI

Classy, floral, spicy, sparkling white of extraordinary finesse and longevity. It's aged in bottle for eight years before release. Long and full on the palate with citrus notes. Drink by 2015.

BIONDI SANTI RISERVA 1988, BRUNELLO DI MONTALCINO

Brunello at its best, from one of Italy's most prized producers. A red with a warm harmony of flavours that will become aristocratically austere with age. Drink by 2018.

VIGNETO BELLAVISTA 2001, CHIANTI CLASSICO, CASTELLO DI AMA

An estate that stands above the rest, not only in altitude, but in quality and its philosophy of production. This red has intense, evolved aromas, ripe fruit, soft silky tannins; it's elegant and classy. Drink by 2016.

MASSETO 2001, TENUTA DELL'ORNELLAIA

Masseto expresses the genius loci of Ornellaia and promises even better as the wine matures. At the moment this red is opulent with hints of cassis, vanilla, and spice. Silky tannins, elegant and seductive. Drink by 2015.

SASSICAIA BOLGHERI 1998, TENUTA SAN GUIDO

Italy's first Supertuscan, Sassicaia is living up to its reputation. Elegant and supple, round, full, and ageworthy, with hints of ripe blackberry, cherry, and spice. Drink this red by 2020.

TREBBIANO D'ABRUZZO 1992, VALENTINI

A white with elaborate aromas yet which epitomises the barren landscape and rusticity of the region. It has uncommon depth, minerality, and ageworthy vitality, layered with flowery, herbal, and intense fruity aromas. Drink by 2015.

TAURASI RADICI RISERVA 1997, MASTROBERARDINO

Radici, meaning "roots", refers to the ancient ties that link Aglianico, the historic red grape that makes this wine, to its landscape. Rich and concentrated with balance between tannins, fruit, and acidity. Ripe cherries with underlying tobacco and spice, and a fine finish. Drink by 2020.

DON ANSELMO AGLIANICO DEL VULTURE 1994, PATERNOSTER

A top Aglianico dedicated to its founder Don Anselmo, produced only in the finest vintages. Ripe blackberries and violets with hints of spice. Firm, sweet tannins, full, warm, and lasting. Drink by 2010.

A little learning...
A few technical words

The jargon of laboratory analysis is often seen on back-labels. It creeps menacingly into newspapers and magazines. What does it mean? This hard-edged wine-talk, unsympathetic as it is to most lovers of wine, is very briefly explained below.

Alcohol content (mainly ethyl alcohol) is expressed in per cent by volume of the total liquid. (Also known as "degrees".) Table wines are usually between 12.5° and 14.5°, though up to 16° is increasingly seen.

Acidity is both fixed and volatile. **Fixed acidity** consists principally of tartaric, malic and citric acids, all found in the grape, and lactic and succinic acids, produced during fermentation. **Volatile acidity** consists mainly of acetic acid, which is rapidly formed by bacteria in the presence of oxygen. A small amount of volatile acidity is inevitable and even attractive. With a larger amount the wine becomes "pricked"– to use the Shakespearian term. It turns to vinegar. Acidity may be natural, in warm regions it may also be added.

Total acidity is fixed and volatile acidity combined. As a rule of thumb, for a well-balanced wine it should be in the region of one gram per thousand for each 10° Oechsle (see above).

Barriques Vital to modern wine, either in ageing and/or for fermenting in barrels (the newer the barrel the stronger the influence) or from the addition of oak chips or – at worst – oak essence. Newcomers to wine can easily be beguiled by the vanilla-like scent and flavour into thinking they have bought something luxurious rather than something cosmetically flavoured. But barrels are expensive; real ones are only used for wines with the inherent quality to benefit long-term. French oak is classic and most expensive. American oak has a strong vanilla flavour.

Malolactic fermentation is often referred to as a secondary fermentation, and can occur naturally or be induced. The process involves converting tart malic acid into softer lactic acid. Unrelated to alcoholic fermentation, the "malo" can add complexity and flavour to both red and white wines. In hotter climates where natural acidity may be low canny operators avoid it.

Micro-oxygenation is a widely used technique that allows the wine controlled contact with oxygen during maturation. This mimics the effect of barrel-ageing, reduces the need for racking, and helps to stabilize the wine.

pH is a measure of the strength of the acidity: the lower the figure the more acid. Wine usually ranges from pH 2.8 to 3.8. High pH can be a problem in hot climates. Lower pH gives better colour, helps stop bacterial spoilage and allows more of the SO_2 to be free and active as a preservative.

Residual sugar is that left after fermentation has finished or been stopped, measured in grams per litre. A dry wine has virtually none.

Sulphur dioxide (SO_2) is added to prevent oxidation and other accidents in winemaking. Some of it combines with sugars etc and is **"bound"**. Only the **"free"** SO_2 is effective as a preservative. **Total SO_2** is controlled by law according to the level of residual sugar: the more sugar, the more SO_2 is needed.

Tannins are the focus of attention for red-winemakers intent on producing softer, more approachable wines. Later picking, and picking by tannin ripeness rather than sugar levels gives riper, silkier tannins.

Toast refers to the burning of the inside of the barrel. "High toast" gives the wine caramel-like flavours.